RETHINKING NEURAL NETWORKS: *QUANTUM FIELDS AND BIOLOGICAL DATA*

RETHINKING NEURAL NETWORKS: *QUANTUM FIELDS AND BIOLOGICAL DATA*

Editor
Karl H. Pribram

With a Keynote By
Sir John Eccles

Proceedings of the First Appalachian Conference on Behavioral Neurodynamics

LEA LAWRENCE ERLBAUM ASSOCIATES, PUBLISHERS
1993 Hillsdale, New Jersey Hove and London

Lawrence Erlbaum Associates, Inc., Publishers
365 Broadway
Hillsdale, New Jersey 07642

Library of Congress Cataloging-in-Publication Data

Rethinking neural networks : quantum fields and biological data / editor, Karl H. Pribram : with a keynote by Sir John Eccles.
p. cm.
Includes bibliographical references.
ISBN 0-8058-1466-3 (pbk. : alk. paper)
1. Neural networks (Neurobiology)--Congresses. I. Pribram, Karl H., 1919- . II. Eccles, John C. (John Carew), Sir, 1903-
[DNLM: 1. Nerve Net--congresses). 2. Models, Neurological--congresses. WL 102 R438 1993]
QP363.3.R48 1993
612.8'2--dc20
DNLM/DLC
for Library of Congress 93-20503
CIP

Books published by Lawrence Erlbaum Associates are printed on acid-free paper, bindings are chosen for strength and durability.

Printed in the United States of America

TABLE OF CONTENTS

Section II. Quantum Neurodynamics

Section III. Nanoneurology

ACKNOWLEDGEMENTS

My initial gratitude is to Daniel Levine, who invited me to a series of conferences in Dallas, Texas, where I met Paul Prueitt and Sam Leven. Prueitt joined the Physics Department at Georgetown University and organized two conferences, where I met several potential contributors to the Appalachian meeting. Leven joined the Center for Brain Research and Informational Sciences at Radford University and subsequently helped plan and initiate financial support for such conferences, of which the Appalachian Conference on Behavioral Neurodynamics is the first.

Leven also introduced me to Paul Werbos and Harold Szu, who provided the major funding for the conference through the International Neural Network Society. At Harold Szu's suggestion, I called Richard Nakamura at the National Institute of Mental Health, who provided the additional funding that allowed a number of students to participate.

Another neural networks scientist introduced to me by Sam Leven was Alianna Maren, who organized colloquia for the Brain Center, bringing to Radford such speakers as Paul Werbos, Harold Szu, Walter Schempp, and Adi Bulsara.

Once the conference planning was seriously under way, Katherine Neville provided inspiration and the organizational support necessary to bring about the conference. The administration of Radford University, through the wonderful coordination efforts of Debbie Brown, pitched in to an extent well beyond the ordinary, to graciously host the participants with student-provided transportation, good food and wine. Without these "behind the scenes" contributors, this conference and its proceedings would not have materialized.

Once the proceedings did materialize, we deliberated and discussed the issue of an appropriate title: Werbos' suggestion won the day.

My heartfelt thanks.

Karl H. Pribram

Radford, Virginia
January 1993

FOREWORD

Three years ago, when Radford University made a commitment to participate in the nation's "Decade of the Brain", economist Sam Leven and I discussed the importance of holding annual meetings to provide a focus for both the experimental and educational endeavors of the University. The conferences were to be modelled on the successful series of symposia on motivation conducted annually at the University of Nebraska. Our concern centered on how brain processes become organized during decision making--that is, on the variety of neural antecedents that determine which course of action is to be pursued.

Shortly thereafter, when it became clear that a sizeable laboratory would be made available for brain research, the administration of the University suggested that a dedication ceremony be planned when the laboratory became functional. An obvious possibility emerged: the dedication ceremonies could serve to inaugurate this series of conferences.

A decision needed to be reached as to the topic for the first conference. While we were engaged in this decision-making process, mathematician Paul Prueitt organized a series of meetings at Georgetown University. These conferences explored the ideas put forward in Pribram's Brain and Perception: Holonomy and Structure in Figural Processing. The data-based mathematical models proposed in this publication begged for implementation in parallel distributed processing neural network programming architectures. These two conferences were successful in bringing together a small group of like-minded scientists. Some of these were invited individually to present their work in more extended form at the Brain Research Center in Radford; others had already interacted with members of the Radford group in the past.

As these interactions gained momentum, Harold Szu and Paul Werbos felt that a more encompassing conference was in order. Szu suggested that it be held at what by now had become the "Center for Brain Research and Informational Sciences" (with the acronym B.R.A.I.N.S.) at Radford. This, then, would serve as the inaugural of a series which Szu baptized "Appalachian Conferences." The International Neural Networks Society (I.N.N.S.) voted to support such a conference and additional aid was provided by the National Institute of Mental Health.

Thus, the organization of the First Appalachian Conference on Neurodynamics came to pass. The focus was to be on processing in biological neural networks taking off from the Epilogue and Appendix A of Brain and Perception. Half of the program would deal with modelling synapto-dendritic and neural ultrastructural processes; the remainder of the program, with laboratory research results, often cast in terms of the models. The interchanges at the conference and the ensuing publication were to provide a foundation for further meetings. These would address how processes in different brain systems, coactive with the neural residues of experience and with sensory input, determine decisions.

The Dendritic Microprocess

The first order of business in a transdisciplinary conference is to describe how the scientists involved go about obtaining their results. The publications presented in Section I aim to accomplish this. In the first paper, I review what can be learned about the functional organization of the receptive fields of neurons from an analysis of the spike trains recorded in the neuron's axon. The mapped receptive fields reflect the effective functional processes occurring in the synapto-dendritic network. In this paper, I review a stepwise path taken in collaboration with Dale Berger, leading from data to a stochastic resonance model and then to congruence with the Gabor elementary function. The next paper, by Bankman, introduces some of the most recent techniques used to analyze the data gathering process, the axonal spike train per se, techniques that are fundamental to any further analysis and attempts at modelling. The paper by Adi Bulsara and his collaborators does the same for the modelling process: it brings up to date the random walk procedure used in the Berger and Pribram analysis by showing how stochastic resonance with added noise can enrich our understanding of the relationship between the essentially quantum field characteristics of the synapto-dendritic network and the essentially discrete axonal spike train.

Quantum Neurodynamics

The papers published in Section II take forward the finding that Hermetians such as Gabor functions are excellent descriptors of receptive field organization in the visual cortex. Kunio Yasue and Mari Jibu had developed a neural wave equation akin to Schroedinger's in their contribution as appendices to my MacEachron lectures published as Brain and Perception. Almost simultaneously, Dawes had also proposed a quantum neurodynamics based on the Schroedinger equation. His contribution here takes these proposals into the realm of practical applications. In the main text of Brain and Perception, I had reviewed the data from my own and other laboratories which showed that the best description of the functional dendritic field of a visual cortical neuron is a Gabor elementary function or related Hermitian. This function Gabor called a "quantum of information" because his mathematics was identical to that which Heisenberg had used in identifying the quantum in microphysics. Bruce MacLennon clarifies a considerable number of issues that involve modelling in neural network architectures, including the use of Gabor wavelets. Walter Schempp brings to bear his mathematical expertise to delineate the relationship between all of these quantum-type formulations and to show their relevance to current engineering and biological concerns. The concluding paper in this section, presented by Paul Werbos, outlines some of the pitfalls that must be avoided when the mathematical formulations found appropriate in one field of inquiry (quantum physics) are applied in another (biological neural networks).

Nanoneurology

An alternative set of methods for exploring the functional organization of the synapto-dendritic processes directly addresses the microarchitecture and microprocesses surrounding the synapse. Sir John Eccles introduced this topic in his keynote address -- more on this presently. In Section III, Stuart Hammeroff and Glen Rein discuss the cellular infrastructures, the operations of the microtubules and the neurochemistry that regulate processing at the synapse. Next, Judy Dayhoff and Harold Szu address the adaptive changes that occur in this microarchitecture as a function of learning. These papers lead us from the essentially linear invertible and reciprocal stochastic resonance processes that guide sensory-motor behavior to an irreversible, largely chaotic or otherwise deterministic modification of the synapto-dendritic microstructure.

Perceptual Processing

The last section returns us to the perceptual process per se. The papers of Walter Freeman, Bruce Bridgeman and Barry Richmond report the research from their laboratories which demonstrates above all that the perceptual act is based not only on current sensory input but also a variety of encoded residues of prior experiences. Furthermore, there is no single neuron that acts as a solitary detector of current input; rather, ensemble processing is what occurs. Richmond explores the nature of the ensemble process in information theoretic terms; Bridgeman in terms of the content of a perception; and Freeman in terms of Chaos theory. Freeman's contribution shows that, at least in the early stages of olfactory processing, no invariant neural pattern can be made out that identifies a particular operant. He suggests that whatever remains constant in recurring experiences must be encoded in some invariant response to an invariant environmental configuration. His data do not preclude the possibility that such invariances become encoded elsewhere in the brain. As detailed in Brain and Perception, in the visual system the shifting patterns coordinate with imaging are processed into objects that demonstrate invariance across images. Reciprocal interactions between striate and the peri and prestriate systems of the brain are involved. As a concluding paper, Harold Szu and his colleagues present a novel technique of growing live neurons on electrons to determine how the resulting connectivity patterns interact to produce efficient processing.

Achievement

The keynote address given by Sir John Eccles brought our various endeavors into focus. In his discussion of the details of the synaptic process, he stated that he is averse to modelling: that if you want to make a brain you don't model it, you make a baby! Despite this bias, at the end of the conference, he told several of us that this was the best conference he had attended in decades. And it turned out that, in fact, Eccles himself had begun his collaboration with Friedrich Beck of the Institut fur Kernphysik of the Technische Hochschule in Darmstadt from which I have his permission to quote as detailed in the Afterword.

Excitement was generated; a thirst for knowledge and for evidence permeated the conference. Charles Peirce, the pragmaticist philosopher, stated that knowing can be achieved in three ways: 1) Through induction, i.e. through the gathering of observations and placing them in some sort of order; 2) Through deduction, i.e. through rigorously formulating and formally manipulating the orderings achieved through induction. However, Peirce noted that neither of these procedures really added to our knowledge base. He suggested that: 3) Only through abduction, the proper use of analogy, could knowledge grow.

Our use of models in this conference was abductive rather than inductive or deductive. As such, we need to examine the text of the proceedings of the conference carefully to see whether we used or abused the use of analogy. Was our use of the processes of quantum microphysics merely a cute exercise in metaphor? Was our use of Schroedinger's equations and Heisenberg's matrices sufficiently based in laboratory observation and experiment? Are the non-linear dynamics of the currently popular chaos theory simply fads we must bear or do these formulations really pose more clearly (and perhaps even answer) questions we only dimly perceived as recently as a decade ago?

There is no question as to our intent. Even Sir John, who has worked the vineyard of synapses all his long and illustrious career, became convinced of the validity of our mathematical procedures as a means for organizing the wealth of accumulated fact about neural processing. Only among behavioral neuroscientists would serious doubts arise. In physics, molecular biology, astronomy and paleontology, theorists, using mathematical formulations, and the gatherers of observations have worked out the "proper" collaborative use of analogy. In large part this has come about by distinguishing what in biology is called homology, a set of proven (tested) relationships among structures, from mere analogy, a correspondence among functions. With regard to neural networks, this distinction comes out to be the difference between pursuing biologically relevant applications (homology) versus implementing more generally useful applications (analogy). This conference showed that, not only it possible to pursue homology, but that the endeavor can be a warm, human and exciting adventure. We very much look forward to Appalachian II.

Karl H. Pribram

Professor Emeritus, Stanford University
James P. and Anna King University Professor
and Eminent Scholar, Commonwealth of Virginia

Radford University
Radford, VA 24142

Keynote

Evolution of Complexity of the Brain with the Emergence of Consciousness

John C. Eccles
Max-Planck-Institut für Hirnforschung
Frankfurt/M - Niederat 71, Germany

Abstract

It has been proposed in a recent publication that before the evolution of the mammalian brain the animal world was literally mindless, without feelings. In the evolution of even the most primitive mammals, the basal insectivores, there came to exist a neocortex with a higher level of neural complexity, particularly in its pyramidal cell structure. Their apical dendrites have an enormous synaptic input and they form bundles as they ascend through the cortical laminae. There are hundreds of thousands of synaptic inputs, through boutons, onto a dendritic bundle, which is the reception unit, named dendron of the cerebral cortex. The axons of the pyramidal cells have a wide distribution in the brain. In this simplified conventional account of the structure of the cerebral cortex there is completely missing the story of the feelings that may be generated by the brain activity.

In developing that story it is necessary to move into a higher level of complexity, the ultramicrosite structure and function of the synapse, as discovered particularly by Akert and associates of Zurich. The boutons of chemical transmitting synapses have a presynaptic ultrastructure of a paracrystalline arrangement of dense projections and synaptic vescicles, a presynaptic vesicular grid. Its manner of operation in controlling chemical transmission opens up an important field of neural complexity that is still at its conception. The key activity of a synapse concerns a synaptic vesicle that liberates into the synaptic cleft its content of transmitter substance, an exocytosis. There are about 50 synaptic vesicles in the presynaptic vesicular grid. A nerve impulse invading a bouton causes an input of thousands of Ca^{2+} ions, 4 being necessary to trigger an exocytosis. The fundamental discovery is that at all types of chemical synapses an impulse invading a single presynaptic vesicular grid causes at the most a single exocytosis. There is conservation of the synaptic transmitter by an as yet unknown process of higher complexity.

The conservation challenge becomes intense when it is recognized that synapses of the cerebral cortex have an exceptionally effective conservation with a probability of exocytosis as low as 1 in 5 to 1 in 4 in response to an impulse invading a hippocampal bouton.

Because of the conservation laws of physics, it has been generally believed that non-material mental events can have no effective action on neuronal events in the brain. On the contrary it has been proposed that all mental experiences have a unitary composition, the units, being unique for each type of experience and being called psychons. It has been further proposed that each psychon is linked in a unitary manner to a specific dendron, which is the basis of mind-brain interaction.

Quantum physics gives a new understanding of the mode of operation of the presynaptic vesicular gird and of the probability of exocytosis. Changes in this probability are brought about without an energy input, so the mind could achieve effective action on the brain merely by increasing the probability of exocytosis, for example from 1 in 5 to 1 in 3. That would give a large neuronal response when the mind through its psychons causes this increment in the hundreds of thousands of presynaptic vesicular grid on specific dendrons. A higher level of neural complexity is thus envisaged in order to lead to an understanding of how the mind can effectively influence the brain in conscious volition without infringing the conservation laws.

1. Introduction

The key concept of my lecture is that in the evolution of the mammalian brain there had come to exist in the neo-cortex levels of complexity in its ultramicrostructure, that we may literally call transcendent because (Eccles, 1992) they opened the brain to the world of conscious feeling. Before that the living world was mindless, as we would now recognize for bacteria, plants and lower animals. We may ask how long? The usual answer would be that all mammals, dogs, cats, monkeys, horses, rats experience feelings and pain and possibly also birds, but not invertebrates and lower vertebrates such as fish and even amphibia and reptiles that have instinctual and learned responses. However, much more experimental testing may be possible in the light of concepts of how animals could use their consciousness as I will mention at the end of the lecture.

We can assume that the mammalian neocortex evolved for the purpose of integrating the greatly increased complexity of the sensory inputs: visual, auditory, tactile, olfactory, gustatory, proprioceptive, so as to give effective behavior. We can now try to understand how the functional structure of the mammalian brain could have properties mediating consciousness of another world from that of matter-energy: the world of feelings, thoughts, memories, intentions, emotions.

We have to concentrate on the neocortex because all other parts of the brain such as the striatum, the diencephalon, the cerebellum, the pons exist in lower vertebrates, reptiles, amphibia and fish that do not exhibit evidence for conscious feelings (Thorpe, 1974, 1978).

2. The mammalian neocortex

In this enquiry we come to the mammalian neocortex that is qualitatively similar to ours, though usually much smaller. It has the same neuronal structure as illustrated in Figs. 1A, B, 2A, which show the most numerous and important neurons, the pyramidal cells (B, C, D, E in Fig. 1A); 3 in Fig. 1B; and 5 are drawn in Fig. 2A with many in shadowy outline. The cortex has six layers (Fig. 2A) and all true pyramidal cells are in laminae V, III, II, each with an apical dendrite and many side branches projecting towards the surface to end as a terminal tuft. A pyramidal cell has a nerve fibre or axon for transmitting information. It projects downwards from the cell, as shown in Figs. 1A, 1B, 2A, 3A and leaves the cerebral cortex. It ends eventually in many branches either elsewhere in the cortex or far more distant sites in the brain.

It is necessary to make some further statements with illustrations on the mammalian neocortex before we come to its transcendent properties. It is composed of an immense number, even thousands of millions, of individual nerve cells that have been illustrated in Figs. 1 and 2 and each is the recipient of information from other nerve cells by means of the fine axonal branches that terminate as synaptic knobs or boutons. There are thousands of excitatory spine synapses on each pyramidal cell, as are partly illustrated by the spines on the pyramidal cell apical dendrites in Figs. 1B and 2A and by the clustered boutons on the apical dendrite and its branches in Fig. 3A. Even that drawing is inadequate in showing the thousands of boutons on the synaptic spines of the apical dendrite of each pyramidal cell and of course also on other cell dendrites and the cell body.

The bouton (pre) of one synapse is shown in Fig. 2B making an excitatory synapse across a synaptic cleft (d) on a dendritic spine and containing numerous synaptic vesicles (sv) filled with 5000 to 10000 molecules of the specific transmitter substance. Some vesicles are clustered along the synaptic surface of the bouton and they are the principal actors in my story.

Nerve impulses are brief signals of about 1 millisecond depolarization passing along nerve fibres to finish in the terminal bouton as in Fig. 2B and as greatly enlarged in Figs. 4 and 6. Transmission across a synapse occurs when an impulse invading the bouton causes a synaptic vesicle to discharge its contents of transmitter substance into the synaptic cleft, as indicated by the curved arrow in F, and so to act on the specific receptor sites across the synapse (e in Fig. 2B) and postsyn. in Fig. 4. For excitatory synaptic transmission in the cerebral cortex we are specially concerned with glutamate as the transmitter with its action in briefly opening ionic channels to decrease momentarily the electric potential across the postsynaptic membrane, so causing a mini-excitatory postsynaptic potential (EPSP) of the dendrite. By electrotonic transmission along the dendrite there is summation of the mini-EPSPs generated by each bouton activated at about the same time. When this occurs for a multitude of boutons (cf. Fig. 3A) the summed mini-EPSPs could result in a membrane depolarization of 10 to 20 mV, which could be enough to generate an impulse in the pyramidal cell that would travel down its axon shown in Figs. 1, 2A, 3A eventually to the many synapses of the cerebral cortex on dendrites of neurons or to other regions of the brain.

This is the conventional macro-operation of the pyramidal cell of the neocortex (Figs. 2A, 3A) and it can be satisfactorily described by classical physics and neuroscience, even in the most complex design of network theory and neuronal group selection (Szentagothai, 1978; Mountcastle, 1978; Edelman, 1989, Changeux, 1985).

It may seem that this generally accepted simplified account of the neuronal mechanism of the neocortex indicates already a high level of complexity in its design. However, this account neglects the conscious feelings that may be generated by the brain activity. In order to move into this field it is necessary to consider in detail the manner of operation of synapses on the pyramidal cells, which is new level of complexity. Furthermore these complex neural structures have been postulated to have mental properties (Edelman, 1989; Crick and Koch, 1990). For example, Changeux (1985) speaks of "consciousness being born". However, Stapp (1991, 1992) asserts that the origin of consciousness cannot be explained by classical physics; quantum physics is necessary. Classical physics is dedicated to matter-energy at all levels of complexity, but is not concerned with the mental world. By contrast quantal physics is closely related to the mental world. So our enquiry into the manner of operation of synapses on pyramidal cells moves into a higher level of complexity in the quest for mind.

3. Organization of the neocortex

There is agreement by Peters of Boston and Fleischhauer of Bonn and their associates that the apical dendrites of the pyramidal cells in laminae V, III and II (Fig. 2A) bundle together as they ascend to lamina I (Figs. 3B and 9). So there are neural receptors units of the cerebral cortex composed of about 100 apical dendrites plus their branches (Fig. 3A) that is called a dendron. The enormous synaptic input into the 70 to 100 apical dendrites bundled into a dendron (Fig. 3B) can be calculated to be much more than 100,000 synapses, if there be on the average about 2000 on each apical dendrite (Fig. 3A).

4. Ultrastructure of synapses

In Fig. 2B there is a general drawing of a cortical synapse, but it is now necessary to describe the ultrastructure as revealed to Akert and associates by the techniques of freeze fracture, electronmicroscopy and selective staining. It is here that we enter into a higher level of complexity. Fig. 4 is a key diagram showing as a central feature a nerve terminal or bouton confronting the synaptic cleft (d in Fig. 2B). The inner surface of a bouton has been recognized in Fig. 2Bc as in assemblage of synaptic vesicles, but now is shown as a beautiful structure with dense protein projections (DP) in triangular array, AZ in Fig. 4, forming the presynaptic vesicular grid (PVG) (Figs. 4,5,6). Fig. 5A is a micrograph of a tangential section of a PVG showing the DP's in triangular array with the lightly seen SV's fitting snugly in hexagonal array as in Fig. 4 and the left inset. Fig. 5B is an interpretative drawing of the dense projections emphasizing the supportive triangularly arranged protein filaments, which are also seen in Fig. 6 and insert, with measurements in Angstroms. The spherical SV's, 50 A to 60 A, with their content of transmitter molecules can be seen in the idealized drawings of the PVG (Fig. 4 and inset to left) with the triangularly arranged DP's, AZ and the hexagonal of the SV's. The SV's are so intimately related to the presynaptic membrane that it dimples outwards to meet them (Fig. 4 to left), and when the SV's are stripped off, these dimples reveal the hexagonal pattern of the presynaptic attachment sites (VAS in Fig. 4 and right inset). The usual number is 40 to 60 SV's in the single PVG of a bouton (Figs. 4 and 6).

The exquisite design of the PVG can be recognized as having an evolutionary origin for chemically transmitting synapses. In a more primitive form it can be seen in synapses of the Mollusc, Aplysia (Kandel et al., 1987) and the fish Mathner cell (Korn and Faber, 1987). Its essential rationale would appear to be conservation of transmitter molecules during intense synaptic usage.

With chemical synaptic transmission not only was there the problem of manufacturing the transmitter and transporting it to the synaptic site of action, where it was packaged in vesicles, but there was also the necessity for conservation. As stated above, there are no more than 40 to 60 vesicles assembled in the PVG ready for liberation in exocytosis. Yet the demand may be caused by presynaptic impulses invading the bouton at about 40/sec. So the necessity for conservation is evident.

5. Exocytosis

A nerve impulse propagating into a bouton causes a large influx of Ca^{2+} ions (Fig. 7A). The input of 4 Ca^{2+} ions activates via calmodulin a synaptic vesicle and may cause it momentarily to open a channel (Fig. 7C) through the contacting presynaptic membrane, as indicated by the curved arrow in Fig. 4, so that its total transmitter content is liberated into the synaptic cleft in a process called exocytosis.

At most a nerve impulse evokes a single exocytosis from a PVG (Fig. 4). This limitation must involve organized complexity of the paracrystalline PVG. It has not yet been explained how exocytosis can be controlled when the nerve impulse causes an influx of Ca^{2+} ions into a bouton that is thousands of times in excess of the 4 required for the calmodulin that generates one exocytosis (McGeer et al., 1987, p. 96).

Exocytosis is the basic unitary activity of the cerebral cortex. Each all-or-nothing exocytosis of synaptic transmitter results in a brief excitatory postsynaptic depolarization, the EPSP. As already described, summation by electronic transmission of many hundreds of these mini-EPSP's is required for an EPSP large enough (10-20 mv) to generate the discharge of an impulse by a pyramidal cell. This impulse will travel along its axon (Fig. 2A) to make effective excitation at its many synapses.

Exocytosis has been intensively studied in the mammalian central nervous system where it is now possible to move to a new level of complexity by utilizing a single excitatory impulse to generate EPSP's in single neurons that were being studied by intracellular recording. Immense difficulties are presented by the background noise that was even as large as the signals being studied (Fig. 8). Fortunately the signal can be repeated many thousand times for effective averaging above the background noise, and special statistical procedures of deconvolution analysis have been devised to extract the probabilities for exocytoses (Redman, 1990).

The initial studies were on the spinal cord, the monosynaptic action on motoneurones by single impulses in the large Ia afferent fibres from muscles (Jack et al., 1981). Recently (Walmsley et al, 1987) it was found that the signal to noise ratio was much better for the neurons projecting up the dorso-spino-cerebellar tract (DSCT) to the cerebellum, and many quantal responses generated by exocytosis on DSCT neurons were studied. The quantal EPSP's had a mean probability of 0,76.

6. Probability of exocytosis

Fig. 8 shows diagrammatically the experimental arrangement for making the most important study on the probability of exocytosis in neurons of the hippocampus, which is a special type of cerebral cortex (Sayer et al., 1989). Advantage was taken of a unique neuronal connection. The axon of a CA3 neuron gives of a branch, a Schaffer collateral (Sch), that makes synapses on the apical dendrite of another neuron, type CA1. A microelectrode inserted into a CA3 neuron (A) can set up the discharge of an impulse that goes by the Schaffer collateral to the CA1 neuron to end there and generate an EPSP that is recorded intracellularly (C). This meticulous technique ensures that the CA1 EPSP is generated by an impulse in a single axon, but as shown on E and F the EPSP's set up by a stimulus at the arrow are superimposed on noise that is even larger than the EPSP. Nevertheless, superposition of many 1000 impulses virtually eliminates the random noise so that smooth EPSP's can be recorded (F and H) and measured to be about 160 μV (Sayer et al., 1990). Moreover the statistical technique of deconvolution analysis enables the determination of the probability of release by a nerve impulse of a single synaptic vesicle, an exocytosis. As in simpler situations this probability of release is always less than one, in fact very low for the hippocampus with average mean values of 0,27, 0,24 and 0,16 for the three completely reliable experiments on the hippocampus (Redman, personal communication 1992). So an impulse invading a bouton induces an exocytosis with a probability as low as 1 in 4 to 1 in 6. This is a fundamentally important finding, introducing a new level of complexity.

The control of exocytosis has been investigated by Professor Heinrich Betz and his associates, who have for several years made an intensive study of the proteins of synaptic vesicles in the hope of understanding the quantal release mechanism. The two highly significant proteins are rather similar, synaptophysin and synaptoporin. However, in their last paper (Marquize-Pouey et al, 1991) they state that "the function of these two homologous proteins in the vesicle membrane is presently unknown." Fig. 7D with legend gives their suggested explanation of exocytosis (Thomas, Knaus and Betz, 1989).

In the dynamic structure of the PVG the dense projections (DP in Fig. 4) are at least as important as the synaptic vesicles but there seems to be no study of them complementary to that of synaptic vesicles by Betz and associates. Elucidation of the paracrystalline structure of the PVG requires detailed knowledge of both components.

The ultimate goal is to account by quantum physics for the low probability of quantal emissions (exocytoses) in response to nerve impulses invading the bouton.

7. Psychons

The hypothesis that the dendron is the neural unit of the neocortex leads on to the attempt to discover the complimentary mental units which interact with the dendron, for example in intention and attention.

Mental experiences, such as feelings, may not be vague nebulous happenings, but may be microgranular and precisely organized in their immense variety so as to bring about accurate description of the type of feeling. For example, the experience could be a special sensation from a spot on the right big toe.

The hypothesis has been proposed (Eccles, 1990) that all mental events and experiences, in fact that the whole of the outer and inner sensory experiences are a composite of elemental or unitary mental events at all levels of intensity. Each of these mental units is reciprocally linked in some unitary manner to a dendron, as is illustrated ideally in Fig. 9 for three dendrons. The three associated mental units are represented as an ensheathing of the three dendrons by designs of solid squares, open squares and dots. Appropriately we can name these proposed mental units as "psychons" (Eccles, 1990). According to the unitary hypothesis (Eccles, 1990) there is a unique linkage of each psychon with its dendron in brain-mind interaction, for example the special feeling in the right big toe.

Psychons are not perceptual paths to experiences. They are the experiences in all their diversity and uniqueness. There could be millions of psychons each linked uniquely to the millions of dendrons (Eccles, 1990). It is the very nature of psychons to link together in providing a unified experience.

8. Generation of neural events by mental events

There has been a long history concerning the manner in which voluntary movements can be generated. Some neuroscientists, taking up a materialistic dogma, deny that the non-material mind can effectively influence the brain so as to cause an intended movement. This materialistic dogma neglects the conscious performance which we experience at every moment, even in the linguistic expression of this dogma!

Ingvar (1990) introduced the term pure ideation that is defined as cognitive events which are unrelated to any ongoing sensory stimulation or motor performances.

He stated that "a study of brain structures activated by pure ideation therefore appears to open up a new approach to understand the human psyche". Ingvar and associates at Lund (1965 onwards) introduced the study of the regional cerebral blood flow (rCBF) to display by cerebral ideography the activity of the brain in pure ideation in all the immense variety generated by the psyche. By radio Xenon mapping Roland et al. (1980) demonstrated that in pure motor ideation of complex hand movements there was activation of the supplementary motor area on both sides (SMA, Fig. 10). By the more accurate technique of PET scanning Raichle and his associates demonstrated a wide-spread patchy activity of the neocortex during specific mental operations in selective attention (Posner et al., 1988).

So extensive experimental studies establish that mental intentions (psychons) can effectively activate the cerebral cortex. This increased neural activity can be accounted for if the psychons caused momentarily an increased probability of the exocytoses generated in a bouton by its incoming nerve impulses (Beck and Eccles, 1992).

The effectiveness of a mental intention causing neural activity has also been well established in the readiness potential (RP) that is recorded by the averaging technique as a slow negative potential over the scalp (Deecke and Lang, 1990). it is largest over the supplementary motor area (SMA, Fig. 10) anterior to the motor cortex (MI in Fig. 10). By exquisitely designed experiments Libet (1990) has discovered that the readiness potential (RP) begins at least 0,5 s before the subject is conscious (W) of willing the movement, which is at the earliest only 0,2 s before the onset of the movement. So it has been concluded that the brain is active about 0,3 sec before the movement is consciously willed (W) by the subject. However, the earlier part of the RP is probably artifactual (Libet, 1990, General Discussion). So it seems that the effective willing (W) of the movement does not occur until about 0,2 sec before the movement. The mental event of willing (W) can be regarded as preceding the neural events in the brain, particularly in the SMA (Fig. 10).

The presynaptic vesicular grid provides a unique structure in the attempt to account for the effective action of mental events on the brain by a process that does not infringe the conservation laws of physics (Beck and Eccles, 1992). A nerve impulse induces an exocytosis in a bouton and an effective mini-EPSP with a mean probability as low as 1 in 5 for the cerebral cortex (Sayer et al., 1989, 1990). This probability requires an explanation by quantum physics. If a mental intention momentarily increased that probability to an average value of 1 in 3, it would have almost doubled the EPSP's for the whole dendron. Thus there would be an effective mind-brain action without infringing the conservation laws (Beck and Eccles, 1992). The very low probabilities of quantal release in the cortex give excellent opportunities for mind-brain interaction in the cerebral cortex. It could be very effective if the psychon's influence was distributed widely to the hundreds of thousands of synapses on a dendron (Fig. 9). So the low probability of quantal emission in the cerebral cortex was of fundamental significance in the origin of consciousness. The complexity of the ultra-design of cortical synapses presents the ultimate scientific challenge.

As has been described (Eccles, 1990, 1992) consciousness gives global experiences from moment to moment of the diverse complexities of cerebral performances, e.g. it would give a mammal global experience of a visual world or a tactual world for guiding its behavior, far beyond what is given by the robotic operations of the visual or tactile cortical areas per se. Thus conscious experiences such as feelings would give evolutionary advantage. This opens up a field of behavioral psychology in which the consciousness of animals could be tested. For example, a reptile such as a tortoise and an insectivore (mammal) such as a hedgehog with its neocortex can be tested to see if the hedgehog displays intelligence when compared to the tortoise, which has no neocortex that could give it consciousness (Eccles, 1992).

It may seem to be a poor evolutionary design for the fundamental performance of brain-mind interaction because of its dependence on a rather indirect action via quantal probability. It would have been expected that mental intentions would directly excite the neurons of the SMA that are precisely concerned in the intended movement. The indirect action by increase of quantal probability would seem to lack precision and speed, which are of paramount importance in motor control. However, once the movement is initiated, it is subject to all the subtle controls of the complex neural machinery of the brain in the conventional neuroscience of motor control.

The hypothesis is that, because the vertebrate brain evolved in the matter-energy world of classical physics, it was mindless, deterministic and subject to the conservation laws. Then, because of the complex design of the mammalian neocortex with its operation of quantal probability, there came to exist experiences of another world, that of the conscious mind, presumably most primitive and fleeting (Eccles, 1992). However, with hominid evolution there eventually came higher levels of conscious experiences as expressed eventually in human culture (Eccles, 1989), and ultimately in Homo Sapiens Sapiens - self-consciousness- which is the unique life-long experience of each human self, and which we must regard as a miracle beyond Darwinian evolution (Lack, 1961; Eccles, 1989).

Fig. 1: Neurons and their synaptic connections. a. Eight neurons from Golgi preparation of the three superficial layers of frontal cortex from a month-old child. Small (B,C) and medium (D,E) pyramidal cells are shown with their profuse dendrites covered with spines. Also shown are three other cells (F,J,K), which are in the general category of Golgi type II with their localized axonal distributions (Ramon y Cajal, 1981). b. The direct excitatory neuron circuit of the specific (sensory) afferents (spec. aff.). Both spiny stellate (sst) with ascending main axon, and apical dendrites of both lamina III and V pyramidal cells (stippled) are probably the main targets (Szentagothai, 1979).

Fig. 2: A. Three dimensional construct by Szentagothai (19798) showing cortical neurones of various types. There are two pyramidal cells in lamina V and three in lamina III, one being shown in detail in a column to the right, and two in lamina 2. B. Detailed structure of a spine synapse on a dendrite (den.t); st, axon terminating in synaptic bouton or presynaptic terminal, pre; sv, synaptic vesicles; c, presynaptic vesicular grid; d, synaptic cleft; e, postsynaptic membrane; a, spine apparatus; b, spine stalk; m, mitochondrion (Grey, 1982).

Fig.3: A. Drawing of a lamina V pyramidal cell with its apical dendrite showing the side branches and the terminal tuft all studded with spine synapses (not all shown). The soma with its basal dendrites has an axon with axon collateral before leaving the cortex. B. Drawing of the 6 laminae of the cerebral cortex with the apical dendrites of pyramidal cells of laminae II, III and V, showing the manner in which they bunch in ascending to lamina I, where they end in tufts. The small pyramids of laminae IV and VI do not participate in this apical bunching (A. Peters, personal communication).

Fig. 4: Schema of nerve terminal (bouton) of mammalian central synapse showing active zone, the presynaptic vesicular grid with geometrical design of dense projections (AZ) in triangular array and of synaptic vesicles (SV) in hexagonal array. One vesicle is shown in exocytosis indicated by arrow in the synaptic cleft. Below is the postsynaptic membrane with particles PA below the cut out. The presynaptic vesicular grid is stripped off to right to display hexagonal arrangement of presynaptic attachments (VAS). Insets to left show presynaptic vesicular grid and to right the vesicle attachment sites (VAS). Modified from Akert et al., (1975).

Fig. 5: A. Tangential section through the presynaptic area. A section of the dense projection and synaptic vesicle pattern, triangular and hexagonal, of the presynaptic vesicular grid is clearly represented. Original photograph, scale of 0,l μ. B. Interpretative drawing of A (Pfenninger et al., 1969).

Fig. 6: Axon terminal or bouton showing dense projections (dp) projecting from the active site with cross linkages forming the presynaptic vesicular grid, PVG, that is drawn in the inset with dimensions (Pfenninger et al., 1969).

Fig. 7: A,B,C. Schematic drawing of a synaptic vesicle filled with transmitter molecules in stages of exocytoses (Kelly et al., 1979). D. Possible functions of synaptophysin. a. Synaptophysin may serve as a transmembrane channel connecting cytoplasm and vesicle interior. b. Synaptophysin participates in fusion pore formation during transmitter release. Docking of synaptophysin (o) to a channel protein (o) in the presynaptic plasma membrane (b) followed by fusion of vesicle and plasma membranes (a). Membrane areas fusing incidentally are dotted. Note that membrane fusion is not required for release. (Thomas et al. 1989).

Fig. 8: A,B,C,D show the experimental arrangement for making probability study on exocytosis of neurons in the hippocampus as described in the text. E are three records recorded as in C in response to a stimulus of a single Sch fibre as in D, F being the average of many thousands responses. G, H as in E,F but for a Sch fibre distributed more distally to the CA1.

Fig. 9: Drawing of three dendrons showing manner in which the apical dendrites of large and medium pyramidal cells bunch together in lamina IV and more superficially, so forming a neural unit. A small portion of apical dendrites do not join the bunches. The apical dendrites are shown terminating in lamina I. This termination is in tufts (cf. Fig. 3A). The other feature of the diagram is the superposition on each neural unit or dendron, of a mental unit or psychon, that has a characteristic marking (solid squares, open squares, solid circles). Each dendron is linked with a psychon giving its own characteristics unitary experience.

Fig. 10: The left hemisphere from the lateral side with frontal lobe to the left. The medial side of the hemisphere is shown as if reflected upwards. F.Rol. is the fissure of Rolando or the central fissure; F.Sylv. is the fissure of Sylvius. The primary motor cortex, M1, is shown in the precentral cortex just anterior to the central sulcus and extending deeply into it. Anterior to M1 is shown the premotor cortex, PM, with the supplementary motor area, SMA, largely on the medial side of the hemisphere.

REFERENCES

Akert, K., Peper, K. and Sandri, C. (1975) "Structural organization of motor end plate and central synapses." In Cholinergic Mechanisms. Ed. P.G. Waser, New York: Raven Press, pp. 43-57.

Beck, F. and Eccles, J.C. (1992) "Quantum Aspects of Brain Activity and the Role of Consciousness." Proc. Nat. Acad. Sci.-submitted.

Changeux, J.P. (1985) Neuronal Man. Paris: Fayard.

Eccles, J.C. (1990) "A unitary hypothesis of mind-brain-interaction in the cerebral cortex." Proc. Roy. Soc. Lond. B 240, pp. 433-451.

Eccles, J.C. (1992) "The Evolution of Consciousness." Proc. Nat. Acad. Science, vol. 89.

Eccles, J.C. (1989) Evolution of the Brain: Creation of the Self. London, New York: Routledge.

Crick, F and Koch, C. (1990) "Towards a neurobiolotical theory of consciousness." The Neurosciences, Seminars in 2, pp. 263-275.

Deecke, L. and Lang, V. (1990) "Movement-related potentials and complex actions: Coordinating role of the supplementary motor area." In The Principles of design and operation of the brain. Eds. J.C. Eccles and O.D. Creutzfeldt. Exp. Brain Res. Series 21 (1990), pp. 303-341.

Edelman, G.M. (1989) The remembered present: A biological theory of consciousness. New York: Basic Books.

Gray. E.G. (1982) "Rehabilitating the dendritic spine." Trends Neurosci. 5, pp. 5-6.

Ingvar, D. (1990) "On ideation and 'ideography'." In The Principles of design and operation of the brain. Eds. J.C. Eccles and D.D. Creutzfeldt. Exp. Brain Res.Series 21, (1990), pp. 433-453 .

Jack, J.J.B, Redman, S.J., Wong, K. (1981) "The components of synaptic potentials evoked in cat spinal motoneurones by impulses in single group Ia afferents." J.Physiol., 321, pp. 65-96.

Kandel, E.R., Klein, M., Hochner, B., Schuster, M., Siegelbaum, S.A., Hawkins, R.D., Glanzman, D.L., Castellucci, V.F. and Abrams, T.W. (1987) "Synaptic modulation and learning: New insights into Synaptic transmission from the study of behavior." In Synaptic Function. Eds. G.M. Edelman, W.E. Gall, W.M. Cowan. A Neurosciences Institut Publications. John Wiley, New York.

Kelly, R.B., Deutsch, J.W., Carlson, S.S. and Wagner, J.A. (1979) "Biochemistry of neurotransmitter release." Ann.Rev.Neurosci. 2, pp. 399-446.

Korn, H. and Faber, D.S. (1987) "Regulation and Significance of Probabilistic release mechanisms at Central Synapses." In New Insights into Synaptic Function. Eds. G.M. Edelman, W.E.Gall, W.M. Cowan. Neurosci Res. Foundation. New York: John Wiley & Sons, pp. 57-108.

Libet, B. (1990) "Cerebral processes that distinguish conscious experience from Unconscious mental functions." In The Principles of design and operation of the brain. Eds. J.C. Eccles and O.D. Creutzfeldt. Exp. Brain Res., Series 21 (1990) Berlin, Heidelberg, New York: Springer Verlag, pp. 185-205, plus general discussion, pp. 207-211.

McGeer, P.L., Eccles, J.C. and McGeer, E. (1987) The molecular neurobiology of the mammalian brain. 2nd ed. New York: Plenum Press.

Marquize-Pouey, B., Wisden, W., Malosio, M.L. and Betz, H. (1991) "Differential expression of Synaptophysin and Synaptoporin in RNA's in the post-natal rat central nervous system." J. of Neuroscience 11, pp. 3388-3397.

Mountcastle, V.B. (1978) "An organizing principle for cerebral function: the unit module and the distributed system." In The Mindful Brain. Cambridge, Mass.: MIT Press.

Peters, A. and Kara, D.A. (1987) "The neuronal composition of area 17 of the rat visual cortex. IV: The organization of pyramidal cells." J. Comp. Neurol. 260, pp. 573-590.

Pfenninger, K., Sandri, C., Akert, K. and Eugster, C.H. (1969) "Contribution to the problem of structural organization of the presynaptic area." Brain Res. 12, pp. 10-18.

Posner, M.I., Petersen, S.E., Fox, P.T., Raichle, M.E. (1988) "Localization of Cognitive Operations." Science 240, pp. 1627-1631.

Ramon y Cajal, S.R. (1911) Histologie du Systeme Nerveux. Paris: Maloine.

Redman, S. (1990) "Quantal Analysis of Synaptic Potentials in Neurons of the Central Nervous System." Physiolog Rev. 70 (1990), pp. 165-198.

Schmolke, C. and Fleischhauer, K. (1984) "Morphological characteristics of neocortical laminae when studied in tangential semi-thin sections through the visual cortex in the rabbit." Anat. Embryol. 169, pp. 125-132.

Roland, P.E., Larsen, B., Lassen, N.A. and Skinhoj, E. (1980) "Supplemental motor area and other cortical areas in organization of voluntary movements in man." J. Neurophysiol. 43, pp. 118-136.

Sayer, R.J., Redman, S.J. and Andersen, P. (1989) "Amplitude fluctuations in small EPSP's recorded from CA1 pyramidal cells in the guinea pig hippocampal slice." J. Neurosci. 9, pp. 845-850.

Sayer, R.J., Friedlander, M.J., Redman, S.J. (1990) "The Time-course and amplitude of EPSP's evoked at synapses between pairs of CA3/CA1 neurons in the hippocampal slice." J. Neurosci. 10 (3), pp. 626-636.

Stapp, H.P. (1991) "Brain-Mind Connection." Foundations of Physics 21, Nr. 12. New York: Plenum Press.

Stapp, H.P. (1992) In Nature, Cognition and System. Ed. Marc Carvallo. Dordrecht: Kluwer Academic Publishers.

Szentagothai, J. (1978) "The neuron network of the cerebral cortex: a functional interpretation." Proc. Roy. Soc. B 201, pp. 219-248.

Szentagothai, J. (1979) "Local Neuron Circuits of the Neocortex." In The Neurosciences Fourth Study Program. Eds. F.O. Schmitt and F.G. Worden. Cambridge, Mass.: MIT Press, pp. 399-415.

Thomas, L., Knaus, P. and Betz, H. (1989) "Comparison of the pre-synaptic vesicle component synaptophysin and gap junction proteins: A clue for neurotransmitter release?" In Molecular biology of neuroreceptors and ion channels. Ed. A. Maeliche. Berlin, Heidelberg: Springer Verlag.

Thorpe, W.H. (1974) Animal Nature and Human Nature. London: Methuen.

Thorpe, W.H. (1978) Purpose in a world of chance. Oxford: Oxford University Press.

Walmsley, B., Edwards, F.R. and Tracey, D.J. (1987) "The probabilistic nature of synaptic transmission at a mammalian excitatory central synapse." J. Neurosci. 7, pp. 1037-1046.

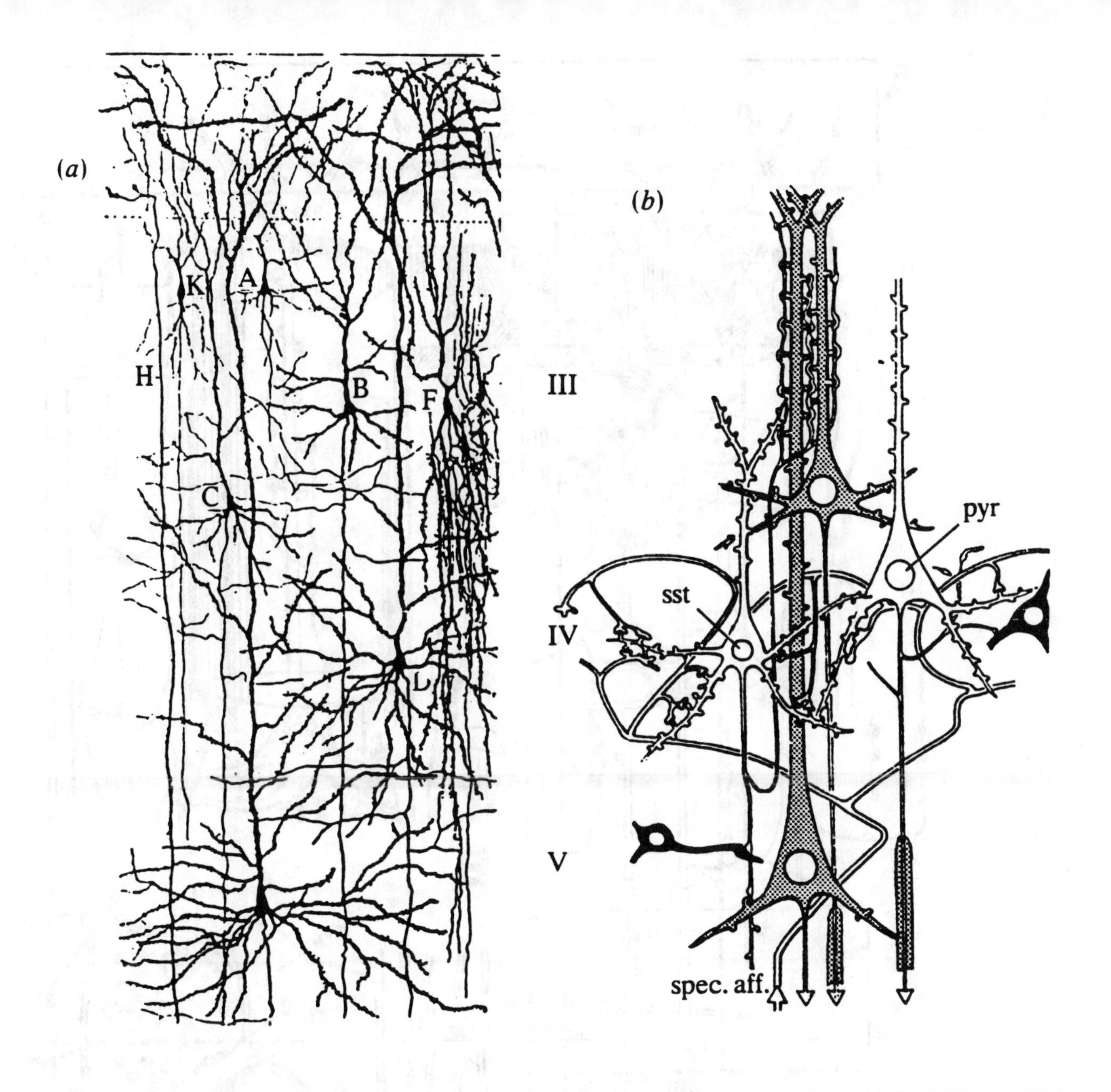

Fig. 1

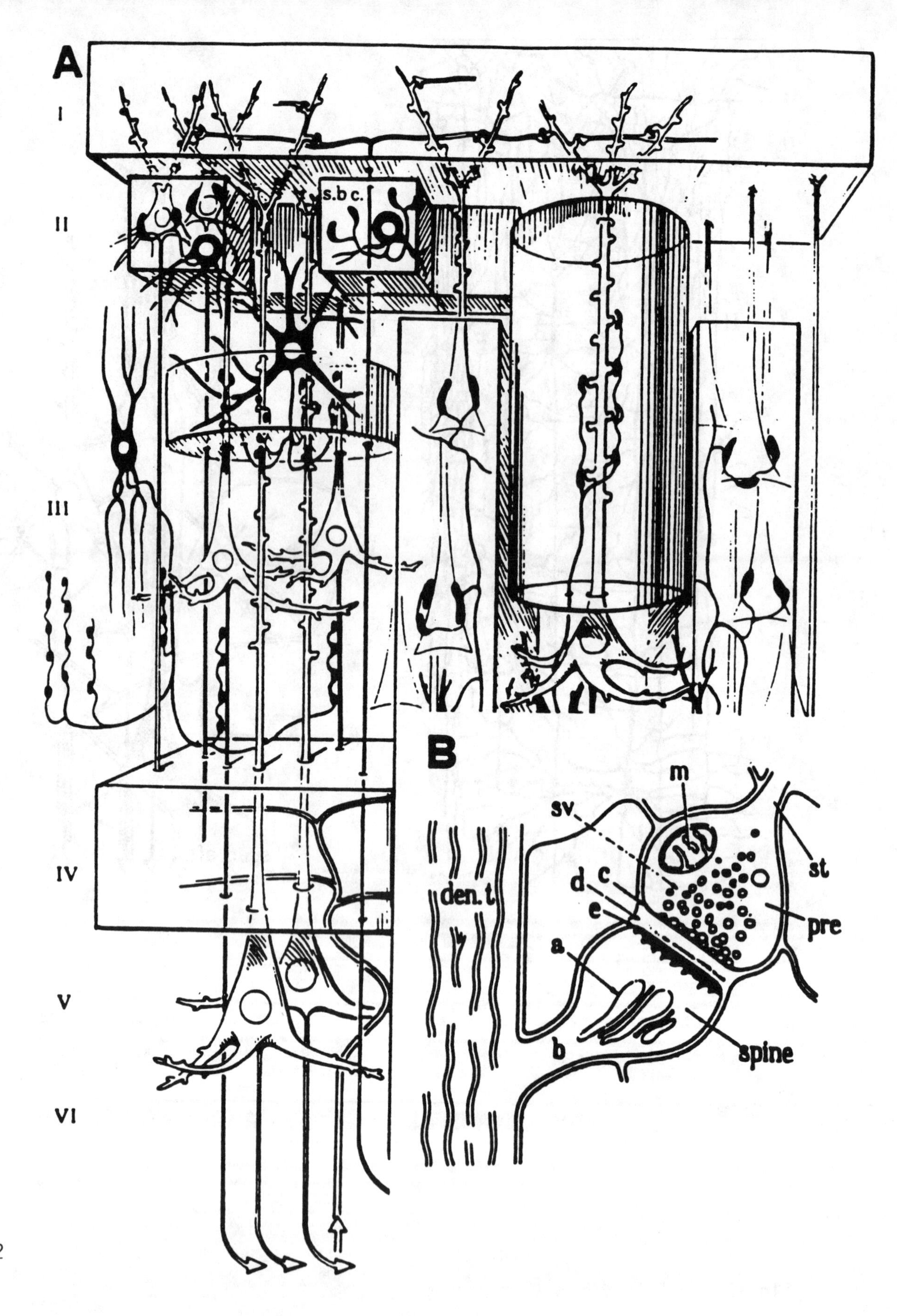

Fig. 2

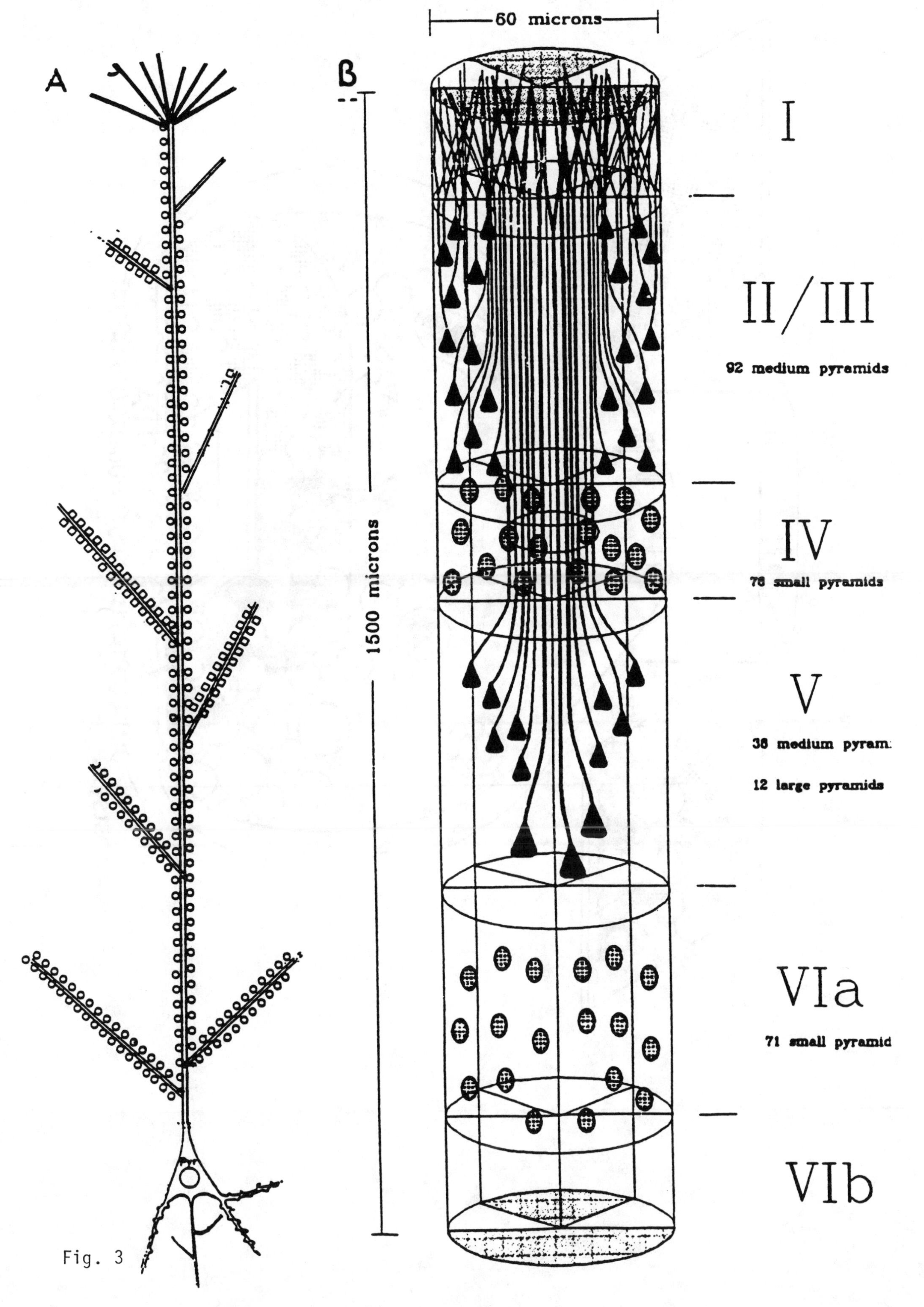
A
B
60 microns
1500 microns
I
II/III
92 medium pyramids
IV
76 small pyramids
V
38 medium pyram
12 large pyramids
VIa
71 small pyramid
VIb

Fig. 3

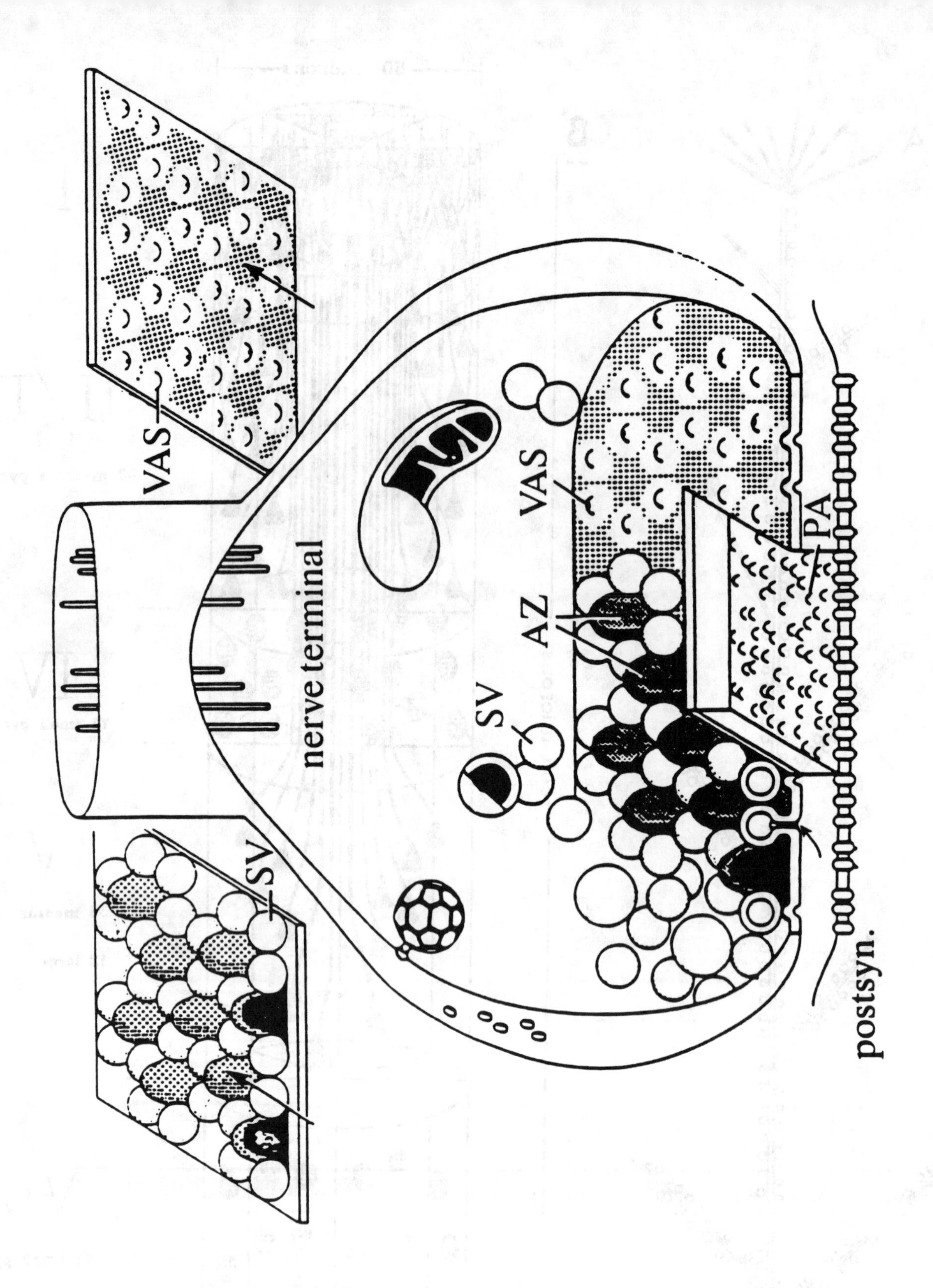

Fig. 4

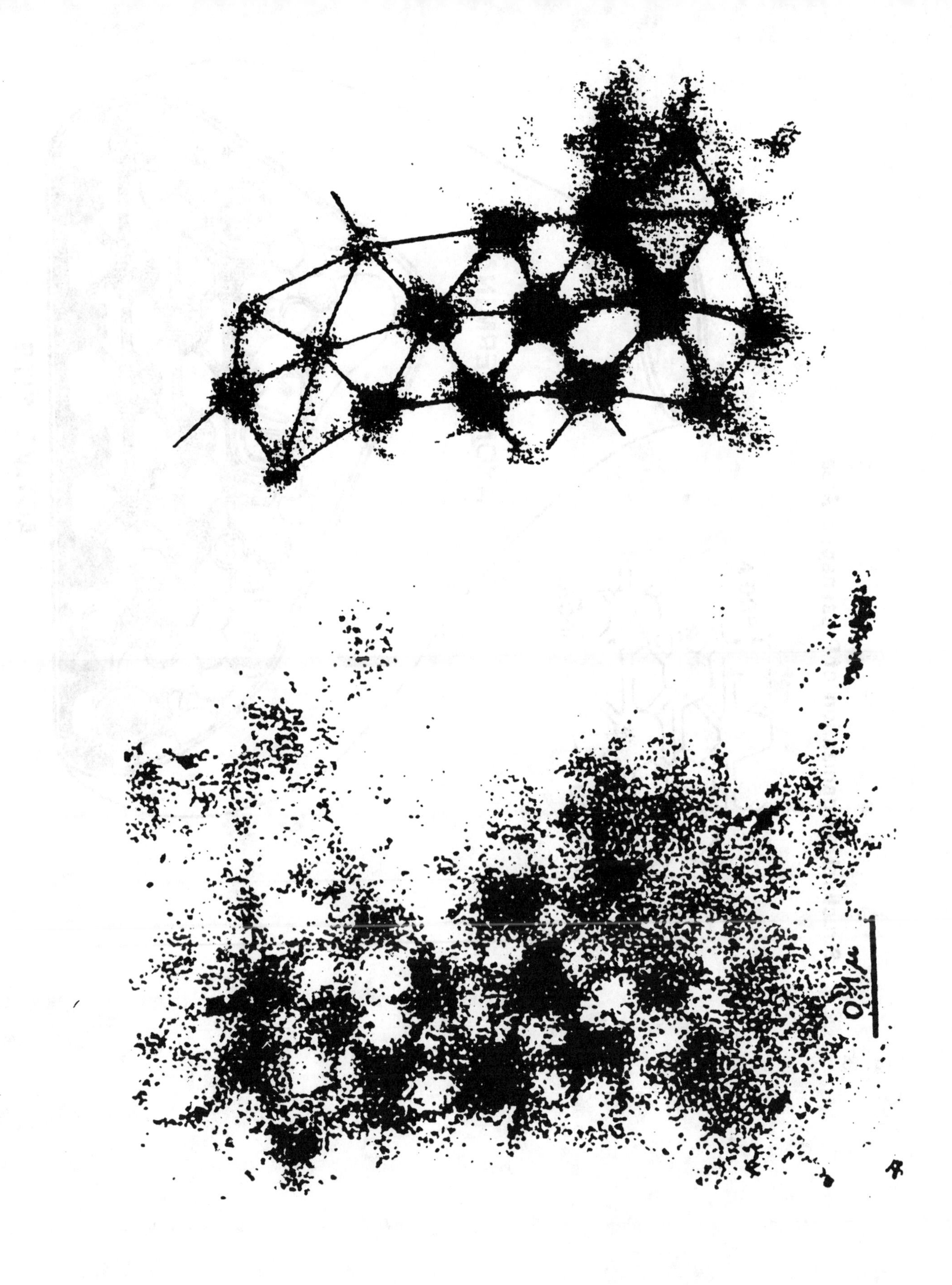

Fig. 5

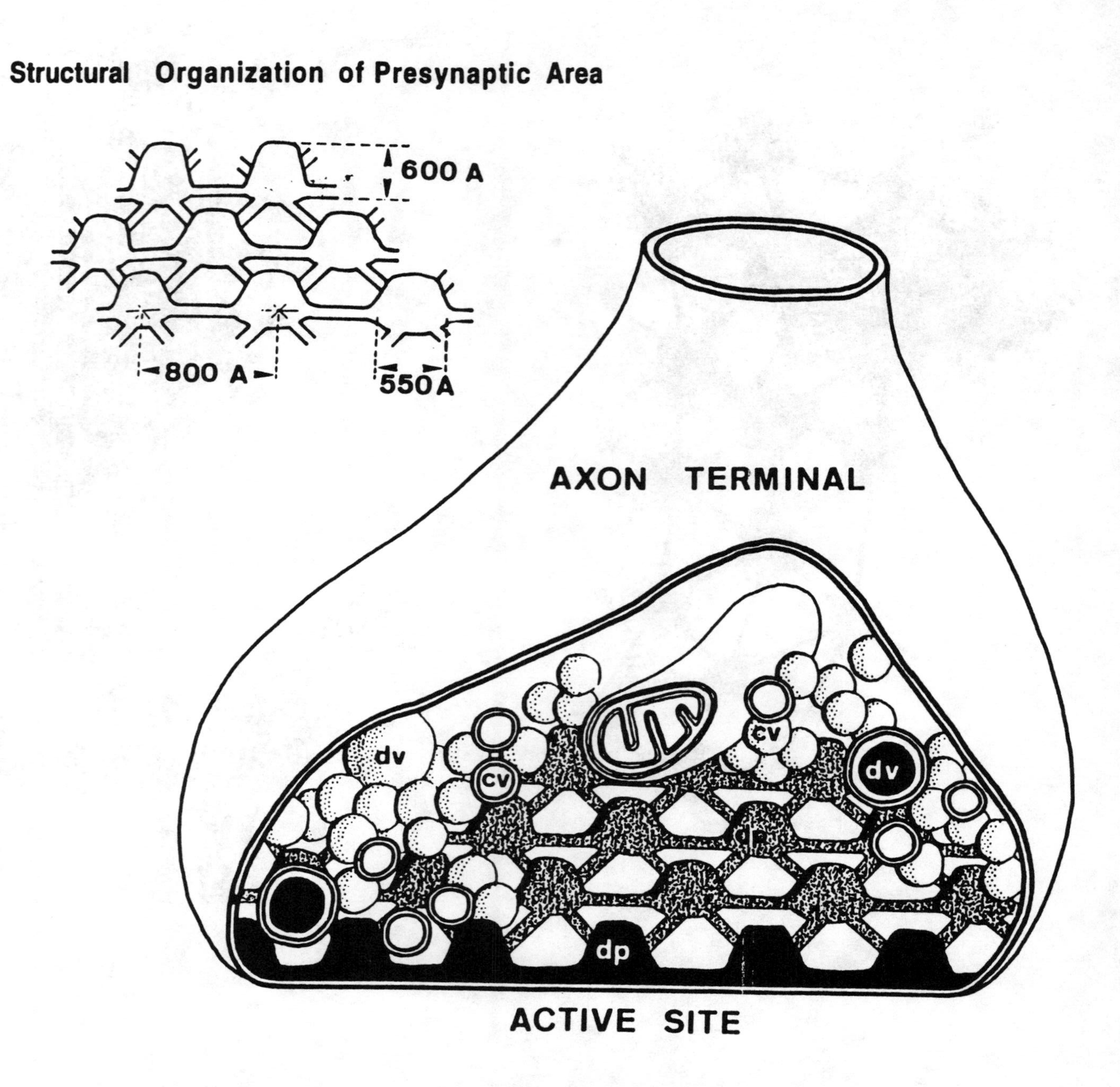
Structural Organization of Presynaptic Area
600 A
800 A
550A
AXON TERMINAL
dv
cv
cv
dv
dp
ACTIVE SITE

Fig. 6

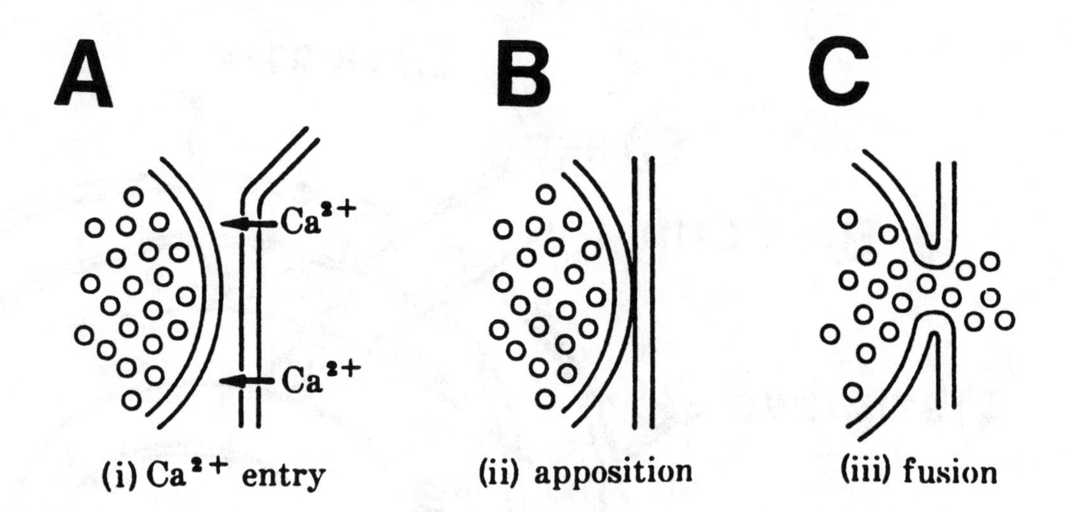
A
B
C
Ca²+
Ca²+
(i) Ca²+ entry
(ii) apposition
(iii) fusion

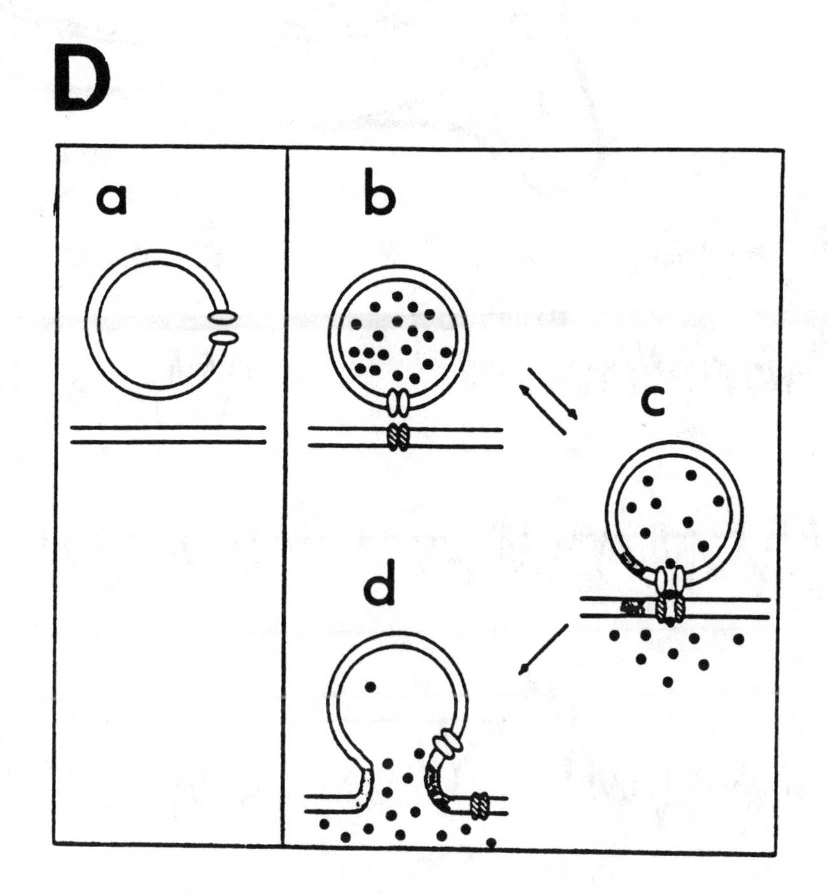
D
a
b
c
d

Fig. 7

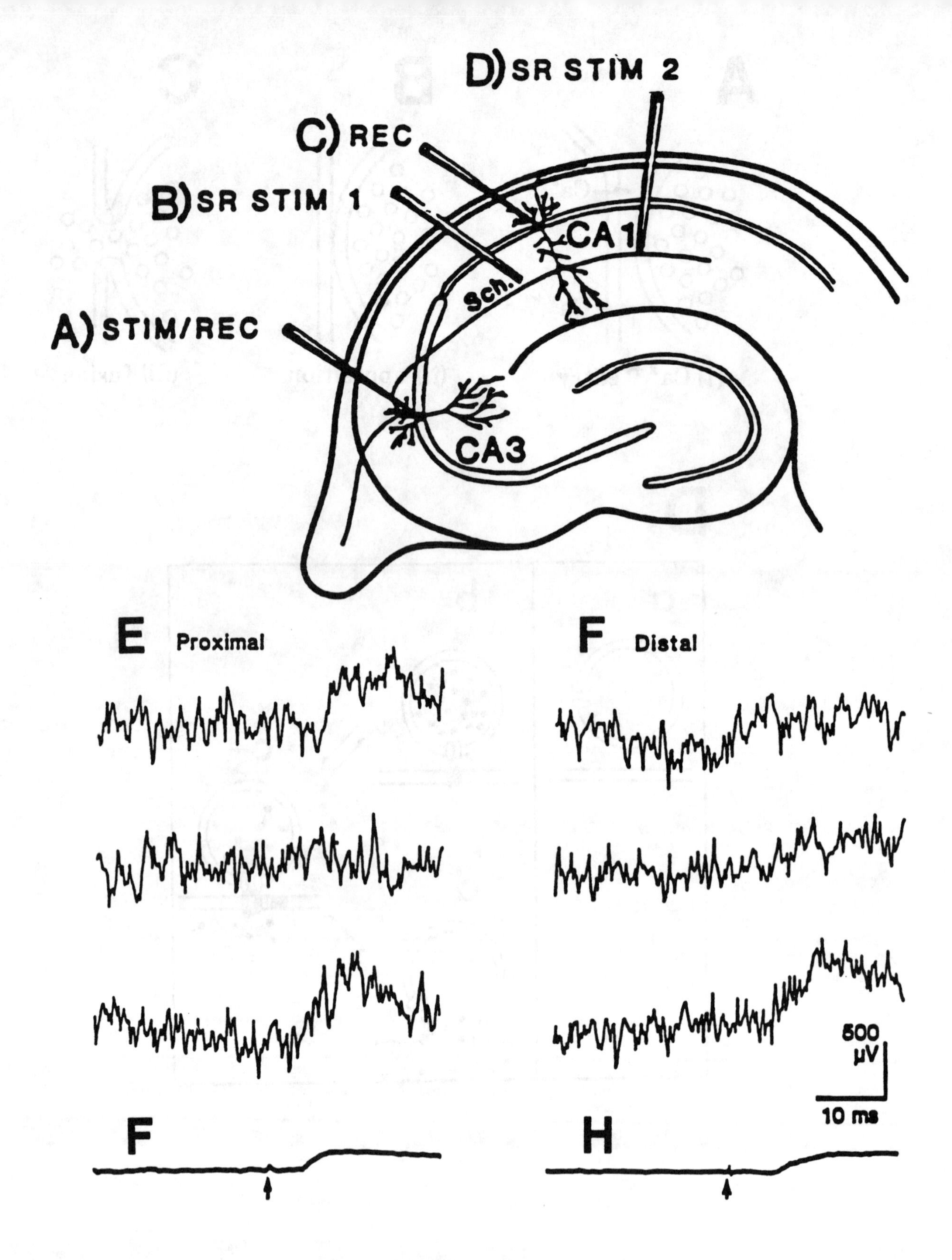

D) SR STIM 2
C) REC
B) SR STIM 1
CA1
Sch.
A) STIM/REC
CA3
E
Proximal
F
Distal
500
µV
10 ms
F
H

Fig. 8

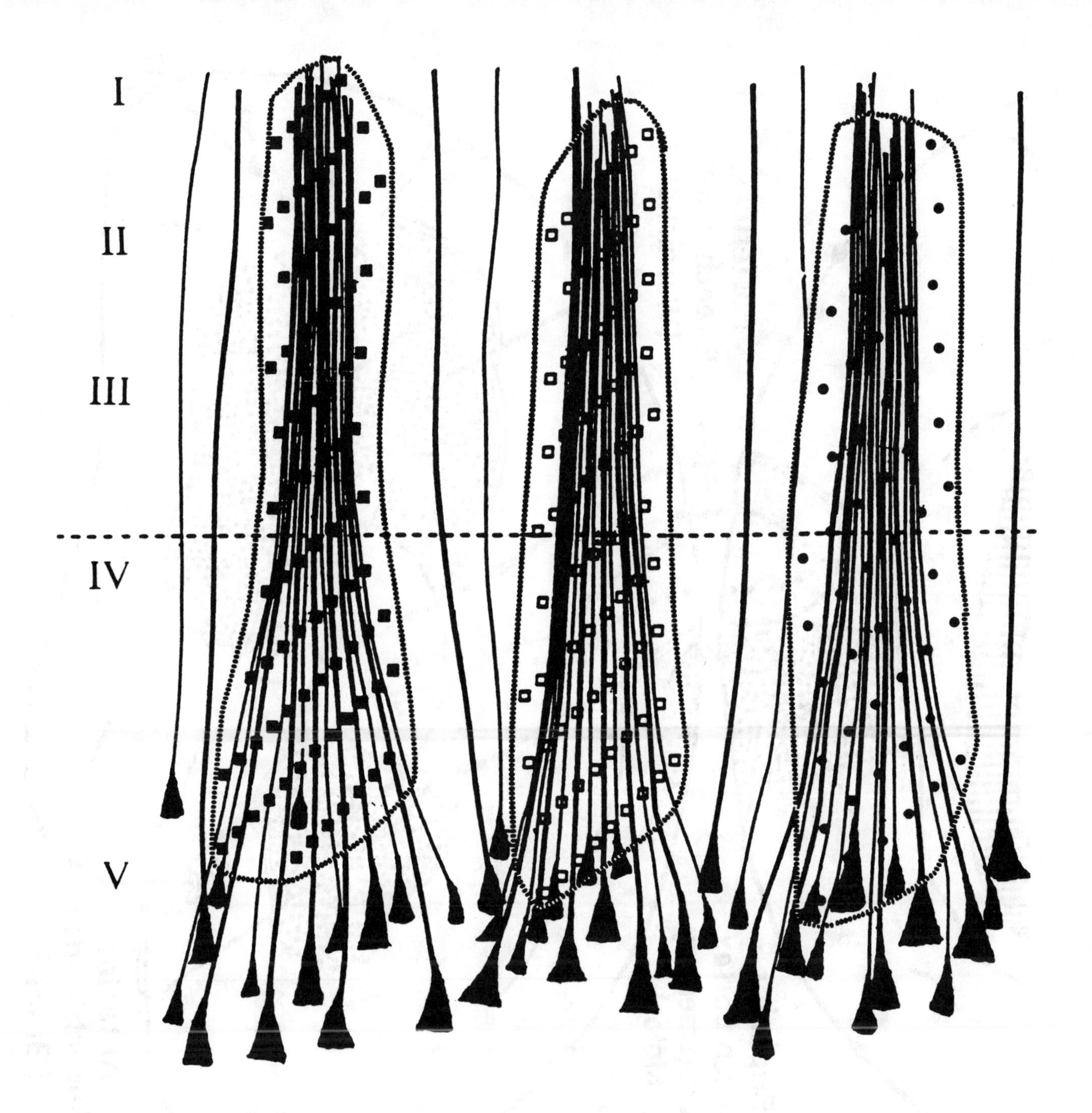

Fig. 9

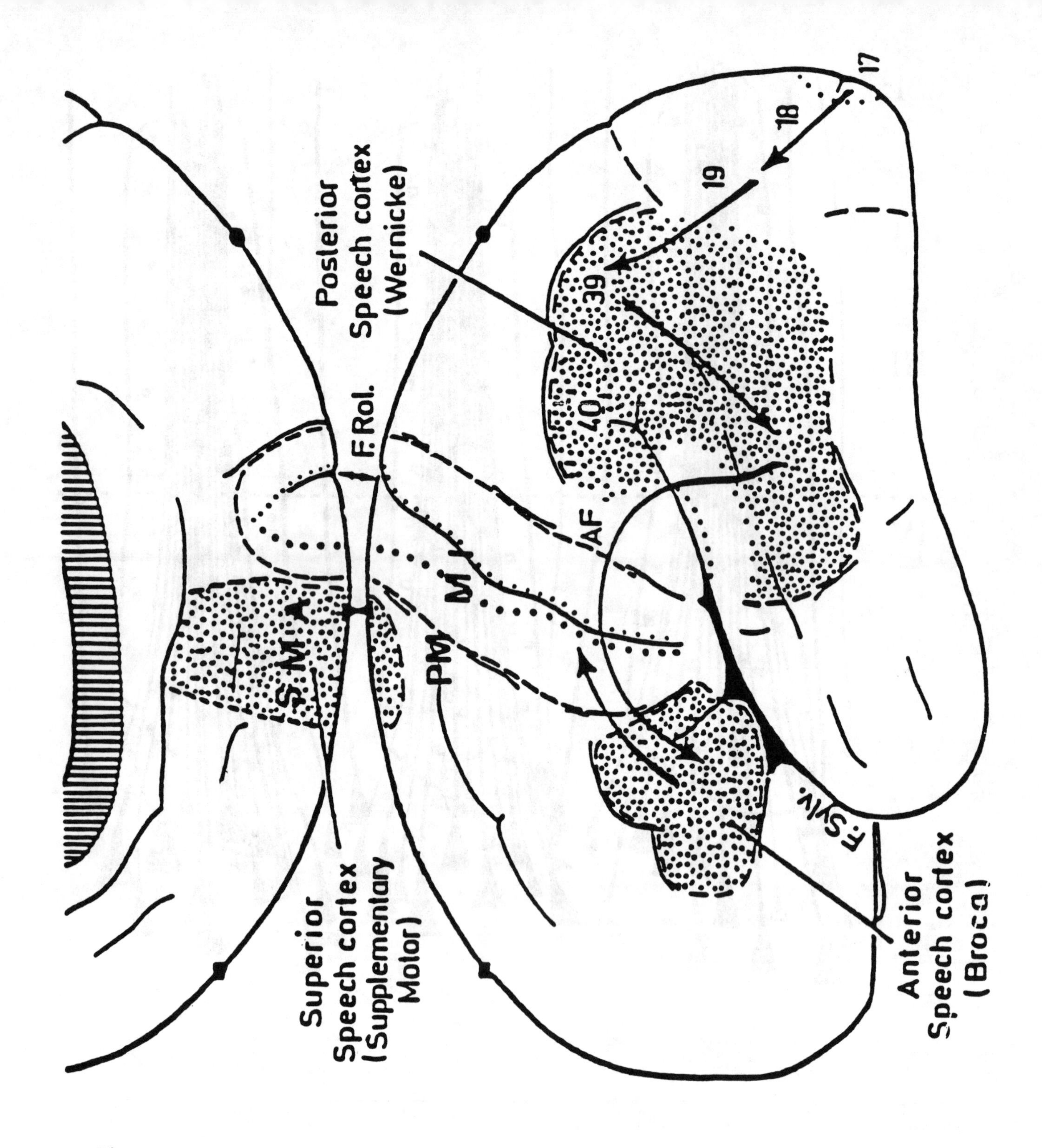

Posterior Speech cortex (Wernicke)
F.Rol.
17
18
19
39
40
AF
M I
PM
S M A
F.Sylv.
Superior Speech cortex (Supplementary Motor)
Anterior Speech cortex (Broca)

Fig. 10

Viewpoint

Neurodynamics and Synergetics

Michael Stadler and Peter Kruse
Institute of Psychology and Cognition Research
University of Bremen, Germany

NEURODYNAMICS AND SYNERGETICS

Michael Stadler and Peter Kruse
Institute of Psychology and Cognition Research
University of Bremen, Germany

Some problems in mind-brain-research

The mind-brain-problem has been discussed by philosophers over more than 2000 years. Today it gains new interest in the sciences, especially in neurobiology and neuropsychology. Although it seems to be a great advantage that this problem may now be reanalysed in the context of empirical investigation instead of being claimed by a rather unfruitful "ignorabimus"-position, there remain some very strong principle embarrassments concerning this topic.

1. Cognitive and brain processes obviously are on totally different scales of system behavior. The elementary dynamics of neuronal brain processes take place in the order of magnitude of 10^{12} to 10^{15} major events per second. In the stream of consciousness, on the other hand, no more than 100 bits/sec of information can be analyzed. The enormous complexity of the neural network is confronted with the unity of mental events.
2. Brain processes consist of myriads of identical action potentials forming global spatial and temporal patterns. The language of the brain is an unspecific "click, click" as Heinz von Foerster (1985) put it. The mental events on the other hand are rich of different sensory qualities and are capable of continuous qualitative changes in a number of dimensions. The unspecifity of neuronal events is confronted with the specifity of meaning in the cognitive sphere.
3. The brain processes seem to be governed by syntactic rules from which structures of any kind but without any observable meaning emerge. On the other hand phenomenal events are always meaningful and make sense for the individual. The syntax of brain processes is confronted with the semantics of mental events. The relations between meanings are organized by different laws than brain processes obey to.
4. The brain processes have well defined elements, the neurons, with well defined connections between one another, the synapses. The phenomenal events on the other hand have no such elements but instead, as the Gestaltists have pointed out, holistic features (Koffka 1935). Any part of the phenomenal field influences and is influenced by all other parts. The - on first sight - relatively discrete functioning on the neuronal level is confronted with the obvious field-like interactions in cognition (Kruse et al. 1987).
5. The most suspicious problem in mind-brain-research seems to be the assumption of causal relationships between material and immaterial events. While most philosophers and natural scientists agree that there are causal effects of the brain processes on the mental events, there is strong scepticism for causal relationships the other way round because such an assumption seems to violate the lawof conservation of energy. As long as one does not dare to assume brain effects caused by mental efforts the mind is only an epiphenomenon of the brain.

Cognitive neurobiologists and psychologists have to keep in mind all these problems when trying to explain brain-mind-relationships.

The synergetic approach

Some of the problems may be solved by using the theoretical and mathematical tools of an new interdisciplinary field of research called "synergetics". Synergetics was founded by Hermann Haken in the early seventies (see Haken 1977) and now has broad interdisciplinary relevance in the natural and even in the social sciences. Synergetics "is concerned with the cooperation of individual parts of a system that produces macroscopic spatial, temporal, or functional structures", as it was defined in the preface to the now about sixty volumes of the "Springer series of synergetics" (1977ff.) edited by Hermann Haken. The synergetic theory was first developed to explain the cooperative phenomena giving rise to laser light. Later it was applied to fluid dynamics to explain the Bénard-instability. Today there are synergetic approaches to explain cooperative phenomena in biological rhythms, movement regulation, preceptual multistability and population dynamics.

The first step of a synergetic analysis is to demonstrate the existence of non-linear phase transitions in a complex system. A phase transition is an autonomous reorganisation of macroscopic order emerging spontaneously from elementary interactions. For this reorganisation certain control parameters can be named which release a sudden phase transition to a higher order state of the system when continuously enhanced. The phase transition is preceded by an autocatalytical destabilisation of the system which is manifested in critical fluctuations and by a critical slowing down of the innersystemic tendency to conserve the existing ordered state. The non-linear behaviour of the system is explained by concurring modes which reach a bifurcation point where one of the modes predominates the others by slaving the elementary components of the process. This predominating mode is called the order parameter. In a synergetic system there is a certain circular causality between microscopic and macroscopic processes. The macroscopic structure emerges from and organizes the microscopic interactions of elementary components of the system.

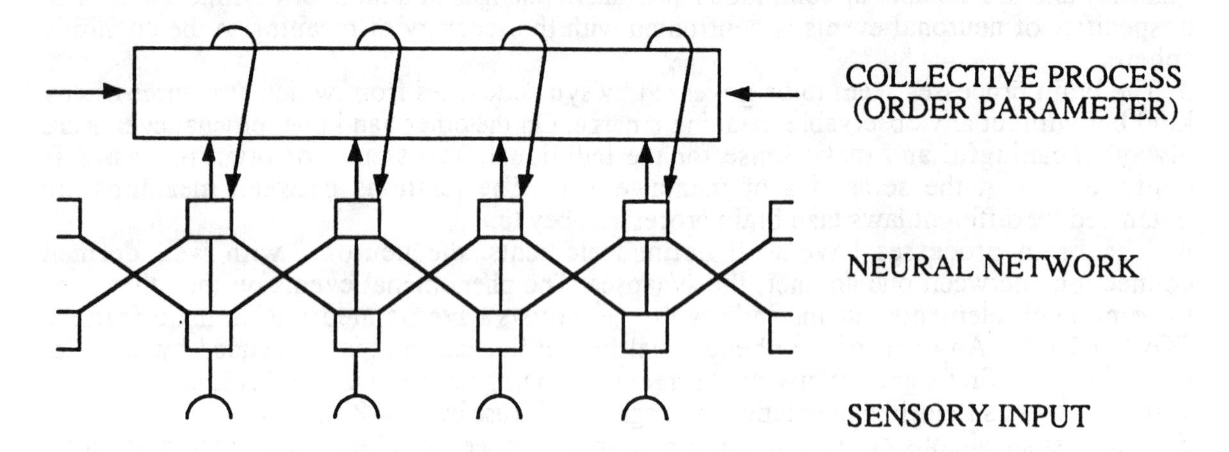

Fig. 1: Micro-macro-relation in mind-brain-dynamics

Applied to mind-brain-dynamics such a circular causal process may be modelled in the following way. The micro processes of the nervous network give rise to a macroscopic collective process, for instance to a temporal synchronicity distributed over more or less distant areas of the brain. This collective process, if it predominates, represents a certain rhythmic pattern, the order parameter, which reinfluences the microscopic processes in the neural network (figure 1).

One of the main results of the synergetic approach is the obvious analogy between pattern formation and pattern recognition (Haken 1991). In the highly developed biological system of the brain pattern formation may be even identical with pattern recognition. This assumption represents an important step towards an empirical handling of the mind-brain-problem. If the macroscopic order parameter, which has emerged from the elementary activity, represents and governs this activity, it may at the same time represent the cognitive process which influences the behaviour of the organism by its nervous processes.

Following the assumption that pattern formation is pattern recognition, one would have overcome some of the problems of the mind-brain-relation mentioned above. The dynamics of perception, thinking and memory need not be reduced to elementary brain processes. The cognitive dynamics may be represented directly by the macrodynamics of the brain. In this case cognitive phenomena may be used as a methodological window for observing and understanding brain activity. The relevance of many different macrodynamic neuronal processes for cognitive phenomena has been claimed in the last fifty years of brain research. Wolfgang Köhler (1949) was the first who ascertained a concretization of such a macroprocess, of the D.C.-fields. His hypothesis was corroborated by Lashley, Sperry, and Pribram who showed that perception is resistant against the disturbance of these fields. Today D.C.-fields are interpreted as an unspecific background activity of the brain (cf. Kruse et al. 1987).

Donald Hebb forwarded the hypothesis that certain cell assemblies might be the substrata of memory and perceptual phenomena. Hebb`s ideas have influenced very strongly the neural network theorists of today. Lashley thought about interference patterns as a distance bridging emergent macroscopic brain process. He influenced Karl Pribram (1971) to formulate his hologram idea of brain functioning which has been elaborated to the holonomic brain theory (1991). In the last years, there was a certain revival in the recognition of the importance of the EEG-rhythms for cognitive processes (Mountcastle 1992). Walter Freeman and later Wolf Singer and the Marburg group around Eckhorn and Reitböck investigated the selforganzing properties of the EEG in the gamma band (cf. Haken and Stadler 1990). The 40 Hz waves seem to be good candidates for figure-ground resolution and they may even be interpreted as attractors for meaning in perception. Finally an interesting hypothesis was brought forward by Sir John Eccles during one of the Elmau-meetings on synergetics about the possibility of immaterial macro processes influencing the material neuronal micro processes in the brain without violating the law of energy conservation. Eccles (1985) proposed macro processes analog to the probability fields in quantum physics as a representation of the mind in the brain.

There are enough unanswered questions about the relation between cognition and brain processes. Even if one accepts the analogy between pattern formation and pattern recognition and the circular interaction between macroscopic and microscopic brain processes as proposed by the synergetic approach, the question, which brain process is the representative of cognition, remains to be answered. Furthermore, there is the philosophical question whether there is a correlation or an identity between brain processes and mind. The possibility of an empirical test of the identity theory as proposed by Herbert Feigel`s autocerebroscope (1958) may be approached by new technical developments. The scenario of a PET or NMR-biofeedback experiment has come into sight. This level of data collection promises to develop fruitful hypotheses and should not be rejected in brain research.

Given the assuption that the brain is a selforganizing system and that cognitive processes are based on the elementary neronal dynamics of the brain, the synergetic approach can be concretized in three empirical hypotheses:

- It is possible to demonstrate non-linear phase transitions in cognition. For example continuous changes in stimulus conditions are able to trigger sudden reorganizations in perception. Perceptual organisation can not be reduced to the properties of the stimulus.
- Stable order in cognition is the result of underlying neuronal dynamics and therefore critically bound to instability. For example any percept is the result of a process of dynamic order formation. Because of the underlying dynamics perception is in principle multistable. Each stable percept can be destabilized and each instable percept can be stabilized.
- Meaning is an order parameter of the elementary neuronal dynamics. For example in the instability of ambiguous displays the basic order formation of perception can be influenced by subtle suggestive cues.

In the following, some examples of perceptual experiments are presented which may demonstrate the psychophysical significance of the synergetic approach.

Structure by iteration

Frederic C. Bartlett described in one of his books (1951) a nice little experiment which showed that an iterative performance may reveal hidden structures in homogeneous areas. Bartlett used the method of serial reproduction to show that a dot on a blank piece of paper seen for a second or so has changed it's position on another blank paper after reproduction. If this reproduced dot is again reproduced by another subject, it will another time be displaced and so on.

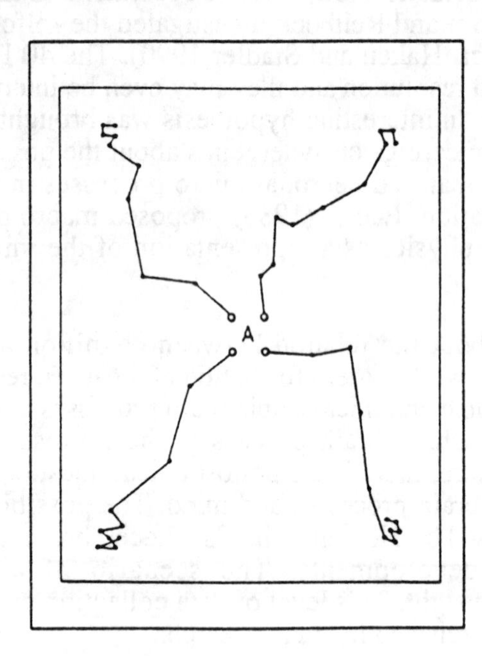

Fig. 2: Phenomenon of the wandering dot

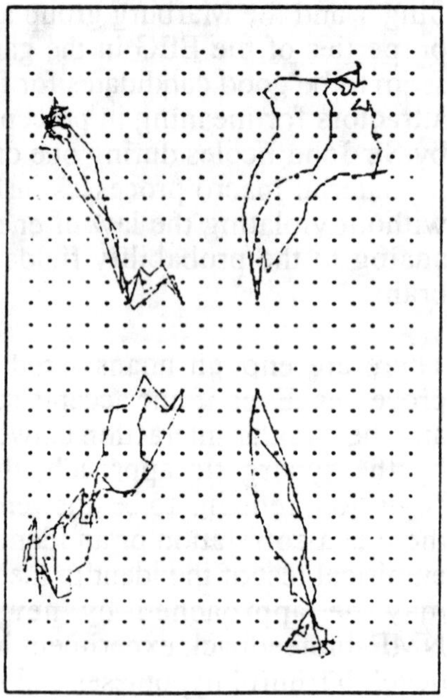

Fig. 7: Simulation of the phenomenon of the wandering dot

We adapted this experiment for our purposes and investigated this phenomenon of the wandering dot systematically (Stadler et al. 1991). In figure 2 some typical trajectories of wandering dots starting from different positions A in the middle of the area are reproduced. It seems, that the dots first take small steps, then longer steps and then diminish their steps again until they have found an attractor near one of the corners of the area from which they dot cannot flee again. The trajectories look as if there is an invisible potential gradient distributed over the area which causes the dots to make these particular movements. Obviously the wandering dots show a non-linear behaviour on this virtual potential gradient and such a behaviour seems to be in contradiction to the linear texture gradients distributed over surfaces as described by J.J. Gibson (1950) and the ecological school (figure 3).

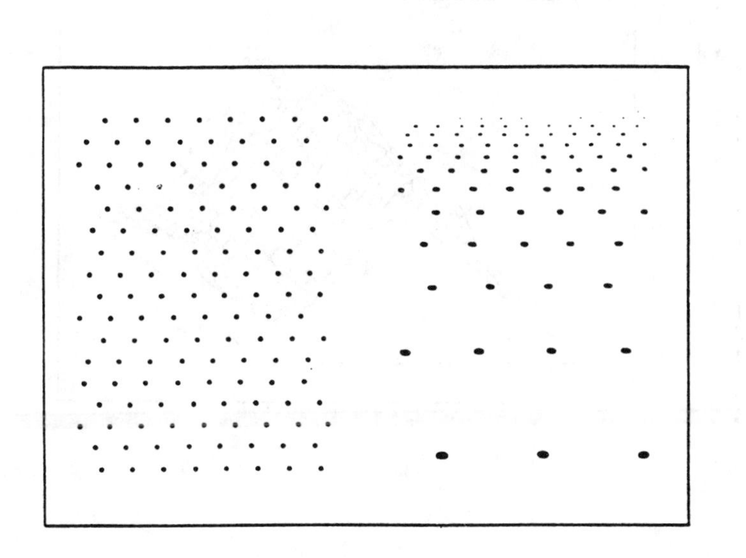

Fig. 3: Texture gradients (Gibson 1955)

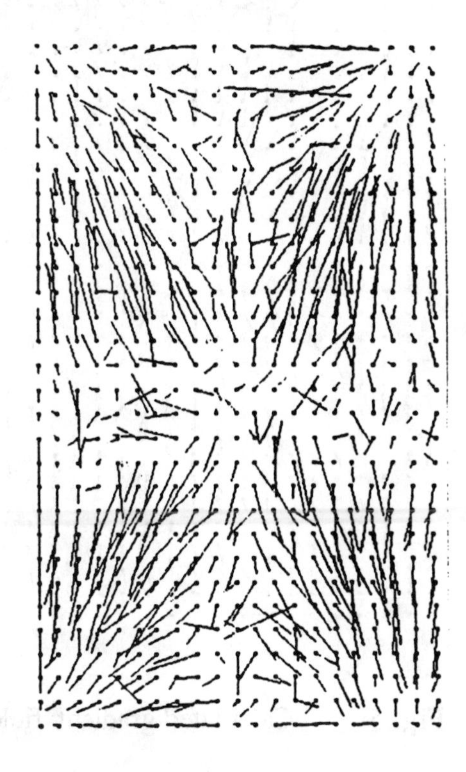

Fig. 4: Displacement vectors of one Subject

Attempts were made in our laboratory to measure the underlying non-linear potential fields. For this purpose first the displacement vectors were collected for a 21x29 dot-position-pattern from 10 Ss. Figure 4 shows the result of one of them. Next the raw vectors of all individual experiments were subjected to a vectorial analysis procedure by which the sources of each vector are integrated over the whole pattern and the circular potential is divided from the gradient potential. (The mathematical procedure is described in Stadler et al. 1991.) Figure 5 shows the calculated vector field of the averaged data of 10 Ss. Here we find already a very regular distribution of the vectors on the field, showing the non-linearities of the field, i.e. the bifurcation saddle in the middle and the attractors near the four corners. Figure 6 shows the gradient potential as a landscape over which the dots move like spherical particles. In figure 7 (see figure 2) a model calculation of these movements is shown, which resembles very good the empirical data of figure 2.

The experiment shows very good the hidden non-linear structure of a homogeneously stimulated perceptual field. Stabilities and instabilities in this field are represented by bifurcation areas (repellers) and attractor areas. The virtual structure, which is effective in perception but not visible, shows directly the field characteristics of the underlying macrodynamic brain process. The properties of stability and instability require more detailed investigation, for they represent system properties which may be analyzed on the brain level as well as on the psychophysical level.

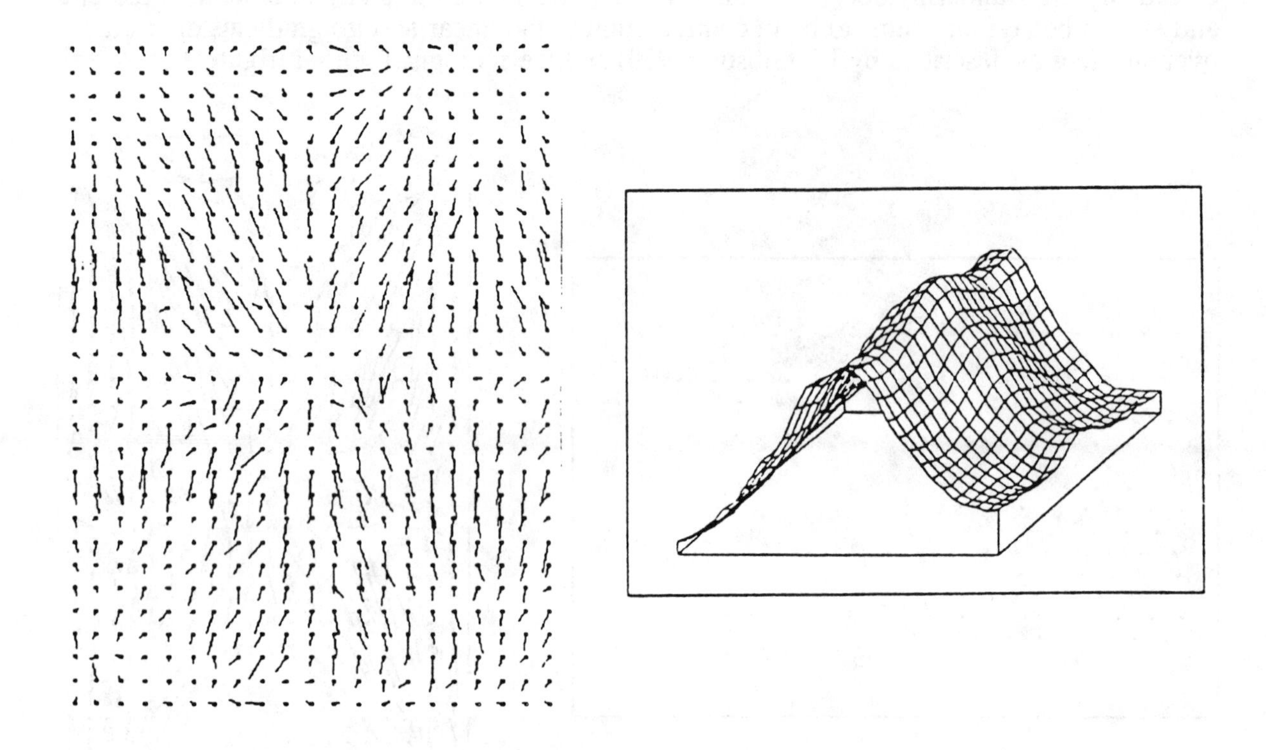

Fig. 5: Calculated gradient field (10 Ss) Fig. 6: Calculated gradient potential

Stability, instability, multistability

Inspite of the apparent stability of our daily perceptions, instability and multistability seems to be a basic feature of all perceptual processes. Figure 8 shows an example in which we can observe directly the fluctuating activity in the visual system on the search for stability. There are obviously different modes (collective processes) which compete for some time and which give the whole pattern a dynamic appearance. Non of the modes is able to predominate as an order parameter. Therefore no pattern is stabilized for more than a few seconds.

Demonstrations of multistability in perception, the so-called reversible figures like the Necker-cube, Rubin's vase/ face-picture, the Maltese-cross, the rabbit/dog-pattern and many others, are very well known in cognition research. Usually there are two predominating stable states which alternate periodically. Figure 9 shows the underlying potential of such a reversible process, as it is used for model calculations by Ditzinger and Haken (1989, 1990).

Fig. 8: Instable visual pattern

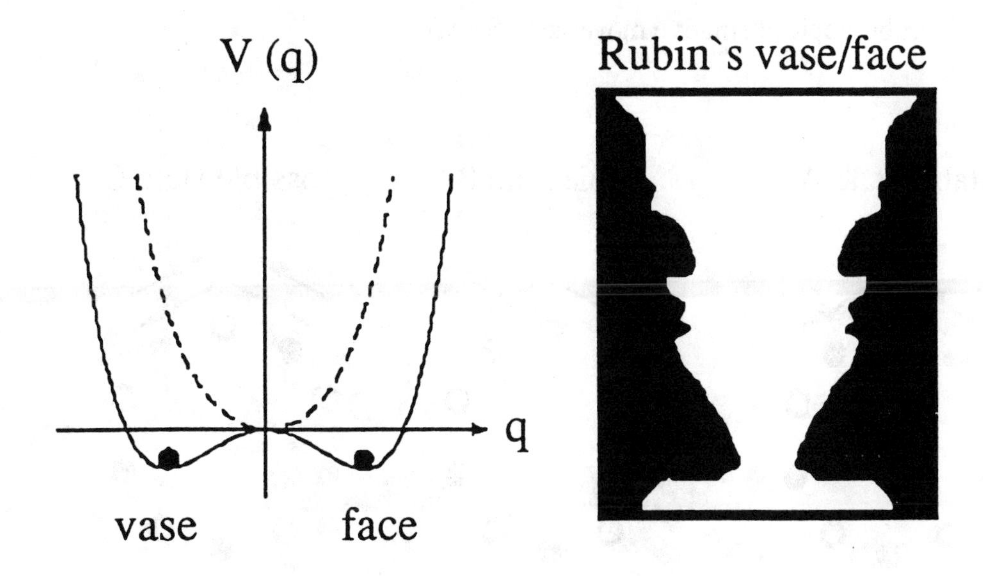

Fig. 9: Reversible pattern and underlying potential (modified from Haken 1991)

In our experiments we preferred dynamic displays to analyse multistable behaviour because in motion perception the systematic variation of a control parameter is easier than in static pictures. Additionally ambiguous apparent movement patterns are very reliable in their dynamic behaviour and the reversion process is well defined for perceivers (see Kruse 1988). Figure 10 and 11 show the two stimulus situations used: the stroboscopic alternative movement (figure 10, SAM) and the circular apparent movement (figure 11, CAM). The change from one alternative to the other shows the phenomenon of hysteresis as it is predicted in the synergetic model for phase transitions (cf. Kruse, Stadler, Strüber 1991). We could demonstrate in a variety of experiments that it is possible to influence the degree of stability or instability of such multistable patterns by contextual and semantic influences.

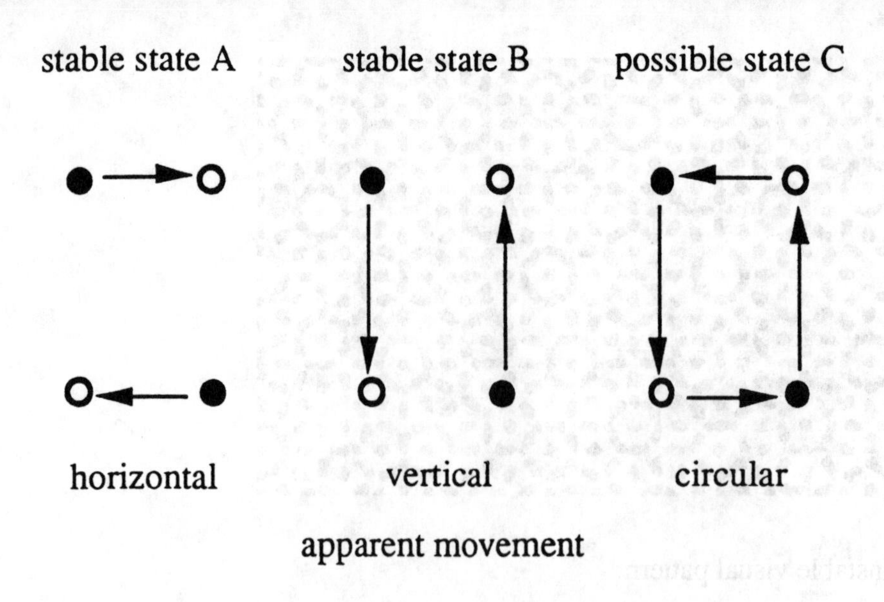

Fig. 10: Stroboscopic alternative movement (SAM)

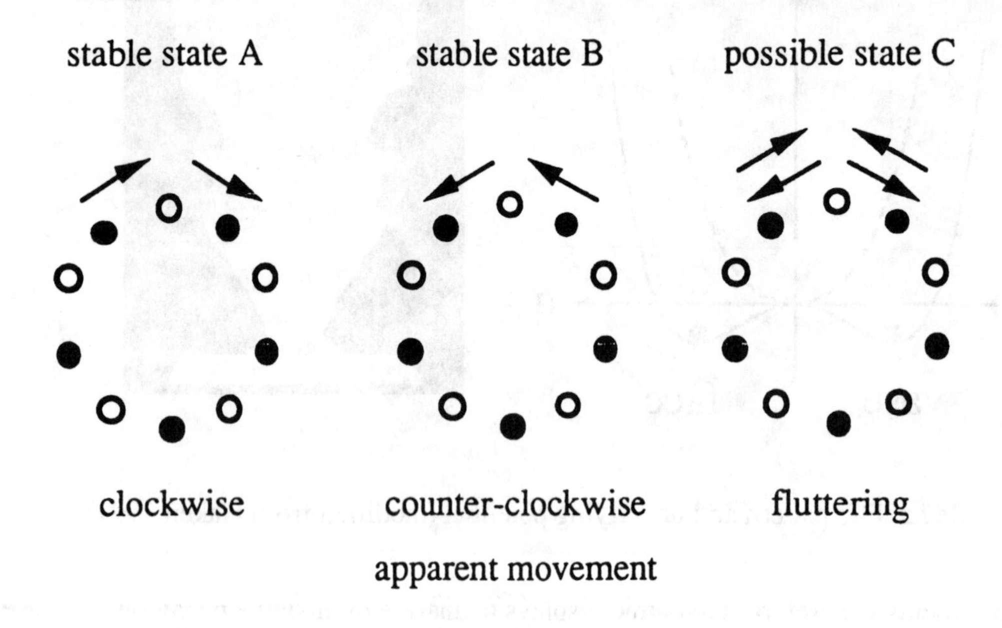

Fig. 11: Circular apparent movement (CAM)

The potential landscape underlying the dynamics of the reversion process can be altered by introducing gestalt factors like common motion (figure 12) or figural identity (figure 13), by perceptual learning, or even by very subtle semantic cues.

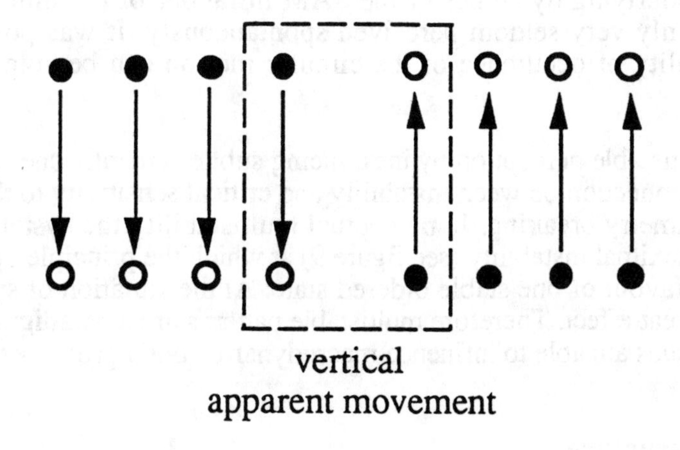

Fig. 12: Stabilizing the multistable SAM by introducing a strong vertical bias (gestalt factor of common motion)

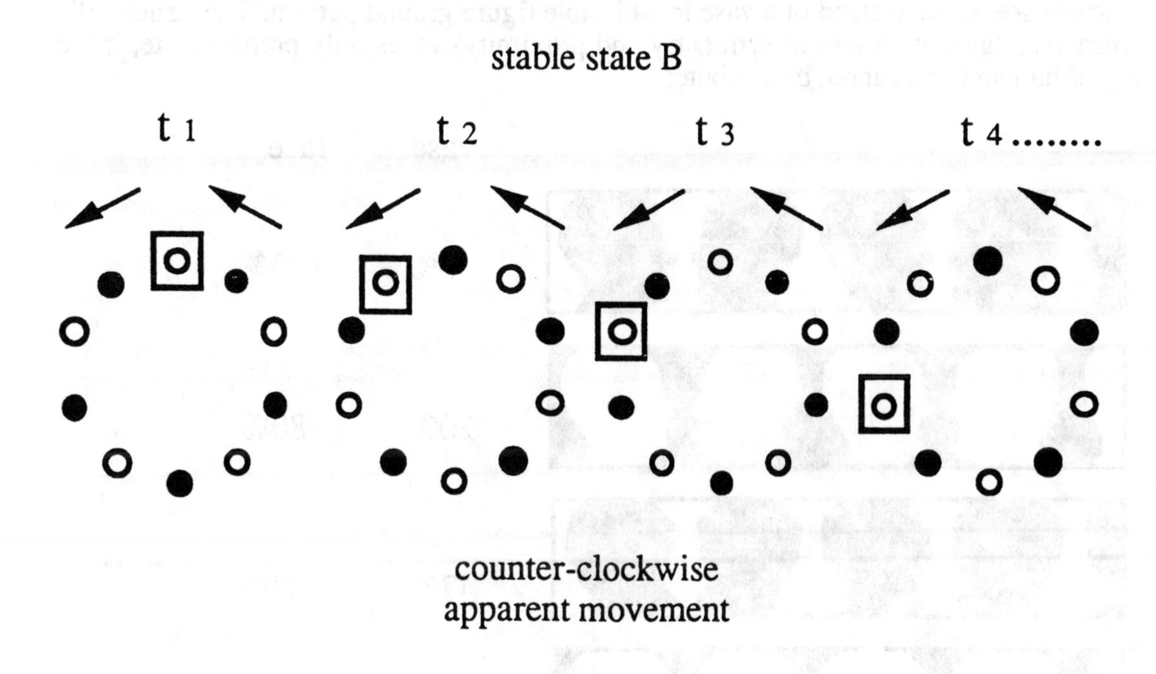

Fig. 13: Stabilizing the multistable CAM by introducing a strong counter clockwise bias (gestalt factor of figural identity)

In the experiment of perceptual learning the bi-stable SAM was further destabilized by enhancing the probability of occurence of the third theoretically possible perceptual alternative (see figure 10). In this experiment the CAM was used in a training session to change the potential landscape of the underlying dynamics of the SAM in favour of the third version "circular motion" which is only very seldom perceived spontaneously. It was possible to demonstrate that the probability of occurence of the circular motion can be significantly enhanced by training.

The aspect of influencing multistable perception by introducing subtle semantic cues supports the theoretically predictable connection between instability and critical sensitivity to the initial conditions in the case of symmetry breaking. In perceptual multistability the system passes again and again the point of maximal instability (see figure 9) at which the principle symmetry of the dynamics is broken in favour of one stable ordered state. At the situation of symmetry breaking little influence has great effect. Therefore multistable patterns are a paradigmatic tool to demonstrate that semantic cues are able to influence macrodynamic brain processes.

Semantic influences on structure

There are many examples in perceptual research showing top down influences from meaning to structure and even to basic sensory qualities in the research program of the so-called "new look" of the late forties and fifties (cf. Graumann 1966). One and the same green-brownish colour, for instance, is judged by many subjects more brown, if it is exposed in the form of a horse and more green if it is exposed in form of a leaf. Figure 14 shows that there is a clear preference to see a face instead of a vase in a bistable figure ground pattern. The structurally more attractive (gestalt factors of symmetry and proximity) vases only predominate, if the meaning of human faces cannot be attributed.

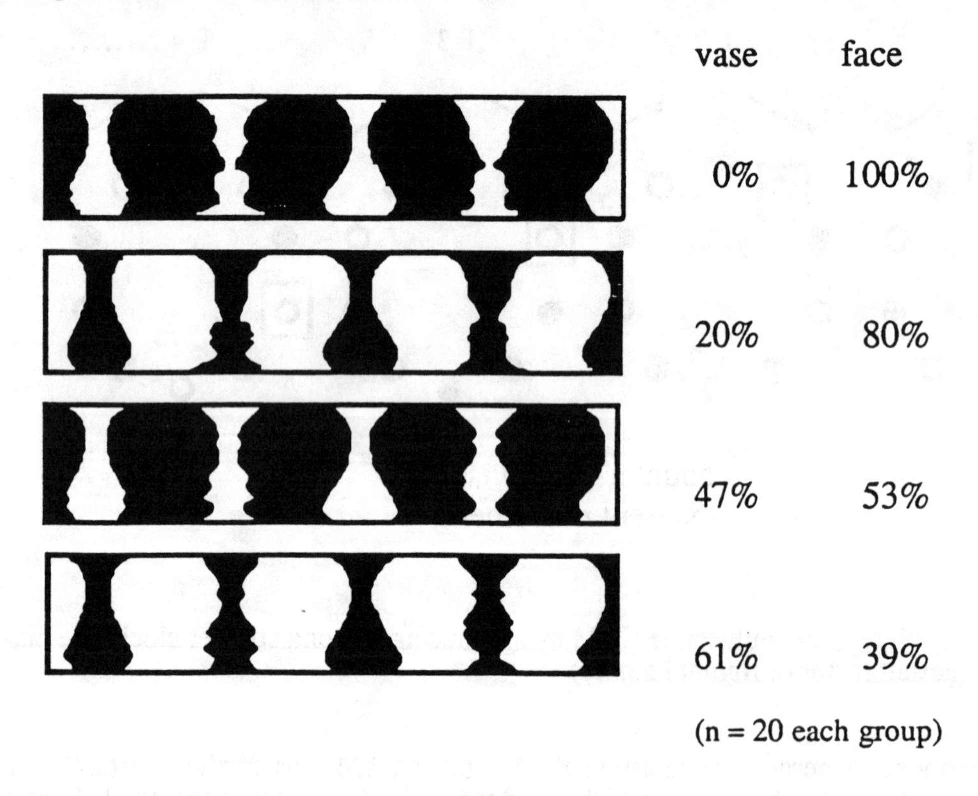

Fig. 14: Meaning predominates structure (figure-ground pattern from Kruse 1986)

For the investigation of semantic bias effects, again the dynamic stimulus patterns SAM and CAM were used. If the CAM, for instance, is composed of arrows pointing in an anti-clockwise direction instead of circular dots, this direction is preferred significantly in the bifurcation situation at first sight. Nearly all subjects see an anti-clockwise rotation of the apparent movement although the clockwise rotation in a directional display is preferred (Figure 15).

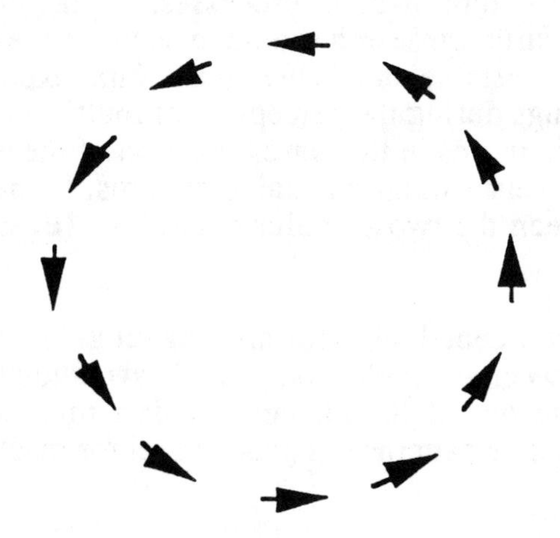

Fig. 15: Semantical bias (using arrows instead of dots for the CAM)

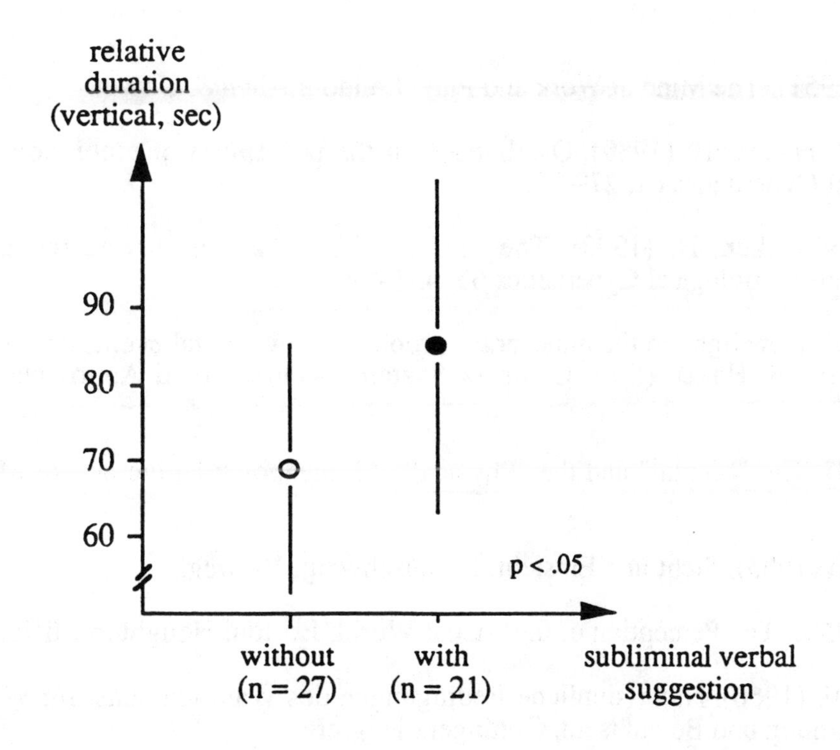

Fig. 16: Effect of subliminal verbal suggestion on the relative duration of the vertical movement version during a 3-minute-presentation of the SAM

Further experiments showed that the instability point of two perceptual alternatives is extremely sensitive to suggestive influences. Even subliminal verbal suggestions, e.g. "up and down like bouncing balls", given to the subjects below the auditive threshold during presentation of the SAM has a significant effect on the relative duration of the movement alternatives (figure 16).

The fact that meaning may influence the structure of brain processes, is predicted by the synergetic model of mind-brain-interaction. Further research should investigate the properties of macrodynamic brain processes during the instable and stable phase. First experiments in that direction demonstrate that EEG recordings during the perception of multistable patterns show a significant enhancement of the 40 Hz waves in the vertex position of the electrodes, which is not found during the perception of very similar but stable patterns. In the occipital EEG there is, however, no difference between the two stimulus conditions (Basar et al. in prep.).

The synergetic approach stimulates new experimental ideas for investigating the mind-brain-interaction on different levels of analysis between neurophysiology and psychology. Thus the concept of order parameters which emerge out of the elementary dynamics and which transform the basic instability into coherent stable patterns is a good model for macrodynamic brain-mind processes.

References:

Bartlett, F.C. (1951). The Mind at Work and Play. London: Allen & Unwin.

Ditzinger, T. & Haken, H. (1989). Oscillations in the perception of ambiguous patterns. Biological Cybernetics 61, 279-287.

Ditzinger, T. & Haken, H. (1990). The impact of fluctuations on the recognition of ambiguous patterns. Biological Cybernetics 63, 453-456.

Eccles, J. (1985). New light on the mind-brain-problem: How mental events could influence neural events. In: H. Haken (Ed.), Complex Systems - Operational Approaches. Berlin: Springer.

Feigl, H. (1958). The "Mental" and the "Physical". Minneapolis: University of Minnessota Press.

Foerster, H. von (1985). Sicht und Einsicht. Braunschweig: Vieweg.

Gibson, J.J. (1950). The Perception of the Visual World. Boston: Houghton Mifflin.

Graumann, C.-F. (1966). Nicht-sinnliche Bedingungen des Wahrnehmens. In: W. Metzger (Ed.), Wahrnehmung und Bewußtsein. Göttingen: Hogrefe.

Haken, H. (1977ff). Springer Series of Synergetics. Berlin: Springer.

Haken, H. (1977). Synergetics. Berlin: Springer.

Haken, H. (1991). Synergetic Computers and Cognition. Berlin: Springer.

Haken, H. & Stadler, M. (Eds.) (1990). Synergetics of Cognition. Berlin: Springer.

Hebb, D.O. (1949). The Organization of Behavior. New York: Wiley.

Köhler, W. & Held, R. (1949). The cortical correlate of pattern vision. Science 110, 414-419.

Koffka, K. (1935). The Principles of Gestalt Psychology. London: Routledge & Kegan Paul.

Kruse, P. (1986). Wie unabhängig ist das Wahrnehmungsobjekt vom Prozeß der Identifikation? Gestalt Theory 8, 141-143.

Kruse, P. (1988). Stabilität, Instabilität, Multistabilität. Selbstorganisation und Selbstreferentialität in kognitiven Systemen. Delfin, 6, 35-57.

Kruse, P., Roth, G. & Stadler, M. (1987). Ordnungsbildung und psychophysische Feldtheorie. Gestalt Theory 9, 150-167.

Kruse, P., Stadler, M. & Strüber, D. (1991). Psychological modification and synergetic modelling of perceptual oscillations. In: H. Haken & H.P. Koepchen (Eds.), Rhythms in Physiological Systems. Berlin: Springer.

Mountcastle, V.P. (1992). Preface to E. Basar and T.H. Bullock (Eds.), Induced rhythms in the brain. Boston: Birkhäuser.

Pribram, K.H. (1971). Languages of the Brain. Englewood Cliffs, N.Y.: Prentice-Hall.

Pribram, K.H. (1991). Brain and Perception. Hillsdale: Lawrence Erlbaum.

Stadler, M., Richter, P.H., Pfaff, S. & Kruse, P. (1991). Attractors and perceptual field dynamics of homogeneous stimulus areas. Psychological Research 53, 102-112.

I. The Dendritic Microprocess

Chapter 1

From Stochastic Resonance to Gabor Functions: An analysis of the probability density function of interspike intervals recorded from visual cortical neurons

Dale Berger and Karl H. Pribram

Center for Brain Research and Informational Sciences
Radford University
Radford, VA

INTRODUCTION

Receptive Fields

The neurophysiologist can readily study the output -- spike trains -- of neurons when they act as channels, but he has only limited access to the functions of the interactive synapto-dendritic process because of the small scale at which the processes proceed. A major breakthrough toward understanding was achieved, however, when Kuffler (1953) noted that he could map the functional dendritic field of a retinal ganglion cell by recording impulses from the ganglion cell's axon located in the optic nerve. This was accomplished by moving a spot of light in front of a paralyzed eye and recording the locations of the spot which produced a response in the axon. The locations mapped the extent of the responding dendritic field of that axon's parent neuron. The direction of response, inhibitory or excitatory, at each location indicated whether the dendrites at that location were hyperpolarizing or depolarizing.

However, spike trains recorded from axons reflect more than the architecture of the functional dendritic field; three separable influences can be identified: 1) those, such as the sensory stimuli which characterize the input to the neuron 2) those which parameterize the properties of the ensemble of dendritic activities of the neuron, and 3) those which directly determine the output of the neuron at the axon hillock (Pribram, Lassonde and Ptito, 1981). The influence of sensory stimuli (influence #1) is obtained, as in the Kufler experiments, by correlating input with spike train characteristics.

For a given stimulus condition a dendritic environment (influence #2) is generated from the excitatory and/or inhibitory character of the dendritic events per se. The assignment of a weighted rate process to the events of this dendritic microprocess reflects their degree of influence on the generating of spikes by the cells being examined. The neuron can thus be conceived as a processor of stochastic dendritic events which displays its computed output as the statistics of the sequence of inter-spike intervals.

In this paper the analysis of neural activity emphasizes properties of the distribution of inter-spike intervals. A random walk with positive drift model for simulating the interspike interval distribution is used to describe the unknown underlying process. This model incorporates two parameters that specify the temporal distribution of the first passage time of a diffusion process. These parameters, the drift coefficient and barrier height, are derived from the measured mean and standard deviation of the actual neural spike train intervals. The model is therefore a device for describing the underlying process.

If the process generating the interspike interval is stationary, without a temporal change in the probability density, an analysis based on a random walk with drift is potentially relevant. An early study indicated the random walk with positive drift yields an excellent fit to experimental data of inter-spike intervals recorded from spontaneous neural activity (Gerstein and Mandelbrot 1964). There are therefore theoretical and experimental reasons to believe the model based on the first-passage time of a random walk with positive drift realistically describes the process generating spike-train statistics.

When the spontaneous activity of neurons measured by extracellular recordings had been analyzed it was observed that the temporal distributions of inter-spike intervals resemble the distribution of the first passage time of a random walk with drift process (Lansky 1983; Lansky and Lanska 1987; Lansky and Radil 1987; Tuckwell 1976; Tuckwell and Cope 1980; Kryokov 1976; Yang and Chen 1978). The forward Kolmogorov form of the Fokker-Planck equation provides a formalism whose solution gives the probability density function of the process (Harrison 1985; Karlin and Taylor 1975). The forward equation is recovered whenever any of several types of random noise are assigned as the inputs to the Hodgkin-Huxley equations (Tuckwell 1986). The distribution for the first passage time of random walk with positive drift has also been referred to as the inverse Gaussian distribution (Wasan 1969; Johnson and Kotz 1970).

When viewed as a neuronal-spike generating process, the membrane potential of the neuron changes from the resting potential to threshold, at which time an action potential is initiated; after a brief refractory period the process is reset to the resting potential to begin another drift toward the threshold. In the formal model of spike generation the resting potential is considered the process origin and the threshold voltage as the absorbing barrier. Drift reflects the voltage change resulting from input current and membranae conductance. It is the probability density function of this process that is observed as the sequence of inter-spike intervals recorded extra-cellularly during the experiment. The spike-generating process is influenced by the collective dendritic activity of the neuron. The model process, which is a representation based on the formalism of the forward equation, provides the statistics describing the spike-rain intervals.

METHODS

Subjects

Subjects were eight adult cats obtained from the cattery at the University of California at Davis. A total of 339 spike trains from 110 visual cortical neurons were recorded. Eight spike trains were of sufficient duration and completeness to be useful for the analysis presented here.

Apparatus

The stimulus, consisting of sine wave gratings of variable spatial frequency, drift velocity and contrast, was displayed on a Tektonix type 602 XY oscilloscope. Orientation of gratings was varied mechanically. The display was maintained at a distance of 50 cm from the subject's head. The neural response was picked up using Haer tungten microelectrodes with impedance from one to six MegaOhms. A combination of an RCA 3140IC chip provided first amplification, constant input current of 5 picoamps, and a low output impedance. This device was fastened via alligator clip directly to the electrode. A large bore hypodermic needle inserted through the animal's scalp provided the ground. The signal was transmitted to the input of a Grass P511 J AC preamplifier with gain set at 10k, low pass at 3 Hz, high pass at 300 Hz, and a 50 Hz notch filter. This combination of settings allowed operation without a Faraday cage although partial screening around the animal's head was sometimes necessary. The output of the Grass amplifier was divided: one output went to an A-to-D converter input of PDB11 computer; another went to an adjustable Schmitt trigger; a third to a Tektronix model 5111A oscilloscope; and a fourth to an audio monitor. The output of the Schmitt trigger, set to fire when a spike appeared above background noise, was in turn sent to the alternate trace of the oscilloscope and audio monitor. A software window discriminator allowed setting two voltage windows for accepting spikes. Two separate records of interspike intervals were thus kept when two units were defined. Interspike interval lengths were rounded to the nearest millisecond.

Surgical Procedures

Craniotomy and implantation of two 6.5 mm tubular electrode chambers were performed under halothane anesthesia and sterile conditions. A ¼"-20 bolt was embedded in a cranial cap made of dental acrylic and fastened to the skull by four to six stainless steel screws. Trephine holes were centered at stereotaxic coordinates posterior 2.0 cm and left and right 0.5 cm. The trephine holes were thus placed over areas 17 and 18, and included, at their medial margins, cells activated by stimuli in the midline of the cat's visual field. It is these cells from which most of the recordings were made.

Experimental Procedures

The animal was allowed to recover from surgery for at least one week. On the morning of the experiment subjects were anesthetized with Ketamine and Valium, intubated, and fastened to the Kopp stereotactic apparatus by the head bolt. Subjects were paralyzed with 10 mg/kg Flaxedil to prevent muscle action. Respiration and temperature were stably maintained; heart rate and anal temperature were recorded every 15 min. Subsequent medication during the experimental session was limited to intravenously administered Valium and Flaxedil, titrated to the condition of the animal: Valium was administered when heart rate began to rise; Flaxedil was administered when hind leg muscle tension began to increase. One electrode chamber was opened and coordinates for the placement of the electrode were determined. Contact lenses with zero correction were inserted in both eyes, the eye ipsilateral to the recorded hemisphere was occluded. The electrode was then set with the stereotax to touch the surface of the brain where a small cut in the dura had been made.

The experimental room was darkened and recording commenced. A Wells hydraulic drive was used to slowly lower the electrode. A small flashlight, masked to project an oblong patch of light onto a ground glass or white paper screen at about 20 cm distance form the cat, was used as a search stimulus. When a responding unit was found an unaltered flashlight was used to illuminate a 50 cm by 38 cm stimulus card with 2.5 cm wide alternating black and white stripes, to hand-map the response of the unit. For this study only spike trains from cells whose receptive fields showed "simple" properties were used. The XY display monitor was positioned at the orientation which provided the best response of the unit. Using maximum contrast (0.8 on a scale were 1 equals maximum brightness on a background of total darkness) the frequency of the sine wave gratings and the velocity of their drift were varied until a maximum response was obtained; the direction of movement of black and white stripes over the visual field was reversed to check for directional selectivity.

<u>Testing Procedures</u>

The intent of the experiment was to contrast the stimulus which included the maximal response (determined by an online sample as the histogram with maximum amplitude) with suboptimal stimuli whose parameters were changed over one dimension at a time. After the optimal stimulus parameters had been determined, the experimental procedure was as follows: Recordings were made while the animal was in darkness; then the optimal condition was displayed twice; then again the dark-condition. After this, the variations of single stimulus parameters were carried out in the following order: variation 1; darkness; variation 1; darkness; variation 2; darkness; variation 2; darkness; variation 3; darkness; variation 3; darkness; etc., until all effective values of that variable were explored. At this point a new stimulus parameter was varied leaving the previously manipulated variable at optimum. The dark conditions preceding and following each comparison made it possible to detect linear drift of the spontaneous firing rate and to search later for stationarity in an analysis of covariance of firing rates. Presenting the optimal condition each time before and after a series of variations allowed for additional tests of stationarity for the conditions with stimulation. The first stimulus variable to be systematically changed was spatial frequency; the next was the velocity of the grating (temporal frequency); systematic changes in orientation and contrast followed if the unit held up long enough. After completion of the procedure search began for a second unit, and the sequence was repeated. When an electrode track was no longer productive the electrode was moved 2 mm laterally, or moved to the other chamber to begin a new search. After about four hours the administration of Flaxedil was discontinued and the animal allowed to recover.

<u>Analytic Procedures</u>

The temporal stability of the distribution of inter-spike intervals is essential to all consideration of reproducibility of experimental results. If this criterion is not met, either some aspect of the experimental preparation is changing, or the instrumentation is not recording the activity correctly. If the conditions of time invariance for the distribution of inter-spike intervals and a low level of first order auto-correlation are met, a two-parameter fit of the data can be based on the random walk with drift model of neural activity. This approach uses the derived values of drift coefficient and barrier that can generate probability densities which have the same mean and variance as the measured spike trains.

Calculated values of mean and standard deviation from the measured inter-spike intervals were determined from the following expressions:

The mean of the measured inter-spike intervals,

$$T_m = \sum_{i=1}^{N} \frac{T_i}{N}. \tag{1}$$

The standard deviation of the measured inter-spike intervals,

$$S_d = \left\{ \sum_{i=1}^{N} \frac{(T_i - T_m)^2}{(N-1)} \right\}^{1/2}. \tag{2}$$

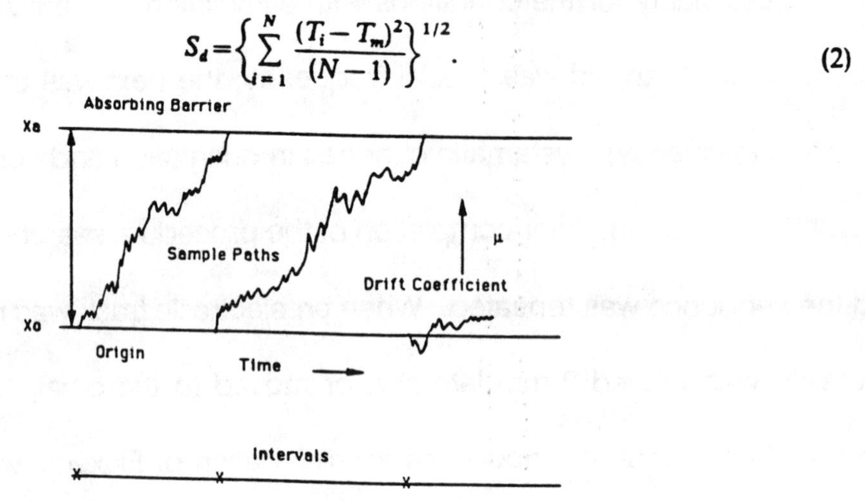

Fig 1. First passage time of random walk with drift is illustrated for positie drift coefficient μ and barrier height $Z = X_a - X_0$. The probability distribution function for the first passage time intervals is determined by these parameters

The random walk with positive drift process is illustrated in Fig. 1. A sample path beginning with the origin at X_0 is seen to advance towards the absorbing barrier at X_a. The distance between the origin and the absorbing barrier, $Z=X_a-X_0$, will always be referred to as the "barrier height" in this paper. The problems are to determine 1) the density of this processing path, 2) its first moment or expectation value, and 3) the second moment from which the variance is calculated. Using sample values for the mean inter-spike interval T_m and the standard deviation S_d then the drift coefficient μ and barrier height Z can be derived for the first passage time of random walk with positive drift process. A normalized diffusion constant, $\sigma^2/2=1.0$, is assumed in the derivation of the drift coefficient and barrier height. This normalization scales the process to ensure the consistency of the units of the derived parameters.

The solution of the forward equation, Eq. (3), is the probability density function of the first passage time of random walk with positive drift.

$$\frac{\partial P}{\partial t}=-\mu\frac{\partial P}{\partial x}+\frac{\sigma^2\partial^2 P}{2\partial x^2}. \tag{3}$$

The probability density function that is a solution of the forward equation is given by:

$$P(\mu, Z, \sigma; t)=\frac{Z}{\sqrt{2\pi}\sigma t^{3/2}}\exp\left\{\frac{-(Z-\mu t)^2}{2\sigma^2 t}\right\}. \tag{4}$$

The first moment or expectation value the second moment and the variance of the probability density function are given by Eqs. (5), (6) and 7).

$$E[t]=\frac{Z}{\mu} \tag{5}$$

$$E[t^2]=\frac{\sigma^2 Z}{\mu^3}+\frac{Z^2}{\mu^2} \quad \frac{\sigma^2}{2}=1.0 \tag{6}$$

$$E[t^2]-E[t]^2=\frac{2Z}{\mu^3}. \tag{7}$$

To obtain derived values of drift coefficient μ and barrier height Z, the sample mean, T_m, is set equal to the expectation value of the probability density function and the sample standard deviation S_d is set equal to the square root of the variance of the probability density function. In this way a calculated probability density function with the same mean and variance of the measured inter-spike interval distribution is obtained. The derived drift coefficient of the model process is given by equation (8) and the derived barrier height is given by Eq. (9).

$$\mu = \frac{\sqrt{2T_m}}{S_d} \tag{8}$$

$$Z = \mu T_m. \tag{9}$$

The main objective of this report is to illustrate the activity of neurons under different stimulus conditions as graphs of Z and μ; this will provide insight into the changes in the spike-generating process. If sufficient stationarity during recording of experimental data is observed it is believed that this method for investigating neural activity will yield a substantially correct description of the inter-spiked interval statistics in a concise form.

EXPERIMENTAL RESULTS

The methods described were applied to the inter-spike intervals of recorded data for eight cells that were under similar experimental conditions. The four conditions can be summarized as follows:

Condition 1. No stimulus presentation and a corresponding spontaneous neural discharge-rate.

Condition 2. Orientation change with the same spatial frequency as Condition 4.

Condition 3. Spatial frequency change with the same orientation as Condition 4.

Condition 4. Condition of orientation and spatial frequency for maximal discharge rate.

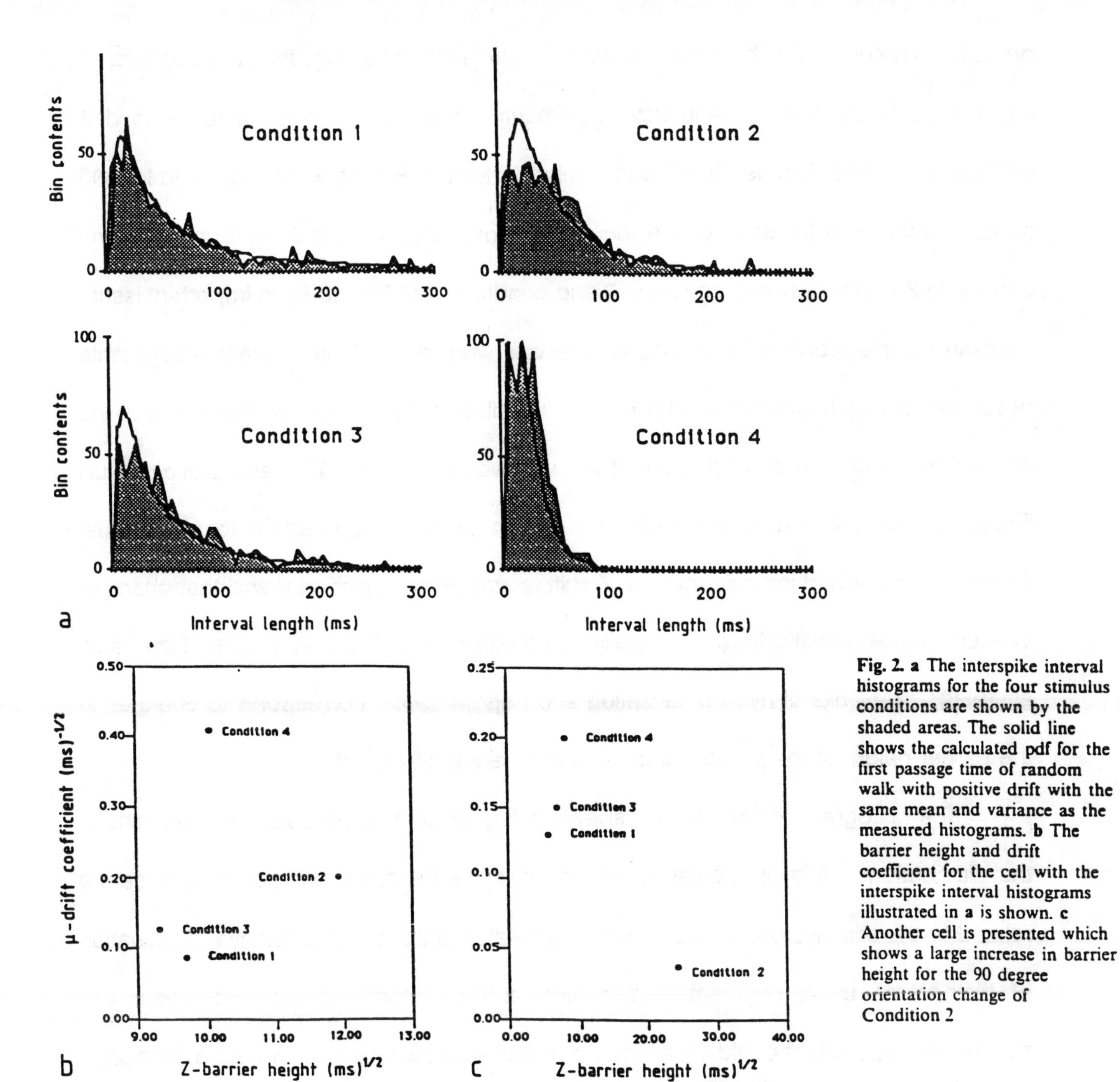

Fig. 2. a The interspike interval histograms for the four stimulus conditions are shown by the shaded areas. The solid line shows the calculated pdf for the first passage time of random walk with positive drift with the same mean and variance as the measured histograms. **b** The barrier height and drift coefficient for the cell with the interspike interval histograms illustrated in **a** is shown. **c** Another cell is presented which shows a large increase in barrier height for the 90 degree orientation change of Condition 2

The inter-spike interval histograms for a selected cell are shown in Fig. 2a. These histograms show that a given stimulus condition results in a unique distribution of inter-spike intervals. Figure 2b illustrates the derived values of drift coefficient μ and barrier height Z for this cell. For condition 2, for which the stimulus orientation is changed by 90 degrees relative to conditions 3 and 4, an increase in barrier height Z is seen for the process. Another cell with an even greater Z shift is shown in Fig. 2c. The condition 3 for change in the spatial frequency is primarily associated with a decrease in drift coefficient μ in both figures. The Z and μ values shown in Fig. 2b were evaluated for 800 measured intervals for each of the four conditions. The statistical significance of the change in Z values between condition 2 and condition 3 of Fig. 2b is an important issue. To examine this problem the measured intervals were divided into ten equal segments of 72 intervals each for both condition 2 and condition 3. The mean and variance of the derived values of Z of each collection of intervals was calculated. The results of a one-tail T-test showed the confidence level for eighteen degrees of freedom to be $T=2.09$, $P<0.05$). This would indicate that the Z shift is statistically significant and that changes in orientation and spatial frequency are indexed separately. (Sillito et al. 1980; Romoa et. al. 1986). The limits of hyperpolarization and depolarization correspond to changes in the barrier height of the process if other factors are unchanged.

The histogram of the intervals shown in Fig. 2a has some peaks and troughs in the distributions. It is of interest to determine if this structure is a permanent feature related to the stimulus conditions or if it an unrelated artifact. An extensive examination of histograms using segmented data and auto-correlograms did not reveal any permanent feature that could be attributed to the representation of relevant information. The structure of the probability density function derived from the measured histograms appears to contain all the significant information in terms of representation of the stimulus. Clearly a sufficiently low rate of temporal change in the stimulus conditions would create variations in the probability density function and auto-correlograms but under the nearly stationary conditions of these experiments no temporal sequences provided evidence for an additional mode of stimulus representation.

THE GABOR FUNCTION

An additional analysis was undertaken to bring the results of the previous analysis into formal register with the functional properties of the dendritic fields of visual cortical neurons described by their Gabor filter response (Pribram and Carlton, 1986). The Gabor elementary function was initially derived from the fact that the dendritic field of a cortical neuron is spatially limited and that edges produce a greater neural response than would be predicted by a simple Fourier transform of the spatial and temporal frequency characteristics of a grating (Marcelja, 1980; Kulikowski et al, 1982). This formulation was supported by the finding that neurons within the same cortical column respond to the cospectrum and quadspectrum, i.e., the quadriture of the phase changes produced by the drifting gratings (Pollen & Ronner, 1980). The formulation was generalized to two dimensions to include the role of orientation of the grating in changing the response of the cortical neuron (Daugman, 1980, 1985, 1988).

Pribram (1991, p. 678) has suggested that the formal model presented above can be related to the Gabor filter function which represents the geometry of the receptive field. The signature of coefficients that characterize drift rate can be conceived to represent the coherence among the frequencies of fluctuations of polarizations in the dendritic receptive field. When these coefficients are cross-multiplied by probabilities which represent amplitudes, boundary conditions are determined by the orientation of the stimulus display. The result is a probability amplitude modulated set of Fourier coefficients which describe a class of four-dimensional informational hyperspaces such as Hermite polynomials constrained by Gaussians, of which the Gabor function is an elementary example.

The drift coefficient and barrier height parameters, functions of spatial distribution and orientation, will now be shown to be consonant with the Gabor elementary function. The analysis is based on the assumption that the inputs to dendritic receptive fields are transformed into a specific drift coefficient and barrier height that in turn produce a characteristic configuration of neuronal-spike interval histogram.

In our previous analysis changes in spatial frequency were indexed solely by changes in drift coefficient, while change in barrier height was determined only by orientation. Here an indexing method is used to simulate the same mode of influencing the distribution of the output. A ten second sequence of intervals is modeled by an algorithm that simulates the inter-spike intervals by a random walk to the moving barrier. The overall behavior of the model can be seen in effects of orientation change (Fig. 2a) and change in spatial frequency (Fig. 2b). The effect of non-optimal orientation on spatial frequency tuning and non-optimal spatial frequency on orientation responses are seen to reflect measured characteristics (Webster and DeValois, 1985).

There is thus a constant set of parameters for the barrier height for a given orientation; the drift coefficient is generated from the spatial frequency. The variations of drift coefficient and the orientation parameters for the barrier height are shown in the following equations.

$$Zo(\Theta) = 2.0 \cos(/\Theta/ - \pi/2) + 3.0 \qquad (11)$$

$$Zt(\Theta) = 2.0 \cos(/\Theta/ - \pi/2) + 3.0 \qquad (12)$$

$$To(\Theta) = 7.0 \cos(/\Theta/ - \pi/2) + 8.5 \qquad (13)$$

$$\mu(\Theta, f) = 0.2 \exp(-2.0\Theta^2) \exp(-4.0(f-1)^2) \qquad (14)$$

In these equations, the inputs are temporally fixed and a continuous stream of outputs of inter-spike intervals are generated by the model neuron. The calculated drift coefficient and barrier height values are then used in the simulation to generate the interspike intervals that constitute the output. Different spatial frequencies of input are used to produce different response rates for different normalized input spatial frequencies. Surrounding flanks simulate inhibition by decreasing the incremental value of the drift coefficient for the edges of the regions examined. This reflects the spatial property of the receptive field and therefore selectivity represents orientation in our simulation. The μ parameters of each neuron are thus determined by the center-excitation, flank-inhibition configuration of the Gabor filter function.

CONCLUSION

As noted in the introduction, spike trains recorded from visual cortex neurons reflect three separable influences: 1) those, such as the sensory stimuli which characterize the input to the neuron 2) those which parameterize the properties of the ensemble of dendritic activities of the neuron, and 3) those which directly determine the output of the neuron at the axon hillock (Pribram, Lassonde and Ptito 1981). Receptive field properties (#2 above) can be characterized as filters resonating to spatial (and temporal) frequencies (DeValois and DeValois 1988) which are specified as sinusoids in the spectral domain. These sinusoids are limited by a Gaussian envelope which reflects the spatial characteristic of the receptive field, specifically, orientation. The result is best described as a Hermitian of which the Gabor elementary function is a basic example. (Marcelja 1980; Pribram and Carlton 1986; Daugman 1988). The analyses undertaken in this study indicates that these two separable characteristics of the receptive dentritic field, responses to changes in spatial frequency and orientation, have different effects on the processes generating neural impulses at the axon hillock.

REFERENCES

Daugman JG (1985) Representational issues and local filter models of two-dimensional spatial visual encoding. In D. Rose & V.G. Dobson (Eds.), *Models of the Visual Cortex*, (pp. 96-107). New York: Wiley.)

Daugman JG (1988) Complete discrete 2-d Gabor transforms by neural networks for image analysis and compression. *IEEE Trans Acoustics, Speech, Signal Processing, 36*: 1169-1179.

De Valois RL, De Valois KK (1988) Spatial vision. Oxford University Press, New York.

Gerstein GL, Mandelbrot B (1964) Random walk models for the spike activity of a single neuron. *Biophys Journal, 4*: 41-68.

Harrison JM (1985) Brownian motion and stochastic flow systems. John Wiley, New York.

Johnson NL, Kotz S (1970) Distributions in statistics: continuous univariate distributions 1. Houghton Mifflin, Boston.

Karlin S. Taylor HM (1975) A first course in stochastic processes. Academic Press, New York.

Kryukov VI (1976) Wald's identity and random walk models for neuron firing. Adv Appl Prob 8:257-277).

Kuffler, S.W. (1953). Discharge patterns and functional organization of mammalian retina. *Journal of Neurophysiology, 16*, 37-39.

Kulikowski, J. J., Marcelja, S., & Bishop, P.O. (1982). Theory of spatial position and spatial frequency relations in the receptive fields of simple cells in the visual cortex. *Biological Cybernetics, 43,* 187-198.

Lansky P (1983) Inferences for the diffusion models of neuronal activity. Math Biosci 67:247-260.

Lansky P, Radil T (1987) Statistical inference of spontaneous neuronal discharge patterns. I. Single neuron. Biol Cybern 55:299-311.

Lansky P, Lanska V (1987) Diffusion approximation of the neural model with synaptic reversal potentials. Biol Cybern 56:19-26.

Marcelja S (1980) Mathematical description of the responses of simple cortical cells. *Journal Optometric Society of America, 70*: 1297-1300.

Pollen, DA, & Ronner, SE (1980) Spatial computation performed by simple and complex cells in the cat visual cortex. *Experimental Brain Research, 41,* A14-15.

Pribram KH, (1991) *Brain and Perception: Holonomy and Structure in Figural Processing.* New Jersey: Lawrence Erlbaum Associates, Inc.

Pribram KH, Carlton EH (1986) Holonomic brain theory in imaging and object perception. *Acta Psychologica, 63*: 175-210.

Pribram KH, Lassonde MC, Ptito M (1981) Classification of receptive field properties. Exp Brain Res 43:119-130.

Romoa AS, Shalden M, Skottun BC, Freeman RD (1986) A comparison of inhibition in orientation and spatial frequency of cat visual cortex. *Nature, 321*: 237-239.

Sillito AM, Kemp JA, Milson JA, Berardi N (1980) A re-evaluation of the mechanisms underlying simple cell orientation selectivity. Brain Res 194:517-520.

Tuckwell HC (1976) On the first-exit time problem for temporally homogeneous Markov processes. *Jour Appl Prob, 13*: 39-48.

Tuckwell HC, Cope DK (1980) Accuracy of neuronal interspike times calculated from a diffusion approximation. J Theor Biol 83:377-387.

Tuckwell HC (1986) Stochastic equations for nerve membrane potential. J Theor Neurobiol 5:87-99.

Wasan MT (1969) First passage time distribution of Browman motion with positive drift (inverse Gaussian distributions), Queen's Paper in Pure and Applied Mathematics no 19. Queen's University, Kingston, Ontario, Canada.

Webster MA & DeValois RL (1985) Relationship between spatial frequency timing and orientation timing of striate-cortex cells. J. Opt. Soc. Am. A. 2, 1129-1132.

Yang GL, Chen TC (1978) On statistical methods in neuronal spike-train analysis. Math Biosci 38:1-34.

This paper is condensed and modified from two published reports:

An analysis of neural spike-train distributions: determinants of the response of visual cortex neurons to changes in orientation and spatial frequency. D. Berger, K. Pribram, H. Wild, and C. Bridges. Experimental Brain Research, 80(1); 129-134.

The relationship between the Gabor elementary function and a stochastic model of the inter-spike interval distribution in the responses of visual cortex neurons. D. H. Berger and K. H. Pribram. Biological Cybernetics, 67; 191-194.

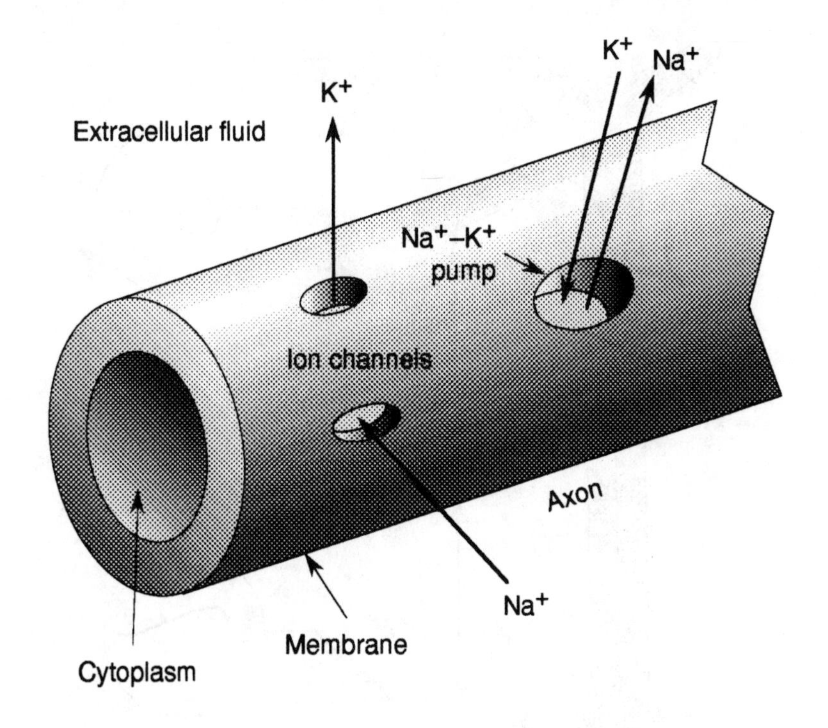

Fig. 1 In the nerve cell is at rest, the electrochemical gradients cause the Na^+ ions to diffuse into the cell and the K^+ ions to diffuse out. The Na-K pump balances these passive fluxes with an active transport of Na^+ ions out and K^+ ions in.

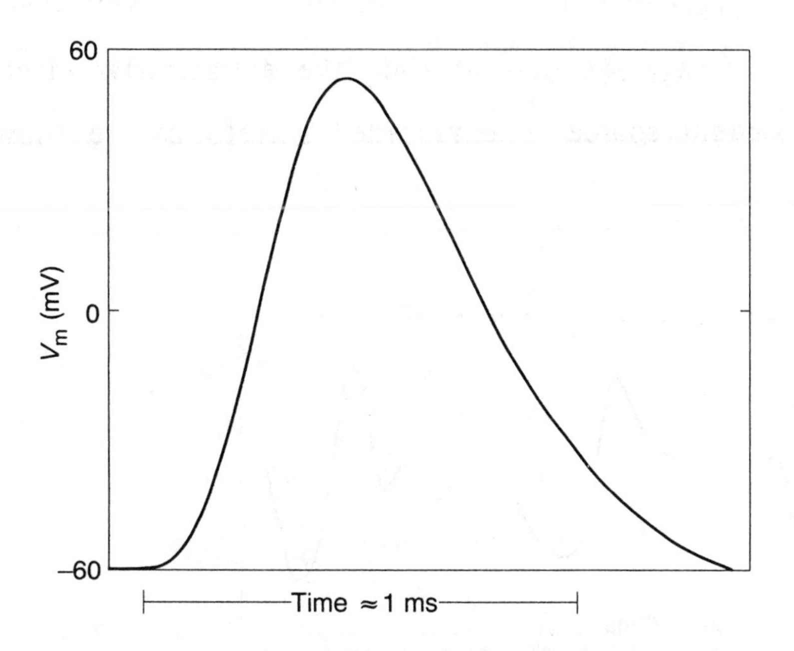

Fig. 2 The action potential waveform.

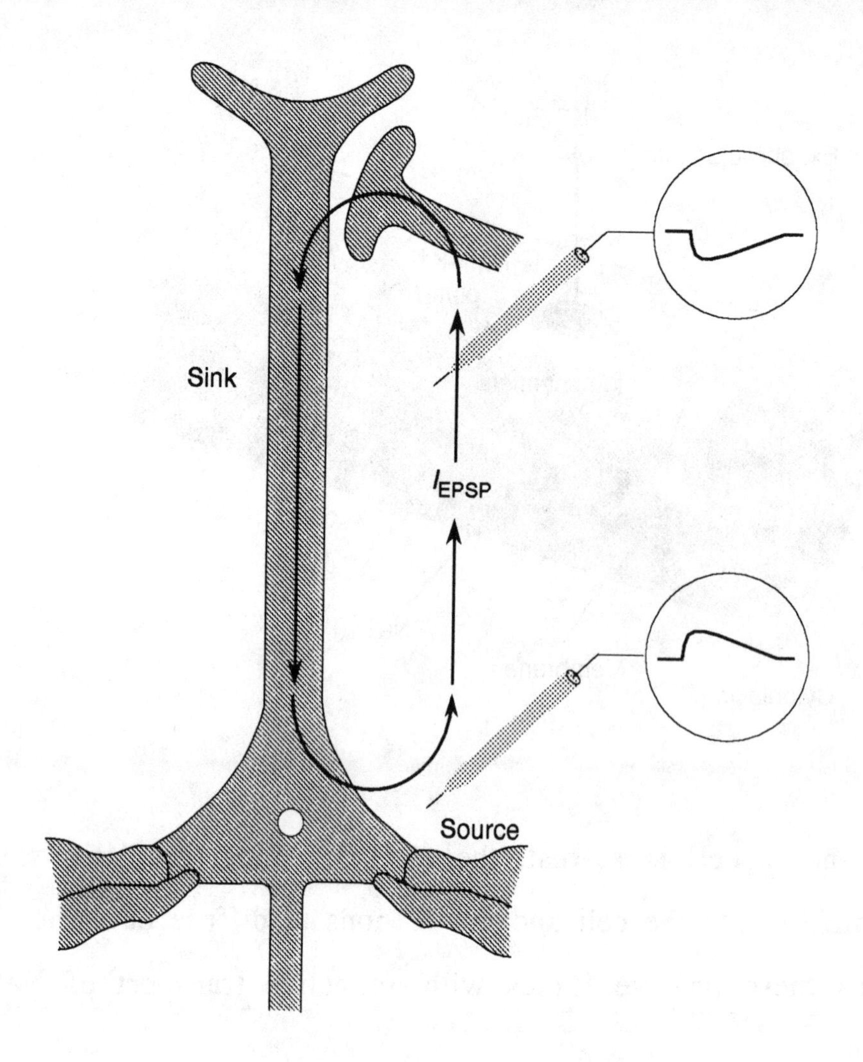

Fig. 3 Current flow (I_{EPSP}) in and around a nerve cell. The extracellular electrode at the top is near the current sink, the extracellular electrode below is near the current source. The recorded waveforms are shown in circles.

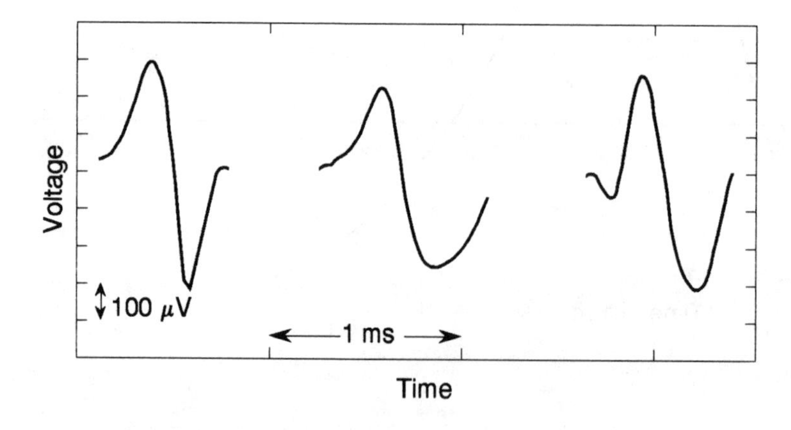

Fig. 4 Examples of extracellularly recorded action potential waveforms.

Chapter 2

Automated Recognition of Action Potentials in Extracellular Recordings

Isaac N. Bankman
Johns Hopkins
Applied Physics Lab
Laurel, MD 20723

AUTOMATED RECOGNITION OF ACTION POTENTIALS IN EXTRACELLULAR RECORDINGS

Isaac N. Bankman
Johns Hopkins, Applied Physics Lab, Laurel, MD 20723

Neuroscience stands at the threshold of a significant expansion owing to the clarity of propitious avenues and the availability of adequate approaches for understanding brain function. Indeed, guiding concepts, experimental techniques, and analytical tools are available for progress in many fields ranging from ion-channels to neural systems studies. In the investigation of sensory and cognitive processes, one of the prerequisites is instrumentation for obtaining reliable recordings of the physiological activity of neuronal assemblies. The concurrent activity of several neurons can be observed with an extracellular electrode that records the action potentials of neurons in the vicinity of the tip. The main advantage over an intracellular electrode is the ability to record from more than one neuron at the same time. The extracellular electrode also allows recording without damaging the neurons and enables longer recording periods. The cost of these benefits is the requirement for sorting the interleaved neural spike trains of several neurons to determine the firing instants of individual neurons. Due to differences in their geometry and the impedances connecting them to the electrode, the depolarization of different neurons is manifested with different transient waveforms in the recording. However, typically, the waveform of a given neuron preserves its general shape during a recording period. Therefore, the activity of individual neurons can be determined by sorting the different types of neural waveforms. An additional challenge in extracellular recordings is the relatively low signal-to-noise ratios (SNR) that can occur in many cases. The background noise is mainly due to the activity of a large number of distant neurons resulting in a considerable overlap between the spectra of waveforms of interest and noise. The neural waveform recognition problem is a typical example of detection and classification of transient patterns embedded in colored noise.

NEURAL DATA

In a nerve cell at rest, a resting potential of about -40 mV to -75 mV across the cell membrane is maintained owing to the steady state distribution of anions and cations. The unequal permeability of the cell membrane to Na^+ and K^+ ions, the higher concentration of K^+ inside and Na^+ outside the cell, and the active Na^+- K^+ pump that retrieves Na^+ from the cell while injecting K^+ (Fig. 1) are all factors that contribute to this potential difference (polarization). When the overall synaptic effect of the other neurons is excitatory, positive charges are injected into the neuron. If the membrane potential at the trigger zone exceeds a critical threshold, an active process changes the permeability of the cell membrane in the trigger zone. This causes the intracellular membrane potential to rise rapidly to about 50 mV. This potential returns to its resting level in about 1 ms, giving rise to the action potential across the membrane of the trigger zone (Fig. 2). Under constant excitation, a neuron can fire repeated action potentials at a rate that can reach about 500 impulses per second (ips). Typical impulse rates are in the range of 10 ips to 100 ips.

The action potential, generated at the trigger zone, is conducted along the axon both passively and actively. During the depolarization, the Na^+ ions that enter the trigger zone passively travel a small distance inside the neuron and excite the membrane of a region adjacent to the trigger zone. The resulting depolarization, in turn, excites a further part of the membrane, causing an active, lossless propagation of the action potential. This process generates a current flow away from the synapse, through the axon and towards the synapse outside the cell (Fig. 3). The current flow outside the cell generates small, transient potential differences across the extracellular fluid in the vicinity of the cell. These potential spikes are typically in the range of 1-100 microvolts and can be recorded with an extracellular electrode.

The shape of an action potential waveform recorded in an extracellular electrode depends on the position of the electrode relative to the neuron. An electrode near the trigger zone (current sink) records a negative deflection that peaks and decays to zero rapidly with a possible overshoot, while an electrode placed away from the trigger zone but close to the axon (current source) records a positive peak and subsequent decay to zero with a possible undershoot (Fig. 3). Recording sites close to the dendritic tree of the neuron produce more complex spike waveforms. Fig. 4 shows some examples of extracellularly recorded neural spikes. The voltage level of neural spikes decreases rapidly with increasing distance between neuron and electrode. In extracellular recordings the signals of interest are the action potential waveforms of several neurons that are close to the tip of the electrode, and the noise process is mainly due to the activity of a large number of neurons that are distant from the electrode tip. Ideally, the electrode would be placed at a location that provides high amplitude spikes from several neurons in the vicinity and low amplitude interference from other neurons. In practice such adjustments are difficult and time consuming, and recordings frequently have very poor SNRs.

The time constant of the depolarization is of the same order of magnitude in most neurons because the membrane capacitance and the axoplasmic resistance do not change considerably from neuron to neuron. Therefore, the spectral content of action potential waveforms is similar in most neurons, and the spectra of signal and noise in extracellular recordings overlap to a large extent. Therefore, discrimination between signal and noise is not possible by simply using a band-pass filter. Furthermore, since the noise process is primarily made of the accumulation of low amplitude spikes, the autocorrelation function of noise has significantly high coefficients at lags as large as the average duration of a neural spike (about 1 ms). This autocorrelation of noise has significant implications for the multidimensional classification that is necessary to recognize the action potentials of different neurons.

ACTION POTENTIAL RECOGNITION METHODS

In order to determine the firing patterns of individual neurons recorded with extracellular electrodes, action potential waveforms that have a sufficiently similar shape have to be identified and classified in the same class to indicate the firing times of the corresponding neuron. Window discriminators, the first instruments for sorting neural spikes, were based on specialized hardware that separated different spike types using their peak amplitude. Subsequently, a large number of algorithms for neural waveform sorting were introduced owing to the availability of digital computers.

In two pioneering interactive off-line computerized systems [1, 2] allowed the user to form a template for each waveform type by selecting and averaging several waveforms of the same type. Classification was based on the mean square difference between a candidate spike and the templates. An attempt was made in [2], to determine whether unclassified spikes were linear superpositions of two or more known spike types. In the following decades, several variants of the template matching approach were suggested [3-14], based on i) different similarity measures such as cross-correlation, Euclidean distance, and city block distance, ii) different sampling rates ranging from 4 KHz to 50 KHz, and iii) different number of samples to represent a spike, ranging from 5 to 69.

Other methods extracted first a small number of features from the spike waveforms and performed classification based on these features. Some of the suggested features were peak amplitude, peak-to-peak amplitude, various duration measures, as well as Fourier coefficients [15-18].

Principal components, a more elaborate and more reliable method for feature extraction has also been applied to neural waveform recognition. The principal components method is based on a set of basis functions derived from the data. An early implementation of this method used tapped delay line filters for computing the projection of the signal on the first 3 principal components [19]. The theoretical and practical aspects of principal components were further investigated in [20-25].

Other methods used for neural spike sorting include the first 8 Fourier coefficients of the spike [26], regression coefficients in fitting a curve to the spike [27], and estimation of the conduction velocity with multiple electrodes [28-30].

It has been difficult to compare the performance of the suggested action potential recognition methods because different data were used by different investigators. An "apparent separation matrix" was proposed for evaluating the quality of neural waveform sorting techniques [31]. The classification power of a set of parameters was determined by computing a measure of separation (dissimilarity) among all waveform types. The root-mean-squared (rms) value of the difference between the cluster centers of the two types in parameter space was used as the measure of separation, computed for each pair of waveform types. Using this evaluation approach, the classification performances of peak amplitude, the first principal component and conduction latency were compared in [32]. In a comprehensive evaluation study [33], the classification performances of peak amplitude, conduction latency, a combination of these two, 32-sample template matching, and principal components, were compared. These evaluations concluded that, in recordings with high SNR, peak amplitude and conduction latency were adequate, but robust classification with minimal noise sensitivity required principal components or template matching.

The general approach in all the methods mentioned above consists of:
a. feature extraction i.e., forming a vector of parameters that represents each action potential in the record,
b. template generation i.e., characterization of the different clusters formed by different waveform types,
c. discrimination i.e., setting decision boundaries used for classification of subsequent waveforms.

Feature extraction

In the standard template matching method the features are the consecutive samples digitized on an action potential. In the principal components method, the features are the projection of the data on a few optimal, orthogonal basis vectors. The most complete information in the digitized domain is conveyed by the consecutive samples of a spike. In the principal components method, the template for each neuron is made of a few coefficients obtained by projection. The advantage of the principal components method is operation in a much lower dimensional space. However, some preprocessing of data is required in the principal components method.

The principal components method, also known as the Karhunen-Loeve Transform (KLT) in the signal processing field represents the data in a transformed space spanned by a set of orthonormal basis vectors derived from the data. Let each waveform be represented by an N dimensional column vector **x**, the covariance matrix of the waveform vectors is:

$$\mathbf{C} = E\{(\mathbf{x} - \mathbf{m})(\mathbf{x} - \mathbf{m})'\}, \tag{1}$$

where,

$$\mathbf{m} = E\{\mathbf{x}\} \tag{2}$$

is the mean vector, E{} is the expected value operator, and (') denotes transposition. The transformation matrix **T** of the KLT, is a square matrix whose rows are the eigenvectors of **C**. The KLT transform **y** of a vector **x** is obtained with:

$$\mathbf{y} = \mathbf{T}(\mathbf{x} - \mathbf{m}), \tag{3}$$

and the covariance matrix of the transformed vectors

$$\mathbf{L} = \mathbf{TCT}' \tag{4}$$

is a diagonal matrix whose elements are the eigenvalues λ_ι of **C**. These eigenvalues, indexed in decreasing size order, are the variances of the transformed data along the corresponding eigenvector. The inverse transform, that can be used to reconstruct **x** from **y**, is equal to the transpose of **T**:

$$\mathbf{x} = \mathbf{T}^{-1}\mathbf{y} + \mathbf{m} = \mathbf{T}'\mathbf{y} + \mathbf{m}. \tag{5}$$

For an arbitrary set of data, the existence of the transformation matrix **T** is guaranteed because **C** is a real, symmetric matrix.

The effective data reduction property of the KLT, used also in image coding, results from the fact that most of the information is often concentrated in the components of **y** which are associated with the largest eigenvalues. If a reduced transformation matrix **R** is built with only the M principal eigenvectors with largest eigenvalues, the mean square error between the original vector **x** and its approximation

$$\mathbf{a} = \mathbf{R'y} + \mathbf{m} \qquad 6)$$

is given by:

$$e = \sum_{i=M+1}^{N} \lambda_i , \qquad (7)$$

the sum of the N-M eigenvalues of the unused eigenvectors. Since this error is minimized by selecting the eigenvectors with largest eigenvalues, the KLT transform is optimal in the least-square-error sense. Although the matrix **T** (or **R**) is not separable, a fast KLT algorithm based on the Fast Fourier Transform has been developed [34].

The minimal number of principal components required for a reliable representation of the signal with reduced dimensionality depends on the data set. In the action potential sorting applications, waveforms initially composed of a large number of samples (20-40) have been represented successfully by 2 principal components for purposes of detection and classification [24, 25] . In general, more than 95% of the pattern's energy is contained in the first two KLT coefficients. This allows very fast processing, as well as monitoring the data and the decision boundaries on a two-dimensional display.

Template Generation

In pattern recognition, characterization of the clusters in feature space can be achieved with several approaches. In the case of action potential recognition, each class (neuron) forms one cluster because the underlying pure waveform, the centroid of the cluster, is practically identical every time that the neuron fires. The Gaussian nature of noise generates an analytically tractable cluster around the centroid. Under these conditions, characterization of the clusters can be achieved conveniently by template matching.

With either standard template matching or principal components, one of the main challenges is to generate the template for each neuron in that recording. This can be performed by analyzing an initial segment of the recording with a simultaneous unsupervised clustering method [35, 36]. This approach provides reliable clusters but introduces a delay in the pattern recognition process. The duration of this delay depends on the rate of arrival of patterns, the clustering algorithm, and the computer speed. If classification has to start with the first pattern, a sequential unsupervised clustering algorithm can be used to circumvent the learning delay. Under relatively high SNR conditions, and when the pattern types are not very similar, this algorithm generates the same clusters as the simultaneous clustering method.

Discrimination

Decision boundaries can either be placed manually or implied by the use of a distance metric and an appropriate acceptance threshold. The distance and its threshold depend on the probability density of the various classes.

Since the amplitude distribution of noise in neural recordings is Gaussian, optimal Bayesian classification can be obtained by setting a decision boundary around the centroid of each cluster with a distance metric that depends on the covariance matrix of noise.

The probability density p(x) of a multivariate normal distribution is:

$$p(\mathbf{x}) = \frac{1}{(2\pi)^{N/2}|C|^{1/2}} \exp[-(\mathbf{x}-\mathbf{m})'C^{-1}(\mathbf{x}-\mathbf{m})/2], \tag{8}$$

where, **x** is the N-dimensional parameter vector, C is the covariance matrix of **x**, |C| is the determinant of C, and **m** is the mean vector. The quantity:

$$d^2_m = (\mathbf{x}-\mathbf{m})'C^{-1}(\mathbf{x}-\mathbf{m}) \tag{9}$$

is the squared Mahalanobis distance between **x** and **m**.

Let the data have K different classes (neurons) represented by ω_i with i = 1,...,K. Since the noise process that corrupts each waveform type is the same, in the action potential classification problem the probability density of each class is identical, around the corresponding centroid vector $\mathbf{m}_i$. Multiclass Bayesian classification is performed with discriminant functions that are based on the class densities and *a priori* probabilities of the classes. A convenient choice of discriminant function is:

$$g_i(\mathbf{x}) = \log(p(\mathbf{x}|\omega_i) + \log P(\omega_i), \tag{10}$$

where, $g_i(\mathbf{x})$ is the discriminant function, $p(\mathbf{x}|\omega_i)$ is the probability density of class i, and $P(\omega_i)$ is the *a priori* probability of class i. The class to which a candidate pattern belongs is determined by computing the values $g_i(\mathbf{x})$ of the discriminant function using the pattern's feature vector **x** for each class i = 1,...,K. The pattern is assigned to the class with the highest discriminant function value. When each class has a multivariate Gaussian distribution, the expression for $g_i(\mathbf{x})$ becomes:

$$g_i(\mathbf{x}) = -(\mathbf{x}-\mathbf{m}_i)'C^{-1}(\mathbf{x}-\mathbf{m}_i)/2 \; - (N\log 2\pi)/2 \; - \; (\log|C|)/2 + \log P(\omega_i). \quad (11)$$

This expression can be further simplified because:

a. the $(N\log 2\pi)/2$ and $(\log|C|)/2$ terms are constants, and

b. in cases where the *a priori* probability of each class is known to be the same or when it is unknown and is assumed to be the same, the $\log P(\omega_i)$ can be ignored.

Disregarding also the division by 2 in the remaining term, the discriminant function becomes:

$$g_i(\mathbf{x}) = -(\mathbf{x}-\mathbf{m}_i)'C^{-1}(\mathbf{x}-\mathbf{m}_i). \quad (12)$$

Therefore, under the conditions stated above, the Bayesian approach consists of selecting the class that generates the lowest Mahalanobis distance between its centroid $\mathbf{m}_i$ and the candidate pattern $\mathbf{x}$. Constant Mahalanobis distance contours are ellipses centered around the mean of each class. In most applications, it is desirable to have the option of leaving some patterns unclassified or rejecting them. To do so, a pattern is classified only if its lowest distance is below an acceptance threshold. This is equivalent to setting an elliptical decision boundary around the mean of each class.

None of the reported action potential recognition applications have used the Mahalanobis distance in classification due to the large amount of computations that it requires: estimation of the covariance matrix and its inversion, then, for each class, a matrix-vector multiplication and a dot product. On the other hand, the Euclidean distance which is considerably faster to compute has been commonly used, but it is equivalent to setting a circular decision boundary and provides suboptimal results. The extent of performance loss due to the use of Euclidean distance depends on the covariance matrix of noise, the noise level of the data and the similarity between different classes. If the noise level is relatively low and the clusters of different classes are sufficiently apart, the Euclidean distance can provide satisfactory results regardless of the covariance matrix of noise. Our recent studies, using 32-sample templates and 5 different waveform classes embedded in typical neural recording noise, showed that if the Euclidean distance between the means of the two closest clusters is more than 14 standard deviations of noise, perfect classification can be obtained. But as the clusters get closer and/or the noise level increases, the performance drops and the loss, referred to the optimal case, can reach up to 30%. This is due to the fact that Euclidean distance is compatible with circular density contours but in many applications, such as the action potential sorting problem, the distributions are elliptical.

In the template matching approach for neural spike sorting, since the variance of each dimension is the same, elliptical distributions result only from the significant autocorrelation in the noise process. This is reflected in the covariance matrix. The higher the autocorrelation in noise, the higher the eccentricity of the elliptical distributions and the lower the performance will be with Euclidean distance.

Whitening

If the density contours were circular, optimal classification could be achieved with the Euclidean distance. This case occurs when the components of the multivariate distribution are uncorrelated or equivalently, when the noise process is white. In this case the covariance matrix C is diagonal with the elements being all equal to the variance of noise σ^2, its inverse C^{-1} is diagonal with elements equal to $1/\sigma^2$, and the discriminant function reduces to:

$$g_i(x) = -(x-m_i)'(x-m_i). \tag{13}$$

This is equivalent to classification with minimal Euclidean distance.

Recently a whitening method for neural recordings, that provided theoretically expected optimal results with the Euclidean distance was reported [37, 38]. This method is based on an autoregressive moving average model of noise and can be implemented on-line with a recursive filter using less than 10 coefficients. The best possible classification performance can be achieved with this approach, under any level of noise.

Fully automated operation

In order to provide a convenient research tool for neuroscientists, especially when multiple extracellular electrodes are used, the recognition algorithms have to be implemented in a fully automated manner. Therefore, setting the acceptance thresholds and designing the whitening filter should be automated. The acceptance threshold for template matching has to be commensurate with the amount of noise in the record. The whitening filter has to be obtained by modeling the noise process in the recording. Hence, both for threshold setting and whitening, a segment of the record that contains only noise has to be extracted first. Since this needs to be achieved at the start of the analysis process when templates and thresholds are not yet available, a specialized algorithm is required. Such an algorithm, based on the normal distribution of noise amplitude, was recently introduced [39]. This algorithm extracts the Gaussian part in a distribution of spike and noise mixture in an iterative manner. It discards short windows (1-2 ms) in the recording until the remaining part of the recording reaches a normal distribution to a desired accuracy. The choice of windows to be discarded is guided by the analysis of remainder distributions at each iteration.

PERFORMANCE TESTS

The classification performance using raw data, whitened data and principal components was evaluated on a test data set built with 5 different physiological action potential waveforms embedded in varying levels of physiological neural recording noise. In order to determine the comparative performance of different recognition approaches, independently from other factors that may affect performance, the evaluation was made using i) prior knowledge of noise-free templates, ii) prior knowledge of occurrence times, and iii) prior knowledge of noise segments and corresponding acceptance thresholds [37, 38]. Each of the 5 templates, made of 32 consecutive samples of the data digitized at 32 KHz, was generated by averaging action potential waveforms from the same neuron, after visual recognition and alignment using a recording with very low noise. The test data set was formed by adding these 5 templates to a recording segment containing only noise at known, multiple locations.

The SNR of a record in these studies was defined as the rms value of the smallest target action potential in the record divided by the standard deviation of noise in the test record. The SNR was varied in a controlled manner by placing the noise-free templates in recording segments of only noise, scaled to obtain the desired SNR.

The thresholds were set to provide fewer than 0.1% exclusion errors in all waveform types. Template matching with Euclidean distance on raw data (without whitening) was 74% correct, at an SNR of 1 and 96% correct at an SNR of 2. On whitened data, template matching with Euclidean distance provided 91% and 100% correct classification at SNRs of 1 and 2 respectively. These results were consistent with theoretical multidimensional discrimination analysis based on normally distributed noise amplitude. As expected, the benefit of whitening was more pronounced at higher noise levels.

In similar tests, aimed to determine the performance of the principal components method independently from other factors that are involved in an on-line operation, prior knowledge of the exact noise-free waveforms to be classified was used to determine the covariance matrix and the principal component vectors. The acceptance threshold was set to yield fewer than 0.1% exclusion errors. When the SNR was above 5, the performance of principal components was 99% correct or more. Between SNRs of 5 and 3, this performance fell to about 95% correct and was only 5% less than the performance of Euclidean distance template matching on whitened data. When the SNR was less than 3, principal components remained about 20% lower in performance than Euclidean distance template matching on whitened data.

The results of template matching and principal components were considerably better than peak amplitude classification which is used in window discriminators. When the threshold was set for fewer than 0.1% exclusion errors, peak amplitude was more than 96% correct when the SNR was above 5 but deteriorated rapidly between SNRs of 5 and 3. When SNR was below 3, the classification performance dropped to 50% or less.

The above results indicated the comparative performance of different features and classification methods. In particular, computational verification of the benefits of whitening at low SNR levels were obtained. In these tests where the goal was to observe the best performance that can be expected from each method on the test data set, several related steps were effected in a controlled manner to prevent loss of performance due to factors other than those tested. These steps included, generation of templates, detection of occurrence time, and setting acceptance thresholds. Further evaluation tests were conducted [41] to determine the overall performance of a fully automated system where all steps were performed by automated algorithms based on template matching and whitening, without human supervision. The templates were generated with a sequential clustering algorithm, events were detected with power threshold crossing followed by matched filtering, and the acceptance thresholds were set by automatically extracting [39] a noise segment from the data. The overall recognition performance obtained with the fully automated approach was above 95% correct when the SNR was 3 or more. Compared to the controlled approach, the fully automated approach degraded more rapidly with decreasing SNR below 3 where its performance was 10-20% below that of the controlled approach. The two main factors that contributed to this drop in performance at low SNR levels were template generation and event detection. The thresholds set by the automated algorithm were adequate at all SNR levels.

DISCUSSION

The advantage of principal components is considerable data reduction and speed, while template matching with Euclidean distance on whitened data is the theoretically optimal approach. In recordings with moderate amount of noise, principal components can provide reliable discrimination. However, reliable resolution of waveform superpositions requires templates of individual action potential waveforms. Resolution of superpositions can be achieved reliably by using an iterative algorithm based on template matching [37].

It is possible that basis functions other than principal components can provide successful classification. A promising candidate that we are investigating, the wavelet transform [40], is especially suited for an efficient representation of transient signals. Since its orthonormal basis functions are independent of the data, the wavelet transform does not require computation of the data covariance matrix and its eigenvectors.

Recently, neural networks have been applied to various pattern recognition problems. Their ability to generate nonlinear, and sometimes disjoint decision regions is the main contribution of neural networks to pattern recognition. In applications where each class has one cluster and when components of patterns are uncorrelated (whitened data), the distribution of each class is spherical around its centroid. In such cases, the required decision boundary is a spherical shell and it can be implemented simply with a template and the Euclidean distance. The nonlinear discriminatory power of neural networks does not provide an advantage for such cases. If the application precludes satisfactory whitening of the data then neural networks may contribute to the solution.

On-line recognition and display of the activity of individual neurons in extracellular electrodes can provide a considerable benefit for neurophysiological research. On-line results can indicate immediately the relevance of the recording site to a given stimulus, or it can guide the choice of appropriate stimulus for a given recording site. On-line and fully automated implementation of robust recognition algorithms is becoming increasingly necessary for reliable and efficient recordings, especially when multiple electrodes are used. A fully automated, on-line recognition system based on floating-point fast computational hardware has been reported [42]. In this system, template matching and whitening is used and the resolution of overlapping action potential waveforms is also addressed.

REFERENCES

1. G. L. Gerstein and W. A. Clark, "Simultaneous Studies of Firing Patterns in Several Neurons," *Science*, vol. 143, pp. 1325-1327, (1964).

2. D. G. Keehn, "An Iterative Spike Separation Technique," *IEEE Trans. Bio-Med. Eng.*, vol. 13, pp. 19-28, (1966).

3. V. J. Prochazka, "Bioelectric Signal Sorter," (JULIA), *Decus Program Library*, Digital Equipment Computer Users' Society, Digital Equipment Corp., Marlboro, Mass., pp. 12-35 (1971).

4. V. J. Prochazka, B. Conrad and F. Sindermann, "A Neuroelectric Signal Recognition System," *Electroenceph. Clin. Neurophysiol.*, vol. 32, pp. 95-97, (1972).

5. J. J. Capowski, "The Spike Program: A Computer System for Analysis of Neurophysiological Action Potentials," *Computer Technology in Neuroscience*, P. B. Brown, ed., Hemisphere Publ. Co., Washington, DC, pp. 237-251, (1976).

6. B. Matthews, "Identifying Action Potential Waveforms in Neurophysiological Recordings," *J. Physiol.* (London), vol. 277, pp. 32P-33P, (1978).

7. E. H. D'Hollander and G. A. Orban, "Spike Recognition and On-line Classification by Unsupervised Learning System," *IEEE Trans. Bio-Med. Eng.*, vol. 26, pp. 279-284, (1979).

8. C. J. DeLuca and W. J. Forrest, "An Electrode for Single Motor Unit Activity During Strong Muscle Contractions," *IEEE Trans Bio-Med. Eng.*, vol. 19, pp. 367-372, (1979).

9. G. J. Dinning and A. C. Sanderson, "Real-time Classification of Multiunit Neural Signals Using Reduced Feature Sets," *IEEE Trans. Bio-Med. Eng.*, vol. 28, pp. 804-812, (1981).

10. R. S. LeFever and C. J. DeLuca, "A Procedure for Decomposing the Myoelectric Signal into its Constituent Action Potentials - Part I: Technique, Theory and Implementation," *IEEE Trans. Biomed. Eng.*, vol. 29, pp. 149-157, (1982).

11. A. Cohen and D. Landsberg, "Adaptive Real-time Wavelet Detection," *IEEE Trans. Bio-Med. Eng.*, vol. 30, pp. 332-340, (1983).

12. R. M. Studer, R.J.P. de Figueiredo and G. S. Moschytz, "An Algorithm for Sequential Signal Estimation and System Identification for EMG Signals," *IEEE Trans. Bio-Med. Eng.*, vol. 31, pp. 285-295, (1984).

13. M. Salganicoff, M. Sarna, L. Sax and G. L. Gerstein, "Unsupervised Waveform Classification for Multi-neuron Recordings: A Real-time Software-based System. I. Algorithms and Implementation," *J. Neurosci. Meth.*, vol. 25, pp. 181-187, (1988).

14. C. Forster and H. O. Handwerker, "Automatic Classification and Analysis of Microneurographic Spike Data using a PC/AT," *J. Neurosci. Meth.*, vol. 31, pp. 109-118, (1990).

15. D. J. Mishelevich, "On-line Real-time Digital Computer Separation of Extracellular Neuroelectric Signals," *IEEE Trans. Bio-Med. Eng.*, vol 17, pp. 147-150, (1970).

16. R. M. Harper and D. J. McGinty, "A Technique for Recording Single Neurons from Unrestrained Animals," *Brain Unit Activity During Behavior*, M. I. Phillips, ed., C. Thomas, Springfield, IL, pp. 80-104, (1973).

17. R. J. Radna and W. J. Vaughn, "Computer Assisted Unit Data Acquisition/Reduction," *Eletroenceph. Clin. Neurophysiol.*, vol. 44, pp. 239-242, (1978).

18. D. Stashuk and H. DeBruin, "Automatic Decomposition of Selective Needle-detected Myoelectric Signals," IEEE Trans. Biomed. Eng., vol. 35, pp. 1-10, (1988).

19. W. B. Marks, "Some Methods of Simultaneous Multiunit Recording," *Proc. Sympos. Information Processing in Sight Sensory Systems,* Cal. Tech., Pasadena, CA (1965).

20. D. H. Friedman, *Detection of Signals by Template Matching*, Dissertation, The Johns Hopkins University, Baltimore, MD (1968).

21. E. M. Glaser and W. B. Marks, "On-line Separation of Interleaved Neuronal Pulse Sequences, Data Acquisition Process," *Bio. Med.*, vol. 5, pp. 137-156, (1968).

22. E. M. Glaser, "Separation of Neuronal Activity by Waveform Analysis," in *Advances in Biomedical Engineering, Vol. 1,* R. M. Kenedt, ed., Academic Press, New York, pp. 77-136 (1971).

23. M. Abeles and M. H. Goldstein, Jr., "Multispike Train Analysis," *Proc. IEEE*, vol. 65, pp. 762-773, (1977).

24. G. L. Gerstein, M. J. Bloom, I. E. Espinosa, S. Evanczuk, and M. R. Turner, "Design of a Laboratory for Multineuron Studies," *IEEE Trans. Systems, Man. and Cybernetics,* vol. 13, pp. 668-676, (1983).

25. S. R. Smith and B. C. Wheeler, "A Real-Time Multiprocessor System for Acquisition of Multichannel Neural Data," *IEEE Trans. Biomed. Eng.*, vol. 35, pp. 875-877, (1988).

26. P. Bessou and E. R. Perl, "Response of Cutaneous Sensory Units with Unmyelinated Fibers to Noxious Stimuli," *J. Neurophysiol.*, vol. 32, pp. 1025-1043, (1969).

27. R. S. Remmel, "A Computerized Discriminator for Action Potentials," *Electroenceph. Clin. Neurophysiol.*, vol. 56, pp. 528-530, (1983).

28. W. M. Roberts and D. K. Hartline, "Separation of Multiunit Nerve Impulse Trains by a Multi-Channel Linear Filter Algorithm," *Brain Res.*, vol. 94, pp. 141-149, (1975).

29. M. N. Oguztoreli and R. B. Stein, "Optimal Linear Filtering of Nerve Signals," *Biol. Cybernet.*, vol. 27, pp. 41-48, (1977).

30. C. Camp and H. Pinsker, "Computer Separation of Unitary Spikes from Whole-Nerve Recordings," *Brain Res.*, vol. 169, pp. 455-479, (1979).

31. W. J. Heetderks, "Criteria for Evaluating Multiunit Spike Separation Techniques," *Biol. Cybernet.*, vol. 29, pp. 215-220, (1978).

32. B. C. Wheeler and W. J. Heetderks, "Separation of Cockroach Giant Action Potentials using Multiunit Analysis Techniques," *Proc. 7th. New. England Bioeng. Conf.*, pp. 310-313, (1979).

33. B. C. Wheeler and W. J. Heetderks, "A Comparison of Techniques for Classification of Multiple Neural Signals," *IEEE Trans. Biomed. Eng.*, vol. 29, pp. 752-759, (1982).

34. A. K. Jain, "A Fast Karhunen Loeve Transform for a Class of Random Processes," *IEEE Trans. Commun.*, vol. 24, pp. 1023-1029, (1975).

35. S. Bow, "Clustering Analysis and Nonsupervised Learning," *Pattern recognition*, Marcel Dekker, New-York, pp. 98-153, (1984).

36. R. Dubes and A. K. Jain, "Clustering Methodologies in Exploratory Data Analysis," *Adv. Comput.*, vol. 19, pp. 113- 228, (1980).

37. I. N. Bankman, K. O. Johnson, and W. Schneider, "Optimal Detection, Classification, and Resolution of Superpositions of Neural Waveforms," *IEEE Trans. Biomed. Eng.*, (in press).

38. I. N. Bankman, K. O. Johnson, and W. Schneider, "Optimal recognition of neural waveforms," *Proc. of the 13th Annual International Conference of the IEEE Engineering in Medicine and Biology Society,* vol. 13, pp. 409-410, (1991).

39. I. N. Bankman, and A. M. Menkes, "Automated Segmentation of Neural Recordings for Optimal Recognition of Neural Waveforms," *Proc. of the 14th Annual Conference of the IEEE Engineering in Medicine and Biology Society,* vol. 14, pp. 2560-2561, (1992).

40. I. Daubechies, "The Wavelet Transform, Time Frequency Localization and Signal Analysis," *IEEE Trans. Infor. Theory.*, vol 36, pp. 961-1005, (1990).

41. A. M. Menkes, I. N. Bankman, and K. O. Johnson, "Simulation of a Fully Automated System for Optimal On-line Recognition of Neural Waveforms in Extracellular Recordings," *Proc. of the 14th Annual Conference of the IEEE Engineering in Medicine and Biology Society,* vol. 14, pp. 2562-2563, (1992).

42. I. N. Bankman, K. O. Johnson, A. M. Menkes, S. D. Diamond, and D. M. O'Shaughnessy, "Automated Analyzer for On-line Recognition of Neural Waveforms in Extracellular Recordings of Multiple Neurons," *Proc. of the 14th Annual Conference of the IEEE Engineering in Medicine and Biology Society,* vol. 14, pp. 2852-2853, (1992).

Chapter 3

Coupled Neural-Dendritic Processes: Cooperative Stochastic Effects and the Analysis of Spike Trains

A.R. Bulsara
NCCOSC-RDT & E Division
San Diego, CA 92152

A.J. Maren
Accurate Automation Corp.
1548 Riverside Drive
Chattanooga, TN 37406

and

Brain Research Center and Computer Sciences Departments
Radford University
Radford, VA 24142

COUPLED NEURAL-DENDRITIC PROCESSES; COOPERATIVE STOCHASTIC EFFECTS AND THE ANALYSIS OF SPIKE TRAINS

A. R. Bulsara

NCCOSC-RDT&E Division, San Diego, CA 92152

A. J. Maren

Accurate Automation Corp., 1548 Riverside Drive, Chattanooga, TN 37406
and
Brain Research Center and Computer Sciences Dept., Radford University, Radford, VA 24142

ABSTRACT

We can create a richer and more neurophysiologically realistic model of neural activity in the brain by developing a model of neural-dendritic coupling, one which expressly accounts for the way in which the many afferent connections into the neural body influence the somatic membrane potential. Such a model would begin to fill the need within the Artificial Neural Network community for neural models which go beyond the current "weighted sum" paradigm for artificial neuron connectivity. Although such models have use in engineering applications, there are many aspects of biological neural-dendritic organization which could enrich artificial neural networks. Moving from simple "axonal" connection weight neural models to neural-dendritic models with a richer structure will allow investigation of both events at the neural level (e.g. inter-spike interval histograms and stochastic resonance) and also potentially at the neural systems level. This will also introduce the possibility of introducing cross-scale interactions into artificial neural systems.

I. INTRODUCTION

The effect of neural-dendritic interactions has so far been only weakly probed in the realm of artificial neural networks and neural modeling. Traditional Artificial Neural Network (ANN) models of interacting neurons use a simple description of neural connectivity. In such simple models, communication between neurons is afforded by artificial axons, and the "strength" of a given neuron-to-neuron connection is given as a "connection weight" between the two neurons. Synaptic plasticity is viewed in terms of the modifiability of connection weight ("axonal") strengths (for a review of ANNs, see Maren, Harston, and Pap, 1990).

A more neurophysiologically realisitic - and interesting - basis for modeling neural systems would take into account the nature of neural-dendritic connectivity. Such considerations for neural systems modeling were advanced as early as 1958 by John von Neumann. In 'The Computer and the Brain,' von Neumann wrote:

...However, the more frequent situation is that the body of a neuron has synapses with axons of many other neurons. It even appears that, occasionally, several axons from one neuron form synapses on another. Thus the possible stimulators are many, and the patterns of stimulation that may be effective have more complicated definitions than the simple "and" and "or" schemes described ... It may well be that certain nerve pulse combinations will

> stimulate a given neuron not simply by virtue of their number but also by virtue of the spatial relations of the synapses to which they arrive... [p. 54]

von Neumann went on to describe the role of synaptic connections on information processing in the brain:

> It is conceivable that in the essentially digitally-organized nervous system the complexities referred to play an analog or at least as "mixed" role. It has been suggested that by such mechanisms more recondite over-all electrical effects might influence the functioning of the nervous system. It could be that in this way certain general electrical potentials play an important role and that the system responds to the solutions of potential theoretical problems *in toto,* problems which are less immediate and elementary than what one normally describes by the digital criteria, stimulation criteria, etc. [p. 59]

In 1991, Pribram extended his earlier outline of local circuit processes of dendro- dendritic connections to describe a "holonomic brain theory" [Pribram, 1991]. Under this conceptualization:

> A microprocess is conceived in terms of *ensembles* of mutually interacting pre- and post-synaptic events distributed across limited extents of the dendritic network. The limits of reciprocal interaction vary as a function of input (sensory and central) to the network - limits are not restricted to the dendritic tree of a single neuron. In fact, receiprocal interaction among pre- and postsynaptic events often occurs at a distance from one another, that is, in a saltatory fashion. [p.16]

It seems, then, that parallel to the traditional neural network approach of modeling neural systems using only "axonal" (weighted sum) connectivity, there has been an awareness that the situation is much more complex, and that a "feltwork" of multiple axo-dendritic and dendro-dendritic (synaptic) connections plays a strong role in neural information processing. This realization has been born out in the investigations of researchers such as Rall [1970], who has developed a detailed model for the influence of local dendritic potentials on the somatic membrane potential. Yet there remains the issue of how we are to couple, in a single model, both the effect of multiple dendritic potentials afferent to a neuron, and the neural membrane potential at the cell body. This task involves a transformation of the signal from wave to pulse, and back to wave again. Walter Freeman has described the information flow process:

> "...At the first stage, pulses coming in to a set of neurons are converted into synaptic currents (patterns of hyper- and de-polarizations) which we call waves. Second, these synaptic currents are operated on by the dendrites of the neurons. This involves filtering and integration over time and space in the wave mode. Third, the wave activity reaching the trigger zones is converted back to the pulse mode. Fourth, it then undergoes transmission, which is translation from one place to another, delay, dispersion in time, etc... Pulse to wave conversion at synapses is commonly thought to be nonlinear, but in fact, in the normal range of cortical operation it is linear... But the operation of wave to pulse conversion is nonlinear, and the trigger zone is the crucial site of transformation that determines the neural gain over the four stages..." [personal communication; Pribram 1991]

Our goal, in this work, is to model the activity of a given neuron as it receives input from various sources, including its own synapses. Hence, we construct a model that couples two levels of description: (1) the activation at the neuron (soma and axon hillock), where we are interested in describing how the membrane potential changes in response to both dendritic input and activation decay and, (2) the activity in a large set of dendritic volumes, each of which is afferent to the neuron. At the dendritic level, we are interested in modeling the overall activity in a small dendritic volume (a 'reductionist' approach). This will be a function of the input into a set of synapses plus decay terms. To accomplish this task, we must identify appropriate time-scales for the activation decay at both the neural and dendritic levels. At the dendritic level, there exist different time constants for synaptic activities corresponding to electrotonic synapses, direct chemically-gated synapses, and second-order chemically gated synapses. The time constant for an electrotonic synapse is very short ($\ll 1ms.$) while the time constant for a direct chemically-gated synapse (which is more common in cortical neurons) may be on the order of a few milliseconds. The effects of both these synaptic activities fall within the purview of the current work; however second-order chemically gated synapses have longer time constants and cannot be treated by our model.

In order to characterize processes at the synaptic level, i.e., to characterize a dendritic volume activation in terms of its relationships to inputs and to activation decay, we set $u_i(i>1)$ to be the total post-synaptic activation of a small *dendritic volume*, which can include several dendritic spines and their afferent connections. The dendritic volume is roughly equivalent to the "dendron" introduced by Eccles [1964]. Pre-synaptic chemically-gated input to the dendritic volume, resulting from action potentials at other neurons, contributes to the total dendritic volume activation. We think of this input as being predominantly due to chemically-gated synaptic transmissions which have time-constants in the 1-5ms. range [Kandel et. al. 1991 pg. 124]. To a great extent, the elicited post-synaptic-potential (PSP) response to afferent spiking is linear. However, the response is bounded from above in the case of excitatory inputs and from below when the inputs are inhibitory. This is due to probabilistic release of quantized packets of neurotransmitter into the synaptic cleft [Eccles, 1981] and to a finite number of channels in the post-synaptic terminus. Further, experimental measurements of excitatory and inhibitory PSPs show that both are maximally within several tens of millivolts of the membrane resting potential [Kandel et. al. 1991]. This also indicates bounding of the PSPs. Bounding also comes about through scalingof the PSP which occurs in the short distance the PSP travels from the synaptic site, at the spine head, to the spine base; simulations indicate that the potential may drop by as much as 95% as a result [Segev et. al. 1992]. Consideration of these combined factors will allow us to model the temporal derivative of the activation or total polarization of a small dendritic volume as an activation decay term plus input terms. The inputs will include the weighted and bounded effects of presynaptic signals from axonal and/or dendritic connections, a weak (low amplitude and frequency) periodic driving force, and noise. As we shall see later, the form for the temporal derivative of the activation in a synaptic volume will be the same as for the neural body itself.

The activation potential which originates in a local dendritic volume and moves through the dendritic arborization towards the soma undergoes two substantial changes [Segev et. al. 1992]. Both changes influence the model that we construct for time-dependent activation at the soma. First, there is a marked attenuation of the maximal signal amplitude, and second, there is a drawing out of the signal waveform. Simulations by Rall and Rinzel [1973], Rinzel and Rall [1974] and Segec et. al. [1992] indicate a strong attenuation if the synaptic PSP as it passes from the originating dendritic volume towards the soma. The final maximal signal amplitude reaching the soma can be less than 1% of the original maximal amplitude, even though the stretched signal duration indicates that a substantial portion of the signal is preserved via temporal integration. This leads us to model the neuronal (i.e. soma) input not as the direct value of the synaptic activation but rather as a bounded function of it. This makes plausible the use of a transfer function such as a sigmoid or hyperbolic tangent, which is so ubiquitous in neural modeling. It is important to point out that the decoupling (to be described in the following section) of the neuro-dendritic stochastic differential equations via the adiabatic theory will be tantamount to a "quasi-linearization" of the dendritic dynamics. Another observation arising out of these simulations is that the PSP signal waveform is greatly stretched as it travels towards the soma. Specifically, an input that may occur in less than $10ms.$ at the synaptic site may have an influence persisting over $100ms.$ at the soma. This is particularly true if the synaptic site is far from the soma. We can summarize this by noting that "...the dendritic tree behaves as a substantial *delay line* for the synaptic inputs [and that] distal inputs are subject to significantly longer neural delays than proximal inputs..." [Segev et. al. 1992]. The notion of different distributions of synaptic input has been stated and experimentally observed as early as the 1960s [e.g. Rall 1970]. In any given neuron, due to the branching nature of the dendritic tree, there will be far more distal inputs than proximal inputs. Thus, to a first approximation, we can model the synaptic inputs under the assumption that the time-constants of events are "stretched" as they move through the dendritic passage to the soma. This allows us to make an adiabatic approximation in treating the activation equations of the dendritic volumes and the neuron.

We turn our attention now to the membrane potential at the neural soma and axon hillock, and note that again we may think of the temporal derivative of the activation as the sum of an activation decay term plus various input terms. We characterize the time constant at the neural soma as the time constant for temporal integration of the inputs from the dendritic volumes. This concept has been used to explain how different neurons can differentially respond to synaptic input that occurs over time; a short time constant provides only a small window for temporal integration, whereas longer time constants allow successive waves of synaptic input to be integrated, thereby providing a greater possibility for producing an action potential [Kandel et. al. 1990, pp 167-68]. Time constants pertaining to the soma and axon hillock have been incorporated into models by Stein et. al. [1974]. The use of long neural time constants is also congruent with the results of Segev et. al. [1992] in that synaptic input is both attenuated and drawn out over time as it reaches the soma. Long time constants for temporal integration would permit the effect of input from a distal dendritic volume to be recovered at the soma. We note that our approach models neural time-dependent activity in terms of its relation to inputs, and neglects the transient spiking behavior of the action potential. It should be noted that a more general description of the dynamics of coupled neurons, having time constants of comparable magnitude to those of their dendritic counterparts, should be developed using a quasi-linear mean field theory, which is a more general approach than the model discussed in this work; such work is currently underway.

To complete our model we assume, in addition to background random noise from chemical and/or electrotonic sources, the presence of a weak periodic modulation of the form $q \sin\omega t$. This may arise via direct communication to other neural layers receiving a periodic stimulus, or to a pacemaker neuron, or via interaction with an ambient chemical bath in which certain neurotransmitters are induced, by either of the former causes, to appear with regularity. We may then write down the N-body stochastic differential equation describing our model neuron coupled to its dendritic "bath" (the coupling itself being weakly nonlinear):

$$C_i \dot{u}_i = \sum_{j=1}^{N} J_{ij} \tanh u_j - \frac{u_i}{R_i} + F_i(t) + q \sin\omega t \, , \qquad (1)$$

where the dot denotes the time-derivative. The $i=1$ index denotes the cell body, with the remaining indices denoting the elemental dendritic volumes. u_1 represents the activation (or membrane potential in a Hopfield-style description) of the soma and R_1C_1 is the activation decay time. Alternatively, we may think of C_1 and R_1 as the input capacitance and trans-membrane resistance respectively. $u_i(i>1)$ represents the total activation of the ith dendritic volume. The noise is taken to be Gaussian delta-correlated having zero mean and variance σ_i^2. The noise sources for the different indices i are uncorrelated. J_{1j}, J_{j1} represent the forward and backward couplings between the cell body and the jth dendritic volume and $J_{ij}(i,j>1)$ represents the coupling between dendritic volumes i and j. We allow the matrix J to be non-symmetric.

The membrane potential $u_1(t)$ has been given different interpretations by different researchers. Because of the complexity of the process being modeled, and because the assumptions that different investigators make in identifying $u_{(t)1}$ with the neural membrane potential are not always obvious, this point is worth clarification. The most common interpretation of $u_1(t)$ in the ANN literature is via the "continuous" model advanced by Hopfield [1984]. This point of view was also advanced earlier by investigators such as Cowan [1970,74] and Clark [1988,89]. In these models, the membrane potential of a generalized neural body is modeled as $u_1(t)$. This is the simplest possible model of a neural-like element, and incorporates only considerations of capacitance and resistance, in analogy to an electrical circuit. This model has been useful in the design of artificial neural networks. However, it requires clarification before it can be applied to a real neural system. Specifically, we must identify how the continuous function $u_1(t)$ relates to the neural membrane potential, which is subject to sharp discontinuities when an action potential is created.

Stein [1965,67] treated the neural activation as a continuous Markov process whose sample paths had discontinuities of the first kind. Solutions to this type of model are difficult due to the nature of the differential-difference dynamics. Also, this approach modeled the inputs to a neuron as discrete current pulses arriving according to a Poisson process. The value of $u_1(t)$ would change instantaneously upon arrival of a distinct excitatory or inhibitory event, and then decay back to a (zero-level) resting state. A more effective model of neural activation requires that the inputs to the neural system be modeled in a continuous manner, consistent with our understanding of the "stretched" arrival of dendritic activations at the neural soma, as has been described by Rall and Rinzel [1973], Rinzel & Rall [1974], Holmes & Rall [1992], and Segev et al. [1992]. In a later work, Stein et al. [1974] identified the activation of the neuron as the rate at which nerve impulses would be fired. While this would allow an intuitive connection between the neural model description and "states", which could be roughly described in terms of the average frequency of firing of an action potential, it does not serve when the model needs to be connected with a more explicit description of neural dynamics, such as the generation of interspike interval histograms. We will return to this point later in this work. Subsequent investigators have developed diffusion models in which the discontinuities in $u_1(t)$ have been smoothed out (see e.g. Tuckwell, 1980 and references cited therein). While more mathematically tractable, such models again treat the arrival of excitatory and inhibitory signals to the neural soma as discrete rather than continuous processes.

For the current work, a more precise identification of the neural membrane potential is needed; one which distinguishes it from the potentials within the dendritic network afferent to the soma, and one which decouples the continuous-time activation changes in the soma that occur in response to input and activation decay from the action potential, whose abrupt nature may be viewed as a reset mechanism of an otherwise continuous process. In our work, the variable $u_1(t)$ refers specifically to the membrane potential at the trigger zone in the neural soma. This is because the interesting dynamics of the soma are generated at the trigger zone, which has a lower threshold than the rest of the soma. However, changes in membrane potential at the trigger zone propagate rapidly both throughout the soma itself, and down the axon as an action potential. We regard the brief depolarization and ensusing hyperpolarization of the action potential (and its corollary within the neural soma itself) as a reset mechanism whose details are not addressed in this work. Our model does, however, address the continuous changes in membrane potential due to dendritic connectivity, activation decay, and other factors.

The disparity in the neural and dendritic time-constants discussed above is incorporated into our model via the constraint,

$$R_i \ll R_1 \quad (i > 1). \tag{2}$$

This constraint will allow us to confidently utilize the slaving principle of Haken [1977] to reduce the system (1). This reduction is carried out in the next section. We also consider, via numerical simulations, the range of validity of the adiabatic elimination technique as well as the bifurcation properties and collective effects that appear in the decoupled neuron dynamics because of the interaction with the dendritic bath. Finally, we discuss switching events (between the firing/quiescent states of the neuron) that arise as a consequence of the interplay between the noise and the periodic modulation... *stochastic resonance*.

II. SINGLE NEURON DYNAMICS

The separation of time-scales embodied in the inequality (2) permits us to apply the slaving principle [Haken 1977] to the coupled system (1). This leads to a closed equation for the soma activation function $u_1(t)$ i.e., the system (1) is decoupled. The proceedure is outlined in the following subsection (refer to Schieve, Bulsara and Davis 1991, Bulsara, Maren and Schmera, 1992 for details) in which we also introduce the effective "potential function" corresponding to the single neuron dynamics. This is followed by an analysis of the bifurcation properties of the reduced model (in the absence of the deterministic modulation $q \sin\omega t$). The remainder of this paper examines the cooperative effects (together with their potential implications in neuroscience) that arise when this modulation term is switched on.

Reduced Neuron Equation

Equation (1) represents a system of globally coupled nonlinear stochastic differential equations, subject to the constraint (2) on the equivalent circuit resistors R_i. The N-dimensional

Fokker Planck equation [see e.g. Stratonovich 1963, Risken 1984; Gardiner 1985] for the probability density function $P(u_1, u_2, ..., t)$ corresponding to the system (1) may be written in the form,

$$\frac{\partial P}{\partial t} = -\sum_i \left\{ \frac{\partial}{\partial u_i}(q_i P) + Q_i \frac{\partial^2 P}{\partial u_i^2} \right\}, \tag{3}$$

where the drift and diffusion terms are defined by

$$C_i\, q_i(u_1, u_2, ... u_N) = -\frac{u_i}{R_i} + J_{ii} \tanh u_i + \sum_{k \neq i} J_{ik} \tanh u_k + q \sin \omega t\,, \tag{4a}$$

and

$$Q_i = \sigma_i^2 / C_i^2 \tag{4b}$$

We have assumed that the noise sources $F_i(t)$ in (1) are uncorrelated i.e., $\langle F_i(t) F_k(t+\tau) \rangle = 0$ (this condition is not, however, crucial to the analytical tractability of the problem) and that they are Gaussian, delta-correlated with zero mean values and variances σ_i^2. Multiplicative noise effects have been considered (for the $q=0$ case) in earlier work [Bulsara, Boss and Jacobs 1989; Schieve, Bulsara and Davis 1991; Bulsara and Schieve 1991] and the effects of multiplicative noise on stochastic resonance in a single (isolated) neuron have been treated by Bulsara et. al. [1991a].

The essence of the slaving principle is that the steady state solution for the probability density function P may be factored as

$$P(u_1, u_2, ... u_N) \equiv h(u_2, u_3, ... | u_1)\, g(u_1), \tag{5}$$

where h is to be interpreted as a conditional probability density for finding $u_{j>1}$ given u_1 (both h and g are normalized to unity). We have assumed that the dendritic bath, by virtue of its faster time-constants, reaches its steady-state configuration far more rapidly than the cell body (described by the activation function u_1). Then we may substitute the factored probability density function (5) into the original Fokker Planck equation (3) and separate it [Haken 1977; Gardiner 1985; Schieve, Bulsara and Davis 1991]:

$$\frac{\partial h}{\partial t} = -\sum_{i>1} \left\{ \frac{\partial}{\partial u_i}(q_i h) + \frac{1}{2} Q_i \frac{\partial^2 h}{\partial u_i^2} \right\}, \tag{6}$$

$$\frac{\partial g}{\partial t} = -\frac{\partial}{\partial u_1} \left\{ A(u_1)\, g(u_1) \right\} + \frac{\sigma_1^2}{2 C_1^2} \frac{\partial^2 g}{\partial u_1^2} \tag{7}$$

where we define the kernel $A(u_1)$ by,

$$A(u_1) \equiv \int \cdots \int du_2 du_3 ... h(u_2, u_3, ... | u_1)\, q_1(u_1, u_2, ...)\,. \tag{8}$$

We first must integrate (6) in the steady state ($t \to \infty$) treating u_1 as constant. This can only be done if the modulation frequency ω is much smaller than all other frequencies in the system. This so-called adiabatic approximation is a cornerstone of stochastic resonance theory [McNamara and Wiesenfeld 1989] and will be made more precise later in this work. For the purposes of integrating (6), we assume the modulation term to be approximately constant. Far more serious, however, is the lack of detailed balance [Risken 1984, Gardiner 1985] when the dimensionality of (6) exceeds unity. In general, a steady state (potential function) solution of (6) cannot be found for this case. However, using a technique due to Stratonovich [1989] we can write down a potential solution of (7) for very small deviations from equilibrium. Specifically, we write $h(u_2, u_3, \cdots u_N / u_1)$ as an $(N-1)$ - dimensional Gaussian, Taylor-expand the terms $\tanh u_{i>1}$ about the equilibrium states $\bar{u}_{i>1}$, and evaluate the kernel $A(u_1)$ defined in (8). The proceedure has been detailed earlier [Schieve, Bulsara, and Davis 1991; Bulsara, Maren and Schmera 1992] and is not repeated here. We finally obtain the stochastic differential equation corresponding to the Fokker Planck Equation (7):

$$\dot{u}_1 = -\frac{dU(u_1)}{du_1} + \delta \sin \omega t + \sqrt{\sigma_e^2}\, F(t), \tag{9}$$

where $\sigma_\epsilon^2 \equiv \sigma_1^2/C_1^2$ and $F(t)$ is Gaussian delta-correlated noise having zero mean and unit variance and we have introduced the (deterministic) potential function that affords us a more elegant mathematical treatment of the dynamics:

$$U(u_1) \equiv \frac{1}{2}\alpha u_1^2 - \beta \ln \cosh u_1 . \tag{10}$$

The coefficients in the above dynamics are given by,

$$\alpha \equiv (R_1 C_1)^{-1} \tag{11a}$$

$$\beta \equiv C_1^{-1}\left[J_{11} + \sum_{i>1} R_i G_i^{-1} J_{1i} J_{i1} \left[1 - \frac{\sigma_i^2 R_i}{2C_i} \right] \right], \tag{11b}$$

$$\delta \equiv \frac{q}{C_1}\left[1 + \sum_{i>1} R_i G_i^{-1} J_{1i} \left[1 - \frac{\sigma_i^2 R_i}{2C_i} \right] \right], \tag{11c}$$

and we have set $G_k \equiv 1 - J_{kk} R_k$. Equation (9) (the so-called "reduced" or "effective" neuron dynamics) constitutes the starting point for our subsequent analyses, u_1 representing the voltage at the soma. We note that it contains (via (11)) the effects of the coupling between the cell body and each of the dendritic volumes. Back-coupling (characterized by the coefficients J_{i1}) effects are included as well as self-feedback terms (characterized by the coefficients J_{ii}). Cross-coupling terms (characterized by products of the form $R_i R_k J_{ik} J_{ki}$; $k, i > 1$) between the dendritic spaces are also present but are neglected. It is important to point out that, in general, the expressions (11b,c) contain higher order terms; these are absent because of the truncation (at second order) of the Taylor expansion of the functions $\tanh u_{i>1}$, consistent with our assumption of small deviations from equilibrium of the dendritic "bath". The detailed analysis [Schieve, Bulsara and Davis 1991] leading up to the expressions (11) shows these terms to be of higher order in $\sigma_i^2 R_i / 2C_i$. We assume that the dendritic noise terms are sufficiently weak so that we always have

$$\frac{\sigma_i^2 R_i}{2C_i} < 1 \quad i > 1, \tag{12}$$

so that the deviations $u_i - \bar{u}_i$ are small. Note also that we have *not* assumed that the matrix **J** is symmetric, in contrast with existing (Hopfield-type) models. In fact, no further assumptions beyond (2) and (12) (both of which are based on very reasonable physical and neurophysiological arguments) as well as the adiabatic assumption of very low modulation frequency ω need be made to obtain the reduced neuron dynamics (9). In the next subsection, we write down the "potential" function corresponding to the reduced neuron dynamics and examine its stability and bifurcation properties. We also present numerical simulation results that elucidate the range of validity of the reduced description (9) when compared to the full dynamics (1).

Steady-State Potential Function; Stability and Bifurcation Properties

It is easy to show, via linear stability analysis, that the dynamics in (9) are globally stable as long as $\alpha \geq 0$. For this case, the potential function $U(u_1)$ is a Liapounov function for the reduced dynamics (9). We note that stability does *not* depend on the properties of the coupling matrix **J** Assuming $\alpha \geq 0$, we can easily show that the potential (10) will be parabolic (with an elliptic fixed point at u_1=0) if $\beta \leq \alpha$ (this includes negative as well as positive values of β). For $\beta > \alpha$, the potential is bimodal (with its minima located at $c \approx \pm(\beta/\alpha)\tanh(\beta/\alpha)$, and a hyperbolic fixed point at c=0) and cooperative stochastic effects come into play. The transition to bimodality (at $\beta = \alpha$) is accompanied by a pitchfork bifurcation in the most probable value of the activation u_1 with the two states (attractors) corresponding roughly to the quiescent and firing states of the neuron. The flow (given by the first term on the rhs of (9)) exhibits the characteristic N-shaped relationship known to exist in excitable cells (see e.g. Rinzel and Ermentrout 1989; Abbott and Kepler 1990). We now consider the effects of the cell body coupling to multiple dendritic volumes on this transition. Throughout the remainder of this work we shall assume, for simplicity, that the noise variances in the elemental dendritic volumes are the same and, further, that all the dendritic time-constants are equal. Specifically, we set $\sigma_i^2 = \sigma_2^2, R_i = R_2$ for all $i > 1$ and $C_i = 1$ for all i. We further assume that the elements of the coupling matrix **J** are drawn from a Gaussian random number set with specified mean and variance. This permits us to loosely identify the particular elements J_{ij}, drawn from the wings of the Gaussian, as associated with couplings to dendritic volumes which occur closer to the cell body.

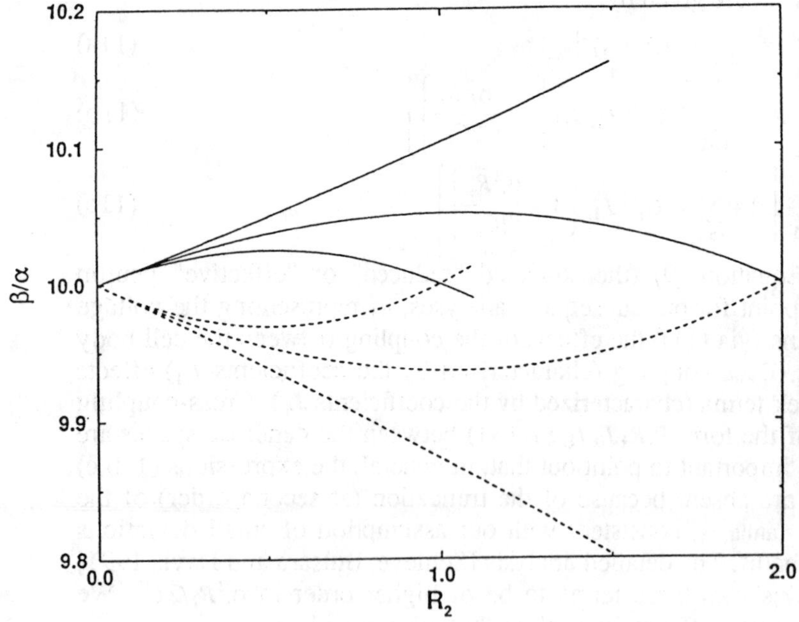

Fig 1. Effective nonlinearity parameter β/α (computed from (11b)) vs. R_2 for $N=100$, $R_1=10$. Solid curves represent $\bar{J}_{1i}=1=\bar{J}_{i1}$ and dendritic noise variance $\sigma_2^2=0,1,2$ reading from the top curve downward. Dotted curves correspond to $\bar{J}_{i1}=-1$ with same values of σ_2^2 reading from the bottom curve upward. $\bar{J}_{ii}=0$, $\overline{J_{ii}^2}=1$ for $i>1$.

Figure 1 is a plot of β/α vs. the dendritic resistance R_2. For this figure we have assumed that the diagonal elements J_{ii} of the coupling matrix are drawn from a Gaussian set having mean zero and unit variance. We further assume that the elements J_{1i} are drawn from a Gaussian set having unit mean and variance, whereas the back-coupling elements J_{i1} can be drawn from a Gaussian set having unit mean and variance as well as from a Gaussian set having a mean of -1 and unit variance. We thus assume that the couplings can be (almost) purely excitatory or a mixture of excitatory and inhibitory. It is important to note that, in general, the elements of **J** can take on any values since the only criterion for global stability is the positivity of the coefficient α. Since, in general, N can be quite large, we must scale the coupling matrix by N to assure that the second term in (10) does not become inordinately large. This is done throughout the remainder of this work. From the expressions (11) we may obtain [Bulsara, Maren and Schmera, 1992], approximately, the threshold value, R_{2c} at which the potential becomes bimodal (all other parameters being fixed). Throughout this work, we set $J_{11}=N$ so that, in the absence of any coupling to the dendritic bath, the cell body behaves like a bistable oscillator characterized by the potential function (10). In figure 1 we have set $J_{11}=10(=N)$ i.e. we assume an excitatory self feedback in the cell body in the absence of any coupling to the dendritic bath. We also set $R_1=10$ so that in the absence of any coupling to the bath, the single (i.e. isolated) neuron potential is bimodal. In the presence of a preponderance of excitatory couplings ($\bar{J}_{1i}=1=\bar{J}_{i1}$ and $\overline{J^2}_{1i}=1=\overline{J^2}_{i1}$) the ratio β/α increases (for nonzero σ_2^2) upto a maximum value, after which it decreases. The opposite effect is seen to occur for the case of a mix of excitatory and inhibitory couplings ($\bar{J}_{1i}=1=-\bar{J}_{i1}$). The curves corresponding to these two realizations of the off-diagonal elements for a given value of σ_2^2 (for the cases in which an extremum exists) cross at the values $R_2=0$ and $2/\sigma_2^2$, yielding the $J_{1j}=0$ result ($\beta/\alpha=J_{11}R_1=10.0$). Beyond this intersection, the inequality (12) is violated and we do not expect the theory to yield accurate results.

We now digress briefly to consider the case in which the potential is monomodal in the absence of any coupling to the dendritic bath (this can be achieved by setting $J_{11}R_1 < 1$), in contrast to the case discussed in the preceding paragraph. Then, one can easily calculate the value of R_2 (for given noise variance σ_2^2 and configuration of the matrix **J**) above which the effective potential is bimodal. Increasing R_2 leads to a transition to bimodality (occurring at $\beta/\alpha=1$) *only* for the case in which the sum $\sum_{i>1} J_{1i}J_{i1}$ is positive (keeping in mind the constraint imposed by the inequality (12)). This may be realized by imposing the same sign on the vast majority of the off-diagonal elements J_{1i} and J_{i1}. Increasing the noise variance σ_2^2 degrades the effect; this is evident from (11b). It is apparent that the coupling to the dendritic bath may actually introduce a phase-transition-like behavior into the neuron dynamics. Effects such as this *coupling-induced bimodality* are a hallmark of multiplicative noise (see e.g. Horsthemke and Lefever 1984) and have been examined in simpler neuron models (for both additive and multiplicative noises) by Bulsara, Boss and Jacobs [1989], and Bulsara and Schieve [1991]. The opposite effect can also occur: depending on the magnitude and sign of each element J_{ij}, a potential that is bistable in the absence of the bath coupling, can be rendered monostable by the dendritic field. This is evident from (11b).

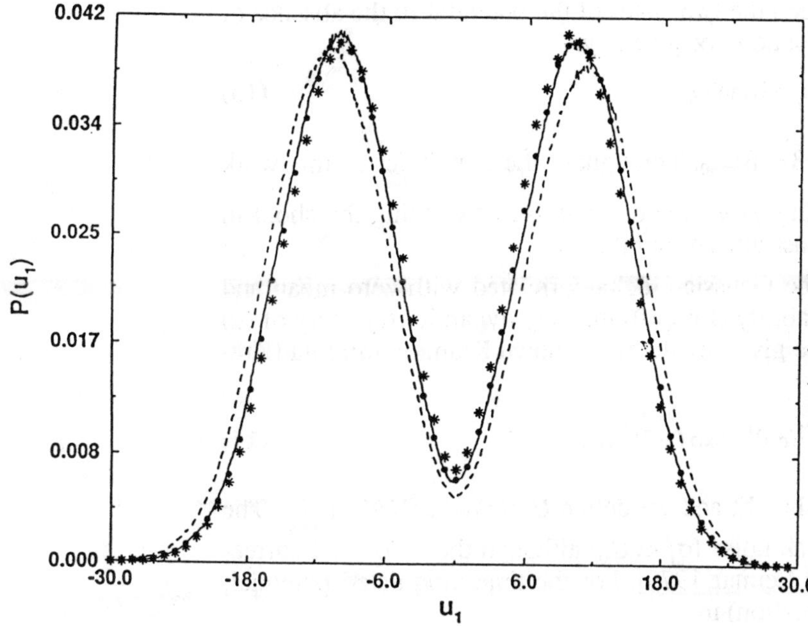

Fig 2. Neuron (cell body) probability density computed via direct integration of (1) and the reduced equation (9) (data points). $(R_1, \sigma_1^2, \sigma_2^2, q, \omega, N) \equiv (10,5,2,0.1,0.1,10)$. $J_{ik}=1=J_{ik}^2$. $J_{ii}=0, J^2=1$ $(i>1)$. $R_2=0.35$ (solid curve and filled data points) and 1.0 (dashed curve and asterisk data points).

Before concluding this subsection, we present the results of numerical simulations aimed at demonstrating the validity of the approximations made in this paper. Figure 2 shows the probability density function corresponding to the "slow" variable u_1. The solid curves (corresponding to simulations of the fully coupled system (1)) have been obtained via direct integration on an HP-Apollo 425T workstation. We consider $N=10$ elements since the simulations become prohibitively time-consuming for larger N values. The system has been integrated through 12,000 periods of the deterministic modulation (after allowing the transients to die out) using a stepsize of 0.015. Noise has been included in the dynamics via the Heun algorithm (see e.g. Greiner et. al. 1988). The data points show the results of integrating the corresponding effective one-body equation (9) using the same routine. In this figure we take $R_1=10$ and consider the case $R_2=0.35$ and 1.0, all other parameters remaining fixed. The agreement between the exact and reduced dynamics is seen to be excellent for $R_2=0.35$. Increasing R_2 to 1.0 still yields reasonably good qualitative agreement although it is apparent that we are very close to the boundary at which (2) ceases to be a good approximation (and we are already in violation of (12)). It is important to point out that, contrary to conventional mean field theories, the adiabatic elimination of fast variables utilized in this work does not necessarily yield better results as the number N of entities increases; rather it depends solely on the separation of time-scales embodied in the inequality (2). Hence, repeating the simulations of figure 2 with larger N is unlikely to shed any fresh light on this aspect of the problem. Increasing N does, however, lead to other changes in the bifurcation properties of the reduced dynamics (9). These changes have been detailed elsewhere [Bulsara, Maren and Schmera 1992] and are not discussed here.

III. THE EFFECT OF WEAK DETERMINISTIC MODULATION; STOCHASTIC RESONANCE

Consider now, the inclusion of the *weak* deterministic modulation term $q\sin\omega t$ in the system (1). We have seen that this term reappears in the reduced equation (9) with a renormalized amplitude δ given by (11c). We assume that the modulation is not strong enough to cause the system to switch between the two states of the potential (12) in the absence of noise, i.e., if the cell body is quiescent in the absence of any external perturbation, the inclusion of the modulation will not cause it to fire unless noise is also present. We define the deterministic switching threshold for our reduced system (9) via the critical value, δ_c, of the renormalized modulation amplitude, above which one would obtain switching between the two states of the potential in the absence of noise ($\sigma_1^2=0=\sigma_2^2$). This critical value is easily found to be given by

$$\delta_c=-\alpha u_c+\bar{\beta}\tanh u_c\,, \tag{13}$$

where we define $u_c\equiv\ln\left[\sqrt{\frac{\beta}{\alpha}}+\sqrt{\frac{\beta}{\alpha}-1}\right]$ and $\bar{\beta}\equiv(\beta)_{\sigma^2=0}$. Throughout the remainder of this work we assume $\delta<\delta_c$. This can be assured by taking $q<q_c$, the deterministic switching threshold in the absence of any bath coupling, within the constraints of our theory.

In the presence of noise (taken here to be Gaussian, delta-correlated with zero mean and variance σ_1^2), there will always be a finite probability (for $q=0$) that any dynamic trajectory of (9) can surmount the barrier with the switching rate given by the well-known Kramers formula [Kramers 1940 and, e.g., Gardiner 1985],

$$r_0=\frac{1}{2\pi}\,[U^{(2)}(0)\,U^{(2)}(c)]^{1/2}\exp(-2U_0/\sigma_1^2)\,, \tag{14}$$

where $U_0\equiv U(0)-U(c)$ is the potential barrier height and we define $U^{(2)}(c)\equiv\left[d^2U/du_1^2\right]_{u_1=c}$. The above formula holds for high damping and weak noise ($\sigma_1^2\ll U_0$) although there do exist corrections to it for intermediate noise [Edholm and Leimar 1979]. For the time-modulated potential, the Kramers rate is modified (as a first approximation) to

$$r(t)=r_0\exp\left[-\frac{2\delta}{\sigma_1^2}\sin\omega t\right] \tag{15}$$

which is valid only for $\omega<<r_0$ (adiabatic approximation). The periodic modulation of the Kramers rate leads to switching events that are coherent with the modulation. If one integrates (9) and computes the power spectral density one obtains a series of sharp peaks located at odd multiples of ω, superimposed on a Lorentzian background. In addition, the total power of the signal plus noise is constant; as the signal strength is increased, the power in the signal peaks grows at the expense of the noise background. Finally, the signal-to-noise-ratio (SNR) passes through a maximum as a function of the noise variance σ_1^2, the maximum occurring at $\sigma_1^2\approx U_0$. Stochastic resonance has been observed in a number of physical systems [see e.g. the review paper by Moss 1992 and references therein]. The theory has been applied to a single (isolated) neuron, taking into account both additive and multiplicative (in the elements of J) noise effects by Bulsara et. al. [1991a]. We now consider the effect of the dendritic coupling, as well as large N effects, on stochastic resonance as it occurs in the reduced dynamics (9).

An approximate expression for the power spectral density for a one-dimensional nonlinear stochastic system of the form (9) has been derived by McNamara and Wiesenfeld [1989]:

$$P(\Omega)=[1-2Z(r_0\zeta)^2](8Zr_0c^2)+4Z\pi(r_0\zeta c^2)^2\delta(\Omega-\omega)$$
$$\equiv \mathrm{N}(\Omega)+\mathrm{S}(\Omega)\,\delta(\Omega-\omega)\,, \tag{16}$$

where we define $Z=(4r_0^2+\Omega^2)^{-1}$ and $\zeta=\delta c/\sigma_1^2$ is a perturbation theory expansion parameter. S and N are, respectively, the signal and noise powers. The above expression provides a good approximation to the power spectral density for $\zeta<1$ and has been derived under an adiabatic (i.e. low-frequency) approximation $\omega \ll U^{(2)}(c)$ that is somewhat less stringent than the $\omega \ll r_0$ approximation introduced earlier. The SNR is then obtained from

$$SNR=10\log\left[\frac{1}{\mathrm{N}(\omega)}\left\{\frac{\mathrm{S}(\omega)}{\Delta\omega}+\mathrm{N}(\omega)\right\}\right], \tag{17}$$

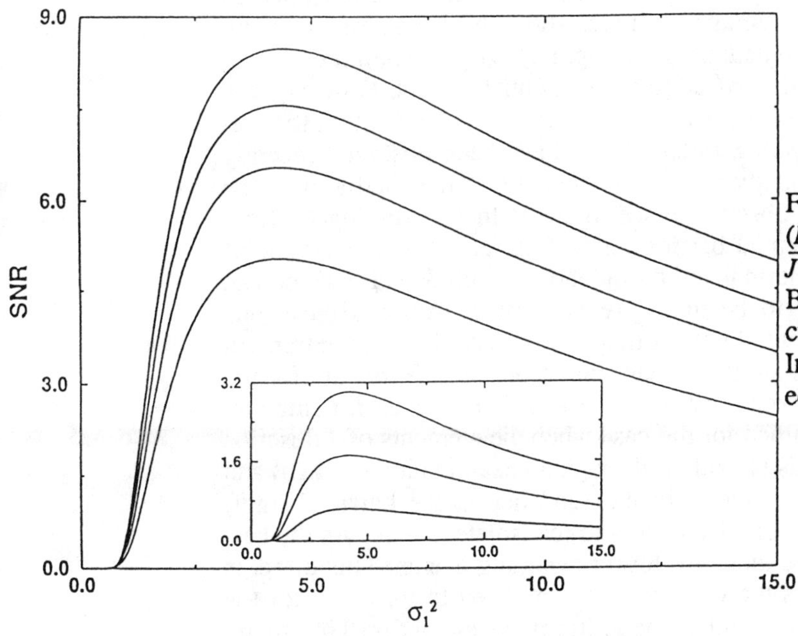

Fig 3. SNR computed from (16) and (17) for $(R_1,R_2,q,\omega,\Delta\omega,N)\equiv(10,0.6,0.1,0.1,0.001,100)$. $\overline{J_{1i}}=1=-\overline{J_{i1}}, \overline{J_{i1}^2}=1=\overline{J_{1i}^2}$. $\overline{J_{ii}}=0, \overline{J_{ii}^2}=1, (i>1)$. Bottom curve: $J_{1i}=0$ (isolated case). Remaining curves: $\sigma_2^2=0$ (top), 1 (middle), and 2 (lower). Inset: the case for no modulation in the cell-body eqn. in the system (1).

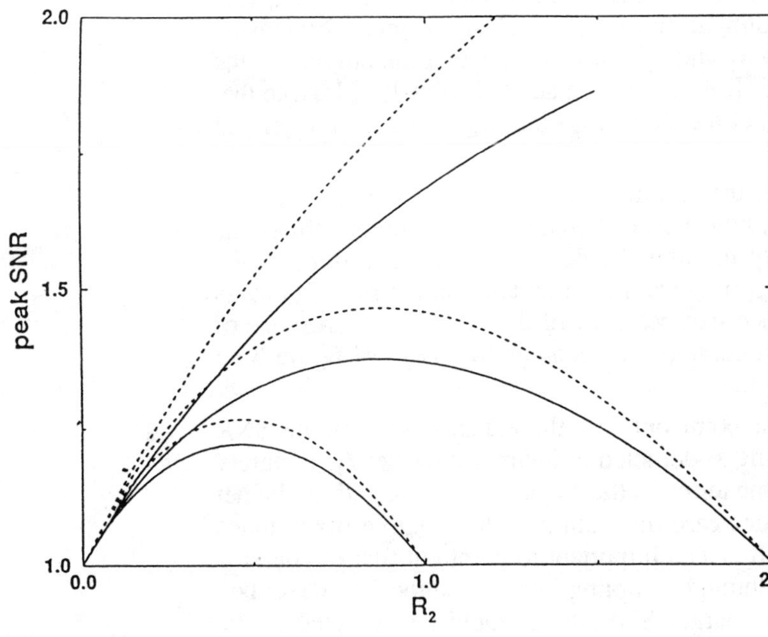

Fig 4. Peak SNR (normalized to its value for $J_{1i}=0$ case) vs. R_2 for $(R_1,q,\omega,\Delta\omega,N)\equiv(10,0.1,0.1,0.001,10)$ and $\sigma_2^2=0$ (top curve), 1 (middle curve), 2 (bottom curve). $\overline{J_{ii}}=0, \overline{J_{ii}^2}=1, (i>1)$.
Solid curves: $\overline{J_{1i}}=1=\overline{J_{i1}}, \overline{J_{1i}^2}=1=\overline{J_{i1}^2}$.
Dotted curves: $\overline{J_{1i}}=1=-\overline{J_{i1}}, \overline{J_{1i}^2}=1=\overline{J_{i1}^2}$.

Here, $\Delta\omega$ is the width of a single frequency bin in the (experimental) Fourier transformation. It is introduced in (17) to make contact with experimental results [Zhou and Moss 1989, 90]. We note, in passing, that the expression (16) contains effects due to the noise and deterministic modulation in both the signal and noise terms, unlike the case for a linear system. Further, by increasing the signal amplitude, the first term on the rhs of (16) can be made smaller in magnitude so that one obtains a decrease in the background noise power. Increasing the noise strength increases the Kramers rate r_0 while decreasing the expansion parameter ζ. The interplay of these two effects lead to the resonance-like curve for the SNR vs. σ_1^2.

In figure 3 we show the SNR for the reduced equation (9). We set $R_1=10$ and $R_2=0.6$. The elements of J are drawn from a Gaussian set with $\bar{J}_{1i}=1=-\bar{J}_{i1}, \bar{J^2}_{1i}=1=\bar{J^2}_{i1}, \bar{J}_{ii}=0, \bar{J^2}_{ii}=1$ and once again, we set the neuron (i.e. cell body) self-feedback coefficient $J_{11}=10(=N)$. For comparison purposes, the bottom curve shows the SNR that would be obtained for the isolated case ($J_{1i}=0, i>1$). Note that the combination of excitatory and inhibitory couplings used in our work has been theoretically predicted and also observed in experiments on the mammalian nervous system [Rall 1970, and references therein]. The remaining curves show the effects of including the dendritic coupling with different values of the bath noise strength σ_2^2. The maximum enhancement is seen to occur for $\sigma_2^2=0$ and then, increasing σ_2^2 degrades this enhancement. However, the coupling to the bath enhances the SNR *even in the presence of dendritic noise* (recall that the inequality (17) imposes an upper limit on the noise). Similar effects have been observed recently [Jung et. al. 1992] in a mean field model of globally (linearly) coupled bistable oscillators. The enhancement of the SNR may be explained by observing (see figure 1) that increasing R_2 from zero causes the ratio β/α (and therefore, the potential barrier height U_0), for this configuration of J, to initially decrease and then increase. The renormalized modulation amplitude δ, however, can only increase since we have taken the set J_{1i} to be mainly excitatory in nature. Hence, one obtains a marked increase in the SNR as the potential barrier height decreases. Past the extremum of β/α in figure 1, the opposite effect occurs. A similar enhancement of the SNR occurs for the case of all the off-diagonal elements of J being excitatory (i.e. $\bar{J}_{1i}=1=\bar{J}_{i1}$). However, for small N, the enhancement will not be as great as that obtained for the case when the elements of J describe a mix of excitatory and inhibitory couplings. This is evident through an examination of (11b) and figure 1; for the case of all excitatory couplings, the ratio β/α (and hence, the barrier height) increases from the values in the isolated case, before decreasing to the isolated value. As the barrier height increases the SNR will decrease since there are fewer switching events. This effect is strikingly demonstrated in figure 4 which shows the peak SNR (normalized to its value for the isolated, i.e., $J_{1j}=0$ case) as a function of R_2 for different dendritic noise strengths. This figure clearly shows that increasing the dendritic noise leads to a lower enhancement in the SNR; also the effects described above for the two different configurations of J are clearly evident. Increasing N leads to an increase in the peak SNR (for given R_2 and σ_2^2); also we find that the curves for the two configurations of J described above, converge [Bulsara, Maren and Schmera 1992]. Note that the curves in figure 4 are peaked (for nonzero σ_2^2) at the same values of R_2 for which the critical curves of figure 1 display their extrema.

Throughout this work, we have assumed that the modulation $q \sin\omega t$ acts on every equation of the system (1). In neurophysiological systems, however, one frequently encounters situations wherein the cell body receives input signals only through the dendritic bath. In this case, the modulation is present only in the equations for $u_{i>1}$ in (1) and the first term on the rhs of (11c) is absent. For this case, one still obtains the resonance-like behavior of the SNR in the presence of the bath (see inset of figure 3) although the lowest curve (corresponding to $J_{1i}=0$) of figure 3 no longer exists.

Before concluding this subsection, we must point out that the enhancement of the SNR through the dendritic coupling will not be as striking as depicted in figure 4 if the set J_{1i} is purely inhibitory. This is evident from (11c). If most of the terms in the summation are negative, the net effect is to decrease δ, while β may increase or decrease depending on the relative magnitudes and signs of the product terms in the summation. It is also important to point out that the dendritic bath may actually *induce* stochastic resonance through coupling-induced bimodality described in the preceding subsection; we may expect to see larger SNRs than would be expected in the absence of the bath, as a consequence.

IV. STATISTICAL ANALYSIS OF FIRING EVENTS

It is important to point out that stochastic resonance (as characterized by the bell-shaped SNR vs. noise variance curve of figure 3) has not yet been directly observed in a living system (although we will ennunciate a possible caveat to this statement at the end of the following subsection). The existence of noise-induced switching in the nervous system would seem, however, to be an eminently reasonable assumption, based on our simple model of the neuron as a noisy bistable switching element. Certainly, noise is ubiquitous in the nervous system; hence one might expect that when sensory neurons are periodically stimulated, the time intervals between successive firing events contain sensory information. These "reset" or "refractory" events correspond to the repolarization of the cell membrane. In fact, this has been well-known to neurophysiologists for many years. In neurophysiological experiments it is common to assemble an ensemble of firing events and fit a histogram to the intervals between the spikes. An example of these Inter-Spike-Interval Histograms (ISIHs), which are quite commonly seen in the neurophysiological literature, is shown in the following subsection. In this subsection we also demonstrate how the salient features of the experimentally observed ISIHs can be easily explained by our bistable model; in fact, we shall see that our model affords the *simplest possible* interpretation of the experimental spike train data. Throughout the rest of this work we show results for arbitrary values of the constants α, β, δ in (9), i.e., we do not consider the particular details of the quantities on the right-hand-sides of equations (11).

The Inter-Spike-Interval Histogram

We now return to our reduced system (9) and consider only the time intervals of the transitions between the potential wells (labeled A and B) while ignoring the intrawell motion (recall that the potential wells correspond, roughly, to the firing and refractory states of the soma). This is tantamount to replacing the detailed dynamics contained in (9) by the equivalent "two-state dynamics" depending only on the barrier height and the locations of the elliptic points of the potential (10). The result is the random "telegraph signal"$x(t)$ ($\equiv u_1(t)$ in the notation of this paper) depicted in figure 5.

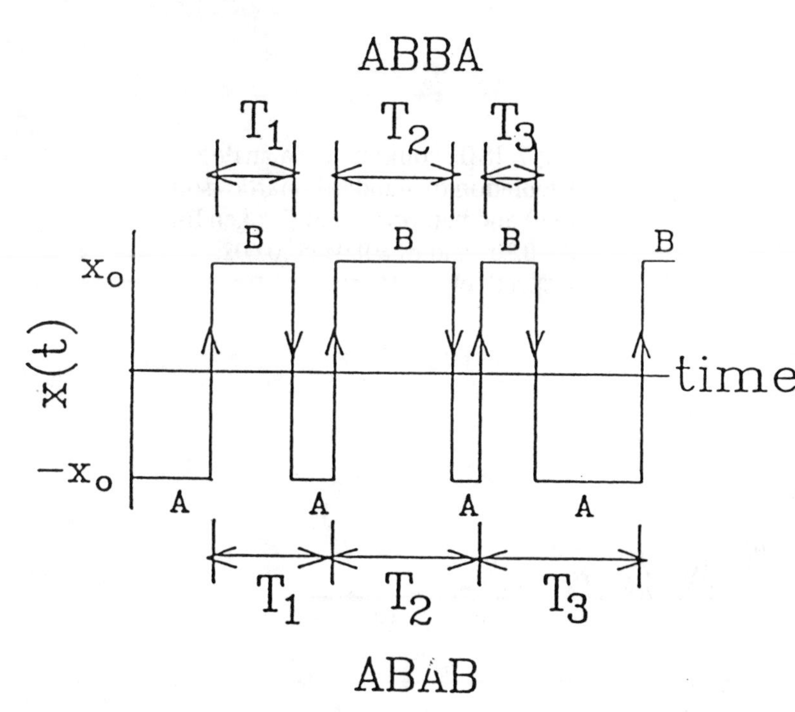

Fig 5. Sample output from two-state device driven by noise plus weak sinusoidal modulation. Stable states at $\pm x_0$ are labelled A and B. The ABBA and ABAB sequences shown, are the only consecutive time-interval sequences available to the two-state system from which ISIHs can be generated.

Two possible (unique) sequences of time interval measurements are possible in this system; they are depicted in figure 5. By measuring these residence times and fitting a histogram to the data, one obtains the probability density of well residence times. This quantity has been found [Longtin, Bulsara and Moss 1991; Longtin et. al. 1992] to reproduce many of the features of experimentally obtained (via direct measurement of the time series $u_1(t)$ corresponding to the firing/resetting of a stimulated neuron) inter-spike-interval histograms (ISIHs). In the presence of

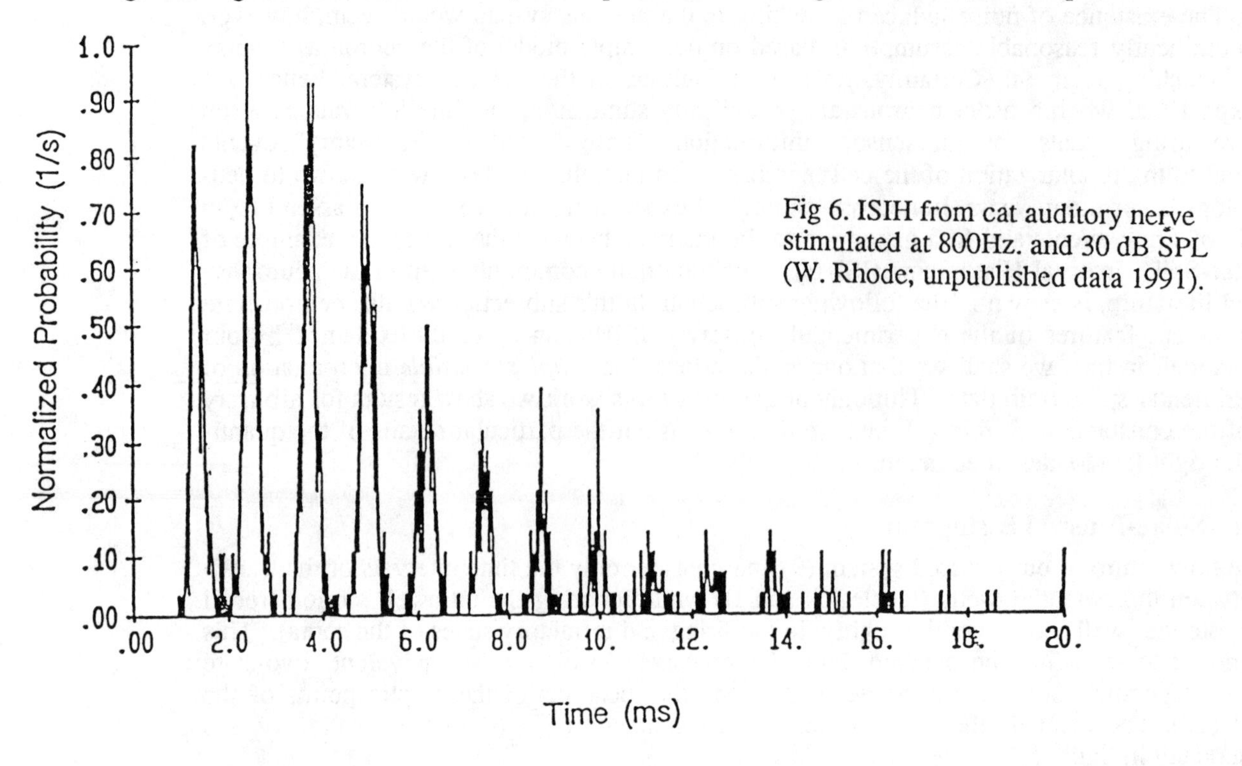

Fig 6. ISIH from cat auditory nerve stimulated at 800Hz. and 30 dB SPL (W. Rhode; unpublished data 1991).

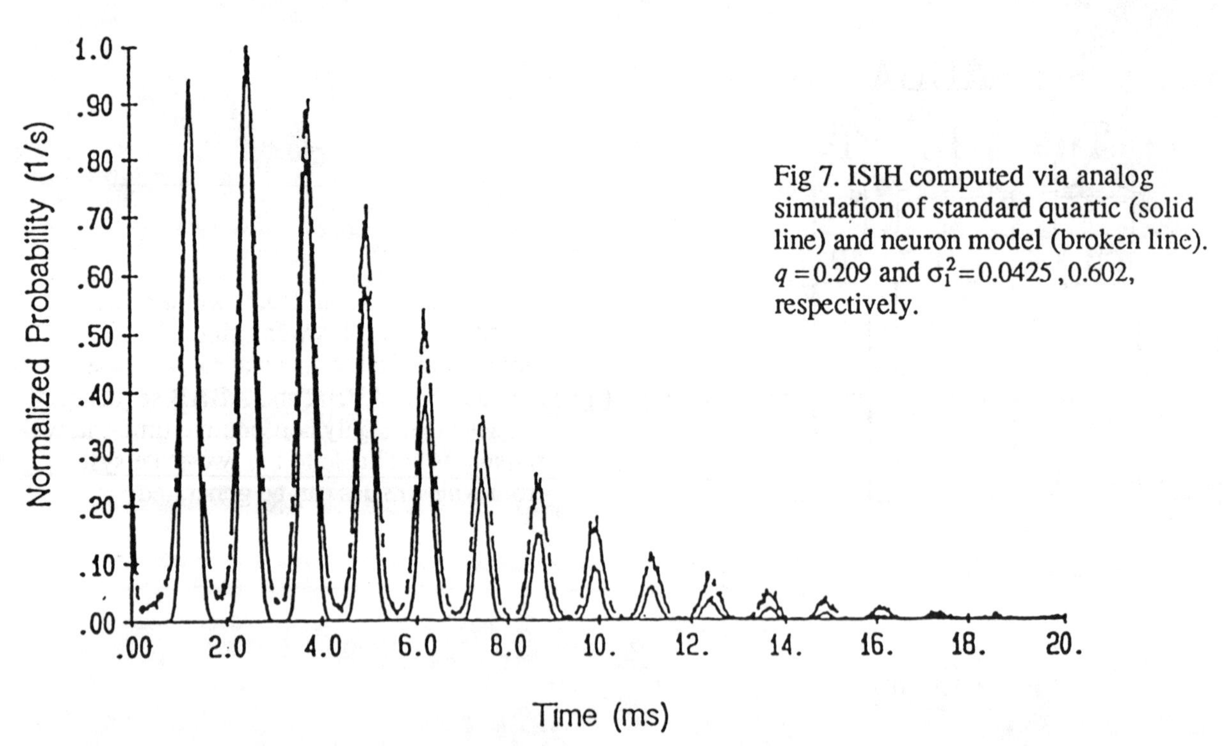

Fig 7. ISIH computed via analog simulation of standard quartic (solid line) and neuron model (broken line). $q = 0.209$ and $\sigma_1^2 = 0.0425, 0.602$, respectively.

the deterministic modulation in (9), the two sequences of figure 5 lead to different ISIHs. The top sequence, referred to as the ABBA process, measures the escape time from well B. It leads to an ISIH with modes located at *odd integer multiples of* $T/2$, T being the modulation period. A theory describing this histogram has recently been developed [Zhou, Moss and Jung 1991]. The bottom sequence (the ABAB process) leads to a histogram with peaks located at *all integer multiples of* T. This is the sequence commonly observed in experiments (and the one that we concentrate on through the remainder of this discussion); it points to the existence of a "reset mechanism" between every pair of spikes. The reset events are identified with the repolarizations of the neuron membrane that occur between successive upstrokes of the action potential and are not directly observable in neurophysiological experiments. In figure 6 we show an experimental ISIH obtained from the single auditory nerve fiber of a cat. This data should be compared with the ABAB ISIH shown in figure 7. The sequence in this figure is obtained via analog simulation of (9) with the potential function U given by (10) as well as the "standard quartic" $U(u_1)=-\frac{1}{2}u_1^2+\frac{1}{4}u_1^4$ (this potential is also bistable). The sequence of peaks in the ISIH implies a form of phase-locking of the neuron dynamics to the stimulus. Starting from its quiescent state, the neuron tries to fire at the first maximum of the stimulus cycle. If it fails to do so, it will fire at the next maximum of the stimulus (i.e. after a complete stimulus cycle) and so on, with a firing event corresponding to a switch between the two states of the potential (10). This "statistical skipping" leads to the sequence of peaks in the ISIH. Decreasing the noise strength (keeping all the other parameters fixed) leads to more peaks in the histogram since skipping becomes more likely. Conversely, increasing the noise tends to concentrate the probability into the first few peaks. For vanishingly small stimulus amplitude, the peaks merge into a Gamma distribution characterizing the ISIH for the spontaneous case [Longtin et. al. 1992]; such a distribution has also been observed experimentally.

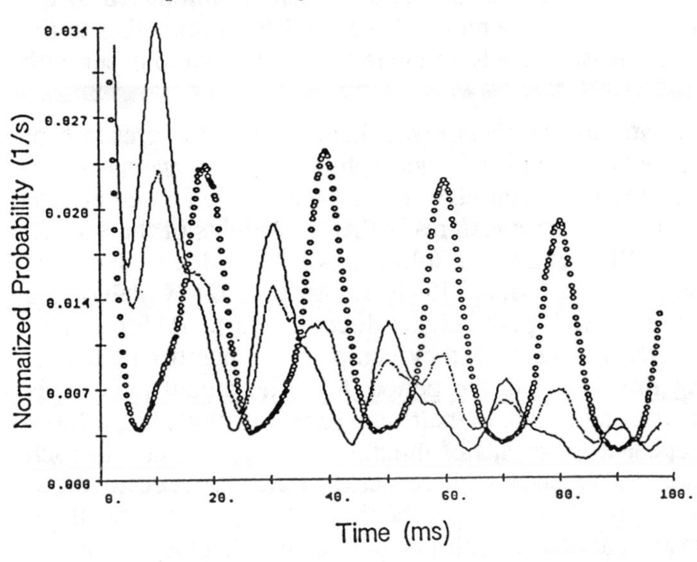

Fig 8. ISIHs computed via numerical simulation of (9) with $(\beta, q, \omega, \sigma_1^2) \equiv (1.6056, 0.304, \pi/10, 0.134)$ and uncertainty (see text) $\Delta t = 0$ (solid curve), 0.1 (dotted curve), and 0.25 (data points). Note the transition from peaks at $nT/2$ to peaks at nT for increasing Δt.

Our model is seen to reproduce all substantive features of the experimental data: in addition to the characteristic T-dependent locations of the successive peaks, the modal decay rates (except for the first few peaks) are exponential. Analog simulations show [Longtin, Bulsara and Moss 1991; Longtin et. al. 1992] that, on a semi-logarithmic scale, the decay constant is proportional to the modulation amplitude δ for fixed noise intensity σ_1^2, with a qualitatively similar relationship obtained between the decay rate and the noise strength for constant δ. This is not too surprising since the noise and signal are on equal footing in (9). We may then speculate that, over a certain (as yet not fully defined) range of parameters, the noise and signal play interchangeable roles in determining the shape of the ISIH. Their roles are not completely reciprocal, however, since the peak-widths in the ISIH are dependent on σ_1^2. Increasing the stimulus amplitude leads to an increase in the heights of the lower lying peaks. This is consistent with experimental observation:

increasing the stimulus amplitude causes the neuron to fire faster. The existence of the non-renewal component in the ABAB sequence can be explained on simple statistical grounds: the firing probability after n cycles can be shown to behave as $\ln P(n) = an + b + \ln(n)$ (a, b constant, $a < 0$) which is linear for large n only. By contrast, the corresponding quantity $\ln P(n)$ for the ABBA sequence is linear for all n. Further, one frequently encounters [Longtin et. al. 1992] (even in the ABAB sequence) an additional small peak at $T/2$ (accompanied by even smaller peaks at $3T/2, 5T/2, ...$) in experimental data. These "anti-phase" peaks may be explained as being caused by short interval multiple barrier crossings induced by white noise; the probability of these "bad switches" is a maximum at $nT/2$. By introducing a coarseness into our measurement of the switching events (i.e. neglecting most of these short interval events), the peaks at $nT/2$ may be reduced. This effect is demonstrated in the numerically computed (via direct simulation of (9)) ISIHs, *corresponding to the ABAB sequence,* shown in figure 8. If one accurately keeps track of all the barrier crossings one obtains a sequence of peaks located at $nT/2$. This sequence begins to disappear (to be supplanted by peaks at nT) as the "uncertainty" Δx in the location of the hyperbolic fixed point of the potential (corresponding to an uncertainty Δt in the residence time measured directly after crossing the hyperbolic point) is increased. It must be pointed out here that little information is conveyed in a computed ISIH about the specific nature of the nonlinearity in (9). However, it appears that the anti-phase peaks are seldom seen in systems described by "hard" potentials e.g. the standard quartic. Hence, it seems reasonable to assume that the potential function describing the bistable neuron is "soft" (i.e. it approaches infinity linearly with the dependent variable u_1 as contrasted to the hard potential which approaches infinity as u_1^4); the potential function (10) fits this description. Effects analogous to those shown in figure 8, are brought about by using non-white noise [Longtin et. al. 1992]. As the correlation time of the noise increases, the peaks at $nT/2$ in the ABAB sequence disappear; the correlations in the noise introduce memory effects that compel the switches to follow the rocking of the potential introduced by the modulation. As the noise correlation time increases, the mean of the ISIH (corresponding to the mean firing period) increases, implying a decrease in the Kramers rate (as is known to occur with increasing the noise color).

The Inter-Spike-Interval histograms are not, by themselves, indicative of the presence of stochastic resonance as an underlying cooperative effect in neurophysiological systems. However, various features of these histograms may lend themselves to an interpretation based on stochastic resonance. Perhaps the most important of these features is that the heights of the successive peaks (excluding the first peak) in the ISIHs of figure 8 follow a bell-shaped resonance-like behavior as a function of noise [Zhou, Moss and Jung 1991; Longtin 1992]. Chialvo and Apkarian [1992] have attempted to relate the ISIH peak heights directly to a SNR. From their telegraph signal (similar to the one depicted in figure 5), they compute the number of barrier crossings (i.e. firing events) with firing time equal to the period T of the modulation. This number, normalized to the total number of firing events in their time series, is plotted as a function of noise variance. The process is repeated for events of duration $2T, 3T, \cdots$, etc. In each case a resonance curve analogous to figure 3 is obtained, with the peaks of the curves occurring at different critical values of the noise intensity. A simple psychophysical experiment by these researchers yields qualitatively similar results, although it must be pointed out that they use *external* noise in their experiment. So far, no experiments using internal noise (i.e. the background noise in the nervous system), have been carried out to demonstrate the presence (or absence) of cooperative stochastic effects of the type described in this work. At least one such experiment, aimed at quantifying stochastic resonance in the mechanoreceptor neurons in crayfish is, however, currently underway [Douglas and Moss 1992; private communication]. At present one can say only that the ISIHs are a consequence of noise-induced switching in sensory neurons, for, while the above observations point to a *possible* manifestation of stochastic resonance at the level of the ISIHs, a precise connection between the histograms and stochastic resonance has not yet been established. Further, it must be pointed out that, although we are able to explain most of the experimentally observed features of the ISIHs using our simple bistable neural model, we have not been able to determine conclusively which of these characteristics are due to the statistical mechanics of bistable systems, and which ones can be ascribed directly to cellular properties that transcend our simple description. Clearly, this is an area which merits considerable further study.

Comparison to Integrate-Fire Models

A stochastic model, similar in spirit to the deterministic integrate-fire model [see e.g. Keener, Hoppensteadt and Rinzel 1981, and references therein] was originally developed [Gerstein and Mandelbrot 1964] to try to explain the experimentally observed ISIH corresponding to spontaneous firing events; as pointed out above, this distribution function is a Gamma distribution. Assuming the underlying dynamics to be time-stationary, a random walk description was invoked, based on the cornerstone requirement of a stable distribution function for the probability density of first passage times corresponding to the dynamics. The state variable u_1 was assumed to execute a biased random walk to an absorbing threshold at which point a firing event was designated to have occurred and the membrane potential u_1 was then instantaneously reset to its starting value (the reset mechanism being purely deterministic unlike our bistable model, in which it is stochastic). The distance between the origin and the threshold is the "barrier height" z (analogous to the height U_0 of the potential barrier in our bistable model) in the Gerstein-Mandelbrot description. Further, it was assumed that the motion in phase space occurs under the influence of a positive drift coefficient μ which was defined by Gerstein-Mandelbrot as the difference between the drift velocities corresponding to excitatory and inhibitory synaptic inputs (it is neurophysiologically reasonable to assume these velocities to be different). Then, assuming the presence of some (as yet unquantified) random background noise which is taken to be Gaussian delta-correlated with zero mean and variance σ^2, one may write down the Langevin equation for this process:

$$\dot{u}_1=\mu+F(t), \tag{18}$$

to which corresponds the Fokker Planck equation

$$\frac{\partial}{\partial t}P(u_1,t)=-\mu\frac{\partial P}{\partial u_1}+\sigma^2\frac{\partial^2 P}{\partial U_1^2}, \tag{19}$$

for the probability density function $P(u_1,t)$. This equation can be readily solved subject to the appropriate boundary conditions and the probability density function of first passage times written down in the form [Gerstein and Mandelbrot 1964],

$$g(t)=\frac{z}{\sqrt{2\pi\sigma^2 t^3}}\exp\left\{-\frac{(z-\mu t)^2}{2\sigma^2 t}\right\}. \tag{20}$$

The density function $g(t)$ reproduces many of the properties of experimentally observed ISIHs for the spontaneous firing case. The mean first passage time to the absorbing threshold is calculated as the first moment of $g(t)$, and its reciprocal yields an average firing rate. Variations of this model incorporating moving boundaries (which mimic refractoriness and are therefore closer to neurophysiological reality) as well as a drift term that is linear in the dependent variable u_1 (the underlying dynamics is, in this case, representative of an Ornstein-Uhlenbeck process), have been studied by Johanessma [1968] and, Clay and Goel [1973].

In order to make even better contact with experimental results, it is necessary to provide reasonably good numerical values for the drift coefficient μ, the "barrier height" z and the background noise variance σ^2 in the above model. A first attempt to do so (while simultaneously providing a test of the goodness of fit of the model to neurophysiological data) was carried out by Berger et. al. [1990]. They carried out an experiment aimed at recording the inter-spike-interval distribution from extra-cellular recordings on the cat visual cortex. Having obtained the experimental ISIHs, they were able to compute the equivalent model quantities μ and z via the mean and standard deviation of the experimentally obtained ISIHs, assuming a fixed background noise variance σ^2. While we do not give any further details of the experiment, it is noteworthy that, once these "self-consistent" values of μ, z and σ^2 were substituted into the first passage time probability density function, an excellent fit of the model (20) to the experimental ISIHs resulted. In a subsequent publication, Berger and Pribram [1992] extended their work to incorporate the effects of spatial frequency variation through the Gabor filter function.

It is instructive to consider the IF model in the presence of a periodic modulation term added to the rhs of the Langevin equation (18). For this case, the Fokker Planck equation (19) may be solved (subject to the absorbing boundary condition at $u_1 = z$) *exactly* using standard techniques [see e.g. Cox and Miller 1972; Gardiner 1985] to yield the probability density function:

$$P(u_1, t) = \frac{1}{\sqrt{2\pi\sigma^2 t}} [e^{-h_1} - e^{h_2} e^{-h_3}] , \qquad (21)$$

where we define

$$h_1(u_1, t) \equiv \frac{(u_1 - \mu t + \frac{q}{\omega} \cos\omega t)^2}{2\sigma^2 t} \qquad (22a)$$

$$h_2(t) \equiv \frac{2z}{\sigma^2 t} (\mu t - \frac{q}{\omega} \cos\omega t) \qquad (22b)$$

$$h_3(u_1, t) \equiv \frac{(u_1 - 2z - \mu t + \frac{q}{\omega} \cos\omega t)^2}{2\sigma^2 t} . \qquad (22c)$$

From (21) and (22), we calculate the first passage time density function via the formula,

$$g(t) = -\frac{d}{dt} \int_{-\infty}^{z} P(u_1, t) \, du_1 , \qquad (23)$$

which yields, after some calculation,

$$g(t) = \frac{1}{\sqrt{2\pi\sigma^2}} \frac{z}{t^{3/2}} e^{-h_1(z, t)} - \frac{zq}{\sigma^2 t^2} (t \sin\omega t + \frac{q}{\omega} \cos\omega t) [\Phi(-\sqrt{h_1(z, t)}) - 1] e^{h_2(t)} , \qquad (24)$$

where $\Phi(x) \equiv \frac{2}{\sqrt{\pi}} \int_0^z e^{-t^2} dt$ is the Error function.

Equation (24) yields a density function showing peaks at the locations nT, similar to the results obtained via the ABAB symmetry of the preceeding subsection. The non-renewal effects introduced earlier, are also present in this model. However, it is difficult to obtain a more precise connection between the bistable model derived earlier in this work and the IF model. Moreover it is unclear how, starting from our fully coupled neuro-dendritic model (1), a *monostable* potential model of the neuron in which firing events are treated as excursions to a boundary, could be obtained; certainly, our "reduced" or "effective" neuron model (9) was rigorously deriveable from (1) under the neurophysiologically reasonable constraints (2) and (12). Another possible problem with IF-type models subject to diffusion has been pointed out by Tuckwell and Cope [1980]. They show that the diffusion model, when compared to the model of Stein [1965], can severely underestimate or overestimate (sometimes by up to 100%) the mean first passage time. The analog of the mean first passage time, in our bistable model, would be the mean duration of an ABAB event. One is tempted to consider a single ABAB event as the sum of two IF events; however, this is not exact. A more detailed comparison of the two models has been given by Longtin et. al. [1992]. Clearly, however, the correspondence between the two approaches is (currently) tenuous at best.

V. DISCUSSION

The central theme of this paper has been the beneficial cooperative effects that result from the coupling of a single neuron (i.e. cell body) to a noisy dendritic bath. This composite system, described by the equations (9)-(11) is the "reduced" or "effective" neuron considered throughout this work. The coupling clearly enhances the information flow (measured by the SNR) through the system and can, for not too large noise parameters, provide signal/information capabilities that are beyond the capabilities of the original (isolated) cell. By making the (neurophysiologically realistic) assumption of the separation of time-scales between the cell body and the dendritic bath, we are able to derive an "effective" or "reduced" neuron dynamics (9) that agrees with the fully coupled N-body system within the constraints of the theory. The approach leads to a macroscopic "potential" function U (defined in (16)) which guarantees global stability of our dynamic system for positive α without having to constrain ourselves to a symmetric coupling matrix $\mathbf{J}$. Our theory is seen to agree well with large numerical simulations of the coupled stochastic differential equations (1), within the bounds imposed by the constraints (2) and (12).

The theory described here enables us to describe a network of nonlinear oscillators with *nonlinear* coupling. However, because of the separation of time-scales, the dendritic bath is tacitly assumed to be very close to its steady state. This leads to the quasi-linearization approximations (9) and (11) and brings our description of the bath closer to other quasi-linear dendritic models [see e.g. Segev et. al. 1989]. In effect, we have assumed that the dendritic patches are only weakly bistable; they are not "strong" threshold devices. These assumptions also bring our approach closer to conventional mean-field theories [see e.g. Amit 1989 for an overview]. Unlike such theories, the current approach does not depend on a large number N of entities to improve its convergence although, as pointed out earlier, in the presence of additional elements in (1) with similar time constants, recourse to a more conventional mean-field approach may be unavoidable. Further, it is interesting to note that the notion of representing the dendritic bath as a tesselation of elemental volumes each described by a quasilinear stochastic differential equation for an activation function u_i $(i>1)$ is similar in spirit to existing compartmental models of dendritic trees (see e.g. Segev et. al. 1989). Our results appear to be independent of the choice of the statistics of the elements of $\mathbf{J}$; repeating the calculations of this paper with the J_{ij} drawn from a uniform distribution yields qualitatively similar results although, as pointed out earlier, Gaussian statistics may be more reasonable from a neurophysiological perspective. In this connection it is worth pointing out that one expects typically small/sparse interactions (characterized by coefficients $J_{ij} \rightarrow 0 \; i,j > 1$) between dendritic volumes so that these coefficients may indeed be reasonably characterized by a sharply peaked (about zero mean) Gaussian. The distribution of the coefficients J_{1j} and J_{j1} (these coefficients characterize the interaction between the soma and the dendritic volumes) is broader. Good agreement between the probability density $P(u_1)$ for the reduced system (9) and the exact system (1) is also obtained for somewhat larger q values and noise strengths (within the bounds of the inequality (12)), although the agreement begins to break down when the adiabatic condition on the frequency is violated. The magnitudes and *signs* of the J_{ij} can be very important in determining the overall sign of the renormalized coefficient β in (11b) and this, in turn, determines the modality of the potential (10). For a monostable potential $(\beta < \alpha)$ the cell body is always quiescent and there are no cooperative effects. The bath coupling can render a monostable potential (for the isolated cell body) bistable, under certain conditions, thereby imparting a firing capability to the neuron; the opposite effect can also occur. This is evident from the definitions (11b,c): changing the dendritic parameters changes the barrier height and the location of the elliptic points of the effective potential (10) that characterizes the soma dynamics, while also renormalizing the modulation amplitude. These changes lead, in turn, to changes in the SNR given by the expressions (16) and (17).

The approach to the processing of information in noisy nonlinear dynamical systems, based on the probability density of residence times in one of the stable states of the potential offers an alternative to the FFT, and has been applied [Longtin, Bulsara and Moss 1991; Longtin et. al. 1992] in the theoretical construction of inter-spike-interval histograms (ISIHs) that describe neuronal spike trains in the central nervous system. This model exhibits remarkable agreement with data obtained in two different experiments some 25 years apart [Rose et. al. 1967; Siegal 1990] as well as with the more recent data of Rhode [1991; unpublished]; figures 6 and 7 demonstrate this agreement. The approach of Longtin et. al. has been contrasted with more conventional theories of ISIHs based on integrate-and-fire (IF) models in which the activation performs a random walk to an absorbing barrier and is then reset to its initial value. In the absence of an absolute refractory period, the two approaches may, in fact, converge with the mean firing rate (computed as the reciprocal of the mean first passage time) in the IF model corresponding, roughly, to the mean duration of a full-cycle switching event in the bistable diffusion model of Longtin et. al. The approach of Longtin et. al., however, seems to offer the most elegant treatment of the ISIH; certainly it permits one to match the model with experimental data (far more closely than corresponding theories based on IF models) for a given stimulus frequency, by changing only one parameter (the signal or noise strength). Further, the bistable description of the neuronal dynamics, that constitutes the cornerstone of the theory of Longtin et. al., is rigorously derivable from the fully coupled neuro-dendritic dynamics (1). Replacing the background noise by low-dimensional chaos appears to produce qualitatively similar results [Ippen et. al. 1992; Longtin 1992; Nicolis, Nicolis and McKernan 1992]. This is especially significant in light of the current interest in chaos and its control [Garfinkel et. al. 1992] in the nervous system. It is worth a brief digression to point out that, for the cell-body, in the bistable regime, the coefficient of the linear term in the dynamics (9) determines the "hardness" of the potential function (10). When α is increased (keeping β fixed and $\beta>\alpha$), the sides of the potential become steeper and the barrier height U_0 decreases; in turn, this leads to an increase in the firing rate, an effect which can be readily seen from the Kramers formula (14). For the case of no modulating signal ($q=0$) the firing rate may be determined approximately from the inverse of the mean first passage time obtained from the ISIH [see e.g. Berger et. al. 1990; Longtin et. al. 1992].

The question may well be asked: "Is the neuron a noisy *bistable* switching element characterized by a 'soft' potential (e.g. (10))?" Certainly, noise (whose effects manifest themselves in the diffusion term in a Fokker Planck description) plays a critical role in the neural dynamics. It is important to point out that the peaks in the ISIHs *cannot exist in the absence of noise*. This provides yet another example of the beneficial aspects of noise in the processing of information by the central nervous system. It also implies the existence [F. Moss 1991-92; private discussions] of a "regulatory mechanism" in which the potential barrier height, U_0 plays a critical role. Given a stimulus (external or internal) $q\sin\omega t$, it is tantalizing to speculate that *neurophysiological systems constantly adjust the coupling coefficients J_{ij} as well as the other dendritic and soma parameters such that the effective potential function characterizing the network admits of more than one minimum. Further, the height U_0 of the potential barrier is internally adjusted in response to the stimulus and background noise characteristics.* This is an important point since, for given stimulus and noise, one obtains well-defined multi-peaked histograms (such as those shown in figures 6 and 7) for only a small range of U_0. The network then operates as a bistable switching element and actually can *use the background noise so that its response* (measured by the SNR or, equivalently, through the ISIH) *is optimized. This implies that the network operates close to the maxima of the stochastic resonance curves of figure 4, while simultaneously obtaining other information about the stimulus (e.g. amplitude and frequency) via the ISIH.* In effect, our construction and interpretation of the ISIH (together with the remarkable ability to explain most of the features of experimentally obtained ISIHs) as a natural outcome of our modelling the neuron as a noisy bistable switching element implies that *the central nervous may measure the stimulus intensity by comparing it to the background noise, using the (internally adjusted) potential barrier height to optimize the measurement* [F. Moss 1991-92; private discussions]. In light of these speculations, our choice of the cell body self feedback coefficient as a function of the dendritic coupling (specifically, we have set the "unscaled" $J_{11}=N$) seems to be reasonable. Allowing the elements of **J** to fluctuate in time (thereby introducing a form of time-dependent "synaptic plasticity" at the neuro-dendritic level) seems to be the logical next step; this is currently under investigation. Throughout this work, the underlying thread has been the positive role of noise; this, in fact, was recognized earlier by Buhmann and Schulten [1986, 87] who found that noise, deliberately added to the deterministic equations governing individual neurons in an artificial network, significantly enhanced the network's performance. They concluded that *"...the noise...is an essential feature of the information processing capabilities of the neural network, and not a mere source of disturbance, better suppressed..."*

ACKNOWLEDGEMENTS

It is a pleasure to acknowledge conversations with Profs. Frank Moss, Karl Pribram, Lauren Gerbrandt, William Hudspeth, Andre Longtin, Wilfrid Rall, Dante Chialvo, A. Vania Apkarian and Stephen Schiff. ARB acknowledges support from ONR under grant numbers N00014- 92-WX24088 and N00014-92-WX24238; AJM acknowledges support from ONR SBIR contract N00014-C-91-0268.

REFERENCES

Abbott LF, Kepler TB (1990) Model neurons: from Hodgkin-Huxley to Hopfield. In Garrido L (ed.) Statistical mechanics of neural networks. Springer, Berlin.

Amit DJ (1989) Modeling brain function. Cambridge Univ. Press, Cambridge.

Berger D, Pribram K, Wild H, Bridges C (1990) An analysis of neural spike-train distributions: determinants of the response of visual cortex neurons to changes in orientation and spatial frequency. Exp. Brain Res. 80:129-134.

Berger D, Pribram K (1992) The relationship between the Gabor elementary function and a stochastic model of the inter-spike-interval distribution in the responses of visual cortex neurons. Biol. Cyb. 67:191-194.

Buhmann J, Schulten K (1986) Influence of noise on the behavior of an autoassociative neural network. In Denker J (ed.) Neural networks for computing. AIP, New York.

Buhmann J, Schulten K (1987) Influence of noise on the function of a "physiological" neural network. Biol. Cyb. 61:313-327.

Bulsara AR, Boss RD, Jacobs EW (1989) Noise effects in an electronic model of a single neuron. Biol. Cyb. 61:211-222.

Bulsara AR, Schieve WC (1991) Single effective neuron: macroscopic potential and noise-induced bifurcations. Phys. Rev. A44:7913-7922.

Bulsara AR, Jacobs EW, Zhou T, Moss FE, Kiss L (1991a) Stochastic resonance in a single neuron model: theory and analog simulation. J. Theor. Biol. 152:531-555.

Bulsara AR, Maren AJ, Schmera G, (1992) Single effective neuron: dendritic coupling effects and stochastic resonance. Biol. Cyb., preprint.

Chialvo DR, Apkarian AV (1992) Modulated noisy biological dynamics: three examples. In Shlesinger MF, Moss FE, Bulsara AR (eds.) Proceedings of the NATO Advanced Research Workshop on Stochastic Resonance and its Applications to Physics and Biology; to appear.

Clark JW (1988) Statistical mechanics of neural networks. Phys. Repts. 158:91-157.

Clark JW (1989) Introduction to neural networks. In Proto AN (ed.) Nonlinear phenmoena in complex systems. North Holland, Amsterdam.

Clay JR, Goel NS (1973) Diffusion models for the firing of a neuron with varying threshold. J. Theor. Biol. 39:633-644.

Cowan JD (1970) A statistical mechanics of nervous activity. In Gerstenhaber M (ed.) Some mathematical questions in biology. Amer. Math. Soc., Providence, RI.

Cowan JD (1974) Stochastic models of neuro-electric activity. In Rice SA, Freed KF, Light JC (eds.) Statistical mechanics. Univ. of Chicago Press, Chicago.

Cox DR, Miller HD (1972) Theory of stochastic processes. Chapman and Hall, London.

Eccles JC (1964) The physiology of synapses. Academic Press, N.Y.

Eccles JC (1981) Do mental events cause neural events analogously to the probability fields of quantum mechanics? Proc. Roy. Soc. B227:411-428.

Edholm O, Leimar O (1979) The accuracy of Kramers' theory of chemical kinetics. Physica 98A:313-324.

Gardiner CW (1985) Handbook of stochastic processes. Springer, Berlin.

Garfinkel A, Spano ML, Ditto WL, Weiss JN (1992) Controlling cardiac chaos. Science 257:1230-35.

Gerstein G, Mandelbrot B (1964) Random walk models for the spike activity of a single neuron. Biophys. J. 4:41-68.

Greiner A, Strittmatter W, Honercamp J (1988) Numerical integration of stochastic differential equations. J. Stat. Phys. 51:95-108.

Haken H (1977) Synergetics. Springer, Berlin.

Holmes WR, Rall W (1992) Electrotonic models of neuronal dendrites and single neuron computation. In McKenna T, Davis J, Zornetzer S (eds.) Single neuron computation. Academic Press, N.Y.

Hopfield JJ (1984) Neurons with graded response have collective computational properties like those of two-state neurons. Proc. Natl. Acad. Sci. 81:3088-92.

Horsthemke W, Lefever R (1984) Noise-induced transitions. Springer, Berlin.

Ippen E, Lindner J, Ditto W (1992) Chaotic resonance: a simulation. In Shlesinger MF, Moss FE, Bulsara AR (eds.) Proceedings of the NATO Advanced Research Workshop on Stochastic Resonance and its Applications to Physics and Biology; to appear.

Johannesma PIM (1968) Diffusion models for the stochastic activity of neurons. In Caianello ER (ed.) Neural networks. Springer, Berlin.

Jung P, Behn U, Pantazelou E, Moss FE (1992) Collective response of globally coupled bistable oscillators. Phys. Rev. A46:R1709-1712.

Keener J, Hoppensteadt F, Rinzel J (1981) Integrate-and-fire models of nerve membrane response to oscillatory input. SIAM J. Appl. Math. 41:503-517.

Kramers HA (1940) Brownian motion in a field of force and the diffusion model of chemical reactions. Physica 7:284-304.

Kandel ER, Schwartz JH, Jessell TM (1991) (eds.) Principles of neuroscience. Elsevier N.Y.

Longtin A, Bulsara AR, Moss FE (1991) Time-interval sequences in bistable systems and the noise-induced transmission of information by sensory neurons. Phys. Rev. Lett. 67:656-659. See also Nature 352:469.

Longtin A, Bulsara AR, Pierson D, Moss FE (1992) Bistability and dynamics of periodically forced sensory neurons. J. Neuroscience, Preprint.

Longtin A (1992) Stochastic resonance in neuron models. Shlesinger MF, Moss FE, Bulsara AR (eds.) Proceedings of the NATO Advanced Research Workshop on Stochastic Resonance and its Applications to Physics and Biology; to appear.

Maren AJ, Harston CT, Pap RM (1990) Handbook of neural computing applications. Academic Press, San Diego, California.

McNamara B, Wiesenfeld K (1989) Theory of stochastic resonance. Phys. Rev. A39:4854-4869.

Nicolis G, Nicolis C, McKernan D (1992) Stochastic resonance in chaotic dynamics. Shlesinger MF, Moss FE, Bulsara AR (eds.) Proceedings of the NATO Advanced Research Workshop on Stochastic Resonance and its Applications to Physics and Biology; to appear.

Moss FE (1992) Stochastic resonance; from the ice ages to the monkey's ear. In Weiss G (ed.) Some problems in statistical physics. SIAM, Philadelphia.

Pribram K (1991) Brain and perception: holonomy and structure in figural processing. Lawrence Erlbaum Assoc., Hillsdale, NJ.

Rall W (1970) Dendritic neuron theory and dendro-dendritic synapses in a simple cortical system. In Schmidt FO (ed.) The neurosciences: second study program. Rockefeller Univ. Press, New York.

Rall W, Rinzel J (1973) Branch input resistance and steady state attenuation for input to one branch of a dendritic neuron model. Biophys. J. 13:648-688.

Rinzel J, Rall W (1974) Transient response in a dendritic neuron model for current injcted at one branch. Biophys. J. 14:759-790.

Rinzel J, Ermentrout B (1989) Analysis of neuronal excitability and oscillations. In Koch C, Segev I (eds.) Methods in neuronal modeling. MIT Press, Cambridge, Mass.

Risken H (1984) The Fokker Planck equation. Springer, Berlin.

Rose J, Brugge J, Anderson D, Hind J (1967) Phase-locked response to low frequency tones in single auditory nerve fibres of squirrel monkey. J. Neurophys. 30:769-793.

Schieve WC, Bulsara AR, Davis G (1991) Single effective neuron. Phys. Rev. A43:2613-2623.

Segev I, Fleshman JW, Burke RE (1989) Compartmental models of complex neurons. In Koch C, Segev I (eds.) Methods in neuronal modeling. MIT Press, Cambridge, Mass.

Segev I, Rapp M, Manor Y, Yarom Y (1992). Analog and digital processing in single nerve cells: dendritic integration and axonal propagation. In McKenna T, Davis J, Zornetzer S (eds.) Single neuron computation. Academic Press, N.Y.

Siegal R (1990) Nonlinear dynamical system theory and primary visual cortical processing. Physica 42D:385-395.

Stein RB (1967) Some models of neuronal variability. Biophys. J. 7:37-68.

Stein RB (1965) A theoretical analysis of neuronal variability. Biophyshys. J. 5:173-184.

Stein RB, Leung KV, Oguztoreli MN, Williams BW (1974) Properties of small neural networks. Kybernetik 14:223-230.

Stratonovich RL (1963) Topics in the theory of random noise, vol. 1. Gordon and Breach, New York.

Stratonovich RL (1989) Some Markov methods in stochastic processes. In Moss F, McClintock P (eds) Noise in nonlinear dynamical systems, vol. 1. Cambridge Univ. Press.

Tuckwell HC, Cope DK (1980) Accuracy of neuronal interspike times calculated from a diffusion approximation. J. Theor. Biol. 83:377-387.

Zhou T, Moss FE, Jung P (1991) Escape-time distributions of a periodically modulated bistable system with noise. Phys. Rev. A42:3161-3169.

II. Quantum Neurodynamics

Chapter 4

The Basics of Quantum Brain Dynamics

Mari Jibu and Kunio Yasue
Research Institute for Informatics and Science
Notre Dame Seishin University
Okayama 700, Japan

1. Motivation

One of the major purposes of this first Appalachian conference is an exposition of several prototypes of quantum neurodynamics, and intensive discussion will be expected to open a new direction in the research activity of BRAINS founded by Dr. Karl Pribram in Radford University. We wish to take part by addressing a small exposition of the basic concepts and ideas of quantum brain dynamics coined originally by Dr. Hiroomi Umezawa catching Pribram's enthusiasm in which the fundamental physical process of the brain can be described within the realm of quantum field theory.

Issues on the research activity in the field of brain science today seem to be arising from the unbalance of research interests between physical science and brain science. In good old days a scientist like Descartes investigated the fundamental law and processes of the brain from the point of view of the fundamental law of the materialistic world he found. Today, scientists are scattered into many different fields and the brain belongs to brain scientists officially.

The brain stands on the very intersection of the materialistic world and the mind world. It seems therefore natural to expect the same order of research activity from physical science as that from brain science. Unfortunately, this is not the case. Knowing very well the fundamental law of materialistic world, that is, quantum mechanics and quantum field theory, physicists are in general not interested in investigating the fundamental process of the brain function, even though their activity comes from that. However, it seems of certain importance that a few great physicists founded once quantum mechanics and quantum field theory have made deep considerations on the brain function. Among them are Bohr, Schrödinger, Pauli, Bohm and Josephson. We can guess their common deep insights:

For better understanding of the fundamental law of the mind world, it may help us to see fundamental processes of the brain as fundamental physical processes from the point of view of the fundamental law of the materialistic world, that is, quantum mechanics and quantum field theory.

2. Emergence of Quantum Field Theory

First of all, it is necessary to understand the conventional way to see the materialistic world. Although the fundamental law of the materialistic world is provided by quantum theory, that is, quantum mechanics and quantum field theory, it is very hard in most cases to investigate the real sophisticated natural phenomena in the materialistic world directly in terms of quantum theory. Therefore, physicists developed an approximative description of the materialistic world given by quantum statistical mechanics, classical statistical mechanics and classical electromagnetism which is valid only for investigating natural phenomena of matters in which all the huge number of atomic ingredients manifest thermal disorder.

It succeeded in describing the fundamental feature of matters in or near thermal equilibrium, and then has been believed accidentally by many scientists to be the most fundamental theory of physics convenient for investigating also such natural phenomena of life as the brain function.

Consequently, the conventional way to see the brain stands on the approximative law of the materialistic world. There, quantum and classical statistical mechanics, classical electromagnetism and quantum chemistry offered us an empirically unified standpoint. Approximative and empirical laws of living matters have been built up by patching many fragmentary results or knowledge obtained in this empirically unified standpoint. Among them are chemical biology, biological physics, physical biology and molecular biology. They do not provide us with a good framework for clarifying the essential aspect of natural phenomena of life, because they gathers only the thermally disordered behaviors of living matters.

The essential aspect of such natural phenomena of life as the brain function may be a fact that they are resulting from certain fundamental processes of fully quantum theoretical nature in which all the atomic ingredients manifest ordered behavior and no longer suffer from thermal disorder. What is needed definitely seems to provide the brain scientists with a proper framework of quantum theory valid for investigating the fundamental process of living matters full of ordered natural phenomena. We call such a framework describing the fundamental physical process of the brain from the point of view of the fundamental law of the materialistic world, that is, quantum mechanics and quantum field theory, "quantum brain dynamics" and abbreviate it by "QBD".

Of course, such a fundamental framework is not restricted to the brain function. It may provide us also with a drastically new way to see life. We call the more general framework in which the fundamental physical process of living matters can be investigated from the fundamental point of view of quantum theory "quantum biodynamics"and abbreviate it also by "QBD". It is time, in September 1992, to declare quantum mechanics and quantum field theory respectable in both brain and life sciences.

3. History of Quantum Brain Dynamics

There may be many different ways to approach to quantum brain dynamics and quantum biodynamics just as you can easily find in other addresses of this conference. It is our principle role to present you the basic concepts and ideas of a long-standing world-wide approach to QBD's coined originally by Umezawa in 1960's.

Let us start from a historical sketch of the development of Umezawa's quantum brain dynamics.

In 1944 Schrödinger emphasized that the essential aspect of natural phenomena of life is to create order in the disordered environment against the second law of thermodynamics. (Schrödinger, 1944) Living matters are matters eating entropy and producing order. Other matters are all subject to the second law of thermodynamics and well described by quantum statistical mechanics. However, quantum statistical mechanics becomes poor in investigating the order-creating process against the second law of thermodynamics. For such aim, we have to work directly with quantum mechanics and quantum field theory, and if necessary introduce a completely new approximation suitable for describing ordered natural phenomena of life. When we apply quantum mechanics or quantum field theory to ordered natural phenomena, it is of extreme importance that we have to use appropriate approximations which may keep the general and fundamental features of such phenomena clear. Certainly, quantum statistical mechanics may not provide us with a good approximation.

Pribram is an outstanding brain scientist who claimed the emergence of incorporating quantum theoretical method of investigation into the brain science about ten years after Schrödinger's deep insight on the long-standing problem "What is life?". He coined the notion of neural holography and called the attention of physicists to the issues. (Pribram, 1960, 1971, 1991)

Catching Pribram's enthusiasm, Ricciardi and Umezawa took the very first step forward into the terra incognita of understanding the summit phenomena of life -brain and consciousness - in terms of quantum field theory. (Ricciardi and Umezawa, 1967) Slightly later Fröhlich coined a quantum theoretical analysis of biological cells and showed the existence of a quantum mechanical collective mechanism like the superconductivity to store energy in biological cells without thermal loss. (Fröhlich, 1968)

In 1978 and 1979 Umezawa and his colleagues in Edmonton proposed a memory mechanism based on the spontaneous symmetry breaking in quantum field theory and triggered the succeeding extensive theoretical investigations by Umezawa schools in Italy and Japan in 1980's and 1990's. (Stuart, Takahashi, and Umezawa, 1978, 1979; Del Giudice, Preparata and Vitiello, 1988; Del Giudice, Doglia, Milani and Vitiello, 1983, 1985, 1986, 1988a, 1988b; Del Giudice, Doglia, Milani, Smith and Vitiello, 1989; Jibu and Yasue, 1991, 1992a, 1992b, 1992c)

The motivation of the research activity of the Umezawa school in Japan on QBD's is to look for answers to the two famous and monumental questions by two Nobel Laureates from the fundamental point of view of quantum mechanics and quantum field theory. Namely, "What if life?" by Schrödinger, and "Do mental events cause neural events analogously to the probability fields of quantum mechanics?" by Sir Eccles. (Eccles, 1986)

Our answers to the questions will be as follows:

Life is a fully quantum mechanical process of creating order in many-body dynamics of biomolecules and water molecules in living matters.

At least, memories are nothing else but macroscopic probability fields (i.e., wave functions) representing dynamical states and cause neural events in accordance to quantum mechanical law.

We wish to organize our address by presenting first the conceptual survey of quantum brain dynamics, then wasting your time by a little bit of quantum biodynamics, and finally showing the details and techniques of quantum field theory needed in quantum brain dynamics.

4. Concept of Quantum Brain Dynamics

Now we will give a conceptual survey of quantum brain dynamics. We start from a naive question, "What is QBD of Umezawa?". The essential idea is that the conventional neuron-synapse dynamics is not fundamental, but some unknown quantum field dynamics is essential in realizing the brain function. In other words, the brain is essentially a microscopic quantum dynamical system with macroscopic spatial extent, that is, quantum field dynamics.

We coin a new picture of brain dynamics with Umezawa that it consists of quantum brain dynamics (i.e., quantum mode) and classical brain dynamics (i.e., classical mode).

Namely, the brain is a mixed physical system of quantum dynamical system and classical dynamical system.

We proceed now to the QBD picture of memory due to Stuart, Takahashi and Umezawa. (Stuart, Takahashi, and Umezawa, 1978, 1979) The basic idea came from indeed Schrödinger's question, "What is life?". Schrödinger suggested that the fundamental process of life is an ordering process such as order creating, negentropy producing, and macroscopic quantum phenomena. In QBD the memory is thought of as a quantum order, and so the memory mechanism is expected to be given by quantum theoretical ordering processes.

According to the basic assumptions of QBD, the brain is a mixed physical system of a quantum dynamical system and a classical one. The former with quantum field theoretical degrees of freedom manifests coherent, ordered and non-thermalized dynamics of a huge number of atomic ingredients. On the contrary, the latter with transmembrane ionic diffusions manifests incoherent, disordered and thermalized dynamics.

As the basic concepts of the quantum mode of QBD, that is, the quantum dynamical system of quantum field theoretical degrees of freedom, the notions of corticon and exchange boson are introduced by Umezawa. They manifest both macroscopic distributed degrees of freedom and microscopic quantum mechanical degrees of freedom and so assumed to suffer from quantum field dynamics. Due to Umezawa's original idea of QBD, the process is effectively not localized. Over a considerable number of neurons, corticons and exchange bosons span certain yet unknown extents of quantum fields.

We get a QBD picture of the brain. The brain tissue in classical picture of cell biology and molecular biology is essentially a macroscopic huge neural network system. However, a much more fine and sophisticated structure appears in the QBD picture. There, the brain tissue consists of the classical dynamical system of classical picture in the macroscopic scale and the quantum dynamical system of corticons and exchange bosons in the microscopic scale.

5. Memory as Quantum Vacuum State

Once accepting this drastically new picture of the brain function an interesting memory mechanism can be proposed in which the quantum dynamical system play the role of memory storing apparatus. The memory inputs of external stimuli are transformed by the classical dynamical system into energy inputs and transmitted to the quantum dynamical system in which certain quantum dynamics of corticons and exchange bosons induced by the energy inputs play the role of memory storage printed on quantum field theoretical degrees of freedom.

For the purpose of maintaining the memory storing mechanism of the quantum dynamical system of corticons and exchange bosons, some basic dynamical features of quantum mode are assumed in QBD. First, dynamics is assumed to be invariant under certain symmetry transformation. Second, the lowest energy state, that is, the vacuum state violates the symmetry property. In other words, the QBD vacuum state is of the spontaneous symmetry breaking type and appears as spatially extended macroscopic ordered state just as the superconducting media.

Under those assumptions, the memory printing process is though of as a phase transition of the quantum dynamical system to a higher ordered state from a less ordered one induced by the energy inputs of external stimuli transmitted by the classical dynamical system of transmembrane ionic diffusions. It is of certain interest to see that such a phase transition of the quantum vacuum state is essential in the development of the early universe. We may be allowed to make an analogy from purely quantum field theoretical point of view that the quantum mode of the brain manifests an evolution like our universe. In this sense, the brain is indeed a universe of one litre space. (Jibu and Yasue, 1991)

Once the external stimuli are stored in the quantum dynamical system as a more ordered dynamical state by the energy induced vacuum phase transition, they are stable against incoherent energy inputs and maintain the long-term memory. There, the memory storage can be recalled by transforming weak external stimuli similar in a sense to the original ones into coherent and small energy inputs through the classical dynamical system. Such coherent energy inputs can induce the creation of coherent wave propagation called a Goldstone mode or Goldstone boson in quantum field theory, even though they are unlimitedly small. The Goldstone boson thus created takes part in the quantum dynamical system and produces a coherent dynamical effect and submit it to the classical dynamical system as coherent outputs which will be enlarged there. This is nothing but the memory recalling process in QBD.

After establishing the mechanism of long-term memory in terms of the QBD vacuum state by Stuart, Takahashi and Umezawa, the conceptual generalization of memory mechanism in QBD in terms of various dynamical states of quantum mode has been made. (Sivakami and Srinivasan, 1983) Various types of memories can be supposed to correspond to different types of dynamical states of the quantum dynamical system. For example, the vacuum state corresponds to a long-term memory, the excited state to an instantaneous memory, the classical state to a metastable memory (i.e., short-term memory), the steady state to an external stimuli maintained memory (i.e., conditioned long-term memory), and the decay of a classical state due to quantum tunnel effect corresponds to the decay of metastable memory.

6. A Physical Picture of Quantum Brain Dynamics

We visited the theoretical realm of QBD and found that it succeeded in providing us with a drastically new physical description of the brain function from the fundamental point of view of quantum mechanics and quantum field theory. Once standing on Umezawa's hypothesis that yet unknown quantum field dynamics of corticons and exchange bosons plays the important role in the fundamental process of the brain, various known results in quantum field theory open new ways to see the brain function in the light of the true fundamental law of the materialistic world. Of course, Umezawa's hypothesis should be verified from the practical point of view, and several questions may arise naturally:

What is QBD?
What is the corticon?
What is the exchange boson?
What are there really in your brain?

Let us look for answers to those questions. What are there in the brain? If we revisit the QBD picture of the brain, we have a brain tissue containing the classical dynamical system and the quantum dynamical system. The former gives us a well-known molecular biological structure of transmembrane ionic diffusions. The essential feature of the QBD picture comes from the hypothesis that overlapping this classical neuron-synapse structure exists some microscopic quantum theoretical degrees of freedom with macroscopic spatial extent. What are there? There are a huge number of water molecules and biomolecules correlated very strongly with each other. Therefore, the quantum theoretical degrees of freedom in question could be the molecular vibrational fields.

We get by inspection a realistic physical picture of QBD. The classical dynamical system consists of transmembrane ionic diffusions and manifests the macroscopic neuron-synapse network. The quantum dynamical system consists of the molecular vibrational field of biomolecules and that of water molecules. Now QBD becomes a specific physical theory in which the theoretical analysis of phase transition dynamics of the molecular vibrational fields of biomolecules and water molecules from the fundamental point of view of quantum mechanics and quantum field theory plays the most important role.

Then, what is the corticon? Corticons are nothing but quanta of the molecular vibrational field of biomolecules. They are quanta with electric polarization confined within the dynamical three dimensional network of protein filaments spanning densely the cytoplasm of dendrites and synapses as well as the extracellular matrices. Due to the theoretical inspections by Fröhlich and Davidov, those quanta with electric polarization may be created and annihilated by the electron-hole supply from the transmembrane ionic diffusion such as the ATP cyclic process. (Fröhlich, 1968; Davydov, 1979, 1982) It opens the possibility for corticons in QBD to interact with the classical dynamical system just as expected.

What is the exchange boson? Exchange bosons are nothing but quanta of the molecular vibrational field of water molecules. They are quanta with electric polarization, too. It is known that water molecules besides the dynamical three dimensional network of protein filaments manifest extremely strong correlation and coherence. Therefore, the molecular vibrational field of such water molecules maintains phonons as its quanta. In other words, exchange bosons in QBD are dipolar phonons typical to the quasi-crystalline structure of a huge number of water molecules.

What is remained for us now is to write down the quantum field theory of the quantum dynamical system of molecular vibrational fields of water molecules and biomolecules. The most important feature of the molecular vibrational fields is that they are invariant under the three dimensional rotation and the vacuum states violate the three dimensional rotational symmetry. This goes well along the basic assumption of QBD.

7. Toward Quantum Biodynamics

The realistic theoretical framework of QBD thus claims that the fundamental process of the brain is given by quantum field dynamics of the molecular vibrational fields of water molecules and biomolecules. This drastically new point of view may not be restricted to the brain tissue. Once applied to other tissues or biological systems it will open a completely new picture of life in quantum biodynamics.

Before proceeding to writing down the details of quantum field theory of the molecular vibrational fields of water molecules and biomolecules, let us waste your time by visiting some ideas of quantum biodynamics.

As we have already mentioned the physical picture of quantum brain dynamics can be well applied to general biological cells including monocellular organs, and we obtain the theoretical framework of quantum biodynamics. There, even a monocelluar organ like an amoeba should be analyzed from the fundamental point of view of quantum field dynamics of the molecular vibrational fields of water and biomolecules.

When one talks about the life he or she is tacitly asked today to use the language of either molecular biology or philosophy. Any major deviation from that custom requires a defense. This is the case for quantum biodynamics.

It is our intention in the deviation to focus on the inherent rich structure of quantum biodynamics which seems to provide us with possible solutions to the totally open problems in modern biology. Among them are the mechanism of anesthesia, the mechanism of meridian flow of Qi in Chinese and Japanese traditional medicine, and the mechanism of biophoton. We believe strongly that in near future those exciting open problems will find solutions within the realm of quantum biodynamics. Keynotes are already there. For example, we know already that anesthetic molecules break the quantum dynamical order of the molecular vibrational fields of water molecules and biomolecules. This may explain an important aspect of anesthesia. In quantum biodynamics it is a natural consequence that the molecular vibrational fields of water molecules and biomolecules interact coherently with the quantized electromagnetic field, and so corticons or exchange bosons may create and annihilate photons.

We may propose a physical picture of Qi as an ordered dynamical state of the molecular vibrational fields of water molecules and biomolecules. There, the Qi flow is nothing but a current of Goldstone bosons in the ordered dynamical state. In Chinese and Japanese traditional philosophy, Qi is the essential being in living matters. So, quantum biodynamics suggests that the quantum order is the essence of living matters just as Shrödinger suggested half a century ago. (Schrödinger, 1944)

8. Calculus in Quantum Brain Dynamics

We present now a detailed technical aspect of quantum brain dynamics. For simplicity we work with the system of units in which the Planck constant divided by 2π and the light speed become unity.

Recall that quantum theoretical degrees of freedom in QBD are given by the molecular vibrational field of biomolecules and that of water molecules. We call the former the B-field and the latter the W-field which manifest spatial extent in the volume V of the whole brain tissue.

It is convenient to work with a spinor representation of the B-field in terms of a two-component spinor field. This is because the molecular vibrational field of biomolecules in QBD arises from the existence of unlocalized electrons or holes along the protein filaments. Let us denote the B-field by

$$\psi_B(\mathbf{x},t) = \begin{pmatrix} \psi_B^+(\mathbf{x},t) \\ \psi_B^-(\mathbf{x},t) \end{pmatrix},$$

where $\psi_B^+(\mathbf{x},t)$ and $\psi_B^-(\mathbf{x},t)$ are spinor components. The electric dipole moment of the B-field is then given by

$$\tilde{\psi}_B(\mathbf{x},t)\sigma\psi_B(\mathbf{x},t),$$

where

$$\tilde{\psi}_B(\mathbf{x},t) = (\psi_B^+(\mathbf{x},t)^* \quad \psi_B^-(\mathbf{x},t)^*)$$

is the adjoint spinor and

$$\sigma = (\sigma_1, \sigma_2, \sigma_3)$$

is a vector with components equal to Pauli spin matrices

$$\sigma_1 = \begin{pmatrix} 0 & 1 \\ 1 & 0 \end{pmatrix},$$

$$\sigma_2 = \begin{pmatrix} 0 & -i \\ i & 0 \end{pmatrix},$$

$$\sigma_3 = \begin{pmatrix} 1 & 0 \\ 0 & -1 \end{pmatrix}.$$

As we have seen the vibrational degrees of freedom of biomolecules are localized within each protein filament. Correspondingly the B-field manifests localization $\psi_B(\mathbf{x},t) \neq 0$ only in each mean position $\mathbf{x} = \mathbf{x}_k$ of N protein filaments. The suffix k takes the integer value from 1 to N. The localized electric poralization is then given by N discrete variables

$$\tau^k = \tilde{\psi}_B(\mathbf{x}_k,t)\sigma\psi_B(\mathbf{x}_k,t)$$

which are proper dynamical variables of corticon localized within the protein filaments.

Since the W-field is the dipolar phonon field of the water molecular vibrations, it is appropriate to work with a vector representation

$$\mathbf{R}_W(\mathbf{x},t) = (R_W^1(\mathbf{x},t), R_W^2(\mathbf{x},t), R_W^3(\mathbf{x},t)),$$

which indicates the local spatial orientation of water molecules in each position of the volume V. According to the canonical quantization procedure in quantum field theory, we introduce a Fourier series expansion of the W-field.

$$\mathbf{R}_W(\mathbf{x},t) = \frac{1}{\sqrt{V}} \sum_{\mathbf{k}} \{\mathbf{A}_W(\mathbf{k},t)e^{i\mathbf{k}\cdot\mathbf{x}} + \mathbf{A}_W^*(\mathbf{k},t)e^{-i\mathbf{k}\cdot\mathbf{x}}\}$$

Without loss of generality we may assume that the W-field manifests a constant polarization in the third direction

$$\mathbf{R}_W(\mathbf{x},t) = \frac{1}{\sqrt{V}} \mathbf{e}_3 \sum_{\mathbf{k}} \{A_W(\mathbf{k},t)e^{i\mathbf{k}\cdot\mathbf{x}} + A_W^*(\mathbf{k},t)e^{-i\mathbf{k}\cdot\mathbf{x}}\},$$

where $\mathbf{e}_3$ denotes a unit vector along the third direction. Then, assuming that the Fourier coefficients $A_W(\mathbf{k},t)$ and $A_W^*(\mathbf{k}',t)$ are creation and annihilation operators subject to the canonical commutation relation

$$\left[A_W(\mathbf{k},t), A_W^*(\mathbf{k}',t)\right] = \delta_{\mathbf{k}\mathbf{k}'},$$

$$\left[A_W(\mathbf{k},t), A_W(\mathbf{k}',t)\right] = \left[A_W^*(\mathbf{k},t), A_W^*(\mathbf{k}',t)\right] = 0,$$

we can pass to the quantum field dynamics of the W-field.

In quantum field theory it is popular to introduce canonical variables and the Hamiltonian operator. So, we introduce canonical momentum operators and canonical coordinate operators related to the creation and annihilation operators as follows.

$$A_W(\mathbf{k},t) = \frac{1}{\sqrt{2}}\left\{\sqrt{K_\mathbf{k}}Q_\mathbf{k}(t) + \frac{i}{\sqrt{K_\mathbf{k}}}P_{-\mathbf{k}}(t)\right\},$$

$$A_W^*(\mathbf{k},t) = \frac{1}{\sqrt{2}}\left\{\sqrt{K_\mathbf{k}}Q_{-\mathbf{k}}(t) - \frac{i}{\sqrt{K_\mathbf{k}}}P_\mathbf{k}(t)\right\}.$$

Here $K_\mathbf{k}$ is a constant inherent to the molecular vibrational field of water molecules. Those canonical variables of the W-field satisfy certainly the canonical commutation relation in quantum field theory.

$$\left[P_\mathbf{k}(t), Q_{\mathbf{k}'}(t)\right] = -i\delta_{\mathbf{k}\mathbf{k}'},$$

$$\left[P_\mathbf{k}(t), P_{\mathbf{k}'}(t)\right] = \left[Q_\mathbf{k}(t), Q_{\mathbf{k}'}(t)\right] = 0,$$

$$P_\mathbf{k}^* = P_{-\mathbf{k}},$$

$$Q_\mathbf{k}^* = Q_{-\mathbf{k}}.$$

Hamiltonian operator is nothing but the total energy of the quantum field dynamics and in most cases it is given by a sum of the free Hamiltonian and the interaction Hamiltonian.

$$H = H_0 + H'.$$

The free Hamiltonian of the molecular vibrational fields, that is, B-field and W-field, is given by

$$H_0 = \frac{1}{2}\sum_{\mathbf{k}}\{P^*_{\mathbf{k}}(t)P_{\mathbf{k}}(t) + K_{\mathbf{k}}{}^2 Q^*_{\mathbf{k}}(t)Q_{\mathbf{k}}(t)\},$$

and the interaction Hamiltonian by

$$H' = \sum_{j=1}^{N}\sum_{\mathbf{k}}\frac{f}{2\sqrt{V}}\left\{\tau_1^j Q_{\mathbf{k}}(t)e^{i\mathbf{k}\cdot\mathbf{x}_j} - \tau_2^j\frac{P_{\mathbf{k}}(t)}{K_{\mathbf{k}}}e^{-i\mathbf{k}\cdot\mathbf{x}_j}\right\}.$$

Here, f denotes the coupling constant between the B-field and the W-field. Since the canonical variables of the B-field are nothing but localized electric dipole moments

$$\tau^k = \tilde{\psi}_B(\mathbf{x}_k,t)\sigma\psi_B(\mathbf{x}_k,t),$$

they are subject to the commutation relation of the type

$$\left[\tau_1^j(t), \tau_2^k(t)\right] = 2i\tau_3^j\delta_{jk},$$

$$\left[\tau_2^j(t), \tau_3^k(t)\right] = 2i\tau_1^j\delta_{jk},$$

$$\left[\tau_3^j(t), \tau_1^k(t)\right] = 2i\tau_2^j\delta_{jk}.$$

In terms of those canonical variables

$$P_{\mathbf{k}}(t),$$

$$Q_{\mathbf{k}}(t),$$

$$\tau^k(t) = \tilde{\psi}_B(\mathbf{x}_k,t)\sigma\psi_B(\mathbf{x}_k,t),$$

and the Hamiltonian operator

$$H = H_0 + H',$$

quantum field dynamics of the B-field and the W-field is given by the Heisenberg equations

$$\frac{d}{dt}Q_{\mathbf{k}}(t) = -i[Q_{\mathbf{k}}(t), H],$$

$$\frac{d}{dt}P_{\mathbf{k}}(t) = -i[P_{\mathbf{k}}(t), H],$$

$$\frac{d}{dt}\tau^j(t) = -i[\tau^j(t), H].$$

Before proceeding to explicit expressions of those Heisenberg equations, it is convenient to see here the symmetry property of the B-field and the W-field. The Hamiltonian remains indeed invariant under the transformation of canonical variables

$$\left.\begin{matrix} P_{\mathbf{k}}(t) \\ Q_{\mathbf{k}}(t) \\ \tau^j(t) \end{matrix}\right\} \to \left\{\begin{matrix} P_{\mathbf{k}}'(t) \\ Q_{\mathbf{k}}'(t) \\ \tau^{j}{}'(t) \end{matrix}\right.$$

given by

$$Q_{\mathbf{k}}'(t) = Q_{\mathbf{k}}(t)\cos\theta - \frac{P_{\mathbf{k}}(t)}{K_{\mathbf{k}}}\sin\theta,$$

$$P_{-\mathbf{k}}'(t) = K_{\mathbf{k}}Q_{\mathbf{k}}(t)\sin\theta + P_{-\mathbf{k}}(t)\cos\theta,$$

$$\tau_1^{j}{}'(t) = \tau_1^{j}(t)\cos\theta + \tau_2^{j}(t)\sin\theta,$$

$$\tau_2^{j}{}'(t) = -\tau_1^{j}(t)\sin\theta + \tau_2^{j}(t)\cos\theta,$$

$$\tau_3^{j}{}'(t) = \tau_3^{j}(t)$$

for a continuous parameter θ. This transformation corresponds to a continuous rotation around the third axis. Such a rotational symmetry property of the B-field and the W-field is strongly related to the constant polarization of the B-field.

Let us write down the Heisenberg equations in QBD. We obtain

$$\frac{d}{dt}Q_{\mathbf{k}} = -i[Q_{\mathbf{k}}, H] = P_{\mathbf{k}} - \sum_{j=1}^{N} \frac{f}{2\sqrt{V}} \frac{1}{K_{\mathbf{k}}} \tau_2^j e^{-i\mathbf{k}\cdot\mathbf{x}_j},$$

$$\frac{d}{dt}P_{\mathbf{k}} = -i[P_{\mathbf{k}}, H] = -K_{\mathbf{k}}^2 Q_{\mathbf{k}} - \sum_{j=1}^{N} \frac{f}{2\sqrt{V}} \tau_1^j e^{-i\mathbf{k}\cdot\mathbf{x}_j},$$

$$\frac{d}{dt}\tau_1^j = -i[\tau_1^j, H] = -\sum_{\mathbf{k}} \frac{f}{\sqrt{V}} \frac{1}{K_{\mathbf{k}}} \tau_3^j P_{\mathbf{k}} e^{i\mathbf{k}\cdot\mathbf{x}_j},$$

$$\frac{d}{dt}\tau_2^j = -i[\tau_2^j, H] = -\sum_{\mathbf{k}} \frac{f}{\sqrt{V}} \tau_3^j Q_{\mathbf{k}} e^{i\mathbf{k}\cdot\mathbf{x}_j},$$

$$\frac{d}{dt}\tau_3^j = -i[\tau_3^j, H] = \sum_{\mathbf{k}} \frac{f}{\sqrt{V}} \left\{ \tau_2^j Q_{\mathbf{k}} e^{i\mathbf{k}\cdot\mathbf{x}_j} + \frac{1}{K_{\mathbf{k}}} \tau_1^j P_{\mathbf{k}} e^{-i\mathbf{k}\cdot\mathbf{x}_j} \right\}.$$

Our task is now to find the vacuum state solution of those Heisenberg equations. In quantum field theory the vacuum state solution corresponds to the time-independent solution of the Heisenberg equation. Let

$$P_{\mathbf{k}}(t) = \overline{P}_{\mathbf{k}},$$

$$Q_{\mathbf{k}}(t) = \overline{Q}_{\mathbf{k}},$$

$$\tau^j(t) = \overline{\tau}^j$$

be such solutions representing quantum field dynamics of the B-field and the F-field in the vacuum state. Then, the Heisenberg equations become

$$0 = \overline{P}_{\mathbf{k}} - \sum_{j=1}^{N} \frac{f}{2\sqrt{V}} \frac{1}{K_{\mathbf{k}}} \overline{\tau}_2^j e^{-i\mathbf{k}\cdot\mathbf{x}_j},$$

$$0 = -K_{\mathbf{k}}{}^2 \overline{Q}_{\mathbf{k}} - \sum_{j=1}^{N} \frac{f}{2\sqrt{V}} \overline{\tau}_1^j e^{-i\mathbf{k}\cdot\mathbf{x}_j},$$

$$0 = -\sum_{\mathbf{k}} \frac{f}{\sqrt{V}} \frac{1}{K_{\mathbf{k}}} \overline{\tau}_3^j \overline{P}_{\mathbf{k}} e^{i\mathbf{k}\cdot\mathbf{x}_j},$$

$$0 = -\sum_{\mathbf{k}} \frac{f}{\sqrt{V}} \overline{\tau}_3^j \overline{Q}_{\mathbf{k}} e^{i\mathbf{k}\cdot\mathbf{x}_j},$$

$$0 = \sum_{\mathbf{k}} \frac{f}{\sqrt{V}} \left\{ \overline{\tau}_2^j \overline{Q}_{\mathbf{k}} e^{i\mathbf{k}\cdot\mathbf{x}_j} + \frac{1}{K_{\mathbf{k}}} \overline{\tau}_1^j \overline{P}_{\mathbf{k}} e^{-i\mathbf{k}\cdot\mathbf{x}_j} \right\}.$$

It is straightforward to find the explicit forms of the vacuum state solution, obtaining

$$\overline{P}_{\mathbf{k}} = 0,$$

$$\overline{Q}_{\mathbf{k}} = -\frac{v}{K_{\mathbf{k}}{}^2} \sum_{j=1}^{N} \frac{f}{2\sqrt{V}} e^{-i\mathbf{k}\cdot\mathbf{x}_j}$$

$$\equiv Q_{\mathbf{k}}^0$$

$$\overline{\tau}^j = (v, 0, 0).$$

Here, v is a nonvanishing constant. Notice that the canonical variables of the B-field takes the same values for all the localized sites. This means that the B-field manifests a strong order globally in the whole volume V.

However, it seems more realistic that the B-field manifests such a strong order as given by constant canonical variables only in a restricted spatial domain in the volume V. Namely, we have a global domain structure of quantum vacuum states in QBD just as we have in quantum cosmology. Different domain shows different order represented by different constant value of the canonical variables of the B-field.

10. Spontaneous Symmetry Breaking and Goldstone Boson

We are in the best position to investigate the spontaneous symmetry breaking property of the vacuum states in QBD. The vacuum state solution in each domain is no longer invariant under the rotational transformation around the third axis even though the Hamiltonian is invariant . In other words, the QBD vacuum state is of the spontaneous symmetry breaking type.

It is this spontaneous symmetry breaking property which provides the molecular vibrational fields of biomolecules and water molecules with a specific mechanism to store the energy inputs in the ordered quantum dynamics. There exist two different reactions of the quantum vacuum states of the B-field and the W-field against the energy inputs. For lower energy case, the domain structure of the vacuum states remains the same but Goldstone bosons are created which correspond to the memory recalling process. For higher energy case, the walls of the domains are in part destructed and consequently several domains become unified and develops into a larger domain of the vacuum state. In this case quantum field dynamics of the B-field and the W-field manifests a phase transition from the less ordered dynamical state to the more ordered one. This corresponds to the memory printing process.

Those two different reactions of the QBD vacuum state can be seen through the calculation of excited mode. We look for the time-dependent solution of the type

$$P_{\mathbf{k}}(t) = \overline{P}_{\mathbf{k}} + \delta P_{\mathbf{k}}(t) = \delta P_{\mathbf{k}}(t),$$

$$Q_{\mathbf{k}}(t) = \overline{Q}_{\mathbf{k}} + \delta Q_{\mathbf{k}}(t) = Q_{\mathbf{k}}^{0} + \delta Q_{\mathbf{k}}(t),$$

$$\tau_1^j(t) = \overline{\tau}_1^j + \delta\tau_1^j(t) = v + \delta\tau_1^j(t),$$

$$\tau_2^j(t) = \overline{\tau}_2^j + \delta\tau_2^j(t) = \delta\tau_2^j(t),$$

$$\tau_3^j(t) = \overline{\tau}_3^j + \delta\tau_3^j(t) = \delta\tau_3^j(t),$$

where

$$\delta P_{\mathbf{k}}(t), \delta Q_{\mathbf{k}}(t), \delta\tau_1^j(t), \delta\tau_2^j(t), \delta\tau_3^j(t)$$

denote small fluctuation variables. Then, the Heisenberg equations up to the first order in fluctuation variables become

$$\frac{d}{dt}\delta Q_{\mathbf{k}} = \delta P_{\mathbf{k}} - \sum_{j=1}^{N} \frac{f}{2\sqrt{V}} \frac{1}{K_{\mathbf{k}}} \delta\tau_2^j e^{-i\mathbf{k}\cdot\mathbf{x}_j},$$

$$\frac{d}{dt}\delta P_{-\mathbf{k}} = -K_{\mathbf{k}}^2 \delta Q_{\mathbf{k}} - \sum_{j=1}^{N} \frac{f}{2\sqrt{V}} \delta\tau_1^j e^{-i\mathbf{k}\cdot\mathbf{x}_j},$$

$$\frac{d}{dt}\delta\tau_1^j = 0,$$

$$\frac{d}{dt}\delta\tau_2^j = -\sum_{\mathbf{k}} \frac{f}{\sqrt{V}} \delta\tau_3^j Q_{\mathbf{k}}^0 e^{i\mathbf{k}\cdot\mathbf{x}_j},$$

$$\frac{d}{dt}\delta\tau_3^j = \sum_{\mathbf{k}} \frac{f}{\sqrt{V}} \left\{ \delta\tau_2^j Q_{\mathbf{k}}^0 e^{i\mathbf{k}\cdot\mathbf{x}_j} + v\frac{1}{K_{\mathbf{k}}} \delta P_{\mathbf{k}} e^{-i\mathbf{k}\cdot\mathbf{x}_j} \right\}.$$

From the third equation we may put

$$\delta\tau_1^j = 0$$

and so the second equation becomes

$$\frac{d}{dt}\delta P_{-\mathbf{k}} = -K_{\mathbf{k}}^2 \delta Q_{\mathbf{k}}.$$

Let us perform the change of variables.

$$\begin{cases} q^j(t) \equiv -\sum_{\mathbf{k}} \frac{1}{K_{\mathbf{k}}} \delta P_{-\mathbf{k}} e^{i\mathbf{k}\cdot\mathbf{x}_j} \\ p^j(t) \equiv -\sum_{\mathbf{k}} K_{\mathbf{k}} \delta Q_{-\mathbf{k}} e^{i\mathbf{k}\cdot\mathbf{x}_j} \end{cases}$$

The new variables $q^j(t)$ and $p^j(t)$ satisfy the canonical commutation relation

$$\begin{aligned} \left[p^j(t), q^l(t)\right] &= -i\sum_{\mathbf{k}} e^{i\mathbf{k}\cdot(\mathbf{x}_j - \mathbf{x}_l)} \\ &= -i\delta_{jl} \end{aligned},$$

and so they are also canonical variables. The Heisenberg equations become

$$\frac{d}{dt} p^j(t) = -K^2 q^j(t) - \frac{f}{2\sqrt{V}} \delta\tau_2^j(t),$$

$$\frac{d}{dt} q^j(t) = p^j(t),$$

$$\frac{d}{dt} \delta\tau_2^j = -fG\delta\tau_3^j,$$

$$\frac{d}{dt} \delta\tau_3^j = fG\delta\tau_2^j - \frac{f}{\sqrt{V}} v q^j(t),$$

where

$$K \equiv \sum_{\mathbf{k}'} K_{\mathbf{k}'} \delta_{\mathbf{k}\mathbf{k}'}$$

and

$$\begin{aligned} G &\equiv \frac{1}{\sqrt{V}} \sum_{\mathbf{k}} Q_{\mathbf{k}}^0 e^{i\mathbf{k}\cdot\mathbf{x}_j} \\ &= -\frac{fv}{2V} \sum_{j=1}^{N} \sum_{\mathbf{k}} \frac{1}{K_{\mathbf{k}}^2} e^{i\mathbf{k}\cdot(\mathbf{x}_j - \mathbf{x}_l)} \end{aligned}.$$

Coupling the first two equations we obtain

$$\frac{d^2}{dt^2}q^j(t) = -K^2 q^j(t) - \frac{f}{2\sqrt{V}}\delta\tau_2^j(t)$$
.

The last two equations yield

$$\frac{d^2}{dt^2}\delta\tau_2^j(t) = -fG^2\delta\tau_2^j(t) + \frac{f^2}{\sqrt{V}}Gvq^j(t)$$
.

Those are coupled second order linear differential equations and so nontrivial solutions exist only when the determinant

$$\begin{vmatrix} \omega^2 - K^2 & -\frac{f}{2\sqrt{V}} \\ \frac{f}{\sqrt{V}}Gv & \omega^2 - f^2G^2 \end{vmatrix} = (\omega^2 - K^2)(\omega^2 - f^2G^2) + \frac{f^2}{2V}vG$$

vanishes, where ω is the angular frequency of the normal mode solution. We obtain finally a secular equation which is a fundamental equation to describe the reaction of the QBD vacuum states against the energy inputs.

We have two different solutions to the secular equation.

$$\omega_-^2 = \frac{1}{2}\left[(K^2 + f^2G^2) - \sqrt{(K^2 + f^2G^2) - f^2G^2(K^2 + \frac{fv}{2VG})}\right]$$
$$\omega_+^2 = \frac{1}{2}\left[(K^2 + f^2G^2) - \sqrt{(K^2 + f^2G^2) - f^2G^2(K^2 + \frac{fv}{2VG})}\right]$$

They are angular frequencies of two different normal mode solutions of the Heisenberg equations. The first normal mode with angular frequency ω_- is called the Goldstone mode or Goldstone boson which represents quantum field dynamics corresponding to a wave propagation with angular frequency ω_-. By the particle-wave duality in quantum field theory, it is nothing but a boson with energy equals to the angular frequency ω_-.

Since the minimum value of the angular frequency is zero, this normal mode solution represents a gapless excitation of the quantum vacuum states which can be induced by unlimitedly small energy inputs. The second solution with angular frequency ω_+ represents a gap excitation of the quantum vacuum states. This normal mode solution of the Heisenberg equations corresponds to the destruction of the walls of the vacuum domain structure and requires the energy inputs higher than the minimum value

$$\omega_+ = \sqrt{f^2G^2 - \frac{fv}{2VG}}$$

of the angular frequency ω_+.

We have found that the vacuum states of quantum field dynamics of the B-field and the W-field is of spontaneous symmetry breaking type and manifest strong order from the fundamental point of view of quantum field theory. It is shown that the vacuum states manifest reaction against the energy inputs from the classical dynamical system by creating the Goldstone boson or developing larger vacuum domains just as expected in QBD.

It seems of certain interest to notice here that such a specific feature of the vacuum states of quantum field dynamics plays the common principal role in quantum cosmology, superconducting media, LASER device, and macroscopic quantum effect.

11. An Outlook

In this address we presented the canonical formulation of quantum field dynamics in QBD due to Stuart, Takahashi and Umezawa. Of course, there exist other formalism of quantum field dynamics of the molecular vibrational fields. Among them are the path-integral formalism of quantum field theory due to the Umezawa group in Italy and the macroscopic wave function formalism of quantum ordered dynamics due to the Umezawa group in Japan to which we belong. (Del Giudice, Preparata and Vitiello, 1988; Del Giudice, Doglia, Milani and Vitiello, 1983, 1985, 1986, 1988a, 1988b; Del Giudice, Doglia, Milani, Smith and Vitiello, 1989; Jibu and Yasue, 1991, 1992a, 1992b, 1992c) We call the latter wave cybernetics and represents quantum field dynamics in QBD in terms of the Josephson network or the Josephson machine.

Since the domain walls play the role of thin layer of insulator, there exists a Josephson current between the neighboring vacuum domains due to the Josephson effect. Thus the domain structure of the QBD vacuum realizes a huge microscopic three dimensional network of Josephson current between neighboring vacuum domains which may be though of as a quantum neural network described by the Sine-Gordon equation.

We hope your head is now in more ordered state than before coming to Radford. Thank you.

Acknowledgement

Today it is difficult to keep one's research activity on one's own purely scientific interest mainly due to the rush of easy financial supports from some military sources (direct and/or indirect). The authors are indebted to Sisters of Namur Notre Dame for helping them to overcome the difficulty. They also wish to thank Professors H. Umezawa, Y. Takahashi, K. Pribram, L. Ricciardi and G. Vitiello for their suggestions and helpful discussions.

References

Davydov A. S. (1979), Physica Scripta *20*, 387; (1982), Biology and Quantum Mechanics, (Pergamon, Oxford).

Del Giudice E., Preparata G. and Vitiello G. (1988), Phys. Rev. Lett. *61*, 1085.

Del Giudice E., Doglia S., Milani M. and Vitiello G. (1983), Phys. Lett. A*95*, 508; (1985), Nucl. Phys. B*251*, 375; (1986), Nucl. Phys. B*275*, 185; (1988a), "Structures, correlations and electromagnetic interactions in living matter: Theory and applications", in Biological Coherence and Response to External Stimuli, Fröhlich H. Ed., (Springer-Verlag, Berlin); (1988b), Cell Biophys. *13*, 221.

Del Giudice E., Doglia S., Milani M., Smith C. W. and Vitiello G. (1983), Physica Scripta *40*, 786.

Eccles, J. C. (1986), Proc. R. Soc. Lond. B*227*, 411.

Fröhlich H. (1968), J. Quantum Chem. *2*, 641.

Jibu M. and Yasue K. (1991), Cosmology of the One Liter Universe, in Japanese, (Kaimei-sha, Tokyo); (1992a), "A Physical Picture of Umezawa's Quantum Brain Dynamics", to be published in the proceeding of EMCSR 1992; (1992b), "Intracellular Quantum Signal Transfer in Umezawa's Quantum Brain Dynamics", to be published in Cybernetics and Systems; (1992c), "Introduction to Quantum Brain Dynamics", in Nature, Cognition, and System, Editor, Carvallo E. (Kluwer Academic, Dordrecht/Boston/London).

Pribram K. H. (1960), in Handbook on Physiology, Neurophysiology II (pp.1323-1344), (American Physiological Society, Washington D. C.); (1971), Languages of the Brain, (Prentice-Hall, Englewood Cliffs); (1991), Brain and Perception, (Lawrence Erlbaum Associates, New Jersey); (1987), "The implicate brain" in Quantum Implications, Eds. Hiley B. J. and David Peat F., (Routledge & Kegan Paul, London).

Ricciardi L. M. and Umezawa H. (1967), Kybernetik *4*, 44.

Schrödinger E. (1944), What is Life?, (Cambridge University Press, Cambridge)

Sivakami S. and Srinivasan V. (1983), J. Theor. Biol. *102*, 287.

Stuart C. I. J. M., Takahashi Y. and Umezawa H. (1978), J. Theor. Biol. *71*, 605; (1979), Found. Phys. *9*, 301.

Chapter 5

Advances in the Theory of Quantum Neurodynamics

Robert L. Dawes
Martingale Research Corp.
100 Allentown Parkway, Suite 211
Allen, TX 75002

ADVANCES IN THE THEORY OF QUANTUM NEURODYNAMICS

Robert L. Dawes
Martingale Research Corp.
100 Allentown Parkway, Suite 211
Allen, TX 75002

Abstract This paper presents a perspective on the theory of Quantum Neurodynamics (QND) that is complementary to that which has been described by Yasue, Jibu and Pribram. We describe a mathematical and computational model of cognitive processes in the form of a neural stochastic filter, i.e., a neural processor whose function is to transform the ensemble of past observations of a system of interest into estimates of the current probability density function for the state of that system. This neural stochastic filter employs the Schroedinger equation for the computation of the essential probability density function and this, in turn provides a model for cognitive phenomena at the behavioral scale. We conclude with a description of the implications of QND for the resolution of certain paradoxes of quantum mechanics.

I. INTRODUCTION

In Appendix A of [13], Yasue, Jibu and Pribram have used variational and probabilistic principles of the holonomic brain theory to derive the linear time-dependent Schroedinger equation as the dynamic descriptor of the interaction between the ionic bioplasma density distribution and the phase patterns of neural membrane potential oscillations. Independently, this author [3-6] has found that the same Schroedinger equation provides the key to the solution, in a parallel distributed neurocomputing architecture, of a large class of nonlinear, nonGaussian stochastic filtering problems, of which the Kalman filtering problem is a very small subset.

We view these two developments as being, respectively, a bottom-up and a top-down perspective on the ultimate principles of neural dynamics. That is, the one is a description of neural membrane dynamics that is consistent with principles of cognitive processing, while the other is a description of cognitive processing that is consistent with the principles of neural membrane dynamics. Interestingly, even though these two perspectives were independently developed, both Pribram's group and this author, again independently, recognized that the only reasonable name to apply to the resulting descriptions should be "Quantum Neurodynamics".

In this paper, we describe our development of the neural stochastic filter based on the use of the Schroedinger equation as the mediator of the essential time-varying conditional probability density function for the state of the observed universe (system). We show that essentially all behavioral response to stimulus is the result of a "flow" of motor pattern signals computed as the probabilistic Expectation of pattern-valued functions of the state (stored in the synapses) with respect to that time-varying ("flowing") probability density function. We then describe how a brain operating on these principles can be expected to perform some well-known but hard-to-model functions, such as inferential reasoning. (Some of this material has been borrowed from my forthcoming paper to appear in the Proceedings of the IEEE Conference on Systems Man and Cybernetics, November, 1992.) Finally, we present the implications of Quantum Neurodynamics for the resolution of certain long-standing paradoxes in the field of quantum mechanics.

II. REVIEW OF STOCHASTIC FILTERING

Stochastic filtering is the mathematical and engineering discipline that deals with the problem of computing estimates for the "hidden" variables of a dynamical system by implementing some formula that operates on the complete time series of prior "observed" signals emanating (presumably) from that system. Knowledge of the "hidden" variables is important, because even though it is obviously only the "observable" quantities that can, by definition, have any impact upon the observer, experience shows that a system can be initialized on separate occasions to be observably identical both times, yet it will subsequently evolve along different trajectories. This affront to our unshakable faith in causality is resolved by arguing that there must have been unobserved (and perhaps unobservable) elements of the system that were different at the beginning of the two experiments. The vector of these additional elements is referred to as the *state* vector of the system.

In order to understand the implications of Quantum Neurodynamics, it is very important at this point for the reader to confront the possibility that, even though both common and uncommon sense insists that the state vector "of" a system represents something that is a real physical part "of" the system, it may "really" be only a component of a MODEL that resides in a computational engine whose purpose is the avoidance of unpleasant surprises. I shall return to this point later.

The essence of stochastic filtering, according to Bucy [1], is the computation of a time-varying probability density function (PDF) for the state of the observed system. What one subsequently does with that PDF is dictated by the nature of the application and the requirements for optimality. For example, if one is only interested in the maximum likelihood (ML) state at a given time, then one merely sorts the set of states in order of probability, and the state with the greatest probability is the winner.

The method used to compute the PDF is dependent on the mathematical nature of the time-series of observed signals, called the *stochastic process.* In practice, the method is usually determined by mathematical simplicity and computational feasibility. Thus, Markov methods are often thought of as stochastic filtering methods, but technically, they only apply to a class of stochastic processes known as Markov processes. Most of the signals presented by sensor systems that observe the physical universe, on the other hand, are not Markov processes but rather martingale processes. (Brownian motion is one of the few stochastic processes in the intersection of the two classes.)

Mathematically, martingale processes are very difficult to describe and understand without a thorough development of probability theory from the measure-theoretic point of view. See Krishnan [12], Kalman, Falb & Arbib [10], and Kallianpur [9]. Heuristically, however, a martingale process is a signal that is accompanied by another mathematical object (the σ-algebra of measurable sets) whose structure increases with time. This increasing structure provides a home in the present time for all the probabilistic information that was contained in the past history of the signal, thus making that past history accessible for operations in the present -- operations such as predictions of the future course of the observed signal.

The Kalman filter is one of the key mathematical methods for making these predictions. Unfortunately, the Kalman filter is limited to a class of martingales that is not representative of the signals presented by the "buzzing, booming reality" of our environment, these being signals generated by linear (or "locally" linear) dynamical systems and corrupted by Gaussian noises. But, it is computable (sometimes), so we make do.

Kailath [8] has described the basic structure of a stochastic filtering algorithm that applies to the Kalman filter and to much more general stochastic filters. He refers to it as the "innovations approach" to stochastic filtering, but we may think of it as the basic structure of the predictor-error-corrector loop. The idea is conceptually straightforward: All the information that we have any right to know about our filter's performance is contained in the difference, or error, between the actual observed signal and the signal that our filter led us to <u>expect</u>. That difference, called the <u>prediction error</u>, and its statistical history, provide the means to reduce the error both in the immediate future and in the (presumably ergodic) statistical future. In the immediate future, the error is used to control the evolution of our computational model so that the computed PDF flows, at least asymptotically, into a distribution that minimizes the discrepancy between expectation and observation. In the more distant future, the error is used to improve both the dynamical and the statistical models of the observed process, so that when another observation with beginnings similar to this one is presented, the subsequent prediction error will be even smaller than before.

Figure 1 in the next section is a predictor-error-corrector loop that is similar to one appearing in Kailath [8] for the Kalman filter. The difference is that in the Kalman filter, the probability density is assumed to be Gaussian, so that it can be completely characterized by a mean vector and a covariance matrix. The computation of those quantities is accomplished by the integration of an iterative matrix Riccati equation at a computational burden that grows as the cube of the order of the system. In Figure 1, the probability density is not assumed to be Gaussian, but rather is given as the squared modulus of the wavefunction of the Schroedinger equation. That probability density is fed back to the input layer, where it is used to compute the conditional expectation of the current observation, y(t). The difference between the expectation and the observation is fed forward to the "classifier layer", where it is used to control the flow of the wavefunction and, hence, of the probability.

III. QUANTUM NEURODYNAMICS

We have described the equations of Quantum Neurodynamics in some detail in [3]. Here, we shall summarize the equations and provide a brief explanation of the neurocomputing architecture, called the Parametric Avalanche (PA), which implements the computations. Figure 1 is a functional diagram of the algorithm, which should be referred to while studying the following equations.

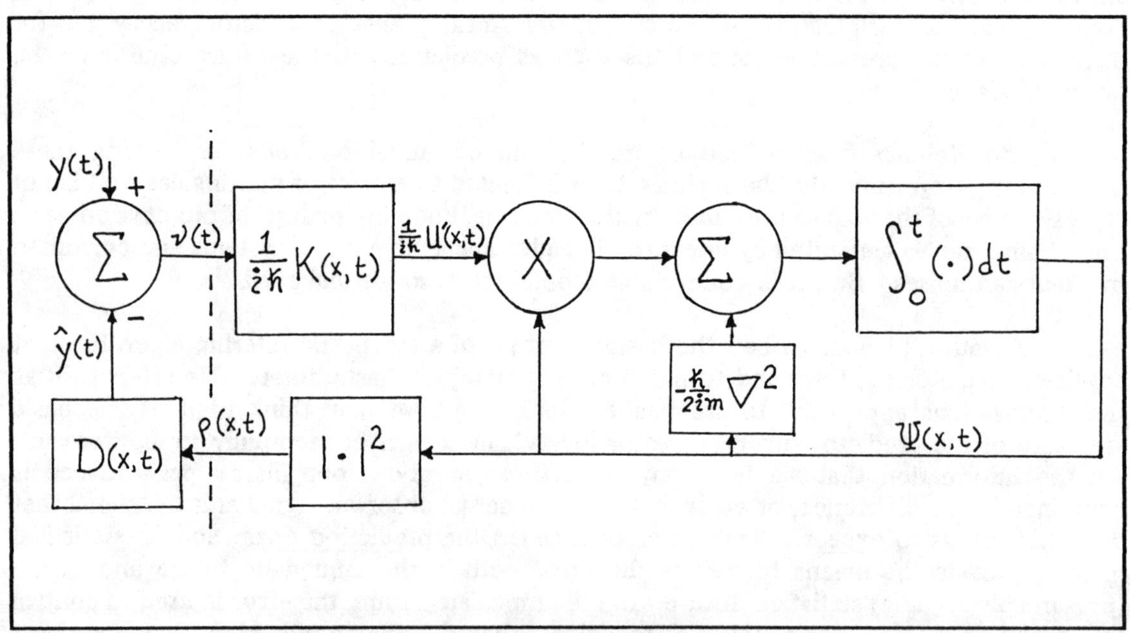

Figure 1: The PA Architecture

Equation (1) is the nonlinear time-dependent Schroedinger equation from quantum mechanics. An excellent review of its properties may be found in [2].

$$i\hbar\frac{\partial\Psi(x,t)}{\partial t} = -(\frac{\hbar^2}{2m})\nabla^2\Psi(x,t)+(U(x,t)+G(|\Psi|^2))\Psi(x,t) \qquad (1)$$

Here, $\hbar$ is Planck's constant divided by 2π, i is the imaginary unit, m is the mass of the particle and ∇^2 is the Laplacian differential operator. The real-valued function U(x,t) is the scalar potential energy field, which we use via (5) as a control input to the equation. This equation has solutions $\Psi(x,t)$ in the form of complex-valued wavefunctions whose envelope (modulus squared) localizes the position of a particle in that this envelope represents a probability density function for the location of the particle in the vector space:

$$\rho(x,t) = |\Psi(x,t)|^2 \qquad (2)$$

This probability density function is used to compute an expectation of the current observation vector y(t) by computing a ρ-weighted average over the state domain Ω of an adaptive pattern-vector-valued function D(x,t) :

$$\hat{y}(t) = \int_\Omega D(x,t)\,\rho(x,t)\,dx \qquad (3)$$

The difference between the actual observation vector $y(t)$ and the expectation is the prediction error vector,

$$\boldsymbol{\nu}(t) = y(t) - \hat{y}(t), \tag{4}$$

which under certain conditions of optimality would be called the *innovations process* [8] of $y(t)$. Such optimality is not practically attainable with this algorithm except, perhaps, after a long sequence of successive applications of the algorithm to the prediction error vector that results from each preceding stage. Such a sequence would implement a constructive Doob-Meyer decomposition of the input stochastic process, and would be a stochastic filtering equivalent of the Gram-Schmidt orthogonalization procedure. Whether optimal or suboptimal, however, $\boldsymbol{\nu}(t)$ is that part of $y(t)$ that cannot be anticipated by this method of computing probabilistic combinations of patterns previously mapped as $D(x,t)$, and it is therefore the part of $y(t)$ that is *novel* with respect to this method.

The linear part of the scalar potential field is the scalar product of another adaptive vector field $K(x,t)$ over Ω with the observation $y(t)$:

$$U(x,t) = - \langle K(x,t) | y(t) \rangle. \tag{5}$$

The nonlinear part of the scalar potential field is obtained from

$$G(|\Psi(x,t)|^2) = \langle K(x,t) \mid \hat{y}(t) \rangle \tag{6}$$

The resulting scalar potential field controls the evolution of the Schroedinger wavefunction through the Ehrenfest theorem of quantum mechanics. According to the Ehrenfest theorem, a gradient in the potential field induces a local flow of the probability in the direction of the gradient with an acceleration that is proportional to the magnitude of the gradient. The nonlinearity arises from the fact that the estimate $\hat{y}(t)$ is dependent on the wavefunction through the feedback loop. This nonlinearity produces wavepackets having the properties of solitons. The vector field $K(x,t)$ is the QND equivalent of the Kalman gain matrix, but it is much easier to interpret: At each state x, the vector $K(x,t)$ is a weighted average of previously observed patterns developed in accordance with the adaptation law (8) below.

The adaptation laws for $D(x,t)$ and $K(x,t)$ are just the antiHebbian and Hebbian laws, respectively, of neurocomputing:

$$\frac{\partial D(x,t)}{\partial t} = -\alpha \rho(x,t) \boldsymbol{\nu}(t) \tag{7}$$

$$\frac{\partial K(x,t)}{\partial t} = \beta \boldsymbol{\nu}(t) \rho(x,t) \tag{8}$$

Antihebbian learning is a well known component of novelty filtering [11], and can be derived as a special case of the delta rule learning law when the threshold function is linear and the desired output of the unit is zero. In Quantum Neurodynamics, the objective of learning is to minimize the novelty in the input stochastic process. That is, based on the fundamental assumption that the observed stochastic process is *ergodic*, learning seeks to ensure that if any previously observed spatiotemporal pattern should recur, then the flow of the wavefunction will be "better" in the sense that the ℓ^{*} norm of the prediction error is closer to zero than it was during the previous observation.

Note that both learning laws are intrinsically "supervised" by the probability density function, so that learning occurs only at those states x where there is substantial prior probability for the observed system to be found. Or, to put it another way, the amount of the current prediction error vector that is averaged into the pattern vector that is stored with the state x is (for each x) proportional to the a-priori conditional probability that the state x is the current state of the system, *given* the current historical ensemble of observations. In effect, since that conditional probability is given by $\rho(x,t)$, fast learning occurs in the wakes of large-amplitude traveling wave packets of the Schroedinger equation, but slow learning occurs at any state where the product $\rho(x,t)\nu(x,t)$ has nonzero mean over time intervals that are large relative to the reciprocal of the learning rate constants.

So far, we have treated the neural stochastic filter as merely a passive observer. Modern systems theory, however, permits us to use such an observer for the generation of forces that interact with the observed system and drive it into compliance with some objective. Although it is customary in control theory textbooks to use the observer for the generation of state estimates which then serve as the input to the controller, it is clear that when the observer computes a state PDF that is more general than the Gaussian density, it would be a waste of available detail to collapse the PDF into a simple state estimate. Instead, the control signal $u(t)$ should be computed as a conditional expectation:

$$u(t) = \int_{\Omega} Y(x,t)\,\rho(x,t)\,dx \tag{9}$$

where $Y(x,t)$ is a (vector) control signal to be applied when the observed system is in the state x. This is a true continuous pattern generator, since the PDF $\rho(x,t)$ flows continuously (or, in a discrete time simulation, as continuously as the temporal quantization will allow), even over the discrete state space dictated by a neural lattice.

At this point, we have not been able to describe a suitable adaptation law for the mapping Y that associates each state (neuron) with a control vector. There are, of course, certain obvious principles that a suitable law must accommodate, such as the principle of least action that results from the antiHebbian law (7). But we have not found a satisfactory way to generate and represent certain necessary signals, such as the reference (desired) trajectory for the controlled system. These remain open and important problems that will probably turn out not to be terribly difficult when approached with the proper technical background.

IV. NUMERICAL SIMULATIONS

The QND equations have been implemented in two spatial dimensions on both PC computers and on a Cogent Research Corp. XTM parallel workstation. Forward Euler integration is used for simplicity, although both backward and symmetric time integration methods have been explored. The Laplacian operator is approximated with a first order (nearest neighbor) kernel. (Incidentally, the first order discrete kernel of the negative Laplacian operator is an "on-center off-surround" operation, so it should not be surprising that many of the properties of cooperative-competetive neural processing algorithms will be found in Quantum Neurodynamics.) More sophisticated numerical methods have been rejected in favor of a spatial randomization method that is compatible with asynchronous neural parallelism and yet still avoids the accumulation of spatial "rasterization" artifacts.

The computational burden of integrating the Schroedinger equation is modest in comparison with the neurocomputing computations. When the neural lattice is laid out in two spatial dimensions, the extra arithmetic is equivalent to the addition of only sixteen additional synapses, plus a small amount of fixed overhead, to each neuron. When the normal synaptic fan-in on each neuron is counted in the hundreds or thousands of synapses, this represents only a small (and bounded) increment.

Numerical integration of the Schroedinger equation on a discrete spatial lattice gives rise to a quantization effect that is equivalent to the introduction of a *viscosity* term. In effect, the solution being produced is not a solution of the original Schroedinger equation, but rather of a modified equation with some fourth-order terms attached.

We thought at first that we would have to compensate for this viscosity with additional computation, but it turned out to be a fortuitous gift, rather than a problem, for the following reason: Our stochastic filtering objective requires that when the scalar potential $U(x,t)$ is stationary, then the wave packet should settle to the local minimum of the field, where the state estimate is optimum. Were it not for the gift of viscosity, however, the wave packet would oscillate forever in the potential well without ever converging asymptotically to the optimum state. Thus, for those who are interested in the asymptotic stability of the algorithm, the viscosity provides Lyapounov stability. Moreover, the viscosity also broadens the class of dynamical systems to which the method of Quantum Neurodynamics applies to include not only the purely Hamiltonian systems, but also the mildly dissipative systems.

These equations have been simulated in the context of the multitarget tracking problem in two dimensional video. They are able to track multiple targets prior to the accumulation of sufficient probability to declare a detection ("track-before-detect"). They track pairs of targets through collision and close approach without any ad-hoc intervention because of their soliton-like properties. And they are able to detect targets at signal to noise ratios down to 0 dB. Furthermore, we have demonstrated that the algorithm is parallelizable through an image tiling procedure, so that it scales gracefully to large-scale images.

These simulations provide persuasive support for the utility of the Parametric Avalanche as a new and powerful stochastic filtering algorithm. In the remainder of this paper, we present a few of the arguments in favor of the utility of the method as a quantitative model of cognitive phenomena.

V. COGNITIVE PHENOMENA

Quantum Neurodynamics provides an explicit, quantifiable model of the mechanisms of consciousness in the higher vertebrates. While a complete model would require a detailed description of the way in which a network of PA modules provides successive decomposition of a stochastic process into 2D (possibly 3D) factors with decreasing stochastic covariance, we can provide examples on a less complicated scale that should prove to be persuasive. At the heart of each of these examples is the following rather bold hypothesis: *Consciousness of a stimulus is mediated NOT by the immediate neuro-synaptic activation, but rather by some mediator of nonlinear wave mechanics that allows probability to flow in response to the neuro-synaptic activation field.* A plausible mediator for these dynamics is the glial matrix, long suspected of serving a greater function than merely taking up space, and known to support the propagation of solitary waves of Ca++ ions. Another is the dendritic medium as modeled by Yasue, Jibu and Pribram [13].

A. "Phi" phenomenon

The "phi" phenomenon occurs when a subject is shown two points of light that flash alternately on and off against a blank background. That is, when one light turns off, the other is immediately turned on. If the two points of light are sufficiently separated in the visual field, they are perceived correctly. But if they are moved close together, the subject percieves erroneously that there is just one light shining constantly and moving back and forth between the two positions.

When a point of light turns on in the visual field, it produces a broad depression in the scalar potential field. (The one-sigma width of the depression will be the sum of the optical point spread and the one-sigma width of the convolutional pattern template.) Probability flows into that depression. When the light turns off, the potential field becomes flat, and the probability disperses (the origin of an after-image). But if another depression is created nearby before the first wave packet can disperse, the wave packet will find itself on a slope and will flow laterally into the adjacent depression. The *conscious perception*, therefore, is that the spot of light itself moved.

B. Multiple Personality

A "personality" is a consistent pattern of responses to stimuli and situations. In QND, the personality of the stochastic filter is determined by the locally homotopic mappings of experience onto the neural domain and by the configuration of discontinuities between homotopic domains.

A conscious train of thought consists of a well-formed wave packet propagating within the neural domain in response to a combination of inputs from a number of sources, including the sensory apparatus and the outputs of other domains at various levels of abstraction. Whenever the probability density corresponding to this wave packet produces an expectation that does not compare well with the actual ensemble of inputs, the result is a potential field gradient (or "barrier", if it is sufficiently steep) that deflects the wave packet toward states associated with less prediction error.

Suppose that when the network's personality is being formed, it experiences a deliberately consistent "diabolical" training in which certain common experiences are interrupted with frustrating or painful intervention. QND learning will encode the painful experience on the trajectory so that it will be properly predicted as a consequence of the prior experience. (Incidentally, QND learning models classical conditioning even though it is simple Hebbian, because of the causal dynamics of the Schroedinger equation.) Whenever the common experience subsequently occurs without the intervention of the diabolical agent, the extreme difference between the expected punishment and the benign experience drives the conscious wave packet away from the states where the pain was stored. This "avoidance" has two consequences, one obvious and the other subtle. The obvious effect is that the deflected wave packet will generate an altered behavior pattern. The subtle effect is that the neurons where the painful patterns are encoded will be prevented from receiving enough probability to allow the patterns to be corrected.

Now suppose that the diabolical training is "extensive", both figuratively and literally. That is, suppose that it succeeds in placing other avoidance patterns into a geometry that surrounds and isolates a large cognitive domain from the rest of the neural network. Subsequently, wavepackets that form in that domain will be trapped there, and that domain will then develop a personality that is distinct from the personality of the exterior domain(s). <u>But the entrapment is not permanent:</u> Quantum tunneling provides a mechanism for penetration of the barrier, after which another distinct personality emerges.

C. Inferential reasoning

"Reasoning", in QND, is the stimulation and control of a wave packet in one region of the cognitive space primarily by the output of another, usually more abstract, region, that is, without significant direct sensory input. Whenever this stimulation initializes a Cauchy problem (establishing the initial wavefunction and its boundary values) for the Schroedinger equation, its subsequent evolution constitutes a "gedankenexperiment".

Suppose the QND network has been exposed to visual observation of a large number of experiments consisting of (say) a que stick propelling a single ball on a billiard table on which there are no other balls. If the learning algorithm builds a global homotopy of the observation space into a region of the cognitive space, it will then be possible to predict the motion of a single ball from initial conditions (position and velocity) distinct from any that were in the training set. But this is only "deductive" reasoning, because it results from minor displacements of learned trajectories into new, qualitatively similar trajectories.

But suppose now that the network conducts a gedankenexperiment in which <u>two</u> wavepackets are initialized in the cognitive domain of the billiard table. (No training example had ever involved the propagation of two balls simultaneously.) And suppose further that these two wavepackets converge upon the same state (position) at the same time. Because of the soliton properties of the QND wavepackets, they will interact with each other, each altering the other's momentum in accordance with the laws of Hamiltonian particle dynamics. They will emerge from the interaction on "bent" trajectories such as had never occurred in any training trial in the middle of the table. This constitutes an inference about the behavior of a system, and this inference can be tested by constructing and performing the corresponding real experiment.

Note that the nonlinear wave mechanics of the Schroedinger equation are necessary for the synthesis of (nontrivial) inferences in this fashion. If we had used, say, the Fokker-Planck equation, which is *linear* in the probability, the two wave packets would have emerged from the superposition without any perturbation from the interaction, as if the other particle's presence had no effect. This constitutes an inference, of course, but it is a null or trivial inference that contains nothing new.

This situation is analogous to the well-known fact that a linear filter cannot create energy at frequencies where there was no energy in the input. Just as the synthesis of new frequencies requires a nonlinear stationary filter, the synthesis of new knowledge requires a nonlinear stochastic filter.

VI. IMPLICATIONS FOR QUANTUM MECHANICS

Earlier in this paper, we emphasized the importance of acknowledging that the hidden variables of a system may actually be hidden in MODELS of the system rather than in the system itself. Quantum Neurodynamics provides a quantitatively explicit and intuitively natural way to accept the physical truth of this assertion. That is, the state of every observed system is truly in the mind of the observer! Why is this important? It is important mainly because Von Neumann and a few other hardy physicists have maintained that, if it were not so patently "absurd", this assumption would resolve the Einstein-Podolsky-Rosen paradox and other related paradoxes of quantum mechanics.

Note, in particular, that Quantum Neurodynamics places the observer in a symmetric, rather than a privileged, relationship to the observed. The act of observing a system does not cause the wavefunction of the system to collapse. Rather, the observation modulates the evolution of the wavefunction over the observer's neural model statespace in accordance with the principles of stochastic filtering and, consequently, in accordance with the principles of information theory. Thus, for example, Schroedinger's cat is NOT in any superposition of states prior to its being observed. The observer's brain carries a wavefunction whose probability is perhaps equally distributed over neurons coded for live cats and dead cats, but prior to opening the box, Schroedinger's cat is merely unobserved. After opening the box, the observation deforms the observer's mental scalar potential field, which redistributes most of the probability onto one or the other of the two neurons (leaving some behind to account for normal skepticism). Then, through a process we call "reasoning", the brain solves an inverse scattering problem for the causal flow that connects the decay or non-decay of the radioactive nucleus to the vial of poison and thence to the hapless cat. Due to the enormous amplification and the attendant noise in this "instrumentation", the solution of this inverse scattering problem is a wavefunction that is still distributed over both the decayed and the non-decayed states of the model nucleus, though perhaps more on one now than on the other. Thus, even if we observe a dead cat, there will always be the lingering suspicion that its life was taken by a stray cosmic particle, or perhaps by some clown in the adjacent laboratory, and the subject nucleus is still there, waiting for its time to split.

Similarly, in the Einstein-Podolsky-Rosen gedankenexperiment, when the observer at one end of the galaxy traps one of the two particles and measures its spin, his measurement redistributes the probability in his own mental statespace to lie mostly (but not totally) over, say, the spin-up state. Then, after a bit of "reasoning", his estimate of the state of the companion particle at the other end of the galaxy flows almost as strongly toward the spin-down state (allowing a little excess uncertainty for clowns). This has no effect on the companion particle and it has no effect on wavefunctions in the other observer's brain. But each observer *expects* that he or she knows what the other will observe, and if that expectation is shown by a subsequent message to be in error, then each observer will have to incorporate that prediction error into a revised model of the universe.

REFERENCES

[1] Bucy, R.S., "Linear and Nonlinear Filtering", Proc. IEEE, 58, No. 6, June 1970.

[2] Bialynicki-Birula, I., and Mycielski, J., "Nonlinear Wave Mechanics", Annals of Physics 100, 62-93 (1976).

[3] Dawes, R.L., "Quantum Neurodynamics: Neural stochastic filtering with the Schroedinger Equation", Proc. IJCNN, Vol I, p. 133, July, 1992.

[4] Dawes, R.L., "Quantum Neurodynamics and the Parametric Avalanche", Technical Report MRC-NASA-89004, Martingale Research Corporation, Allen, TX, August, 1989.

[5] Dawes, R.L., "Quantum Neurodynamics: A New Neural Network Paradigm for Knowledge Representation, Cognition, and Control", Technical Report MRC-NSF-89003, Martingale Research Corporation, Allen, TX, July, 1989.

[6] Dawes, R.L., "Adaptive Control and Stabilization with the Parametric Avalanche", Technical Report MRC-ARDEC-89002, Martingale Research Corporation, Allen, TX, April, 1989.

[7] Ho, Y.C., and Lee, R.C.K., "A Bayesian Approach to Problems in Stochastic Estimation and Control", IEEE Trans. Automat. Contr., vol. AC-9, pp. 333-339, Oct. 1964.

[8] Kailath, T., "The Innovations Approach to Detection and Estimation Theory", Proc. IEEE, vol 58, No. 5, May 1970.

[9] Kallianpur, G., Stochastic Filtering Theory, Springer-Verlag, 1980.

[10] Kalman, R.E., Falb, P., and Arbib, M., Topics in Mathematical System Theory, McGraw-Hill, New York, 1969.

[11] Kohonen, T., Self-Organization and Associative Memory, Springer Verlag, New York, 1984.

[12] Krishnan, V., Nonlinear Filtering and Smoothing: An Introduction to Martingales, Stochastic Integrals and Estimation, John Wiley & Sons, New York, 1984.

[13] Pribram, Karl, Brain and Perception, Holonomy and Structure in Figural Processing, Erlbaum, Hillsdale, NJ, 1991.

[14] Sorenson, H.W. (Ed.), Kalman Filtering: Theory and Application, IEEE Press, New York, 1985.

[15] Yashin, A., "Continuous-Time Adaptive Filtering", IEEE Trans. on Automatic Control, Vol AC-31, No. 8, August 1986.

Chapter 6

Information Processing in the Dendritic Net*

Bruce MacLennan†

Abstract

The goal of this paper is a model of the dendritic net that: (1) is mathematically tractable, (2) is reasonably true to the biology, and (3) illuminates information processing in the neuropil. First I discuss some general principles of mathematical modeling in a biological context that are relevant to the use of linearity and orthogonality in our models. Next I discuss the hypothesis that the dendritic net can be viewed as a linear field computer. Then I discuss the approximations involved in analyzing it as a dynamic, lumped-parameter, linear system. Within this basically linear framework I then present: (1) the self-organization of matched filters and of associative memories; (2) the dendritic computation of Gabor and other nonorthogonal representations; and (3) the possible effects of reverse current flow in neurons.

---

*Based on a presentation at the 2nd Annual Behavioral and Computational Neuroscience Workshop, Georgetown University, Washington DC, May 18–20, 1992.

†Computer Science Department, University of Tennessee, Knoxville TN 37996; `maclennan@cs.utk.edu`.

Chapter 6

[illegible]

Abstract

[illegible]

1 Goal

My goal is a model of the dendritic net that:

- is mathematically tractable,
- is reasonably true to the biology, and
- illuminates information processing in the neuropil.

The approach is different from previous approaches, which lack at in least one of these desiderata. For example, at least from the time of Hodgkin and Huxley we have had differential equations that describe the dynamics of ion flows across neural membranes. Unfortunately, these equations are much too complex and at much too low a level to tell us much about the representation and processing of information in the brain. At the other extreme, we have the neural network models, beginning with McCulloch and Pitts and continuing through modern PDP models. Although these have a relatively tractable mathematical theory and are at a high enough level to explicate information processing, they deviate from the biology in many important respects (Crick & Asanuma 1986; Shepherd 1990a). First, by treating dendrites as no more than the input wires to neurons, they ignore the important role that the dendrites play in neural information processing. Second, by treating neurons as simple discrete time systems with no spatial structure, they ignore much of the important spatiotemporal signal processing that occurs in the nervous system.[1] In this I follow Shepherd (1990, p. 20):

> The vast majority of neural network simulations — in particular, connectionist models — consider individual nerve cells to be single node, linear integration devices. They thus neglect the effect of dendritic, synaptic, and intrinsic membrane properties on the function of individual cells. An important goal of the study of synaptic organization is therefore to identify the specific operations that arise from these properties and incorporate them into more realistic network simulations of specific brain regions.

[1]See Roberts & Bush (1981), especially the papers by Bullock, Rall and Shepherd.

2 Some Principles of Mathematical Modeling

Before describing the model, I suggest two principles to guide the mathematical modeling of the nervous system, the *Complementarity Principle* and the *Robustness Principle.* Like other scientific principles, such as the Verification Principle, these are neither synthetic nor analytic, and so they can be established neither empirically nor deductively. Rather, they should be considered normative principles that must be assessed pragmatically by their long-term consequences for the scientific enterprise.

The Complementarity Principle

> *If your theory predicts different outcomes depending on whether you use discrete mathematics or continuous mathematics, then you've got the wrong theory.*

In simple terms, this principle says that continuous mathematics should be equivalent to discrete mathematics with fine grid, and that discrete mathematics should be equivalent to continuous mathematics with steep transitions. Its practical consequence is that we can move between the two as convenient. Although this may seem obvious enough, it's worthwhile to be reminded of it, since psychology is periodically infected by debates about whether cognition is *really* digital or *really* analog, which are prone to degenerating into medieval scholasticism. The point is, that *mathematical* differences between the discrete and the continuous can't be relevant to our enterprise. What is relevant is whether the phenomena look more discrete or more continuous at our level of analysis. Since all we intend is an approximation to reality, the essential point is that we may use discrete mathematics to approximate the continuous as closely as we like, and vice versa. In stronger terms, we may put this as

The Ontological Argument (or Nobel Prize Argument): If you have a theory that predicts different macroscopic phenomena depending on whether space, time or other physical variables are *really* discrete or *really* continuous, then you have a design for an experiment that will tell us, not just another approximation to the structure of the physical universe, but an absolute and final answer to it. If this is so then you should immediately abandon whatever you are doing and set up that experiment, because you will almost surely earn a Nobel prize.

In the absence of such a theory the complementarity principle applies: continuous mathematics is equivalent to approximately-continuous, discrete mathematics, and conversely, discrete mathematics is equivalent to approximately-discrete, continuous mathematics. Thus we can move back and forth between the two as convenient.

So much for the Complementarity Principle; consider now:

The Robustness Principle

> *No biological process can depend on an absolute mathematical property.*

This principle may be justified by

The Argument from Noise: Thermal noise and other sources of error and imprecision limit the accuracy of biological processes. For example, if a biological process depended on two things being *exactly* equal or something having *exactly* the correct value, it could never work in a real biological context. Another example: orthogonality, as normally defined in mathematics, is an absolute property: two vectors either are or are not orthogonal; closeness to orthogonality is not relevant.[2] A biological process could not depend on whether two vectors are exactly orthogonal (versus nearly orthogonal). Certainly, given the one or perhaps two digits of precision of axonal signalling, the most we could expect is neuronal processes that depend on orthogonality to within a few percent of their inner products.

One conclusion we can draw from the Robustness Principle is that representations in the brain cannot depend on whether a set of representing functions is an orthogonal basis or a nonorthogonal basis; the most that we can assume is approximate orthogonality. In other words, we're much better off assuming representations are nonorthogonal and then talking about degrees of orthogonality. Another example: the infinite, but vanishingly small, support of the Gabor elementary functions is not a significant problem compared to the finite support of other wavelet families. Finally, and most importantly for the model presented here, we cannot expect a biological system to depend on exact linearity, but approximate linearity is reasonable.

[2] Notions of approximate orthogonality, such as ϵ-orthogonality, have been proposed, most recently by Kainen (1992), and are discussed below.

To emphasize the point of the Robustness Principle, I will digress to consider the precision of computation in the nervous system. First consider signalling by action potential density. The Gabor Uncertainty Principle with 1 kHz bandwidth implies that N msec. are required to distinguish N values (MacLennan 1991). Therefore it takes 10 msec. to transmit an analog value with one digit of precision, and 100 msec. for a value with two digits. Hence we can expect at most 1 to 2 digits precision in axonal signalling.

Next consider the transmission of analog values across a chemical synapse. Since releases of neurotransmitter are quantal, and an action potential releases 100–200 quanta (Shepherd 1988, p. 36), we can expect only about 2 digits precision from a chemical synapse.

Electrical synapses are not well understood and seem to be rare in the mammalian brain. Nevertheless, the quantal change in conductance is about 5 times that of a chemical synapse (120 pS vs. 20–40 pS[3]), suggesting that it is even lower precision (but quicker) (Shepherd, 1988, pp. 70–2, 128–9; Neher, 1992; Sakman, 1992).

Membrane juxtaposition also results in nonsynaptic electrical field potential effects, sometimes called *ephapses*, especially between dendrites (e.g., Shepherd 1988, pp. 123–4, 1990, pp. 48–50). These interactions are difficult to study, but it seems safe to say that since they are very weak (about 10 mV at most), thermal and electrical noise will keep the precision low.

In conclusion I claim:

> *1% to 10% is "close enough for brain work."*

Of course, the foregoing should not be interpreted as an argument against the attempt to find deep mathematical principles underlying neural processes. There are many instances in the history of science where taking the mathematics seriously pointed the way to future discoveries; special relativity and Dirac's postulation of the positron are examples. In the area of neuroscience we can cite the discovery of Gabor receptive fields. On the other hand, there have also been cases where mathematically obvious generalizations have apparently been ignored by Nature (the magnetic monopole?). Thus:

> *We should take our mathematical models seriously —*
> *but not* **too** *seriously.*

[3]The abbreviation pS stands for picosiemen, a unit of conductance equal to 1000 megohm^{-1}.

3 The Dendritic Model of Computation in the Brain

The view I take in this paper is that the neuron is predominantly a transducer, and that computation is implemented by linear processes in the dendritic net. The approach is mainly based on Karl Pribram's (1991) ideas, but also on Gordon Shepherd's notion that the synapse should be viewed as the basic computing element of the brain.

3.1 Shepherd's Microcircuits

Since the mid 1960s Shepherd has stressed the importance of dendritic interactions, and has shown the presence of microcircuits even within a single dendritic spine (e.g., Shepherd 1972, 1978, 1988, 1990). The simplest example is the *reciprocal synapse* that occurs between mitral cells and granule cells in the olfactory bulb. The reciprocal synapse comprises an inhibitory and an excitatory synapse that transmit in opposite directions. Thus a depolarization wave spreading through the mitral-cell dendrite can activate the excitatory synapse to the granule-cell dendrite, thereby causing a depolarization wave to spread though the granule-cell dendrite. The latter depolarization activates the inhibitory synapse, which suppresses the original depolarization of the mitral cell. Thus we have a negative feedback loop implemented within a dendritic spine, about one micron in diameter. The effect is that of an *operational amplifier*, one of the basic components of an analog computer (Fig. 1).

Microcircuits of this kind have been found now in many areas of the brain, including the thalamus, the basal ganglia of the cerebrum and the midbrain, the motor area of the cerebral cortex, the trigeminal nerve, and the suprachiasmatic nucleus, as well as in retinal amacrine and bipolar cells. The conclusion that Shepherd draws is that significant computing takes place in the dendrites, including in microcircuits in individual dendritic spines. If, as Shepherd suggests, we take the synapse as the basic computational unit of the brain, then we find that the computational resources of the brain are much greater than we would suppose from counting neurons. Since there are about 300 million (300×10^6) synapses per cubic mm of cortex (but only 50 000 neurons), the human brain comprises some 60 trillion (60×10^{12})

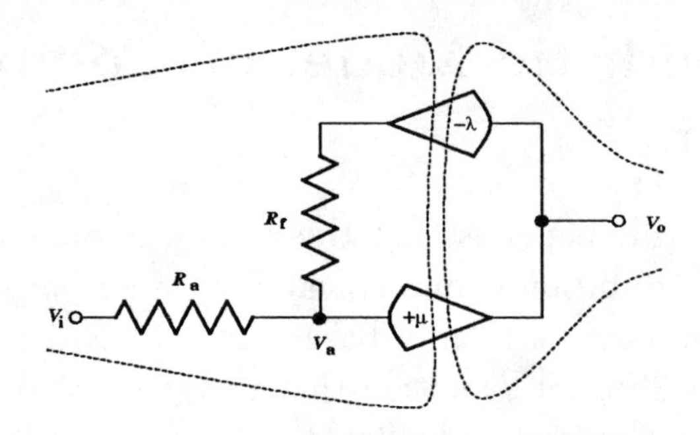

Figure 1: A reciprocal synapse between two dendrites provides negative feedback, in effect implementing an operational amplifier, one of the principal components of an analog computer.

synapses, but only 10 billion neurons (Beaulieu & Colonnier 1983; Shepherd 1990, p. 7).[4]

3.2 Pribram's Neural Wave Equation

Pribram's *holonomic brain theory* (1991) is a development of his earlier holographic hypothesis (1971). Its main points can be summarized as follows: (1) The neural (axonal) net is regular and sparsely connected. That is, in contrast to the full or random interconnection of most PDP models, axon bundles make topology-preserving projections from one area to another. (2) On the other hand, the dendritic net (neuropil) is randomly and densely connected. In fact, if one looks at the neuropil, it appears to be a dense feltwork of dendrites, with cell bodies and axons embedded in this matrix (Fig. 2). Thus PDP models are more similar to the dendritic net than to the axonal net. (3) The foregoing implies that the function of the axons is *communication*, since they make regular projections and impulses are ideally suited to long-distance transmission. (4) On the other hand, the function of the dendrites is *computation*, since they are ideally suited (as we will show below) to subtle, spatiotemporal analog interactions. (5) Indeed, the dendritic net may be viewed as a medium for linear wave interactions. (6) Nonlinearity enters only at axon hillock.

[4]These microcircuits are also sensitive to the geometry of the dendritic tree, since the propagation of the electrical wave is influenced by membrane capacitance, ion conductances, dendritic diameter and many other factors.

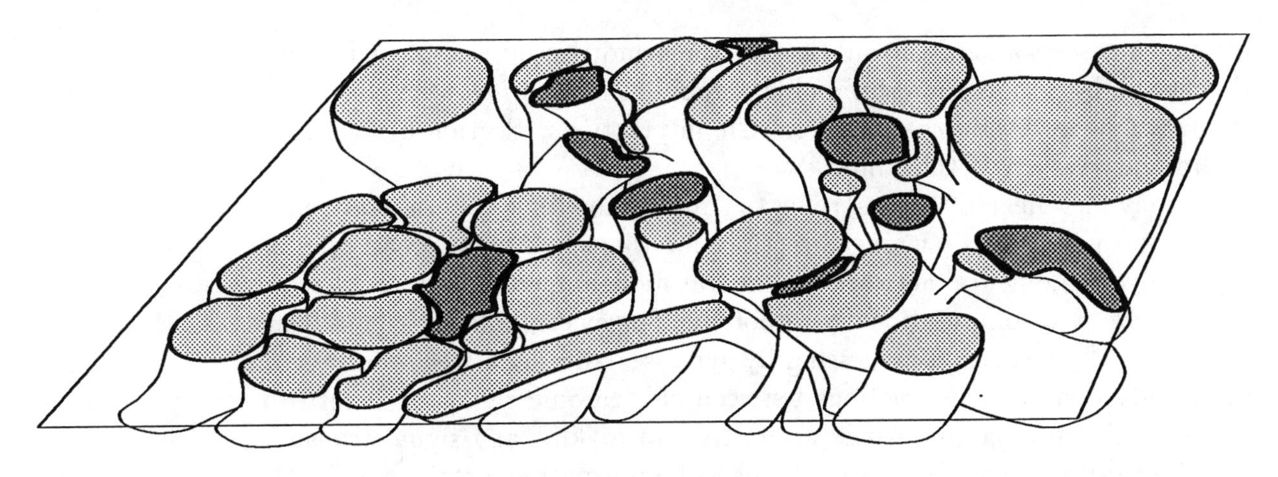

Figure 2: Visualization of neuropil. The figure depicts a cross-section through the neuropil (rat cerebral cortex), magnified approximately 3500 times. Notice the dense packing, allowing for both chemical and electrical interactions. Darker areas represent axons, lighter represent dendrites. Black bands represent synapses (both symmetric and asymmetric). Several dendritic spines are also visible.

3.3 Motivation for Linear Systems Approach

In the Appendices of his 1991 book Pribram, together with Kunio Yasue and Mari Jibu, has presented a neural wave equation for the dynamics of wave interactions in dendritic networks. Several plausible assumptions lead to a wave equation formally identical to that used in quantum mechanics, but this is a two-edged sword: it is very suggestive, and allows the application of many of the mathematical tools developed for quantum theory, but it inherits all the mathematical intractability of quantum mathematics. Analytical results require gross simplifying assumptions, such as a toroidal topology for the dendritic membrane. Many of the results are hard-won, and come as much from the structure of the underlying Hilbert space as from the neural wave equation.

Consideration of these difficulties has led me to try a simplification. By replacing the linear partial differential equations of the neural wave equations by linear ordinary differential equations relating membrane properties at discrete sites, the dendritic net can be viewed as a *dynamic lumped parameter system*. This places it squarely within linear systems theory, an extremely well-understood mathematical framework. Although this approximation misses some of the subtlety of the dendritic interactions, I believe that it will be a more powerful tool for probing the *function* — in contrast to the merely the *dynamics* — of dendritic interactions. Section 6 gives some preliminary results of this kind.

It may be objected that in trying to simplify the linear neural wave equation, I am going in the wrong direction, for there is a widespread opinion, especially in the neural network and neural modeling communities, that linear systems are computationally impotent. For example, Poggio and Torre (1981) say, "information processing by synapses and dendrites must rely on essentially nonlinear interactions between electrotonic signals if it is to be nontrivial," and, "nonlinearities are critical in making any signal transduction interesting from the point of view of information processing." Also Reichardt & Poggio (1981, p. 187) say "every nontrivial computation has to be essentially nonlinear, that is, not representable (even approximately) by linear operators." While I am very sympathetic to the importance of nonlinear systems, I think we may have sold short the information processing capabilities of linear systems. For example, in a forthcoming paper David Wolpert and I show that a linear field computer can simulate a Turing machine (Wolpert & MacLennan submitted), which is hardly trivial and uninteresting information processing.[5]

4 Are Neurons Linear?

4.1 Dendritic Nets

Before we can apply linear systems theory to the dendritic net we must address a factual question: Are synapses linear? Or, more in a accord with the Robustness Principle: Are synapses approximately linear? This question is surprisingly hard to answer from the literature, although Koch & Poggio (1987) is valuable. It is obvious that the synapse cannot behave linearly at high neurotransmitter concentrations since either the receptors become

[5]So that there is no mystery how this is possible, let me simply point out that if the states of a machine are represented by orthogonal vectors, then any deterministic state transition is a simple linear operator (a sum of outer products). The nonlinearities occur in the input coding, not in the computation or input. (This is not, however, the construction used in Wolpert & MacLennan submitted.)

saturated or the neurotransmitter becomes depleted (Koch & Poggio 1983, p. 462). Thus the dependence must become sublinear at the upper end, probably approximately logarithmic.

At low conductances, the postsynaptic potential depends linearly on the synaptic conductance induced by the presynaptic potential (Koch & Poggio 1983, p. 462; Shepherd 1990, p. 427).[6] Although Shepherd claims that we do not know whether synapses operate in their linear range, in simulated dendrites the linear region seems to extend to 10 000 pS (Shepherd 1990, p. 427). Since the quantum of conductance change is on the order of 20–40 pS, and an AP releases less than 200 quanta (8000 pS), it appears likely that synapses will usually be linear. Koch & Poggio (1983, p. 471) suggest that a dendritic spine is in its linear range when the conductance change is less than 10% of the input admittance of the spine head (i.e., a conductance change of less than about 10 000 pS). Furthermore, Koch & Poggio (1985, p. 653) suggest that linear operation can be enhanced by having the input distributed to several sites that are somewhat decoupled in their electrical behavior. Indeed we find that a cortical cell will often make 5–10 synapses with each neuron to which it projects (Shepherd 1990, p. 399), thus improving linearity. Overall we can tentatively conclude that a synapse often behaves linearly, but saturates at high levels. By the Robustness Principle, we can treat the synapse as approximately linear.[7]

---

[6]Synaptic communication can be decomposed into three components: (1) the relation between presynaptic depolarization and the amount of neurotransmitter released, (2) the relation between quantity of neurotransmitter released and the number of postsynaptic ion channels opened, and (3) the relation between the number of ion channels opened and postsynaptic voltage and current. All three seem to be approximately linear except for saturation. However, (1) can be nonlinear due to facilitation and fatigue (Berne & Levy 1983, p. 60). Nonlinearities enter in (3) because the increased conductance partly depolarizes the membrane, which results in decreased driving potential (Koch & Poggio 1983; Rall & Segev 1987, p. 611; Shepherd 1990, p. 427); for modest depolarizations it is approximately linear (see above).

[7]The chemical synapse operates as voltage-controlled voltage-source or as a voltage-controlled current-source depending on the ratio of the stimulus-induced synaptic conductance to the conductance of the spine neck (Koch & al. 1992). The chemical synapse can also be thought of as a voltage amplifier; a typical gain is 3 (in the linear range), but gains as low as 0.3 and as high as 50 have been observed (Koch & Poggio 1987, pp. 648–649). Chemical synapses can also function as both positive and negative resistances, since presynaptic depolarization can cause postsynaptic hyperpolarization (Poggio & Koch 1985).

4.2 The Axon Hillock

Although my primary concern is with dendritic computation, it will be worthwhile to consider the linearity of the axon hillock. Conventional neural network models are based on the assumption that axonal impulse rate is related to soma depolarization by a sigmoidal or "squashing" function, that is, by a saturating linear function such as $y = \tanh(x)$. However, this model diverges from the biology in several respects (Shepherd 1990, pp. 411–413). First, due to neural adaptation the pulse rate typically decreases during the spike train. For example, if we consider the relation of interspike interval to depolarizing current in certain pyramidal cells, the same depolarizing current will produce a 280/sec. rate for the first interspike interval, but 120/sec. for the second, and only 40/sec. for the fifth. Second, the relation is flatter for later intervals than for earlier. Thus 0.3 nA current leads to a 60/sec. change in rate for the second intervals, but only 40/sec. for the fifth. Finally, the rate/current relation is more linear for later intervals, with the first interval displaying a somewhat irregular (not even monotonic) sigmoidal shape. Although in some cases the axon hillock may function as an approximately linear amplitude to pulse rate converter, for others the relation will be nonlinear. Whether or not a particular neuron's hillock can be treated as linear will therefore depend on its usual operating range.

Shunting inhibition may be a mechanism for nonlinear synaptic interactions, and a basis for multilinear computation, as described in MacLennan (1987, 1990, this volume); for example, Shepherd (1990, p. 417) claims that in effect these inhibitory synapses divide (multiply by a fraction). However, the simulation studies of Koch & al. (1983) suggest that shunting inhibition is more likely to function as a veto of distal excitatory connections; elsewhere they discuss possible multiplicative effects of excitatory and inhibitory synapses on a single spine (Torre & Poggio 1978, 1981), but these effects depend on rather precise timing of signals and placement of synapses.

Nonlinear effects may also enter into the "addition" of inputs from separate spines. However, if the spine neck resistance is high, then the currents are small and combine linearly (Jack & al. 1975, pp. 192–213; Koch & Poggio 1983, pp. 468–469, 1985, pp. 651–653; Shepherd 1990, pp. 465–473). A final source of nonlinearity is the generation of action potentials in the dendrites (Eccles 1957, p. 270; Jack & al. 1975, pp. 213–218; Shepherd 1990, pp. 428–429, 465); although I leave these out of this model, they might be accommodated in the same way as approximately linear axon hillocks (see below).

5 The Linear Systems Model

5.1 Spatiotemporal Fields

Out of the many properties of nervous tissue, we can expect some to be relevant to information processing and others not. Significant quantities likely include membrane depolarizations, ionic currents, transmembrane charges, etc., but may also include others, such as flow rates in microtubules. In contrast with other mathematical models of the detailed dynamics of neural tissue (e.g., Deutsch & Micheli-Tzanakou 1987; Jack & al. 1975; Koch & Poggio 1985), I will not be particularly concerned with the physical quantities that the variables represent. For my purposes, it is not so important to have a final list of the relevant variables; it is important only that they vary approximately continuously (cf. Complementarity) and have approximately linear dynamics.[8]

For mathematical convenience, I assume a discrete set of variables, $\psi(k,t) = \psi_k(t)$, for k in $1, \ldots, N$. These could be, for example, depolarizations at synapses. However, the number of synapses is sufficiently large (say, 5000 to 200 000) that I will often view the variables as $\psi(x,t)$ with x varying over a continuum D, that is, as spatially-continuous time-varying fields, $\psi(t)$.[9] The Complementarity Principle permits this. Further, since we usually take time also to vary continuously, we are really dealing with spatiotemporal fields, $\psi(x,t)$.

Although it is useful to think of the variables as spatiotemporal fields, it is critical that we treat them mathematically as discrete variables, since

[8]The basic theory of information processing presented here would hold for any continuous quantities with approximately linear interactions. For example, this could include certain aspects of the dynamics of the cytoskeleton, as described by Dayhoff and Hameroff (see also Hameroff 1987). In addition to ionic currents in the microtubules, it could include MAP-induced field effects in the average position of vibrating tubulin sidearms. This follows also from the general correspondence between electrical and chemical networks (Oster & al. 1971; Poggio & Koch 1985).

[9]A basic tenet of field computation, as I have defined it (1987, 1990), it that the number of computational units be sufficiently large that it may be treated as a continuous quantity. Thus the Complementarity Principle may be applied. It should be noted that my variety of field computation deals predominantly with nonholonomically constrained fields, as opposed to the holonomically constrained fields familiar from physics (cf. Kugler, these proceedings). However they have in common that they deal with physical quantities varying continuously over a region of space.

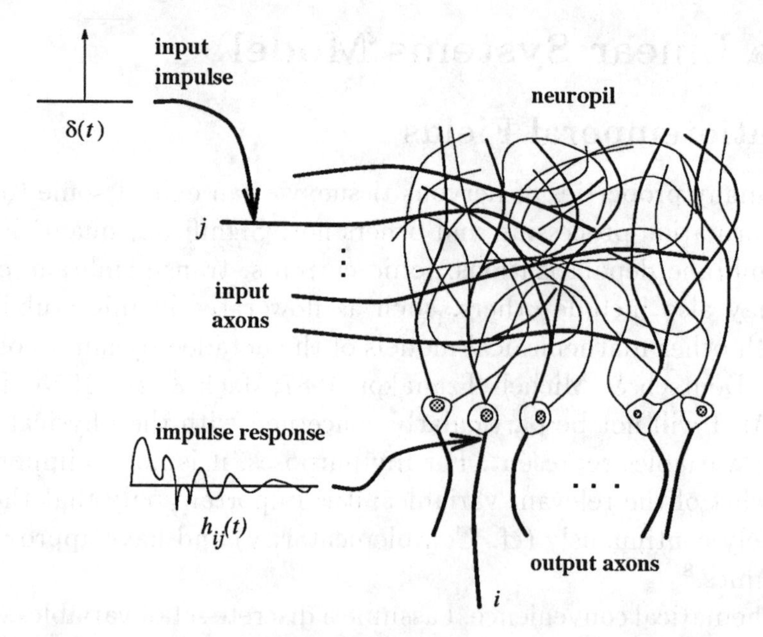

Figure 3: Resonance model of dendritic computation. A dendritic net can be thought of as a large system of coupled resonators with many resonance modes. Input signals arriving on axons activate some of these modes. The resulting signals are integrated in neuron somas and translated into spike trains for transmission to other dendritic nets.

that is the basic simplification over the neural wave equation. Technically, it means that we are viewing the dendritic net as a *lumped parameter system.* In concrete terms, we are viewing the neuropil as a network of discrete summers, multipliers, integrators and differentiators operating on variables of several kinds (e.g., concentrations of different ions). However we can use as fine a division as we choose. Such systems are especially well understood, because they have rational transfer functions.

5.2 Resonance Model

We can think of the overall dynamics of the dendritic processes in terms of a *resonance model* (Fig. 3). The idea is that the dendritic net can be thought of as a large system of coupled resonators with many resonance modes — on the order of the number of synapses (5000 to 200 000), as will be shown below. The input signal drives the net and activates some of these resonances.

The soma, acting analogously to an antenna, integrates the internal signals over space and time. Thus integrated, the activated resonances, if they are sufficiently strong, may trigger action potentials at the axon hillock.

5.3 Dynamic Equation

The *coupling coefficients* of the differential equations are assumed constant. These coefficients include the synaptic efficacies, membrane capacitances, spine-neck diameters, etc. Thus I assume no learning or development during dendritic processing. In effect I analyze the dendritic net at two time scales: the fast scale deals with dendritic resonance, the slow scale with learning. (I will show later an example of how learning is handled.) Next is a mathematical description of the dynamics of dendritic resonance. Readers familiar with linear systems theory will probably want to skip to Section 6 (Examples of Dendritic Information Processing).

A system of higher-order differential equations can be reduced to first order by introducing additional variables ψ_k. Thus the n-th order differential equation

$$\psi^{(n)} = G[t, \psi, \psi^{(1)}, \psi^{(2)}, \ldots, \psi^{(n-1)}]$$

becomes a system of first-order equations:

$$\begin{aligned}
\dot{\psi}_{n-1} &= G(t, \psi, \psi_1, \psi_2, \ldots, \psi_{n-1}) \\
\dot{\psi}_{n-2} &= \psi_{n-1} \\
&\vdots \\
\dot{\psi}_1 &= \psi_2 \\
\dot{\psi} &= \psi_1.
\end{aligned}$$

Henceforth, without loss of generality, I restrict my attention to first-order equations.

The behavior of a dendritic net is determined by three spatiotemporal fields (or sets of variables): (1) the inputs φ_j, normally thought of as depolarizations of the boutons of incoming axons, (2) the outputs ω_i, normally thought of as depolarizations at the axon hillock of outgoing axons, and (3) the state variables ψ_k, which include all properties of the dendritic net relevant to information processing (including those introduced in the reduction to first-order equations). (See Fig. 4.) We will sometimes write the equations

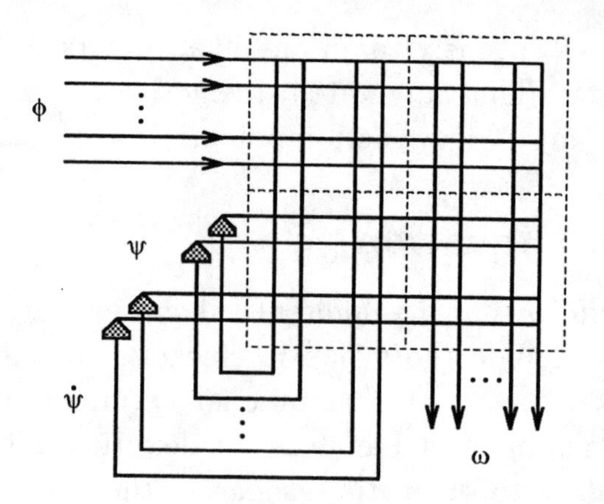

Figure 4: Schematic diagram of dendritic net. Input comes from the left, output leaves at the bottom. Shaded triangular figures are integrators. Intersecting lines within dotted boxes represent connections from horizontal lines to vertical lines with constant efficacies (weights).

in terms of time-varying discrete variables, e.g., $\psi_k(t)$ or $\psi(k,t)$, and other times in terms of time-varying fields, e.g., $\psi(t)$.

The state field $\psi(t)$ is driven linearly by the input field $\varphi(t)$:

$$\dot{\psi}(k,t) = D_{k1}\varphi(1,t) + D_{k2}\varphi(2,t) + \cdots + D_{kn}\varphi(n,t) + \text{other terms},$$

or, more compactly,

$$\dot{\psi}(t) = D\varphi(t) + \text{other terms}.$$

The output field is a sum of the input and state fields:

$$\begin{aligned} \omega(k,t) \;\; = \;\; & E_{k1}\varphi(1,t) + E_{k2}\varphi(2,t) + \cdots + E_{kn}\varphi(n,t) + \\ & G_{k1}\psi(1,t) + G_{k2}\psi(2,t) + \cdots + G_{kp}\psi(p,t). \end{aligned}$$

That is:

$$\omega(t) = E\varphi(t) + G\psi(t).$$

The state field is also driven by feedback from itself:

$$\dot{\psi}(k,t) = \text{input drive} + F_{k1}\psi(1,t) + F_{k2}\psi(2,t) + \cdots + F_{kp}\psi(p,t).$$

That is:

$$\dot{\psi}(t) = D\varphi(t) + F\psi(t).$$

The feedback matrix F determines the dynamics of system and hence its resonances.

In summary, the field evolution equations for a dendritic net are:

$$\begin{aligned}\dot{\psi}(t) &= D\varphi(t) + F\psi(t),\\ \omega(t) &= E\varphi(t) + G\psi(t).\end{aligned}$$

By Complementarity, these equations may be interpreted either as system of linear first order ordinary differential equations or as a linear integro-differential equation.

5.4 Laplace Transform Analysis

The system of differential equations can be solved in the usual way by taking the Laplace transform of the evolution equation:

$$\begin{aligned}s\Psi(s) - \psi(0) &= D\Phi(s) + F\Psi(s),\\ &\quad \text{where } \Psi(s) = \mathcal{L}\{\psi(t)\}\\ &\quad \text{and } \Phi(s) = \mathcal{L}\{\varphi(t)\}.\end{aligned}$$

($\mathcal{L}\{\}$ is the Laplace transform.) Define the transformed transition matrix:

$$R(s) = (s\mathrm{I} - F)^{-1},$$

and then the transformed solution is given by:

$$\Psi(s) = R(s)[D\Phi(s) + \psi(0)].$$

For understanding the signal processing properties of the net it is useful to consider its *forced response*, which is its response with no stored energy. Thus we set $\psi(0) = 0$, and the transformed output is:

$$\Omega(s) = E\Phi(s) + GR(s)D\Phi(s).$$

Define the *transfer function matrix*:

$$H(s) = E + GR(s)D,$$

and then the system function in the transformed domain is:

$$\Omega(s) = H(s)\Phi(s).$$

Suppose all the inputs are clamped at zero except the jth input, $\varphi(j,t)$, and consider output i, $\omega(i,t)$. The transforms of this input/output pair determine $H_{ij}(s)$:

$$H_{ij}(s) = \Omega(i,s)/\Phi(j,s).$$

This is the transform of the *impulse response*, $h_{ij}(t)$, which can be convolved with the input to yield the output:

$$\omega(i,t) = h_{ij}(t) * \varphi(j,t).$$

(Throughout this paper "$*$" is the convolution operation.) In particular, if φ_j is a Dirac delta (impulse) function, then:

$$\omega(i,t) = h_{ij}(t).$$

That is, injecting an impulse into input j causes the signal $h_{ij}(t)$ at output i. This is only approximate, since a nerve impulse (an action potential) is a poor approximation to a delta function; nevertheless it suggests the general form of the output (h_{ij} blurred by convolution with the action potential).

To determine the potential number of resonances of a dendritic net, recall that the inverse of a matrix is its adjoint divided by its determinant, and write the transformed transition matrix:

$$R(s) = \frac{\mathrm{adj}(s\mathrm{I} - F)}{|s\mathrm{I} - F|}.$$

There will be poles (infinities) wherever $s\mathrm{I} = F$, that is, at any s that is an eigenvalue of F. Thus the eigenvalues of F are its resonances, that is, the complex frequencies at which the resonances occur. Since F is $p \times p$ matrix, where p is the number of state variables, F has up to p eigenvalues, and so the dendritic net has up to p resonances. But the number of state variables is at least the number of synapses in the dendritic net, which is on the order of 5 000 to 200 000 for each neuron. Therefore I conclude that a typical dendritic net could have 10^4 to 10^6 resonances, which suggests a vast pattern recognition capacity for a dendritic net.

6 Examples of Possible Dendritic Information Processing

6.1 Gabor Coefficients and Dendritic Iteration

The Gabor elementary functions of time (for a given Δt) are defined (Gabor 1946):

$$\gamma_{mn}(t) = \exp\left[-\pi \frac{(t - n\Delta t)^2}{2(\Delta t)^2}\right] \exp\left(\frac{2\pi i m\, t}{\Delta t}\right).$$

There is considerable evidence (summarized in MacLennan 1991) that Gabor functions of space and (perhaps) time are representational primitives in visual cortex. If this is so, then the visual cortex has to find the Gabor coefficients c_{mn} such that:

$$\varphi(t) = \sum_{mn} c_{mn}\gamma_{mn}(t).$$

Unfortunately, the Gabor functions are not orthogonal, and so the coefficients c_{mn} cannot be computed by a simple inner product, $\langle \gamma_{mn}, \varphi \rangle$. One way to determine the Gabor coefficients is by performing gradient descent in error of representation (Daugman 1988):

$$E(c) = \left\| \varphi - \sum_{mn} c_{mn}\gamma_{mn} \right\|^2.$$

This can be accomplished by the linear system:

$$\begin{aligned}
&\dot{c} = Fc + D\varphi \\
&\qquad \text{where } D = \eta G^{\mathrm{T}} \\
&\qquad \text{and } F = -\eta G^{\mathrm{T}} G \\
&\qquad\qquad \text{where } G = (\ldots, \gamma_{mn}, \ldots) \\
&\qquad\qquad \text{and } \eta \text{ is the adaptation rate.}
\end{aligned}$$

Thus $F_{jk} \propto \langle \gamma_j, \gamma_k \rangle$ for some enumeration γ_j of the Gabor functions γ_{mn}. This system is an iterative correction $(-\eta G^{\mathrm{T}} G)$ of the inner product (ηG^{T}). We have seen that such a linear system is a simple computation for a dendritic net. The same approach works for many other nonorthogonal representations.[10]

[10] It should be noted that Gabor (1946) showed that the optimal real, as opposed to complex, basis functions are derivatives of Gaussians, which is the same as saying Gaus-

Iteration is generally considered too slow for biological neural networks, since neuronal signalling limits its speed to 10 to 100 msec./iteration. However, we can see that iteration in dendritic nets is much faster, since the delay of a chemical synapse is only about 0.5 msec. Thus dendritic iteration may be 20 to 200 times as fast as neuronal iteration. Since electrical synapses are essentially delayless, they may mediate even faster computational processes. Thus dendritic computation opens up an entire new range of possible neural information processing algorithms.

6.2 Orthogonality in High-dimensional Spaces

It will become apparent that I will be making considerable use of matched filters, which compute the inner products of patterns, and I will also be considering Hebb-like (i.e. correlational) learning rules. It is widely believed in the neural net community that inner-product pattern matching and Hebbian learning are weak, since nonorthogonal patterns result in excessive crosstalk. Therefore I digress to consider the issue of orthogonality in high-dimensional spaces; recall that the input dimension of a dendritic net is on the order of hundreds of thousands.

I begin with an argument sketched in Hamming (1986), which demonstrates that if we pick randomly any two of the 2^n bipolar vectors in n-dimensional space $\{-1, 1\}^n$, then they are almost surely nearly orthogonal. Specifically, with increasing n the cosine of the angle between them approaches 0 almost certainly (by the weak law of large numbers). Alternatively, if we normalize these vectors, then their inner product approaches zero almost certainly:

$$\mathbf{X}^{\mathrm{T}}\mathbf{Y} = \sum_k \pm 1/n,$$

where $\mathbf{X}$ and $\mathbf{Y}$ are random bipolar vectors of the form

$$(\pm 1, \pm 1, \ldots, \pm 1)^{\mathrm{T}} / \sqrt{n}.$$

Since dendritic computation is predominantly analog, we need to consider extensions of Hamming's result to continuous-valued vectors. Let $\mathbf{X}$ and $\mathbf{Y}$

sians times Hermite polynomials or Gaussians times Hermite functions (Stork & Wilson 1990). This set of functions has the added advantage that those defined at a fixed (spatial or temporal) location are orthogonal.

be random vectors in $\mathbf{R}^n$ with zero mean and standard deviation proportional to $1/n$ (thus maintaining normalization on the average). Of course the expectation value of $\mathbf{X}^{\mathrm{T}}\mathbf{Y}$ is 0, but it is also easy to see that its variance is $1/n^3$:

$$\mathrm{Var}\{\mathbf{X}^{\mathrm{T}}\mathbf{Y}\} = \sum \mathcal{E}\{X_k^2\}\mathcal{E}\{Y_k^2\} = \sum \frac{1}{n^2}\frac{1}{n^2} = \frac{1}{n^3}.$$

Once again the weak law of large numbers tells us that with increasing n the inner product will almost surely be 0.

We have seen that neural computation and communication is limited to about two digits of precision — most likely even less. Therefore a matched filter in the dendritic net will be unable to distinguish orthogonal vectors from vectors whose inner products are less then ϵ, where ϵ is at least 0.01. Therefore I will consider sets of vectors that are *ϵ-orthogonal*, that is, vectors whose inner product is less than ϵ.[11] For simplicity I assume the vectors are normalized and that $\epsilon \in (0,1)$. Kainen (1992) has shown that for fixed ϵ the number of ϵ-orthogonal n-dimensional vectors increases exponentially in n. In particular, if $N(n)$ is the number of n-dimensional ϵ-orthogonal vectors, then

$$(1-\epsilon^2)^{-1/2} \leq \lim_{n\to\infty} N(n)^{1/n} \leq (1-\epsilon)^{-1/2}.$$

For example, if $\epsilon = 0.1$, then

$$1.00504 \leq \lim_{n\to\infty} N(n)^{1/n} \leq 1.0541.$$

We can see that asymptotically

$$1.0541^n \geq N(n) \geq 1.00504^n,$$

approximately. For example, for $n = 5000$ we have the lower bound $N(5000) \geq 8.2 \times 10^{10}$; for $n = 10\,000$ we have $N(10\,000) \geq 6.7 \times 10^{21}$. So, linear algebra tells us that a 5000-dimensional space has 5000 orthogonal vectors, but we see that it has 82 billion 0.1-orthogonal vectors. By not requiring exact orthogonality we greatly increase our representational resources.[12]

---

[11]Over the last two decades several investigators have independently invented ϵ-orthogonality; citations can be found in Kainen (1992).

[12]If we pick $\epsilon = 0.01$, the bounds are much less impressive, since we get $8.2 \times 10^{10} \geq N(5000) \geq 1.28$ and $6.7 \times 10^{21} \geq N(10000) \geq 1.65$. It may be that this ϵ is too close to perfect orthogonality. More likely, the problem may simply be that the formula gives very loose bounds. If so, the results for $\epsilon = 0.1$ are even more impressive.

Suppose that inner products less than ϵ are indistinguishable from inner products equal to zero. Then an outer-product associative memory could hold $N(n)$ associated pairs, which we have seen can be much greater than the expected capacity, n pairs. However, this requires the stimulus patterns to be drawn from an ϵ-orthogonal set. This could be accomplished either by a self-organizing process,[13] or by random selection of vectors perhaps followed by a Gram-Schmidt process.

In conclusion, it is well-known that many simple, efficient neural information processes work best on nearly orthogonal representations, since orthogonality decreases crosstalk. But in a space of high dimension, randomly chosen representations will almost always be nearly orthogonal. Thus, in the context of the brain, which is insensitive to slight deviations from orthogonality, nonorthogonality will take care of itself.

6.3 Matched Filters

The inner product $\langle \zeta, \varphi \rangle$ is maximized for identical normalized signals ζ and φ, which makes it a popular way means of pattern matching in neural networks.[14] The inner product can also be expressed as the final value of a reverse convolution (essentially a correlation):

$$\langle \zeta, \varphi \rangle = \zeta(T - t) * \varphi(t)|_{t=T} \,. \qquad (1)$$

This is called a *matched filter* for the pattern ζ. Under reasonable assumptions, matched filters are optimal in maximizing signal-to-noise ratio at time T (e.g., see Cooper & McGillem 1986, Sec. 9.5). A matched filter has an impulse response that is the time-reverse of the pattern for which it is tuned:

$$h(t) = \zeta(T - t).$$

From the Eq. 1 for the inner product, we can see that if a dendritic net implements a matched filter, then an action potential will be generated at

[13]The problem of finding an ϵ-orthogonal set is equivalent to the problem of packing s-spheres into a related space (the n-dimensional elliptic space), where $s = (1/2) \arccos \epsilon$ (Kainen 1992). This should be easy so long as we don't try to pack the spheres too tightly.

[14]For notational clarity, these derivations apply to scalar in / scalar out nets, but can be easily extended to fields.

time T if the match exceeds the threshold at the axon hillock. If this threshold is a little less than the norm of ζ (and input φ is approximately normalized), then the matched filter acts as a pattern recognizer for ζ.

There are several ways that we may interpret the output of a matched filter. First, it may be interpreted as the inner product of *spatiotemporal* fields ζ, φ:

$$\omega(T) = \langle \zeta, \varphi \rangle.$$

Second, it may be interpreted as the sum of the pairwise *temporal* correlations of input signals φ_j and stored patterns ζ_j:

$$\omega(T) = \sum_j \langle \zeta_j, \varphi_j \rangle.$$

Finally it may be interpreted as the *temporal* integration of the running *spatial* inner products:

$$\omega(T) = \int_0^T \zeta(t) \cdot \varphi(t) \mathrm{d}t.$$

Each of these interpretations may be informative in different circumstances.

One of the simplest ways of implementing a matched filter is a *tapped-delay line* or *transversal filter*:

$$\omega(t) = \sum_{jk} W_{jk} \zeta_j(t - \tau_k),$$

where the τ_k are delays. This formula is essentially a (discrete) convolution. The self-organization of a matched transversal filter can result from a simple Hebb-like rule. Suppose the firing of ω causes W_{jk} to move toward the last value it transmitted (a mechanism for this is described in Section 6.4):

$$\Delta W_{jk} = c \zeta_j(t - \tau_k).$$

Then each weight approaches the average value that it transmits when ω fires:

$$W_{jk} \longrightarrow \mathcal{E}\{\zeta_j(t - \tau_k) \mid \omega \text{ fires}\}.$$

Thus the dendritic net becomes a filter matched for $\mathcal{E}\{\zeta \mid \omega \text{ fires}\}$, the expected input that causes ω to fire. If there is lateral inhibition among a number of dendritic nets of this form, then they will tend to become matched filters for distinct spatiotemporal patterns.

Although the transversal filter is simple, it is more efficient (fewer synapses) to make use of the dynamic properties of dendritic feedback. This can be accomplished by an autoregressive implementation of a matched filter:

$$\psi(t) = \sum_i F_i \psi(t - \tau_i) + \sum_j D_j \varphi(t - \tau_i).$$

We can adapt the weights by using the Feintuch (1976) approximate gradient descent algorithm:

$$\begin{aligned} \dot{F}_i &= k[\zeta(T-t) - \psi(t)]\psi(t - \tau_i), \\ \dot{D}_j &= k[\zeta(T-t) - \psi(t)]\varphi(t - \tau_i). \end{aligned}$$

This is a simple "delta rule." An even better approach is to implement the self-organization of the poles and residues of a recursive filter (described in Section 6.6).

Successive layers of self-organizing matched filters will adjust to recognize spatiotemporal patterns at higher levels of abstraction. The higher levels are characterized by longer stored pattern lengths (i.e. larger T in the impulse response $\zeta(T - t)$), which is simply the temporal analog of the successively wider receptive fields found in higher vision areas. Conversely, as shown in the next section, triggering of higher-order patterns will flow backward to generate expectations for lower-order patterns, in effect priming the matched filters.

6.4 Action Potential-Triggered Antidromic Dynamics

An AP (action potential) causes an electric wave to spread electrotonically from the axon hillock back into the dendritic net (Shepherd 1988, p. 137). This *antidromic* electrical signal is transferred efficiently into the dendritic spines (Koch & Poggio 1983, p. 461; Shepherd 1990, p. 464). (See Fig. 5.) To a first approximation this can be treated mathematically as the injection of an impulse (Dirac delta function) at the axon hillock. Since we are putting a signal into the "output" of the dendritic net, we need to know the *antidromic dynamics* of the neuron.

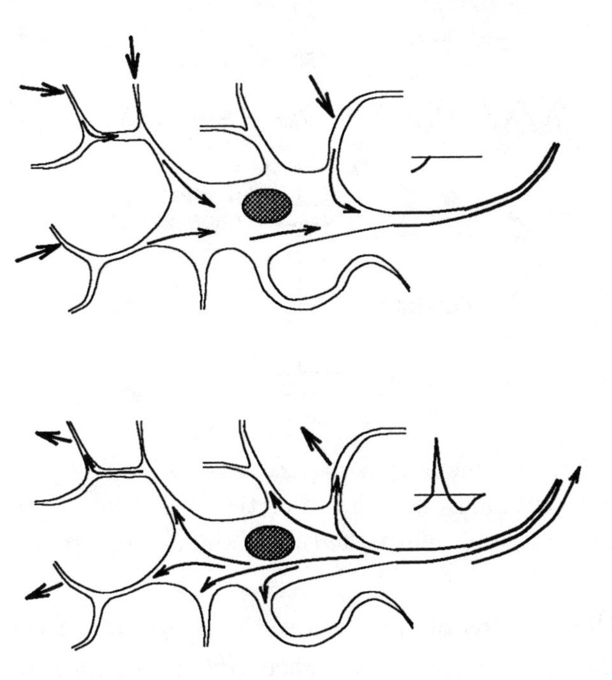

Figure 5: Antidromic electrotonic spread. Converging electric waves from dendritic net are summed in soma. If an action potential is triggered, current is efficiently transferred back into dendritic spines.

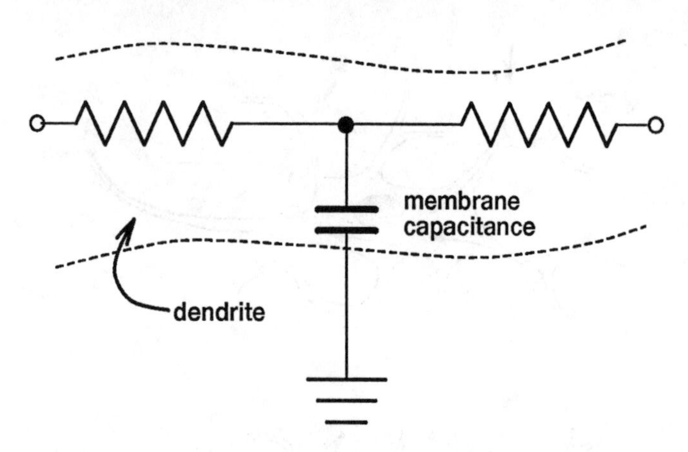

Figure 6: The dendritic membrane capacitance as a reversible (but leaky) integrator. An electrical wave from either direction will charge the capacitance, and so cause the total charge to reflect the (approximate) integral of the signal.

To enable the analysis of the *antidromic dynamics* of the dendritic net, I will assume that the integrators are *reversible* or *reciprocal.* In other words, putting a signal into the output of an integrator causes its integral to appear at the input. This is in fact a reasonable assumption, because integration is usually a result of the membrane capacitance, which may be charged by a electrical wave coming from either direction (Fig. 6). This assumption is also valid for many chemical accumulation processes. For the same reasons we will assume that multipliers (connection strengths) are reciprocal, since they are often a result of electrical resistance, which has the same affect in either direction. Reciprocity (reversibility) does not apply automatically to chemical or electrical synapses, which are usually nonreciprocal or *rectifying* (Koch & Poggio 1987, pp. 649–650), but we ignore this complication for now.[15]

Under the foregoing assumptions it is easy to show that the reversed equations are:

$$\begin{aligned} \varphi &= \psi D + \omega E, \\ \dot{\psi} &= \psi F + \omega G. \end{aligned}$$

[15]It is probably best handled by decomposing F into two matrices, F^{R} and F^{D}, one of which is reversible, the other not. Under some conditions electrical synapses exhibit reciprocity (Koch & Poggio 1987, p. 650).

The transfer function matrix is the transpose of that of the original system:

$$\Phi(s) = H(s)^{\mathrm{T}}\Omega(s).$$

Now we consider the antidromic dynamics in the special case where the dendritic net implements a matched filter (again assuming φ, ω and ζ are scalars). For a matched filter the transfer function is:

$$H(s) = e^{sT}\mathrm{Z}(-s).$$

For the antidromic impulse response, set the output to the transform of a delta function, $\Omega(s) = 1$. Therefore, the antidromic impulse response is:

$$\Phi(s) = e^{sT}\mathrm{Z}(-s).$$

In other words, the signal at the "input" is exactly the pattern to which the matched filter is tuned:

$$\varphi(t) = \zeta(T - t).$$

We have seen that for a matched filter, the pattern for which it is tuned is produced at the dendritic terminals. There are several effects this could have. First, it could trigger or enhance learning (e.g., by a Hebbian rule) by delivering extra current to the activated dendrites. (I showed above how this could function in the self-organization of transversal filters.) Second, the antidromic spread could generate an expectation for the stored pattern by partially depolarizing the dendritic spines, in effect "priming" the dendrites. Such priming could proceed top-down through many levels of successively less abstract matched filters, thus providing a mechanism for top-down expectations. Finally, the antidromic electrotonic flow may implement a kind of pattern completion, since if a partial pattern succeeds in triggering an AP, it will succeed in regenerating the complete pattern at the input terminals. (However, these theoretical predictions have not been tested by simulation using realistic APs.)

In summary, the generation of an AP at the output of a dendritic net will cause production of that output's impulse response at the input terminals of the net. This could be a mechanism for triggering learning, for generating expectations, and for pattern completion. It assumes that (1) integrators and multipliers are reciprocal; (2) the AP can be modeled as a Dirac delta function.

6.5 Spectral Density Analysis

If, as indicated in Berger, Pribram et al. (1990, 1992), the statistical properties of the impulse train are more significant than the actual phase relations, then the spectral density may be more relevant than the Laplace transform as a description of impulse spike trains. Their investigation shows that the results of dendritic computation are encoded in the statistics of spike trains. Specifically, the results determine the barrier height and drift coefficient of a random walk that determines the mean and standard deviation of the interspike intervals. This suggests that spike trains should be treated as random processes, so I turn to the spectral density, which is a powerful tool for such analysis.

The *autocorrelation* of a signal $\varphi(t)$ describes its temporal periodic structure, and is defined:

$$R_\varphi(t) = \varphi(t) * \varphi(-t).$$

The autocorrelation of white noise is a delta function, since it has no periodic structure. The *spectral density* of a signal ω is simply the Fourier transform of its autocorrelation:

$$S_\varphi(s) = \mathcal{F}\{R_\varphi(t)\} = \mathcal{F}\{\varphi(t) * \varphi(-t)\}.$$

Thus the spectral density of white noise is a constant. By the convolution theorem we can express the spectral density as the product of the direct and reversed Fourier transforms:

$$S_\varphi(s) = \Phi(s)\Phi(-s).$$

The spectral density of the output of a linear system is the product of the spectral density of its input and a spectral density transfer function,

$$S_\omega(s) = S_h(s)S_\varphi(s),$$

which is given by $S_h(s) = H(s)H(-s)$, the spectral density of the impulse response of the system. Thus we see that the spectral density transfer function of a matched filter,

$$S_h(s) = \mathcal{F}\{\zeta(-t) * \zeta(t)\} = S_\zeta(s),$$

is simply the spectral density of the pattern to which it is tuned. More accurately, the spectral density is given by $\mathcal{F}\{\zeta(T-t) * \zeta(t-T)\}$, but the phase is ignored by the spectral density:

$$\mathcal{F}\{\zeta(T-t) * \zeta(t-T)\} = e^{sT}\mathrm{Z}(-s)\, e^{-sT}\mathrm{Z}(s) = \mathrm{Z}(-s)\mathrm{Z}(s).$$

As we've seen, the autocorrelation of white noise $W(t)$ is an impulse function, $R_W(t) = c\delta(t)$, and its spectral density is thus a constant, $S_W(s) = c$. Therefore the spectral density of the output of a matched filter that is given white noise is:

$$S_y(s) = S_h(s)S_W(s) = S_\zeta(s)c.$$

Thus the white-noise response is proportional to the spectral density of the pattern to which the matched filter is tuned. In other words, we can discover a matched filter's "expectation" by probing it with white noise.

We've seen that white noise input to a matched filter causes it to reproduce a signal with the same spectral density as the pattern to which it is tuned. I mention briefly the possible significance of this for understanding certain perceptual phenomena. It is well known that experimental subjects in sensory deprivation tanks often experience hallucinations. Further, people often report hearing "radio or TV sounds" in the white noise of forced-air heaters, air conditioners, etc., but cannot identify precisely what they are hearing. In these situations white noise may be showing us the signals to which sensory systems are tuned.

It's noteworthy that many divinatory practices, ancient and modern, rely on: (1) preventing sensory input (covering ears, closing eyes), thus causing the automatic gain control to increase sensitivity; then (2) providing white noise input (rustle of leaves or water, voices of a crowd, reflective or blank surface, etc.); then (3) looking or listening for something relevant. By activating higher-order matched filters with white noise, these practices could expose top-down expectations, concerns, etc. in the mind of the practitioner.

6.6 Self-organization of Recursive Matched Filters

I suggested above that a more efficient use of dendritic processing resources uses recursive (as opposed to transversal) filters, but now we need to consider their self-organization by biologically plausible mechanisms. Suppose we want to construct a matched filter for ζ of the form:

$$\begin{aligned}\dot{\psi} &= F\psi + D\varphi,\\ \omega &= G\psi.\end{aligned}$$

where G is a row vector and D is a column vector. (For simplicity I will restrict my attention to filters with scalar input and output.) I will assume that there are enough state variables ψ_k to match ζ reasonably well (e.g., at least twice as many as the number of poles of ζ, so that we can have a second order differential equation for each pole).

There are several ways a filter of this kind can self-organize, but the simplest is based on the generalized Fourier series. To have a matched filter for the signal ζ, complete with its phase relations, it's necessary that the impulse response be $h(t) = \zeta(T - t)$, where T is the duration of pattern ζ. Therefore, suppose that ρ_k is an orthonormal system over $(0, T)$ and that $h(t) = \zeta(T - t)$ has the generalized Fourier series:

$$\zeta(T - t) = \sum_{k=0}^{\infty} c_k \rho_k(t),$$

where

$$c_k = \int_0^T \zeta(T - t)\rho_k(t)\mathrm{d}t. \tag{2}$$

The goal is to extract the Fourier coefficients c_k of $\zeta(T - t)$ from a training presentation of ζ to the network. Now observe that by Eq. 2 the coefficients are given by the values at $t = T$ of convolutions:

$$c_k = \zeta(t) * \rho_k(t)\big|_{t=T}.$$

Therefore, if the training signal is presented to filters with impulse responses $h_k(t) = \rho_k(t)$, then their outputs at time T will be the Fourier coefficients. If these coefficients are used as the weights on the filters, then the total impulse response will be

$$h(t) = \sum_{k=0}^{n} c_k h_k(t) = \zeta(T - t),$$

as desired.

This transfer of the Fourier coefficients into the weights could be triggered by an antidromic electrotonic pulse, for example (Fig. 7). More specifically,

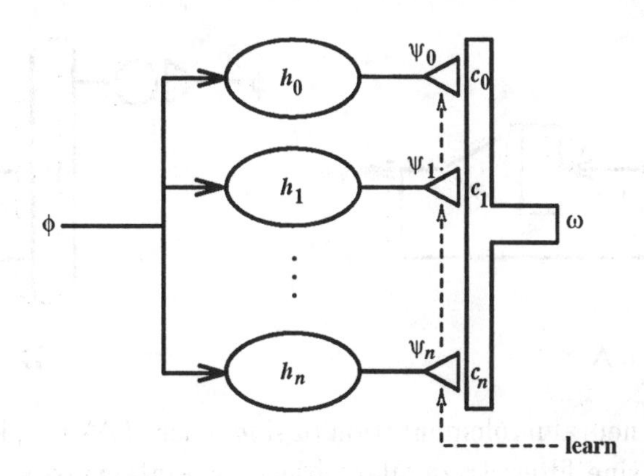

Figure 7: Adaptive recursive filter. In the simplest form the filters h_k have impulse response equal to orthonormal basis functions ρ_k. At time T after a signal ζ is input, the output activities of these filters, ψ_k, are the Fourier coefficients of $\zeta(T - t)$. A learning trigger, for example, an antidromic impulse from the postsynaptic neuron or a learning signal from a third source, can cause these ψ_k to become the synaptic efficacies c_k, thus matching the filter to ζ.

at time T the presynaptic activity, as reflected in depolarization or neurotransmitter release, for example, is proportional to the corresponding Fourier coefficient. All that is necessary to match the network to the signal ζ received up to that point is to cause that activity to determine the synaptic efficacy. Although all the information comes from the presynaptic side, the trigger to cause the efficacy change could be an antidromic electrotonic pulse on the postsynaptic side, or indeed a signal from a third location. Thus the overall scheme is compatible with various kinds of Hebbian learning.

Next consider the dendritic implementation of the filters themselves. The most familiar basis fields ρ_n are the trigonometric functions:

$$\begin{aligned}\rho_0(t) &= 1,\\ \rho_{2k}(t) &= \cos(2\pi kt/T),\\ \rho_{2k-1}(t) &= \sin(2\pi kt/T).\end{aligned}$$

These filters are implemented by simple second order equations:

$$\begin{aligned}\ddot{\rho}_{2k} &= \dot{\varphi} - \nu_{2k}^2 \rho_{2k},\\ \dot{\rho}_{2k-1} &= \varphi - \nu_{2k-1}^2 \int \rho_{2k-1} \mathrm{d}t,\end{aligned}$$

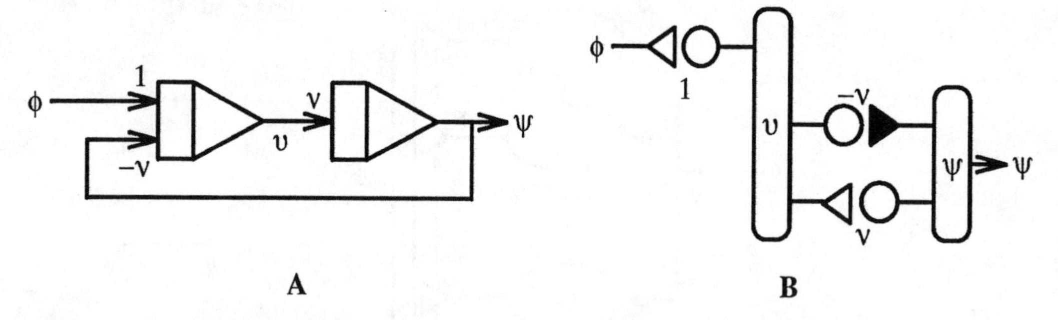

Figure 8: Possible neural implementation of sine filter. (**A**) Typical analog circuit implementation of sine filter; triangular objects are integrators, whose inputs are summed with the indicated weights. (**B**) Possible dendritic implementation of the analog circuit shown in (A). Graded potentials are input on dendritic spines and are summed and temporally integrated in the dendritic trunks or the soma. Integrated sums are transferred into presynaptic dendrites or axons. Open triangles are excitatory synapses; filled triangles are inhibitory.

where $\nu_k = 2\pi k/T$. These filters have a comparatively simple implementation in dendritic circuits; nonlinear saturation effects ensure stability (Figs. 8, 9).

The sine filters ρ_{2k-1} can be dispensed with in many cases, since the cosine filters ρ_{2k} are sufficient to recover the spectral density of the signal without its phase, which, as we've seen, may be the usual case.

The regular patterns of weights in the $\boldsymbol{\nu}$ vector may seem biologically implausible. However, if $\boldsymbol{\nu}$ is a uniformly random vector over the same range, the results are not much worse, in spite of there being no guarantee that the filters are orthogonal.

7 Conclusions

In this paper I have argued that (1) mathematical models are at best approximately realized in nervous systems, and so we should take them seriously, but not *too* seriously; (2) linear dynamical systems are useful models of information processing in dendritic nets; (3) iterative processing is feasible in dendritic nets, and an example is the computation of Gabor coefficients; (4) dendritic nets can easily self-organize into matched filters for spatiotemporal fields; (5) white noise may stimulate recall of stored patterns; and (6) impulse-triggered reverse electrotonic spread may facilitate learning and gen-

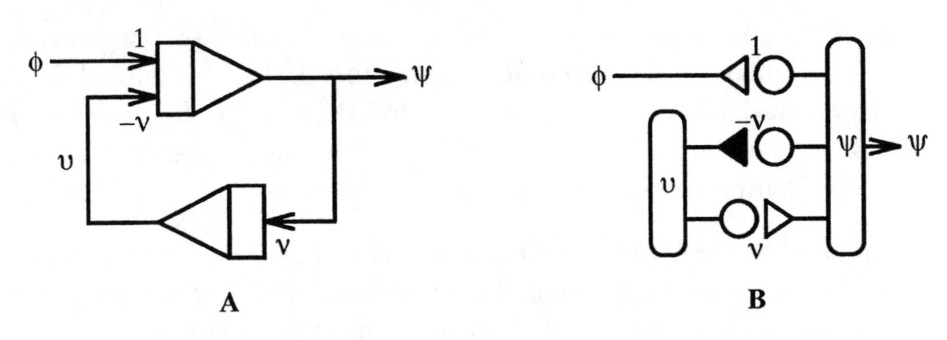

Figure 9: Possible neural implementation of cosine filter. (A) Typical analog circuit implementation of cosine filter. (B) Possible dendritic implementation of the analog circuit shown in (A).

erate top-down expectations. Overall we have seen that the dendritic net, although approximately linear, may be a powerful processor of information.

8 References

Beaulieu, C., & Colonnier, M. (1983). The number of neurons in the different laminae of the binocular and monocular regions of area 17 in the cat. *J. Comp. Neurol*, **217**: 337–344.

Berger, D., Pribram, K., Wild, H., & Bridges, C. (1990). An analysis of neural spike-train distributions: determinants of the response of visual cortex neurons to changes in orientation and spatial frequency. *Experimental Brain Research*, **80**: 129–134.

Berger, D. H., & Pribram, K. H. (1992). The relationship between the Gabor elementary function and a stochastic model of the inter-spike interval distribution in the responses of visual cortex neurons. *Biological Cybernetics*, **67**: 191–194.

Berne, R. M., & Levy, M. N. (Eds.) (1983). *Physiology*. St. Louis MO: C. V. Mosby.

Cooper, G. R., & McGillem, C. D. (1986). *Probabilistic methods of signal and system analysis*, 2nd ed. New York NY: Holt, Rinehart and Winston.

Crick, F. H. C., & Asanuma, C. (1986). Certain aspects of the anatomy and physiology of the cerebral cortex. In: J. L. McClelland & D. E. Rumelhart (Eds.), *Parallel Distributed Processing: Explorations in the Microstructure of Cognition*, Vol. 2, *Psychological and Biological Models.* Cambridge MA: MIT Press.

Daugman, J. G. (1988). Complete discrete 2-D Gabor transforms by neural networks for image analysis and compression. *IEEE Transactions on Acoustics, Speech and Signal Processing*, **36**: 1169–1179.

Deutsch, S., & Micheli-Tzanakon, E. (1987). *Neuroelectric systems.* New York NY: New York University Press.

Eccles, J. C. (1957). *The physiology of nerve cells.* Baltimore MD: Johns Hopkins Press.

Feintuch, P. L. (1976). An adaptive recursive LMS filter. *Proceedings of the IEEE*, **64**: 1622–1624.

Gabor, D. (1946). Theory of communication. *Journal of the Institution of Electrical Engineers, III*, **93**: 429–457.

Hameroff, S. R. (1987). *Ultimate computing: Biomolecular consciousness and nanotechnology.* Amsterdam: North Holland.

Hamming, R. W. (1986). *Coding and information theory.* Englewood Cliffs NJ: Prentice-Hall.

Jack, J. J. B., Noble, D., & Tsien, R. W. (1975). *Electric current flow in excitable cells.* Oxford UK: Clarendon Press.

Kainen, P. C. (1992). Orthogonal dimension and tolerance. Unpublished report, Washington DC: Industrial Math.

Koch, C., & Poggio, T. (1983). A theoretical analysis of electrical properties of spines. *Proceedings Royal Society London B*, **218**: 455–477.

Koch, C., & Poggio, T. (1987). Biophysics of computation: Neurons, synapses, and membranes. In G. M. Edelman, W. E. Gall & W. M. Cowan (Eds.), *Synaptic Function* (pp. 637–697). New York NY: Wiley.

Koch, C., Poggio, T., & Torre, V. (1983). Nonlinear interactions in a dendritic tree: Localization, timing, and role in information processing. *Proceedings National Academy Sciences USA*, **80**: 2799–2802.

Koch, C., Zador, A., & Brown, T. H. (1992). Dendritic spines: Convergence of theory and experiment. *Science*, **256**: 973–974.

MacLennan, B. J. (1987). Technology-independent design of neurocomputers: The universal field computer. In M. Caudill & C. Butler (Eds.), *Proceedings, IEEE First International Conference on Neural Networks* (Vol. 3, pp. 39–49). New York NY: Institute of Electrical and Electronic Engineers.

MacLennan, B. J. (1990). *Field computation: A theoretical framework for massively parallel analog computation; parts I - IV* (report CS-90-100). Knoxville TN: University of Tennessee, Computer Science Department.

MacLennan, B. J. (1991). *Gabor representations of spatiotemporal visual images* (Report No. CS-91-144). Knoxville TN: University of Tennessee, Knoxville, Computer Science Department; submitted for publication.

MacLennan, B. J. (in press-a). Characteristics of connectionist knowledge representation. *Information Sciences*, to appear.

MacLennan, B. J. (in press-b). Continuous symbol systems: The logic of connectionism. In D. S. Levine and M. Aparicio IV (Eds.), *Neural Networks for Knowledge Representation and Inference.* Hillsdale NJ: Lawrence Erlbaum.

MacLennan, B. J. (this volume). Field computation in the brain. This volume.

MacLennan, B. J., & Pribram, K. H. (in preparation). Neural computation without sigmoids.

Neher, E. (1992). Ion channels for communication between and within cells. *Science*, **256**: 498–502.

Oster, G., Perelson, A., & Katchalsky, A. (1971). Network thermodynamics. *Nature*, **234**: 393–399.

Poggio, T., & Koch, C. (1985). Ill-posed problems in early vision: From computational theory to analog networks. *Proceedings Royal Society London B*, **226**: 303–323.

Poggio, T., & Torre, V. (1981). A theory of synaptic interactions. In W. E. Reichardt & T. Poggio (Eds.), *Theoretical approaches in neurobiology* (pp. 28–38). Cambridge MA: MIT Press.

Poggio, T., Torre, V., & Koch, C. (1985). Computational vision and regularization theory. *Nature*, **317**: 314–319.

Pribram, K. H. (1971). *Languages of the brain: Experimental paradoxes and principles in neuropsychology.* Englewood Cliffs NJ: Prentice-Hall.

Pribram, K. H. (1991). *Brain and perception: Holonomy and structure in figural processing.* Hillsdale NJ: Lawrence Erlbaum.

Rall, W., & Segev, I. (1987). Functional possibilities for synapses on dendrites and dendritic spines. In G. M. Edelman, W. E. Gall & W. M. Cowan (Eds.), *Synaptic Function* (pp. 605–636). New York NY: Wiley.

Reichardt, W. E., & Poggio, T., (Eds.). (1981). *Theoretical approaches in neurobiology.* Cambridge MA: MIT Press.

Roberts, A., and Bush, B. M. H. (1981). *Neurones without impulses: their significance for vertebrate and invertebrate nervous systems.* Cambridge UK: Cambridge University Press.

Sakmann, B. (1992). Elementary steps in synaptic transmission revealed by currents through single ion channels. *Science*, **256**: 503–512.

Shepherd, G. M. (1972). The neuron doctrine: A revision of functional concepts. *Yale Journal of Biology and Medicine*, **45**: 584–599.

Shepherd, G. M. (1978). Microcircuits in the nervous system. *Scientific American*, **238**: 92–103.

Shepherd, G. M. (1988). *Neurobiology*, second edition. New York NY: Oxford University Press.

Shepherd, G. M. (Ed.). (1990). *The Synaptic organization of the brain*, third edition. New York NY: Oxford University Press.

Shepherd, G. M. (1990a). The significance of real neuron architectures for neural network simulations. In E. L. Schwartz (Ed.), *Computational Neuroscience* (pp. 82–96). Cambridge MA: MIT Press.

Stork, D. G., & Wilson, H. R. (1990). Do Gabor functions provide appropriate descriptions of visual cortical receptive fields? *Journal of the Optical Society of America A*, **7**, 8 (August 1990): 1362–1373.

Torre, V., & Poggio, T. (1978). A synaptic mechanism possibly underlying directional selectivity to motion. *Proceedings Royal Society London B*, **202**: 409–416.

Torre, V., & Poggio, T. (1981). An application: A synaptic mechanism possibly underlying motion detection. In W. E. Reichardt & T. Poggio (Eds.), *Theoretical approaches in neurobiology* (pp. 39–46). Cambridge MA: MIT Press.

Wolpert, D. H., & MacLennan, B. J. (submitted). A computationally universal field computer which is purely linear.

Chapter 7

Field Computation in the Brain

Bruce MacLennan
Computer Science Department
University of Tennessee, Knoxville TN

Abstract

We begin with a brief consideration of the *topology of knowledge.* It has traditionally been assumed that true knowledge must be represented by discrete symbol structures, but recent research in psychology, philosophy and computer science has shown the fundamental importance of *subsymbolic* information processing, in which knowledge is represented in terms of very large numbers — or even continua — of *microfeatures.* We believe that this sets the stage for a fundamentally new theory of knowledge, and we sketch a theory of continuous information representation and processing. Next we consider *field computation*, a kind of continuous information processing that emphasizes spatially continuous *fields* of information. This is a reasonable approximation for macroscopic areas of cortex and provides a convenient mathematical framework for studying information processing at this level. We apply it also to a linear-systems model of dendritic information processing. We consider examples from the visual cortex, including Gabor and wavelet representations, and outline field-based theories of sensorimotor intentions and of model-based deduction.

1 Topology of Knowledge

1.1 The Assumption that Knowledge is Discrete

For the ancient Greeks the *knowable* and the *sayable* were nearly identical. Socrates is quite explicit: "what we know we must surely be able to tell" (*Laches* 190c), but the idea goes much further back and is nearly inherent in the Greek language: *logos* simultaneously means word, language, thought, reason, explanation, calculation and meaning. Socrates likely came out of the Pythagorean tradition, which reduced the universe to numbers (especially ratios, another meaning of *logos*), and which *calculated* by the mechanical manipulation of formal arrangements of pebbles (*calculi*, in Latin). Through Plato and Aristotle this led to the idea that true knowledge could be reduced to a deductive structure in which inference is represented by the mechanical rearrangement of patterns of discrete symbols. The search for a calculus for knowledge representation and inference was continued by such figures as Lull, Hobbes, Leibniz and Boole.

These efforts reached a kind of culmination in the twentieth century. The development of practical symbolic logics by Peano, Russell, Whitehead and others created the real possibility of putting knowledge in the form of a calculus. Within just a few decades, however, inherent theoretical limitations of calculi were discovered by Gödel, Turing, Löwenheim, Skolem and others. In order to do this they investigated the mechanical manipulation of discrete symbols, and so laid the foundation for the theory of digital computation.

The twentieth century also brought the technological means — the electronic digital computer — for manipulating large discrete-symbol structures at high speed. The theory that knowledge can and must be reducible to calculi then found its home in AI (artificial intelligence), which attempted to apply it to practical problems. The emerging discipline of cognitive science also adopted this view of knowledge in its information processing model of cognition. The assumption that knowledge representation and processing is equivalent to the formal manipulation of discrete symbols was accepted, almost without question, until the mid-1980s, when finally its limitations, both as a technology and a model of cognition, could no longer be ignored.

There is no need to rehearse here the arguments in favor of *connectionist* knowledge representation over the traditional, symbolic approaches. I will observe only that connectionism brings with it a recognition of the role of flexible, context-sensitive information processing as a foundation upon which rest the more symbolic processes. Thus discrete, or approximately discrete, symbol manipulation is viewed as an emergent phenomenon grounded in continuous, or approximately continuous, subsymbolic processes.

We believe that, although there have been many demonstrations of the power of connectionist knowledge representation, its progress is impeded by the lack theoretical construct that captures the essence of connectionist knowledge representation. We have attempted to fill this gap by developing the idea of a *simulacrum*, a model of continuous information representation and processing that fills a role in connectionist epistemology analogous to that filled by the idea of a *calculus* in traditional epistemology (MacLennan in press-a, in press-b, subm.-c). It attempts to answer the question, "What, if not symbols, can be a medium for knowledge representation and processing?" The simulacrum is postulated as the central concept of the theory of continuous computation.

1.2 Theory of Continuous Computation

It must be remarked that a simulacrum, like a calculus, is an idealization of reality. Just as a calculus is taken to be perfectly (i.e. topologically) discrete, so a simulacrum is taken to be perfectly continuous (the mathematical formalization is below). For example, in the conventional theory of (discrete) computation, we assume certain processes are unproblematic, such as the separation of a token from the background or the classification of a token as to its type. Thus, we don't consider the possibility that a Turing machine could misidentify the tape symbol under its read head, although this would be a significant issue for a real (vs. ideal) Turing machine. Similarly, in the theory of continuous computation we assume the continuity of the spaces, maps and processes, even though in practice they might be represented in terms of discrete charge carriers, for example. For both calculi and simulacra the relevant question is whether the real system is sufficiently close to the ideal that the differences may be ignored. In the following we present the simulacrum as an idealized model of continuous computation.

The central idea in the theory of simulacra is the *image*, which is the vehicle of continuous information representation; images correspond to the symbols, formulas and other structures of calculi. The images in a simulacrum belong to one or more *image spaces*, which determine their topology. Examples of images include the set of all visual images (of bounded area and amplitude) and the set of all auditory images (likewise bounded). On the other hand, a single real number can be considered an image, and an interval of the real line is perhaps the simplest image space. Image spaces satisfy the following postulates.[1]

[1]These postulates are tentative; our familiarity with simulacra is too slight to permit

Postulate 1 *Image spaces are path-connected metric spaces.*

Some implications of this postulate are (1) that images have quantifiable degrees of similarity, (2) that any image is reachable from any other in the space by a continuous process of transformation, and (3) that image spaces have at least the cardinality of the real numbers.

Postulate 2 *Image spaces are separable and complete.*

This postulate is introduced mainly for mathematical convenience; it ensures that images can be approximated by convergent sequences and that the limits of these sequences are in the space. One important consequence of this postulate is that image spaces are topologically equivalent to subsets of Hilbert spaces, which allows us to apply the theory of field computation (see below).[2]

Postulate 3 *Maps between image spaces are continuous.*

One implication of this is that syntactic relations between images are continuous and inherently fuzzy.

Just as in idealized discrete computers the state transitions are taken to occur at discrete time intervals (even though in fact the underlying physical processes proceed continuously), so likewise in idealized continuous computers, states are taken to change continuously (even though some implementations might approximate this with small discrete steps). We define a *formal process* to be one that depends only on the form of the image representing the state of the system; the process is not affected by any meaning that may be associated with the images.

Postulate 4 *Formal processes in simulacra are continuous functions of time and process state.*

The preceding postulates deal with simulacra as *formal* systems, that is idealized computational processes that depend on the *form* of images but not on any interpretation of them; they are the postulates of *uninterpreted simulacra* or *continuous formal systems.* Now we turn to *interpreted simulacra*, which can be considered *continuous symbol systems.* Thus as the

a definitive formalization. Justification for the postulates is in MacLennan (in press-a, in press-b).

[2]This follows from a theorem of Urysohn which shows that any metric space with a countable base is homeomorphic to a subset of $\mathcal{L}_2$ (Nemytskii & Stepanov 1989, p. 324).

interpretation of a calculus is required to be *systematic*, in particular, to be *compositional*, to respect the constituent structure of the formulas, so also we require systematicity of the interpretations of simulacra, in particular, that interpretations be continuous.[3] Thus:

Postulate 5 *Interpretations of simulacra are continuous.*

There are many open questions in the theory of continuous computation. One immediate question is whether the famous undecidability and uncomputability results of Gödel and Turing apply. Interestingly, some of these questions cannot even be asked in a consistently continuous context, so the problems must be reformulated.[4] Another issue is the existence of *universal machines* for continuous computation. Although it's well-known that under various idealizing assumptions artificial neural networks can simulate Turing machines, and Wolpert & MacLennan (subm.) present a purely-linear continuous-computer with Turing power, we think that there are probably other notions of computational universality that are more appropriate to the theory of continuous computation (MacLennan 1987a).[5]

Another open problem — in continuous computation as well as discrete — is how representations can come to have meanings. Of course, human beings can impose interpretations on otherwise uninterpreted computational systems. But a central philosophical question for computational theories of cognition is whether representations can acquire meanings on their own, so-called *original intentionality*, as opposed to having meanings attributed by a outside observer, *derived intentionality* (e.g., Dennett 1987, 1988). Harnad (1990, in press) has called this the *symbol grounding problem.* Although he thinks it applies only to digital computers and not to analog computers, elsewhere (e.g. MacLennan subm.-c) we argue that grounding is just as much of an issue for continuous (analog) computers as for discrete (digital)

[3] Indeed, systematicity in both cases is equivalent to continuity, since respect for constituent structure is just continuity under the appropriate topology for discrete, hierarchically structured formulas (Scott 1970, 1971, 1973; Scott & Strachey 1971).

[4] See MacLennan (in press-a, in press-b) for a discussion and preliminary results. Other formulations of the problems can be found in Blum & al. (1989, 1988), Pour-El & Richards (1979, 1981, 1982) and Stannett (1990).

[5] See also McCulloch & Pitts (1943), Pollack (1987), Hartley & Szu (1987), Franklin & Garzon (1990), and Garzon & Franklin (1989, 1990) for discussion of computational universality in a continuous context.

computers. As should be clear from the preceding discussion, the constraints of systematic interpretation are no less for continuous computational systems than for discrete, and the solution of the symbol grounding problem does not hinge on the continuous/discrete distinction.[6]

Finally, one of the most important open problems, from the standpoints of both psychology and artificial intelligence, is to understand the emergence of quasidiscrete symbolic processes from the underlying, continuous subsymbolic processes (MacLennan 1992b, in press-a, in press-b). This is the dual problem of that which traditional, symbolic AI was unable to solve: the reduction of continuous information representation and processing (including tacit knowledge, perceptual understanding, sensorimotor skill and associative memory) to discrete symbol manipulation. It resulted in the *cognitive inversion* of the "old AI" (MacLennan 1987b, 1988): it was most successful where humans are least successful (e.g., formal deduction), but least successful where people — and even lower animals — are most successful (e.g., pattern recognition). However, the goal of the "new AI" should not be limited to a connectionist implementation of traditional discrete symbol manipulation (a neural network implementation of LISP); rather we term the symbol processing of the new AI *quasidiscrete* because it has an ineluctable admixture of the continuous, which imparts to it the flexibility characteristic of human symbol use.

2 Field Computation

2.1 Overview of Theory

Evidence is accumulating that Hilbert spaces provide a central theoretical framework in which to construct a theory of neurodynamics and cognition. In addition to the neural wave equation developed by Pribram, Yasue and Jibu (Pribram 1991), we have Urysohn's theorem, cited above, which implies that image spaces are topologically equivalent to subsets of Hilbert spaces. We also expect Hilbert spaces to provide the basis for understand-

[6]We have proposed a different solution to the problem of original intentionality, in which conventional representations acquire meaning through shared relevance to a community that is ultimately grounded in inclusive fitness (MacLennan 1992a; MacLennan & Burghardt subm.). Harnad's notion of grounding would be derivative from this.

ing the emergence of symbolic cognition from subsymbolic processes, since the continuous and the discrete meet mathematically in Hilbert space ($\mathcal{L}_2$ is homeomorphic to ℓ_2); recall that the square wave is an infinite superposition of sinusoids. Finally we have found Hilbert spaces to be the most convenient theoretical framework in which to construct our theory of *field computation*, to which we now turn.

It is necessary to remark on the meaning of *field* as used in the phrase 'field computation' (MacLennan 1987a; MacLennan 1990), which is somewhat broader than current usage in physics, but corresponds to Faraday's. Informally, we define a *field* to be a *spatially extended continuum of quantity.* This seems to be an especially useful basis for understanding the neurodynamics of cognitive processes, as recognized by the Gestalt psychologists (e.g. Köhler 1940, Ch. II). We'll illustrate the idea with several examples before giving a formal definition.

Perhaps the simplest example of a field is the distribution of light intensity over the rods in the retina. Although we know the number of rods is finite, it is sufficiently large (10^8) that they may be treated as a continuum and analyzed through the theory of field computation (MacLennan 1987a). The value of the field φ at retinal position $\mathbf{p}$, $\varphi(\mathbf{p})$, is a scalar representing the light intensity.

A more complex example is provided by the activity of the cones, since there are three kinds of these, and so the activity of the cones is represented by a vector field $\boldsymbol{\varphi}$. The vector $(x, y, z) = \boldsymbol{\varphi}(\mathbf{p})$ represents the activities (x, y and z) of the three kinds of cones at location $\mathbf{p}$.

The preceding examples were two-dimensional fields, that is, quantities defined over a two-dimensional continuum (the retina). One dimensional fields are also common in the nervous system; for example, the instantaneous activities of hair cells in the cochlea define a one-dimensional field $\varphi(f)$, where f is the frequency of the sound. We consider later fields of dimension greater than two.

It's obvious that the fields we've mentioned are *time-varying*, and we have argued elsewhere (MacLennan 1991) for the importance of their temporal structure. Therefore, we often find it convenient to view a time-varying spatially-extended field $\varphi(\mathbf{x})$ as a *spatiotemporally-extended field* $\varphi(\mathbf{x}, t)$. This often yields a considerable theoretical simplification and greater insight into the neural processes, as we'll show later.

Although we've illustrated fields with examples from sensory systems, they are just as prevalent in motor systems and in higher cognitive areas, as will also become apparent later.

Now we define fields more formally. Readers uninterested in the mathematical details, which are routine, may wish to skip to the next section. We capture the requirement for continuous extension by stipulating that a field φ is a continuous function defined between two continua $\varphi : \Omega \to \Omega'$, where, as usual in topology, a *continuum* is a *nontrivial compact connected set.* Most commonly the domain Ω will be a closed and bounded subset of a Euclidean space, such as a finite interval of the reals, or a disk or rectangle in the plane. The range Ω' will most often be a closed and bounded subset of the real numbers, but complex-valued and vector-valued fields also occur. Finally, it is usually realistic and convenient to restrict our attention to *finite energy* (i.e., $\mathcal{L}_2$) functions, so we can assume fields belong to a Hilbert space.

If φ is a field over Ω and K is a field over $\Omega' \times \Omega$, then we define a kind of product $K\varphi$, which is the continuous analog of a matrix-vector product:

$$K\varphi = \psi, \quad \text{where } \psi(s) = \int_{\Omega} K(s,t)\varphi(t)\mathrm{d}t.$$

If K is finite energy ($\mathcal{L}_2$) then this product defines an *integral operator of Hilbert-Schmidt type with kernel K.* In MacLennan (subm.-a) we have argued that excitatory synapses and hyperpolarizing inhibitory synapses are *effectively linear*, and so they may be viewed as computing a field product of this kind (Fig. 1A). The field of synaptic efficacies defines the kernel of the operator.

We extend the product notation in the obvious way to more than one argument field. Suppose M is a field over $\Omega \times \Omega_1 \times \cdots \times \Omega_n$ and that φ_k is a field over Ω_k, $k = 1, \ldots, n$. The product is defined:

$$M\varphi_1\varphi_2\cdots\varphi_n = \psi,$$

where

$$\psi(s) = \int_{\Omega_n} \cdots \int_{\Omega_2} \int_{\Omega_1} M(s, t_n, \ldots, t_2, t_1)\varphi_1(t_1)\varphi_2(t_2)\cdots\varphi_n(t_n)\mathrm{d}t_1\mathrm{d}t_2\cdots\mathrm{d}t_n.$$

The result is a *multilinear operator of Hilbert-Schmidt type with kernel M*; *multilinear* means that it is linear in each of its n arguments.

Notice that the multilinear operator is reduced to the simple product by writing

$$M\varphi_1\varphi_2\cdots\varphi_n = \{\cdots[(M\varphi_1)\varphi_2]\cdots\varphi_n\}.$$

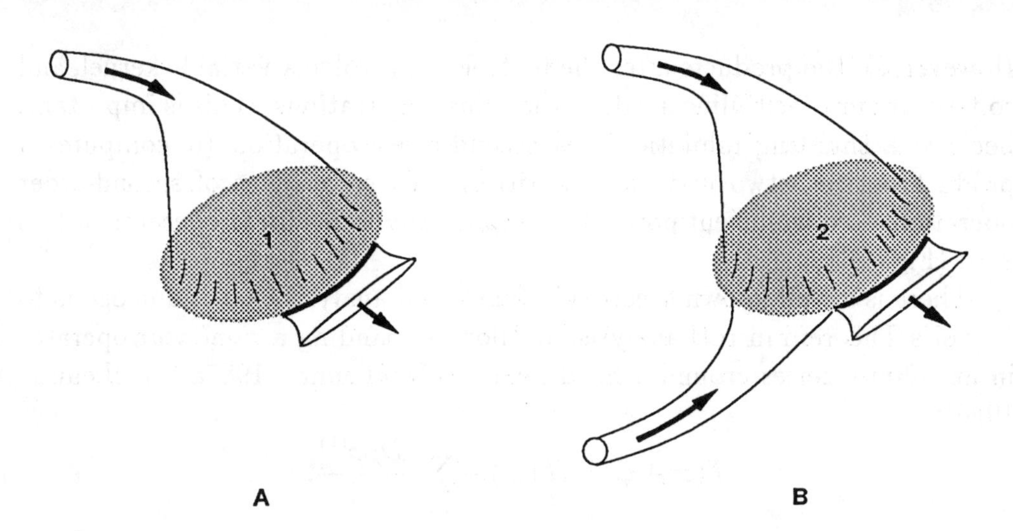

Figure 1: Linear and Bilinear Synaptic Fields. **A.** Excitatory synapses and hyperpolarizing inhibitory synapses can define a linear interaction field L operating on an incoming field φ, $\psi = L\varphi$. More generally these synapses implement an affine field transformation, $\psi = K + L\varphi$. The input and output fields may be defined by spike densities or graded polarizations. (The figure '1' indicates a first-order interaction field.) **B.** Shunting inhibition permits an approximate multiplication between two graded potentials, thus giving a second-order (bilinear) interaction between two fields, $\psi = M\varphi\xi$. More generally such a synaptic field implements a second order interaction, $\psi = K + L_1\varphi + L_2\xi + M\varphi\xi$. The input fields must be graded potentials, but the output field may be represented by graded potentials or spike density. (The figure '2' indicates a second-order interaction field.)

However, all the products after the first, $M\varphi_1$, involve a variable kernel, and so they are in effect bilinear rather than linear operations. This is important, because a shunting inhibition is a second-order operation (it computes a product between two variable quantities), and so a series of second-order operations is of sufficient power to compute any multilinear operator of this kind (Fig. 1B).

There is a well-known theorem in functional analysis that is analogous to Taylor's Theorem in real analysis. It allows expanding a *nonlinear* operator in an infinite series around a fixed field ϖ (MacLennan 1987a; MacLennan 1990):

$$T(\varpi + \varphi) = T(\varpi) + \sum_{k=1}^{\infty} \frac{D_k \varphi^{(k)}}{k!},$$

where

$$D_k \varphi^{(k)} = D_k \underbrace{\varphi\varphi \cdots \varphi}_{k}.$$

The fields D_k are the derivatives of the operator T evaluated at ϖ, $D_k = \mathrm{d}^k T(\varpi)$; these fields give locally-multilinear approximations to T.[7] Although this expansion is "locally good" around ϖ, more often we would like expansions that satisfy global criteria of goodness. Therefore we consider general "polynomial" multilinear expansions of the form:

$$T(\varphi) = K_0 + K_1\varphi + K_2\varphi^{(2)} + K_3\varphi^{(3)} + \cdots.$$

The kernels K_k are chosen to satisfy or optimize some global criterion, such as minimum error over a training set.

As we've seen, nonlinear operators can be approximated by field "polynomials" of the form $\psi = \sum_k K_k \varphi^{(k)}$, which can be reduced in turn to a sum of first- and second-order interactions. In MacLennan (1987a) we argued that this provides a theoretical basis for universal field computation analogous to the Universal Turing Machine in the theory of discrete computation.[8] Therefore it is especially interesting that first- and second-order interactions can be computed by synaptic fields (Fig. 1), since this suggests that the layers of a

[7] Under the assumptions of field computation, the Fréchet and Gâteaux derivatives are identical (MacLennan 1990).

[8] In Wolpert & MacLennan (subm.) we show that there is a completely linear field computer that is computationally universal in the sense of Turing.

neural network may be computing successively higher-order approximations to a nonlinear operator, and series-parallel projections of a field may have a kind of computational universality (Fig. 2).

2.2 Neuronal Field Computation

In this section we'll consider briefly how a number of neural processes can be understood from the standpoint of field computation. For this purpose we will distinguish *neuronal information processing* from *dendritic information processing.* The activity of relatively large cortical areas (i.e., those typically identified anatomically and given names or numbers) can be characterized in terms of *neuronal activity fields.* Most obviously, if $\mathbf{x}$ is the coordinate vector of a neuron in some area Ω, then $D(\mathbf{x})$ could represent the instantaneous spike density of the neuron. Alternately we may view this as a spatiotemporal field (signal or wave) $D(\mathbf{x}, t)$.

Another way of understanding neuronal information processing is in terms of the somatic potential, which represents the integration of a neuron's inputs. Thus we may take $V(\mathbf{x})$ to be the potential of the soma of the neuron with coordinates $\mathbf{x}$. It may be the case that in many areas and in most circumstances, the spike-density field is approximately proportional (up to neuronal precision) to the somatic-potential field, $D(\mathbf{x}) = kV(\mathbf{x})$. This will be the case except for neurons that operate frequently in saturation (i.e., at their minimum or maximum firing rates; see MacLennan subm.-a).

It may be objected that neural cortex is not continuous, but composed of discrete neurons, and of course this is true. But a square centimeter of cortex contains approximately 15 million neurons, which is a large enough number to allow the application of continuous mathematics. It is a central tenet of field computation (MacLennan 1987a, 1990) that it does not matter whether the spatial distribution of a quantity is *really* continuous or *really* discrete; to be considered a field it is sufficient that it approximate a continuum well enough to apply continuous mathematics. We believe that for the practical purposes of biological modeling and computer technology, all that matters is whether a phenomenon *looks* continuous or discrete, a methodological tenet

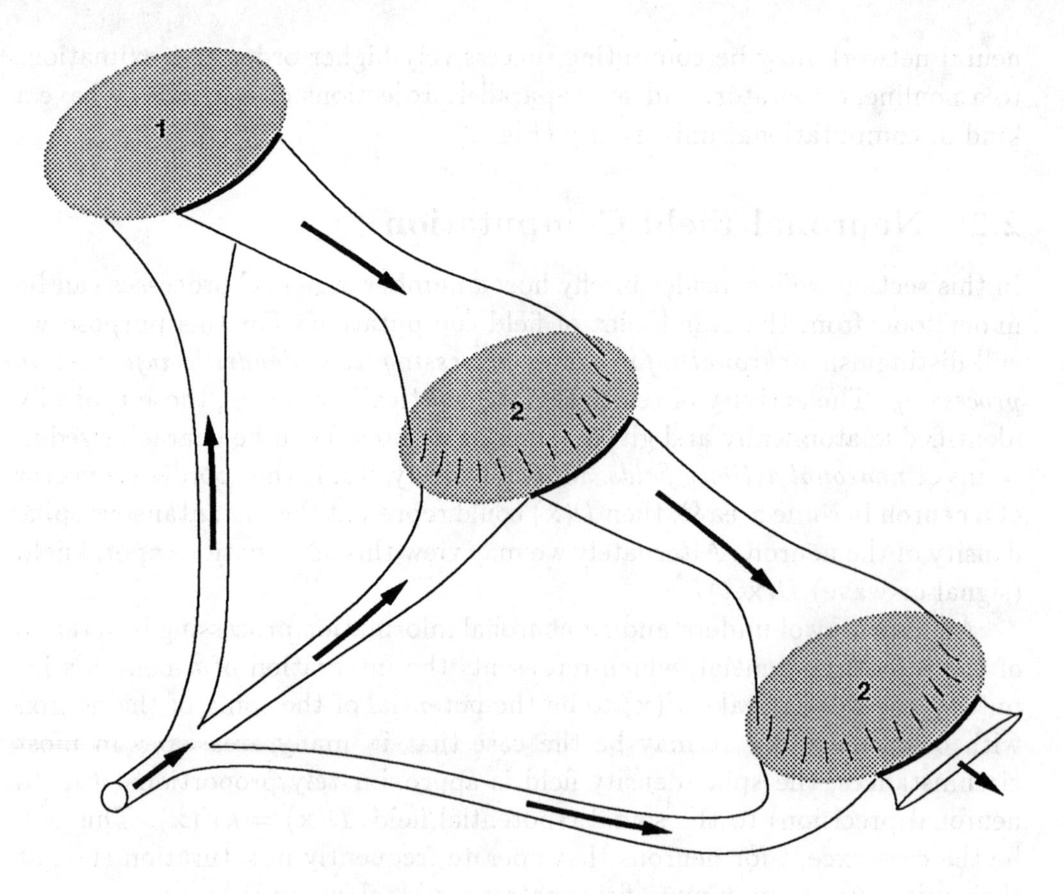

Figure 2: Higher-Order Field Computation in Neural Networks. By projecting in parallel to sequential second-order interaction fields, a neural network may implement a higher-order field polynomial approximating an arbitrary nonlinear operator. Therefore the class of networks of this form exhibit a kind of computational universality. In this case the three-layer network implements the third-degree operator $\psi = K_0 + K_1\varphi + K_2\varphi^{(2)} + K_3\varphi^{(3)}$.

called the *Complementarity Principle* (MacLennan subm.-a). We may put it:

> *Continuous models should be practically indistinguishable from approximately-continuous discrete models, and vice versa.*

It has been remarked that neural networks in the brain — as opposed to most PDP models — are neither random nor fully connected (Crick & Asanuma 1986; Pribram 1991, pp. 5–7). Much more common are *neurotopic maps*, topology preserving maps from one cortical area to another.

For an example of neuronal field computation we may take the coordinate transformation that occurs between the retina and its first projection (VI, area 17) in the primary visual cortex.[9] The retinal hemifield is most easily represented in polar coordinates (r, θ), where r represents the radial position from the center of the retina, and θ represents the angle measured clockwise from the horizontal radius of the hemifield (Fig. 3A). Thus $r \in \mathrm{P} = [0, r_{\max}]$, where $r_{\max}$ is the radius of the retina, and $\theta \in \Theta = [-\pi/2, \pi/2]$.

The projection from the retinas to area 17 is *topology preserving* in that regions adjacent on the retina remain adjacent on the cortex. However, there is a *metric distortion* since much more cortical space is devoted to the center of the retina than to the periphery. Indeed, to a first approximation the arrangement of area 17 is as shown in Fig. 3B, which shows logarithmically less cortical distance with increasing distance from the retinal center.[10] If we let (ρ, ϕ) be the coordinates in visual cortex of the point corresponding to the retinal point at (r, θ), then we see that (ignoring scale factors), $\phi = \theta$ and $\rho = \log r$. Thus the retina-to-cortex map distorts an image φ by applying the transformation:

$$T(\varphi) = \psi, \quad \text{where} \quad \psi(\log r, \theta) = \varphi(r, \theta).$$

Following Baron (1987, pp. 181–186) we note that if we represent retinal position by Cartesian coordinates (x, y), then the coordinate transformation

[9] Although this transformation apparently occurs in the projection of the retinal ganglion cells onto the LGN (Berne & Levy 1983, p. 127), we'll take it to be between the retina and VI. Recall that the right visual hemifields of both eyes project to VI in the left hemisphere, and vice versa.

[10] For the time being we are ignoring orientation and velocity sensitivity of cortical cells; they will be considered later.

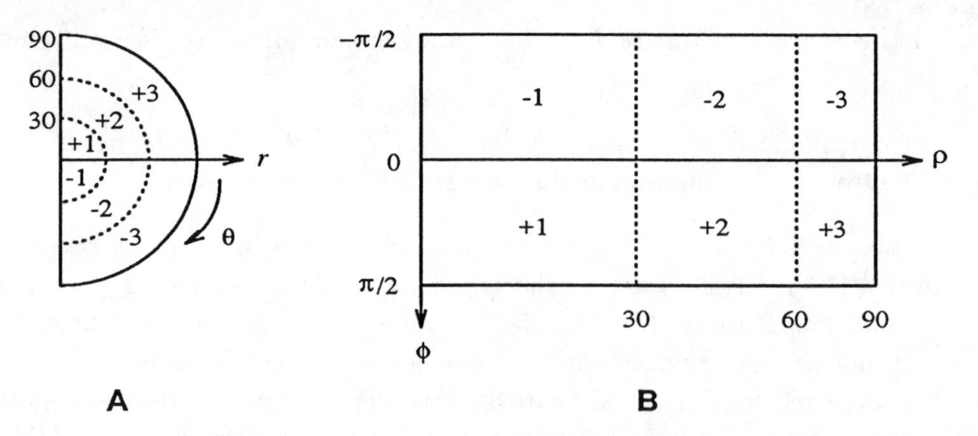

Figure 3: Hemifield Coordinates. **A.** The figure shows the coordinates of the right visual hemifield of either eye. The particular convention chosen for the angles is for convenience in mapping to area 17 (VI) of the visual cortex. **B.** A schematic representation of the retinotopic map of the right hemifields in area 17 (VI) of the left visual cortex. The ρ axis is along the calcarine fissure, from the back of the brain forward (left to right) on the medial surface of the cortex. Radial positions are mapped approximately logarithmically, $\rho = \log r$. Overall the relation between the two coordinate systems is a complex logarithm.

can be expressed

$$\rho = \log \sqrt{x^2 + y^2}, \qquad \phi = \tan^{-1}(y/x).$$

If we express both systems of coordinates by complex numbers, $z = x + iy$, $\zeta = \rho + i\phi$, then this *logmap transformation* is simply a complex logarithm, $\zeta = \log z$. The corresponding field transformation is

$$T(\varphi) = \psi, \text{ where } \psi(\zeta) = \varphi(\exp \zeta).$$

The logmap transformation has many information-processing advantages for the visual system (Baron 1987, Ch. 8; Schwartz 1977). In particular, rotations and scale changes of centered retinal images correspond to simple translations of the cortical image.

2.3 Dendritic Field Computation

Shepherd (e.g., 1972, 1978, 1988, 1990a, 1990b) has argued that the synapse, rather than the neuron, should be considered the basic computational element of the brain, and that spatiotemporal relations in the dendritic tree are crucial to understanding synaptic information processing. Further, Pribram (1991, pp. 5–7) has argued that PDP models are a better description of information processing in dendritic nets, which have dense, random interconnection patterns, rather than in neural nets, with their regular topology.

The fields involved in dendritic information processing are predominantly electrochemical fields. Specifically, if $\mathbf{x}$ represents the location of an active site in the dendritic arbor, such as a synapse, then $\varphi(\mathbf{x})$ most commonly represents the membrane potential, but it could also represent the concentration of a chemical species, such as an ion or neurotransmitter. Of course, there has been much work, from Hodgkin and Huxley's day, that models the detailed dynamics of these processes, but that is not our concern here. Since we are interested in the general structure of information processing in the brain, it is sufficient that such fields exists; we would like to understand their possible role in information representation and processing.

The electrochemical dynamics of nervous tissue is without doubt complex, so the challenge is to find simplifying approximations that capture the essence of information processing and avoid irrelevant detail. To this end we have been investigating a *linear system* model of dendritic information processing (MacLennan subm.-a; MacLennan & Pribram in prep.). The mathematical advantages of a linear model are obvious, but do we have any basis for assuming it? We believe that the evidence supports linear models of both excitatory synapses and hyperpolarizing inhibitory synapses, and bilinear models of shunting inhibition (MacLennan subm.-a; MacLennan & Pribram in prep.). Although there is widespread opinion that linear systems are computationally impotent (e.g., Poggio & Torre 1981; Reichardt & Poggio 1981), we show below that dynamic linear systems can accomplish significant information processing (cf. also Wolpert & MacLennan subm.).

We also consider the present theory a simplification of the neural wave equation developed by Pribram, Yasue and Jibu (Pribram 1991, Apps. A–G), which is also a linear model. Specifically, by assuming a discrete set of interaction sites, the model becomes a *lumped-parameter* system, which means that its dynamics can be described by ordinary differential equations rather than partial differential equations. A significant simplification results from this assumption, which is justified by our Complementarity Principle, and we anticipate that this simplification will help us to go beyond the dynamics of dendritic interactions, and to understand their *function*.

Let ψ be some time-varying field relevant to dendritic information processing (membrane polarization at synapses would be an example). Based on the linear-system assumption, we take its dynamics to be defined by a nth-order integro-differential equation with kernels F_k:

$$\psi^{(n)} = \sum_{k=0}^{n-1} F_k \psi^{(k)} + \text{input drive}.$$

As usual this equation can be reduced to a system of first-order equations by introducing additional field variables ψ_k corresponding to the time-derivatives of ψ:

$$\begin{aligned} \psi &= \psi_0, \\ \dot{\psi}_k &= \psi_{k+1}, \quad k = 0, \ldots, n-1, \\ \dot{\psi}_{n-1} &= \sum_{k=0}^{n-1} F_k \psi_k + \text{input drive}. \end{aligned}$$

If these state variables are combined into a field-vector $\boldsymbol{\psi} = (\psi_0, \ldots, \psi_{n-1})$ and the kernels $F_0, \ldots, F_{n-1}$ into a kernel-vector F, then the system can be described by a single field-vector differential equation:

$$\dot{\boldsymbol{\psi}} = F\boldsymbol{\psi} + \text{input drive}.$$

To complete our description of the linear system, we must describe how it is driven by the input φ and how it in turn drives the output ω. Then we have a linear system of the form (Fig. 4):

$$\begin{aligned} \dot{\boldsymbol{\psi}} &= D\varphi + F\boldsymbol{\psi}, \\ \omega &= E\varphi + G\boldsymbol{\psi}. \end{aligned}$$

Such a system will exhibit *resonances*, the number of which is on the order of the size of the state fields, that is on order of the number of interaction sites. Since there may be 5 000 to 200 000 synapses in the dendritic arbor of a single neuron, it's not implausible to assume that such a dendritic net may have thousands of resonances. We consider elsewhere some kinds of information processing that such a system can implement, including the self-organization of hierarchically-structured spatiotemporal matched filters (MacLennan subm.-a).

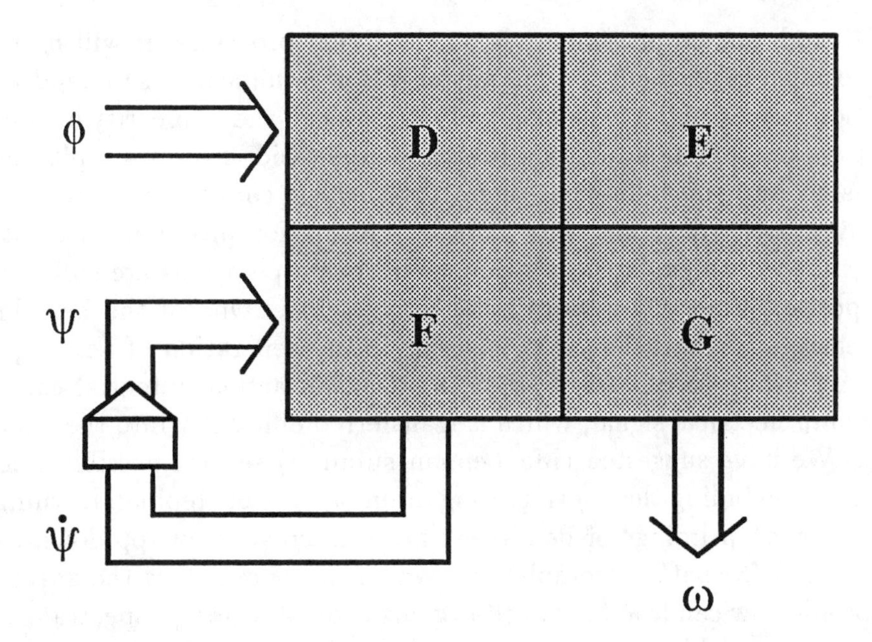

Figure 4: The Dendritic Net as a Dynamic Linear System. The input field φ drives both the state fields ψ through kernel D and the output field ω through kernel E. Kernel F determines the feedback among the state fields, and kernel G governs the contribution of the state fields to the output field. The house-shaped figure represents a field integration (with respect to time) of the state fields.

Although our emphasis here is on the linear processes, it will be worthwhile to say a little about the functional role of nonlinearities in dendritic information processing. We have already mentioned the bilinearity of shunting inhibition; one possible function it could serve (aside from a simple and-not gate) is to implement bilinear operators such as convolutions and correlations over both space and time, whose information-processing potential is manifest. Also, as explained previously, bilinear operations are sufficient for an important kind of computational universality. One of the best known nonlinearities in the behavior of neurons is the generation of action potentials. According to Shepherd (1988, p. 137), an action potential causes an *antidromic* electrical signal, which is transferred efficiently into the dendritic spines. We have suggested (MacLennan subm.-a) several possible roles for this signal, including the (1) triggering or enhancing of Hebbian learning, (2) the top-down "priming" of dendrites (i.e., the creation of top-down expectations), and (3) pattern completion. We've also shown how the antidromic electrotonic flow can lead to the self-organization of recursive spectral-density matched-filters, which have many possible applications in neural information processing.

Hameroff (1987) has suggested that Boolean and automata-like processes could occur in the cytoskeletons of neurons, and that this could be "where the action is" so far as information processing is concerned. We suggest that field computation may be a better model of cytoskeletal processing — if it exists — since the large number of elements (~1625/micron) makes the microtubule a good approximation to a field.[11] Local values of the field could be represented, for example, by rate of conformational change of the microtubule-associated proteins. The question remains, of course, whether the dynamics are approximately linear, but if they are, then much of the theory presented here would apply unchanged.

[11]Microtubules are composed of spirals of tubulin dimers, 13 around the circumference, which are 8 nm long in the direction of the axis (Hameroff 1987, p. 106). Therefore, a one-micron length of microtubule contains 1000nm / 8nm spirals, each containing 13 dimers; $13 \times 1000/8 = 1625$.

3 Gabor-like Representations

In this section we will consider some Gabor-like field representations that may be important in sensory and motor systems.

3.1 Vision

3.1.1 Spatial Gabor Wavelets

There is now considerable evidence that the receptive fields of simple cells in the primary visual cortex correspond (up to synaptic precision) to the even- or odd-symmetric parts of two-dimensional Gabor functions $\gamma_{\mathbf{q}}$, which suggests that Gabor functions are the representational primitives of the primary visual cortex.[12] (See MacLennan 1991 for a review.)

The problem is that the Gabor functions are not orthogonal, so the coefficients $c_{\mathbf{q}}$ of a Gabor expansion of a field φ,

$$\varphi = \sum_{\mathbf{q}} c_{\mathbf{q}} \gamma_{\mathbf{q}},$$

cannot be computed by a simple inner product, $c_{\mathbf{q}} \neq \langle \varphi, \gamma_{\mathbf{q}} \rangle$. Nevertheless, inner products with Gabor functions are what the simple cells seem to compute.[13]

Although there are theoretical reasons to expect representation in terms of Gabor functions (they are optimal in terms of the Gabor Uncertainty Principle), we must keep in mind that they are mathematical objects and cannot

[12]An N-dimensional Gabor function is a Gaussian-modulated complex-exponential,

$$\gamma_{S\mathbf{pu}}(\mathbf{x}) = \exp\{-\pi \| S(\mathbf{x} - \mathbf{p}) \|^2\} \exp[2\pi i \mathbf{u} \cdot (\mathbf{x} - \mathbf{p})].$$

All the vectors are N-dimensional. The parameter $\mathbf{p}$ determines the function's location in N-space; the wave vector $\mathbf{u}$ determines its modulatory frequencies, or position in N-dimensional spectral space, and the orientation of the function in N-space. The parameter S is a diagonal matrix which defines the function's *aspect ratio*, or shape in N-space. When it is not necessary to distinguish the parameters, we simply write $\gamma_{\mathbf{q}}(\mathbf{x})$. The Gabor functions form an *anisotropic (oriented) wavelet family.*

[13]This is an oversimplification, as noted in MacLennan (1991, n. 23). The input to area 17 is from the retina via the LGN, which have already represented the image in terms of radial basis functions (center-surround receptive fields). Therefore, the Gabor receptive fields observed in striate cortex reflect the combined effect of retina, LGN and area 17 on the image.

be instantiated perfectly in the biology. Therefore, objections against the Gabor functions, such as that they have noncompact support, are not relevant in a biological context. It's true that the Gaussian envelope extends to infinity, but 99.7% of its area is within three standard deviations of its mean, and 99.994% within four. Thus the Gabor functions are practically indistinguishable from functions with compact support. The conclusion we draw is that the theory is underdetermined by the biology, and so we can choose to model the receptive fields by Gabor functions, if it is mathematically convenient to do so.

Another problem with the Gabor functions is that they are complex-valued, and therefore not representable by real-valued membrane potential, spike densities, etc. Although there is evidence (Pollen & Ronner 1981) that simple cells occur in conjugate pairs with receptive fields representing the (real valued) odd- and even-symmetric parts of the Gabor function, Stork & Wilson (1990) have objected that these real functions do not minimize the Gabor uncertainty, and therefore that they should not be given special status. The real-valued functions that achieve the minimum are the Hermite functions, as shown by Gabor and proved more carefully by Stork & Wilson. Nevertheless, the Hermite functions are sufficiently like the real parts of the Gabor functions, that even this difference may be insignificant.

Although Gabor functions are nonorthogonal and so cannot be a basis, under biologically plausible conditions they do form a *frame*, for which the inner products fulfill a similar role to that for bases (MacLennan 1991). Thus one possibility is that the higher levels of the visual system simply operate in terms of a nonorthogonal representation. Just because orthogonality is mathematically convenient doesn't imply that it's biologically convenient. As Daugman (1988) observed, nonorthogonality is ubiquitous in sensory and motor systems, which we should expect from the *Robustness Principle* (MacLennan subm.-a):

> *No biological process can depend on an absolute mathematical property.*

This tells us that biological processes cannot depend on exact orthogonality. In fact, approximate orthogonality is in many ways preferable to exact orthogonality (Kainen submitted; MacLennan subm.-a). Further, given the imprecision of biological computation, the correction of coefficients by relaxation (such as described below) can be expected even for formally orthogonal representational primitives.

In MacLennan (1991) we argued that such a relaxation process was unlikely in neural networks in which signaling is mediated by impulses, since the rate of information transmission is too slow, but that it was feasible in local circuits in dendritic nets, where signaling may be mediated by graded potentials. In MacLennan (subm.-a) we showed that dendritic iteration can be expected to proceed 20 to 200 times as fast as neuronal iteration, and furthermore that dendritic nets have the computational power to implement a linear system that relaxes to the coefficients of a nonorthogonal representation, such as the Gabor (see also MacLennan & Pribram in prep.). In this linear system, the driving matrix D is proportional to the array of elementary fields $\varrho_{\mathbf{q}}$,

$$D_{\mathbf{q}} = \eta \varrho_{\mathbf{q}},$$

for example even- or odd-symmetric Gabor functions, which correspond with the observed receptive field profiles. The feedback matrix or interaction field F is proportional to all the inner products between the elementary fields (i.e., the Gram matrix),

$$F_{\mathbf{qr}} = -\eta \langle \varrho_{\mathbf{q}}, \varrho_{\mathbf{r}} \rangle,$$

and has a decorrelating effect which takes care of the nonorthogonality.

Pattison (1992) has independently proposed the same relaxation algorithm for Gabor or other nonorthogonal representations, but claims that it could be implemented in neural networks. In particular he assumes that the coefficients are represented by instantaneous firing frequencies, but neglects the finite interval — given by the Gabor Uncertainty Principle — required to represent a coefficient to a given precision (MacLennan 1991, subm.-a; MacLennan & Pribram in prep.). In fact, approximately 10^k msec. are required for k digits of precision. Nevertheless he estimates that the relaxation process will require at least 50 msec. per iteration, which he concedes is inconsistent with simple cell response times observed by Jones & Palmer (1987). We suggest that the inconsistency is eliminated by assuming that the relaxation takes place through graded interactions in the dendritic net, which have a delay of about 1 msec.

We consider briefly the representation of the Gabor coefficients in visual cortex. We've already seen that the logmap transformation converts retinal coordinates (r, θ) into VI coordinates (ρ, ϕ); recall Fig. 3. If the VI field were simply a representation of light intensity at the retina, then it would be a scalar field over the two-dimensional domain $P \times \Theta$, but we've seen that it's a scalar field over three dimensions: two for retinal location and one for Gabor-field orientation.[14] The possible orientations of the receptive fields range from 0 to 2π so we define $\Phi = [0, 2\pi]$; it is not simply $[0, \pi]$ since the odd-symmetric receptive fields are asymmetric across their edge. Therefore, VI must represent a scalar field defined over three-dimensions, $P \times \Theta \times \Phi$. How can this be represented in the essentially two-dimensional cortex?

This is a standard problem in field computation (MacLennan 1990), and there are a number of ways of mapping a higher dimensional field into a lower dimensional space. One is to simply cut up the field along one or more of the dimensions, and arrange the resulting lower-dimensional fields next to one another. This is exactly what we find in the orientation columns of striate cortex. The orientations $[0, 2\pi]$ run through an entire cycle in a space of about 2mm and repeats thereafter (Baron 1987, p. 153). Therefore, wherever the mathematical function requires a field of dimension greater than two, we expect to see a striate or columnar structure in the cortex.

This arrangement has another useful effect in that it leads to texture (oriented spatial frequency) being represented is a similar way to color: the orientation columns are arranged similarly to the *cortical pegs* or *blobs* that respond to color (Shepherd 1988, pp. 348–349). This is reasonable since both texture and color are "extended" properties.

3.1.2 Spatiotemporal Gabor Wavelets

The research which led to the Gabor representation (Gabor 1946) was motivated in part by the observation that our perception of sound is simultaneously of duration and pitch. Thus the Gabor representation captures the local temporal structure of the sound. The preceding discussion of vision can be interpreted to mean that our visual perception is simultaneously of extension and texture (oriented spatial frequency). Thus the Gabor representation captures the local spatial structure of a scene. On the other hand, we also have an immediate visual awareness of motion, and we know that some cells in the visual cortex respond to motion, so we might wonder if our

[14]There is actually a fourth dimension, representing spatial frequency and receptive-field size, which are closely correlated. For simplicity this will be ignored.

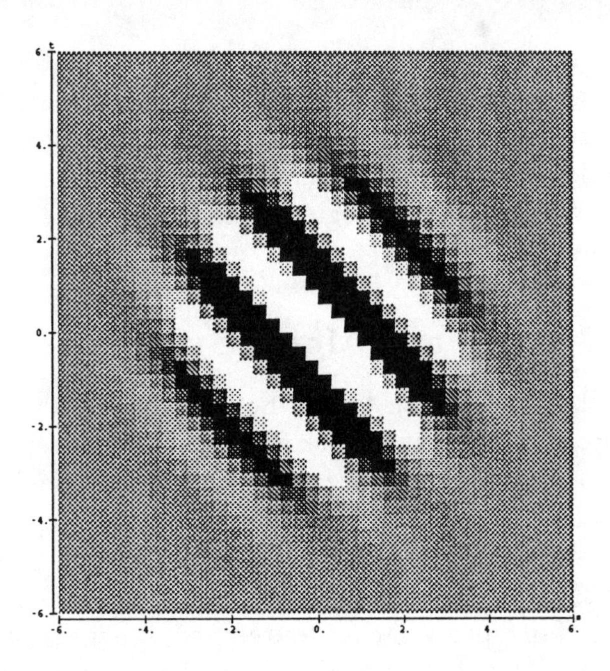

Figure 5: Depiction of Spatiotemporal Gabor Function. The figure shows a slice through the even (cosine) part of a 3D Gabor function. The vertical axis represents time and the horizontal axis is along the spatial orientation of the function. This filter is selective for fringes of a specific frequency moving at a specific velocity in a localized region of space and time. This particular filter responds maximally to fringes with a frequency $1/\sqrt{8}$ moving with a velocity of 1 to the left (arbitrary units).

visual system uses a Gabor representation in both the spatial and temporal domains.

In MacLennan (1991) we suggest three-dimensional Gabor functions, with two space dimensions and one time dimension, as possible representational primitives in vision. In addition to orientation in space, these functions may be oriented in space-time, which gives them receptive fields responsive to textural motion localized in space and time (Fig. 5). Temporal localization suggests that visual system operates cyclically, which is compatible with the use of relaxation to calculate Gabor coefficients. The idea is that the basic cycle is (1) acquire the image; (2) calculate its Gabor coefficients by relaxation; (3) forward the coefficients on to the next stage of processing. It's possible that the frequency of this cycle is the alpha rhythm, which is the principal rhythm of the occipital cortex. It might seem that representational primitives oriented in space-time are of only theoretical interest, but in fact they have a simple neural implementation in terms of spatial Gabor functions, analogous to the well-known construction of moving-edge detectors from static-edge detectors. Although spatiotemporal Gabor functions seem to be consistent with neurophysiological data, more research is needed to establish their presence.

3.2 Other Sensory and Motor Systems

The ability of Gabor and similar locally-Fourier representations to capture temporal structure suggests that we look for them in other sensory and motor systems; perhaps they are a general representational principle in the brain. For example, observe that an auditory signal, from the cochlea on, is represented by a spatiotemporal wave, in which instantaneous frequency — the local Fourier transform — is mapped to spatial location. Therefore, 2D spatiotemporal Gabor functions will capture temporal changes of intensity and pitch — what we might call the rhythm and melody of the sound.

Temporal structure is also very important in motor activity, and so we will consider the possibility of Gabor-like representations there. It is reasonable to treat as a field the activity of a large system of motor neurons or of a region of motor cortex. Motor control is then accomplished by generating an appropriate spatiotemporal wave (in a feedback loop, of course). Since such a signal may be represented as a linear superposition of Gabor-like functions, we will investigate the effect of such a representation of motor signals.

Considered as a *generative field* rather than a receptive field, a Gabor-like function amounts to an amplitude-controlled, time-bounded rhythm generator (Fig. 5). More concretely, a Gabor function γ_{q} generates, during a given time interval Δt, a burst of waves of a given frequency and direction across a field of motoneurons (such as a somatotopically mapped region). Higher levels of motor control have the task of generating the Gabor coefficients. More global control mechanisms can adjust the size of the Gabor functions, which affects both their frequency and their spatial and temporal extent.

4 Cognition

In this section we touch on the role field computation may play in higher cognitive function; our focus will be on *intentionality*.

4.1 Intentions

4.1.1 History

The notions of *intentionality* and *intention* are central to the modern philosophy of the mind, so it will be useful to review the meanings of these terms before considering *intentional fields*.

The basic meaning of Latin *intendo* is to stretch toward, point at, or to direct one's mind toward, and at least from the time of Cicero the related noun *intentio* could refer to acts of stretching, reaching or concentrating one's attention (*Oxford Latin Dict.*, s.vv.). The basic idea is an active process of directing the mental faculties.

The Medieval Schoolmen chose *intentio* to translate Arabic *ma'nā* (a meaning, thought, signification or notion) in the works of Avicenna. Later, Ockham defined an intention as "something in the soul capable of signifying something else," or more briefly, a sign in the mental discourse (*Summa Logicae* I § 12). Although this definition is limited by Ockham's linguistic view of cognition, it captures the idea that an intention is a mental representation that refers to something outside of itself (either in the world or in another mental representation).

Brentano (in his *Psychology from an Empirical Standpoint*) resurrected the medieval notion of intention, and used it to refer to the ability of consciousness to refer out of itself and be directed toward something, that is, the characteristic of consciousness that it is consciousness *of* something. Husserl borrowed the term from Brentano and used it with this sense. In accord with its methodological biases, Anglo-American philosophy gave intentionality a linguistic interpretation. An intentional proposition is one which has another proposition as its content, and so it expresses a certain "attitude" toward that proposition.

All these definitions have in common the idea of *selecting* or "foregrounding" some aspects of a mental representation with respect to others, which are left in the background. A "mental sign" picks out some aspect of the external or internal world (in Scholastic terms, a first or second intention); in Brentano and Husserl's terms, consciousness is directed at some aspects of experience; in linguistic terms, an intentional expression has a particular content. The essence of selection is a decrease in entropy, for by making some things more likely to be processed relative to others, we shift the probability distribution away from the uniform distribution, which has maximum entropy, to a nonuniform, lower entropy distribution (MacLennan 1988, pp. 172–173). Thus an intention organizes a representation with respect to an intended functional role. Intentions, as understood here, are closely related to the focus of attention (Pribram 1991, pp. 119–120, 219).

4.1.2 Field Representation

Next we will consider a possible theory of intentions in terms of field computation. We define an *intentional field* to be a $[0, 1]$-valued field over any domain Ω. If φ is any field over the same domain Ω as an intentional field ν, and $F(\nu, \varphi)$ is an operation on the pair of fields (ν, φ), then ν is called an *intention of type F toward φ*.[15] This definition reflects the fact that an essential part of an intention is its *function* or *end*; it is an intention to treat something in a particular way (e.g., to notice it, to be surprised by it, to fear it, to avoid it, to orient toward it, to seize it). Thus the operator F represents the function of the intention, which I call its *kind.* (In biological terms, F might correspond to a specific brain area and ν to a field over that area.) Each intention also has a particular *content*, which is the region of the image towards which the operation is directed; the content is given by the pair of fields (ν, φ). The intention field ν can be interpreted as a probability distribution selecting certain regions of φ for more-likely processing by F. In this sense an intention functions like a continuous analog of a programming-language pointer.

Some examples may make this idea clearer. Visual intentions are characteristic responses or attitudes to the content of the visual field. Thus we may be surprised, either by the presence of some object or by its absence. Also, we may react to perceived objects with fear or with comfortable familiarity. These are not purely visual intentions, since they typically involve

[15] I will generally use ν (from νοέω = intend, discern, notice, remark) for intentional fields. Similarly I will generally use φ (from φάνταcμα = mental image) for fields representing images of any other sort.

nonperceptual evaluations. Purer examples include the tracking of a moving object, or the sudden focus of our attention on an unexpected movement. It is clear in both of these how the relevant intention field could be computed from relatively low level perceptual fields.[16] Auditory intentions are similar, including, for example, the ability to focus on a particular sound, such as a voice, among many other sounds.

For an example of a nonperceptual intention, consider our awareness of an object not visible to us (e.g. behind our back, in a closet). We suppose that spatial awareness is represented in several frameworks, such as the egocentric, centered on the body, and the allocentric, centered elsewhere (Bryant 1990; Bryant et al. 1992; Franklin & Tversky 1990), and that these representations are not unlike abstract sensorimotor representations. Spatial intentions then refer to locations within these spaces, and establish functional relations with those locations (e.g., intent to move an arm to that place, noting presence or absence of an object in that place). Spatial intentions may be translated from one reference frame to another in the same way as images.

Orienting reactions can be understood in this context. An unexpected sight, sound or touch creates a perceptual intention (ν, φ) in a functional area F. The intentional field ν is translated from sensoricentric to egocentric coordinates in the same way as a perceptual image. This "surprise" intention has the functional role of being translated into an intention to move, which can be used to compute a spatiotempral motor field to control the motion.

4.2 Abstract Reason

Johnson-Laird and Byrne have argued that abstract reason is accomplished by manipulating mental models rather than formal symbols (Johnson-Laird & Byrne 1991, in press). We suggest that these models are just abstract, multimodal sensorimotor images, including intentions (MacLennan subm.-b), and we anticipate that manipulation of mental models can be described in terms of field computation. To give a very rough idea, we consider one of the formal logic problems studied by Johnson-Laird & Byrne:

---

[16]For example, the spatiotemporal Gabor representation makes it easy to detect sudden changes in the motion in a local area. We simply apply a low pass filter to eliminate slow changes. Of course that's not the whole story, since animals also habituate to rapid changes.

There is a cross if and only if there is a circle. There is not a cross. What follows?

Let φ be an (abstract) image of both the cross and the circle. Let ν_{xp} be an intentional field indicating that the cross is present, and ν_{op} that the circle is present. Then $\nu_{\mathrm{p}} = \nu_{\mathrm{xp}} + \nu_{\mathrm{op}}$ is an intention referring to both and indicating their presence.[17] To show the absence of the objects, we postulate intentional fields ν_{xa} and ν_{oa}, and their sum $\nu_{\mathrm{a}} = \nu_{\mathrm{xa}} + \nu_{\mathrm{oa}}$.

The first premiss (the biconditional) results in the construction of two models, $(\nu_{\mathrm{p}}, \varphi)$ and $(\nu_{\mathrm{a}}, \varphi)$, which are held in working memory (as fields in prefrontal cortex).

The second premiss, "there is not a circle," results in the model $(\nu_{\mathrm{oa}}, \varphi)$. In an attempt to merge this with each of the previous models, it's found to be incoherent with the first, since the intentions ν_{oa} and ν_{p} treat φ inconsistently (as can be seen by noting $\nu_{\mathrm{oa}}\nu_{\mathrm{p}} \neq 0$). The only other model, that the cross and circle are both absent, is consistent with the second premiss, so it is the conclusion (or, more accurately, the model that the conclusion expresses).

5 Conclusions

We have argued that the limitations of the traditional representation of knowledge as discrete symbols can be avoided by a reformulation in terms of continuous images. We proposed the *simulacrum* as a topological model of continuous knowledge representation and processing, and discussed *field computation* as a specific instance of it. We showed that both neuronal and dendritic information processing can be understood in the context of field computation. In the course of this we considered the possible role of spatiotemporal Gabor wavelet representations in sensorimotor systems, and suggested a field representation of intentions. Overall we hope that this paper has shown the potential contribution of continuous computation — and especially field computation — toward understanding the mind and brain.

[17]In fact, these intentions mean that these are the only allowed models in which these things are present; thus they include Johnson-Laird & Byrne's "exhaustive representation tag"; there are other intentions, not discussed here, that do not bear that tag (i.e., they have a different functional role).

6 References

Baron, R. J. (1987). *The cerebral computer: An introduction to the computational structure of the human brain.* Hillsdale NJ: Lawrence Erlbaum.

Berne, R. M., & Levy, M. N. (Eds.). (1983). *Physiology.* St Louis MO: C. V. Mosby Company.

Blum, L. (1989). *Lectures on a theory of computation and complexity over the reals (or an arbitrary ring)* (Report No. TR-89-065). Berkeley CA: International Computer Science Institute.

Blum, L., Shub, M., & Smale, S. (1988). On a theory of computation and complexity over the real numbers: NP completeness, recursive functions and universal machines. *The Bulletin of the American Mathematical Society,* **21**: 1–46.

Bryant, D. J. (1992). A spatial representation system in humans. *PSYCOLOQUY,* **3**(16) space.1.

Bryant, D. J., Tversky, B., & Franklin, N. (1992). Internal and external spatial frameworks for representing described scenes. *Journal of Memory and Language* **31**: 74–98.

Crick, F. H. C., & Asanuma, C. (1986). Certain aspects of the anatomy and physiology of the cerebral cortex. In: J. L. McClelland & D. E. Rumelhart (Eds.), *Parallel distributed processing: Explorations in the microstructure of cognition, Vol. 2: Psychological and biological models* (pp. 333–371). Cambridge MA: MIT Press.

Daugman, J. G. An information-theoretic view of analog representation in striate cortex. In: E. L. Schwartz (Ed.), *Computational Neuroscience* (pp. 403–423). Cambridge MA: MIT Press.

Dennett, D. (1987). *The intentional stance.* Cambridge MA: MIT Press.

Dennett, D. (1988). The intentional stance. *Behavioral and Brain Sciences,* **11**: 495–546.

Franklin, S., & Garzon, M. (1990). Neural computability. In: O. M. Omidvar (Ed.), *Progress in neural networks* (Vol. 1, pp. 127–145). Norwood NJ: Ablex.

Franklin, N., & Tversky, B. (1990). Searching imagined environments. *Journal of Experimental Psychology: General*, **119**: 63–76.

Gabor, D. (1946). Theory of communication. *Journal of the Institution of Electrical Engineers*, **93 (III)**: 429–457.

Garzon, M., & Franklin, S. (1989). Neural computability II (extended abstract). In: *Proceedings, IJCNN International Joint Conference on Neural Networks* (Vol. 1, pp. 631–637). New York NY: Institute of Electrical and Electronic Engineers.

Garzon, M., & Franklin, S. (1990). Computation on graphs. In: O. M. Omidvar (Ed.), *Progress in neural networks* (Vol. 2, Ch. 13). Norwood NJ: Ablex.

Hameroff, S. R. (1987). *Ultimate computing: Biomolecular consciousness and nanotechnology.* Amsterdam: North Holland.

Harnad, S. (1990). The symbol grounding problem. *Physica D*, **42**: 335–346.

Harnad, S. (in press). Grounding symbols in the analog world with neural nets: A hybrid model. *Think.*

Hartley, R., & Szu, H. (1987). A comparison of the computational power of neural network models. In: M. Caudill & C. Butler (Eds.), *Proceedings, IEEE First International Conference on Neural Networks* (Vol. 3, pp. 17–22). New York NY: Institute of Electrical and Electronic Engineers.

Johnson- Laird, P. N., & Byrne, R. M. J. (1991). *Deduction.* Hillsdale NJ: Lawrence Erlbaum.

Johnson-Laird, P. N., & Byrne, R. M. J. (in press). Precis of *Deduction. Behavioral and Brain Sciences*, in press.

Jones, J. P., & Palmer, L. A. (1987). The two-dimensional spatial structure of simple receptive fields in cat striate cortex. *Journal of Neurophysiology*, **58**: 1187–1211.

Kainen, P. C. (submitted). Orthogonal dimension and tolerance.

Köhler, W. (1940). *Dynamics in Psychology.* New York NY: Liveright.

MacLennan, B. J. (1987a). Technology-independent design of neurocomputers: The universal field computer. In: M. Caudill & C. Butler (Eds.), *Proceedings, IEEE First International Conference on Neural Networks* (Vol. 3, pp. 39–49). New York NY: Institute of Electrical and Electronic Engineers.

MacLennan, B. J. (1987b). *Field computation and nonpropositional knowledge* (Report NPS52-87-40). Monterey CA: Naval Postgraduate School, Computer Science Department.

MacLennan, B. J. (1988). Logic for the new AI. In: J. H. Fetzer (Ed.), *Aspects of Artificial Intelligence* (pp. 163–192). Dordrecht NL: Kluwer Academic Publishers.

MacLennan, B. J. (1990). *Field computation: A theoretical framework for massively parallel analog computation; parts I – IV* (report CS-90-100). Knoxville TN: University of Tennessee, Computer Science Department.

MacLennan, B. J. (1991). *Gabor representations of spatiotemporal visual images* (Report No. CS-91-144). Knoxville TN: University of Tennessee, Knoxville, Computer Science Department; submitted for publication.

MacLennan, B. J. (1992a). Synthetic ethology: An approach to the study of communication. In: C. G. Langton, C. Taylor, J. D. Farmer and S. Rasmussen (Eds.), *Artificial Life II* (pp. 631–658). Redwood City, CA: Addison-Wesley.

MacLennan, B. J. (1992b). *Research Issues in Flexible Computing: Two Presentations in Japan* (Report No. CS-92-172). Knoxville TN: University of Tennessee, Knoxville, Computer Science Department.

MacLennan, B. J. (in press-a). Characteristics of connectionist knowledge representation. *Information Sciences*, to appear.

MacLennan, B. J. (in press-b). Continuous symbol systems: The logic of connectionism. In: D. S. Levine and M. Aparicio IV (Eds.), *Neural Networks for Knowledge Representation and Inference.* Hillsdale NJ: Lawrence Erlbaum.

MacLennan, B. J. (submitted-a). Information processing in the dendritic net.

MacLennan, B. J. (submitted-b). Visualizing the possibilities (review of Johnson-Laird & Byrne 1991).

MacLennan, B. J. (submitted-c). Grounding analog computers (commentary on Harnad in press).

MacLennan, B. J., & Burghardt, G. M. (submitted). Synthetic ethology and the evolution of cooperative communication.

MacLennan, B. J., & Pribram, K. H. (in preparation). Neural computation without sigmoids.

Nemytskii, V. V., & Stepanov, V. V. (1989). *Qualitative theory of differential equations.* New York NY: Dover; also (1960) Princeton NJ: Princeton University Press.

McCulloch, W.S., and Pitts, W. (1943). A logical calculus of the ideas immanent in nervous activity. *Bulletin of Mathematical Biophysics*, **5**: 115–133.

Pattison, T. R. (1992). Relaxation network for Gabor image decomposition. *Biological Cybernetics*, **67**: 97–102.

Poggio, T., & Torre, V. (1981). A theory of synaptic interactions. In: W. E. Reichardt & T. Poggio (Eds.), *Theoretical approaches in neurobiology* (pp. 28–38). Cambridge MA: MIT Press.

Pollack, J. B. (1987). *On connectionist models of natural language processing* (Ph.D. dissertation). Urbana IL: University of Illinois; also report

MCCS-87-100, Las Cruces NM: New Mexico State University, Computing Research Laboratory.

Pollen, D., & Ronner, S. (1981). Phase relationships between adjacent simple cells in the visual cortex. *Science*, **212**: 1409–1411.

Pour-El, M. B., & Richards, I. (1979). A computable ordinary differential equation which possesses no computable solution. *Annals of Mathematical Logic*, **17**: 61–90.

Pour-El, M. B., & Richards, I. (1981). The wave equation with computable initial data such that its unique solution is not computable. *Advances in Mathematics*, **39**, 215–239.

Pour-El, M. B., & Richards, I. (1982). Noncomputability in models of physical phenomena. *International Journal of Theoretical Physics*, **21**: 553–555.

Pribram, K. H. (1991). *Brain and perception: Holonomy and structure in figural processing.* Hillsdale NJ: Lawrence Erlbaum.

Reichardt, W. E., & Poggio, T., (Eds.), *Theoretical approaches in neurobiology.* Cambridge MA: MIT Press.

Schwartz, E. L. (1977). Spatial mapping in the primate sensory projection: Analytic structures and relevance to perception. *Biological Cybernetics*, **25**: 181–194.

Scott, D. S. (1970). Outline of a mathematical theory of computation. In: *Proceedings of the Fourth Annual Princeton Conference on Information Sciences and Systems* (pp. 160–176). Princeton NJ: Princeton University, Department of Electrical Engineering.

Scott, D. S. (1971). The lattice of flow diagrams. In: E. Engeler (Ed.), *Symposium on the Semantics of Algorithmic Languages* (pp. 311–366). Berlin: Springer-Verlag.

Scott, D. S. (1973). Lattice-theoretic models for various type-free calculi. In: P. Suppes, L. Henkin, A. Joja & G. C. Moisil (Eds.), *Logic, Methodology and Philosophy of Science IV* (pp. 157–187). Amsterdam NL: North-Holland.

Scott, D. S., & Strachey, C. (1971). Towards a mathematical semantics for computer languages. In: J. Fox (Ed.), *Proceedings of the Symposium on Computers and Automata* (pp. 19–46). New York NY: Polytechnic Institute of Brooklyn Press.

Shepherd, G. M. (1972). The neuron doctrine: A revision of functional concepts. *Yale Journal of Biology and Medicine*, **45**: 584–599.

Shepherd, G. M. (1978). Microcircuits in the nervous system. *Scientific American*, **238**: 92–103.

Shepherd, G. M. (1988). *Neurobiology*, second edition. New York NY: Oxford University Press.

Shepherd, G. M. (Ed.). (1990a). *The synaptic organization of the brain*, third edition. New York NY: Oxford University Press.

Shepherd, G. M. (1990b). The significance of real neuron architectures for neural network simulations. In: E. L. Schwartz (Ed.), *Computational Neuroscience* (pp. 82–96). Cambridge MA: MIT Press.

Stannett, Mike (1990). X-machines and the halting problem: Building a super-Turing machine. *Formal Aspects of Computing*, **2**: 331–341.

Stork, D. G., & Wilson, H. R. (1990). Do Gabor functions provide appropriate descriptions of visual cortical receptive fields? *Journal of the Optical Society of America A*, **7**: 1362–1373.

Wolpert, D. H., & MacLennan, B. J. (submitted). A computationally universal field computer which is purely linear.

Chapter 8

Analog VLSI Network Models, Cortical Linking Neural Network Models, and Quantum Holographic Neural Technology

Walter Schempp

Dedicated to the memory of
Karl S. Lashley
whose intuition anticipated neural holography, and
Karl H. Pribram
whose experimental and theoretical work
realized that intuition

Abstract

Quantum neural holography is implemented in a program which bridges the gap between neurophysiology and models of neural network engineering. The thrust of the program is to describe mathematically the neurodynamical functional connectivity of analog association among stimulus-evoked coherent neural wavelets. It represents the basic function of cortical neural network models. Quantum neural holography represents a fundamental change from the standard connectionist models used in Artificial Neural Network (ANN) theory in that it reconciles the linear and highly nonlinear dynamical systems aspect of neurodynamics. A quantum geometry underlying ANNs is needed to explain the local-global duality of adaptive signal processing going on within cortical neural network models. In addition, deterministic chaotic activity patterns and synaptic plasticity must be accounted for if the modelling is used for learning.

To initially realize such a model, the computational neuroanatomy of the retina is utilized. The retina forms a multilayered precortical perceptual transducer which collects and preprocesses the information that reaches the visual cortex. To emulate biophysical neural network computation by the analog VLSI implementation technology, an analog model of the first stages of retinal processing has been constructed on a single silicon chip by CMOS VLSI circuitry and applied to machine vision. The purpose of this paper is to study the exactly solvable hexagonal resistive networks which model the horizontal cell layer of the retina. An outlook to free-space multilayer architectures of hybrid optoelectronic interconnection network models is also given. It is shown that the parallel shift register stage used in the horizontal and vertical scanner of the silicon retina implementation is in correspondence to the S-SEED technology in the hybrid optoelectronic implementation of interconnection network models. Specifically, analog VLSI networks are considered. These networks are implemented by dynamical holographic interconnects using analog synaptic weights.

Contents

ANDREAE VESALII· 755
DE CORPORIS HVMANI FABRICA LIBER
SEPTIMVS, CEREBRO PRINCIPIS ANIMALIS'QVE
facultatum sedi, & sensuum organis dedicatus: moxq; in initio omnes
propemodum ipsius figuras, uti & duo proximè praece-
dentes libri, commonstrans.

PRIMA SEPTIMI LIBRI
FIGURA

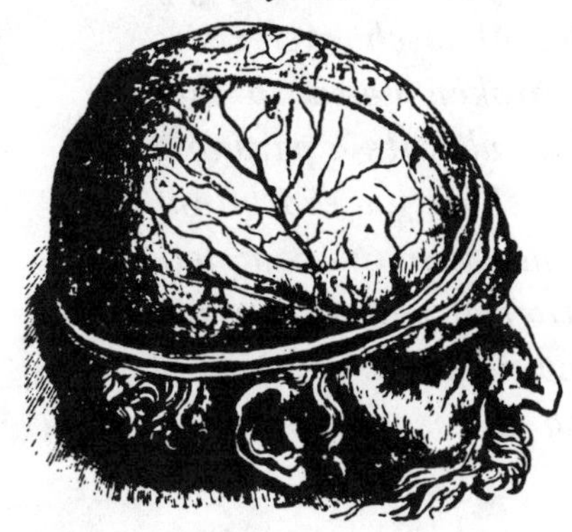

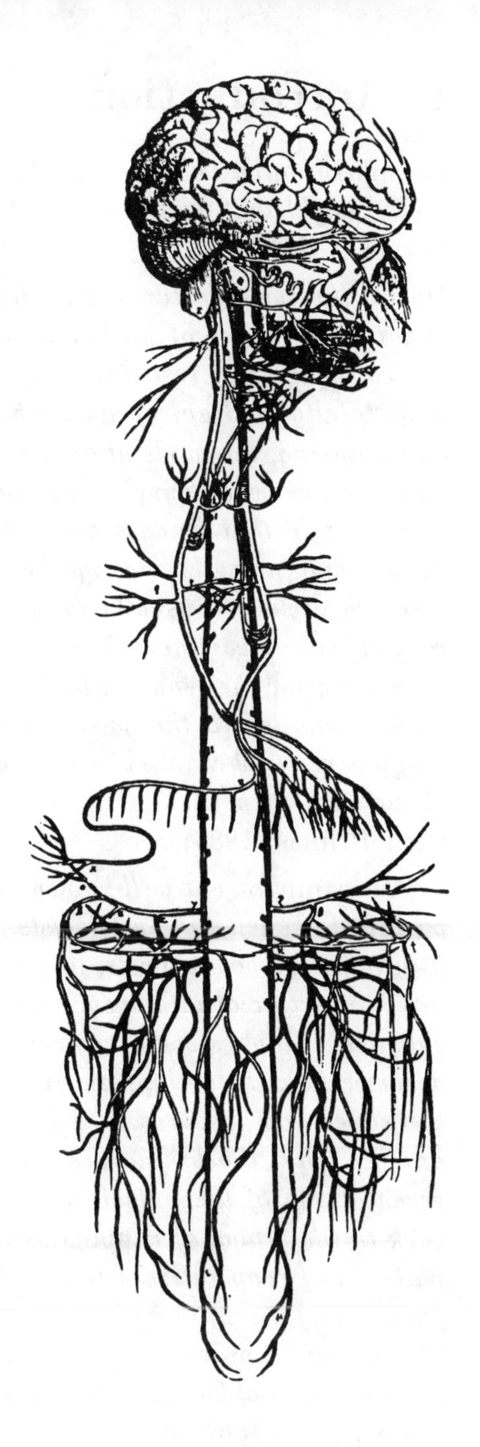

The picture of the human brain and nervous system on the title page was taken from Andreas Vesalius' *De humani corpora fabrica*, published in Basel in 1543. Vesalius (born in 1514 in Brussels, died in 1564 on a trip to Jerusalem) was Professor of Anatomy in Padua and personal physician to Karl V and Philipp II. His large illustrated volumes, based on extensive dissection, gave medicine an enduring anatomical foundation.

Reproduced with kind permission of the Städel'sche Kunstinstitut in Frankfurt am Main, for which we cordially thank Dr. Margret Stuffmann

1 Introduction

Formalism often is viewed as standing on its own, without regard for applications insight that breathes life into it.
Carver A. Mead (1989)

One of the worst features of modern science is the high degree of specialization and the exclusion of all historical and philosophical aspects. It is bad that the contemporary research programs force so many researchers in one area to be totally ignorant of most other areas. The ways of thinking, experiencing and behaving, the mode of activity exhibited by contemporary science strikingly reminds one what Shapiro *has called the paranoid style. It is characteristic of this style that bridges between related problems are broken down so that things remain neatly and rigidly separated. Scientists who cultivate a paranoid research style are usually extremely acute and intense, show an exorbitant respect for compartmentalizations and computers, and firmly demand complete autonomy for their narrowly fixed ideas ... The separation of philosophy and science has led to the so-called realistic world view and to the blindness of many experts who are entirely unaware of the abstracting and isolating nature of modern science.*
Hans Primas (1983)

To paraphrase a well-known political aphorism, the brain is much too important to be left to physiologists. There are numerous psychiatrists, cognitive psychologists, behaviorists, linguists, philosophers, anthropologists, and proponents of artificial intelligence who describe what the brain does; and there are chemists, biophysicists, zoologists, embryologists, and neuroanatomists who describe how it develops and what it is made of. The task of physiologists is to deduce how it works. ... There appears to be consensus among those who analyze what the brain does that one of its main functions is to make representations of the outside world. This idea in various forms can be traced back to the school of Hippocrates. ... *Complex information is encoded in the patterns of cooperative activity of many neurons, and the meaning is derived from transformation and combinations of previous input. I will call this form of representation an image as distinct from a signal. Examples are the direct-current fields of* Köhler, *the "excitational cluster" of* Horridge, *the "statistical ensemble" of* John, *and the neural holographic image of* Pribram.
Walter J. Freeman (1981)

The Central Nervous System (CNS) is usually considered as an organ in which neurons actively respond to specific stimuli from the external environment, and other neurons control muscles acting upon the environment. The link between the two is formed by a highly efficient spatio-temporal neural network within which an adaptive signal processing goes on, involving memory storage and information retrieval. Adaptability means the ability of a spatio-temporal neural network architecture to actively respond to the stimuli originating from complex-valued tempered distributions T representing physical objects in the environment in which the network is embedded in such a way that network performance is improved. This view of stimulus-evoked neuron responses, however, is not adequately characterized as a passive reaction of neurons to stimuli. It implicitly presupposes the knowledge of an internal sensory order ([95, 9]) and an internally generated deterministic chaotic activity pattern ([88]) of perceptual coding. In this view, the role of neurodynamical activity is to create in an adaptive way an internal sensory representation of individual situations occurring in the environment that serves to control motor output.

How the CNS generates internal sensory representations of its external environment has fascinated scientists and philosophers ever since mankind began to reflect on its own nature. The twentieth century saw the emergence of various localization theories which assigned specific cortical functions to specific cytoarchitectonically defined areas of the cortex cerebri. At the same time Lashley put forward a holistic point of view. Lashley considered the whole brain as a neurodynamical functional unit designed for cooperative processing.

Pribram brought these two aspects of brain function together by showing which brain functions are localized and which are distributed ([60]). The search for the engram has focussed on the lowest level of description, namely, to the elementary components of the cortical circuitry: molecules, synapses and neurons, excluding neuroglial cells. This approach has its roots in the nanobiology of the dendritic trees. At the system theoretic level of present-day neuroscience, however, the fundamental problem is to mathematically describe the internal sensory order which determines adaptive signal processing and to relate this order to synaptic plasticity modelled as deterministic chaotic activity patterns ([19, 55]). The internal sensory order and the internally generated deterministic chaotic activity patterns design the internal sensory representation of the CNS.

Due to the progress made in simultaneous, multiple-channel, extracellular recording techniques and in vivo real-time photonic sensor methods in conjunction with large-scale data processing, it is only in the past few decades that speculations on the internal sensory order of perceptual coding could be replaced by precise and experimentally testable neural network hypotheses. The fundamentals of these various mathematical models of spatio-temporal neural networks and the technological implementations of their neurodynamical functional organizations culminated in the idea that phenomenal consciousness is coordinate with quantum neurodynamical processes. Thus quantum mechanics seems to be a much richer theory than initially expected. Yet most of the models remained untested at the level of neurophysiology and unimplemented at the level of quantum holographic neural technology because not enough is presently known about the role played by quantum mechanical coherent states for the internal semantic representation of the external environment.

A universal feature of the neuroanatomical organization of the vertebrate sensory system is that the visual, auditory, somatosensory, and olfactory systems are organized according to an internal sensory order in terms of spatial projections of a peripheral receptor multi-input array to higher processing sites of the cortex cerebri. According to computational neuroanatomy, cerebral cortices are two-dimensional layers of neurons that are vertically segregated into laminae constituting an architecture which can be regarded a type of multi-input/multi-output system. The cerebral cortex receives two classes of inputs:

(i) Specific afferents from sense organs are relayed through specific thalamic nuclei before reaching the primary cortical projection areas. For instance, visual afferents are transmitted through the lateral geniculate nucleus to area 17 of the occipital lobe, auditory signals are transmitted through the medial geniculate nucleus to the supratemporal plane, somatosensory information is transmitted via the nucleus ventralis posterolateralis to the postcentral gyrus.

(ii) Non-specific afferents reach the cortex from the mesencephalic reticular formation. The reticular formation is the term applied to a network of neurons and nerve fibers extending from the caudal medulla to the dienecephalon. A common feature of all of these neurons is that they form a widely distributed network of synaptic contacts. The reticular formation is organized into different nuclei with specific afferent and efferent connections. It is co-innervated via axon collaterals from all sensory afferents ascending from the periphery to the cerebral cortex. Moreover, it receives afferents from the cortex, the basal ganglia, and the cerebellum. The mesencephalic and the dienecephalic reticular formation projects rostrally to the cerebral cortex and influences the cortical processing of specific sensory afferents. The pathways comprise the ascending reticular activating system which is known to play an essential role in arousal, wakefulness, and attention. There is a second site where the reticular formation influences the processing of primary afferents: the thalamic relay nuclei. The nucleus reticularis thalami, a thin sheet of neurons, surrounds the dorsal thalamus and inhibits the thalamic relay nuclei. Its control function is, in turn, affected by collaterals of thalamo-cortical pathways, by colloterals from cortico-thalamic projections and by inhibitory afferents from the mesencephalic reticular formation. For review see [65].

Within the cerebral cortex, primary visual, auditory, and somatosensory fields each have reciprocal connections with adjacent unimodal association areas which, in turn, project to contiguous secondary unimodal association fields. These unimodal associated sensory fields were discovered in primates by Pribram in the late 1940's and early 1950's. See [56, 57, 58] for review. Their function is to establish the sensory order in terms of invariances among iterations of sensory input. In vision, this leads to the perception of objects and subsequently their classification ([59, 61, 64, 63]). The unimodal association areas are, in turn, reciprocally connected to a number of polymodal sensory areas lying in the parietal, temporal, and frontal lobes. Their function is described as a crossmodal association and synthesis. The polymodal association areas project to the inferior parietal lobe which has been termed a supramodal area. Polymodal and supramodal regions have connections to the limbic system. These connections provide the anatomical substrate by which motivational states influence cortical processing of sensory stimuli ([23]).

The neuroanatomical architecture suggests that information from different layers can be combined in a very systematic way. Unlike conventional computer hardware, however, neural circuitry ([1]) though to some extent hardwired, is continually modified by short and long range lateral local circuit connectivity. In addition, extraneuronal glial signaling ([13, 27]) forces one to abandon the neuron doctrine which is currently the basis of the standard connectionist models in artificial neural system theory. Massive parallelism and reciprocity are a prevailing principle of cortical connectivity.

Among the human senses, vision ranks high in its importance for the individual. Actually a major part ($> 75\%$) of cortical activities are concerned with visual processing. A third of the human cerebral cortex is given over to the computations underlying the perception of depth, colour, motion, and visual recognition. At the level of the striate cortex, neurons respond to oriented, elongated stimuli with well-defined velocity, direction of movement, binocular disparity, ocular dominance, and color.

To understand the basic rules of biological vision, it is helpful, therefore, to study the receptotopic structure of vertebrate retina as an outpost of the cortex cerebri. The retina forms not only a multi-input pixel array of detectors sensitive to single photons but it acts also as a neural preprocessor for computing weighted spatio-temporal averages and segregating objects of visual scenes with overlapping contours from each other and from background. Higher levels of retinal functions include the detection of oriented light-intensity edges, edge enhancement, adaption and gain control, spatial-frequency matched filtering, tracking novelty filtering, time series analysis, and statistical optimization. All of this is accomplished without the generation of nerve inpulses. Retinal processing proceeds by virtue of the interactions among hyperpolarizations and depolarizations which do not achieve the threshold for impulse propagation until the retinal ganglion cell layer is reached. At the ganglion cell layer the propagation of nerve impulses allows communication via the optic nerve to the various visually active structures in the brain.

The tangential network in the retina is a flat mesh of dense processes that are highly interconnected by resistive gap junctions. Any given cell is locally and globally connected with many others, and there is a great deal of overlap among interconnected cells. Therefore the horizontal layer of the retinal architecture may serve as a biological paradigm of the parallel computations that can be performed by modular self-adaptive Artificial Neural Network (ANN) models and their various analog and digital implementations.

Information processing in the cerebral cortical layers may be considered as pattern recognition. According to computational neuroanatomy, the basic principle of ANN models designed for pattern recognition and completion can be formulated as follows: Define a hierarchical multilayer geometry to compute the analog stimulus interaction of the ANN as weighted spatio-temporal

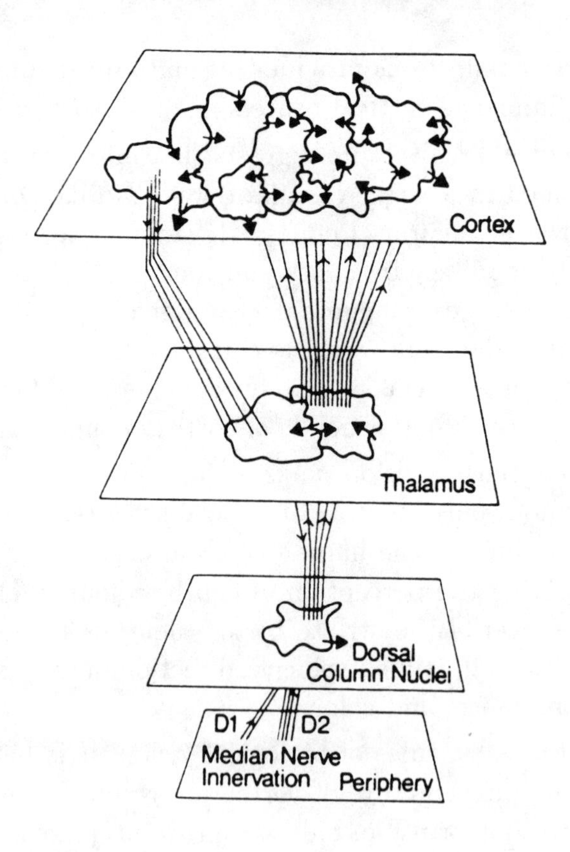

Figure 1: A cortical multilayer architecture

averages over the layers. In this way the difficulties that originate from using only the levels of activity in individual neurons to encode the information will be avoided and a cooperative organization form of neural collectives arises. Presently there are three main categories of architectures available for these neural computations:

1. Analog electronic architectures computing averages by CMOS VLSI circuitry,

2. Analog photonic architectures recording interference patterns of coherent wavelets,

3. Hybrid digital-optoelectronic architectures based on free-space photonic processing.

ANNs are fascinating objects where many different structures meet with highly interesting applications in machine vision and robotics. The mathematical modeling of cortical encoding procedures ([39, 63, 66, 79, 90]) and their practical implementations by interconnection network models, however, is just at the beginning. It is one of the purposes of this paper to focus on the analog VLSI implementations of ANNs and to give an outlook to the hybrid optoelectronic implementation technology.

The hybrid implementations of digital-optical processing (HyDOP) systems use free-space photonics for dynamical interconnect and digital electronics for routing and control. The photonic devices and architecture provide high, effective computational rates by incorporating massive parallelism while the digital electronic components enhance the precision and dynamic range of the HyDOP system. The trade-off between the processing speed and the dynamic range of the system is fundamental to the design of HyDOPs. Typical HyDOP architectures use a small number of components that can be packaged in desktop-size units. Power requirements usually are less than 60 W, computational rates vary from 500 giga-operations per second to about 500 tera-operations per second. Photon shot noise can be minimized by time integration on the photosensor until it is saturated. At this point the photosensor can be dumped to a digital accumulation buffer for further integration, resulting in an improvement in output dynamical range. Because HyDOPs are not general-purpose computers, they offer as neurocomputer architectures additional economy by replacing complex software with relatively simple and robust hardware. In particular they offer an economic alternative to large supercomputing systems.

A hybrid optoelectronic recording of stationary interference patterns of stimulus interaction coherent neural wavelets which reflect cerebral cortex activities with a contribution from the glia cells [13] has been described in the papers [33, 27]. The minute changes in the amount of light reflected from the exposed brain are detected by a charge-coupled device (CCD) camera. A CCD array consists of an array of gates laid over a suitably doped silicon substrate. Incident photons create electron hole pairs, and the photoelectrons collect in the potential wells defined by the gate electrodes. This two-dimensional array of potential wells (pixels) is the parallel register. Phase switching controls the readout process of the CCD array. By switching the voltage on these electrodes, the charge accumulated in the potential wells can be shuffled sequentially to a serial register and then to an output node that forms the input of a low-noise preamplifier circuit ([5]). The amount of reflected light given off during rest is subtracted from the amount produced during an activity, such as talking. This difference is computer enhanced to provide the high-resolution images displayed by Figures 2, 3. In this way, complementary information is obtained that is hard or impossible to obtain with microelectrode techniques.

2 Linearity

Although a cell's response function is in general nonlinear, visual neurophysiologists have found that for many cells, a linear summation approximation is appropriate.
Ralph Linsker (1988)

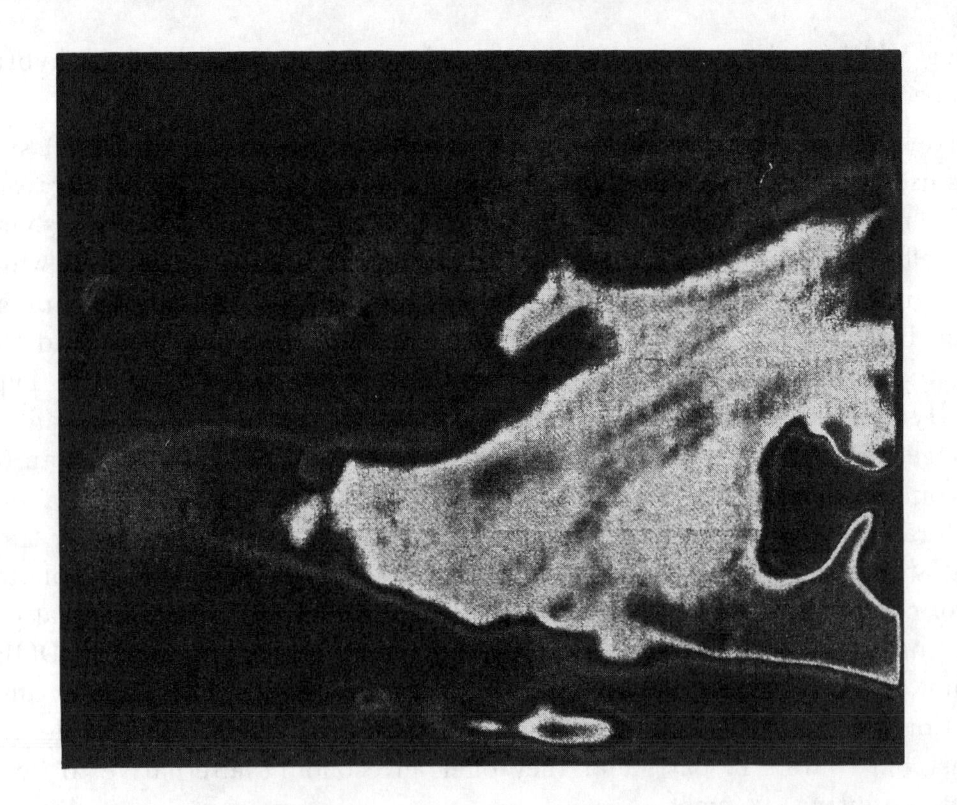

Figure 2: Optical image of brain obtained during tongue movement

Figure 3: Optical image of epileptiform activity in stimulated area of the brain

The single most important principle in the analysis of electrical circuits with components of linear characteristics is the principle of linear superposition. Provided there exists a reference value for voltages, the ground to which all node potentials revert when all sources are reduced to zero, it can be formulated as follows:

Linear Superposition Principle. *For any network containing resistors and voltage sources, the solution for the network is the solution for the network in response to each voltage source individually, with all the other voltage sources reduced to zero.*

Thus the solution for the network determining the voltage at every node and the current through every resistor and including the effects of all voltage sources is the sum of the solutions for the individual voltage sources.

To maintain the linear superposition principle for certain categories of ANNs with components of nonlinear characteristics, linearization can be performed by introducing an infinite number of variables. In particular, an application of the method of covering linearization provides exactly solvable interconnection network models ([78]). Because the procedure of covering linearization preserves the relative phase of coherent wavelet responses, it avoids the superposition catastrophe of cortical encoding ([20, 85, 86]). The recently developed symmetric self electro-optic-effect device (S-SEED) technology ([54, 12]) for ANN implementation which integrates photosensors and quantum-well modulators with transistor circuits has the capability to provide both optical inputs and outputs for VLSI circuitry. Most of the work on S-SEEDs has concentrated on devices for digital HyDOP applications. The devices, however, have also analog modes to implement two-port model neurons. Their greatest strength is that changing states is a function of the relative phase and not of the absolute intensity of the two input beams so that one light beam forms the reference for the other one. The optical inputs and outputs are based on quantum-well absorptive structures consisting of many very thin layers of two different semiconductor materials. The hybrid optoelectronic architectures based on processing arrays of S-SEEDs offer a solution for high-performance free-space digital photonic systems that are highly connection-intensive. The routing within the interconnection network architecture can be all optically controlled by dynamically combining S-SEED two-port model neuron arrays via an amacrine beam-steering module with planar arrays ([41]) of integrated, individually addressed, mutually coherent, surface-emitting micro-laser diodes (SELDAs) to generate focal-plane structures that are photonically and competitively coupled in HyDOPs with local electronics processing cells.

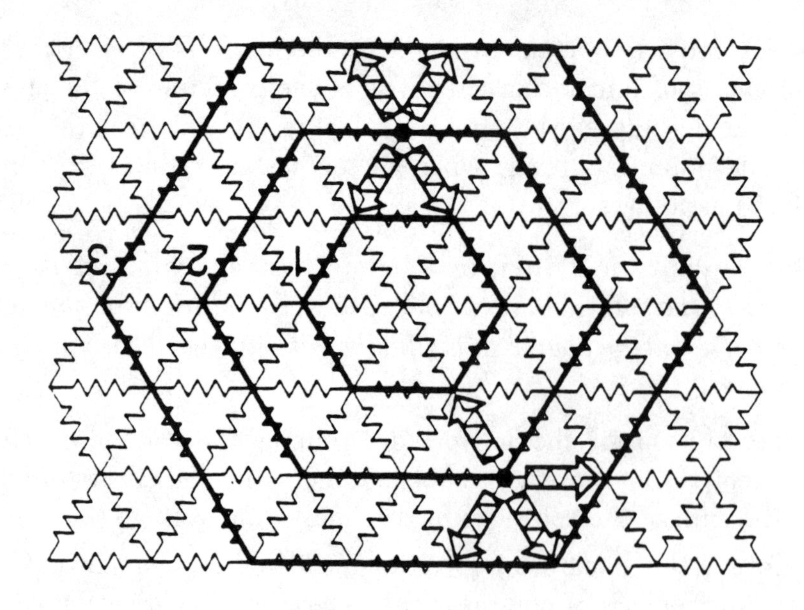

Figure 4: Concentric hexagons in a triangular resistive network

3 Nonlinearity

Signal transmission with its attendant gain control necessitates the introduction of nonlinearities. But pulse to wave conversion at synapses once more linearizes the system. Thus the unconstrained dendritic computational microprocess is essentially linear.
Karl H. Pribram (1991)

Real-time, small, power-lean and robust analog computers are making a limited comeback in the form of highly dedicated, smart visionchips.
Christof Koch (1992)

One may well ask why execute vision algorithms on programmable digital computers when the signals themselves are self-adaptive wavelets and therefore analog signals which allow resonance linking by phase coherence? Indeed, the quantum neurodynamical functional connectivity model of analog stimulus-response association by coherent neural wavelets has recently come to the forefront of attention with the experimental discovery by several labs of cooperatively synchronized neural activity in the visual cortex ([18, 87]). Why not exploit the mature electronics technology presently available to implement analog special purpose vision systems?

In analog VLSI implementation technology, discrete two-dimensional resistive networks are arranged in a regular array by interconnection of nearest neighbors. The retina is modeled by a triangular network of nearest neighbor couplings. Each node is connected with his 6 neighbors by a resistance R.

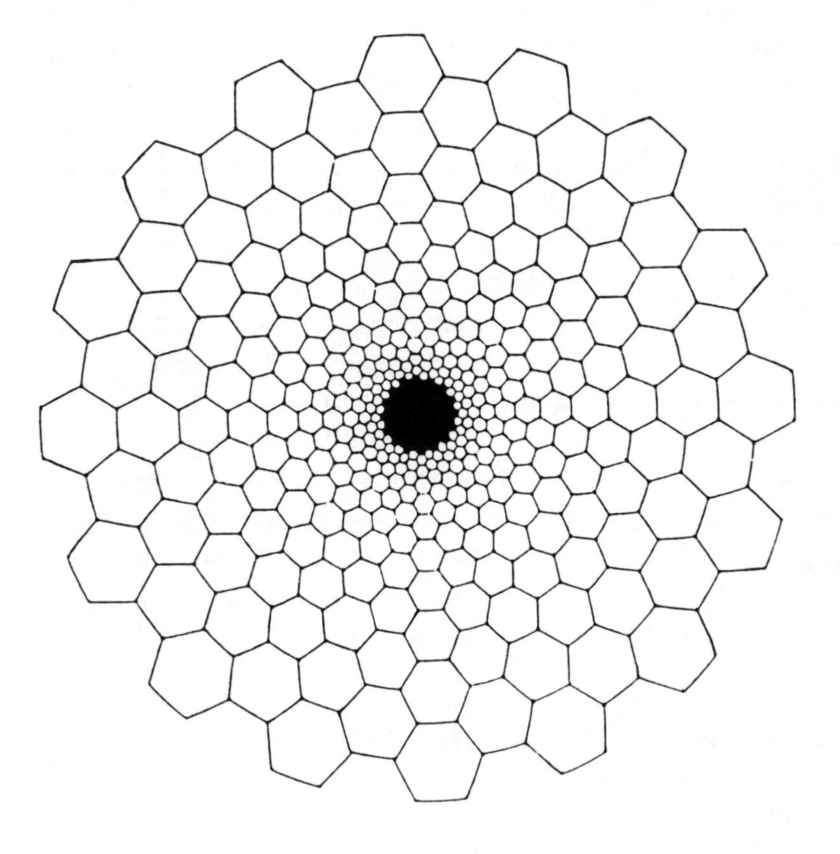

Figure 5: An idealized retina

Moreover, each node is connected to ground which acts as a reference, by a conductance G. Figure 4 displays the hexagonal resistive network. Note that the hexagonal lattice is dual to the triangular lattice.

The silicon retina implemented by complementary metal-oxide-silicon (CMOS) VLSI technology ([2, 51, 52, 53, 37, 45]) yields results remarkably similar to those obtained from the biological paradigm. A photoreceptor whose output voltage is proportional to the logarithm of the incoming light intensity is coupled via the conductance G to drive the resistive network specified above. The output of the silicon chip is proportional to the voltage difference between the logarithmic photoreceptor circuit and the network. Thus the silicon retina as a whole chip models the layer of photoreceptors, the outer-plexiform layer of horizontal cells located just below the photoreceptors, and the layer of bipolar cells of the mammalian retina. The retinal ganglion cell layer forms the multi-output layer of the retina.

Figure 5 displays an idealized retina which represents in the radial direction a logarithmically deformed version of the hexagonal resistive network. According to computational neuroanatomy, the deformation is performed by a log-polar transformation which improves pattern-recognition systems by making them less sensitive to the rotation and scaling of their targets ([82]).

It is often argued that conversion from photonics to electronics and back to photonics is an inefficient procedure. It usually is. The inefficiencies often result, however, from the fact that the hybrid system is not integrated. It is therefore very important that synthetic perceptual systems can be implemented by analog VLSI technology. The retinal image of a visual scene consists of a two-dimensional continuous distribution of grey levels, whereas the retina chip consists of an array of pixels, and a scanning arrangement for reading-out the results of retinal computing. The output of any pixel can be accessed through the scanner, which is made up of a vertical scan register and a horizontal scan register along the sides of the chip. Each scan register stage has 1-bit of shift register, with the associated signal-selection circuits. The main pixel array is made up of alternating rows of rectangular tiles arranged to form a hexagonal pattern. The scanner along the vertical side allows any row of pixels to be selected, the scanner along the horizontal side allows the output current of any selected pixel to be gated onto the output line where it is sensed by the offchip current-sensing amplifier.

4 Circular Approximation

With respect to sensory driven aspects of perception the models point to the importance of successive iterations of the process.
Karl H. Pribram (1991)

When considering the circular approximation of the retinal ANN, a center in the network specified in §3 and displayed by Figure 4 supra has been fixed. It is assumed that the voltage is constant around the perimeters of concentric hexagons ([21]). The concentric hexagon n contains $6n$ nodes from the pixel array on its perimeter. Six of these nodes are vertices of the hexagon n, and the remaining $6(n-1)$ ones are located along its edges. Each of the 6 vertex nodes makes 3 outside connections, i.e., 3 connections to hexagon $n+1$, while each of the other $6(n-1)$ nodes makes only 2 connections.

The total number of connections between the concentric hexagons n and $n+1$ is therefore $12n+6$. Since each link in the triangular mesh corresponds to a resistance R, the impedance between the two neighboring hexagons n and $n+1$ is

$$\frac{R}{12n+6}.$$

Similarly, the impedance connecting hexagon n to hexagon $n-1$ is

$$\frac{R}{12n-6}.$$

Moreover, there are equal conductances from each node to ground, making a net admittance of

$$6nG$$

from hexagon n to ground.

Introduce the parameter $a = RG$. By hypothesis, the potential, say V_n, is constant along hexagon n. Kirchhoff's current law then yields the finite-difference equation for the steady-state node voltage:

$$(2n+1)V_{n+1} - n(4+a)V_n + (2n-1)V_{n-1} = 0$$

The boundary conditions of the difference equation are

$$\begin{cases} V_0 \text{ is given,} \\ V_n \text{ is bounded as } n \to \infty. \end{cases}$$

A global analysis of the voltages V_n for the circular approximation is performed by the generating function

$$F(z) = \sum_{n \geq 1} V_n z^n, \quad z \in \mathbf{C}.$$

It follows from elementary complex function theory that F is a holomorphic function on the open unit disc $|z| < 1$ of the complex plane $\mathbf{C}$. In the engineering terminology, the function F forms the z-transform of the node voltages $(V_n)_{n \geq 1}$. It satisfies the first-order inhomogeneous linear differential equation $(' = \mathrm{d}/\mathrm{d}z)$

$$2\left(z^2 - (2+\frac{a}{2})z + 1\right) F'(z) + (z - \frac{1}{z})F(z) = V_1 - zV_0.$$

The right hand side includes the unknown voltage V_1. The problem is to compute V_1 in terms of V_0 in order to apply the three-term-recurrence for the circular approximation to calculate the node voltages $(V_n)_{n \geq 1}$ step-by-step.

The factorization of the quadratic term reads

$$Q(z) = z^2 - (2+\frac{a}{2})z + 1 = (z - r_+)(z - r_-)$$

where

$$r_- = 1 - \frac{2}{1+\sqrt{1+8L^2}}, \qquad L = \frac{1}{\sqrt{a}} \geq 0$$

so that

$$0 \leq r_- \leq 1, \quad r_+ r_- = 1, \quad r_+ \geq 1.$$

The homogeneous linear differential equation takes the form

$$2Q(z)\Phi'(z) + (z - \frac{1}{z})\Phi(z) = 0.$$

The solution of the homogeneous equation

$$\Phi(z) = \sqrt{\frac{z}{|Q(z)|}}$$

is singular at $z = r_-$. The ansatz

$$F(z) = \Phi(z) f(z)$$

gives

$$2Q(z)\Phi(z)f'(z) = V_1 - zV_0$$

and

$$\begin{cases} f(z) = \dfrac{1}{2} \displaystyle\int_0^z \text{sign } Q(\zeta) \frac{V_1 - \zeta V_0}{\sqrt{\zeta |Q(\zeta)|}} \, \mathrm{d}\zeta \\ f(r_-) = 0 \end{cases}$$

for real values of z. Thus

$$V_1 \int_0^{r_-} \frac{1}{\sqrt{\xi Q(\xi)}} \, \mathrm{d}\xi = V_0 \int_0^{r_-} \frac{\xi}{\sqrt{\xi Q(\xi)}} \, \mathrm{d}\xi$$

with singularities at $z = 0$ and $z = r_-$. In the next step we perform the singularities absorbing substitution

$$\xi = r_- \sin^2 \Theta.$$

Hence,

$$\frac{V_1}{V_0} = r_+ \left(1 - \frac{E(r_-^2)}{K(r_-^2)}\right)$$

where K, E are the complete elliptic integrals of the first and second kind, respectively,

$$\begin{cases} K(r_-^2) = \displaystyle\int_0^{\pi/2} \frac{1}{\sqrt{1 - r_-^2 \sin^2 \Theta}} \, \mathrm{d}\Theta, \\ E(r_-^2) = \displaystyle\int_0^{\pi/2} \sqrt{1 - r_-^2 \sin^2 \Theta} \, \mathrm{d}\Theta. \end{cases}$$

The elliptic integrals for the parameter value r_-^2 can be evaluated by the algorithm of the arithmetic-geometric mean. Set

$$a_0 = 1 \qquad b_0 = \cos r_-^2 \qquad c_0 = \sin r_-^2$$

$$a_j = \tfrac{1}{2}(a_{j-1} + b_{j-1}) \qquad b_j = \sqrt{a_{j-1} b_{j-1}} \qquad c_j = \tfrac{1}{2}(a_{j-1} - b_{j-1})$$

Starting from the product $a_{j-1}b_{j-1}$, the number b_j of the jth iteration loop can be computed by an iteration subloop of Newton linearizations:

$$b_{jk} = \frac{1}{2}\left(b_{jk-1} + \frac{a_{j-1} b_{j-1}}{b_{jk-1}}\right) \quad k \geq 1$$

The algorithm of successive linearizations corresponds to the retinal strategy of superposing average computations in a multilayer architecture. If we have $c_N \approx 0$ in the Nth step of the algorithm, $N \geq 1$, then

$$\begin{cases} K(r_-^2) = \dfrac{\pi}{2a_N}, \\ E(r_-^2) = K(r_-^2)\left(1 - \frac{1}{2}\sum\limits_{0 \leq j \leq N} 2^j c_j^2\right). \end{cases}$$

Thus in the circular approximation, the node voltages $(V_n)_{n \geq 1}$ are obtained by an algorithm of successive averaging. The asymptotic analysis of the node voltages is based on the ansatz with a constant V

$$V_n \sim V\frac{r_-^n}{\sqrt{n}} \quad \text{as } n \to \infty.$$

Now V can be expressed in terms of elliptic integrals by a procedure of singularities absorbing substitution similar to the treatment of V_1 above:

$$V = \frac{1}{\sqrt{\pi(1-r^2)}}\left(V_0 E(1-r_-^2) - r_- V_1 K(1-r_-^2)\right)$$

An application of the Legendre relation yields

$$V = \frac{V_0}{2K(r_-^2)}\sqrt{\frac{\pi}{1-r_-^2}}$$

where, as before, r_- denotes the zero of Q in the interval $[0, 1]$. Recall that r_- depends on the free parameter $a = RG$ in the three-term-recurrence.

Two-dimensional networks compute a spatial average that is a nearly ideal way to derive a reference with which local signals can be compared. If currents are injected at many nodes, the network performs an automatic weighted average: the farther away the inputs are, the less weight they are given. The interconnection density of the silicon system, however, is limited by the total amount of wire required to accomplish the spatial average computation. The hardwiring aspect contributes to the lack of flexibility which forms one of the principal drawbacks of analog CMOS VLSI circuitry. Another drawback is that neurons are not integrated circuits ([40]). However, it is not the existence of a function done by a neural element that cannot, from the point of view of a VLSI system designer, be simulated by electronic components. It is, rather, the neurodynamical functional organization principles which suggest to abandon the technology of smart VLSI visionchips and to look for alternative implementations of biophysical neural network models.

5 Transition to Quantum Neurodynamics of Spatio-Temporal Neural Network Models

My key point is that the cerebral cortex cannot be effectively portrayed as a network of single neurons analogous to transistors. There must exist entities

that transcend the neuron by virtue of widespread synaptic action among neurons. The assembled evidence indicates that macroscopic, cooperative activity does exist in the brain, that it is mediated by synaptic transmission and not by chemical diffusion or electrical fields, and that it participates in operations performed on sensory input to the brain.
Walter J. Freeman (1983)

Bohr *used to say that if you aren't confused by quantum physics, then you haven't really understood it.*
John A. Wheeler (1980)

Biophysical ANN models implemented for pattern recognition purposes by hybrid optoelectronic neural technologies have to transduce by adaptive filter coupling the information carried by photons and detected as photonic bombardments by the retinal receptor multi-input array into the combined phase and amplitude information transmitted by stimulus-evoked coherent neural wavelets. Indeed, several independent lines of experimental evidence concerning the structure of neural information processing to resolve the superposition problem, the constraints of neural signal transmission, and conditions of use-dependent synaptic plasticity lead to the postulate of temporal coding of neural activity, and to the significance of cooperative phase-linked synchrony at a millisecond time scale. Neural signaling is primarily operating by means of electromagnetic transmission. Physically, the theories that as of today ultimately describe electromagnetic signal propagation are quantum mechanics and quantum field theory. It is another purpose of this paper to mathematically describe the basically quantum mechanical transformation from imaging to adaptive signal processing going on in cortical linking neural network models, along with synaptic plasticity. Thus ANN theory opens a *novel* pathway to the world of quantum neurodynamics. This approach which is based on the modeling of highly nonlinear dynamical systems by circle maps is a converse to the current tendency to recast quantum physics in terms of information theory with the goal to include semantics and finally to include phenomenal consciousness into quantum physics.

The Heisenberg geometry underlying the quantum neurodynamical functional connectivity model of analog stimulus-response association by stimulus-evoked coherent neural wavelets corresponds to the computational paradigm of spatio-temporal neural network architectures. It leads to the idea that visual awareness and phenomenal consciousness actually are quantum neurodynamical processes. Unfortunately not enough is presently known about the role played by quantum mechanical coherent states for the internal semantic representation of the external environment. It is known, however, that the transactional interpretation of quantum mechanics ([14]) which includes the von Neumann collapsing of the state vector is an epistemic interpretation. Epistemic interpretations refer to the knowledge of modes of reactions of systems ([9]). The transactional interpretation of quantum mechanics admits an extension to an ontic interpretation of quantum mechanics ([67, 68, 69]).

Notice that the ontic interpretation refers to the objects themselves, independently of any perturbations caused by observers. In this context, the notion of object means the most general ontological expression for entities which need not to be localized in space, and which persist when not perceived, the notion of object means the expression for entities having individuality and properties, and which retain their identity in the course of the time. A combination of both of the interpretations of quantum mechanics expressed by nonlocal wavelet packets and ontic states allow to bridge the gap between syntax and semantics which is of so importance for the controversial discussion of the problem of artificial intelligence ([36]).

6 Temporal Encoding by Coherent Neural Wavelets

Brain function is neither analog nor digital, as these terms are defined for computer usage. Pulse trains that appear to be digital are in fact analog, and sums of dendritic current that appear to be analog are in fact time-segmented by bifurcations into discrete wave packets.
Walter J. Freeman (1991)

In neurobiology, if enough current is injected into the dendritic network, then the neuron will release neurotransmitter from any output synapses it has on its dendrites. Due to the quantal nature of neurotransmitter release and the role of phase coherency in the cortical encoding procedure ([17, 18, 20, 26, 32, 35, 72, 81, 85, 86, 87, 89, 90]), a quantum theoretic approach to self-adaptive wavelets and their modulatory interactions is appropriate. This idea leads to consider L^2 harmonic analysis on the Heisenberg nilpotent Lie group N and the associated Weyl operational calculus as the mathematical fundament of cortical self-organization in the quantum neurodynamical functional connectivity model of analog stimulus-response association by stimulus-evoked coherent neural wavelets. In particular, the dendritic membrane can be identified with a linear metaplectic manifold to explain the basic cortical self-organization principles by the multilayer geometry of the unitary dual of N ([62, 63, 75, 76, 78, 79]). The coadjoint action of N on the planar layers of this multilayer architecture solves the binding problem of synthetic perceptual systems ([81, 85, 86]) by phase coherence. Indeed, each of these planar coadjoint orbits in $\mathrm{Lie}(N)^*$ can be interpreted as a N-homogeneous data page in a stack of layers where N admits a presentation by real unipotent matrices ([75])

$$\begin{pmatrix} 1 & x & z \\ 0 & 1 & \xi \\ 0 & 0 & 1 \end{pmatrix} \quad (x \in \mathbf{R}, \xi \in \mathbf{R}, z \in \mathbf{R}).$$

In the matrices presenting the Heisenberg group N, the entry ξ denotes the

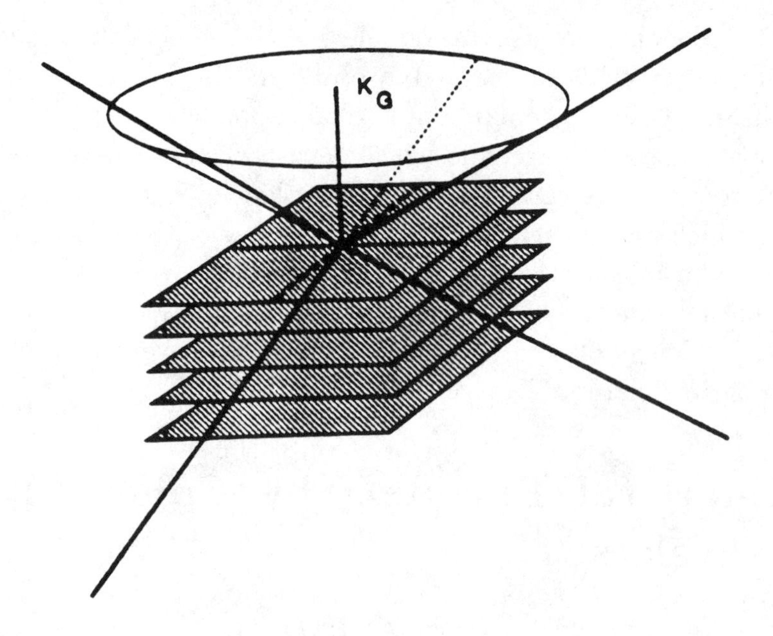

Figure 6: Coadjoint orbits in Lie$(N)^*$

phase shift of the cooperatively synchronized coherent neural wavelets, and the entry x is the dual variable associated to ξ in the phase plane that performs a shift of the temporal coding of neural activity ([52, 51]). Thus the real variable x adjusts the timing in order to achieve cooperative synchronization.

Basic Synchronization-Coherence Principle. *The real variables* (x, ξ) *form a* Fourier *duality pair.*

The preceding principle suggests to combine the pair (x, ξ) of real variables by the complex variable $w = x + i\xi$ and to embed the complex plane $\mathbf{C}$ into N.

Complex Phase Plane Evaluation Principle. *The elements* $w = x + i\xi$ *of the complex phase plane* $\mathbf{C} \hookrightarrow N$ *define phase coherence by the evaluation of cooperative synchrony at phase-locked frequencies* $\nu \neq 0$.

In an associative memory implemented by a cross-linking interconnection ANN, the phase shift ξ encodes the degree of association between coherent stimulus components whereas the amplitude of self-adaptive wavelets encodes the significance of cooperatively synchronized signal components ([72]). The neurodynamical functional connectivity model of analog stimulus-response association by stimulus-evoked coherent neural wavelets forms the fundament of quantum holographic neural technology ([18, 91, 92, 93]).

Because the one-dimensional center C of N is given by the normal subgroup of matrices

$$\begin{pmatrix} 1 & 0 & z \\ 0 & 1 & 0 \\ 0 & 0 & 1 \end{pmatrix} \quad (z \in \mathbf{R}),$$

and the commutator map $N \times N \rightarrow N$ takes values in C, the real Lie group N is nilpotent of step two. Considered as the vertical coordinate, the third entry z gives rise to the central extension

$$0 \rightarrow C \rightarrow N \rightarrow \mathbf{C} \rightarrow 0$$

of the flat phase plane $N/C \cong \mathbf{C}$ with the real horizontal coordinates (x, ξ) of $w \in \mathbf{C}$ under the vector space group structure. Thus N is the universal covering group of the central extension of $\mathbf{C}$ by the circle group $\mathbf{T}$. Under the natural fibration, N forms a principal line bundle over the phase plane $\mathbf{C}$ written

$$\begin{array}{ccc} C & \rightarrow & N \\ & & \downarrow \\ & & \mathbf{C} \end{array} .$$

The vector space dual C^* of C parametrizes the stack of transverse layers (Figure 6) which represent the affine planar coadjoint orbits in $\text{Lie}(N)^*$ associated to the unitary dual of N.

In the SEED technology, the concept of diode-biased SEED (D-SEED) allows to photonically shift the energy levels associated to the planar layers. Moreover, let L now denote the three-dimensional uniform lattice of unipotent matrices with integer entries

$$\begin{pmatrix} 1 & x & z \\ 0 & 1 & \xi \\ 0 & 0 & 1 \end{pmatrix} \quad (x \in \mathbf{Z}, \xi \in \mathbf{Z}, z \in \mathbf{Z}).$$

The stroboscopic lattice L of parallel processes is embedded as a discrete cocompact subgroup into N and the Heisenberg group N projects onto the compact Heisenberg stroboscopic nilmanifold $N \backslash L$ which forms a principal circle bundle over the compact two-dimensional collapsed torus $\mathbf{T}^2$ ([96, 75]). The fiber bundle $N \backslash L$ over the base manifold $\mathbf{T}^2$ gives rise to the diagram

$$\begin{array}{ccc} \mathbf{T} & \rightarrow & N \backslash L \\ & & \downarrow \\ & & \mathbf{T}^2 \end{array} .$$

The decisive step is to consider the compact Heisenberg stroboscopic nilmanifold $N \backslash L$ as the stroboscopically enfolded Heisenberg nilpotent Lie group N. Due to the periodization, the projection $N \rightarrow N \backslash L$ performs a time averaging and induces a parallel shift register action by N on $N \backslash L$. With respect to normalized Lebesgue measure, the complex Hilbert space $L^2(N \backslash L)$ modeled on the compact Heisenberg stroboscopic nilmanifold $N \backslash L$ admits an orthogonal

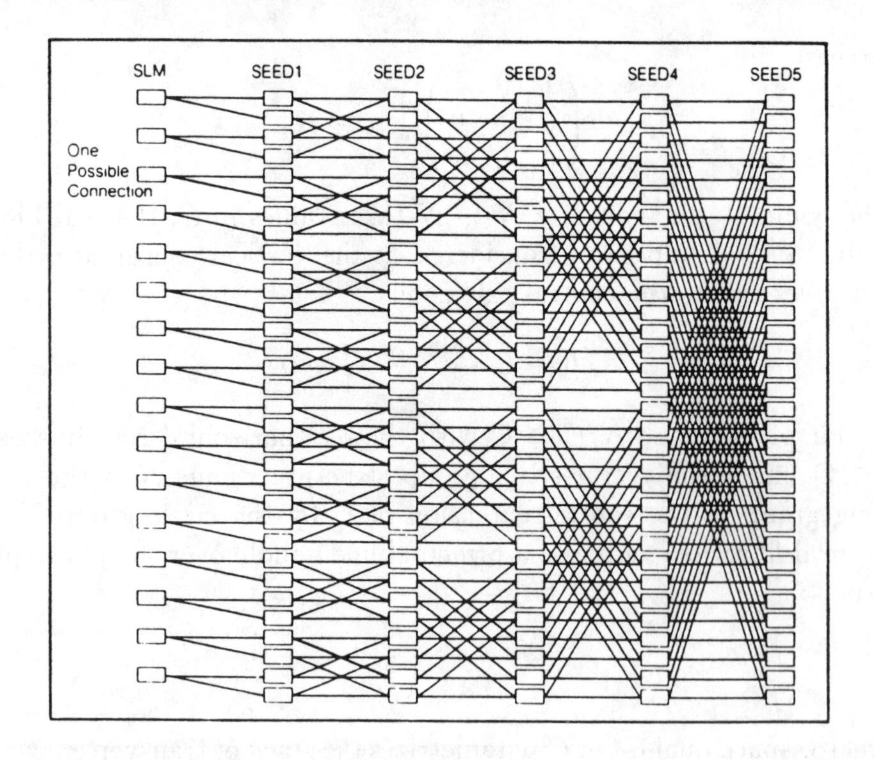

Figure 7: An extended generalized shuffle network

direct sum decomposition into primary homogeneous components $(M_n)_{n\in\mathbf{Z}}$ of multiplicity $|n|$ with respect to the parallel shift register action of N. The Fourier decomposition of L^2 harmonic analysis on $N\backslash L$ reads ([74])

$$L^2(N\backslash L) = \widehat{\bigoplus_{n\in\mathbf{Z}}} M_n.$$

Notice the Hilbert space isomorphisms $M_0 \cong L^2(\mathbf{T}^2)$ and $M_1 \cong L^2(\mathbf{R})$. The complex Hilbert subspace $L^2(\mathbf{T}^2) \hookrightarrow L^2(N\backslash L)$ coincides with its anti-space ([83]). For all integers $n \geq 1$, the Hilbert subspace $M_n \hookrightarrow L^2(N\backslash L)$ forms the anti-space of the Hilbert subspace $M_{-n} \hookrightarrow L^2(N\backslash L)$.

The parallel shift register stage used in the horizontal and vertical scanner of the silicon retina implementation is in correspondence to the S-SEED technology in the hybrid free-space digital photonics implementation of ANNs. Though a young technology, the architecture of planar two-dimensional processing arrays of S-SEEDs offers within HyDOPs a large-scale connectivity that cannot be achieved in the more mature electronics technology of hardwired VLSI circuitry ([76]).

At the time of writing, S-SEED arrays are at the point of early commercial availability. Figure 7 displays S-SEED arrays stacked in planar layers. The strengths of the S-SEED technology include the ability to provide lower signal energy per interconnection, lower onchip power dissipation per connection, lower crosstalk between different connections, lower interconnection skew, high connection density, and massive parallelism. This is quite different from conventional integrated-system silicon chips. Because the dividing line between photonics and electronics becomes indistinct, the SEED technology poses challenges as well as opportunities.

7 Amacronics

The field of micro-optics is about to explode. ... As the new lenses make their way into applications ranging from conventional image-forming optics to integrated-circuit interconnections and machine vision, designers are finding themselves in an unaccustomed situation: limited not by materials or manufacturing techniques but only by their own creative vision.
Wilfrid B. Veldkamp (1992)

The neurobiological model of the retinal multilayer architecture can be emulated in even more elaborate cross-linking interconnection ANNs by current analog VLSI manufacturing technology used to etch integrated circuits on silicon wafers. Steps in producing binary optical elements consist in (i) computer-generation of a microlithography mask which is placed over substrate, (ii) contact-printing of mask pattern into photoresist, (iii) removing of exposed photoresist, (iv) ion-milling or reactive-ion etching to transfer pattern into substrate, (v) removing of remaining photoresist. The process is repeated to produce multistep pattern. Binary diffractive holographic elements ([50]) interconnect the cells of multi-input arrays of photodetectors stacked in planar layers, as are the cells of the retina and the affine planar coadjoint orbits in $\mathrm{Lie}(N)^*$ associated to the unitary dual of N, which are parametrized by the transverse line C^* and log-polar coordinates. The log-polar coordinate system of computational neuroanatomy ([82]) will be transferred in a natural way from the Lie algebra of N, the real three-dimensional Heisenberg algebra $\mathrm{Lie}(N)$, to the complex phase plane $\mathbf{C} \hookrightarrow N$ by the global diffeomorphism

$$\log : N \to \mathrm{Lie}(N).$$

Integrated, individually addressed, mutually coherent SELDAs (Figure 8) and micro-optics (Figure 9) pass the low-level image to another semiconductor chip ([22, 41, 49]) whose sensors might be sensitive, for instance, to the orientation or texture of image features. A stack of image-processing circuits ultimately conveys a largely quantum holographic description of a visual scene in almost the same way that the visual cortex conveys its local feature information by cooperatively synchronized neural activity to the rest of the cerebral cortex. The wavelet amplitudes of the cooperatively synchronized signal components encode significance, and the phase shifts in the cross-linking ANN do encode the degree of association between coherent stimulus components. For the circuits of the ANN the term "amacronics" has been coined, because they emulate the motion-detection, edge enhancement, and dynamic range reduction function

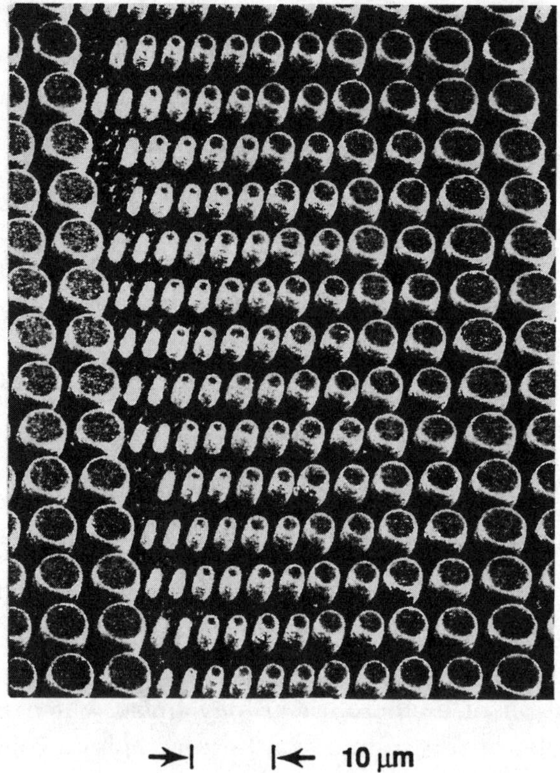

Figure 8: SELDA

of the amacrine cells of the retina. These cells are examples of axonless neurons and are located within the retinal inner-plexiform layer just above the ganglion cell bodies. Although for pattern recognition problems amacronic architectures have been developed with the parallel processing power of several Cray computers, biological vision has thus far proved superior to any presently available analog VLSI implementation that mimics its sensory structure. It can be safely stated that no natural or artificial system in which information is handled surpasses human vision in complexity and efficiency.

8 Magnetoencephalography - Squid Imaging

Biomagnetische Felder lassen sich vor allem dann messen, wenn es um massive elektrische Entladungen großer Zellverbände geht, wie z.B. bei der Herzaktivität, wo ein ganzer Muskel gleichzeitig erregt wird. Beim Gehirn ist dies nun gerade normalerweise nicht der Fall. Die 10^{10} *cerebralen Neurone arbeiten zwar in Arealen zusammen, jedoch nur flüchtig, für wenige* 100 ms, *und je nach Aufgabe räumlich an ganz verschiedenen Stellen. So wird das Magnetenzephalogramm bisher nur bei zwei Fragestellungen in der Neurophysiologie und Neurologie klinisch mit gewissem Erfolg verwendet. Dies ist einmal die Lokalisation epileptischer Foki, wo Massenentladungen von kortikalen Neuronen auftreten. ... Zum anderen sind es die durch natürliche Sinnesreize evozierten cerebralen Felder, wie sie in der Diagnostik normaler und gestörter afferenter Leitungsbahnen verwendet werden. ... Zusammenfassend*

Figure 9: Array of integrated hololenslets

sei gesagt, daß die Magnetenzephalographie zwar ein technisch außerordentlich aufwendiges Verfahren darstellt, das ohne Einsatz entsprechender Rechnerressourcen nicht möglich ist. ... Gemeinsame Anstrengungen sind somit gefragt von Physikern, Radiologen, Physiologen und klinischen Anwendern. Gelingt diese Kooperation, dann allerdings dürfte die Magnetenzephalographie dem konventionellen Elektroenzephalogramm schon bald überlegen sein!
B. Bromm (1991)

What can the MEG *tell us about the manner in which perceptual information is generated and used by large areas of cortex? We have known now for several decades how sensory information is carried to the various primary sensory receiving areas by action potentials, how it is analyzed by local neuronal circuits in subcortical and cortical neurons that are commonly described as "feature detectors". We are far from knowing how these sensory data are linked together with past experience, so as to form perceptions, that then serve as the raw materials for conscious experience. The* MEG *is not yet important for this task, but it will inevitably become so. ...Advances in design of multichannel arrays of* MEG *will open a golden age for the study of neural mechanisms in human perception.*
Walter J. Freeman (1991)

Let $L \hookrightarrow N$ denote the stroboscopic lattice. The compact Heisenberg stroboscopic nilmanifold $N \backslash L$ gives rise to the diagram

$$\begin{array}{ccc} \mathbf{T} & \rightarrow & N \backslash L \\ & & \downarrow \\ & & \mathbf{T}^2 \end{array}$$

of a principal circle bundle over the compact two-dimensional collapsed torus $\mathbf{T}^2$. It determines the transition from periodic-to-quasiperiodic-to-deterministic-chaotic quantum neurodynamics (Theorem 7 infra).

Coupled Circle Map Principle. *The compact Heisenberg stroboscopic nilmanifold $N \backslash L$ implements the coupled circle maps of quantum neurodynamics. The fibers of the compact collapsed base manifold $\mathbf{T}^2$ of $N \backslash L$ define the coupling terms.*

Notice that one-dimensional maps can be simulated more efficiently than differential equations. The globally coupled circle maps implemented by $N \backslash L$ can be used to simulate the cross-correlation of phase even when the signal of the single neuron is chaotic. If the circle map admits a single discontinuity, the behavior of the neuron depends on the sign of the discontinuity. If the discontinuity is positive (no overlap), the dynamics is either periodic or quasiperiodic. If the discontinuity is negative (non-zero overlap), the dynamics is chaotic both in the sense of positive topological entropy and positive Lyapunov exponents ([10, 44]). The quantum neurodynamics of the full neural network is then understood in terms of coupled discontinuous circle maps.

The possibility to choose chaotic states of the circle maps permits to distinguish a large number of objects, i.e., build a number of different neural assemblies ([8, 28, 34]) provided the network is sufficiently large that show no correlation between the neurons belonging to different objects but perfect correlation within the same neural assembly (Figure 11). The number of different neural assemblies is limited by the resolution of the phase variable and the length of the considered time interval ([6]).

It turns out that the nonlinear dynamical behaviour of a Josephson tunnel junction used in Supraconducting Quantum Interference Device (Squid) imaging to measure extremely weak magnetic fields in the femtotesla range (Figure 10) and in cyroelectronics ([7]) can be described in terms of a circle map. Recent advances in Squid design using multiple ultrasensitive magnetic flux detectors arranged in spatial arrays make it possible to record magnetoencephalograms (MEGs) simultaneously from extensive areas of cortex. Notice that the magnetic fields of brain function are an order of 10^{-4} smaller than magnetic fields produced by the heart ([97]). Band pass filtering and spatial filtering allow to extract perceptual information from the γ activity for measurement and display.

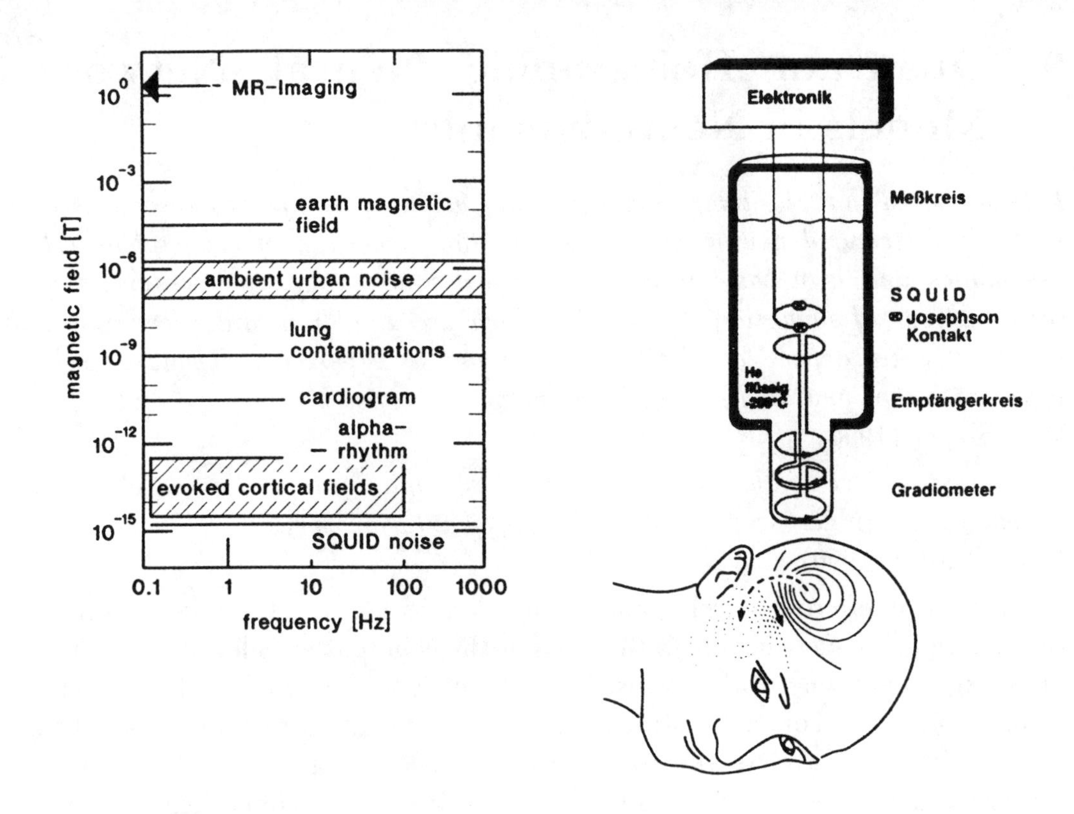

Figure 10: Squid Imaging

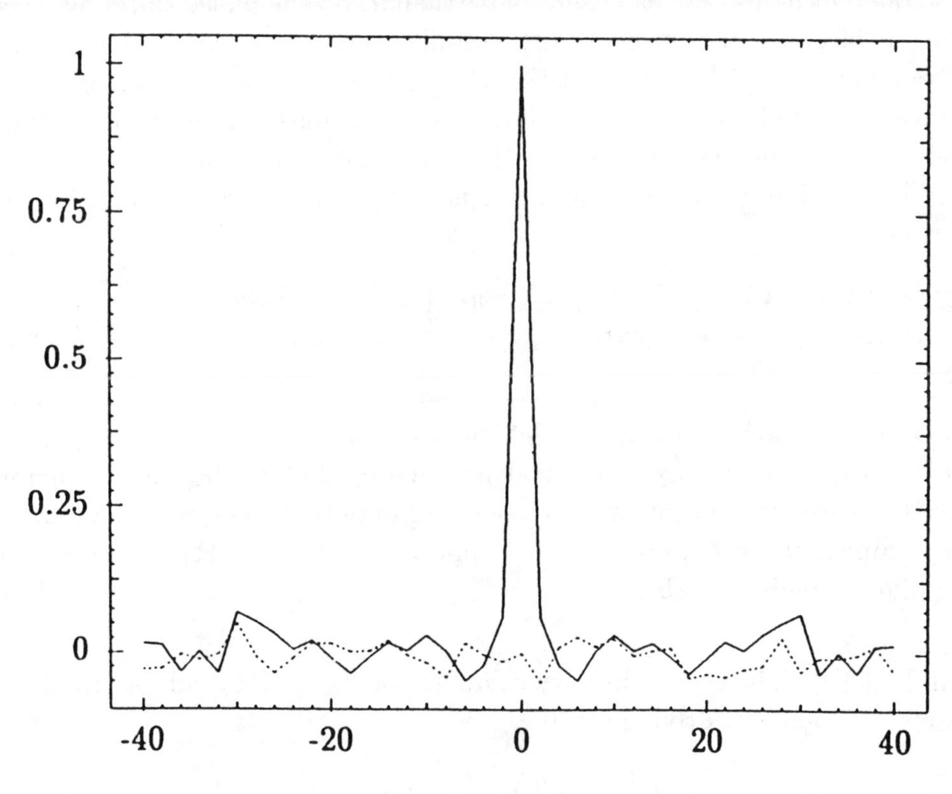

Figure 11: The cross-correlation of the phases for two neurons that are in the same assembly (solid line) and for two neurons that are in different assemblies (broken line)

9 Quantum Holographic Neural Network Models in Neurodynamics

It is proposed that the temporary synchronization of oscillatory responses of spatially distributed neuron clusters serves the formation of cooperating cell assemblies and is a basic feature of cortical processes. ... Use-dependent modifications of synaptic transmission which presumably mediate learning in the adult brain depend on similar mechanisms as experience-dependent self-organization of neuronal connectivity during development.
Wolf Singer (1990)

Nowadays, we know that there are microscopic systems having classical properties and macroscopic systems having quantal properties.
Hans Primas (1990)

Inspection of cross-correlograms of spike trains leads to the following neural linking principle which is at the basis of the coherent wavelet revolution in biophysical neural network models. It finally leads to the dynamical functional connectivity model of analog stimulus-response association by stimulus-evoked coherent neural wavelets and to a mathematical description of the internal sensory order of perceptual coding. Because the local connections between cortical neurons are mediated by unmyelinated axons with slow propagation speeds, the effect of time delays on the cooperative phase-linked synchronization of coherent neural wavelets and, in particular, on the phase shifts between the output of different neurons has to be taken into account. Similar to electrical engineering ([38]) and acoustics ([42]), the measurement of phase as a spectral distribution and its correlation with response in the time domain has not received in neurophysiology the attention which has been devoted to amplitude. The behavior of phase is not apparent from an inspection of amplitude alone.

Basic Neural Linking Principle. *Stimulus-evoked coherent neural wavelets tend to cooperatively synchronize in a shifted phase if they synchronize at all.*

In order to mathematically model the basic neural linking principle, let $\nu \in C^* - \{0\}$ denote a fixed spectral parameter. Let U_ν be an irreducible unitary linear representation of the Heisenberg nilpotent Lie group N modeled in the complex Hilbert space $L^2(\mathbf{R})$. Suppose that $(U_\nu, L^2(\mathbf{R}))$ is associated to the planar coadjoint orbit

$$z^* = \nu$$

of N in $\mathrm{Lie}(N)^*$. The central unitary character of $(U_\nu, L^2(\mathbf{R}))$ adopts the form of a time independent driving term

$$U_\nu|C : \begin{pmatrix} 1 & 0 & z \\ 0 & 1 & 0 \\ 0 & 0 & 1 \end{pmatrix} \mapsto e^{2\pi i \nu z} \quad (\nu \neq 0).$$

Let $< . \mid . >$ denote the standard scalar product of the complex Hilbert space $L^2(\mathbf{R})$ of square integrable neural signals on the whole real line $\mathbf{R}$. Composition of the canonical projection $N \to N/C \cong \mathbf{C}$ with the unitary linear operator

$$U_\nu(\begin{pmatrix} 1 & x & z \\ 0 & 1 & \xi \\ 0 & 0 & 1 \end{pmatrix}) : L^2(\mathbf{R}) \to L^2(\mathbf{R})$$

yields the mapping

$$\mathbf{C} \ni w = x + i\xi \mapsto < U_\nu(\begin{pmatrix} 1 & x & 0 \\ 0 & 1 & \xi \\ 0 & 0 & 1 \end{pmatrix})\psi \mid \varphi >$$

which denotes the temporal cross-correlation function of the cooperatively synchronized coherent neural wavelets $\psi, \varphi \in L^2(\mathbf{R})$. Introducing the Liouville area form

$$\frac{i\nu}{2} \mathrm{d}w \wedge \mathrm{d}\bar{w} = \nu \, . \, \mathrm{d}x \wedge \mathrm{d}\xi \quad (\nu \neq 0)$$

of the complex plane $\mathbf{C}$, the holographic encoding transform explicitly adopts by time integration the spatio-temporal form

$$\mathbf{C} \ni w = x + i\xi \mapsto (\int_{\mathbf{R}} e^{2\pi i \nu \xi t} \psi(t+x)\bar{\varphi}(t)\mathrm{d}t) \, . \, \nu \mathrm{d}x \wedge \mathrm{d}\xi .$$

Because the signal φ is actually involved by its complex conjugate version $\bar{\varphi}$ and the non-linear mapping $\varphi \mapsto \bar{\varphi}$ represents the time mirror, the preceding quantum holographic encoding transformation sets up the cross-correlation of ψ with its phase-linked synchronized response $\bar{\varphi}$ in different cortical areas. It is this relation which naturally involves quantum mechanics in brain activity via the experimentally well established temporal cross-correlation coding of spatio-temporal neural network models linked by cooperative synchronization. Thus the neurodynamical functional connectivity model of analog stimulus-response association by stimulus-evoked coherent neural wavelets refers to quantum mechanics ([15]) rather than the existence of cells "deep in the brain" of single quantum sensitivity (Roger Penrose). Summarizing it follows the

Main Organization Principle. *In spatio-temporal neural network architectures, coherent neural wavelets temporally encode by cooperative synchronization of spatially distributed neural assemblies a quantum mechanical organization form.*

In view of the preceding main organization principle, the mathematical structure given by the Heisenberg group N and the associated Weyl operational calculus permit to include the powerful methods of quantum physics into adaptive signal processing going on within spatio-temporal neural network models. They describe the internal sensory order ([95, 9]) of perceptual coding which designs the internal sensory representation of the CNS acting as a macroscopic quantum system. Specifically the non-commutativity of the group N allows to mathematically describe neural holograms as interference patterns for information expression and storage generated by the analog stimulus-response association of stimulus-evoked coherent neural wavelets.

Quantum Holographic Superposition Principle. *Neural holograms are generated by sesquilinear superposition of analog stimulus-response patterns*

$$\{< U_\nu(\begin{pmatrix} 1 & x & 0 \\ 0 & 1 & \xi \\ 0 & 0 & 1 \end{pmatrix})\psi \mid \varphi > | w = x + i\xi \in \mathbf{C}\} \quad (\nu \neq 0)$$

of stimulus-evoked coherent neural wavelets $\psi, \varphi \in L^2(\mathbf{R})$.

The Poisson summation formula on $\mathbf{R}$, or equivalently the uniform sampling theorem on $\mathbf{R}$ or the Plancherel formula on $\mathbf{T}$ ([73]), are living on the compact Heisenberg stroboscopic nilmanifold $N \backslash L$ via the stroboscopic lattice model of N in an analogous way as do the Fourier transform and the chirplet transform ([48]) on the Heisenberg group N via the Schrödinger model $(U_1, L^2(\mathbf{R}))$ of N. Note that $(U_1, L^2(\mathbf{R}))$ is unitarily isomorphic to the parallel shift register action of N on the Hilbert subspace $M_1 \hookrightarrow L^2(N \backslash L)$. Consider neurons as spike train correlation detectors (Figure 11). According to the resolution of the phase variable, choose a sequence of spike-free windows representing in the Hilbert subspace $M_0 \hookrightarrow L^2(N \backslash L)$ the stroboscopically unfolded compact base manifold $\mathbf{T}^2$ of $N \backslash L$. An application of the parallel shift register action of N implies by superposition the following neural form of the quantum mechanical indeterminacy principle. It diminishes the value of single-unit recording techniques and emphasizes the importance of multiple-channel cross-correlation analysis for neural data.

Theorem 1. *It is impossible to assign precisely predictable space-time coordinates to neural events.*

Another formulation of the basic quantum dynamical limitation of knowledge reads as follows.

Corollary. *The information content of neural holograms will be completely erased when the precise space-time coordinates of neural events are known.*

Thus, if coordinates are assigned to neural events, then for a given stroboscopic lattice $L \hookrightarrow N$, the same neural event may have different coordinates and, for similar reasons, different neural events may have the same coordinates. In other words, coordinates may have probable than precise meaning: The mere threat of obtaining precise information about the space-time coordinates of neural events actually destroys the neural holograms.

The converse of the Corollary supra forms the principle of quantum eraser which in extremis can be considered as a synaptic plasticity phenomenon in spatio-temporal neural networks.

Theorem 2. *By completely erasing the information content of neural holograms, the precise space-time coordinates of neural events can be retrieved.*

Corollary. *Information erasing neural signals are formed by short-time impulses.*

The key point of quantum neurodynamics is

Theorem 3. *The local-global duality of spatio-temporal neural network architectures is reversible.*

The preceding quantum neurodynamical results go far beyond the standard Heisenberg uncertainty principle ([11, 76]) which implies that time resolution and spectral resolution are mutually exclusive. Indeed, the global and local uncertainty inequalities presently available are all out-performed by Poisson summation when the local-global duality of neural network models is studied. In quantum holography, the stroboscopic enfolding of N by $N \backslash L$ and the stroboscopic unfolding of the compact base manifold $\mathbf{T}^2$ of $N \backslash L$ form a technique of analog stimulus-response association by stimulus-evoked coherent wavelets which is not directly achievable through the dynamical interaction of electromagnetic fields. It is the stroboscopic enfolding-unfolding process which forms the mathematical fundament of the quantum eraser principle for spatio-temporal neural network architectures. To understand this principle we will take a short detour from modelling neural networks as they operate in the retina and the brain and consider somewhat simpler operations of the neural networks of the heart.

10 The Sudden Cardiac Death Syndrome

It appears that all human hearts are subject to bombardment by electrical impulses. Only some hearts, however, develop fibrillation. ... Work with single cells, however, has been of only limited help in understanding fibrillation. The reason is that fibrillation is a disorder of the organization of the heartbeat rather than a malfunction of the individual fibers: it affects the timing of activity in the heart fibers with respect to one another. Indeed, it is probable that in the fibrillating heart each fiber is responding in the usual way, but the pattern of electrical impulses has been disturbed, resulting in a loss of cooperative phase-linked synchronization. ... In many instances when an autopsy is done, there is no perceptible clinical reason for the drastic interruption of the normal coordination of the heart.
Arthur T. Winfree (1983)

At rest the human heart muscle contracts roughly with frequency 1 Hz. The intrinsic beat in the sinus node, a pacemaker located near the top of the right atrium (Figure 12) that determines the resting heartbeat rate can be accelerated or retarded by impulses carried by nerves coming from the medulla oblongata in the lower brainstem, various ganglia, and the internal organs such as the lungs. Such nerves infiltrate the entire cardiac tissue, but their endings are particularly dense in the neural pacemaking system. For example, the nervus vagus can have a considerable effect on local rates of contraction and on the coordination of the entire heart activity. The neural pacemaking system which cooperatively synchronizes the heart's contractions is formed by the sinus node and the atrioventricular node, a second pacemaker located between the right atrium and the right ventricle. Under conditions of weak coupling mutual pacemaker cell synchronization results from the effects of the action potentials of each cell on the diastolic depolarizations of the other cell ([100]).

When applied to the heart's spatio-temporal neural network, the principle of quantum eraser has an awful consequence: The sudden cardiac death ([47]). For this syndrome, nervous impulses to the heart are of critical importance. If an electrical input stimulus is applied to a patch of the heart tissue in a moment that is not precisely determined in advance, then the dangerous ventricular fibrillation phenomenon will never be observed. In this case the information content of the patterns of intrinsic electrical stimuli is preserved and the cooperative synchronization of the heart muscle fibers remains essentially unaffected. With the exception of a shift of the usual rhythm ahead or back, most of the external electrical impulses actually have no lasting effect on the subsequent contractions. In particular, the interval between impulses after the external stimulus does not change. If, however, a small electrical input stimulus arrives at a certain position during the vulnerabel time interval of the heartbeat rhythm, the information content is completely erased by the marker so that the cooperative synchronization of the heart muscle fibers and their cooperative organization stop. Although the sinus node has a regular intrinsic discharge, the heartbeat timing of mammalians is not controlled by regular trains of impulses. Therefore, the detection of the vulnerable time interval needs a systematic study of pulse train recordings and a corresponding space-time variation of the external electrical stimuli to cover the interval between contractions. Indeed, the key point is that the contraction of the heart is spatially distributed and the timing of firings and strength of stimuli delivered by the spatio-temporal neural network of Purkinje cells vary considerably even across short distances. In the Purkinje fibers which control the neural pacemaking impulses passing into the ventricular muscle and hence the contractions of the ventricles, a cell drives a follower cell if it is active in cooperative phase-linked synchrony with many other cells which contact the same follower cell for rapid pulse conduction. After having completely erased the information content of the neural hologram by marking the vulnerable time interval with a brief electrical impulse of proper magnitude and timing, the heart starts with chaotic convulsions which after five minutes imply almost certainly the exitus. Although the ventricular fibrillation actually can be reversed, every year several hundered thousand people are killed by the spatio-temporal disorganization of the normal coordinated contraction

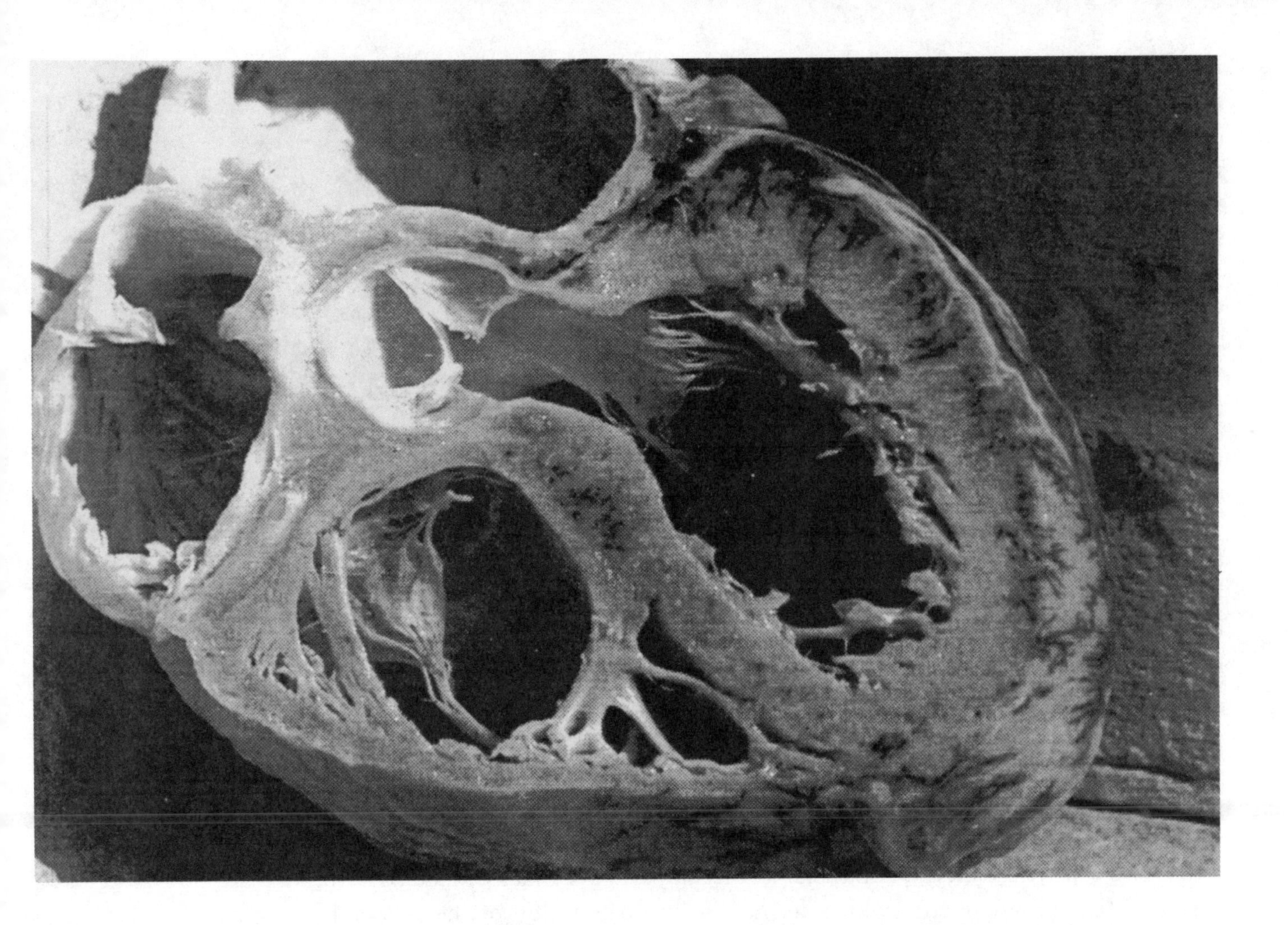

Figure 12: The heart - computer generated

of heart muscle fibers. Therefore the sudden cardiac death syndrome is one of the major challenges to contemporary cardiology. Note that the stimulus employed will never cause erasion of information and hence ventricular fibrillation unless it is properly timed within the cycle of heartbeats. The loss of phase information that results in the arrhythmia catastrophe of violent and disorganized activity is of genuine neural quantum holographic origin. The implantation of a cardioverter defibrillator (ICD) can reverse ventricular fibrillation.

11 The Heisenberg Geometry

Ubi materia, ibi geometria.
Johannes Keppler (1571-1630)

The geometry which the boundary of the ball inherits from the biholomorphic geometry of the ball has been called "Heisenberg *geometry" although* Heisenberg *contributed less to this geometry than did* É. Cartan.
William H. Goldman (1989)

To return to our main theme, another consequence of neural holography is, that when a specific input stimulus is repeated after the organism has been exposed to other input stimuli, the pattern is again unique, it does not necessarily match the specific pattern that was produced on the original occasion by that input stimulus. Thus a specific constellation of features does not always lead to the emergence of the same assembly of coherently co-active neurons. This observation has impact on the geometry of the Heisenberg space, the one-point compactification of the Heisenberg nilpotent Lie group N realized by the set $\mathbf{C} \times \mathbf{R}$ of pairs (w, z) where $w = x + i\xi \in \mathbf{C}, z \in \mathbf{R}$, under the group law

$$(w_1, z_1).(w_2, z_2) = (w_1 + w_2, z_1 + z_2 - \mathrm{Im}(w_1.\bar{w}_2)).$$

Let the unit ball $\mathbf{B}^2 \subset \mathbf{C}^2$ be endowed with the geometry of the Bergmann metric. Then the Heisenberg space can be naturally identified with the boundary $\partial\mathbf{B}^2$ of the complex hyperbolic 2-space $\mathbf{B}^2$. The group N acts simply transitively on $\partial\mathbf{B}^2$, and the complement of a point p_∞ in the boundary $\partial\mathbf{B}^2$ of complex hyperbolic space $\mathbf{B}^2$ has the natural structure of a Heisenberg group. Thus the locally compact metric space $\partial\mathbf{B}^2 - \{p_\infty\}$ forms a geometric realization of N. The geometry that $\partial\mathbf{B}^2 = \mathbf{S}_3$ inherits from the biholomorphic geometry of $\mathbf{B}^2$ has been called Heisenberg geometry.

In Heisenberg geometry, geodesics of $\partial\mathbf{B}^2$ are bounded by pairs of distinct points in Heisenberg space. The boundary of a complex geodesic is called a chain. Chains are represented graphically by ellipses whose vertical Euclidean projections are Euclidean circles. The boundary of a totally real geodesic 2-plane is called an $\mathbf{R}$-circle. Chains and $\mathbf{R}$-circles form the one-dimensional objects of the Heisenberg geometry. The equidistant surfaces meet $\partial\mathbf{B}^2$ in surfaces, the spinal spheres, which decompose into the union of the two endpoints of the vertices and a family of chains, the slices of the spinal surface. Figure 13 and Figure 14 display the slices and meridians of a spinal sphere and the chain through its vertices. The slices are the latitudinal curves and the vertices are the poles ([29, 30, 31]).

The square integrability mod C of $(U_\nu, L^2(\mathbf{R}))$ $(\nu \neq 0)$ or equivalently the planar coadjoint orbit condition imply the neural filtering principle or

Sharp Frequency Selection Principle. *For coherent neural wavelets $\psi, \varphi \in \mathcal{S}(\mathbf{R})$, the identity*

$$\iint_{\mathbf{R}\oplus\mathbf{R}} < U_\nu(\begin{pmatrix} 1 & x & 0 \\ 0 & 1 & \xi \\ 0 & 0 & 1 \end{pmatrix}) \psi \mid \varphi > \overline{< U_{\nu'}(\begin{pmatrix} 1 & x & 0 \\ 0 & 1 & \xi \\ 0 & 0 & 1 \end{pmatrix}) \psi \mid \varphi >} dx d\xi = 0 \quad (\nu \neq \nu')$$

holds.

As a consequence, only those of the simultaneously co-active wavelet inputs will have a chance to improve the synaptic gain which oscillate in precise synchrony with the target cell. Moreover, the traciality follows from the square integrability mod C of $(U_\nu, L^2(\mathbf{R}))$ $(\nu \neq 0)$, too.

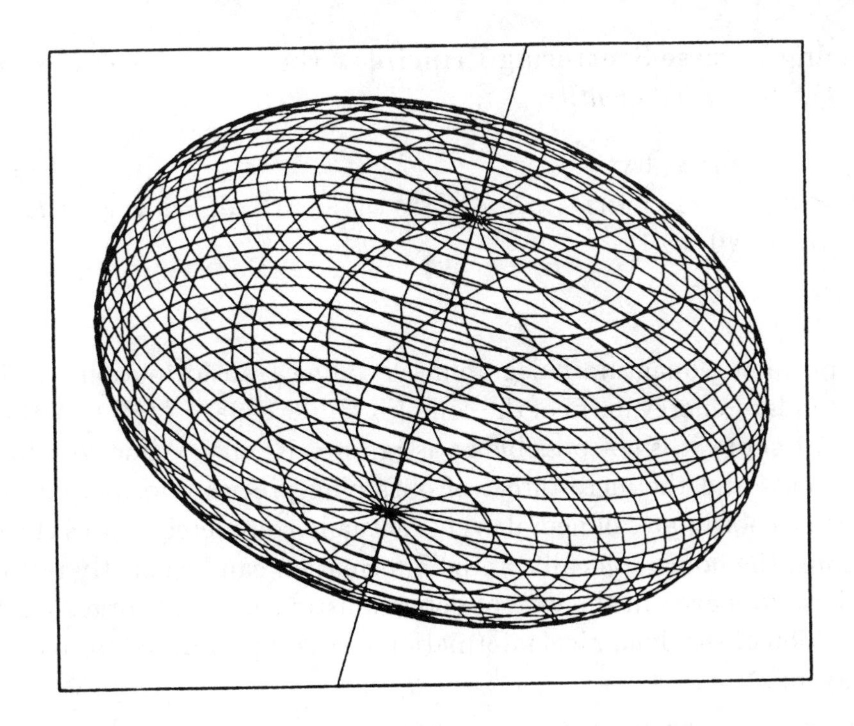

Figure 13: Slices, meridian and complex spine of a vertical spinal sphere

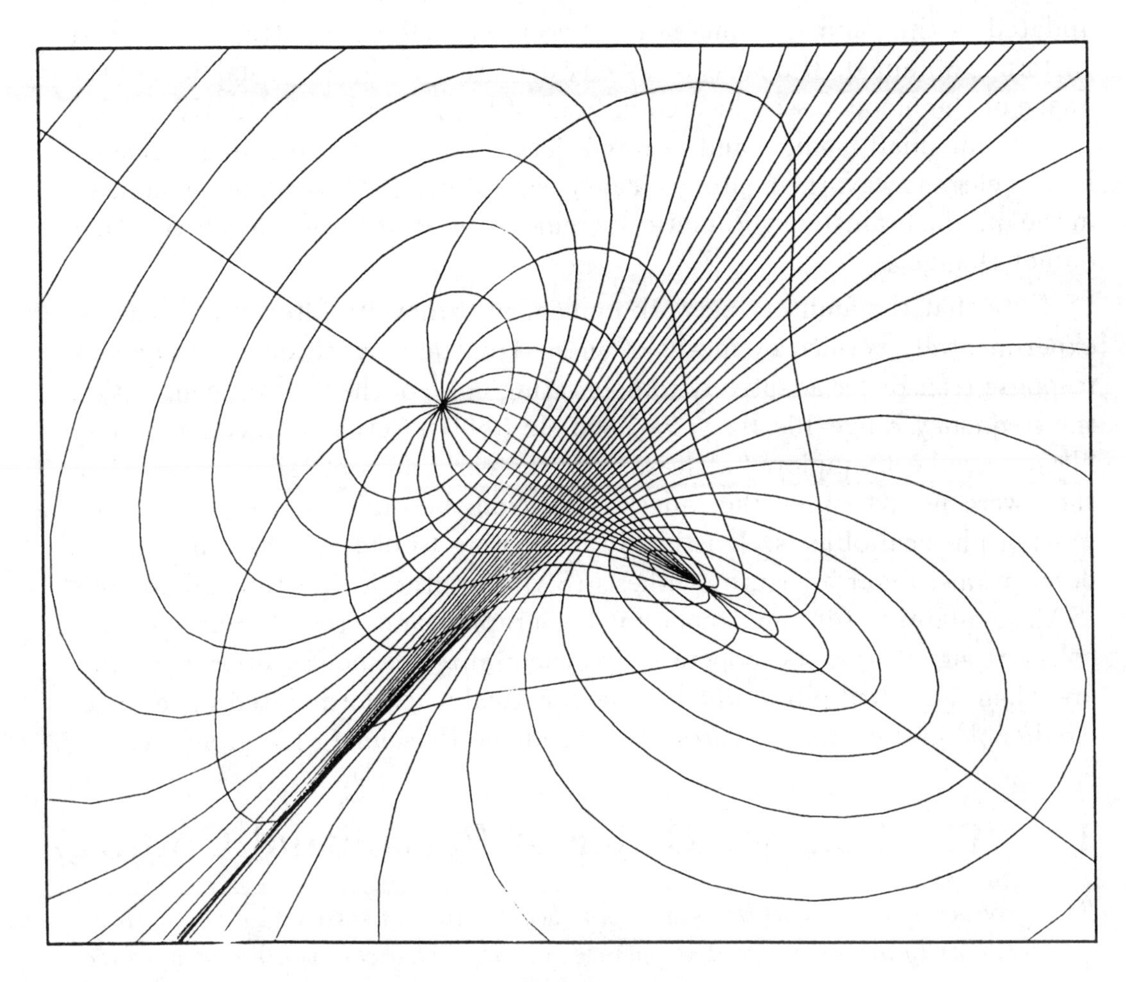

Figure 14: Slices and meridians of a spinal sphere passing through infinity

Reproducing Inverse Scattering Principle. *For coherent neural wavelets $\psi, \varphi \in \mathcal{S}(\mathbf{R})$, the tracial identity*

$$\iint_{\mathbf{R}\oplus\mathbf{R}} < U_\nu(\begin{pmatrix} 1 & x & 0 \\ 0 & 1 & \xi \\ 0 & 0 & 1 \end{pmatrix})\psi \mid \varphi > e^{-2\pi i \nu \xi t}\, \bar{\psi}(t+x)\, \mathrm{d}x \mathrm{d}\xi = \| \psi \|^2 \, \bar{\varphi}(t)$$

holds.

In the preceding quantum holographic decoding transformation, $\| \, . \, \|$ denotes the standard energy norm of the complex Hilbert space $L^2(\mathbf{R})$. Although by Theorem 1 supra it is not possible to assign precise space-time coordinates to neural events and the mere threat of obtaining precise information about the space-time coordinates of neural events actually completely erases the neural holograms, the holographically stored information can be exactly retrieved without phase loss even in the case of deterministic chaos (Theorem 7 infra). The recollection of the dynamical information traces is performed by averaging over the layers $z^* = \nu$.

Due to the autotracing property of phase conjugate signals, the reproducing scattering identity reflects the tracking novelty filter implementation of holograms by four-wave mixing ([3, 4]). The reference pattern is continually updated in time and the difference between one reference pattern and a test pattern is obtained. Humans use novelty detection to rid the visual field of the image of the blood vessels located in front of the retina by constantly moving the eyes in small tremors and in rapid, jerky movements, so called saccades. In this elegant way, the ponto geniculo occipital wavelets which are generated in the middle brainstem automatically remove the image from the objects that do not change.

Note that the auditory network implements a novelty filter, too as can be experimentally verified by means of an electronically synchronized frequency response transducer adaptively compensating noise of the environment within the frequency range 100 Hz $\leq \nu \leq$ 800 Hz ([80]). Actually tracking novelty filters have been employed at least since the early days of radar vision when they were used to keep the radar screen from becoming cluttered by non-moving physical objects. It is highly interesting to observe that the various descriptions, radar aperture synthesis (SAR), synthetic aperture microscopy (SAM), adaptive filtering, quantum holography, and cross-correlation of a coherent signal with its cooperatively synchronized response, diverse as they are when described physically, become identical when formulated in terms of irreducible unitary linear representations of the Heisenberg Lie group N.

12 The Sensory Order of Perceptual Coding

The process of experience thus does not begin with sensations or perceptions, but necessarily precedes them: it operates on physiological events and arranges

them into a structure or order which becomes the basis of their 'mental' significance; and the distinction between the sensory qualities, in terms of which alone the conscious mind can learn about anything in the external world, is the result of such pre-sensory experience. We may express this also by stating that experience is not a function of mind and consciousness, but that mind and consciousness are rather products of experience. ... All that we can perceive is thus determined by the order of sensory qualities which provides the "categories" in terms of which sense experience can alone take place. ... Another interesting consequence following from our theory is that a stimulus whose occurrence in conjunction with other stimuli showed no regularities whatever could never be perceived by our senses. This would seem to mean that we can know only such kinds of events as show a certain degree of regularity in their occurrence in relations with others, and that we could not know anything about events which occurred in a completely irregular manner.
Friedrich A. von Hayek (1952)

Since ancient times, people have recognized the importance of chaos, while they have searched for the order.
Kunihiko Kaneko (1986)

Let the unitary group $\mathbf{U}(L^2(\mathbf{R}))$ of the standard complex Hilbert space $L^2(\mathbf{R})$ be endowed with the strong operator topology, i.e., the weakest topology such that the point evaluations

$$\mathbf{U}(L^2(\mathbf{R})) \times L^2(\mathbf{R}) \ni (V, \psi) \mapsto V(\psi) \in L^2(\mathbf{R})$$

are continuous mappings. Then the embedding $\mathbf{C} \hookrightarrow N$ of the complex plane $\mathbf{C}$ into N by setting $w = x + i\xi$ induces via the linear Schrödinger representation U_1 of N the homeomorphism

$$w \mapsto U_1(w, 0)$$

of $\mathbf{C}$ onto its image within the topological group $\mathbf{U}(L^2(\mathbf{R}))$. Let

$$G = \{ V \in \mathbf{U}(L^2(\mathbf{R})) \mid V \circ U_1(w, z) \circ V^{-1} = U_1(w', z),\ w \in \mathbf{C},\ z \in \mathbf{R} \}$$

where $w' = \sigma(V)w$ depends upon w and V and the points z of the center C of N are left fixed. Then the mapping $\sigma(V) : \mathbf{C} \to \mathbf{C}$ is a homeomorphism. More precisely, $\sigma(V) \in \mathbf{SL}(2, \mathbf{R})$ for all $V \in G$ is area preserving, and $\sigma : G \to \mathbf{SL}(2, \mathbf{R})$ is a Lie group homomorphism. As usual, the special linear group $\mathbf{SL}(2, \mathbf{R})$ on two real variables (x, ξ) denotes the Lie group of unimodular $\mathbf{R}$-linear mappings $\mathbf{C} \to \mathbf{C}$ which can be geometrically thought of as a three-dimensional hyperboloid embedded in $\mathbf{R}^4$. Let $\mathbf{Mp}(1, \mathbf{R})$ denote the commutator group of G. Then $\mathbf{Mp}(1, \mathbf{R})$ is called the metaplectic group. The restriction of σ to $\mathbf{Mp}(1, \mathbf{R})$ is a twofold covering of $\mathbf{SL}(2, \mathbf{R})$ giving rise to the exact sequence

$$1 \to \mathbf{Z}_2 \to \mathbf{Mp}(1, \mathbf{R}) \to \mathbf{SL}(2, \mathbf{R}) \to 1.$$

The realization $\mathbf{Mp}(1,\mathbf{R}) \subset \mathbf{U}(L^2(\mathbf{R}))$ is called the oscillator or metaplectic representation $(W, L^2(\mathbf{R}))$ of $\mathbf{Mp}(1,\mathbf{R})$. In terms of the projector $\mathbf{Mp}(1,\mathbf{R}) \ni \tilde{\sigma} \mapsto \sigma \in \mathbf{SL}(2,\mathbf{R})$, the covariance identity ([96, 74, 75]) reads

$$W_{\tilde{\sigma}} \circ U_1(w,z) \circ W_{\tilde{\sigma}}^{-1} = U_1(\sigma(w),z), \quad w \in \mathbf{C},\ z \in \mathbf{R}.$$

Basic Covariance Principle. *Changes in coherent neural wavelets performed by the action of the unitary operator $W_{\tilde{\sigma}}$ in $L^2(\mathbf{R})$ induce changes of the neural holograms in terms of the area preserving linear mapping $\sigma \in \mathbf{SL}(2,\mathbf{R})$.*

Notice that covariance and traciality are the basic principles of quantum holography.

It is a well known fact that the family of matrices

$$\begin{pmatrix} a & 0 \\ 0 & a^{-1} \end{pmatrix}, \begin{pmatrix} 1 & b \\ 0 & 1 \end{pmatrix}, \begin{pmatrix} 0 & -1 \\ 1 & 0 \end{pmatrix}$$

with real entries $a \neq 0$ and b generates the group $\mathbf{SL}(2,\mathbf{R})$ of area preserving $\mathbf{R}$-linear mappings $\mathbf{C} \to \mathbf{C}$. The one-parameter groups $\{\exp t\sigma \mid t \in \mathbf{R}\}$ generated by this family of matrices σ can be enumerated by the categories of profiles listed in Figure 15 infra. They display the wrappings of the real lines $\{t\sigma \mid t \in \mathbf{R}\}$ which interpolate sequences of points that are contiguous with respect to analog stimulus-response association by stimulus-evoked coherent neural wavelets.

In order to visualize these categories of profiles which include attractors by a simple experimental test, consider a randomly distributed pattern of dots in the plane and reproduce up to a uniform scaling factor the identical dot pattern on a planar transparency. When the two patterns are slowly moved, the various profiles become apparent as predicted. In the case of a non-uniform scaling factor, additional profiles (Figure 16) appear so that the classification of the solutions of autonomous systems of linear differential equations becomes complete.

Theorem 4. *The oscillator representation $(W, L^2(\mathbf{R}))$ of $\mathbf{Mp}(1,\mathbf{R})$ defines the internal sensory order of perceptual coding.*

13 Bouton Exocytosis

The essential feature is that the effective structure of each synapse is a paracrystalline presynaptic vesicular grid, which acts probabilistically in quantal release.
John C. Eccles (1985)

The conscious action of the brain could hardly be understood if the brain were in its entirety functioning on the basis of classical physics. Also, the relative

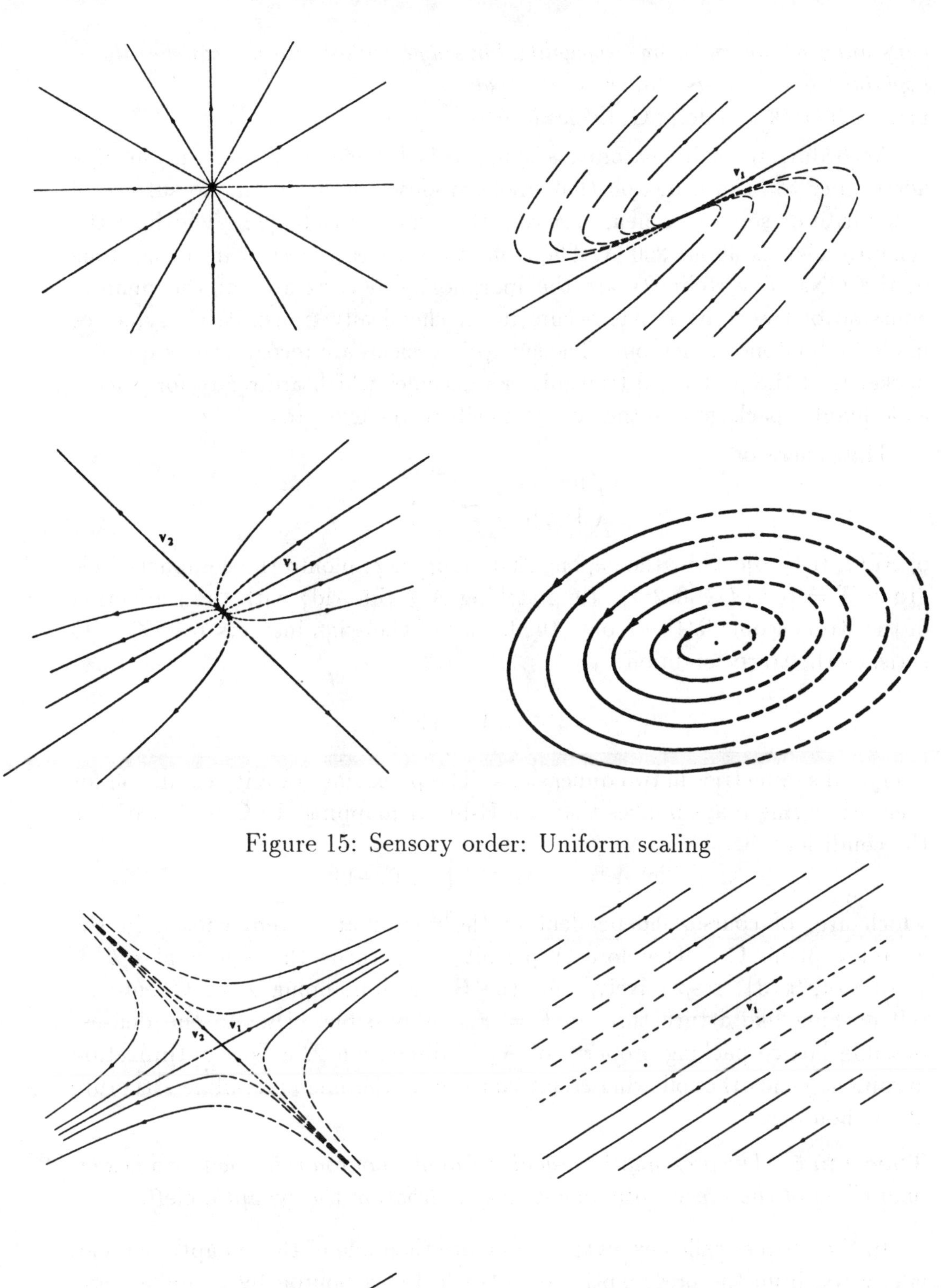

Figure 15: Sensory order: Uniform scaling

Figure 16: Sensory order: Non-uniform scaling

constancy of the emission probability for single bouton release can hardly be explained on the basis of thermal fluctuations.
Friedrich Beck and John C. Eccles (1992)

According to neuroanatomy, a synapse is formed by an expansion of a nerve fiber to form a bouton that makes a close contact with the surface of a dendrite or soma of a neuron across the synaptic cleft. The width of the synaptic cleft is about 200 Å. The synaptic vesicles observed in all boutons in the CNS of vertebrates are the morphological correlates of the quantal emission of transmitter that occurs in all chemically transmitting synapses made by boutons on neurons. The synaptic vesicles are recognized as quantal packages of the performed transmitter molecules which are ready for release as a quantal package into the synaptic cleft in the exocytosis.

The generator

$$\begin{pmatrix} 0 & -1 \\ 1 & 0 \end{pmatrix} = i \in \mathbf{C}$$

of $\mathbf{SL}(2, \mathbf{R})$ projects by the exponential mapping exp onto the compact circle group $\mathbf{T} = \{e^{it} \mid t \in [0, 2\pi[\}$. Its matching $A \notin \{\mathrm{id}, -\mathrm{id}\}$ with the projection of the stroboscopic lattice L onto the lattice of Gaussian integers $\mathbf{Z} \oplus i\mathbf{Z} \hookrightarrow \mathbf{C}$ satisfies the trace condition

$$-2 < \mathrm{tr}\, A < +2$$

of crystal symmetries in two dimensions. The preceding stability condition for area preserving maps implies that the $\mathbf{R}$-linear mapping $A : \mathbf{C} \to \mathbf{C}$ satisfies the conditions

$$\det A = 1, \quad \mathrm{tr}\, A \in \{-1, 0, +1\}$$

which are, of course, independent of the coordinate sytem chosen in the complex plane $\mathbf{C}$. Therefore A permits only turns through angles $\theta \in \{\pi/3, \pi/4, 2\pi/3\}$, respectively. For the $\mathbf{R}$-linear mapping A of $\mathbf{C}$ onto itself nothing like a turn through $\theta = \pi/5$ is possible. Due to the densest possible lattice packing property of A_2 in dimension 2, a flow optimization argument yields the following result concerning the fine crystalline structure of the boutons.

Theorem 5. *The presynaptic vesicular grid of a bouton is formed by a hexagonal tiling of the presynaptic membrane confronting the synaptic cleft.*

In the process called exocytosis, no more than one of the synaptic vesicles is emitted from the presynaptic vesicular grid of a bouton by a single nerve impulse propagating into the bouton ([8, 16]). This process which consists of the opening of a channel in the presynaptic vesicular grid and the discharge of the vesicle's transmitter molecules into the synaptic cleft forms the basic unitary activity of the cerebral cortex. The crystalline structure of the presynaptic vesicular grid established in Theorem 5 supra makes it possible to have long-range interactions between the constituents, as is well known from ordered quantum systems. There are about 40 vesicles altogether in the crystalline structure which do not act independently, but rather immediately after one vesicle is triggered for releasing its content the interaction between them blocks further exocytosis. The relaxation time for the blocking process is of the order of femtoseconds ([8]).

14 Adaptive Filter Coupling in the Dendritic Tree

These synchronous oscillations can, for example, support a preattentive boundary completion process, as occurs during visual boundary segmentation; an attentive resonant state, as occurs during visual object recognition; either preattentive or attentive adaptive filtering operations during more general processes of cortical feature detection and short term memory representation.
Stephen Grossberg (1991)

The complex vector space $L^2(\mathbf{R})^\infty$ of smooth vectors for the oscillator representation $(W, L^2(\mathbf{R}))$ of $\mathbf{Mp}(1, \mathbf{R})$ endowed with the $\mathcal{C}^\infty$ topology is isomorphic to the Schwartz space $\mathcal{S}(\mathbf{R})$ of complex-valued functions which are defined and infinitely differentiable on the whole real line $\mathbf{R}$ and which have the additional property, regulating their decrease at infinity, that all their derivatives rapidly tend to zero at infinity, faster than any polynomial. Let $\mathcal{S}(\mathbf{R})$ be equipped with its standard Fréchet space topology and identify by the canonical isomorphism the completed tensor product $\mathcal{S}(\mathbf{R})\hat{\otimes}\mathcal{S}(\mathbf{R})$ with $\mathcal{S}(\mathbf{C})$. Let a physical object which is embedded in its environment be given by the tempered distribution $T \in \mathcal{S}'(\mathbf{C})$ and extend the linear Schrödinger representation $(U_1, L^2(\mathbf{R}))$ of N from the point measure ϵ_w on $\mathbf{C} \cong N/C$ to T. The extension admits the tempered distribution kernel $K_1(T) \in \mathcal{S}'(\mathbf{C})$ computed by the Weyl operational calculus. It defines the adaptive filter coupling by the rule

$$K_1(T)_w = \bar{\mathcal{F}}_2 T_v,$$

where $\bar{\mathcal{F}}_2$ denotes the distributional partial Fourier cotransform with respect to the imaginary part $\xi = \text{Im}\, w$ of $w \in \mathbf{C}$, and $v = (x + \xi) + i\xi$ is associated to $w = x + i\xi$ in $\mathbf{C}$. Adopting obvious notation, the restriction identity reads

$$K_1(\epsilon_w) = U_1(w, 0) \quad (w \in \mathbf{C}).$$

Adaptation to environmental changes is called learning. The point is the following variant of the Schwartz Kernel Theorem ([83]) which extends the classical learning matrix concept of adaptive filter coupling.

Transducer Principle. *The tempered distribution learning kernel $K_1(T) : \mathcal{S}(\mathbf{R}) \to \mathcal{S}'(\mathbf{R})$ transforms by adaptive filter coupling the planar coordinates of the complex-valued tempered distribution $T \in \mathcal{S}'(\mathbf{C})$ into the phase-plane coordinates of the Weyl quantizing symbol $K_1(T) \in \mathcal{S}'(\mathbf{C})$ associated to T.*

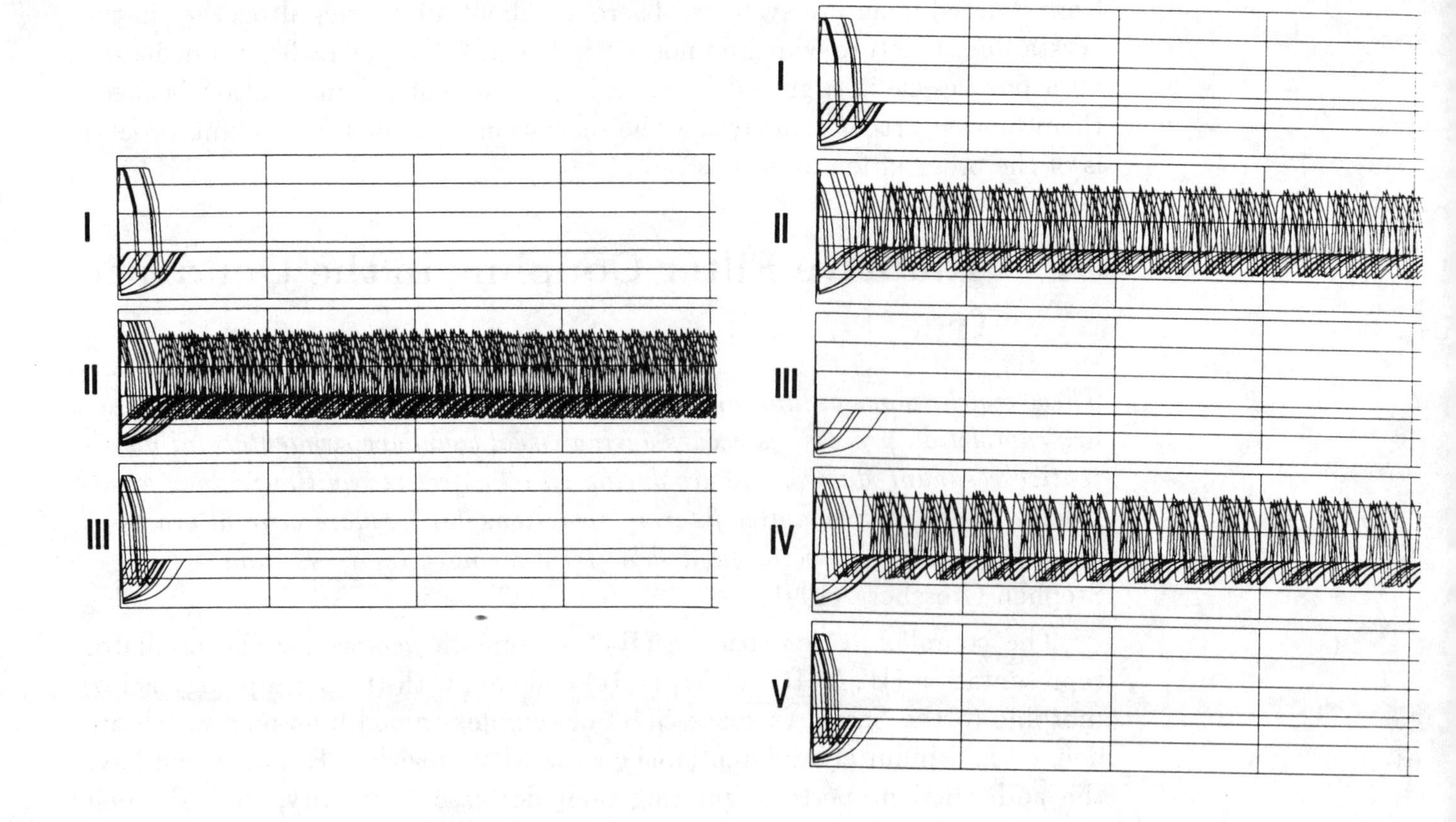

Figure 17: Uncoupled single and double bar input

Each adaptive filter coupling unit represents either the output signal from the dendritic tree of a cell or another cell that sends excitatory connection to this cell. Figures 17 and 18 display how the adaptive filter coupling for single and double bar input ([35]) gives rise to rapid synchronization of oscillatory activity along the bars. Experiments performed with the HNeT emulator system which is based on quantum holographic neural technology ([18, 91, 92, 93]) reveal speed up factors of 10 to 100 times compared to standard learning paradigms of ANN theory.

To simulate local circuits, let $\psi = h_m$, $\varphi = h_n$ be the normalized quantum mechanical harmonic oscillator wavelets of order $m \geq 0$ and $n \geq 0$, respectively. Define the cross-correlation

$$H_{m,n} : \mathbf{C} \ni w \mapsto < U_1(w,0)h_m \mid h_n >$$

and, moreover, let $K_{m,n}$ denote the complete bichromatic graph of $m+n$ vertices and $\Phi_{m,n}$ the associated matching polynomial. From neural network engineering it is well known that the complete bichromatic graphs $K_{m,n}$ form the underlying linking neural networks of the committee machine. The neural assembly $K_{m.n}$ represents a cooperative self-organizing functional unit of coherently co-active neurons whose mechanism of formation constrains all cells within it to share a receptive field. It follows

$$H_{m,n}(w) = \frac{(-1)^n}{\sqrt{m!n!}} e^{-(\pi/2)w\bar{w}} \Phi_{m,n}(w) \quad (m \geq n \geq 0)$$

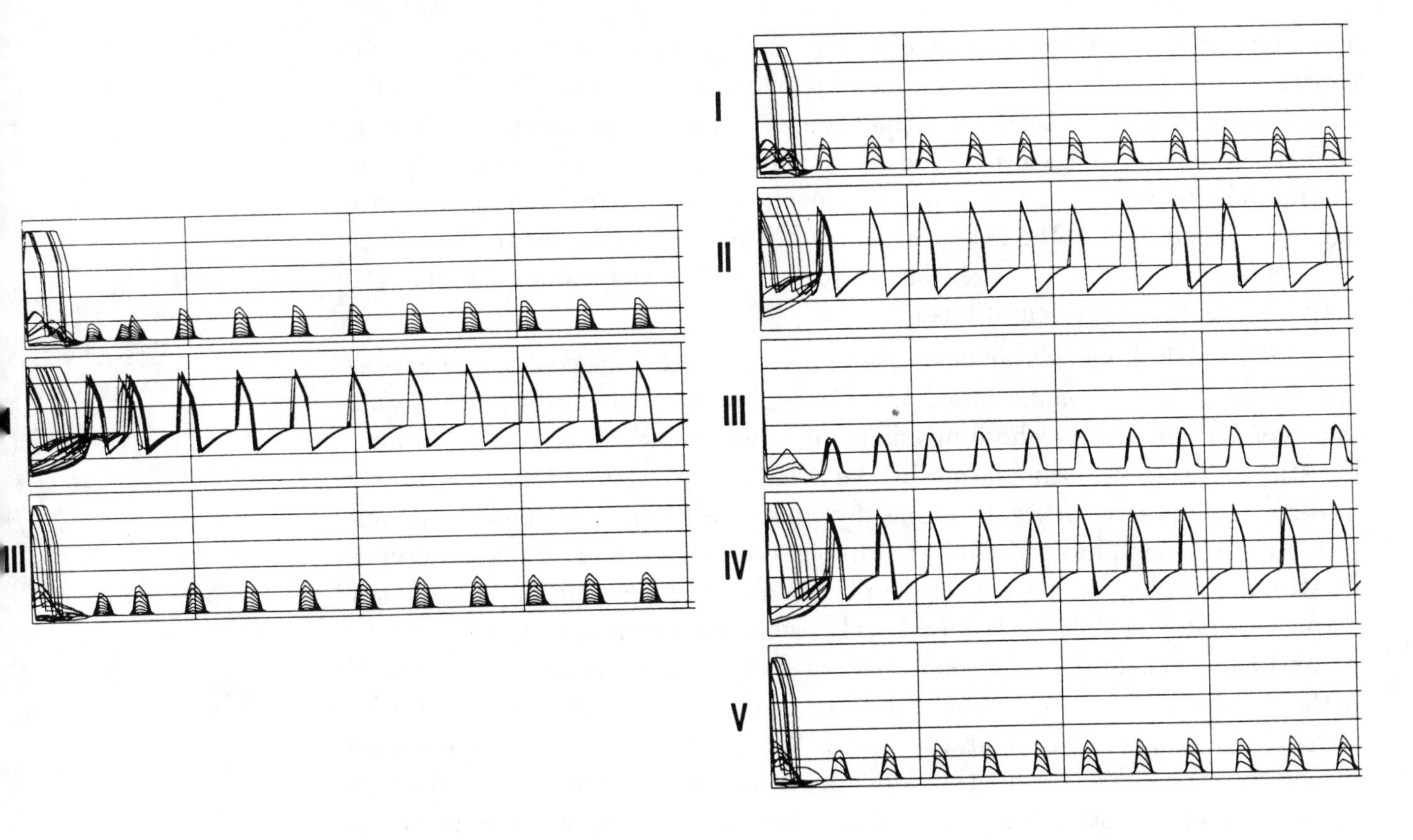

Figure 18: Adaptive filter coupling for single and double bar input

for $w \in \mathbf{C}$. Due to the square integrability mod C of $(U_1, L^2(\mathbf{R}))$ it follows from the orthonormality relations

$$< H_{m,n} \mid H_{m',n'} >= \begin{cases} 1 & m = m' \text{ and } n = n' \\ 0 & \text{elsewhere} \end{cases}$$

and the fact that the linear injections

$$\mathcal{S}(\mathbf{C}) \hookrightarrow L^2(\mathbf{C}) \hookrightarrow \mathcal{S}'(\mathbf{C})$$

have everywhere dense images the

Neural Assembly Coding Principle. *For all $T \in \mathcal{S}'(\mathbf{C})$ the neural assembly selection formula*

$$K_1(T) = \lim_{\substack{M \to \infty \\ N \to \infty}} \sum_{\substack{0 \leq m \leq M \\ 0 \leq n \leq N}} < H_{m,n}, K_1(T) > H_{m,n}$$

holds with respect to the weak or strong dual topology of the space $\mathcal{S}'(\mathbf{C})$ of complex-valued tempered distributions on the complex phase plane $\mathbf{C} \hookrightarrow N$.

Thus the adaptive filter kernel $K_1(T) \in \mathcal{S}'(\mathbf{C})$ computed by the Weyl operational calculus is a linear superposition of local linking neural networks with adaptively modulated synaptic weights. Initially, the strengths of the synaptic connections are assigned randomly according to a Gaussian distribution. The generation by interaction with the external environment of neural assemblies $K_{m,n}$ that are associated to $H_{m,n}$ and provide a complexity beyond a critical threshold level is at the edge of phenomenal consciousness ([23, 24]). Whenever this level is surpassed, phenomenal states must necessarily occur. Deficits in phenomenal consciousness occur if the rate of neural assembly formation falls below the critical threshold level. Thus a critical production rate of neural assemblies is the necessary and sufficient condition for the existence of phenomenal states. Awareness is the result of the system's capacity to actively generate representations ([23]).

The local linking neural networks $K_{m,n}$ of coherently co-active neurons are not built-in neuroanatomical assemblies, but neurodynamical functional local connectivity units whose membership is determined in the model of analog stimulus-response association by the synaptic strengths. They constantly undergo cooperative reorganizations by adaptive filter coupling. However, it needs to be emphasized that the presence or absence of phase coherence in stimulus-evoked single neuron responses actually does neither prove nor disprove that spatially distributed cell assemblies discharge in cooperative phase-linked synchrony. The existence of neural wavelets per se is thus of little diagnostic value for the validation of the temporal encoding concept by stimulus-evoked coherent neural wavelets. What really matters is cooperative phase-linked synchrony and the dependence of cooperative synchronization probability on the stimulus configuration. But these features can only be assessed by multiple-channel recording from several units simultaneously. Nevertheless, neural wavelets are of high interest because they indicate organized cooperative neurodynamical activity in spatio-temporal neural networks.

Two different spatially overlapping stimuli can be represented by two independently synchronized assemblies of cells and individual clusters of neurons can switch between different neural assemblies depending upon stimulus configuration. If cells with overlapping receptive fields but different orientation preferences are activated with a single moving light bar they cooperatively synchronize their responses even if some of these clusters are suboptimally activated. However, if such a cluster of cells is stimulated by two independent stimuli which move in different directions, they no longer form one coherently co-active neural assembly but split into two independently synchronized cell assemblies, those clusters joining the same synchronously co-active neural assembly that have a preference for the same stimulus. Thus the two stimuli become represented by two spatially interleaved but temporally segregated neural assemblies. Neural assemblies representing the same stimulus cooperatively synchronize their responses while no consistent correlations exist between the neural activities of assemblies representing different stimuli. It follows from the neural assembly coding principle that local response parameters of the individual neural clusters such as the amplitude or the interference patterning of the responses are unaffected by changes in the global configuration of the stimuli. Thus it is not possible to predict from the responses of individual neural clusters whether they were activated by one coherent stimulus or by several different stimuli. The only cue for this distinction is provided by the evaluation of cooperative synchrony of the responses of the co-activated neural clusters. These results indicate that response synchronization between simultaneously co-activated neural clusters depends not only on the features preference of the respective clusters but also on stimulus configuration. One methodological caveat following from this is that cross-correlation analysis does not reliably reflect neuroanatomical connectivity ([86]).

Because the interactions in linking neural network models encode the degree of association, the preceding line of reasoning establishes the following cognition principle valid for the quantum neurodynamical functional connectivity model of analog stimulus-response association by stimulus-evoked coherent neural wavelets.

Theorem 6. *A perceptual cognitive code is performed in spatio-temporal neural networks by the analog association between stimulus-evoked interactions.*

A change of frequencies as indicated by the transition of learning kernels

$$K_1(T) \mapsto K_\nu(T) \quad (\nu \neq 0)$$

is performed by choosing the scaled quantum mechanical harmonic oscillator wave functions

$$\psi : t \mapsto h_m(\sqrt{|\nu|}.t), \quad \varphi : t \mapsto h_n(\sqrt{|\nu|}.t)$$

as model neural wavelets. The associated Hamiltonian

$$\frac{1}{\nu}\frac{\mathrm{d}^2}{\mathrm{d}t^2} - 4\pi^2 \nu t^2$$

has a pure point spectrum and yields for the eigenfunctions $\psi, \varphi \in \mathcal{S}(\mathbf{R})$ the eigenvalues

$$-2\pi(\operatorname{sign}\nu).(2m+1), \quad -2\pi(\operatorname{sign}\nu).(2n+1),$$

respectively. The coefficients of the expansions of $K_\nu(T)$ and $K_1(T)$ satisfy the identity

$$< H_{m,n}, K_\nu(T) >= \frac{1}{\sqrt{|\nu|}} < H_{m,n}, K_1(T) >$$

associated to $K_{m,n}$ for degrees $m \geq 0$ and $n \geq 0$, respectively. It follows

Corollary. *In the coherent co-activation of spatially distributed neurons, the amplitude of the wavelets decreases with increasing frequency $|\nu|$. Rapidly oscillating neural assemblies comprise fewer neurons than slowly oscillating neural assemblies.*

The macroscopic cooperative neural activity in the brain is analogous to the property of temperature reflecting the kinetic energy of molecules in a gas.

As temperature is defined in thermodynamics for the ensemble and not for the single particle, so sensory information is defined for the neural assembly and not for the single neuron or neuroglial cell. Like temperature, the interactive condition can be regarded as a distribution. Once the limit cycle activity is induced it destabilizes millions of neurons and neuroglial cells, drives them into coherent rhythmic activity, and directs their organized output onto widely disseminated target neurons. It generates a new image that incorporates an input image with pre-existing patterns that are collated residues of previous images and with more general factors relating to the state of the brain and body. In a process of self-organization it creates an image of a sensory event in a context of past experience and present expectation. This outcome satisfies a fundamental postulate in neuroscience, which holds that psychodynamics is an expression of neurodynamics. Ultimately they must conform. It follows that neurodynamics is a member of the family of dynamics, yet it differs from its siblings in its substrate and postulates as much as quantum mechanics differs from thermodynamics and hydrodynamics. This is because the state variables of neural holography do not represent concentrations of matter and energy directly but indirectly via their expressions in dendritic and axonal activity patterns.

15 Nonlinear Quantum Neurodynamics

Experimentalists such as myself are working with noisy and high dimensional nonautonomous systems, so that proof that brains or parts of brains are chaotic is not only unlikely but illusory.
Walter J. Freeman (1992)

One of the most robust properties of the brain is its capacity to generate low-amplitude fluctuations in electrical and magnetic potential that are detected within the brain and at the surface of the scalp as brain waves or the electroencephalogram (EEG). The brain waves persist so strongly during life that their absence is used as a sure sign of brain death. EEGs are so sensitive to behavioral state that they serve as indicators of the levels of sleep and anesthesia, of abnormalities of consciousness and perception, and of emotional arousal. But they are extremely difficult to read because they manifest deterministic chaos in brain dynamics. The route to deterministic chaos ([94]) goes via an asymmetric coupling condition.

Theorem 7. *The quantum neurodynamical activity pattern of the neural assemblies* $(K_{m,n})_{m \geq n \geq 0}$ *is periodic for* $m = n$, *quasiperiodic for* $m \neq n$ *and* $m \equiv n \bmod 2$, *and deterministic chaotic for* $m \not\equiv n \bmod 2$.

Switching from the polarized cross-section N/C to the isotropic cross-section to C in N yields the bosonic Fock model of N ([75]). An application of the theory of infinite-dimensional Hilbert-Schmidt Grassmannians to the symmetric coupling case $m = n$ allows to reduce the Kadomtsev-Petviashvili hierarchy KP of soliton theory by the affine Lie algebra A_2^1 to the KP_2 hierarchy which contains the exactly solvable Korteweg-de Vries time-evolution equation KdV ([76]). Thus the A_2 symmetry reduction yields

Corollary. *In the symmetric coupling case $m = n$, the quantum neurodynamics activates solutions of the* KdV *hierarchy of soliton theory.*

Due to the underlying algebra of anticommutation relations, it follows that the soliton solutions in the KdV model behave like fermions.

Particularly low frequency oscillations in the δ range of 0.5 Hz $\leq \nu \leq$ 4 Hz are observed during slow wave sleep, but also during pathological states such as coma or anesthesia. Oscillatory activity in the ϑ range of 6 Hz to 7 Hz is prominent in limbic structures such as the septum, the hippocampus, and the entorhinal cortex during states of attentive arousal. Oscillatory activity in the 10 Hz range, also known as α activity, occurs during drowsiness or states of relaxation and is particularly pronounced over occipital cortical areas. Up to this frequency range, oscillatory activity is of large amplitude and can readily be recorded with macroelectrodes indicating that the discharges of a large number of neurons are cooperatively synchronized and phase-locked to these frequencies. This, however, contrasts with the low amplitude and high frequency oscillations in the EEG which characterize high levels of arousal and attention. During these states the Fourier spectrum of the EEG covers a broad range of frequencies extending from 10 Hz to 60 Hz. This pattern is commonly referred to as desynchronized EEG and is thought to reflect temporally incoherent activity of spatially distributed neuron assemblies. However, analysis based on refined methods such as digital filtering and intracerebral recording with microelectrodes has revealed the presence of coherent oscillatory activity also under conditions characterized by desynchronized EEG. These investigations have disclosed oscillatory activity in the β and γ range, i.e., at frequencies from 15 Hz to 30 Hz, and 30 Hz to 60 Hz. These high frequency oscillations occur spontaneously both in humans and higher mammals such as cats and monkeys when the subjects are in a state of focussed attention or when they are performing new and complicated motor acts. Oscillatory components in the γ frequency range are also contained in field potential responses evoked by sensory stimuli. This has been demonstrated to be the case for the cortical responses following acoustic and visual stimulation, for visual responses in the optic tectum of pigeons, and for the event-related wavelets which are thought to reflect high level cognitive processes to selective attention. Particularly regular and prominent field potential oscillations in the range of 40 Hz occur also in the olfactory bulb during the inspiration phase of the respiration cycle.

There is thus ample evidence from a variety of brain structures, especially those showing a laminar organization such as the neocortex, the tectum, and the olfactory bulb that assemblies of cells engage in high frequency cooperative synchronous activity even during states when the EEG is desynchronized. With the exception of the olfactory bulb, however, the amplitudes of these high frequency oscillations are usually small indicating that the assemblies of neurons engaged in such cooperative synchronous activity are small.

These observations indicate that neurons in cortical networks have the tendency to engage in cooperative synchronous activity in different distinct frequency bands whereby the probability of occurrence of cooperative synchronous activity in a particular frequency range depends upon the central state of the brain, on the presence of sensory signals, and on the occurrence of motor acts. This raises the problem as to the functional significance of these cooperative phase-linked synchronization phenomena. As far as synchronization in the low frequency band up to 6 Hz is concerned, it is commonly held that such states of global synchrony are inappropriate for information processing. At these low frequencies very large populations of cells discharge unisonously and these self-generated rhythmic discharges are only little influenced by sensory stimuli. The fact that such large scale synchronization in the low frequency band occurs in sleep and in coma and anesthesia seems to support this notion. It should be emphasized, however, that there have been proposals for a functional significance of low frequency wavelets in natural sleep in relation to processes of memory organization and consolidation. The situation is different for the high frequency wavelets in the β and γ band because these are particularly pronounced in awake performing brains, appear to occur in a less global scale, and show close relations with sensory and motor processes ([86, 84]).

16 The Schrödinger Fiber Bundle

Several independent lines of argumentation concerning the nature of neuronal representations, the constraints for signal transmission and conditions of use-dependent synaptic plasticity all lead to the postulate of a temporal code. All emphasize the significance of synchrony at a millisecond time scale. This in turn requires a temporal structure in neuronal response that allows first for the distinction of synchronous from asynchronous states with high temporal resolution and second for the establishment of cooperative synchrony over large distances.
Wolf Singer (1992)

It is highly unlikely that memory consists of the establishment or facilitation of a specific neural pathway in which firing constitutes remembering.
E. Roy John (1980)

For $\nu \neq 0$ let the complex phase plane $\mathbf{C} \hookrightarrow N$ be equipped with the Liouville area form $\frac{i\nu}{2} dw \wedge d\bar{w}$. Then it can be identified with the layer $z^* = \nu$ in $\mathrm{Lie}(N)^*$ which carries the symplectic form $\nu . dx \wedge d\xi$. In order to define the distributional learning kernel $K_1(T) \in \mathcal{S}'(\mathbf{C})$ independent of the symplectic frames at $w \in \mathbf{C}$, Theorem 3 supra suggests to construct the semi-direct product of the Lie groups $\mathbf{Mp}(1, \mathbf{R})$ and N. The resulting six-dimensional real Lie group is called the Schrödinger group

$$S = \mathbf{Mp}(1, \mathbf{R}) \times N,$$

the action of $\mathbf{Mp}(1, \mathbf{R})$ on the normal subgroup N of S being naturally defined by the covariance identity of the oscillator representation $(W, L^2(\mathbf{R}))$. The linear Schrödinger representation $(U_1, L^2(\mathbf{R}))$ of N admits a natural extension from N to S, also denoted by $(U_1, L^2(\mathbf{R}))$, by the oscillator representation $(W, L^2(\mathbf{R}))$ of $\mathbf{Mp}(1, \mathbf{R})$. The complex vector space $L^2(\mathbf{R})^\infty$ of smooth vectors in $L^2(\mathbf{R})$ is the same whether $(U_1, L^2(\mathbf{R}))$ is regarded as a unitary representation of N or S, namely the complex Schwartz space $\mathcal{S}(\mathbf{R})$ on the whole real line $\mathbf{R}$. Construct the principal $\mathbf{SL}(2, \mathbf{R})$ bundle E of symplectic frames over the base manifold $\mathbf{C}$ written

$$\begin{array}{ccc} \mathbf{SL}(2, \mathbf{R}) & \rightarrow & E \\ & & \downarrow \\ & & \mathbf{C} \end{array} .$$

Let $\tilde{E}$ denote the unique covering of E. Then $\tilde{E}$ forms the principal $\mathbf{Mp}(1, \mathbf{R})$ bundle of metaplectic frames over $\mathbf{C}$ written

$$\begin{array}{ccc} \mathbf{Mp}(1, \mathbf{R}) & \rightarrow & \tilde{E} \\ & & \downarrow \\ & & \mathbf{C} \end{array} .$$

In the next step of geometrization, introduce the fibered product

$$E^{\mathcal{S}'} = \tilde{E} \times_{\mathbf{Mp}(1,\mathbf{R})} \mathcal{S}'(\mathbf{R}).$$

Then $E^{\mathcal{S}'}$ forms a fiber bundle over $\mathbf{C}$ with fiber $\mathcal{S}'(\mathbf{R})$ giving rise to the diagram

$$\begin{array}{ccc} \mathcal{S}'(\mathbf{R}) & \rightarrow & E^{\mathcal{S}'} \\ & & \downarrow \\ & & \mathbf{C} \end{array} .$$

The Schrödinger fiber bundle $E^{\mathcal{S}'}$ over $\mathbf{C}$ admits the fiber subbundles

$$E^{\mathcal{S}} \hookrightarrow E^{L^2} \hookrightarrow E^{\mathcal{S}'}$$

over the base manifold $\mathbf{C}$ with the fiber injections

$$\mathcal{S}_w \hookrightarrow L^2_w \hookrightarrow \mathcal{S}'_w$$

at the point $w \in \mathbf{C}$. The complex vector space $\mathcal{S}'_w$ of tempered distributions is formed by the symplectic spinors ([46]) at $w \in \mathbf{C}$. Because the natural representation of the Schrödinger group S on $\mathcal{S}'_w$ is actually independent of the metaplectic frame chosen in $\tilde{E}_w$ at $w \in \mathbf{C}$, the space $\mathcal{S}'_w$ is isomorphic to the complex vector space $\mathcal{S}'(\mathbf{R})$ of tempered distributions on the whole real line $\mathbf{R}$. The isomorphism

$$\mathcal{S}'_w \rightarrow \mathcal{S}'(\mathbf{R}) \quad (w \in \mathbf{C})$$

restricts to an isomorphism of $\mathcal{S}_w$ onto $\mathcal{S}(\mathbf{R})$ and a complex Hilbert space isomorphism of L^2_w onto $L^2(\mathbf{R})$ for all $w \in \mathbf{C}$.

Theorem 8. *The complex phase plane* $\mathbf{C} \hookrightarrow N$ *can be identified with the neural hologram plane at the point* $w \in \mathbf{C}$.

In particular, the Weyl quantizing symbol $K_1(T) \in \mathcal{S}'(\mathbf{C})$ associated to $T \in \mathcal{S}'(\mathbf{C})$ gives rise to a linear mapping

$$\mathcal{S}_w \to \mathcal{S}'_w \quad (w \in \mathbf{C})$$

which is independent of the metaplectic frame chosen in $\grave{E}_w$. Moreover, the aforementioned isomorphisms of the fibers $\mathcal{S}'_w$ of the Schrödinger fiber bundle $E^{\mathcal{S}'}$ onto $\mathcal{S}'(\mathbf{R})$ combined with the reproducing inverse scattering formula for the holographic transform at the point $w \in \mathbf{C}$ implies the fractal self-identity of neural holograms.

Corollary 1. *In spatio-temporal neural network architectures, the entire information globally encoded by the neural hologram can be reconstructed from any fraction of the neural hologram.*

The fractal self-identity of neural holograms has been established by neurological surgery experiments which have shown that 98 % of the visual tracts bilaterally can be taken out and still patterned vision is preserved ([62, 63]). The redundancy of the information expressed and stored in neural holograms implies large immunity to input distortion. The fractal self-identity is dual to the principle of quantum eraser outlined in Section 9 supra.

Corollary 2. *Information retrieving neural signals are activated by coherently expanded neural wavelets.*

The fundamental local-global duality of spatio-temporal neural network architectures is reflected by the distinction between erasing impulses and retrieving signals.

On the other hand, experiments in contemporary neurophysiology have shown great precision in the extraction of certain features about the external environment by specific feature extractor cells or about the position of particular muscles by cells in the motor system. This demonstration of functional specificity on the input and the output sides suggests localization of function. At the same time, real-life experience provides many examples of patients who have suffered localized brain damage due to stroke, other diseases, or injury and have shown permanent functional deficits. Appropriate weighting of the fibers $\mathcal{S}'_w$ of the Schrödinger fiber bundle $E^{\mathcal{S}'}$ according to the local signal-to-noise ratio, however, leads to the statistical configuration theory ([43]) which reconciles the localizationist and nonlocalizationist views of brain function. It adapts Lashley's law of equipotentiality to the experimental findings and establishes that the difference between brain regions is not all-or-none qualitative mediation of specific sensory, motor, or other functions, but the weighted quantitative representation of different functions, each with its specific local signal-to-noise ratio ([43]). Within the last few years, chaos physics has developed a totally new view of the noise problem.

17 Linking in Cortical Neural Network Models

Recent critics on neural modeling have argued that conventional neural modeling does not account for deeper effects from quantum physics. ... In any event, quantum effects are most likely to be visible in specific molecules in the brain with small energy differences between vibrational states (such as vision pigments). ... These effects could also be understood better if efforts were made to exploit them in areas like optical and molecular computing.
Paul J. Werbos (1992)

Computational neuroscience is an approach to understanding the information content of neural signals by modeling the CNS at various different structural scales, including the biophysical, the circuit, and the systems levels. Neural network computation forms a new scientific and engineering paradigm concerned with non-programmable adaptive information processing systems that develop their own algorithms in cooperatively synchronized stimulus-evoked response to their environment. It is important to observe that in this context computation has a meaning different from large-scale computing, because it derives from the computer metaphor the idea that the neural network computes in the sense of representing, processing, and storing information. The paradigm shift in the concept of computing has led to the emergence of such promising devices as molecular computers ([66, 70, 71, 98, 99]).

The current approach to neurocomputing is a very simplified one based on hierarchical multilayer geometries of computational neuroanatomy. Neuroboard and neurochips like the silicon retina chip provide satisfactory results in some areas. From the aspect of the influence of the environment, the modulatory interaction *coherent stimulus components - coherent neural wavelet - phase-linked synchronized response - neural hologram - revived neural wavelet* has to be considered as an intelligent hardware unit. Of major importance is the neurocontrol mechanism provided by the cross-correlation function. It includes the phase to encode the degree of association between coherent stimulus components and relates cortical linking network models by the neurodynamical functional connectivity model of analog stimulus-response association to quantum mechanics.

In clinical neurology, the very first recordings of the electrical activity of the brain, performed more than sixty years ago with scans from the scalp, have revealed prominent oscillatory activity. Since then and for several decades the study of oscillatory patterns in the EEG and in field potentials recorded with intracerebral macroelectrodes has remained a major research field of experimental neurophysiology. Analyzing the temporal structure of these wavelet patterns has established close correlations between the frequency spectrum of the neural wavelets and changes in the central state of the brain. Different stages of sleep and arousal as well as abnormal states such as coma and anesthesia could be identified by relying exclusively on the spectral decompositions of frequencies in the EEG. However, once it became possible to record the activity of individual neurons, interest in temporal structures and field potentials declined. The discovery that the firing rate of neurons in peripheral structures of the CNS reflected the intensity of sensory stimuli and the speed and force of muscle contractions introduced the notion of rate coding. The evidence of a close relation between the position of a neuron in the brain and its dynamical functional properties led to the concept of place coding. The message conveyed by a neuron was thought to be defined entirely by the amplitude of the response and its provenance. As a consequence, in single unit studies timing as a coding variable received relatively little attention. This is reflected by the fact that neuron responses to sensory stimuli or activities occurring in relation to motor acts are commonly averaged over successive trials in order to improve the signal-to-noise ratio. This averaging procedure destroys the temporal structure in the activation pattern that is not precisely locked to the stimulus-evoked response or the motor response. Thus temporal codes were neither attended to nor were they discoverable with the commonly applied methods of single unit analysis.

Since a few years, however, a dramatic change in attitude and interest can be observed in computational neuroscience. The neural paradigm shifted again towards timing as a coding variable and analog stimulus-response association by stimulus-evoked coherent neural wavelets is now considered as important a code as relations between response amplitudes of spatially distributed neural assemblies.

In correspondence to the experimental neurophysiological research work, hypotheses about the role of temporally cross-correlated neural activity have a history of acceptance and rejection by the computational neuroscience community starting with the nets of McCulloch's model neurons ([10]). McCulloch neural network models require exactly clocked operations, and the early enthusiasm about their logic and arithmetic capabilities was soon followed by criticisms of their neurophysiological implausibility. In fact, strict pulse periodicity was never observed in neural signals since the timing of neural events is unpredictable. Nevertheless, neural information processing based on temporal signal cross-correlation appeared to be particularly suitable for dealing with problems in pattern recognition if the neural representation of object regions are characterized by correlated activity, region filtering, and figure-ground segregation can be achieved by the superposition of arrays of synchronized gates.

Neural holographic models of visual functions gained strong neurophysiological support by the experimentally well established discovery of the collective phenomenon of stimulus-dependent oscillatory neural ensemble activity in the visual system by various laboratories. The discoveries of stimulus-evoked oscillations in the visual cortex of cat and monkey and the discovery of phase-linked synchronized responses in different visual areas and of isolated cortical correlation patches within a single cortical area and between different areas indicate that correlated neural ensemble activity is a local as well as a global phenomenon in the visual system.

A similar model based on parallel phase-linked synchronized response holds for the cerebellar cortex which acts as a neurocontroller of muscle coordination and the learning of rote movements. The key point is that self-organization based on cooperative phase-linked synchronization of cell assemblies leads to the selective stabilization of intracortical interconnections which extend between neuron clusters whose activation patterns show statistical correlation. Development studies have shown that these intrinsic tangential connections essentially appear postnatally by passing through a phase of exuberant proliferation during which they are particularly numerous and far-reaching. Subsequently, the excitatory tangential interconnections become pruned. The process of pruning which provides selectivity is controlled by experience. Thus cooperative phase-linked synchronization of distributed neural responses is crucial not only for signal transmission by stimulus-evoked coherent neural wavelets but also for the processes of use-dependent synaptic plasticity.

The functional role of temporally structured responses in synaptic plasticity is the same as that in neural assembly coding. It serves to resolve superposition problems by providing a temporal coding to express association. Thus considerations on neural assembly coding and on synaptic plasticity both lead to the same postulate of a temporal code that relies on synchrony at a millisecond scale. Connections between cells which have repeatedly been part of an neural assembly strengthen and consolidate. According to the concept of temporal coding the signature for cells belonging to an assembly is the synchronization of their temporal structure responses. As synchrony between pre- and postsynaptic neural activation is at the same time the condition which favours strengthening of synaptic connection, the same temporal code which serves to distinguish the neurons of an assembly can thus be used to distinguish the connections which need to be reinforced in order to stabilize a neural assembly ([86]).

18 Conclusions

An analog parallel model of computation is especially interesting from the point of view of the present understanding of the biophysics of neurons, membranes and synapses.
Tomaso Poggio (1985)

The principle basis of operation within current ANN models defines an ability to generalize functions of pattern classification. Providing these patterns are well separated, it is possible to use gradient descent network models to learn categories and interpret how to separate them. Following this learning process, input patterns are classified according to the degree with which they fall into these categories.

The ability of the visual system to recognize objects in spite of the enormous number of possible shape variations cannot be explained in terms of template matching or object-filtering; the number of templates or filters required would be too large. Adopting a more general point of view, biological organization processes are far too complex to hope that a relatively complete understanding of how a perceptual system like the retina and the visual cortex function will soon emerge. But the basic principles of organization of biophysical ANNs can be understood without one's knowing in detail how the components of the CNS actually work. Furthermore, the same principles can be used to implement ANNs in any of several different technologies. Among these technologies, free-space photonics has many attractive features such as the large bandwidths of optical signals, the high connectivity of holographic image processing, and the quantum holographic implementation of nonlinear dynamics including deterministic chaos. The use of theoretical neural network models that embody biophysically-motivated rules and constraints is a powerful tool in the development and study of synthetic perceptual systems that demonstrate high data capacity, operate in a massively parallel way, and require no explicit programming. The resulting parallel process of cooperative phase-linked synchronized stimulus-evoked oscillatory responses is non-local with respect to spatial distance, resistant to ablation, and adaptable, the characteristics that suggests a fundamental diversion from conventional ANN design by the neural quantum holographic model. Coherent neural wavelet analysis reveals not only what we know about the neurodynamical functional connectivity model of analog stimulus-response association but what is in principle knowable.

19 Outlook

MacKay *was, to our knowledge, one of the first who argued that "temporal coding has the enormous advantage over spatial coding that a signal can be broadcast over a wide area, by the simplest means, without losing its identity," and..."it can be picked out of a welter of other activity by a subsystem alert to it. The vulnerability of a temporally organized system to local damage could be relatively small, since the spatio-temporal patterns of activity are cooperative states of many elements."*
Reinhard Eckhorn (1991)

The neurodynamical functional connectivity model of analog stimulus-response association by stimulus-evoked coherent neural wavelets has been implemented by the HNeT emulator system operating from a transputer processing hardware platform. The multiprocessor board is capable of performing up to 512K holographic based interconnections per second for real time applications. This board, termed Super computing Expansion Board (SEB), utilizes eight transputers and a programmable link adapter permitting the serial data link for each transputer node to be interconnected in a programmable manner. A

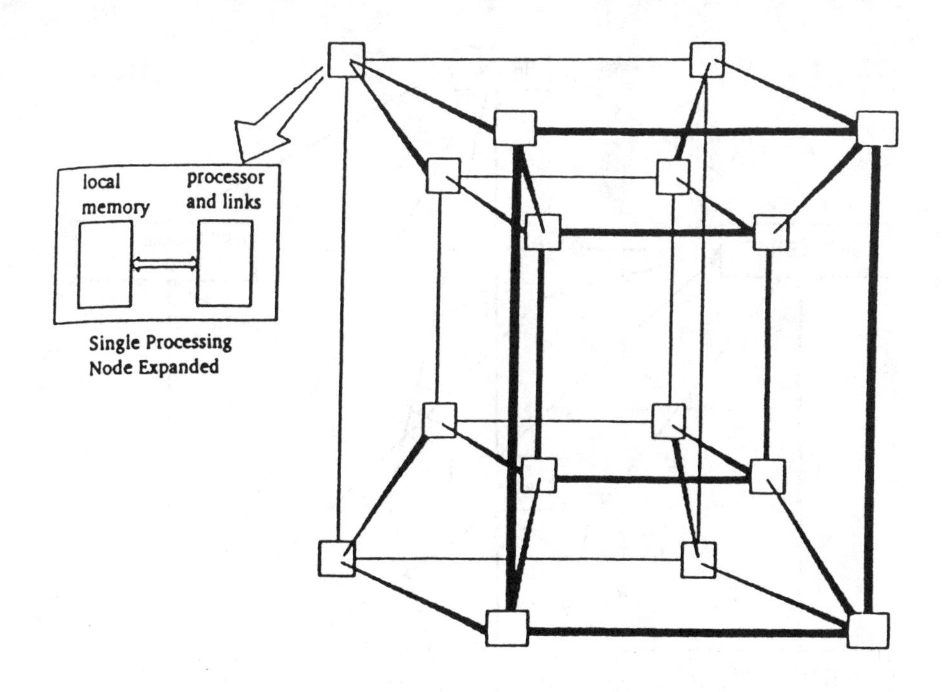

Figure 19: Structure of hypercube parallel processing

parallel data transfer scheme from the host bus that has been incorporated in the SEB permits fast transfer of data from the host application to all transputer nodes. Two SEBs configure the inter-transputer serial communication links of a 16 node hypercube (Figure 19). An application proceeds in two steps, first configuring the neural engine within each processing node, followed by the execution step. The programmable link adapter permits reconfiguration of the transputer serial links in order that each transputer node may be connected in sequence to the host machine during the configuration stage. Following the configuration stage, the link adapter reestablishes a hypercube structure for the inter-transputer serial communication links. Interrupt control of the neural engine, and data transfer during the execution step is facilitated by the I/O bus and memory access facilities ([91, 92, 93]).

Applications include analog control for navigational and robotic systems as well as trend analysis of technical stock price/index movements.

In order to obtain additional evidence in support of the computational neuroscience hypothesis that cooperative stimulus-evoked response synchronization serves as a code for neural information processing, experiments are needed in which causal relations can be established between the occurrence of response synchronization in specific neural assemblies and particular functions, that need to be assessed at the behavioural level. This requires to record simultaneously from several selected cortical areas of awake behaving animals with techniques that allow to assess cooperative response synchronization with high temporal resolution. With the techniques presently available the num-

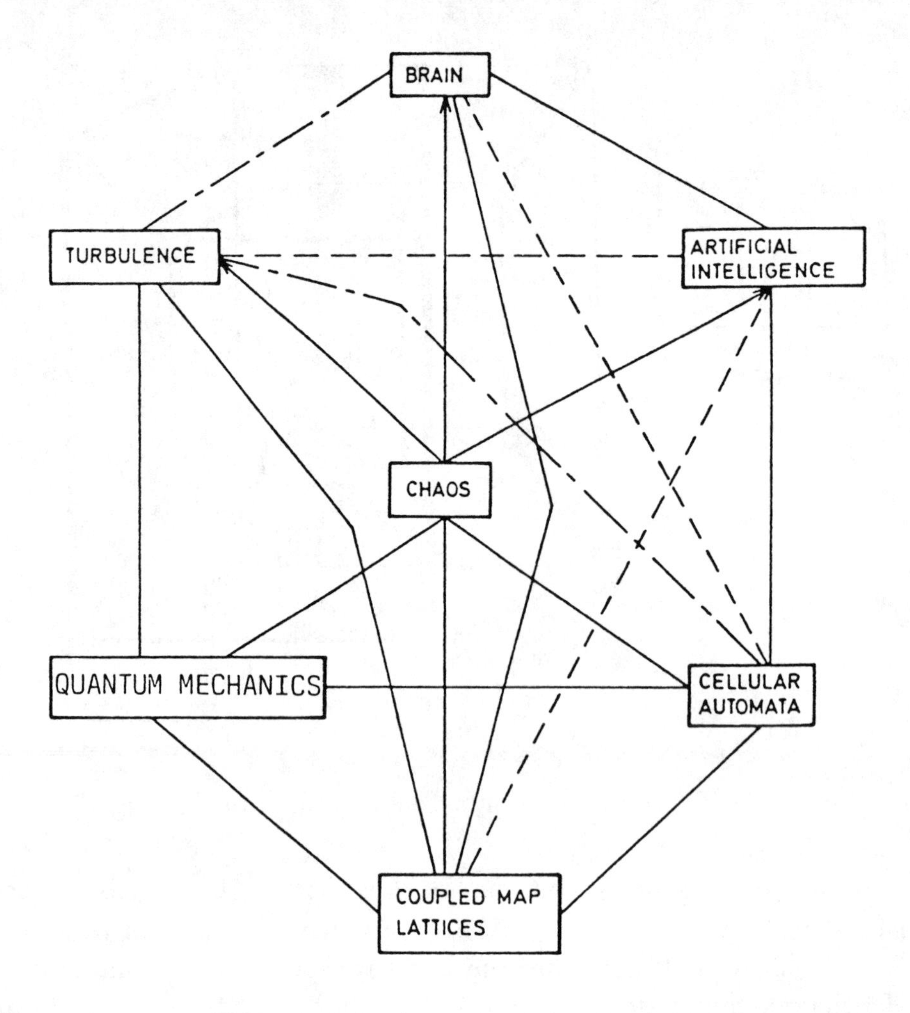

Figure 20: Research program

ber of recording sites that can be simultaneously examined in spatio-temporal neural networks is bound to remain small. Until new techniques become available, relations between synchronization and behaviour will be detectable only for conditions where synchronization is maintained long enough to become detectable even if only a few neurons can be looked at simultaneously ([86]).

The final goal of these neurophysiological experiments should be in support of the idea that visual awareness and phenomenal consciousness actually are quantum neurodynamical processes implemented by nonlinear dynamical systems and deterministic chaos (Figure 20). Quantum mechanics, however, has a basic built-in limitation of knowledge that goes far beyond the standard Heisenberg uncertainty principle. As a consequence, the quantum holographic approach to neurodynamics rigorously establishes that the brain cannot completely explain itself. To express this phenomenon in terms of a paradox, when the brain threatens to completely explain its quantum neurodynamical function it actually finishes to function. Thus some secrets of the cortical activities will be shrouded for ever. Advances in multichannel high temperature Squid techniques ([25]) combined with advances in the theory of nonlinear dynamics and chaos, however, will substantially decrease the amount of secrets.

Acknowledgments. The author is grateful to Dr. Helena Eccles and Sir John C. Eccles for valuable discussions during the First Appalachian Conference on Behavioral Neurodynamics: Processing in Biological Neural Networks at the Center for Brain Research and Informational Sciences at Radford University. Moreover he wishes to express his thanks to Dr. Karin von Radziewski and Dipl. Math. Ludger Knoche for their expert assistance in preparing the TEX-file.

References

[1] Abeles, M.: Local Cortical Circuits. Springer-Verlag, Berlin, Heidelberg, New York 1982

[2] Allen, T., Mead, C., Faggin, F., and Gribble, G.: Orientation selective VLSI retina. Visual Communications and Image Processing '88, T.Russell Hsing, ed., Proc. SPIE 101, 1040-1046 (1988)

[3] Anderson, D.Z., Feinberg, J.: Optical novelty filters. IEEE J. Quantum Electronics 25, 635-647 (1989)

[4] Anderson, D.Z., Lininger, D.M., and Feinberg, J.: An optical tracking novelty filter. Opt. Lett. 12, 123-125 (1987)

[5] Barbe, D.F., Baker, W.D., and Davis, K.L.: Signal processing with charge-coupled devices. Charge-Coupled Devices, D.F. Barbe, ed., 91-145, Springer-Verlag, Berlin, Heidelberg, New York 1980

[6] Bauer, M., Martienssen, W.: Coupled circle maps as a tool to model synchronisation in neural networks. Network 2, 345-351 (1991)

[7] Bauer, M., Krueger, U., and Martienssen, W.: Experimental studies of mode-locking and circle maps in inductively shunted Josephson junctions. Europhys. Lett. 9, 191-196 (1989)

[8] Beck, F., Eccles, J.C.: Quantum aspects of brain activity and the role of consciousness. Proc. Natl. Acad. Sci. USA 89 (1992)

[9] Bouillon, H.: Ordnung, Evolution und Erkenntnis. J.C.B. Mohr (Paul Siebeck), Tübingen 1991

[10] Bressloff, P. C., Stark, J.: Neuronal dynamics based on discontinuous circle maps. Phys. Lett. A 150, 187-195 (1990)

[11] Chen, H.-L., Schempp, W.: The uncertainty inequality in quantum holography, Bohr's indeterminacy principle, and synchronized neural networks. General Inequalities 6, W. Walter, ed., 411-422, Birkhäuser Verlag, Basel, Boston, Berlin 1992

[12] Chirovsky, L.M.F., Focht, M.W., Freund, J.M., Guth, G.D., Leibenguth, R.E., Przybylek, G.J., Smith, L.E., D'Asaro, L.A., Lentine, A.L., Novotny, R.A., and Buchholz, D.B.: Large arrays of symmetric self-electro-optic effect devices. OSA Proc. on Photonic Switching, Vol. 8, H.S. Hinton, J.W. Goodman, eds., 56-59 (1991)

[13] Cornell-Bell, A.H., Finkbeiner, S.M., Cooper, M.S., and Smith, S.J.: Glutamate induces calcium waves in cultured astrocytes: Long-range glial signaling. Science 247, 470-473 (1990)

[14] Cramer, J.G.: The transactional interpretation of quantum mechanics. Rev. Mod. Phys. 58, 647-687 (1986)

[15] Doty, R.W.: Forebrain commissures and the unity of mind. Machinery of the Mind, E.R. John, ed., 3-13, Birkhäuser Verlag, Boston, Basel, Berlin 1990

[16] Eccles, J.C.: New light on the mind-brain problem: How mental events could influence neural events. Complex Systems - Operational Approaches in Neurobiology, Physics, and Computers. H. Haken, ed., 81-106, Springer-Verlag, Berlin, Heidelberg, New York, Tokyo 1985

[17] Eckhorn, R., Dicke, P., Kruse, W., and Reitboeck, H.J.: Stimulus-related facilitation and synchronization among visual cortical areas: Experiments and models. Nonlinear Dynamics and Neuronal Networks, H.G. Schuster, ed., 57-75, VCH Publishers, Weinheim, New York, Basel, Cambridge 1991

[18] Eckhorn, R., Reitboeck, H.J., Arndt, M., and Dicke, P.: Feature linking via stimulus - evoked oscillations: Experimental results from cat visual cortex and functional implications from a network model. International Joint Conference on Neural Networks, Vol. I, 723-730, IEEE/INNS Washington D.C. 1989

[19] Edelman, G.M.: Neural Darwinism. The Theory of Neuronal Group Selection. Basic Books Publishers, New York 1987

[20] Engel, A.K., König, P., Kreiter, A.K., Gray, C.M., and Singer, W.: Temporal coding by coherent oscillations as a potential solution to the binding problem: Physiological evidence. Nonlinear Dynamics and Neuronal Networks, H.G. Schuster, ed., 3-25, VCH Publishers, Weinheim, New York, Basel, Cambridge 1991

[21] Feinstein, D.I.: The hexagonal resistive network and the circular approximation. Caltech Computer Science Technical Report Caltech-CS-TR 88-7. Computer Science Department, California Institute of Technology 1988

[22] Feldman, M.R., Guest, C.C.: Holograms for optical interconnects for very large scale integrated circuits fabricated by electron-beam lithography. Opt. Eng. 28, 915-921 (1989)

[23] Flohr, H.: Brain processes and phenomenal consciousness. A new and specific hypothesis. Theory & Psychology 1, 245-262 (1991)

[24] Flohr, H.: Qualia and brain processes. Emergence or Reduction? Essays on the Prospects of Nonreductive Physicalism. A. Beckermann, H. Flohr, and J. Kim, eds., 220-238, Walter de Gruyter, Berlin, New York 1992

[25] Foglietti, V.: Multichannel instrumentation for biomagnetism. Superconducting Devices and Their Applications, H. Koch, H. Lübbig, eds., 487-501, Springer-Verlag, Berlin, Heidelberg, New York, London, Paris, Tokyo, Hong Kong, Barcelona, Budapest 1992

[26] Freeman, W.J.: What are the state variables for modeling brain dynamics with neural networks? Nonlinear Dynamics and Neuron Networks, H.G. Schuster, ed., 243-255, VCH Publishers, Weinheim, New York, Basel, Cambridge 1991

[27] Frostig, R.D., Lieke, E.E., Arieli, A., Ts'o, D.Y., Hildesheim, R., and Grinvald, A.: Optical imaging of neuronal activity in the living brain. Neuronal Cooperativity, J. Krüger, ed. 30-51, Springer-Verlag, Berlin, Heidelberg, New York, London, Paris, Tokyo, Hong Kong, Barcelona, Budapest 1991

[28] Gernert, D.: Non-classical interactions in generalized neural nets. Cognitive Syst. 1, 39-47 (1985)

[29] Goldman, W.M.: Life in the Heisenberg group. Manuscript, Department of Mathematics, University of Maryland at College Park, MD 1989

[30] Goldman, W.M.: Complex Hyperbolic Geometry. Final preliminary version, Department of Mathematics, University of Maryland at College Park, MD 1992

[31] Goldman, W.M., Phillips, M.B.: HEISENBERG: Exploring geometry at the boundary of the complex hyperbolic plane. Manuscript, Department of Mathematics, University of Maryland at College Park, MD 1988

[32] Gray, C.M., Engel, A.K., König, P., and Singer, W.: Temporal properties of synchronous oscillatory neuronal interactions in cat striate cortex. Nonlinear Dynamics and Neuronal Networks, H.G. Schuster, ed., 27-55, VCH Publishers, Weinheim, New York, Basel, Cambridge 1991

[33] Grinvald, A.: Real-time optical mapping of neuronal activity. Ann Rev. Neurosci. 8, 263-305 (1985)

[34] Grössing, G.: Is quantum theory relevant for the description of brain functions? Cognitive Syst. 3, 289-304 (1992)

[35] Grossberg, S., Somers, D.: Synchronized oscillations during cooperative feature linking in a cortical model of visual perception. Neural Networks 4, 453-466 (1991)

[36] Harnad, S.: Minds, machines and Searle. J. Expt. Theor. Artif. Intell. 1, 5-25 (1989)

[37] Harris, J., Koch, C., Luo, J., and Wyatt, J.: Resistive fuses: Analog hardware for detecting discontinuities in early vision. Analog VLSI Implementation of Neural Systems, C. Mead, M. Ismail, eds., 27-55, Kluwer Academic Publishers, Boston, Dordrecht, London 1989

[38] Heyser, R.C.: Loudspeaker phase characteristics and time delay distortion: Part 1. J. Audio Eng. Soc. 17, 30-41 (1969)

[39] Hoffman, W.C.: The visual cortex is a contact bundle. Applied Math. and Comp. 32, 137-167 (1989)

[40] Hoppensteadt, F.C.: Signal processing by model neural networks. SIAM Rev. 34, 426-444 (1992)

[41] Jewell, J.L., Lee, Y.H., Scherer, A., McCall, S.L., Olsson, N.A., Harbison, J.P., and Florez, L.T.: Surface-emitting microlasers for photonic switching and interchip connections. Opt. Eng. 29, 210-214 (1990)

[42] Johannesma, P., Aertsen, A., Cranen, B., and Van Erning, L.: The phonochrome: A coherent spectro-temporal representation of sound. Hearing Res. 5, 123-145 (1981)

[43] John, E.R.: Multipotentiality: A statistical theory of brain function - evidence and implications. The Psychobiology of Consciousness, R.J. Davidson, J.M. Davidson, eds., 129-146, Plenum Publishing Corporation, New York 1980

[44] Keener, J.P.: Chaotic behavior in piecewise continuous difference equations. Trans. Amer. Math. Soc. 261, 589-604 (1980)

[45] Koch, C.: Implementing early vision algorithms in analog networks: An overview. Applications of Neural Networks, H.G. Schuster, ed., 3-23, VCH Publishers, Weinheim, New York, Basel, Cambridge 1992

[46] Kostant, B.: Symplectic spinors. Symposia Math., Vol. XIV, 139-152, Academic Press, New York, London 1974

[47] Lown, B.: Sudden cardiac death. Circulation 60, 1593-1599 (1979)

[48] Mann, S., Haykin, S.: Adaptive "chirplet" transform: an adaptive generalization of the wavelet transform. Opt. Eng. 31, 1243-1256 (1992)

[49] Marrakchi, A., Hubbard, W.M., Habiby, S.F., and Patel, J.S.: Dynamic holographic interconnects with analog weights in photorefractive crystals. Opt. Eng. 29, 215-224 (1990)

[50] McKee, P., Wood, D., Dames, M.P., and Dix, P.: Fabrication of multiphase optical elements for weighted array spot generation. Practical Holography V, S.A. Benton, ed., Proc. SPIE 1461, 17-23 (1991)

[51] Mead, C.A., Mahowald, M.A.: A silicon model of early visual processing. Neural Networks 1, 91-97 (1988)

[52] Mead, C.: Analog VLSI and Neural Systems. Addison-Wesley, Reading, MA 1989

[53] Mead, C.: Adaptive retina. Analog VLSI Implementation of Neural Systems, C. Mead, M. Ismail, eds., 239-246. Kluwer, Boston, Dordrecht, London 1989

[54] Miller, D.A.B.: Quantum-well self-electro-optic effect devices. Optical and Quantum Electronics 22, S61-S98 (1990)

[55] Pearson, J.C., Finkel, L.H., and Edelman, G.M.: Plasticity in the organization of adult cerebral cortical maps: A computer simulation based on neuronal group selection. J. Neurosci. 7, 4209-4223 (1987)

[56] Pribram, K.H.: Toward a science of neuropsychology (method and data). Current Trends in Psychology and Behavioral Sciences, R.A. Patton, ed., 115-142, University of Pittsburgh Press, Pittsburgh 1954

[57] Pribram, K.H.: Neocortical function in behavior. Biological and Biochemical Bases of Behavior, H.F. Harlow, C.N. Woolsey, eds., 151-172, University of Wisconsin Press, Madison, Wisconsin 1958

[58] Pribram, K.H.: The intrinsic systems of the forebrain. Handbook of Physiology, Neurophysiology II, J. Field, H.W. Magoun, and V.E. Hall, eds., 1323-1324, American Physiological Society, Washington, DC 1960

[59] Pribram, K.H.: Some dimensions of remembering: Steps toward a neuropsychological model of memory. Macromolecules and Behavior, J. Gaito, ed., 367-393, Appleton-Century Crofts, New York 1972

[60] Pribram, K.H.: Localization and distribution of function in the brain. Neuropsychology after Lashley, J. Orbach, ed., 273-296, Lawrence Erlbaum Associates, Inc., New York 1982

[61] Pribram, K.H.: Convolution and matrix systems as content addressable distributed brain processes in perception and memory. Human Memory and Cognitive Capabilities, F. Klix, H. Hagendorf, eds., 541-558, Elsevier Science Publishers, North-Holland 1986

[62] Pribram, K.H.: Prolegomenon for a holonomic brain theory. Synergetics of Cognition, H. Haken, M. Stadler, eds., 150-184, Springer-Verlag, Berlin, Heidelberg, New York 1990

[63] Pribram, K.H.: Brain and Perception: Holonomy and Structure in Figural Processing. Lawrence Erlbaum, Publishers, Hillsdale, NJ 1991

[64] Pribram, K.H., Carlton, E.H.: Holonomic brain theory in imaging and object perception. Acta Psychologica 63, 175-210 (1987)

[65] Pribram, K.H., McGuinness, D.: Attention and para-attention processing: Event-related brain potentials as tests of a model. Psychophysiology and Experimental Psychopathology, Annals of the New York Academy of Sciences 658, D. Friedman, G. Bruder, eds., 65-92, New York Academy of Sciences, New York 1992

[66] Pribram, K.H., Schempp, W.: The dendritic membrane as a linear metaplectic manifold (to appear)

[67] Primas, H.: Chemistry, Quantum Mechanics and Reductionism. Second Edition, Springer-Verlag, Berlin, Heidelberg, New York, Tokyo 1983

[68] Primas, H.: The measurement process in the individual interpretation of quantum mechanics. Quantum Theory without Reduction, M. Cini, J.-M. Lévy-Leblond, eds., 49-68, Adam Hilger, Bristol, New York 1990

[69] Primas, H.: Time-asymmetric phenomena in biology: Complementary exophysical descriptions arising from deterministic quantum endophysics. Open Systems & Information Dynamics 1, 3-34 (1992)

[70] Rebane, A., Ollikainen, O.: Error-corrective optical recall of digital images by photoburning of persistent spectral holes. Opt. Commun. 83, 246-250 (1991)

[71] Rebane, A., Bernet, S., Renn, A., and Wild, U.P.: Holography in frequency selective media: hologram phase and causality. Opt. Commun. 86, 7-13 (1991)

[72] Reitboeck, H.J., Eckhorn, R., Arndt, M., and Dicke, P.: A model for feature linking via correlated neural activity. Synergetics of Cognition, H. Haken, M. Stadler, eds., 112-125, Springer-Verlag, Berlin, Heidelberg, New York 1990

[73] Schempp, W.: Gruppentheoretische Aspekte der digitalen Signalübertragung und der kardinalen Interpolationssplines I. Math. Meth. in the Appl. Sci. 5, 195-215 (1983)

[74] Schempp, W.: Radar ambiguity functions, the Heisenberg group, and holomorphic theta series. Proc. Amer. Math. Soc. 92, 103-110 (1984)

[75] Schempp, W.: Harmonic analysis on the Heisenberg nilpotent Lie group, with applications to signal theory. Pitman Research Notes in Math., Vol. 147. Longman Scientific and Technical, Harlow, Essex 1986

[76] Schempp, W.: Bohr's indeterminacy principle in quantum holography, self-adaptive neural networks, cortical self-organization, molecular computers, magnetic resonance imaging, and solitonic nanotechnology. Nonlinear Image Processing III, E.R. Dougherty, J. Astola, C.G. Boncelet, Jr., eds., Proc. SPIE 1658, 297-343 (1992)

[77] Schempp, W.: Quantum holography, synthetic aperture radar imaging and computed tomographic imaging. Quantum Measurements in Optics, P. Tombesi, D.F. Walls, eds., 323-343, Plenum Press, New York, London 1992

[78] Schempp, W.: Analog VLSI networks. Numerical Methods of Approximation Theory, Vol. 9, D. Braess, L.L. Schumaker, eds., 285-300, Birkhäuser Verlag, Basel, Boston, Berlin 1992

[79] Schempp, W.: Quantum holography and neurocomputer architectures. J. Math. Imaging and Vision 2, 279-328 (1992)

[80] Schempp, W.: The auditory novelty filter. Manuscript (to appear)

[81] Schillen, T.B., König, P.: Temporal coding by coherent oscillation as a potential solution to the binding problem: Neural network simulations. Nonlinear Dynamics and Neuronal Networks, H.G. Schuster, ed., 153-171, VCH Publishers, Weinheim, New York, Basel, Cambridge 1991

[82] Schwartz, E.L.: Computational anatomy and functional architecture of striate cortex: A spatial mapping aproach to perceptual coding. Vision Res. 20, 645-669 (1980)

[83] Schwartz, L.: Sous-espaces hilbertiens d'espaces vectoriels topologiques et noyaux associés (noyaux reproduisants). J. Analyse Math. 13, 115-256 (1964)

[84] Sheer, D.E.: Sensory and cognitive 40-Hz event-related potentials: Behavioral correlates, brain function, and clinical application. Brain Dynamics, E. Başar, T.H. Bullock, eds., 339-374, Springer-Verlag, Berlin, Heidelberg, New York, London, Paris, Tokyo, Hong Kong 1989

[85] Singer, W.: Search for coherence: A basic principle of cortical self-organization. Concepts Neurosci. 1, 1-26 (1990)

[86] Singer, W.: Synchronization of cortical activity and its putative role in information processing and learning. Ann. Rev. Physiol. (in print)

[87] Singer, W., Gray, C., Engel, A., König, P., Artola, A., and Bröcher, S.: Formation of cortical cell assemblies. Cold Spring Harbor Symposia on Quantitative Biology, Vol. 55, 939-952 (1990)

[88] Skarda, C.A., Freeman, W.J.: Chaos and the new science of the brain. Concepts in Neurosci. 1, 275-285 (1990)

[89] Sompolinsky, H., Golomb, D., and Kleinfeld, D.: Phase coherence and computation in a neural network of coupled oscillators. Nonlinear Dynamics and Neuronal Networks, H.G. Schuster, ed., 113-130, VCH Publishers, Weinheim, New York, Basel, Cambridge 1991

[90] Sporns, O., Tononi, G., and Edelmann, G.M.: Dynamic interactions of neuronal groups and the problem of cortical integration. Nonlinear Dynamics and Neuronal Networks, H.G. Schuster, ed., 205-240, VCH Publishers, Weinheim, New York, Basel, Cambridge 1991

[91] Sutherland, J.G.: A holographic model of memory, learning and expression. Int. J. Neural Syst. 1, 259-267 (1990)

[92] Sutherland, J.G.: A transputer based implementation of holographic neural technology. Transputing '91, P. Welch et al., eds., 657-675, IOS Press, Amsterdam 1991

[93] Sutherland, J.G.: The holographic neural method. Fuzzy, Holographic, and Parallel Intelligence, B. Souček and the IRIS Group, eds., 7-92, J. Wiley and Sons, New York, Chichester, Brisbane, Toronto, Singapore 1992

[94] Thatcher, R.W.: Brain stimulation of comatose patients: A chaos and nonlinear dynamics approach. Machinery of the Mind, E.R. John. ed., 376-401, Birkhäuser Verlag, Boston, Basel, Berlin 1990

[95] Von Hayek, F.A.: The Sensory Order. An Inquiry into the Foundations of Theoretical Psychology. University Chicago Press, Chicago, London 1952, Midway Reprint 1976

[96] Weil, A.: Sur certains groupes d'opérateurs unitaires. Acta Math. 111, 143-211 (1964), Collected Papers, Vol. III (1964-1978), 1-69, Springer-Verlag, Berlin, Heidelberg, New York, Tokyo 1985

[97] Weinberg, H., Robertson, A.W., Crisp, D., and Johnson, B.: Magnetic fields of the brain resulting from normal and pathological function. Machinery of the Mind, E.R. John, ed., 479-511, Birkhäuser Verlag, Boston, Basel, Berlin 1990

[98] Werbos, P.J.: The cytoskeleton: Why it may be crucial to human learning and to neurocontrol. Nanobiology 1, 75-95 (1992)

[99] Wild, U.P., Rebane, A., and Renn, A.: Dye-doped polymer films: From supra-molecular photochemistry to the molecular computer. Adv. Mater. 3, 453-456 (1991)

[100] Ypey, D.L., VanMeerwijk, W.P.M., and DeHaan, R.L.: Synchronization of cardiac pacemaker cells by electrical coupling. Cardiac Rate and Rhythm, L.N. Bouman, H.J. Jongsma, eds., 363-395, Martinus Nijhoff Publishers, The Hague, Boston, London 1982

Walter Schempp
Lehrstuhl für Mathematik I
Department of Mathematics
University of Siegen
D-5900 Siegen
GERMANY
schempp@hrz.uni-siegen.dbp.de

[9?] Weinberg, H., Robertson, A.W., [illegible] and Johnson, B.: Magnetic [illegible] Components [illegible] of the [illegible] [illegible] Boston, [illegible]

[illegible] [illegible] [illegible] [illegible] [illegible]

[illegible] [illegible] [illegible] supra[illegible] [illegible] [illegible]

[100] [illegible] and [illegible] [illegible] [illegible] [illegible] [illegible] [illegible] [illegible] [illegible] The Hague, [illegible]

[illegible]
[illegible] Mathematik [illegible]
Department of Mathematics
University of [illegible]
D-[illegible]
GERMANY
[illegible]

Chapter 9

Quantum Theory & Neural Systems: Alternative Approaches and a New Design

Paul J. Werbos
Room 1151, National Science Foundation
Washington, D.C. 20550

Quantum Theory and Neural Systems: Alternative Approaches and a New Design

Paul J. Werbos
Room 1151, National Science Foundation*
Washington D.C., 20550

ABSTRACT

This paper tries to identify at least some connections between all of the talks presented orally at this conference. First, it reviews several approaches to linking quantum theory and neural systems (biological or artificial). Next, it shows how Pribram's notion of "dendritic field" systems can be interpreted without quantum theory, to yield a "third class" of neural network, combining some of the best features of the multilayer perceptron (MLP) and of more association-based learning systems. Finally, it describes some alternative views of the mind/body problem, as discussed at this conference.

EXISTING WAYS TO USE QUANTUM THEORY IN STUDYING NEURAL SYSTEMS

Broadly speaking, one may identify three ways to use quantum theory to study or enhance neural systems:

(1) Direct use of quantum theory to study or design the physical substrate of neural systems. (See Penrose[1], Deutsch[2], Hammeroff, Yasue, (Eccles).)

(2) Use of quantum theory as a formal "metaphor." More precisely, this includes the use of quantum theory as a source of equations to be used to describe or specify information processing at a level higher than that of the true quantum substrate. (See Pribram[3], Dawes, Jahn.)

(3) Use of quantum field theory (QFT) as a source of formal mathematical tools, which can be used to analyze the properties of classical systems. (See Werbos, the companion paper.)

The Physical Substrate Approach

The first approach fits the true, classical, "reductionist" recipe for how to use quantum theory properly. In the classical approach, we observe that the brain is made up of electrons, protons, photons, etc. QFT is our best description of how such particles behave. Therefore, we can use QFT to predict how the components of the brain will behave, building up from the lowest physical level. We can try to generate predictions which are truly interesting from the viewpoint of brain science and information processing. Even though this approach is thoroughly

* The views expressed here are those of the author, not those of NSF. The ideas and the text were developed on the author's personal time.

classical, so far as it goes, people like Penrose and Hammeroff have used it to generate very interesting and heretical hypotheses about the brain.

Hammeroff has argued that classical microbiology (including neuroscience) has treated the inside of the cell as a "bag of water," relying on mathematical tools and assumptions due to classical chemical kinetics. ("Compartment models" in neuroscience could be seen as multiple bags of water.) He has promoted a new science of "nanobiology" which, among other things, would begin to use concepts from solid-state physics (which are based in turn on quantum theory) to help us understand events within the cell. As with any true venture into the unknown, no one can say for sure what will emerge from this effort. It is certain, however, that the issues at stake are of central importance to the understanding of intelligence[4]. They clearly warrant more attention and support than they have received to date. The calculations by Yasue presented at this conference may be seen as one among several strands of analysis which could feed into the efforts of Hammeroff and his colleagues.

Penrose and Deutsch have presented even more heretical ideas, relying on technical aspects of QFT to be discussed in the companion to this paper ("Chaotic Solitons, Computing and Quantum Field Theory").

Quantum Theory as a Metaphor

Both Dawes and Pribram have expressed some discomfort with the term "metaphor," which may conjure up images of poetry and of figures of speech. Here, I use the term "metaphor" as it is used in artificial intelligence: it refers to the effort to understand one domain of knowledge by borrowing structures, images or equations from completely different domains, and hoping that one will find parallels or isomorphisms.

As an example, let us imagine that we build a computer system as follows. First, we obtain a million digital chips, a million processing units comparable to the famous 80486 chips from Intel or to Transputer chips. We organize them into a three-dimensional array, 100 by 100 by 100. Each chip is connected only to its immediate neighbors. (This is called a "systolic" array or a "systolic architecture.") This gives us a completely digital supercomputer, a "fifth generation" massively-parallel processor (MPP), which can be described completely without any use of quantum theory. Nevertheless, we can program this computer to simulate a three-dimensional Schrodinger equation. (The Schrodinger equation is the dynamic equation at the core of quantum theory.) Following ideas like those of Dawes, we may hope to use such a simulation to help us perform useful computations, which may or may not have neural analogues.

The design of Dawes (as presented here) can make use of a three-dimensional Schrodinger equation because it focuses on the specialized problem of tracking the location of a target in three dimensions. However, one could generalize this to tracking across a more generalized set of prototypes (possible states of the environment), in an associative memory; in effect, this would try to combine more general notions of nonlinear filtering and system identification[5] with notions of associative memory or local learning networks. The effort to make such a combination would clearly be of interest, whether or not it follows Dawes' particular approach.

If the set of prototypes were not three-dimensional, then one could not continue to use the three-dimensional Schrodinger equation. However, Dawes has hinted in the past at the possibility of using Kohonen's topological mapping techniques to force the prototypes into a three-dimensional pattern. The computational costs and benefits of this are unclear. Within the brain, I find it hard to imagine any real need to force a three-dimensional ordering so artificially, on a large scale, given that the brain is not limited to a systolic architecture globally. But on a millimeter-level scale, one might argue that three dimensional field effects in the brain do require some effort to map neural signals into a three-dimensional topology.

In the appendices to [3], Pribram, Yasue and Misu describe the possibility that relatively higher-level structures such as dendrites and membranes may be able to implement something like a three-dimensional Schrodinger equation, based on field effects in the brain. This, in turn, raises the possibility that they might be performing calculations similar to those described by Dawes. Pribram does not use the term "metaphor," but he clearly does make distinctions similar to those above.

QFT As a Source of Tools

The companion paper to this one shows a third way that one might use quantum theory: as a source of mathematical tools. More precisely, the mathematical ideas of operator fields, Fock space, etc., can be used very precisely to answer questions about "classical systems" -- systems which can be specified well enough by use of partial differential equations (PDE).

The biologist and the engineer should be warned that these mathematical tools are **not yet ready** for straightforward, off-the-shelf application to practical problems. (See [5] for advanced neural net tools now useful in engineering.) Efforts along these lines would be like hitting an ant with the proverbial heavy-lift sledge-hammer. On the other hand, the further development of these tools by those who understand the mathematics could be of immense importance. The companion paper argues that such developments could actually feed back to QFT itself, and deepen our understanding of the quantum substrate of reality.

Figures 1 and 2 at the end of this paper illustrate the basic ideas here.

Figure 1 represents the two-way interaction between engineering and neuroscience which underlies the neural network profession. Back in the early 1970s, when I argued for this kind of 2-way interaction (including such concepts as backpropagation and adaptive critics), this idea was treated as radical, unacceptable heresy -- even by some people now trying to take credit for it. Now, figure 1 represents a large profession with many practical applications to its credit[5]. The International Neural Network Society (INNS) claims about 4,000 members worldwide.

Figure 2 represents the new heresy proposed by my companion paper, a new science which is virtually devoid of population. As in neural networks, I propose a flow of information from the left to the right, extracting mathematical principles from a vast domain (QFT) which no one fully understands. In the middle -- with chaotic solitons (i.e., chaos in four dimensions) -- clean mathematical principles and definitions, supported by computer simulations, can be used to refine and extend these principles. These extensions can then be brought back to QFT, so as to illuminate QFT more deeply and to allow the extraction of further principles.

Recent experiments by Mandel[6] show that a simple unattended and unmonitored computer can function as an "observer" in quantum-mechanical measurements just as well as any biological organism. In my view, this gives substantial support to observer-free versions of quantum theory advocated in the companion paper.

In the 1970s, my work alone was certainly not enough to develop the entire science of neural networks. In like manner, the companion paper by itself is certainly not enough to exhaust the potential of this new science. (Ueda has suggested the term "chaoitons" or "quantum chaoitons" to define the new science.) Additional research is desperately needed, and could have a huge impact on future technology.

TWO TYPES OF SCHRODINGER EQUATION: A WARNING TO THE BIOLOGIST

Discussions of quantum theory in biology often gloss over an extremely important distinction -- the distinction between two types of Schrodinger equation.There are at least two different Schrodinger equations one reads about very often:

$$i\dot{\Psi}(\underline{x}) = a\,\Delta\,\Psi(\underline{x}) + V(\underline{x})\Psi(\underline{x}) \tag{1}$$

$$\dot{\Psi}(\text{Fock space}) = iH\Psi(\text{Fock space}) \tag{2}$$

Equation 1 is basically the original equation proposed by Schrodinger.
In this equation, the complex number $\Psi(\underline{x})$ represents the state of a force field, the electron field, at the point $\underline{x}$ in three-dimensional space. The equation states that the change of Ψ over time, $\dot{\Psi}$, equals the sum of two terms: (1) $a\Delta\Psi$, which represents the sum of various derivatives of Ψ, and is purely linear; (2) $V(\underline{x})\Psi(\underline{x})$, where V is called the "potential field." V represents the effect of other force fields (such as the electric field), and is assumed to be constant over time.

When equation 1 was first written down, it generated considerable excitement on the part of Einstein, DeBroglie, etc. It began to appear as if all the particles and forces of nature could be described in terms of field equations (PDE) over three-dimensional space. Equation 1 did an excellent job of predicting the spectrum (the energy levels) of hydrogen, a simple atom with only one electron.

Unfortunately, equation 1 was never able to predict the spectrum of helium, which has two electrons. After years of effort across the world, an obscure physicist approached equation 1 with the kind of apparent misunderstanding which commonly gets people thrown out of graduate school: he decided to insert two coordinate vectors, $\underline{x}_1$ and $\underline{x}_2$, to represent the two electrons of helium. (Schrodinger, etc., postulated that Ψ represents a single force field; thus, two electrons would be represented by two "bumps" or local maxima in the function Ψ.) Thus he modified equation 1, and solved it for Ψ as a function of six dimensions. The success of this strange procedure was the pivotal event in shaping modern physics.

Modern quantum theory -- quantum field theory (QFT) -- is based on equation 2, not equation 1. The function Ψ is defined over "Fock space" -- an infinite-dimensional space to be described more precisely in the companion paper. Atomic spectra have been studied very, very extensively, and there is no known way to reconcile equation 1 with the measured higher-order terms. Equation 1 is valid for describing a single particle, against a fixed background potential; any interaction between particles invalidates it. Therefore equation 1 is not a valid basis for describing interactive systems at the quantum level.

Many discussions in biology focus on the three-dimensional Schrodinger equation, equation 1. For example, the appendix to [3] describes how field effects through the dendrites of neurons could implement a three-dimensional Schrodinger equation. In fact, this result is not all that surprising. Most engineers would accept that neurons or silicon could implement any linear system which could be represented as:

$$\dot{\underline{\Psi}}(t) = A\underline{\Psi}(t) \ , \tag{3}$$

where the vector $\underline{\Psi}$ represents the set of values of Ψ across different points in space, and where A is a systolic matrix (a matrix which only connects neighboring points). Equation 1 is just a special case of equation 3. If we accept that neurons and computers can emulate any linear systolic system, then our real challenge is this: can we find a learning rule which describes how A (or $V(\underline{x})$) changes over time, in order to make the system compute something interesting?

A COMPUTATIONAL INTERPRETATION OF PRIBRAM'S DENDRITIC FIELD IDEA

Backpropagation -- the most widely used algorithm for artificial neural networks (ANNs) -- was first developed by translating certain ideas from Freud into workable computational mathematics[4,7]. This section will try to translate Pribram's concepts of dendritic field processing into mathematics. No quantum theory of any kind is required in this translation.

In [3], Pribram has restated the familiar argument that the McCulloch-Pitts model of the neuron, which underlies MLPs, is oversimplified. Going beyond that argument, he conveys an elegant picture of how he thinks neural processing works, especially for assemblies of large cells in the cerebral cortex working together to process visual images. He rejects the idea that individual neurons work by themselves to compute their outputs. Instead, he proposes a three-step processing scheme for groups or assemblies of cells:

(1) The group receives inputs from elsewhere, as in conventional models.

(2) The "important processing" goes on at a dendritic level, which obeys something like equation 3, but with a global field $\underline{\Psi}$ interpenetrating all the cells and the extracellular medium as well.

(3) The cell bodies and axons serve as simple "read-out devices," each performing a simple nonlinear transformation (like the usual "sigmoid" function s) of field strengths at the axon hillock.

Pribram states that the dendritic level involves very complex processing, and that it must settle down dynamically before the group is ready for read-out. The papers by Schempp and by MacLennan at this conference provide qualitative support for this view, based on work in psychology and in theoretical computer science, respectively.

Looking at this picture from a static point of view, without learning, it would appear to offer nothing new. Even if the dendritic level -- level 2 -- were extremely complex, its linearity would insure that the field strengths at the axon hillock, after settling down, would still be a linear combination of the inputs. Thus in a formal sense we could still write:

$$\text{net}_i = \sum W_{ij} * (\text{input})_j \,, \tag{4}$$

exactly as we do now in MLPs[5]. (In this equation, "net_i" represents the field strength or voltage at the axon hillock of neuron number i. The asterisk indicates multiplication.) We would lose the interpretation of W_{ij} as a synapse strength, but the mathematical relations between inputs and outputs of every neuron in the group would still be exactly the same as with MLPs.

Even before we consider learning, we might argue that the dendritic model does allow one additional feature beyond equation 4: it allows for a kind of internal memory or time-lagged recurrence inside the dendrites. However, the concept of time-lagged recurrent networks and "sticky neurons" has already been fully assimilated into parts of the neuroengineering literature [5, chapters 3 and 10]. Likewise, the results by Richmond at this conference appear to involve substantial time delays (circa 100 ms), and would fit quite well with the models of time-lagged recurrent nets discussed in [5]. In fact, Richmond's observation that such effects are much stronger in visual cortex than elsewhere fits very well with our theory that the cerebral cortex as a whole is the primary site of "working memory" implemented by time-lagged recurrent networks [5, 4 p.92]. The kinds of structures described by Stadler at this conference could also fit easily within the known framework of recurrent networks.

From the viewpoint of learning, however, the dendritic field model does open up some important new possibilities. For the dendritic layer, we may modify equation 3 slightly to:

$$\dot{v}_i = -\sum A_{ij} v_j + \text{input}_i \ , \qquad (5)$$

where v_i refers to something like the voltage in the dendritic field in the location where input number i comes in, and where A is a symmetric matrix. (For example, resistances between points i and points j on a dendrite would normally form a symmetric matrix.) For the read-out layer, we might assume:

$$\text{net}_i = \sum B_{ij} v_j \qquad (6)$$

$$\text{output}_i = s(\text{net}_i) \ , \qquad (7)$$

where s is the usual sigmoid function[5].

Equation 5 is nothing but a linearized Hopfield net, whose final settling value is well-known:

$$\underline{v} = A^{-1} \ \underline{\text{input}} \qquad (8)$$

Equations 5 and 6 together yield:

$$\underline{\text{net}} = BA^{-1} \ \underline{\text{input}} \qquad (9)$$

Equation 9 has exactly the same form as multiple regression in statistics! In statistics, it is well-known that a perfect use of past data can be achieved, in observation-by-observation learning, simply by accumulating a covariance matrix A and a cross-covariance matrix B on an observation-by-observation basis; thus if we have a neural system which can afford to maintain an entire matrix A and a matrix B, and use equation 9, then we could use it to implement perfect learning in the linear case. This would be achieved by the following learning rules:

$$\text{new } A_{ij} = \text{old } A_{ij} + (\text{input})_i * (\text{input})_j \qquad (10)$$

$$\text{new } B_{ij} = \text{old } B_{ij} + (\text{target})_i * (\text{input})_j \ , \qquad (11)$$

which look very much like local Hebbian learning rules. In equation 11, $(\text{target})_i$ is the desired output for neuron number i. (See the discussion of supervised learning in [5].)

In actuality, dendritic systems would not be able to update a full A and B matrix. (Notice that the systolic constraint has been neglected here.) However, a local or systolic pattern of connections could still be very powerful. Crucial to this power is the fact that a single input can actually enter the dendritic field in several places, due to the usual proliferation of axon collaterals and multiple synapses. These phenomena appear less important in the McCulloch-Pitts model, but here they play a crucial role -- which is encouraging, in light of their importance in biology. The empirical work reported by Szu at this conference, on the factors which influence the sparse pattern of connectivity in sophisticated neurons, will be important to a more detailed understanding of these aspects.

The linear version of this concept would be "perfect" and elegant in learning a linear relationship between inputs and outputs of the neural assembly. However, the nonlinear aspects cannot be ignored. If an assembly were made up of single, complex dendritic neurons, then it is easy enough to build a system which tries to minimize:

$$\sum_i (\text{target}_i - s(\text{net}_i))^2 \tag{12}$$

by minimizing:

$$\sum_i (s^{-1}(\text{target}_i) - \text{net}_i)^2 * (\frac{\partial s}{\partial \text{net}_i})^2 \tag{13}$$

One could simply use $s^{-1}(\text{target}_i)$ as the target for net_i, and continue to use equations 10 and 11 modified as follows:

$$\text{new } A_{ij} = \text{new } A_{ij} + (\text{input})_i * (\text{input})_j * (\text{attention}) \tag{14}$$

$$\text{new } B_{ij} = \text{old } B_{ij} + (\text{target})_i * (\text{input})_j * (\text{attention}) \tag{15}$$

$$\text{attention} = (\frac{\partial s}{\partial \text{net}_i})^2 \tag{16}$$

This would not give perfect learning, insofar as the attention factor should change, logically, as A and B change; however, it should be far more efficient than the usual gradient-based designs. For the sake of greater robustness, one might imitate ridge regression [5, chapter 10] by initializing A to the identity matrix, or by adding kI to it after the fact, where k is an adjustment parameter to be adapted over time. Likewise, one could still insert variable learning rates[5], trust regions[8], etc, to fine-tune the process, as with MLPs and backpropagation.
For a unified assembly of neurons, equation 16 would be modified to reflect the sum of attention across the various neurons, weighted by some measure of the importance of each neuron's output at the present time. This would imply an attention parameter determined in part by local information (as in equation 16) and in part by inputs from other locations (as in the paper by Desimone at this conference).

From an engineering point of view, this kind of Linearizing Processing Element (LPE) might have several advantages. Conventional Hebbian learning is hardly ever used in practical engineering, because the global version only works in the linear case and with pre-orthogonalization (which is nonbiological because it reduces fault-tolerance and eliminates redundancy), while the local version is somewhat more expensive than other local learning rules. An LPE-based system would probably learn much more rapidly than the usual MLP. Unlike the conventional local learning networks (of which CMAC and RBF are most popular[5]), it would provide a piecewise-linear image of the input-output mapping, rather than a piecewise-flat image; in high-dimensional spaces, the former should be far superior to the latter, when fully developed. The ultimate, ideal supervised learning system would probably use the principle of "syncretism" [5, chapter 3] to combine all three types of network -- MLP, LPE and local -- in an optimal way; however, the LPE might be an important member of the set.

There are certain interesting similarities between the LPE and the Extended Kalman

Filtering learning schemes of people like Feldkamp and Puskorius of Ford Motor Company[9]. Those authors have argued very strongly that maintaining second-order information can be well worth the cost, even in certain engineering applications where the cost is very high. If this were true, then biological systems -- which might use local field effects to avoid paying a higher cost -- might well be expected to exploit such effects.

From a biological viewpoint, this kind of learning model is still extremely speculative. It may apply to a few groups of cells, or to none. I have assumed a frequency or graded code for the output of an LPE (which an engineer would use), but Bulsara has suggested that we need to pay attention to the local noise variables near the axon hillock which could make such a code really work for neurons outputting discrete spikes.

CONSCIOUSNESS, INTELLIGENCE AND THE MIND/BODY PROBLEM: SOME ALTERNATIVE VIEWS

Background

A major motivation for studying the brain and neurodynamics is the hope that this study will help us better understand the human mind. Pribram, among others, has spent decades trying to develop better connections between psychology -- the science which studies the mind -- and neuroscience, which studies the brain. Efforts in these directions ultimately cannot avoid the obvious question: what, precisely, is the relation between the mind and the brain?

The mind/brain issue has plagued us for centuries, in part for religious reasons. In the Judeo-Christian tradition, the mind is often associated with the soul as opposed to the brain. In Western materialism, the mind and brain are treated as more or less the same thing. This past year, the President has endorsed a platform which tells us that we should all proceed from a Judeo-Christian viewpoint, without question. On the other hand, some famous scientists have suggested that we should all proceed from a purely materialist point of view, and work hard to discredit and disestablish all those who seriously consider any alternative. If one were a naive, disinterested party, one might conclude that no one really knows what the truth is here as yet, and that a diversity of views should be examined. Certainly, as a society, we must learn to cope with this diversity in a more constructive manner.

In practice, the serious examination of alternative views is often impossible, because many people believe so firmly in the Bible or in classical materialism that they simply are not willing to think about alternatives. At this workshop, however, a more open atmosphere prevailed, and there were serious exchanges between alternative points of view. This section will try to summarize these exchanges.

In [4] and [10], I have tried to explore what neural networks might tell us about the human mind and about ethics, in detail, conditional upon the two or three major alternatives discussed here.

Dualism versus Materialism

The discussion of the mind/body problem began with the keynote address by Sir John Eccles. In this address, Eccles introduced the debate between dualism and materialism as views of the mind/brain relation. Eccles' views are highly controversial; however, as the discoverer of the synapse, a major pioneer in mapping out the cerebellum, and an early neural modeler (prior to McCulloch and Pitts and Least Mean Square learning), he cannot be lightly discounted.

Eccles described several versions of materialism, including very extreme forms which clearly appear untenable. (Some of these extreme versions have been widely disseminated in the neural net community!) He focused his more serious attention on the "identity" theory, which he regards as the most tenable form of materialism: the view that states of the mind are equivalent to (identical with) configurations of the brain. Many treatises on "consciousness" have appeared lately espousing this point of view, including recent work by John Taylor.

As an alternative, Eccles advocated dualism" -- the view that the human mind exists in one "world," the material universe in another, and that the mind communicates with the brain by perturbing the probabilities of events whose occurrence is indeterminate in QFT. Several speakers at the conference tried to identify the "psychons" (units of mind) in Eccles' theory with specific quantum mechanical effects in the brain; however, Eccles would not accept the identification of "psychons" themselves with any effects in the material universe.

At one point, Eccles pointed to the flexing of one's finger as an example of a voluntary movement, directly ordered by the mind itself, through an act of free will which cannot be understood in materialist terms. Based on this example, he proposed -- albeit very, very tentatively -- that the mind interacts with the brain specifically by perturbing the output probabilities from "crystalline" presynaptic structures in motor cortex. He proposed that this arrangement applies only to mammals -- those creatures who do in fact have a modern six-layer cortex with columnar structure. Citing his books, he even suggested that materialism was a "superstition" (i.e., an apriori belief held without evidence), inconsistent with the latest broad knowledge about neuroscience.

Alternative Forms of Dualism

The discussion of dualism was confused by the existence of several versions of dualism. One view would treat the mind or soul as totally unknowable, mysterious phenomena, not subject to any kind of natural law or mathematical principle. However, many participants argued that cognitive science and other branches of psychology have been making great progress recently, and that it would be foolish to give up on trying to understand the phenomenon of mind this early. Certainly, the phenomenon of mind is not totally unknowable, and certainly it is human nature to make an effort to understand such phenomena better. It still makes sense to strive towards a totally explicit (i.e. mathematical) understanding -- subject to the caveat that we do not stake our existence on achieving a complete understanding by any fixed date. So long as we continue our striving, it may not be necessary or possible to establish whether our striving will ultimately be successful. In summary, some dualists might accept (at least provisionally) that mathematical laws might exist which govern both "worlds."

In this discussion, it was noted that Penrose [1] has questioned the ability of any "algorithm" to replicate true "consciousness." However, Penrose proposes that consciousness is rooted instead in certain phenomena in QFT. Such phenomena may or may not be "algorithmic," but they are certainly governed by mathematical laws of some kind.

The Materialist View

The materialist reply to Eccles consisted of two parts: (1) the claim that materialism can fit the empirical data as well as dualism; (2) the claim, based on Occam's Razor, that materialism should be strongly preferred over dualism, when both fit the data equally well.

Regarding the data, it is easy to see that one does not need to postulate a soul in order to explain simple actions like moving a finger. It is easy to build up computer systems (presumably without souls) capable of directing such movements in a rational fashion. In fact, damage to cortical systems higher than the motor cortex is well known to interfere with the quality of a human's decision to flex or not to flex a finger, even when motor cortex is intact. This last fact seems to rule out the idea that motor cortex itself is the sole mind-brain interface; however, Eccles was quite tentative in suggesting that idea, and the question of dualism does not rise or fall with that one example.

Without further details about Eccles' books, it was not possible to discuss the other examples which that book might contain. However, there has been tremendous progress in artificial neural networks in the past few years; it now seems clear that we can build systems with substantial capabilities in terms of planning, emotion and (probably) language [4,5,7,10]. The most advanced engineering designs have surprising parallels to the empirical results of Freeman, including high-frequency recurrent components embedded within lower-frequency systems.

Could these kinds of designs actually fit what we have observed regarding the mind? Cognitive science has made great progress in recent years, but even such basic phenomena as emotions have been relatively neglected, not because of difficulties in explanation, but because of difficulties (practical, ethical and political) in experimentation on human beings. The phenomena observed in the laboratory do appear explicable in simple neural-network terms, but many phenomena are hard to observe in the laboratory. In animal behavior, a wider range of experiments is possible, including classical (Pavlovian) and instrumental (Skinnerian) conditioning. In that area, Harry Klopf has developed a neural net model (surprisingly similar to the design used by White and Sofge [5] in engineering applications) which can explain all 36 basic experiments he has identified in classical and instrumental conditioning.

If a materialist explanation appears potentially good enough to explain all of the phenomena we have seen in the laboratory, and if artificial systems are growing in capability without any apparent limit (at least in terms of raw intelligence), then one may argue that there is no empirical basis for choosing between materialism or dualism. However, Occam's Razor suggests that we should strongly prefer the simpler theory when both fit the data equally well. Occam's Razor is especially strong when one theory is equivalent to another, except for the addition of a lot of additional hypotheses (e.g. another "world").

D.O.Hebb, in the classic book which helped inspire the entire neural network field[12], attributed great importance to Occam's Razor. For example, he argued that an unbiased scientist would actually tend to accept the claim from parapsychology that psychic phenomena have a better than fifty-fifty chance of being real, empirically; however, from Occam's Razor, he would nevertheless reject the possibility. A similar argument would apply to dualism. Recent work on learning and induction [5, chapter 10] goes much further in explaining Occam's Razor and its fundamental importance.

A Third Viewpoint: Monism

Some participants argued for a third point of view, intermediate between dualism and materialism. The data available in the laboratory do not require the existence of a "soul," but some of the subtler phenomena described by Jung and other psychiatrists (based on some degree of clinical experience) would be very hard to fit into the classical formulations of materialism, rooted in atoms and electromagnetic interactions. (Some would go further, and include "historical" data from formal, organized religious traditions, but the intense conflicts and contradictions between such traditions reduce the value of that evidence in this particular context.)

Given the imprecise nature of such empirical information, one would not expect a consensus among rational scientists as to the reality of such phenomena; however, it is not obviously crazy to consider that the observations of Jung and others might have some degree of empirical validity. Based on Hebb's point, it still might be very hard to justify beliefs in another "world" governed by different mathematical laws; however, the Occam's Razor "cost" of being open to such phenomena would be much less if (like Penrose) we relate them to the likelihood of very strange, imperfectly understood physical phenomena. In the correct application of Occam's Razor [5, chapter 10], we do not simply "rule out" theories based on apriori expectations; we always attribute some nonzero probability to each alternative, and we multiply the empirical probability terms by the apriori probability to get an overall score. Therefore, if one increases the apriori plausibility by assuming that the "soul" may be due to unknown phenomena in this cosmos, then the probability of some kind of soul hypothesis would be greater.

In the earliest stages of this discussion, Pribram introduced the term "monism" (from the Vedas) to describe an alternative viewpoint along these lines. The key concepts of monism are that there does exist some kind of "soul," but that mind, soul and brain are all embedded in one greater universe, subject to (mathematical) natural law.

The Vedas argue that the greater universe is one vast Mind, of which the material universe is an epiphenomenon or local condensation. The Copenhagen school of physics has often argued that the universe now looks more like a Mind than a Machine, and there have been serious models of physics which implement this by trying to represent QFT as a neural network model[11]. The companion paper suggests, as an alternative, that QFT might be represented as an outcome of a simpler, neoclassical PDE system. In either case, we must admit that there are many phenomena not understood as yet in physics -- such as missing neutrinos, false vacuum, dark matter, and redshift anomalies -- which affect the energy balance of the universe in a fundamental way. Where there is energy, there is some possibility of life, both in known and unknown forms. It is conceivable, then, that "soul" could be an emergent biological phenomenon in a greater universe, and that "mind" as we know it could be an emergent phenomenon of a symbiosis between soul and brain; if so, our consciousness or sense of self would be located at least partly in the brain.

In many ways, the monist view reminds me of the play Back to Methuselah, which George Bernard Shaw considered his best. In that play, Shaw portrays the story of the "ultimate" artificial intelligences. He calls them "Romeo" and "Juliet." The point is that human beings tend to identify very strongly with certain phenomena -- such as emotion -- which do not in any way require the existence of "soul." Likewise, it is hard for me to see how consciousness or intelligence as such require such a concept.

East Asian Views and Computer Souls

Some of the most interesting reactions to this discussion came from Asian participants, who had unique perspectives and insights. Jibu, for example, had ideas about how to connect the idea of "qi" or "ki" with quantum theory; however, she did not have time to elaborate on the details. Another participant noted that Chinese culture tends to accept the idea of "soul," but assumes that all living things have "souls."

This raised the further question about the issue of computers and souls.

None of the three viewpoints discussed here -- materialism, dualism or spiritual monism -- are inherently limited to human beings. For example, if Eccles were right that quantum probabilities are the key to manifesting the soul, then properly designed optical computers would be more suitable for that purpose than any organic brain. There are indeed a few people in artificial intelligence who are striving for the replacement of all human life by silicon (though they rarely state this in public). From what we have learned so far about the mind, I would argue that such attitudes must be based on neurotic instabilities (similar, in a way, to notions described in Vonnegut's Sirens of Titan). Nevertheless, the required technologies are now coming into sight, and there are some management forces which would simply like to maximize the associated hardware possibilities. In general, there are crucial opportunities and crucial hazards for the human race in all of these technologies, and those of us who understand the big picture have a strong duty to channel these forces into channels we can live with (literally).

REFERENCES

1. R.Penrose, The Emperor's New Mind: Concerning Computers, Minds and The Laws of Physics. Oxford U. Press, 1989.
2. David Deutsch, Quantum Computing, Physics World, June 1992.
3. K. Pribram, Brain and Perception: Holonomy and Structure in Figural Processing. Erlbaum, 1991.
4. P.Werbos, The Cytoskeleton: why it may be crucial to human learning and to neurocontrol, Nanobiology, Vol. 1, No. 1, 1992.
5. D.White & D.Sofge, Handbook of Intelligent Control: Neural, Fuzzy and Adaptive Approaches. Van Nostrand, 1992.
6. J.Horgan, Quantum philosophy, Scientific American, July 1992.
7. P.Werbos, Neural networks and the human mind: new mathematics fits humanistic insights. In IEEE Proceedings on Systems, Man and Cybernetics, IEEE, 1992.
8. J.Dennis & R.Schnabel,Numerical Methods for Unconstrained Optimization and Nonlinear Equations. Prentice-Hall, 1983.
9. G.V.Puskorius & L.A.Feldkamp, Decoupled extended Kalman filter training of feedforward layered networks. In Proceedings of the International Joint Conference on Neural Networks, IEEE, 1991.
10. P.Werbos, Neurocontrol, neurobiology and the mind: new developments and connections. In IEEE Proceedings on Systems, Man and Cybernetics, IEEE, 1991.
11. D.Finkelstein, Superconducting causal nets, International Journal of Theoretical Physics, Vol.27, No. 4, 1985.
12. D.O.Hebb,The Organization of Behavior, Wiley, 1949.

WHAT IS NEUROENGINEERING?

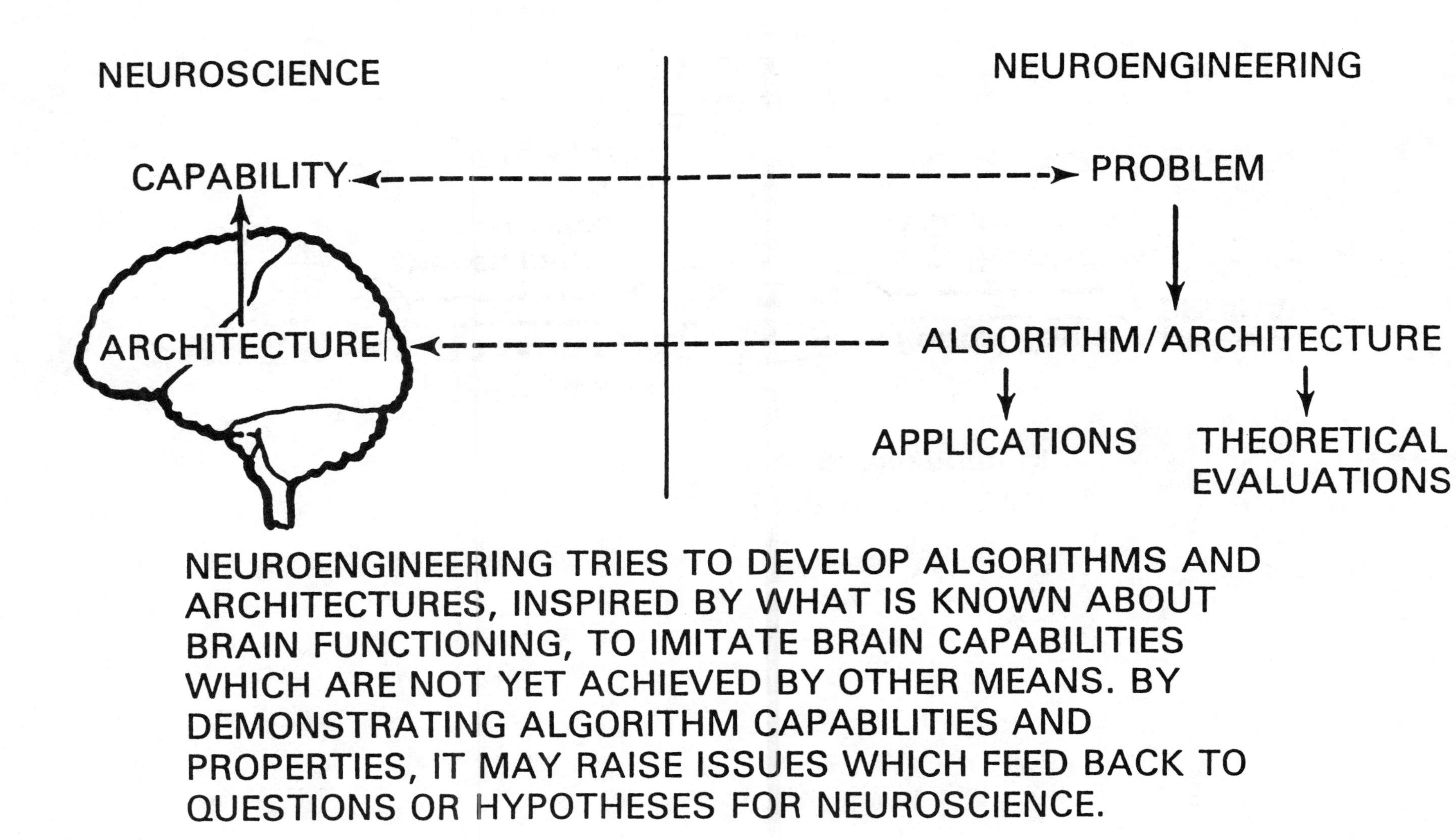

NEUROENGINEERING TRIES TO DEVELOP ALGORITHMS AND ARCHITECTURES, INSPIRED BY WHAT IS KNOWN ABOUT BRAIN FUNCTIONING, TO IMITATE BRAIN CAPABILITIES WHICH ARE NOT YET ACHIEVED BY OTHER MEANS. BY DEMONSTRATING ALGORITHM CAPABILITIES AND PROPERTIES, IT MAY RAISE ISSUES WHICH FEED BACK TO QUESTIONS OR HYPOTHESES FOR NEUROSCIENCE.

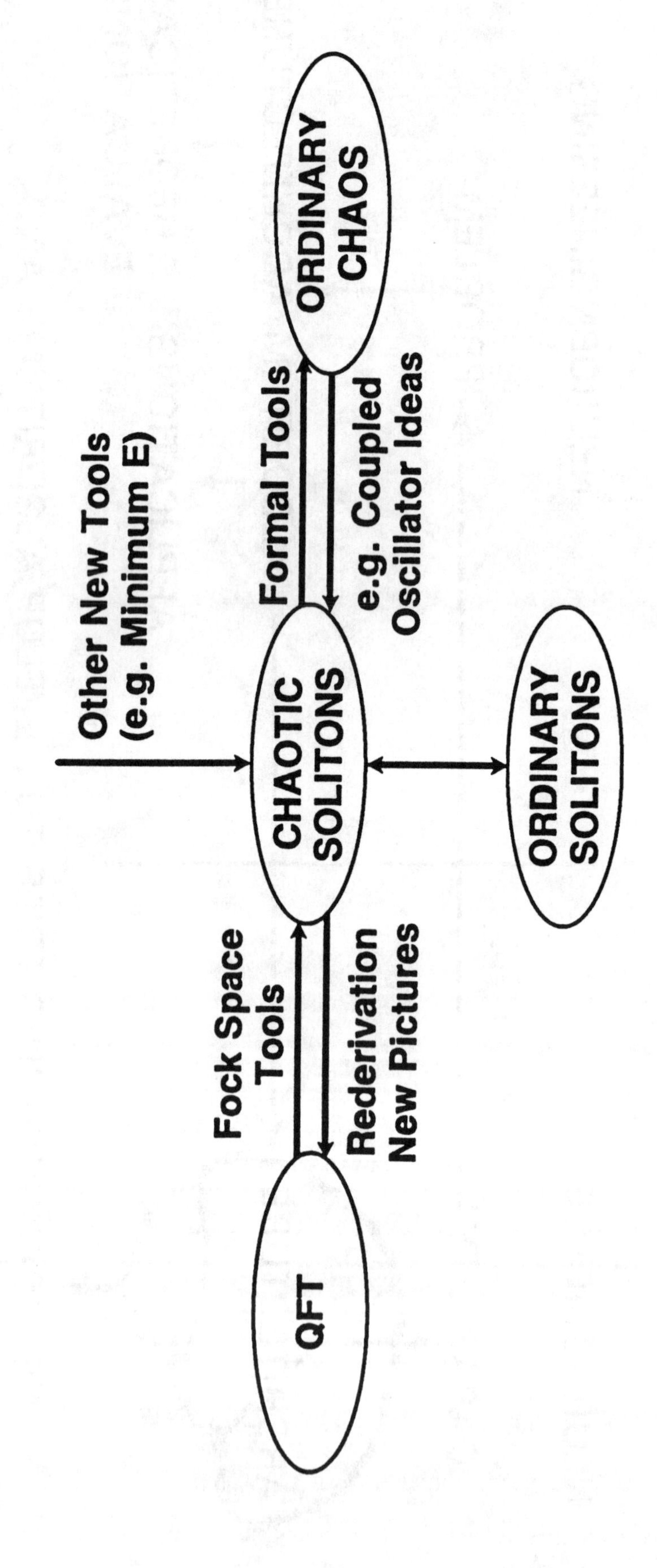

QFT
Fock Space
Tools
Rederivation
New Pictures
CHAOTIC
SOLITONS
Other New Tools
(e.g. Minimum E)
ORDINARY
SOLITONS
Formal Tools
e.g. Coupled
Oscillator Ideas
ORDINARY
CHAOS

III. Nanoneurology

Chapter 10

Nanoneurology and the Cytoskeleton: Quantum Signaling and Protein Conformational Dynamics as Cognitive Substrate

Stuart Hameroff,[1] Judith E. Dayhoff,[2] Rafael Lahoz-Beltra,[1,3] Steen Rasmussen,[4] Ezio M. Insinna,[5] and Djuro Koruga[1]

[1]Advanced Biotechnology Laboratory
Department of Anesthesiology
The University of Arizona Health Sciences Center
Tucson, Arizona 85724 USA

[2]Systems Research Center
University of Maryland
College Park, MD 20742 USA
Naval Surface Warfare Center
Dahlgren, Virginia

[3]Department of Applied Mathematics
Complutense University of Madrid
Madrid 28040, SPAIN

[4]Center for Nonlinear Studies
and Theoretical Division (T-13), MS-B258
Los Alamos National Laboratory
Los Alamos, New Mexico 87545 USA
Santa Fe Institute
Santa Fe, New Mexico

[5]2, Allee Duperrey
93330 Nuilly S/Marne
FRANCE

Abstract

The brain is a hierarchical system which extends below the level of neurons and synapses to intra-neuronal processes. Complex symphonies of molecular activities, these processes determine neuronal architecture, synaptic function and plasticity, and are orchestrated and controlled by the cytoskeleton. Networks of protein polymers which include microtubules ("MT"), actin, intermediate filaments, and centrioles, the cytoskeleton is a dynamic scaffolding in which microtubule-associated proteins ("MAPs") cross-link MT, other cytoskeletal structures, organelles, membranes and receptors. Linked to external events by membrane receptors, structural proteins, ion fluxes, second messengers and protein kinases, cytoskeletal activities can provide a cognitive substrate in cells ranging from single-cell organisms such as Paramecium to human cortical neurons. We propose a set of models for computing within MT and cross-bridging MAPs in which signals and information are represented and transmitted via propagated quantum dipole-coupled conformational changes of these structures' subunits which locally interact via "cellular automata-like" transitions. Cytoskeletal automata (based on quantum dipole-coupled, coherent 10^{-9} to 10^{-11} sec protein subunit conformational excitations) may recognize and adapt to neuronal membrane and synaptic events by changing conformational patterns, modifying MAP-MT connections (and thus neural architecture and synaptic function) and retrograde signaling. These cytoskeletal functions may subserve dendritic processing in neuronal ensembles, provide feedback signaling analogous to back-error propagation in artificial neural networks, link neuronal processes to quantum effects and provide a molecular substrate for cognition.

Introduction

By what mechanisms and at what evolutionary level of complexity do intelligent, adaptive behaviors emerge in biological systems? Some 19th century biologists (e.g. Washburn, Binet, Titchner and Darwin) perceived the irritability and avoidance reactions of single-cell organisms to be simple, basic level correlates of cognitive functions in higher organisms (Jaynes, 1976). Modern neuroscience, however, generally predicates adaptive, intelligent behavior on the complexity and variability of connections among assemblies of multiple neuronal cells. Although attention has been directed at mechanisms of information processing at the level of individual neurons (e.g. Scott, 1977), accepted principles of learning, memory and higher cognitive functions rely on connectionism: quantitative synaptic formation and efficacy of new synaptic connections. However, the mechanisms which mediate neuronal synaptic efficacy and formation from invertebrates to humans, and those which mediate adaptive behaviors in single-cell organisms have common features which may represent a basic level of cognitive function. Namely, these mechanisms depend to a great extent on the membrane-linked actions of the cytoskeleton: intracellular networks of dynamic polymers [e.g. microtubules ("MT"), actin, intermediate filaments, microtubule-associated proteins ("MAPs"), centrioles, etc. (Figure 1)] which regulate and orchestrate cellular activities.

Single-Cell Intelligence

Adaptive behavior in Paramecium

In daily pond life, Paramecium samples regions of its environment by using its own cilia to create vortices of current. If the stimulus is favorable (i.e. bacterial food), the slipper shaped cell swims towards the food and begins to feed. If the stimulus is judged to be injurious, paramecia swim backwards by reversing the strokes of their cilia, turn toward one side, and swim forward in a new direction. Numerous stimuli can elicit such "reflex-like" responses to chemical, mechanical, pressure, fluid flows, gravity, temperature, electrical, and light stimulation (Wichterman, 1985). In the "rebounding reaction," a neutral obstacle is encountered and the organisms swim along it with their anterolateral side, then finally pass it swimming away at a new angle (Figure 2). Paramecia mating behavior involves associating with a partner, aligning and coupling of their single-cell bodies, and exchange of cytoplasmic "pro-nuclei" material (Figure 3). Other activities of paramecia have been ascribed to learning in that they may involve memory, conditioned reflexes, reinforcement, associations and behavior modification based on previous experience (e.g. Gelber, 1958). For example, a number of studies have observed paramecia swimming and escaping from capillary tubes in which they could turn around. In general, results showed that with practice the ciliates took successively less and less time to escape, indicative of a learning mechanism (French, 1940; Applewhite and Gardner, 1973; Fukui and Asai, 1976). Many other experiments suggest paramecia can learn to swim in patterns and through mazes and have a short-term memory, although some of these behaviors depend on their environment (Applewhite, 1979). The learning and memory conclusions have been challenged (Dryl, 1974), but avoidance, rebounding, habituation, and attraction/avoidance responses are adaptive behaviors at least comparable to reflexes in multicellular organisms containing specialized nervous systems. How does Paramecium perform such complex tasks without benefit of a brain or a single synapse?

Adaptive behaviors in Paramecium involve observable motor functions which are performed by coordinated actions ("metachronal waves") of hundreds of cilia (Figure 4a). Hair-like appendages comprised of 9 microtubule doublets arranged in a ring around a central microtubule pair, cilia are membrane-bound extensions of the cytoskeleton in cells ranging from protozoa to human epithelium. They may have sensory function in that their perturbation is transmitted to the cell, and several modes of ciliary motor movement can occur: non-cyclic (inclination) and cyclic (power stroke) bending, and changing rates of circular motion (beating frequency). These movements, utilized in avoidance, rebounding and attraction/avoidance behaviors by paramecia, as well as sweeping of mucus, dust and dead cells by human respiratory epithelial cells, are ascribed to contractile motor-like microtubule-associated proteins such as dynein which are attached at periodic intervals on ciliary microtubule doublets. These dyneins (powered by consumption of ATP: "ATPase") contract sequentially to effect a sliding of microtubule doublets along one another. Coherent sliding of the 9 doublets manifest functional ciliary movement. Membrane potentials (both bipolar and graded) in the ciliary and cell surface membranes are coupled to dynein ATPase activation by "second messenger" cyclic AMP and transmembrane calcium ion [Ca^{++}] flux. This coupling, however, cannot explain numerous significant questions regarding the complexity of ciliary regulation. For example, how does [Ca^{++}] act to induce 9 MT doublets to perform different sliding programs in sequence, and to perform the sequences differently at different levels of ciliary cross section? How can intraciliary [Ca^{++}] reprogram doublet sliding to maintain polarity of the cycle, but with power stroke redirected? Perhaps most interestingly, how are the activities of hundreds of cilia orchestrated to perform complex pivoting, spinning and circling of the entire cell in response to external influences?

These phenomena may be explained by signaling, information processing and working memory in paramecia microtubules--both ciliary and intracellular. Atema (1974) proposed that signal transduction in sensory cilia involved propagating conformational changes along ciliary microtubule subunits, and Lund (1933) and Rees (1933) showed that MT within paramecia were "conductile," and transmitted information. (Arguments for propagative signaling, coherent conformational excitations and information processing in microtubules and microtubule networks will be presented later in this paper.) Complex coordination of multiple ciliary beating ("metachronal patterns") are apparently coordinated from within the cell's cortical ectoplasm which contains cytoskeletal basal bodies and a hexagonal array of cytoskeletal fibrils ("infra-ciliary lattice") to which the cilia are anchored (Figure 4b). This peripheral network is in turn interconnected to internal microtubules and other cytoskeletal structures. Several authors (e.g. Lund, 1933; 1941) identified a central region to which these cytoskeletal structures connect, and proposed that this centralized location was the focal point of integration of sensory input and control of motor response (Figure 5). This "neuromotorium" was seen by some authors as the "brain" of Paramecium; in essence it is a confluence of cytoskeletal structures. Thus the cytoskeleton may be viewed as the nervous system of the Paramecium, with signaling and information processing occurring via traveling conformational changes of microtubule polymer subunits. Metachronal patterns of ciliary beating are reversibly inhibited by the general anesthetic chloroform (Parducz, 1962), suggesting some functional link to cognition in higher organisms.

Adaptive behavior in cortical neurons

External events which initiate adaptive responses via ciliary and/or membrane perturbation in Paramecium are similar to receptor binding of neurotransmitter molecules in neuronal synapses. Each triggers second messenger cascades, which include G proteins, [Ca^{++}], adenyl cyclase, cyclic AMP, etc. These transducing elements, in turn, respond by activation of dynein ATPases and cytoplasmic kinases such as Ca^{++}-calmodulin protein kinase, protein kinases A and C etc. Among the responses of these kinases are phosphorylation/dephosphorylation of cytoskeletal elements such as microtubule associated proteins ("MAPs") and intermediate (neuro) filaments which can reconfigure intra-neuronal structural architecture. In Paramecium, adaptive behaviors involve complex activities of cilia; in neurons they include cognitive functions such as learning and memory which apparently involve regulation of synaptic strengths.

Models of learning in mammalian NMDA (n-methyl-d-aspartate) hippocampal neurons (i.e. long term potentiation: "LTP") involve pre- and post-synaptic enhancement of synaptic function. Silva et al (1992a; 1992b) have shown calcium-calmodulin kinase to be essential for LTP. Aszodi et al (1991) have demonstrated protein kinase A to be involved in learning. Halpain and Greengard (1990) have shown that post-synaptic activation of NMDA receptors induces rapid dephosphorylation of dendrite-specific MAP2. Aoki and Siekevitz (1988) linked learning to protein kinase C mediated MAP2 phosphorylation/dephosphorylation, and Theurkauf and Vallee (1983) demonstrated that

IAP2 phosphorylation/dephosphorylation consumed a huge proportion of brain iochemical energy. Bigot and Hunt (1990) showed that NMDA and other excitatory amino cid neurotransmitters caused redistribution of intraneuronal MAPs and Rasenick et al 1990) and Wang and Rasenick (1991) have shown that G proteins directly link with nicrotubule proteins. Kwak and Matus (1988) showed that denervation caused long-lasting changes in MAP distribution, and Desmond and Levy (1988) showed that LTP involved cytoskeletal-mediated shape changes in dendritic spines. Lynch and Baudry (1987) have proposed that proteolytic digestion of the sub-synaptic cytoskeleton, followed by its structural reorganization, correlate with learning and Friedrich (1990) has formalized a learning model of synaptic cytoskeletal restructuring. Synaptic regulation, both in learning and steady state, also depends on material (enzymes, receptors, neurotransmitters, etc.) synthesized in the cell body and transported along axons and dendrites by contractile MAPs attached to MT ("axoplasmic transport": Figure 6). Similar mechanisms involving actin, synapsin, and other cytoskeletal polymers are involved in neurotransmitter release (Figure 7).

Thus varied adaptive behaviors in cells ranging from paramecia to mammalian cortical neurons (reversal of ciliary beating, altered synaptic structure and efficacy, induction of genetic responses, etc.) share a common feature. In each the cytoskeleton provides the "missing link," a communication network among membrane, second messenger and nuclear genetic elements (in neurons this may traverse a rather large distance). The role of the cytoskeleton, however, is generally held to be passive and subservient. Cytoskeletal components are considered to constitute merely the cell's structural scaffolding and mechanical conveyor belt system controlled by membrane regulated ion fluxes, second messengers, and genetic influences. Despite this prejudice, there are reasons to believe that cytoskeletal activities may underlie intelligence and cognition in cells ranging from lowly paramecia to human cortical neurons. We will discuss those reasons, and describe mechanisms by which cytoskeletal microtubules could conduct and transform information.

Microtubules and the Cytoskeleton

Eukaryotic cells from single-cell protozoa to cortical neurons are comprised of protoplasm, which in turn consists of membranes, organelles, nuclei, and the bulk interior medium of living cells: cytoplasm. Nineteenth century light microscopists described cytoplasm as containing or consisting of "reticular threads", "alveolar foam", or "watery soup" (Burnside, 1974). Development of the electron microscope through the 1960s did not initially illuminate the substructure of cytoplasm because the commonly-used fixative (osmium tetroxide) was dissolving fine structure and the cell was still often perceived to be a "bag of watery enzymes." In the early 1970s with the advent of glutaraldehyde fixation, delicate tubular filamentous structures were found in virtually all cell types and they came to be called microtubules (MT). Originally thought to provide merely structural, or bone-like support, MT and other filamentous structures such as actin, intermediate filaments and centrioles were collectively termed the "cytoskeleton." Recognition that complex, dynamic activities of MT and other cytoskeletal elements were essential for organization, movement and growth of cellular cytoplasm finally brought the cytoskeleton out of the closet.

Parallel arrayed MT are interconnected by cross-bridging proteins (i.e. MT associated proteins: "MAPs") to other MT (Figure 2), organelles and smaller filamentous proteins (actin, intermediate filaments, etc.) to form a dynamic gel whose cellular activities (i.e. mitosis, growth, differentiation, locomotion, exocytosis, phagocytosis, synapse modulation, dendritic spine formation, cytoplasmic movement, neurotransmitter release, etc.) are essential to the living state. Orientation and directional guidance of these cytoskeletal functions depend on centrioles: cylindrical assemblies of nine MT triplets (structurally similar to cilia) arranged in pairs oriented perpendicular to each other. These centriole pairs, which constitute the focal point of the centrosome, or cell center, organize the array of cytoplasmic MT during interphase, duplicate at mitosis to nucleate the two poles of the mitotic spindle and establish orientation and architecture for the next generation of cells (Figure 3).

Of the various filamentous structures which comprise the cytoskeleton, MT are the most prominent, best characterized and appear best suited for dynamic information processing. MT are hollow cylinders 25 nanometers (10^{-9} meters: "nm") in diameter whose lengths may span meters in certain neurons. MT cylinder walls are assemblies of 13 longitudinal protofilaments which are each a series of subunit proteins known as tubulin. Each tubulin subunit is a polar, 8 nm dimer which consists of two slightly different classes of 4 nm, 55 kilodalton monomers known as α and ß tubulin (Figures 8a; 13a). The tubulin dimer subunits within MT are arranged in a hexagonal lattice which is slightly twisted, resulting in differing neighbor relationships among each subunit and its six nearest neighbors (Figure 8b). MT, as well as their individual dimers, have dipoles with negative charges localized toward α monomers (De Brabander, 1982). Thus MT are "electrets": oriented assemblies of dipoles which are predicted to have piezoelectric properties (Athenstaedt,

1974; Mascarenhas, 1974).

Contractile or enzymatic MAPs may be attached to MT at specific tubulin dimer sites; MAP attachments can thus result in various helical patterns on MT surface lattices (Burns, 1978; Kim et al, 1986). Conformational changes occur in tubulin (Engelborghs, 1992), including one in which one monomer shifts 29 degrees from the dimer's vertical axis.

Genes for α and ß tubulin are complex, multi-gene families which give rise to varying tubulin isozymes. During evolution some tubulins have been highly conserved for basic cell functions, however extensive MT heterogeneity exists in complex cells due to genetic diversity, expression, post-translational modifications, MAPs, and assembly patterns. For example, two-dimensional gel electrophoresis has shown 17 different varieties of ß tubulin exist in mammalian brain MT, whereas fewer exist in other tissues (Lee et al, 1986). Tubulin structure may be altered also by "post-translational" modification: enzymatic alteration (usually addition or removal of amino acids such as glycosylation or detyrosination) triggered by intracellular events including second messenger activities. Post-translational modification of the cytoskeleton may serve to "hard-wire" information into long-term memory. The diversity of tubulin in Paramecium occurs primarily due to extensive post-translational modification, which may provide "recognition signals" (Adouette et al, 1991), specific behavior, and/or learning and memory.

MT self-assembly and disassembly are dynamic, complex processes whose states depend on various factors including temperature and calcium ion concentration. Oriented by centrioles, MT polymerization determines the architecture and form of cells which can quickly change by MT depolymerization and reassembly in another direction (Figure 6).

GTP, an energy-providing analog of ATP, binds to free, unpolymerized tubulin; GTP-tubulins then self assemble to form MT in an entropy driven process. Within assembled MT, GTP hydrolyzes to GDP, imparting energy into the MT lattice via tubulin conformational changes. MT whose ends are comprised of GTP-tubulin are stable and will continue to grow. MT whose ends are comprised of GDP-tubulin are unstable and will depolymerize rapidly. As GTP is hydrolyzed to GDP within MT, GDP-tubulin is exposed at MT ends and, unless stabilized by MAPs, centrioles or other structures, MT rapidly disassemble. Free GDP-tubulin is reconverted to GTP-tubulin which becomes available for reassembly. *In vitro*, this "dynamic instability" (Kirschner and Michison, 1986) results in erratic alterations between growing and shrinking phases; *in vivo* "selectionist" activity occurs in which MT networks can adaptively probe or retreat in cellular appendages including axonal and dendritic growth cones and developing synapses (e.g. Reinsch et al, 1991; Sabry et al, 1991).

Recent works concerning labile cytoplasmic MT have shown that special MT spatial structures or patterns may form *in vitro*, under the maintenance of a sustained energy source (GTP hydrolysis), suggesting that MT may be dissipative structures (Tabony and Job, 1990 and 1992). Mandelkow et al even observed how dynamic, spatially oscillating MT patterns may form *in vitro* in the presence of tubulin and GTP (Mandelkow et al, 1989).

Contractile MAPs such as dynein and kinesin participate in ciliary bending as well as intra-neuronal ("axoplasmic") transport which moves material within axons and dendrites and plays a major role in maintaining and regulating synapses. Other MAPs form structural bridges and stabilize MT, preventing their disassembly and some may be phosphorylated by second messengers. Thus MAP-MT interactions help determine cell architecture and dynamic function.

Cytoskeletal Information Processing?

The cytoskeleton has a justified existence in terms of providing structural support and transport. Why invoke an additional, unproven responsibility as the cell's on-board computer? One reason is a lack of satisfactory alternative explanation for real-time, intra-cellular organization. The standard explanations of membrane depolarizations, ion fluxes, diffusion of signal molecules and genetic regulation require faith in an organized soup. The cytoskeleton provides a solid state network which interconnects all the other elements; it is well situated to be the cell's nervous system.

A second reason is a line of evidence which, at least circumstantially, links the cytoskeleton with cognitive function. For example, Mileusnic et al (1980) correlated production of MT subunit protein ("tubulin") and MT activities with peak learning, memory and experience in baby chick brains. Cronley-Dillon et al (1974) showed that when baby rats begin their critical learning phase for the visual system (when they first open their eyes), neurons in the visual cortex begin producing vast quantities of tubulin. Tubulin production is drastically reduced when the critical learning phase is over (when the rats are 35 days old). In gerbils exposed to cerebral ischemia, Kudo et al (1990) correlated the amount of reduction in dendritic MAP-2 with the degree of cognitive impairment. Bensimon and Chernat (1991) found that selective destruction of brain MT by the drug colchicine caused cognitive defects in learning and memory which mimic the clinical symptoms of Alzheimer's disease, in which the cytoskeleton becomes entangled. Geerts et al (1992) showed that sabeluzole, a memory-enhancing drug, increases fast axoplasmic transport. Matsuyama and Jarvik (1989) have proposed that Alzheimer's is a disease of MT and MAPs. In specific hippocampal regions of the brains of schizophrenic patients, Arnold et al (1991) found distorted neuronal architecture due to a lack of 2 MAPs (MAP-2 and MAP-5).

Further suggestion for cytoskeletal computation and/or information storage stems from the spatial distribution of discrete sites (or states) in the cytoskeleton. For example, tubulin subunits in closely arrayed MT have a density of about 10^{17} per cm^3, which is very close to the theoretical limit for charge separation (Gutmann, 1986). Thus cytoskeletal polymers have maximal density for information representation by charge, and the capacity for dynamically coupling that information to mechanical and chemical events via cooperative conformational states.

Some documented cytoskeletal functions do, by themselves, exhibit adaptive behaviors relying on molecular logic. For example, in "dynamic instability", MT can alternate erratically between growing and rapidly shrinking phases. This mechanism ("a generator of diversity") is utilized for probing and reorientation within cells ranging from growing neurons to motile amoeboid movement in macrophages. Such adaptive behavior (in which a stabilizing factor may be considered a positive attraction stimulus) can be observed *in vitro* without membrane or genetic input and can also be computer simulated (Hotani et al, 1992). A final reason is that the cytoskeleton appears structurally well suited for information processing tasks; it resembles computer technology, and computers offer a particularly apt metaphor for cognition.

Computers: Technology Evolving Towards Cognition

In addition to processing and storing information, they can simulate brain functions. Classical attempts at "artificial intelligence" have involved complex rules and algorithms embedded in serial processors and manipulating symbols (e.g. Fodor and Pylshyn, 1988). More recently, computers are evolving towards more efficient modes of information processing which reflect newer understanding of brain function. Three such modes are artificial neural networks ("ANNs"), molecular computing and cellular automata.

Artificial Neural Networks (ANNs)

ANNs are parallel computer architectures which feature layers of nodes ("neurons") interconnected by variable strength connections ("synapses"). Mirroring current understanding that learning occurs by strengthening of specific synaptic connections within a neuronal network, connection strengths in ANNs are the critical parameter which adjusts information flow. By presenting data to an input layer and an expected output to an output layer, ANNs can adaptively learn by a series of trials; they are adaptable rather than programmable. Like the brain, ANNs are good at pattern recognition and abstract analysis, but poor at large scale number crunching. Hopfield (1980) showed that information within ANNs settles into a series of stable energy states much like rain water falling on mountains flows through valleys into lakes and rivers. Similarly, dynamic patterns of neuronal network activity ("attractors") have been likened to mental states in the brain; depending on the rainfall (input), a given information state (i.e. memory, conscious image, thought) would be a given pattern.

In models of the brain, synapses have been compared to variable switches, and the brain to a computer containing such switches. However, the analogy falters in several areas. First, neurons and their synapses are too complicated to be considered simple switches. Neurons must integrate information from thousands of synapses by using analog functions such as dendritic morphology, slow wave potentials, branch point conductances and others. Adjustment of synaptic strength is, by itself, a complex physiological phenomenon. Thus, rather than 40 billion switches, the brain should be viewed as being composed of 40 billion computers! Extensive dendritic-dendritic interactions and dendritic microprocessing have great importance, as emphasized by Pribram (1991) who stresses the need to look away from the neuron as the functional unit in cognition. Another flaw in the brain/ANN analogy is the problem of supervised learning. For example, what agent presents the expected output to the output layer, and how is the running difference between output and expected output (the "error") transmitted back to the connections to vary their weights accordingly? In the most common form of neural networks, this is at least partially accomplished by "back-error propagation" in which the difference is conveyed retrograde to the primary flow of information. [Ironically, the original idea for back-propagation (Werbos, 1974) was based on Freud's concept of feedback/reward.] Because neuronal membrane depolarization is unidirectional and because reciprocal connections do not widely occur, back-error propagation has not been considered a biological phenomenon. These inconsistencies can be at least partially resolved by consideration of the cytoskeleton--already involved in synaptic plasticity and other intra-neuronal functions (Werbos, 1992; Dayhoff et al, this volume).

In a larger sense, the problem of "agency" represents the essence of the brain/mind "problem." Where, and by what mechanism (? by "whom") do perception, self, consciousness occur? Computation at the molecular level offers possible suggestions.

Molecular Computing

Computers are also evolving downward towards molecular and even atomic level switches and storage elements. Since Feynmann's famous 1959 treatise "There's plenty of room at the bottom," a variety of molecular materials have been proposed as switches and information storage sites (as well as molecular scale machines). Materials proposed for molecular computation include tetrahydraquinones, polyacetylenes, optically active rhodopsins, porphyrins, fullerenes, proteins and many others (Carter, 1984; Hong, 1990). Unlike present day semi-conductor based computers in which electron flow conveys information, some molecular computing paradigms are envisioned to utilize packets of conformational energy described as solitons or phonons. In addition to smaller size leading to greater computational density, molecular elements can self-assemble as well as take advantage of quantum effects, phase transitions, resonances and other effects. These in turn could yield emergent phenomena comparable to imaginative ideas and higher cognitive functions up to and including perception, self, and consciousness.

Quantum computation may involve non-locality and non-algorithmic processes (e.g. Penrose, 1989; Deutsch, 1985; Insinna, 1992; Jibu and Yasue, this volume), which could account for cognitive phenomena otherwise difficult to explain. Possible quantum effects in the cytoskeleton will be considered later in this chapter. Molecular interactions relevant to computation may be described in the context of cellular automata (Carter, 1984; Milch, 1986).

Cellular Automata

Computation at any level involves interactive signals or patterns in a lattice structure. General descriptions of such systems (which include computers as special cases) in which complex behavior results from collective activities of simple subunits are called cellular automata. ("Cellular" was originally meant to connote the mistaken notion of cells in the biological sense as indivisible subunits.) Von Neumann's (1966) original cellular automaton consisted of a large number of identical "cells" connected in a uniform pattern. The essential features of cellular automata are as follows: 1) at a given time, each cell is in one of a number of states (usually two for simplicity). 2) The cells are organized according to a fixed geometry. 3) Each cell communicates only with other cells in its neighborhood; the size and shape of the neighborhood are the same for all cells. Depending on geometry, the number of neighbors may be 4 (rectangular), 6 (hexagonal), 8 (rectangular with corners) or more neighbors per subunit or cell. 4) There is a universal clock. Each cell may change to a new state at each tick of the clock depending on its present state and the present states of its neighbors. The rules for changing state are called the transition rules of the cellular automata. At each clock tick (or "generation") the behavior of each cell depends only on the states of its neighbors and its own state. Simple neighbor transition rules can lead to complex, dynamic patterns. For example cellular automata patterns can exhibit chaos, fractal dimensions, partial differential equations, and computation. Patterns which move through the lattice unchanged are called "gliders"; Von Neumann proved mathematically that gliders travelling through a sufficiently large cellular automaton can solve virtually any problem.

Wolfram (1984) observed that mechanisms for information processing in natural systems are more similar to those in cellular automata which are highly parallel, than to conventional computers. The "results" are given by the configuration obtained; the "medium is the message". Further, "it is common in nature to find systems whose complexity is generated by the cooperative effect of many simple identical components." Conrad (1974) used the concept of "molecular" automata within neurons (in the context of cyclic AMP fluxes) as an information processing system subserving synaptic connectionism. We have applied cellular automata principles to the dynamic conformational states of tubulin within cytoskeletal microtubules in an attempt to understand and explain the real-time control, self-organization, communication and computation in living cells. As a "clocking" mechanism, we consider coherent conformational excitations.

Protein Conformational Dynamics

Proteins are vibrant, dynamic structures in physiological conditions. A variety of techniques have shown that proteins and their component parts undergo conformational motions over a wide range of time scales from 10^{-15} seconds to many minutes, and energy scales from 0.1 to 100 kilocalories per mole (Karplus and McCammon, 1984). Very rapid (10^{-15} sec) changes occur in protein side chains or local regions, whereas slow changes may be due to binding of ligands such as oxygen to hemoglobin, and extremely long lasting changes can be induced by post-translational modifications such as glycosylation or detyrosination. Collective conformational transitions in which proteins move globally occur in the nanosecond (10^{-9} sec) to 10 picosecond (10^{-11} sec) time scale. Related to cooperative movements of smaller regions and charge redistributions, these global changes are linked to protein function (signal transduction, ion channel opening, enzyme action etc.) and may be triggered by factors including phosphorylation, ATP or GTP hydrolysis, ion fluxes, electric fields, ligand binding, and "allosteric" influences by neighboring protein conformational changes. In the case of tubulin within MT, nanosecond range conformations can represent information: "programmable" finite states which can be influenced by dynamic neighbor interactions and other factors.

Atema (1974) proposed that ciliary sensory transduction occurred by propagated conformational changes in MT-tubulin, and Roth and Pihlaja (1977) suggested that MT-tubulin conformational states described patterns of information determined by MAP binding sites. They assumed five possible conformational states for each tubulin subunit (based on drug binding studies) which could be induced by proximity of MAP binding and transmitted, cooperative allosteric effects. Propagated conformational changes implied in these models are presently unobservable and therefore untestable due to a lack of appropriate nanoscale technologies (although scanning tunneling, atomic force and related microscopies may soon be capable). However, Vassilev et al (1985) showed that MT/tubulin bridges can couple two membranes; depolarization of one caused depolarization of the other only when interconnected by MT/tubulin. The authors concluded that either ionic or conformational signals occurred along MT in living cells. Theoretical approaches which encompass propagating protein conformational changes include collective, elastic self-trapping modes such as solitons, coherent phonon excitations, and polarization waves.

Self-trapping modes consider the nonlinear balance between energy dispersion and attractive forces which can allow, under proper circumstances, quantized traveling packets of energy and information. Solitons are such packets which have been observed to travel with minimal dissipation in water (canal waves, ocean tidal waves) and optical fibers (carrying information such as telephone data). Conformational solitons have been theoretically predicted to occur in biological materials such as actin-myosin (Davydov,1974), DNA (Yakushevich and Scott, 1990) and MT (Sataric et al, 1992; Manka and Ogrodnik, 1992). These theoretical cases predict that energy is supplied by hydrolysis of ATP or GTP, and that the energy/information packet is utilized in muscle contraction, DNA replication, and MT signaling and polymerization, respectively.

A comparable approach was taken by Fröhlich (1975, 1970) who proposed that protein conformational changes are triggered by charge redistributions such as dipole oscillations within specific hydrophobic regions of proteins. [Such protein hydrophobic regions are also where general anesthetic gas molecules are thought to act, presumably by preventing protein conformational responsiveness (Franks and Lieb, 1991)]. Fröhlich (1970) further proposed that a set of proteins (and associated water molecules) connected in a common physical structure and electromagnetic field such as within a polarized membrane (or polymer electret like a microtubule) may be excited coherently if biochemical energy such as protein phosphorylation or ATP or GTP hydrolysis were supplied. Coherent excitation frequencies on the order of 10^9 to 10^{11} Hz (identical to the time domain for functional protein conformational changes, and in the microwave or gigaHz spectral region) were deduced by Fröhlich who termed them acousto-conformational transitions, or coherent phonons. Other implications of Fröhlich's model include superconductivity, metastable states (longer-lived conformational state patterns stabilized by local factors), long range (non-local) communication, and polarization waves (traveling regions of dipole coupled conformations out of phase with the majority of coherently excited states).

Fröhlich's concept of coherent excitations in biomolecules including MT may be understood in the context of coherent light emission in lasers, based on similar principles of nonequilibrium physics (Haken, 1983). A solid-state laser consists of a rod of material with a mirror on each side. When light is shone on it, the atoms constituting its specially doped material are excited through the absorption of the energy of the incoming light waves and some of their electrons are thrown out of their regular orbits into energetically higher ones. After a very short period of time (10^{-8} sec) those electrons fall back into their orbits, irregularly emitting some light radiation. The excitation of the electrons is uncoordinated and the emitted light consists of several frequencies with a random phase relationship. Up to this point the laser behaves like a common lamp which emits a wide light spectrum.

If the light pumping energy into the rod is increased, the laser material is pushed farther from its equilibrium state (possibly analogous to supplying sufficient biochemical energy to the cytoskeleton). Above this threshold, the atoms start emitting light in a correlated fashion. All electron jumps from their energetically higher orbits back into the original ones are synchronized as if they were simultaneously obeying the same order. It is as if every single atom "knows" about its neighboring atoms so that it can imitate their behavior; a highly coherent light beam is emitted by the rod. Initially, many fluctuating modes or waveforms are present in the rod (as many vibrational frequencies may be in a MT below biochemical excitation). Abruptly a symmetry-breaking phenomenon occurs and a single mode attains supremacy, spreading out over the entire system.

Experimental evidence for Fröhlich-like coherent excitations in biological systems includes observation of GHz-range phonons in proteins (Genberg et al, 1991), sharp-resonant non-thermal effects of microwave irradiation on living cells (Grundler and Keilman, 1983, 1992), GHz induced activation of MT pinocytosis in rat brain (Neubauer et al, 1990), and long-range regularities in cytoskeletal structures, such as the super-lattice attachment pattern of MAPs on MT (Kim et al, 1986). Samsonovich et al (1992) have shown that experimentally observed patterns of MAP attachment sites on MT can be simulated and possibly derive from self-localized coherent phonon excitations.

Molecular Automata in Microtubules: Models of Cytoskeletal Information Processing

To explore the capabilities for cytoskeletal signaling and information processing, we have used computer simulation to apply principles of coherent protein dynamics, "cellular" (molecular) automata and microtubule structure.

Single Microtubule Automata

"Cellular" (molecular) automata require a lattice whose subunits can exist in two or more states at discrete time steps, and transition rules which determine those states among lattice neighbor subunits. Tubulin conformations within MT lattices can provide such states, and neighbor-tubulin interactions (represented by dipole coupling forces) may provide appropriate transition rules. A rough estimate for the time steps, assuming one coherent "sound" wave across the MT diameter (Φ ~ 25 nm) and $V_{sound} = 10^{3}$ m/s, yields a clocking frequency of approximately 4×10^{10} Hz, and a time step, of 2.5×10^{-11} sec. Thus Fröhlich's coherent excitations can provide a "clocking frequency" for MT conformational automata (Hameroff et al, 1989; Rasmussen et al, 1990).

Conformation of individual tubulin subunits at any given time depends on "programming" factors including initial conformational state, primary genetic structure, binding of water, ions, or MAPs, bridges to other MT, post-translational modifications, phosphorylation state, and mechanical and electrostatic dipole forces among neighboring subunits. We consider only electrostatic dipole forces among neighboring tubulin subunits. Figure 8b shows a 7-member MT automata neighborhood: a central dimer surrounded by a tilted hexagon of 6 neighbor dimers. The two monomers of each dimer share a mobile electron which is oriented either more toward the α-monomer ("alpha state") or more toward the ß-monomer ("beta state") with associated changes in dimer conformation at each time step. The net electrostatic force from the six surrounding neighbors acting on a central dimer can then be calculated as:

$$f_{net} = \frac{e^2}{4\pi\epsilon} \sum_{i=1}^{6} \frac{Y_i}{r_i^3}$$

where y_i and r_i are defined as illustrated in Figure 4b, e is the electron charge, and ϵ is the average protein permittivity. Neighbor electrostatic dipole coupling forces are shown in

Figure 8c.

To simulate MT automata, cylindrical MT structure is displayed as 2-dimensional rectangles whose edges (adjacent protofilaments) are contiguous. To avoid boundary conditions, end borders also communicate so that a torus is modeled. MT subunit dimer loci are in either α state (white) or β state (black). At each "nanosecond" time step, forces exerted by 6 surrounding neighbor subunits are calculated for each dimer. If the net force exceeds a threshold, a transition ($\alpha \rightarrow \beta$, $\beta \rightarrow \alpha$) occurs. For example, a threshold of ± 9.0 means that net neighbor forces greater than $+9.0 \times 2.3 \times 10^{-14}$ Newtons (Figure 8c) will induce an alpha state, and negative forces of less than $-9.0 \times 2.3 \times 10^{-14}$ Newtons will induce a β state. Threshold may represent temperature, pH, voltage gradients, ionic concentration, genetically determined variability in individual dimers, binding of molecules including MAPs and/or drugs to dimer subunits, etc. Effects of varying thresholds on MT automata behavior are shown in Figure 9. Behaviors include gliders, traveling and standing wave patterns, oscillators, linearly growing patterns, and frozen patterns (perhaps suitable for memory). Asymmetrical thresholds ($\alpha \rightarrow \beta \neq \beta \rightarrow \alpha$) result in bidirectional gliders.

Assuming MT automata gliders and patterns exist, what functions could they have? They could represent information being signaled through the cell. Glider numerical quantities and patterns may manifest signals, binding sites for ligands, MAPs or material to be transported. Frozen patterns may store information in a memory context, information may become "hardened" in MT by post-translational modifications, and/or MT automata patterns could transfer and retrieve stored information to and from neurofilaments via MAPs.

MT automata gliders travel one dimer length (8 nm) per time step (10^{-9} to 10^{-11} sec) for a velocity range of 8 to 800 meters per sec., consistent with propagating solitons or phonons as well as nerve membrane potentials. Thus traveling MT automata patterns or gliders (equivalent to solitons, phonons or Fröhlich depolarization waves) may propagate in the cytoskeleton in concert with membrane depolarizations and ion fluxes. Long range cooperativity, resonances and phase transitions among spatially arrayed MT automata patterns may occur, and membrane related voltages, ion fluxes or direct links could induce transient waves of conformational switching or lowered threshold along parallel arrayed MT. Consequently, inputs and activities of a particular cell could directly elaborate patterns within that cell's MT automata, phenomena important in emergent cognitive and behavioral functions ranging from simple organisms to human brains.

MT-MAP Network Formation

Architecture and functions of cells depend heavily on cytoskeletal lattices, consisting largely of MT-MAP networks. MAPs stabilize MT, preventing disassembly and promoting assembly. We investigate MT stabilization by MAP binding on adjacent, parallel MT as an initial step in construction of a MT-MAP network.

We assume that MAP attachments on MT assume periodic distributions (Figure 10a) and MAP binding to a specific tubulin increases its affinity to its six surrounding neighbors; this neighborhood then becomes resistant to disassembly (Figure 10b). Maintaining a periodic distribution of MAPs, only a finite number of MAP attachment sites are available for each region on a MT. The number of MAPs per region and their particular location(s) within that region may be related to the reduction of the free energy value which, in turn, may be related to the stabilization of MT sub-assemblies. Using a "mobile finite automata" technique, Figure 10c shows a number of MAP distributions and their calculated free energy values. The efficiency in free energy reduction depends on and determines both MAP location and number.

Learning Via Optimization of MAP Connection Sites

We next consider adaptive behavior in simple MT-MAP automata networks demonstrating input/output learning found in artificial neural networks ("ANNs"). Two MT automata are interconnected via MAP connections capable of transmission of signals (sequences of α or β conformational states) from one MT to another. MAP connection sites vary randomly in an evolutionary optimization process, and two inputs and one output are defined as regions on the two MT (Rasmussen et al, 1990). For two different sets of MT1 and MT2 input pairs (automata patterns), a desired or correct output pattern is predefined. After each sequence of time steps (sufficient for patterns to propagate from the input areas to the output area, with transmission across MAP connections) the output area pattern is compared to the desired output pattern using a mathematical formulation of error called the "Hamming distance" ("H_d": the number of digit positions in which two binary words of the same length differ). Allowing random MAP connection topologies between the two MT, the most efficient topology (that which yields the lowest Hamming distance) is selected as the "mother system" after each time step sequence. At the next step other "daughter" topologies are randomly created. When one daughter performs better than the original system (lower Hamming distance), this connection topology becomes the mother system for the next generation.

Figure 11 shows an MT network with 2 MAP connection topologies which evolved to recognize specific input/output pairs. Because of perturbation-stable glider patterns, the MT network is also able to "associate" patterns, that is produce correct outputs from inputs which are similar, but not identical, to the original output-coupled inputs (Rasmussen et al, 1990).

MT-MAP Network Recognition Via Membrane Coupled MAP Regulation

This model system considers MAPs attached at fixed loci between 2 MT automata as switches ("open" or "closed"); each MAP's state ("open" or "closed") is determined by membrane receptor activation (i.e. by binding of neurotransmitter molecules to post-synaptic neuronal receptors) coupled to the MAPs by second messengers (e.g. G-proteins, [Ca^{++}], cyclic AMP, protein kinases, MAP phosphorylation, etc.).

This model network was used in a training and recognition exercise in which characteristics of virus structure were expressed in 3 binary categories as inputs to the receptors (Hameroff et al, 1992). Training sets and MT2 automata outputs for the four virus patterns are shown in Figure 12.

Artificial Neural Network Models Utilizing Cytoskeletal Signaling

Artificial neural networks (ANNs) are computer designs for learning and computation based on processing units that are inspired by biological neurons. Although some ANN activities seem biologically plausible, those that require backwards feedback along each forwards connection have not appeared biologically plausible without retrograde internal signals within neurons (i.e. axon to dendrite). ANN paradigms that utilize backwards feedback include back-error propagation, sigma-pi and RCE architectures, and adaptive resonance theory. Backwards feedback across synapses in biological neurons has now been shown likely to occur via nitric oxide (e.g. Barinaga, 1992). Backwards neuronal feedback signals, if provided by membrane potentials, would require each forwards connection to have a complementary backwards neuronal synaptic connection. If provided by retrograde axoplasmic transport, backwards feedback signals would be rather slow.

The cytoskeleton may be capable of carrying fast conformational feedback signals backwards through a network of neurons, permitting some ANN models to be considered biologically plausible. These concepts are developed fully in Dayhoff et al (this volume).

Symmetry and Coding in Microtubules

There exist 32 possible symmetrical arrangements of sphere packing to form a cylinder, and many of these exist in biological systems such as viruses (Erickson, 1973). In MT, tubulin monomers are arranged in the Oh (6/4) symmetry group, which can manifest either hexagonal packing (screw symmetry) or cubic packing (Koruga, 1984). Transition between hexagonal and cubic packing may correlate with propagating conformational changes such as phonons, solitons, automata gliders, etc. In MT, two types of spheres (α and β tubulin) are linked such that they differ by 13 monomers in their axial alignment (Figure 13b); from information theory, this arrangement corresponds to a binary code of length n = 13 and distance d = 5. Coding theory accordingly predicts a binary error correcting codes with 64 codewords (MacWilliams & Sloane, 1977). Consequently, Koruga (1992) defined a latent MT bioinformation code $K_1(13,2^6,5)$. For transmission over distances, the 6 binary dimers could be coded to give a 4 dimer terinary sequence code $K_2(24,3^4,13)$. This code could result from interaction among 24 tubulin monomers and MAPs and suggests functional significance to arrangement of MAP attachments and cellular (e.g. neuronal) architecture.

MT can exist as cylindrical assemblies of from 7 to 17 protofilaments; however in the vast majority of experimental observations, they exist as 13 protofilaments. By examining normalized packing density and consideration of Curie symmetry, Koruga (1986) showed that 13 protofilaments were optimal for information processing. Thus, crystallographic symmetry and coding theory support a cognitive function for MT and cytoskeletal networks.

Quantum Theory and the Cytoskeleton

A quantum mechanical view of reality, in which probabilistic rather than precise behaviors occur, may be relevant to the brain/mind. "Perhaps our minds are qualities rooted in some strange and wonderful feature of those physical laws which actually govern the world we inhabit" (Penrose, 1989). Thus, despite the fact that quantum theorists differ greatly in their interpretations and that quantum theory itself may be a "stop-gap . . . until science gives us a more profound understanding of Nature" (Penrose, 1989), quantum effects may be relevant to the brain/mind.

Where and how could quantum effects (e.g. complementarity, indeterminacy of states, wave/particle duality, non-locality, acausality, observer effects on collapse of wave functions, etc.) interact with the brain mind? Eccles has proposed (e.g. this volume) that quantum indeterminacy results in probabilistic, acausal neurotransmitter vesicle release from pre-synaptic boutons, and Penrose (1989) has suggested quantum effects on neuronal function. However, the coherent structure and molecular, nanoscale dimensions of cytoskeletal components such as MT may be most appropriate for quantum level effects. While such effects could occur at larger and smaller scale levels of brain organization, it is the level of the cytoskeleton at which nonlinear, non-equilibrium dissipative dynamics occurs, single electron (or proton) events can couple to protein conformational states, coherent excitations can cooperatively lead to long-range order, and symmetry is most relevant.

Particular features of a device needed to detect spontaneous, parallel occurring quantum transitions and to act as a ground element for a parallel-to-serial conversion (non-local, acausal-to-local, deterministic) may be defined:

1) The device should possess the capability of amplifying microscopical changes or transitions occurring at the quantum level and of displaying them on a macroscopical scale. This could involve either only a few components with many degrees of freedom or energetic states, or numerous components with limited states or energetic levels (for instance, binary). The device should obey the laws of entropy; its components should, for example, be in continuous uncoordinated motion or randomly oscillating before the occurrence of the synchronistic event or state-vector reduction.

2) After the occurrence of the event, the device (or system) should display

discrete meaningful patterns or meaningful groupings of its components, either through their positions or their energetic states, each component or state carrying a "bit" of information. The "emerging" patterns should be coherent and stable; they should exclude incidental or transient random coherence.

3) The global features of the device/system, for instance its physical constraints, should contribute to limiting the number of possible patterns. This means that the system should be a limiting factor in order to set forth a finite number of possibilities and enable the translation (recognition) of the emerging coherent patterns into meaningful results.

Such devices occur as nonequilibrium dissipative systems. Two such systems are nonequilibrium structures described by Prigogine and Haken, and Fröhlich's coherent excitations. Prigogine and Haken demonstrated that coherent behavior can emerge from chaos in a system working far from thermodynamic equilibrium, that is progressing from order to disorder. The emergence of dissipative structures is the result of random microscopic fluctuations occurring in the system. Because of inherent non-linearities, these fluctuations are not dampened, but are amplified and impose a new order upon the whole system.

Descriptions of dissipative structures in living systems have largely focused on readily observable reaction diffusion such as metabolic oscillations of ATP concentrations in the glycolytic cycle (Goldbeter and Nicolis, 1976; Goldbeter and Caplan, 1976), wavelike aggregation of the slime mold Dyctostelium discoideum being regulated by cAMP oscillations (Goldbeter and Segel, 1977), and regulation of enzymatic activity for glucose metabolism in the bacterium Escherichia coli depending on the activity of the lac operon (part of the bacterial genome) (Nicolis and Prigogine, 1977). In eukaryotic cells, the existence of a continuous biochemical oscillator regulating and synchronizing cellular division has been proposed (Kauffman and Wille, 1977; Nicolis and Prigogine, 1977), although cell cycles and clocking may be regulated by cytoskeletal vibrations (e.g. Puiseux-Dao, 1984).

Another description of emergence of coherence is Fröhlich's suggestion that biological molecules, if maintained in a nonequilibrium state at constant temperature and steady external energy supply, would start behaving in coherent fashion under the effect of longitudinal frequency modes (Fröhlich, 1968, 1970, 1975a, 1975b). Through strong excitation, some polar groups of these molecules would be stretched, producing large dipole moments and entering a metastable state comparable to that of dipoles in ferromagnetic materials. If further excited, the oscillating dipoles would condense into the lowest energy state, displaying coherent oscillations of a single mode as well as long-range interactions and correlations. Water molecules bound at biomolecular surfaces would also oscillate coherently and cooperatively. Vitiello (1992) and Jibu and Yasue (this volume) show that such ordered water on cytoskeletal surfaces provides symmetry in cytoplasm which, when perturbed, can yield quantum phenomena such as bosons and vibrational phonon quanta suitable for signaling, coherence and long-range effects.

Prigogine's or Haken's nonequilibrium structures and Fröhlich's coherent vibrational modes are similar phenomena and may be considered as identical in terms of their results. In both cases, chance (probabilities) and deterministic laws seem to coexist, each of them contributing in an equal manner to the emergence of new complex order and of global coherence. Peat (1988) has suggested examining such systems as probable substrates for synchronistic (non-local) quantum events. Coherently oscillating cytoskeletal networks and microtubules may be dissipative systems suitable for quantum detection, amplification, and stabilization.

Causality is founded on sequential events, probably because our brains work mostly in serial fashion when it comes to comprehension of events. Perhaps our brains (in particular, coherently oscillating cytoskeletal MT) discriminate, detect, and serialize synchronistic and non-local, parallelly-distributed discrete quantum states which spontaneously and simultaneously emerge (from what Jung referred to as the "collective unconscious"). This assertion is supported by facts such as short dreams containing such enormous quantities of information that hours are usually needed in order to put it into serial description. Often we don't know which is the beginning or the end of a dream, possibly because of a parallel-to-serial conversion mechanism existing in our conscious processes. The same thing happens with intuitive ideas, which are "received" in a short glimpse and whose interpretation sometimes needs days to be correctly, or serially, ordered. Comprehension of intuitive ideas seems to be a genuine sequential process of our psyche. It enables us to transpose synchronistic unconscious and parallelly received events into finite space-time coordinates, establish value scales and coherently order the received data according to some basic logic (causal and sequential) rules. Again, the parallel, non-local emergence of information and the serial process we suggest here complies with the new holonomic (non-local and holistic) theories of the brain such as the one suggested by

Pribram (1991).

One global feature of a dissipative system capable of quantum detection is limiting the number of possible patterns, enabling recognition of meaningful results. Insinna (1992) has suggested that the possible states of MT dynamical systems ("basins of attraction") correspond with archetypal images as described by Jung. Wuensche (1992) shows that basins of attraction for cellular automata can be calculated and represented (Figure 14) and suggests that such attractors, which exist in multidimensional state space, are the cognitive substrate of the automata ("the ghost in the machine"), in that they represent their catalogue of behaviors. Perhaps the mind/brain relationship may be considered analogous to that of the attractor/automata. If so, the mind may be considered to exist in state space (or some high-dimensional space) comparable to "World 2" proposed by Eccles.

Another quantum aspect is that of wave interference. Pribram (1972; 1991) considers interference of coherent waves as a substrate for consciousness ("holography"). Coherent excitations of MT and their subunits may result in coherent waves (e.g. coupled to calcium ions causing sol-gel transformations) in the cytoplasm. Such coherent calcium coupled waves have been imaged in living cells (Lechleiter et al, 1991). Holographic imaging may result and represent "agent" or cognitive imagery in cells, including neurons, and, collectively, the brain/mind (Figure 15).

Conclusion

Conformational automata in the cytoskeleton could process information in living cells and provide a molecular substrate for cognitive functions. Thus we portray the cytoskeleton as the cell's nervous system, with microtubules serving as processors or signal carriers and MAPs as molecular cross-bridge connections ("synapses"). In the brain, each neuron's cytoskeleton could be viewed as a "fractal-like" sub-dimension in a hierarchy of adaptive networks.

We have explored only a few facets of the possible parameter space for MT-MAP information processing: subunit coupling strength ("threshold"), initial conformational patterns (to a limited extent), MAP attachment sites, and MAP transmission between two MT. Other possible parameters include MAP quantity and variety, whether MAPs attach to MT in series or parallel (e.g. along the same protofilament or different protofilaments within a given MT), clocking frequency and degree of coherence, quantity and genetic heterogeneity of MT, neurofilaments and other cytoskeletal structures, ligand binding, quantum effects, resonances, phase transitions, "coded" MAPs, and MAP attachment sites determined by MT free energy minimization, phonon maxima or specific automata patterns. Thus, cytoskeletal conformational automata imply an enormous information processing capacity. For example, the information processing capacity of a human brain based on consideration of conventional neural synaptic transmissions as fundamental switches (e.g. Moravec, 1987) can be estimated as 100 billion neurons each with over 1000 synapses "switching" 100 times per second to yield approximately 10^{16} "bits" per second. Considering the simplest case of cytoskeletal conformational automata (2 conformational states per MT subunit switching at 10^{-9} sec intervals, 10^{4} MT subunits per cell) yields about 10^{13} bits per second per cell (neuron or paramecium) and 10^{23} bits per second in human brain, permitting ample parallel redundancy. To this may be added (or multiplied) the additional possible parameters previously mentioned. Of these, phase transitions (in which totally new characteristics emerge within a dynamical system) may have the most interesting relevance to cognition. For example, thoughts, imagery, and mental representations may emerge at critical levels of coherence and resonance among MT automata patterns (and their dipoles) within neuronal dendrites. Such a system can also resolve the apparent dichotomy (Fodor and Pylshyn, 1988) between symbolic and connectionist methods of cognitive representation. MT automata patterns are symbols which are related to connectionist processing at higher and lower hierarchical levels (i.e. neuronal networks and MAP/MT networks, respectively). At still higher levels, symbols may re-emerge.

Coupling of neural protein conformational states to dipole events (mobility of individual electrons) can bring cognitive science to the quantum level. Circumstantial supportive evidence stems from the demonstration that general anesthetic gases, notable for their reversible inhibition of consciousness, reversibly inhibit the mobility of electrons (Hameroff and Watt, 1983). Authors such as Penrose (1989) have argued that consciousness must be related to quantum theory, and that the duality/equivalence of brain/mind will ultimately rely on the duality/equivalence of particle/wave. Insinna (1992) has argued that this complementarity/indeterminacy manifests in the cytoskeleton and that MT are dissipative systems which detect and amplify quantum effects, and that conformational patterns are dynamical attractors which relate to Jungian archetypes. Coupling among biomolecules and their electron/phonons is notable because it occurs at the smallest and fastest scale in which biology is organized. We suggest that coherent (quantum dipole coupled) protein conformational states are the fundamental level in the brain's organizational hierarchy, that the next level is the logical interaction of these states in cytoskeletal automata, and above these are dendritic processing, neurons, neural nets, centers, homunculi, regions, lobes, etc. Below the level of cytoskeletal protein conformation may reside coherent cytoplasmic (Ca^{++} coupled/sol-gel) holographic interference patterns. Such evanescent imagery distributed within neurons and among dendritic and neuronal groups could provide a mechanism for representation of reality, self and (at least rudimentary) consciousness in biological systems ranging from single-cell paramecia to the human brain.

ACKNOWLEDGEMENTS

Stuart Hameroff is partially supported by NSF Grant No. DMS-9114503. Judith E. Dayhoff is supported by the Naval Surface Warfare Center, Dahlgren Virginia, and the Institute for Systems Research, University of Maryland. Rafael Lahoz-Beltra is supported by Ministerio de Educacion y Ciencia in Spain under Fulbright/MEC (1989-1991) and FPI/MEC (1991-1992) grants.

The authors thank Michael Rush and Kristine Doll for technical support, Alwyn Scott, Alexei Samsonovich and Paul Prueitt for scientific advice, and Karl Pribram for his beacon-like inspiration.

REFERENCES

1. Adouette A, Delgado P, Fleury A, Levilliers N, Laine MC, Marty MC, Boisvieux-Ulrich E & Sandoz D, Microtubule diversity in ciliated cells: evidence for its generation by post-translational modification in the axonemes of Paramecium and quail oviduct cells. *Biol Cell* 71:227-245, 1991.

2. Amos LA & Klug A, Arrangement of subunits in flagellar microtubules. *J Cell Sci* 14:523-550, 1974.

3. Aoki C & Siekevitz P, Plasticity in brain development. *Sci Am* (December 1988), 34-42.

4. Applewhite PB, Learning in protozoa. In: Biochemistry and Physiology of Protozoa, Volume 1, ed. M Levandowsky & SH Hutner, Academic Press, 341-355, 1979.

5. Applewhite PB & Gardner FT, Tube escape behavior of paramecia. *Behav Biol* 9:245-250, 1973.

6. Arnold SE, Lee VMY, Gur RE & Trojanowski JQ, Abnormal expression of two microtubule-associated proteins (MAP2 and MAP5) in specific subfields of the hippocampal formation in schizophrenia. *Proc Natl Acad Sci* 88:10850-10854, 1991.

7. Aszodi A, Muller V, Friedrich P & Spatz HC, Signal convergence on protein kinase A as a molecular correlate of learning. *Proc Natl Acad Sci* 88:5832-5836, 1991.

8. Atema J, Microtubule theory of sensory transduction. *J Theor Biol* 38:181-190, 1973.

9. Athenstaedt H, Pyroelectric and piezoelectric properties of vertebrates. *Ann NY Acad Sci* 238:68-93, 1974.

10. Barinaga M, Is nitric oxide the retrograde messenger? *Science* 254:1296-1297, 1991.

11. Bensimon G & Chernat R, Microtubule disruption and cognitive defects: effect of colchicine on learning behavior in rats. *Pharmacol Biochem Behavior* 38:141-145, 1991.

12. Bigot D & Hunt SP, Effect of excitatory amino acids on microtubule-associated proteins in cultured cortical and spinal neurons. *Neurosci Lett* 111:275-280, 1990.

13. Burns RB, Spatial organization of the microtubule associated proteins of reassembled brain microtubules. *J Ultrastruct Res* 65:73-82, 1978.

14. Burnside B, The form and arrangement of microtubules: an historical, primarily morphological review. *Ann NY Acad Sci* 253:14-26, 1974.

15. Carter FL, The molecular device computer: point of departure for large scale cellular automata. *Physica* 10D:175-194, 1984.

16. Cohen J, Beisson J, The cytoskeleton. In Paramecium, ed. HD Gortz, Springer-Verlag, Berlin, 363-392, 1988.

17. Conrad M, Molecular automata. In: Lecture Notes in Biomathematics, Vol.4: Physics and Mathematics of the Nervous System, eds. M Conrad, W Guttinger and M Dal Cin, Springer-Verlag, Heidelberg, 419-430, 1974.

18. Cronly-Dillon J, Carden D & Birks C, The possible involvement of brain microtubules in memory fixation. *J Exp Biol* 61:443-454, 1974.

19. Davydov AS, The theory of contraction of proteins under their excitation. *J Theor Biol* 38:559-569, 1973.

20. De Brabander M, A model for the microtubule organizing activity of the centrosomes and kinetochores in mammalian cells. *Cell Biol Intern Rep* 6:901-915, 1982.

21. Desmond NL & Levy WB, Anatomy of associative long-term synaptic modification. In: Long-Term Potentiation: From Biophysics to Behavior, eds. PW Landfield and SA Deadwyler, 1988.

22. Dewdney AK, Computer recreations. *Sci Am* 252, May:18-30, 1985.

23. Dryl S, Behavior and motor responses in Paramecium. In: Paramecium--A Current Survey, ed. WJ Van Wagtendonk, Amsterdam, Elsevier, 165-218, 1974.

24. Dustin P, Microtubules, 2nd Revised Ed., Springer, Berlin, 442, 1984.

25. Engelborghs Y, Dynamic aspects of the conformational states of tubulin and microtubules. *Nanobiology* 1:97-105, 1992.

26. Erickson RO, *Science* 181:4101, 1973.

27. Fodor JA & Pylyshyn ZW, Connectionism and cognitive architecture, critical analysis. In: Connections and Symbols, eds. S Pinker and J Mehler, MIT Press, Cambridge, MA, 3-71, 1988.

28. French JW, Trial and error learning in Paramecium. *J Exp Psychol* 26:609-613, 1940.

29. Friedrich P, Protein structure: the primary substrate for memory. *Neurosci* 35:1-7, 1990.

30. Fröhlich H, Long-range coherence and energy storage in biological systems. *Int J Quantum Chem* 2:641-9, 1968.

31. Fröhlich H, Long range coherence and the actions of enzymes. *Nature* 228:1093, 1970.

32. Fröhlich H, The extraordinary dielectric properties of biological materials and the action of enzymes. *Proc Natl Acad Sci* 72:4211-4215, 1975.

33. Fröhlich H, Evidence for Bose condensation-like excitations of coherent modes in biological systems. *Physics Letters* 51:A-1, 1975.

34. Fröhlich H, Coherent excitations in active biological systems. In: Modern Bioelectrochemistry, eds. F Guttmann and H Keyzer, Plenum Press, New York, 241-261, 1986.

35. Fukui K & Asai H, Spiral motion of Paramecium caudatum in a small capillary glass tube. *J Protozool* 23:559-563, 1976.

36. Geerts H, Nuydens R, Nuyens R, Cornelissen F, De Brabander M, Pauwels P, Janssen PAJ, Song YH & Mandelkow EM, Sabeluzole, a memory-enhancing molecule, increases fast axonal transport in neuronal cell cultures. *Experimental Neurology* 117:36-43, 1992.

37. Gelber B, Retention in Paramecium aurelia. *J Comp Physiol Psych* 51:110-115, 1958.

38. Genberg L, Richard L, McLendon G & Dwayne-Miller RJ, Direct observation of global protein motion in hemoglobin and myoglobin on picosecond time scales. *Science*, 251:1051-1054, 1991.

39. Goldbeter A & Nicolis G, An allosteric model with positive feedback applied to glycolitic oscillations. *Progress in Theoretical Biology* 4:65-160, 1976.

40. Goldbeter A & Caplan SR, Oscillatory enzymes. *Ann Rev Biophys Bioengin* 5:449-473, 1976.

41. Goldbeter A & Segel LA, Unified mechanism for relay and oscillation of cyclic AMP in Dictyostelium Discoideum. *Proc Nat Acad Sci USA* 74:1543-1547, 1977.

42. Gortz HD, Paramecium, Springer-Verlag, Berlin, 1988.

43. Grundler W & Keilmann F, Sharp resonances in yeast growth prove nonthermal sensitivity to microwaves. *Phys Rev Lett* 51:1214-1216, 1983.

44. Gutmann F, Some aspects of charge transfer in biological systems. In: Modern Bioelectrochemistry, eds. F Gutmann & H Keyzer, Plenum Press, New York, 177-197, 1986.

45. Haken H, Synergetics. An Introduction. Springer Verlag, Berlin, 1983.

46. Haken H, Erfolgsgeheimnisse der Natur. Ullstein Verlag, Frankfurt, 1990.

47. Halpain S & Greengard P, Activation of NMDA receptors induces rapid dephosphorylation of the cytoskeletal protein MAP2. *Neuron* 5:237-246, 1990.

48. Hameroff SR, Ultimate Computing: Biomolecular Consciousness and Nanotechnology, North-Holland, Amsterdam, 1987.

49. Hameroff SR, Dayhoff JE, Lahoz-Beltra R, Samsonovich A & Rasmussen S, Conformational automata in the cytoskeleton: models for molecular computation. *IEEE Computer* (Special Issue on Molecular Computing), in press, 1992.

50. Hameroff SR & Watt RC, Do anesthetics act by altering electron mobility? *Anesth Analg* 62:936-940, 1983.

51. Hameroff SR & Watt RC, Information processing in microtubules. *J Theor Biol* 98:549-561, 1982.

52. Hameroff SR, Smith SA & Watt RC, Automaton model of dynamic organization in microtubules. *Ann NY Acad Sci* 466:949-952, 1986.

53. Hameroff SR, Rasmussen S & Mansson B, Molecular automata in microtubules: basic computational logic for the living state? In: Artificial Life, the Santa Fe Institute Studies in the Sciences of Complexity, Vol. VI, ed. C Langton, Addison-Wesley, Reading, MA, 521-553, 1989.

54. Hameroff SR, Dayhoff JE, Lahoz-Beltra R, Samsonovich AV & Rasmussen S, Conformational automata in the cytoskeleton: models for molecular computation. *IEEE Computer* (in press, 1992).

55. Hebb DO, The Organization of Behavior, Wiley, New York, 1949.

56. Hirokawa N, Molecular architecture and dynamics of the neuronal cytoskeleton. In: The Neuronal Cytoskeleton, ed. RD Burgoyne, Wiley Liss, 5-74, 1991.

57. Hopfield JJ, Neural networks and physical systems with emergent collective computational abilities. *Proc Natl Acad Sci* 79:2554-2558, 1982.

58. Hotani H, Lahoz-Beltra R, Combs B, Hameroff S & Rasmussen S, Microtubule dynamics, liposomes and artificial cells: in vitro observation and cellular automata simulation of microtubule assembly/disassembly and membrane morphogenesis. *Nanobiology* 1: 61-74, 1992.

59. Insinna EM, Synchronicity and coherent excitations in microtubules. *Nanobiology* 1(2):191-208.

60. Jaynes J, The Origin of Consciousness and the Breakdown of the Bicameral Mind, London, Alan Payne Penguin Books, London, 1976.

61. Karplus M & McCammon JA, Protein ion channels, gates, receptors. In: Dynamics of Proteins: Elements and Function, Ann Rev Biochem, ed. J. King, Benjamin/Cummings, Menlo Park, 263-300, 1983.

62. Karplus M & McCammon JA, Protein structural fluctuations during a period of 100 ps. *Nature* 277:578, 1979.

63. Kauffman S & Wille JJ, *J Theor Biol* 55:47, 1975.

64. Kim H, Jensen CG & Rebhund LI, The binding of MAP-2 and tau on brain microtubules *in vitro*. In: Dynamic Aspects of Microtubule Biology, ed. D Soifer, 218-239, 1986.

65. Kirschner M & Mitchison T, Beyond self assembly: from microtubules to morphogenesis. *Cell* 45:329-342, 1986.

66. Koruga D, Microtubule screw symmetry: Packing of spheres as a latent bioinformation code. *Ann NY Acad Sci* 466:953-955, 1984.

67. Koruga D, Neuromolecular computing, *Nanobiology* 1:5-24, 1992.

68. Kudo T, Tada K, Takeda M & Nishimura T, Learning impairment and microtubule-associated protein 2 (MAP-2) decrease in gerbils under chronic cerebral hypoperfusion. *Stroke* 21:1205-1209, 1990.

69. Kwak S & Matus A, Denervation induces long-lasting changes in the distribution of microtubule proteins in hippocampal neurons. *J Neurocytol* 17:189-195, 1988.

70. Lasek RJ, The dynamic ordering of neuronal cytoskeletons. *Neurosci Res Prog Bull* 19:7-31, 1981.

71. Lechleiter J, Girard S, Peralta E, & Clapham D, Spiral calcium wave preparation and annihilation in Xenopus laevis oocytes. *Science* 252:123-126, 1991.

72. Lee JC, Field DJ, George HJ & Head J, Biochemical and chemical properties of tubulin subspecies. *Ann NY Acad Sci* 466:111-128, 1986.

73. Lund EE, A correlation of the silverline and neuromotor systems of Paramecium. *University of California Publication in Zoology* 39(2):35-76, 1933.

74. Lynch G & Baudry M, Brain spectrin, calpain and long-term changes in synaptic efficacy. *Brain Res Bull* 18:809-815, 1987.

75. MacWilliams FJ & Sloane NJA, The Theory of Error Correcting Codes. North-Holland, Amsterdam, 674, 1977.

76. Manka R & Ogrodnik B, Soliton model of transport along microtubules. *J Biol Physics*, in press.

77. Mascarenhas S, The electret effect in bone and biopolymers and the bound water problem. *Ann NY Acad Sci* 238:36-52, 1974.

78. Matsumoto G & Sakai H, Microtubules inside the plasma membrane of squid giant axons and their possible physiological function. *J Membr Biol* 50:1-14, 1974.

79. Matsuyama SS & Jarvik LF, Hypothesis: Microtubules, a key to Alzheimer's disease. *Proc Nat Acad Sci* 86:8152-8156, 1989.

80. Milch JR, Computer based on molecular implementation of cellular automata. Proceedings Third Molecular Electronics Device Workshop, ed. Forrest Carter, Naval Research Laboratory, Washington, D.C., 1987.

81. Mileusnic R, Rose SP & Tillson P, Passive avoidance learning results in region specific changes in concentration of, and incorporation into, colchicine binding proteins in the chick forebrain. *Neur Chem* 34:1007-1015, 1980.

82. Moravec HP, Mind Children. University Press, San Francisco, 1987.

83. Neubauer C, Phelan AM, Keus H & Lange DG, Microwave irradiation of rats at 2.45 GHz activates pinocytotic-like uptake of tracer by capillary endothelial cells of cerebral cortex. *Bioelectromagnetics* 11:261-268, 1990.

84. Nicolis G & Prigogine I, Self-Organization in Nonequilibrium Systems. John Wiley & Sons, New York, 1977.

85. Ochs S, Axoplasmic Transport and Its Relation to Other Nerve Functions, Wiley-Interscience, New York, 1982.

86. Parducz B, On a new concept of cortical organization in Paramecium. *Acta Biol Acad Sci Hung* 13:299-322, 1962.

87. Peat FD, Synchronicity. Bantam, New York, 1987.

88. Penrose R, The Emperor's New Mind, Oxford Press, Oxford, 1989.

89. Pribram KH, Languages of the Brain: Experimental Paradoxes and Principles. Brandon House, New York, 1971.

90. Pribram KH, Brain and Perception: Holonomy and Structure in Figural Processing. Hillsdale, NJ, Lawrence Erlbaum, 1991.

91. Puiseux-Dao S, Environmental signals and rhythms on the order of hours - role of cellular membranes and compartments and the cytoskeleton. In: Cell Cycle Clocks, ed. LN Edmunds Jr., Marcel-Dekker Inc., New York, 351-363, 1984.

92. Raes M, Involvement of microtubules in modifications associated with cellular aging. *Mutation Research* 256:149-168, 1991.

93. Rasenick MM, Wang N & Yan K, Specific associations between tubulin and G proteins: participation of cytoskeletal elements in cellular signal transduction. In: The Biology and Medicine of Signal Transduction, ed. Y Nichizuka et al, Raven Press, New York, 381-386, 1990.

94. Rasmussen S, Karampurwala H, Vaidyanath R, Jensen KS & Hameroff S, Computational connectionism within neurons: A model of cytoskeletal automata subserving neural networks. *Physica D* 42:428-449, 1990.

95. Reeke GR & Edelman GM, Selective networks and recognition automata. In: Computer Culture: The Scientific, Intellectual, and Social Impact of the Computer, ed. HR Pagels, Ann NY Acad Sci 426:181-201, 1984.

96. Reinsch SS, Mitchison TJ & Kirschner M, Microtubule polymer assembly and transport during axonal elongation. *J Cell Biol* 115(2):365-379, 1991.

97. Roth LE & Pihlaja DJ, Gradionation: hypothesis for positioning and patterning. *J Protozoology* 24:2-9, 1977.

98. Sabry JH, O'Connor TP, Evans L, Toroian-Raymond A, Kirschner M & Bentley D, Microtubule behavior during guidance of pioneer neuron growth cones in situ. *J Cell Biol* 115(2):381-395, 1991.

99. Samsonovich A, Scott A & Hameroff SR, Acousto-conformational transitions in cytoskeletal microtubules: implications for neuro-like protein array devices. *Nanobiology* (1992), in press.

100. Sataric MV, Zakula RB & Tuszynski JA, A model of the energy transfer mechanisms in microtubules involving a single soliton, *Nanobiology*, in press.

101. Schulman H & Lou LL, Multifunctional Ca^{2+}/calmodulin-dependent protein kinase: domain structure and regulation. *Trends Biochem Sci* 14:62-66, 1989.

102. Scott AC, Neurophysics, Wiley, New York, 1977.

103. Silva AV, Stevens CF, Tonegawa S & Wang, Deficient hippocampal long-term potentiation in α-calcium-calmodulin kinase II mutant mice. *Science* 257:201-206, 1992.

104. Silva AV, Paylor R, Wehner JM & Tonegawa S, Impaired spatial learning in α calcium calmodulin kinase II mutant mice. *Science* 257:206-211, 1992.

105. Smith SA, Watt RC & Hameroff SR, Cellular automata in cytoskeletal lattices. *Physica* 10D:168-174, 1984.

106. Soifer D, Factors regulating the presence of microtubules in cells. In: Dynamic Aspects of Microtubule Biology, ed. D Soifer, Ann NY Acad Sci 466:1-7, 1986.

107. Stebbings H & Hunt C, The nature of the clear zone around microtubules. *Cell Tissues Res* 227: 609-617, 1982.

108. Tabony J & Job D, Microtubular dissipative structures in biological auto-organization and pattern formation. *Nanobiology* 1(2):131-147, 1992.

109. Theurkauf WE & Vallee RB, Extensive cAMP-dependent and cAMP-independent phosphorylation of microtubule associated protein 2. *J Biol Chem* 258:7883-7886, 1983.

110. Vassilev P, Kanazirska M & Tien HT, Intermembrane linkage mediated by tubulin. *Biochem Biophys Res Comm* 126:559-565, 1985.

111. Vitiello G, Coherence and electromagnetic fields in living matter. *Nanobiology* 1(2):221-228, 1992.

112. Vivier E, Morphology, taxonomy and general biology of the genus Paramecium. In: The Biology of Paramecium, ed. WJ Van Wagtendonk, Elsevier, Amsterdam, 1-89, 1986.

113. Von Neumann J, Theory of self-reproducing automata. ed. AW Burks, Urbana, University of Illinois Press, 1966.

114. Wang N & Rasenick MM, Tubulin-G protein interactions involve microtubule polymerization domains. *Biochemistry* 30:10957-10965, 1991.

115. Werbos PJ, The cytoskeleton: why it may be crucial to human learning and to neurocontrol. *Nanobiology* 1(1):75-95, 1992.

116. Werbos PJ, Beyond regression: New tools for prediction and analysis in the behavioral sciences. Ph.D. thesis, Harvard University, 1974.

117. Wichterman R, The Biology of Paramecium, New York, Plenum, 1985.

118. Wolfram S, Cellular automata as models of complexity. *Nature* 311:419-424, 1984a.

119. Wolfram S, Universality and complexity in cellular automata. *Physica D* 10:1-35, 1984b.

120. Wright R, The On/Off Universe. The Information Age. *The Sciences*, May/June:7-9, 1985.

121. Wuensche A, Basins of attraction in disordered networks. In: Artificial Neural Networks, 2, ed. I Aleksander and J Taylor, Elsevier, Amsterdam, 1325-1344, 1992.

122. Wuensche A & Lesser M, The Global Dynamics of Cellular Automata, Santa Fe Institute, Santa Fe, 1992.

LEGENDS

Figure 1
Electron micrograph of quick frozen, deep etched neuronal MT polymerized with MAPs. Scale bar: 100 nm. (From Hirokawa, 1991)

Figure 2
Rebounding reaction of paramecium towards external stimulus. (1-3) short-lasting ciliary reversal; (3-5) pivoting and circling; (6) swimming in new direction. (From Dryl, 1974)

Figure 3
Mating behavior in paramecium. The single-cell organisms align with partners and exchange pro-nuclear material. (From Vivier, 1986)

Figure 4
Left: Scanning electron micrograph (rapid fixation) of paramecium showing protruding cilia. Arrows demonstrate ciliary movement in metachronal waves.
Right: Diagram showing paramecium polygonal infraciliary lattice with cilia (ci), containing 9 + 2 sets of microtubules including peripheral microtubule (pm) doublets. ms: median septum, al: alveoli, tt: trichocyst tips, ps: parasomal sacs, ff: fine fibrils, kf: kinetodesmal fibrils. This illustrates how cilia (sensory and motor) are connected to intra-cellular cytoskeleton. (From Wichterman, 1985)

Figure 5 (1-3)
1. Immunofluorescence image of sub-membrane infra-ciliary MT lattice in de-ciliated paramecium. ci: few cilia remain despite de-ciliation; bb: basal bodies: cortical lattice attachments for cilia; mr: microtubule ribbons: scale bar: 10 μm (10^4 nm).
2. Immunofluorescence image of acetylated ("post-translationally modified) α tubulin in paramecium interior. ci: cilia (poorly labelled); cvr: contractile vacuole roots; pof: post-oval fibers; scale bar: 10 μm.
3a &b. Immunofluorescence images of internal microtubules in paramecium. a. General view. b. Enlargement of posterior part of same cell. Arrow: MT spanning from cortical lattice to internal system. Dense region of MT in center of posterior region includes MT organizing center, centriole and described as "neuromotorium"--Paramecium's central nervous system. Scale bar: 10 μm. (From Cohen and Beisson, 1988)

Figure 6
Axoplasmic transport: vesicle transported through axoplasm by contractile activities of dynein and kinesin MAPs (arrows) attached to MT. Such transport maintains and regulates synapses. Scale bar: 100 nm. (From Hirokawa, 1991)

Figure 7
Schematic of cytoskeletal structures in synapse. Top: Pre-synaptic axon with MT, synapsin, neurotransmitter vesicles. Bottom: Post-synaptic dendrite with receptors, linking proteins, filaments/MT. (From Hirokawa, 1991)

Figure 8
a. MT Structure from x-ray crystallography (Amos and Klug, 1974). Tubulin subunits are 8nm dimers comprised of α and ß monomers. b. MT automata neighborhood: left, definition of neighborhood dimers; center, α and β monomers within each dimer; right, distances in nm and orientation among lattice neighbors. c. Relative net forces for all configurations.

Figure 9
a. MT automata models with MT displayed as rectangular grids (Rasmussen et al, 1990). Black elements are β conformational state tubulin dimers; white elements are α states. (a) Top: Three successive time steps for four objects ("dot glider", "spider glider", "triangle glider", "diamond blinker") at threshold ± 1.0, moving downward, leaving traveling wave patterns. Below: Three time steps for a "dot" and three other gliders at higher threshold ± 9.0. The gliders travel downward without a wake. b. Ten successive time steps of MT automata with asymmetric thresholds: α to β threshold is -20.0; β to α threshold is +2.0. The initial conditions (not shown) were α seeds on β background. A β bus glider (black kinky pattern) moves upward as a new α glider (white line) moves downward.

Figure 10
Simulation of MAP connections and MT network initiation. a) Some possible MAP connection sites and connection topologies, b) MT disassembly until stabilized by MAPs, c) MT MAP quantity and connection topologies which promote neighbor MT assembly and stability. Three possible "rows" of MAP connection sites are considered, negative free energy values were calculated and shown in rectangles.

Figure 11
a) MTA net learning process. The connection topology with MAPs at dimer locations MT_1: (60,6) → MT_2: (55,2) and MT_1 (47,4) → MT_2 (41.3) satisfies an input output map (not shown) with $H_{d=0}$. Dynamics shown at time steps a) 0, b) 43, and c) 66. b) Same MT net at later stage of learning process. Topology with MAPs at dimer locations same as left with additional MT_1 (28,7) → MT_2 (29,5) satisfies both input output maps with $H_d = 0$. Dynamics shown at time steps a) 0, b) 26, and c) 66 after third MAP. Thresholds for MT1 and MT2 were ± 5.9 and ± 9.0 respectively.

Figure 12
Temporal evolution of MT automata patterns at 2, 4, 6 and 8 time steps with MT2 automata patterns for 4 viruses studied. a) MAP-left closed, MAP right open, b) MAP left open, MAP right closed c) both MAPs closed d) both MAPs open.

Figure 13

a. Left: Apparent tertiary structure of tubulin dimer. GTP_e: exchangeable GTP site; GTP_n: non-exchangable GTP site. Right: Arrangement of tubulin in MT.
b. MT in unrolled plane. Numbers in each monomer indicate its position in axial direction.

Figure 14

Basin of attraction for one-dimensional cellular automaton, representing all possible behaviors. (From Wuensche anad Lesser, 1992)

Figure 15

Coherent excitation of MT causing calcium ion waves, coherent sol-gel patterns which can interfere in a holographic mechanism.

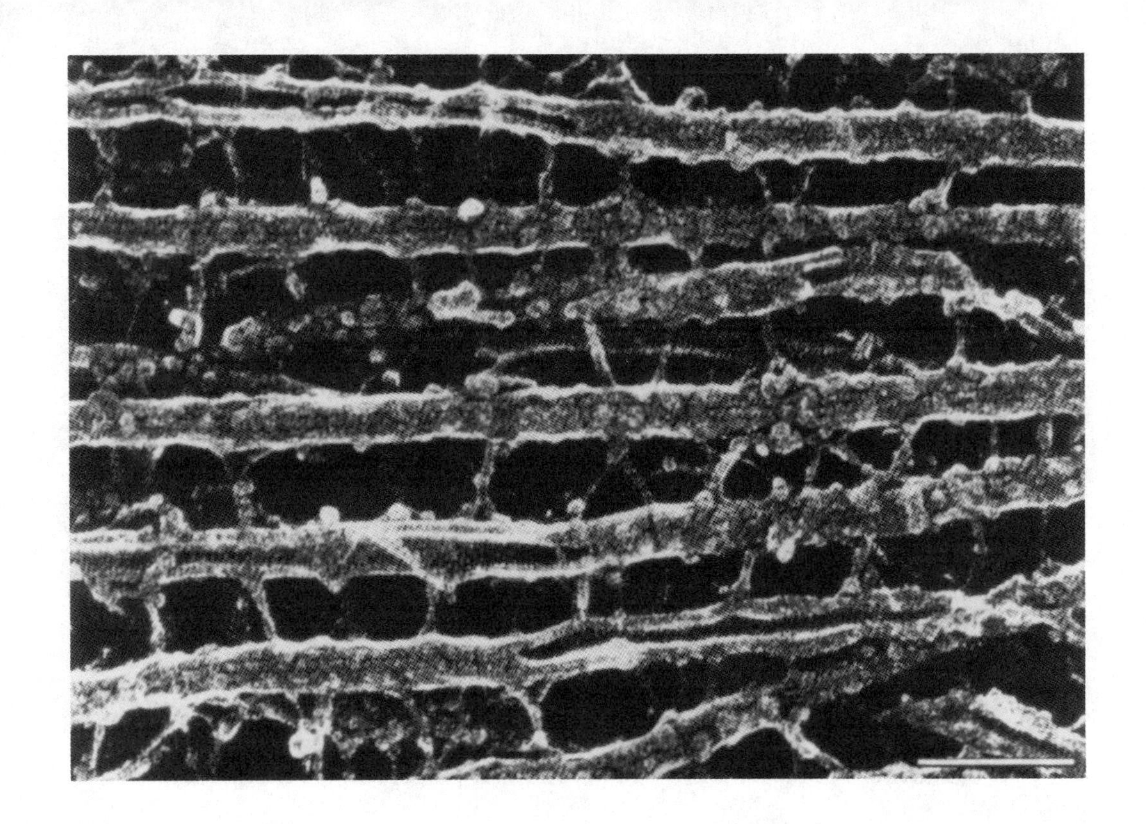

Figure 1

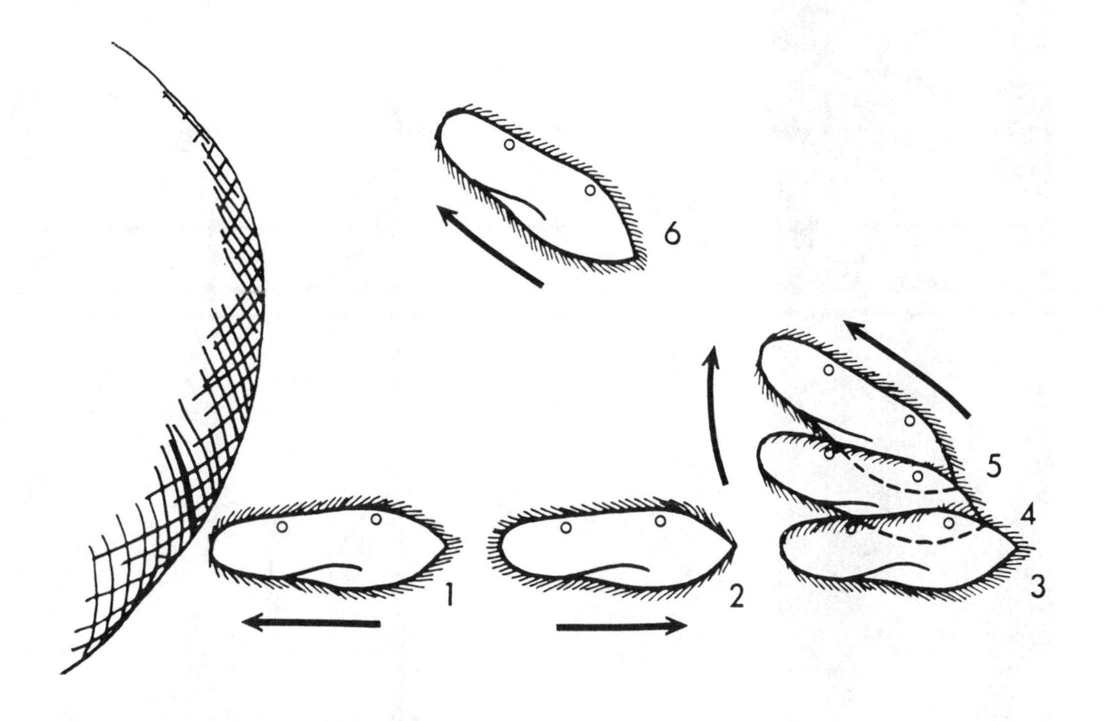

Figure 2

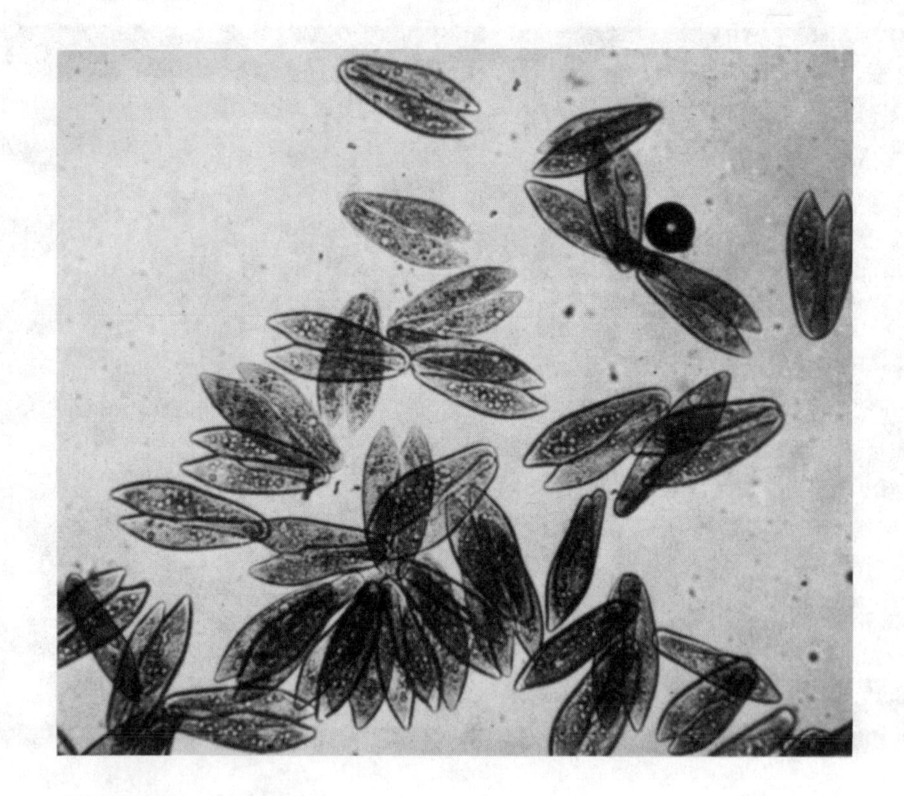

Figure 3

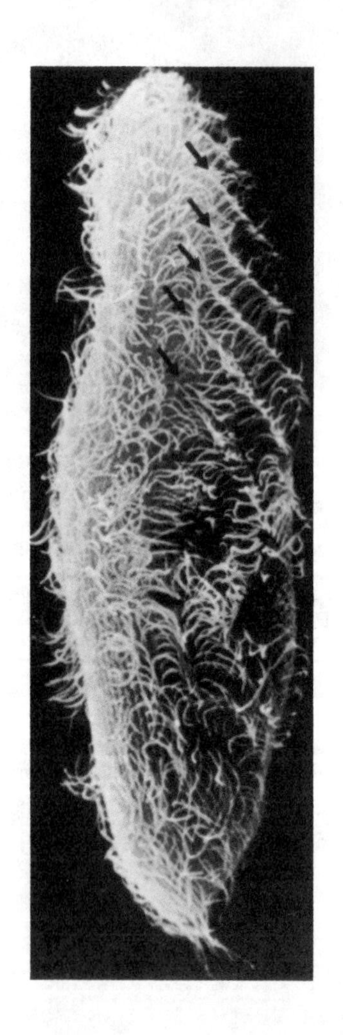

Figure 4 (left)

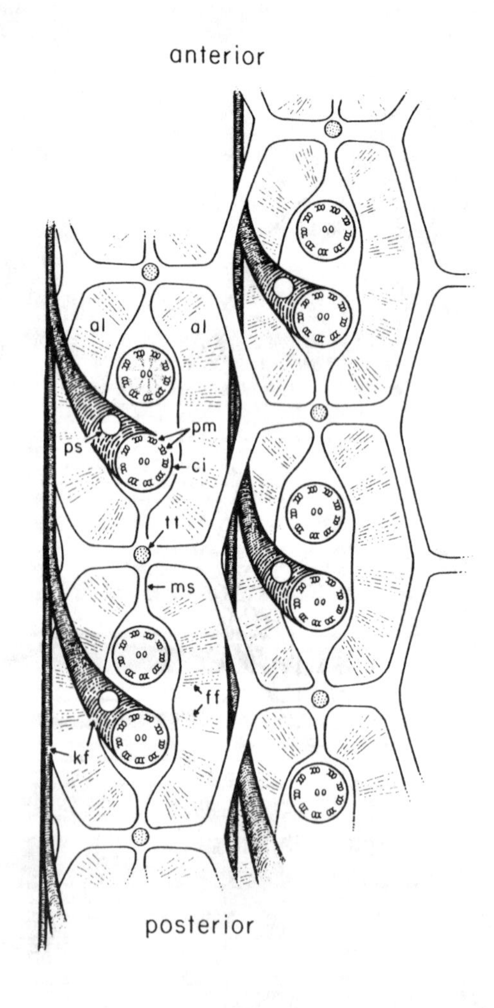

Figure 4 (right)

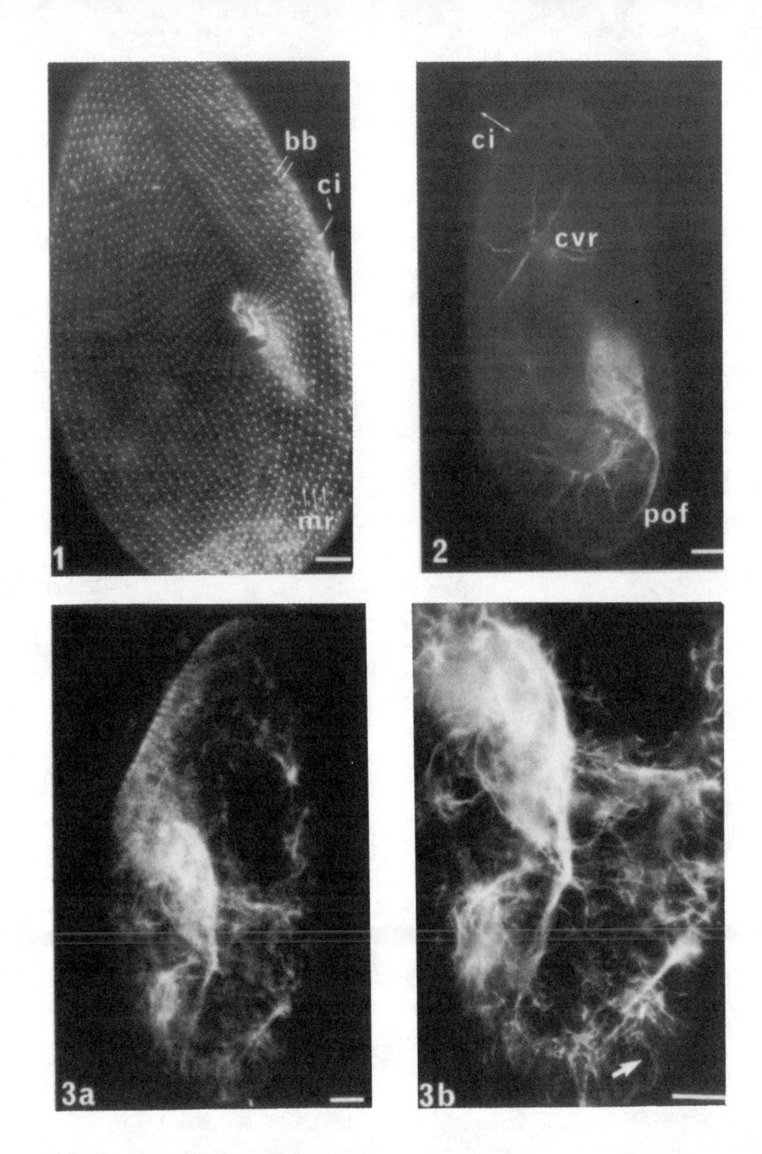

Figure 5

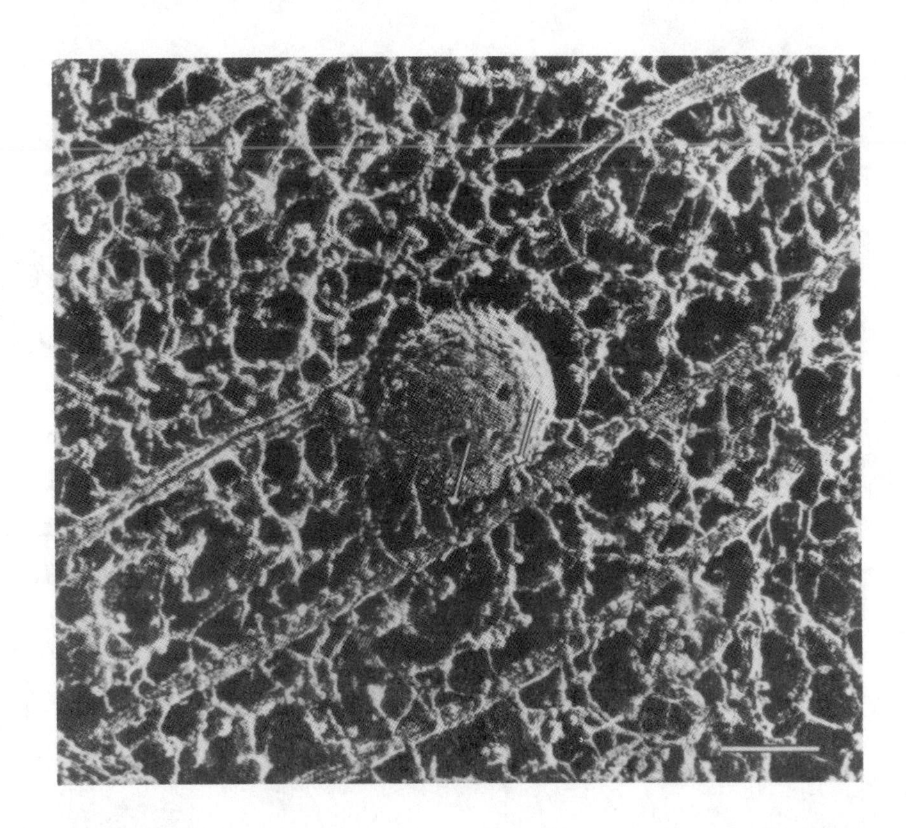

Figure 6

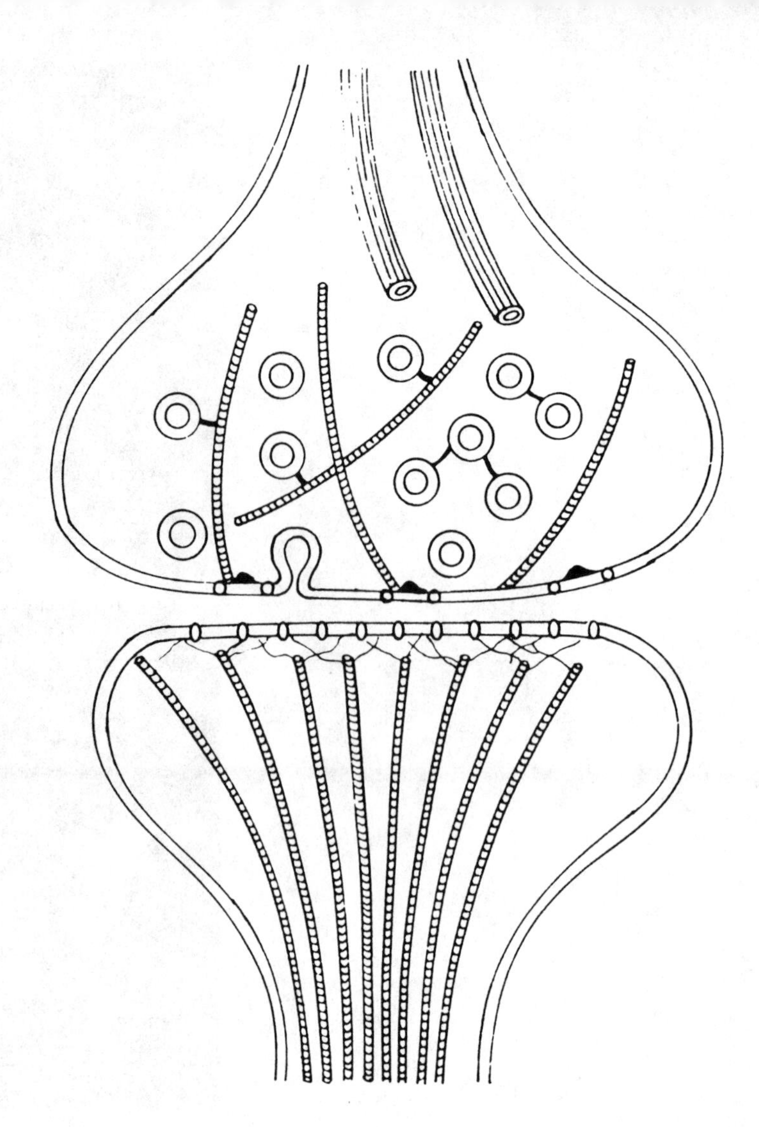

Figure 7

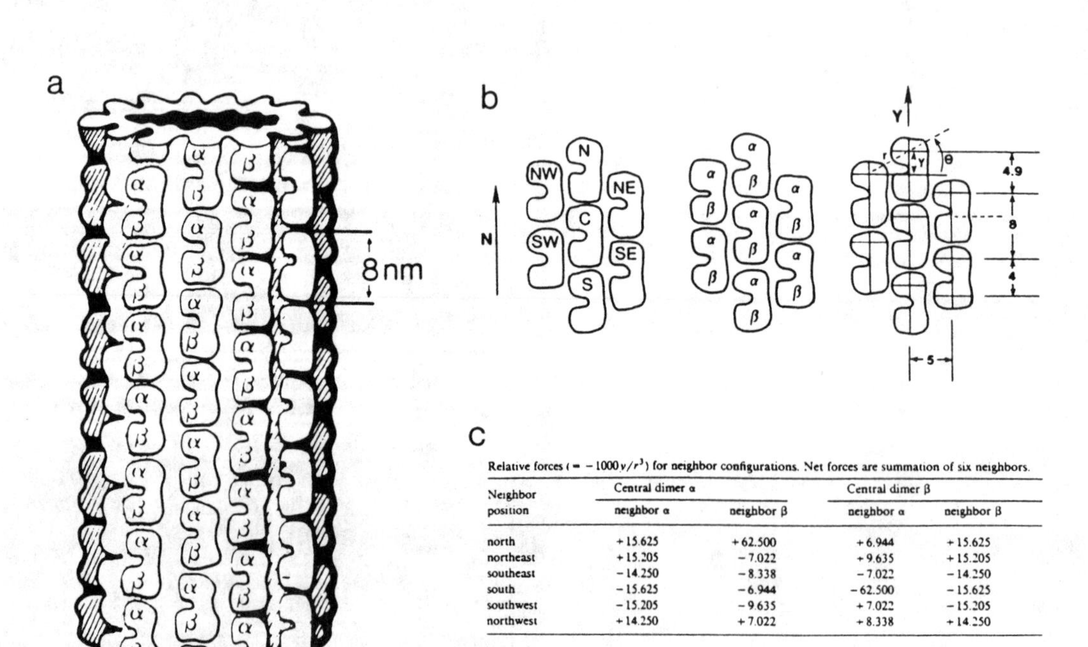

Relative forces ($= -1000v/r^3$) for neighbor configurations. Net forces are summation of six neighbors.

Neighbor position	Central dimer α		Central dimer β	
	neighbor α	neighbor β	neighbor α	neighbor β
north	+15.625	+62.500	+6.944	+15.625
northeast	+15.205	−7.022	+9.635	+15.205
southeast	−14.250	−8.338	−7.022	−14.250
south	−15.625	−6.944	−62.500	−15.625
southwest	−15.205	−9.635	+7.022	−15.205
northwest	+14.250	+7.022	+8.338	+14.250

Figure 8

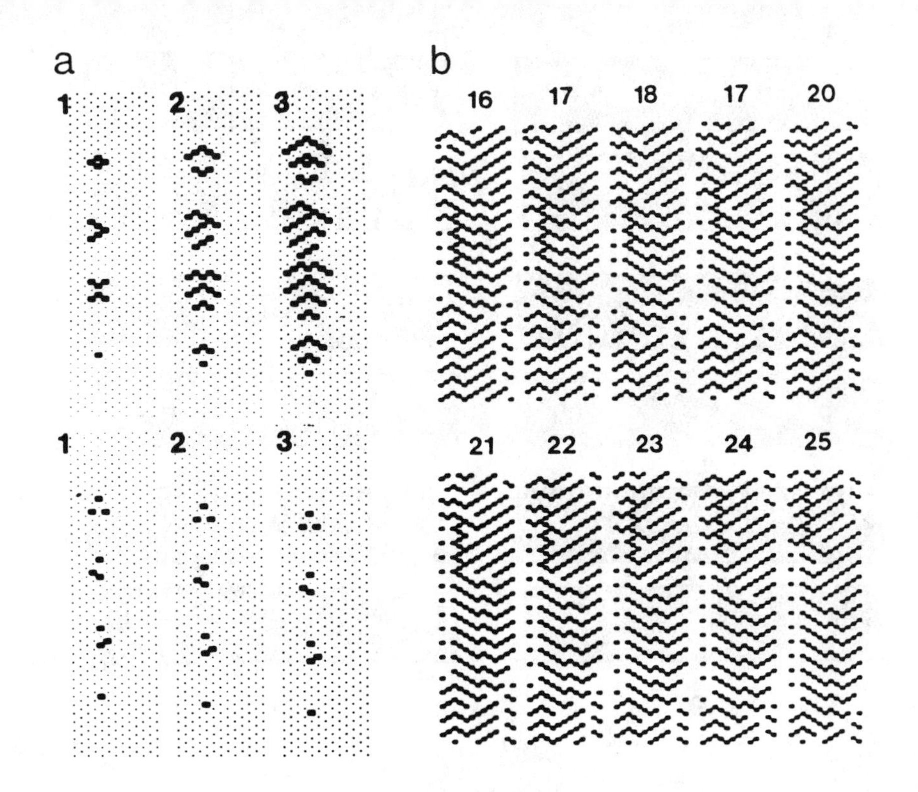

Figure 9

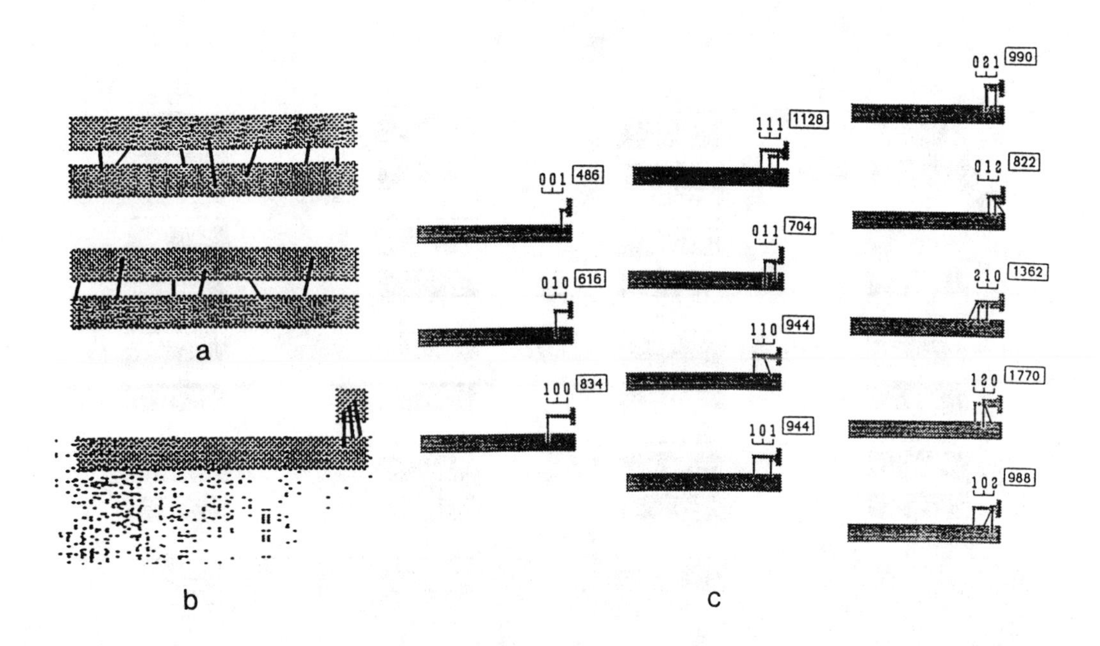

Figure 10

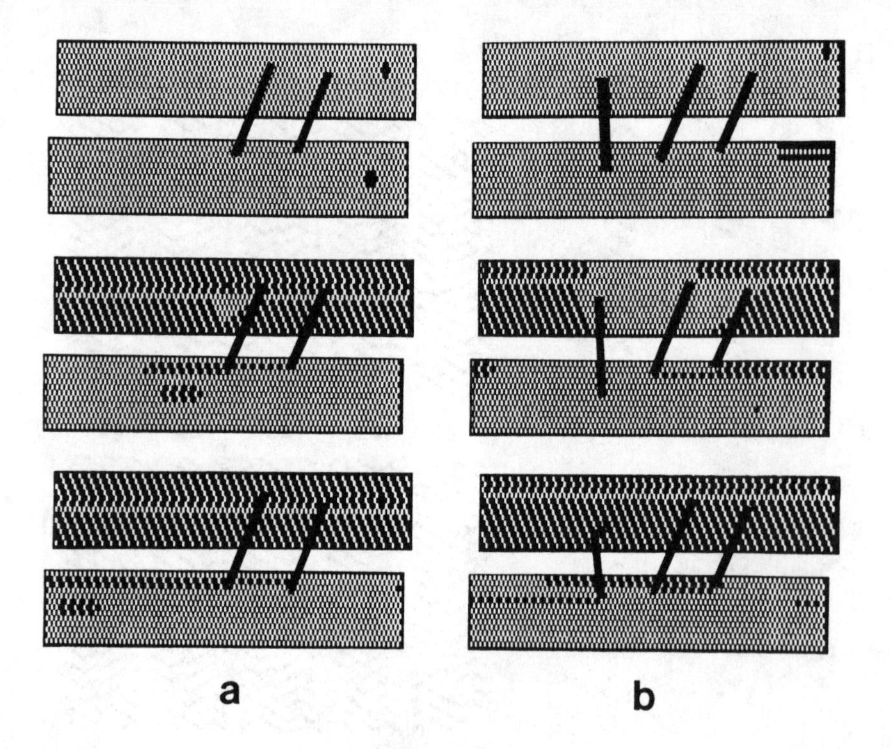

Figure 11

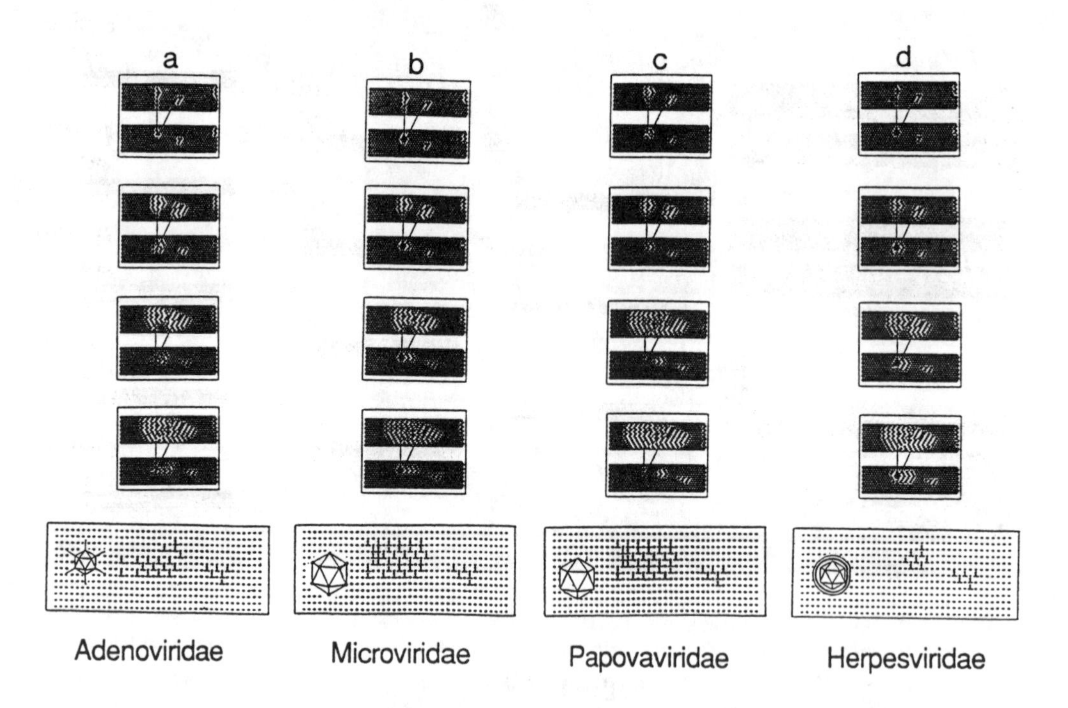

Figure 12

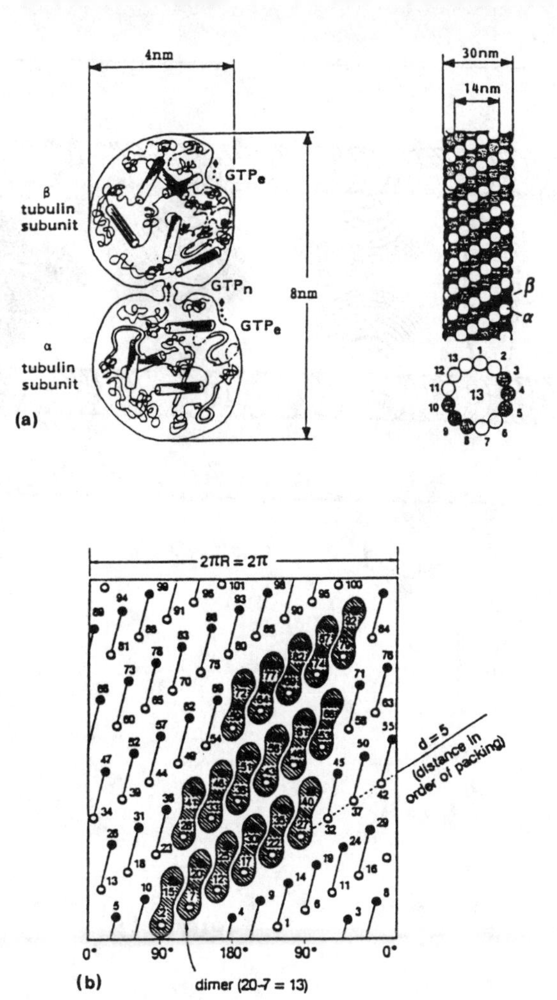

Figure 13

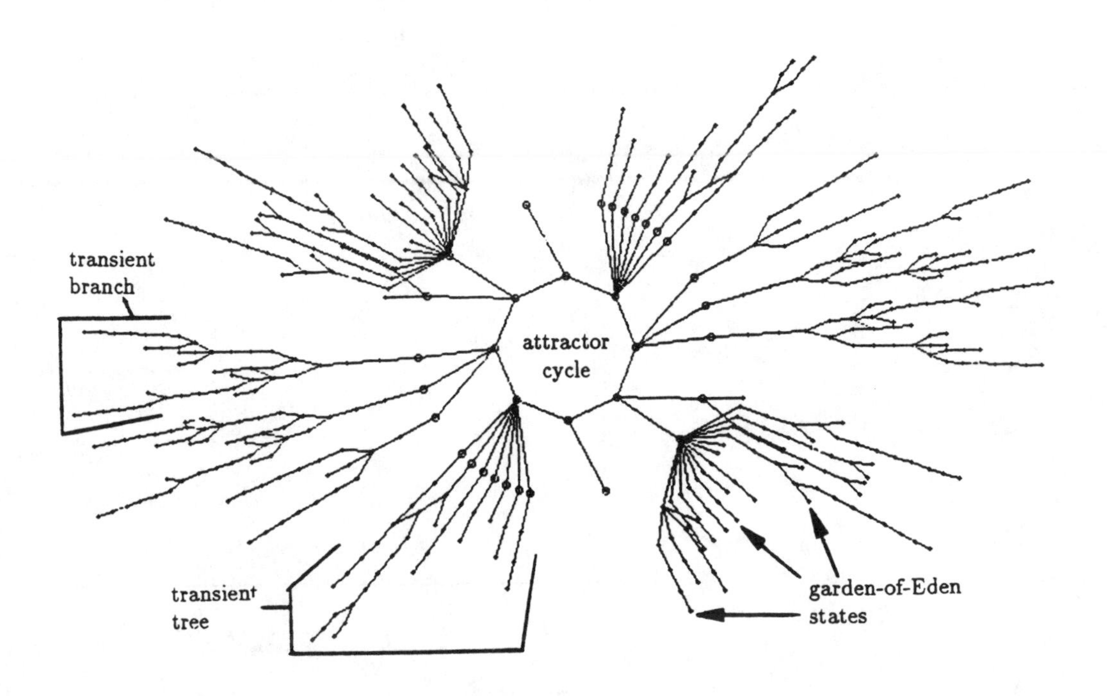

Figure 14

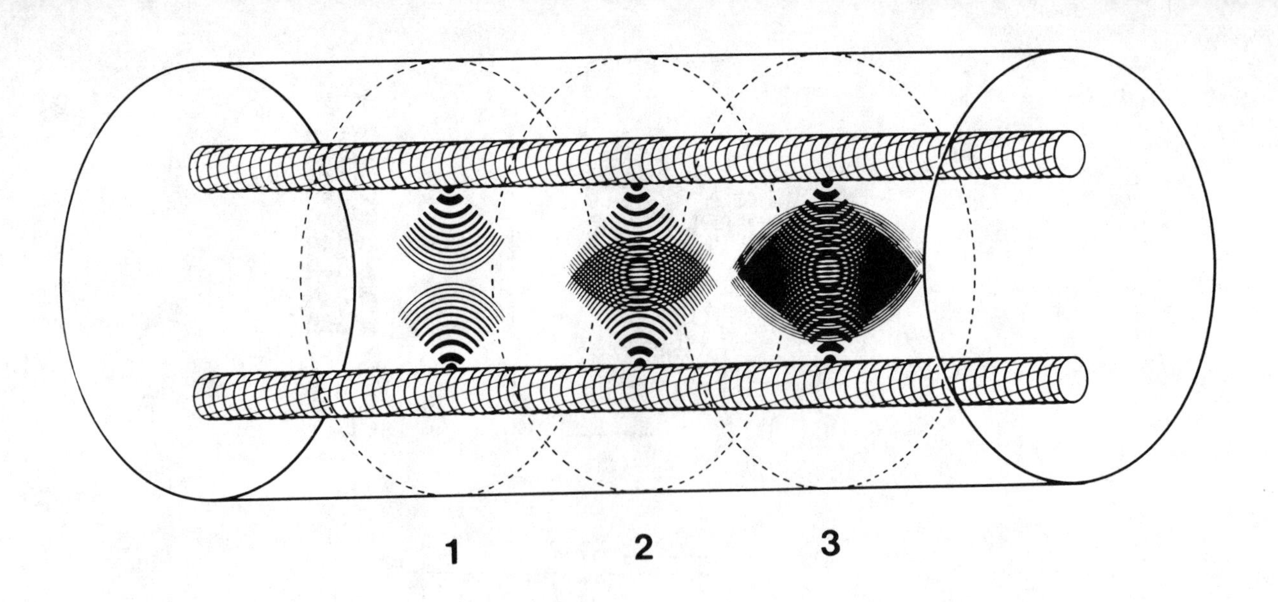

Figure 15

Chapter 11

Modulation of Neurotransmitter Function by Quantum Fields

Glen Rein
Quantum Biology Research Labs
P.O. Box 60653
Palo Alto, CA 94306

MODULATION OF NEUROTRANSMITTER FUNCTION BY QUANTUM FIELDS

Glen Rein

Quantum Biology Research Labs
P.O. Box 60653
Palo Alto, CA. 94306

INTRODUCTION

Holographic models of the brain (1) require a non-linear, coherent interaction between neuronal networks and/or between pre and post synaptic neurons. Coherence in biological systems has traditionally been explained in terms of long range electromagnetic (EM) correlations between physically separated oscillating electric dipoles whether occurring within a molecule, between molecules or between dipole clusters occurring in a distinct cellular or anatomical structures (2,3).

An alternative explanation has been proposed involving an anomalous connection between two superconductors which are physically separated (4). Such Josephson effects have recently been demonstrated in biological systems (4,5) and have therefore been proposed as an explanation for intercellular coherence (4).

Using quantum field theory, it has been predicted that Josephson junctions generate quantum potential fields (6) and that these fields in turn modulate the quantum connection in a Josephson junction (7). It is proposed here that quantum fields also mediate the interaction between superconductors in biological systems. In addition it is proposed that endogenous quantum fields in the brain mediate the communication between physically separated superconducting neurons or brain regions, thereby accounting for the brain's inherent coherent properties. Quantum fields may therefore constitute of new energetic regulatory system which modulates higher brain functions. The quantum field system would be distinct from endogenous EM fields which are well known to influence a variety of neurochemical and electrical processes in the brain (8).

To test this hypothesis, quantum potential fields were generated by a modified toroid antennae and exposed to nerve cells in tissue culture. The ability of exogenous quantum fields to influence neurotransmitter function is presented as evidence for the role of endogenous quantum fields in the brain. The role of such endogenous quantum fields will also be discussed as an explanation for EEG coherence in the brain.

MATERIALS AND METHODS

Quantum potential fields were generated using a mobius antennae which is based on a patented modification of a flat toroid coil (9). The mobius antennae consists of a flat copper coil containing a magnetic film loop of 42 turns with each turn being twisted 180 degrees from the previous turn. Such a twisted coil is a non-inductive electrical mobius resistor. The mobius coil forms a diamagnetic air dielectric when connected to a 3 V lithium battery inside a stainless steel container which acted as a Faraday cage. A quartz crystal oscillator was used to generate a digital pulse with a frequency of 32 kHz. A counter chip then stepped down the 32 kHz signal to a binary electrical signal with a peak frequency of 256 Hz which was coupled to the mobius coil. The exact orientation of the mobius coil relative to the crystal oscillator is not described in the patent.

Although the inherent non-dichotomous topology of mobius antennae makes it difficult to model the field dynamics accurately, the presence of in electric (E) field is predicted in the absence of magnetic B or H fields. The magnetic field could not be detected when measured using a specially designed magnetometer (Alphametrics Inc., Los Angeles, CA) sensitive to 10^{-5} G with a spectral range from 1-30 Hz.

The E field was measured using a specially designed electrometer (ELF International, St. Francisville, Ill) which allowed measurements in the absence of a Faraday cage shield. The electrometer contained a capacitance-type pickup with the cathode connected to the stainless steel container surrounding the mobius shield device and the anode connected to a two stage high gain Darlington amplifier giving a 10,000 to 1 amplification. The frequency domain of the electric field emitted from the mobius shield device was measured using peak frequency analysis with a one second averaging basis. At 1 cm from the mobius shield device the amplitude of the electric field was 3 uV/cm and its frequency spectra peaked at 256 Hz with subharmonics into the ELF region. The amplitude or frequency spectra of the E field did not change significantly when the mobius coil was removed from the mobius shield device. The biological responses were determined for the unmodulated E field, obtained by removing the mobius coil from the crystal oscillator circuit, as compared with the quantum modulated E field obtained when the mobius chip was included in the circuit.

The biological target for studying the effects of a mobius antennae was the PC12 neuronal cell line. PC12 cells have been well established as a model neuronal system since its neurotransmitter functions have been well characterized (10,11). Furthermore, the author has previously shown that noradrenergic transmission in these cells is influences by weak EM fields (10,12).

PC12 cells were grown in tissue culture as previously described (10). Cultures were placed 1 cm from the mobius antennae and exposed to the mobius antennae, with or without the mobius coil, for 10 minutes and 30 minutes. During exposure the petri dishes were separated by the stainless steel barrier partition between the two sides of a double CO2 incubator. At the beginning of each experiment tritium labelled noradrenaline was added to the culture dishes as previously described (10). After exposure to the mobius antennae the cells were harvested and assayed for norepinephrine uptake as previously described (10). Specific activities were calculated as total intracellular radioactive cpm relative to the total intracellular protein.

RESULTS AND DISCUSSION

The results which are presented in Table 1 indicate that after 10 minutes of exposure, no statistical difference in noradrenaline uptake was observed between cells exposed to a classical E field and those exposed to an E field modulated by the quantum fields generated by a mobius antennae. However, after 30 minutes a statistically significant difference in noradrenaline uptake was observed between the two experimental conditions ($p = 0.05$ and $t = 2.77$ using a paired t-test analysis).

TABLE 1

EFFECT OF A 256 Hz MOBIUS FIELD ON NORADRENALINE UPTAKE IN A CULTURED NERVE CELL LINE

SPECIFIC ACTIVITY
cpm/mg protein

	10 min		30min	
	EF	QF	EF	QF
	1111	1137	7032	5009
	880	1079	4520	4041
	1076	1110	9033	6035
			4277	3592
			4117	3500
$\overline{X}$	1022	1109	5796	4435
SEM	72	17	955	480

Specific activity results were calculated as the mean of duplicate determinations for 3-5 independent experiments. EF refers to unmodulated electric field and QF refers to the quantum modulated EF obtained when the mobius coil was included in the circuit.

Extremely low frequency (ELF) electromagnetic fields similar to those naturally occurring in the brain have been demonstrated to influence neurochemical, neurophysiological and electroencephalographic parameters in the brain (8). The author has previously reported the effects of pulsed magnetic fields on noradrenaline release (12) and uptake (13) using PC12 nerve cells in culture. Endogenous EM fields in the brain are believed to form a regulatory network which mediates electrochemical events in the brain (8). In addition to this regulatory network, it is proposed here that endogenous quantum fields in the brain serve a similar regulatory role at the quantum level. It is further proposed that quantal changes regulate the EM level which in turn mediate the biochemical events associated with neural transmission. This hypothesis is supported by the observed effect of time varying quantum fields on noradrenaline uptake reported here.

Quantum fields associated with quantum potentials have been described using quantum field theory. Quantum potentials are mathematically described in terms of the magnetic vector potential and the electrostatic scalar potential. Since classical EM fields can be mathematically derived from quantum potentials (14), quantum fields may be considered to underlie EM fields. Aharonov and Bohm (15) first predicted that these mathematical descriptors, which arise out of a nonlinear solution of the Schroedinger equation (14), would have macroscopic effects. It was subsequently shown that even in the absence of classical magnetic fields, quantum potential fields caused a shift in the wave function of electrons (16). Therefore, quantum fields can be measured with electron interferometers utilizing Josephson junctions.

The use of solenoid-generated DC quantum fields in these studies has more recently been extended to the generation of time-varying quantum fields from toroid, mobius and caduceus antennae (6,17-20,21). Although the gravitational and thermal anomalies associated with these coils have been measured (21), the possibility that quantum fields may interact with biological systems has received little attention.

Flannigan used an 8 Hz magnetic pulse to drive a mobius antennae and observed a shift in the electrical conductivity of the skin over acupuncture points (20). The author used a caduceus coil driven by a complex RF signal to stimulate the proliferation of peripheral blood lymphocytes in tissue culture (22).

These studies used unconventional coil windings to cancel the local EM fields (23) thereby generating time varying quantum potential fields. The mobius antennae used in this study is a modification of a donut shaped toroid resistor. Non-inductive toroid resistors are commonly used in RF and MW electronics circuits to eliminate inductance from resistor elements and to minimize magnetic field loses by containing the B and H fields within the toroid (24). They have also been used by NASA in high speed computer circuitry used in space craft (24).

Jennison has mathematically characterized the properties of

radiation trapped in phase-locked cavities (25). Application of an external electromotive force to such a system accelerates it so its velocity increases in a non-linear "staircase" manner and is maintained when the stimulus is removed. This relativistic effect was accounted for by the presence of two orthogonal standing waves in phase-locked quadrature and shown to be dependent on the configuration and distribution of the wave fields trapped in the cavity. Similar field dynamics may be occurring with toroid resistors which also trap magnetic fields.

Toroid resistors can also act as antennae. Since magnetic fluxes are contained within them, the magnetic field outside the torus is zero. The presence of quantum potential fields in the absence of magnetic fields has been predicted (15) and demonstrated (16).

A mobius coil is a topological modification of a toroid coil which is folded back on itself, thereby allowing current to flow in opposite directions. Thus in addition to containing the magnetic fields, the mobius resistor will cancel them. This same principle is used in bifilar coils common in electrical engineering.

Mobius resistors have similar field properties as a toroid coil since the toroid configuration is contained within the mobius winding. Although both coil windings will generate a quantum field, the particular mobius configuration used in this study will also generate an E field. In contrast to a torus, however, the unique topology of the mobius resistor bucks and cancels magnetic fields contained within the coil. Since the magnetic field vectors along a mobius coil reverse at the twist, half the vectors are oriented upward and half are oriented downward. Therefore, considering the whole system, the vectors sum to zero (17). Due to the self-canceling configuration it has been proposed that mobius antennae emit a novel form of energy (26). This novel form of energy will be referred to as the mobius field.

The first application of self-canceling coils was accomplished by Tesla at the turn of the century. Tesla's magnifying transmitter used two coils where oscillations were phased to create opposing magnetic fields (27). He demonstrated that such a coil could transmit energy, which he referred to as non-Hertzian, over long distances without losses (28).

The presence of such novel mobius field has been predicted by Seike who used the quantum field theory to characterize the field dynamics in mobius antennae (17). This type of analysis is referred to as Topological Electronics. Using the magnetic flux associated with a mobius and the electrical potential across a resistor, Seike has solved Maxwell's equations and obtained a solution which describes the imaginary component of the electrostatic scalar potential and the imaginary component of the corresponding magnetic field. The ohmic loss of resistance is calculated to be a negative value indicating that the imaginary current absorbs (rather than emits) heat and is associated with the presence of negative energy. This conclusion is consistent with the negative energy associated with an electron derived from the Dirac equation (29). Using special relativity theory, Seike further derives a description of the resultant imaginary electric field emitted by a mobius resistor and the real magnetic field contained within it. The equations predict the interchange of energy between these two fields will generate an imaginary magnetic field.

Quantum fields generated from a toroid antennae would be expected to contain the same spectral frequency information as the input current driving the toroid coil. Quantum fields and mobius fields associated with a mobius antennae, on the other hand, will have a unique and complex set of harmonics based on constructive and destructive interference of certain frequencies when the magnetic fields are canceled. The mobius antennae used in this study will also emits an E field with the same frequency signature of the driving current. Due to the close association of EM and quantum fields, the E field can be considered a carrier wave for the more complex harmonic associated with the quantum field and/or mobius field. This is similar to the classical concept of frequency modulation in electrical engineering.

This study was designed to distinguish potential biological effects of the E field and the quantum frequency modulated E field. An unmodulated E field was generated by removing the mobius coil from the crystal oscillator circuit. The validity of such a comparison was demonstrated by the identical E field amplitudes and frequencies measured with and without the mobius coil. Thus, the quantum modulation could not be measured using a standard spectrum analyzer. Nonetheless there was a significant difference in the biological response between the two devices. Since it is known that EM fields can inhibit noradrenaline uptake (13), an untreated control was not used in this study. Nonetheless the results indicate that there was a 24% inhibition of noradrenaline uptake, above and beyond whatever E field effect may have occurred, when the quantum and/or mobius fields were present. These results indicate for the first time that quantum fields can have a direct effect on neuronal cells and supports the hypothesis that these fields are an underlying regulatory system which effects higher brain function by altering neurotransmitter function.

The results also support the hypothesis that endogenous quantum fields in the brain allow anatomically distal sites to interact with each other and can account for coherence in EEG measurements. This is an alternative hypothesis to the classical explanation that coherent excitations in biological systems arise from EM communication between oscillating electric dipoles (3).

Intercellular communication between neurons via quantum fields is based on recently observed superconductivity in biological systems (5). Superconduction of electrons (without the generation of heat) has been predicted and observed for enzymes (30) and organic compounds like cholesterol (31) at physiological temperatures. Since cholesterol is relatively abundant in lipid bilayers in nerve cells, it has been proposed that superconductivity plays a role in nerve function (5). Additional evidence is suggested by the known ability of strong electric fields to induce superconductivity in organic polymers, since such fields are associated with the generation of action potentials (32). Finally, certain neuronal processes show negative temperature coefficients which can not be explained in terms of classical electrochemistry (33). Since electron tunneling between superconductors shows negative temperature coefficients (33), superconduction may explain this anomalous behavior of neurons.

Quantum tunneling of electrons between two superconductors has been offered as an explanation for the anomalous behavior of interacting superconductors forming a Josephson junction (34). An energetic interaction between the pre and post synaptic neurons has been postulated to be mediated via quantum tunneling (35). In turn quantum tunneling can be mathematically described in terms of quantum fields, at least in non biological systems (36). Since quantum fields cause a shift in the phase of current passing through a Josephson junction (6), quantum fields generated from a mobius antennae could modify the coherent interaction between two superconducting neurons. Although this study doesn't measure the ability of neurons to emit quantum fields, the results indicate that they are sensitive to quantum fields. It is therefore possible that quantum fields mediate a new type of synaptic communication between neurons.

DelGiudice has proposed that Josephson effects need not be limited to communication between superconductors, but will apply to interactions between separated coherent domains in biological systems (4). Using quantum field theory, DelGiudice has modeled these interactions and shown them to be "non-Maxwellian" in nature. He further demonstrated that these quantum interactions could be explained in terms of quantum fields (37). In support of this hypothesis, DelGiudice and Smith (4) used dielectrophoresis measurements on yeast cells in suspension to show unusual current-voltage relationships characteristic of those occurring in a Jospheson junction. This nonlinear ohmic behavior was further correlated with a physiological process, cell growth. The authors conclude that physically separated cells, each acting as coherent domains, exhibit phase-locked Josephson behavior and can communicate via quantum coherent interactions.

Similar interactions are likely to occur between individual neurons which display coherent interactions among the glycoproteins in their plasma membranes (38). This new form of non-synaptic intercellular communication between two neurons would be mediated by endogenous quantum fields in the brain.
DelGiuidice's hypothesis may also be extended to interactions between brain regions since it has recently been reported that coherency in the brain can be anatomically localized to specific brain regions in the hippocampal cortex (39). These more global interactions offer a new explanation for brain coherence.

Such global coherent interactions, which are likely to be mediated by endogenous quantum fields, may also be explained in terms of nonlocality. Quantum fields have been used to explain non-local action at a distance (36) arising out the Einstein-Podolsky-Rosen paradox (40) which requires the instantaneous transfer of information between two physically separated electrons. With more complex systems, interactions between each pair of particles depends on the quantum state of all the particles in the system (36). Bohm further describes the information within the quantum potential forming a common pool of information which organizes and makes coherent the individual components of the whole system. With respect to brain function information may be imparted to endogenous quantum fields by specific frequency spectral patterns associated with nerve firing. It is predicted that exogenous quantum fields generated by a mobius antennae could modulate this frequency information thereby altering global coherent interactions and/or local interactions between neurons. The mobius antennae offers a new tool for studying the quantum energetic regulatory network in the brain.

REFERENCES:

1. Psaltis D, Brady D, Gu XG et al. Holography in artificial neural networks. Nature 343:325 (1990).

2. Frohlich H. (ed) Biological Coherence and Response to External Stimuli, Springer, N.Y. (1988)

3. Josephson BD. Adv Phys 14:419 (1965)

4. Del Giudice E, Doglia S, Milani M et al. Magnetic flux quantization and Josephson behavior in living systems. Physica Scripta 40:786 (1989)

5. Cope FW. A review of the applications of solid state physics concepts to biological systems. J Bio Phys 3:1 (1975).

6. Gelinas RC. Apparatus and method for transfer of information by means of a curl-free magnetic vector potential field. US Patent 4,432,098 Feb 14, 1984.

7. Gelinas RC. Apparatus and method for modulation of a curl-free magnetic vector potential field. US Patent 4,429,288 Jan 31, 1984.

8. Adey WR. Tissue interactions with non-ionizing electromagnetic fields. Physiol Rev 61:435 (1981).

9. Puharich HK. Method and means from shielding a person from the effects of ELF magnetic waves. U.S.Patent 616-183 June 1, 1984

10. Greene LA, Rein G. Release, storage and uptake of catecholamines by a clonal cell line of NGF responsive phaeochromocytoma cells. Brain Res 129:247 (1977).

11. Greene LA, Rein G. Synthesis, storage and release of acetylcholine by a noradrenergic phaeochromocytoma cell line. Nature 268:349 (1977).

12. Dixey R, Rein G. Noradrenaline release potentiated in a clonal nerve cell line by low-intensity pulsed magnetic fields. Nature 296:253 (1982).

13 Rein G, Korins K, Pilla A. Inhibition of neurotransmitter uptake in a neuronal cell line by pulsed electromagnetic fields. Proc 9th Bioelectromag Soc. June (1987).

14. Bohm D. A suggested interpretation of quantum theory in terms of hidden variables. Phys Rev 85:166 (1952).

15. Aharonov Y, Bohm E. Significance of electromagnetic potentials in the quantum theory. Phys Rev 115:485 (1959).

16. Tonomura A et al. Evidence for Aharanov-Bohm effect with magnetic field completely shielded from electron wave. Phys Rev Lett 56:792 (1986).

17. Seiki S. The Principles of Ultra-Relativity, Ninomiya Press, PO Box 33, Uwajima City, Ehime (798), Japan, 10th ed., Dec. 1990.

18. Wekroma AG. The use of magnetic vector potentials for the treatment of materials. FRG Patent 3938511.6 Nov.19, 1989.

19. Davis RL. The mobius coil as a non-inductive electrical resistor. US Patent 3,267,406 May 1, 1964.

20. Flannigan P. Normalization of electroacupuncture imbalances using a mobius coil. Electric Engineer Times Oct 29, p38 (1979)

21. Aspen HA. Principles underlying regenerative free energy technology. Proc 26th Intersoc Energy Convers Engineer Conf 4:358 (1991).

22. Rein G. Utilization of a cell culture bioassay for measuring quantum potentials generated from a modified caduceus coil. Proc. 26th Intersoc Energy Convers Engineer Conf 4:400 (1991).

23. McClain JW. Cancellation of internal forces. Amer J. Phys 47:1005 (1979).

24. Resistors with a real twist. Electronics Illustrated, p. 76, Nov. 1969.

25. Jennison RC. Relativistic phase-locked cavities as particle models. J Physics A: Math Gen 11:1525 (1978)

26. Johnson GL. Searches for a new energy source. IEEE Power Engineer Rev. January p20 (1992).

27. Sector HW. The Tesla high frequency oscillator. Electrical Experimenter 3:615 (1916)

28. Tesla N. Transmission of energy without wires. Scient Amer Suppl. 57:23760 (1904).

29. Dirac PAM. Quantum theory of the electron. Proc Royal Soc London A117:610 (1928).

30. Ahmed NAG, Smith CW. Superconductivity of lysozyme in solution. Collective Phenomena 3:25 (1978).

31. Goldfein S. Superconductivity in organic polymers. Physiol Chem Phys. 6:261 (1974).

32. Cope FW. Superconductivity of nerves. Physiol Chem Phys. 6:405 (1974).

33. Cope FW. Negative temperature coefficients in neurons. Physiol Chem Phys 3:403 (1971).

34. Solymar L. Superconductive Tunneling and Applications, Chapman and Hall, N.Y. (1972).

35. Burden SJ, McKay RD. Quantum mechanics of synapses.Cell 63:7 (1990).

36. Bohm DJ, Hiley BJ. On the intuitive understandinng of nonlocality as implied by quantum theory. Found Phys 5:93 (1975).

37. DelGiudice E, Preparata G, Vitiello G. Water as a free dipole laser. Phys Rev Lett. 61:1085 (1988).

38. Adey WR, Lawrence AF. Nonlinear Electrodynamics in Biological Systems. Plenum, N.Y. (1984).

39. Bullock TH, Buzsaki G, McClune MC. Coherence of compound field potentials reveals discontinuities in the hippocampus. Neurosci 38:609 (1990).

40. Bohm DJ, Hiley BJ. Nonlocality in quantum theory understood in terms of Einstein's nonlinear field approach. Found Phys 11:529 (1981).

Chapter 12

THE NEURONAL CYTOSKELETON: A COMPLEX SYSTEM THAT SUBSERVES NEURAL LEARNING

Judith Dayhoff
Systems Research Center, University of Maryland
College Park, MD 20742

-

Stuart Hameroff
Advanced Biotechnology Laboratory
Dept Anesthesiology, University of Arizona
College of Medicine, Tucson, AZ 85724

-

Charles E. Swenberg
Armed Forces Radiobiology Research Institute
Bethesda, MD 20889-5145

-

Rafael Lahoz-Beltra
Advanced Biotechnology Laboratory
Dept Anesthesiology, University of Arizona
College of Medicine, Tucson, AZ 85724

-

Corresponding author: Judith Dayhoff

October 6, 1992

Abstract

The neuronal cytoskeleton, scaffolding for neuronal cell shape and framework for intracellular communication, adds a unique and powerful dimension to the capabilities of biological neurons to compute, adapt, and learn. Potential capabilities of this network of protein polymer strands bridge the gap between detailed and complex biological neurons and their simplified counterpart, the biologically inspired artificial neural network. Intracellular signaling, biologically plausible by several cytoskeleton-mediated mechanisms, could play a key role in neuronal learning paradigms and synaptic adaptation, and have the potential of providing signals from axon to dendrite, from synapse to nucleus, or between membrane sites along dendrites. We propose a model for neuronal learning via cytoskeletal signaling, and identify specific biophysical mechanisms that could plausibly implement this model. Cytoskeletal signaling mechanisms are proposed for transmission along protein polymer strands such as microtubules, actin filaments and neurofilaments, and cross-bridge proteins transfer signals between strands. The proposed cytoskeletal signaling provides a key element in a biologically plausible model for back-propagation of learning signals as synaptic weights are trained. Biophysical sites for each step in an error-correcting learning paradigm are suggested, and cytoskeletal signaling can be modeled by cellular automata or moving ionic waves. Thus the cytoskeleton, anchored to synaptic proteins, furnishes a protein molecular level of processing in the neural network and could imbue the network with key learning and adaptational capabilities.

1 Introduction

The cytoskeleton is a rich structural network that includes microtubules (MT), actin filaments and neurofilaments, membrane coupling proteins and microtubules associated proteins (MAPs) that crosslink MTs to each other and to other cell structures. Cytoskeleton provides physical and structural support to the cell, a role that is particularly critical in the nerve cell, as the extensive branching of both axons and dendrites is important to the presence and location of synaptic connections. Cytoskeleton also provides a communication and transport substrate between remote cell parts, as particles are carried along MTs by specialized motor proteins. In most cells, the MTs connect the cell center (centriole) to the cell periphery in a radial pattern. In nerve cells the MTs have evolved a striking adaptation in that the microtubular lattice extends into the extremities of the axons and the dendrites, and some MTs may bypass the cell center. These internal highly ordered structures allow not only for the mechanical transport of material particles, but possibly the transmission of information utilizing fast signaling mechanisms such as traveling conformational waves (changes) and ionic cable properties. Cytoskeletal signaling provides a medium for internal neuronal signaling that could play a key role in biological learning.

Cytoskeletal signals could provide the missing link for the biological implementation of many learning models, including back-error propagation. In a back-propagating neuronal model, error signals would be propagated internally within neurons along cytoskeleton, from axons to dendrites. Other learning paradigms, such as the sigma-pi and RCE architectures, and adaptive resonance theory (ART), could also be implemented in a biologically plausible fashion with putative cytoskeletal signaling (Dayhoff et al, 1992a). The sigma-pi paradigm, like back propagation, employs error feedback signals as does the RCE architecture. ART utilizes two-way activation propagation and when signals in the forwards and backwards directions are mutually reinforcing, resonance, or recognition, occurs.

In neurons, the cytoskeleton interacts dynamically with other cell structures and mechanisms, such as synapses, membranes, protein conformational changes, and ionic movements, as biological neurons are extremely complex. Neurons employ a wide variety of anatomical and biophysical structures and mechanisms to perform their dynamic roles in neural information processing. Complex anatomy and physiology include the spatial arrangement of axons and dendrites, their branching topologies, the location of cell bodies and the interconnection configuration among cells. Field interactions, molecular-level structures such as membrane channels, receptors, voltage and time dependent channel conductances, membrane resistance and capacitance, receptor binding and conformational changes, and ionic diffusion also play roles in neural processing.

The chemical synapse formed between neurons has been identified as the primary neuronal structure associated with learning and memory. The synapse responds in a complex dynamical manner to not only its primary neurotransmitter but also to a host of neuromodulators. Experimental evidence indicates that synapses also have reverse transmitters - molecules such as nitric oxide (NO) that travel from post-synaptic sites to pre-synaptic membranes. Thus each synapse is a vast electrochemical factory, and as a consequence of the transmitters and modulators, a synapse can exhibits a history-dependent plasticity, adaptation, and learning. As a result, each synapse has tremendous potential for computational activity. Synapses dynamically interact with internal processes within the cell, including the cell cytoskeleton, and synaptic components such as receptor molecules and transmitter vesicles are typically anchored to cytoskeletal protein strands.

Recent models have suggested that the cytoskeleton - the structural support system within cells - might be capable of transmitting signals and could do so internally within a nerve cell (Rasmussen et al, 1990). A variety of candidate mechanisms have been proposed for cytoskeletal signal propagation, including particle transport and traveling conformational changes (Hameroff, 1987; Hameroff et al, 1989; Rasmussen et al, 1990). Movement of ions along actin filaments or MTs, or actual movements of the MTs themselves have also been proposed (Dayhoff et al, 1992). Experiments have shown that actin filaments and MTs act as cables in communicating between separated membrane patches (Cantiello and Kim, 1992; Vassilev et al, 1985).

In this paper, we propose a plausible model for learning by back-error propagation in biological neurons. Forwards propagation occurs as action potentials propagate signals along branching axons and transmit those signals across axo-dendritic synapses, whereupon post-synaptic neurons sum their incoming signals. Back-error propagation is proposed to occur via signals within intraneuronal cytoskeletal filaments or microtubules. These signals modify the effective strengths of synapses during learning via the biophysical interaction between cytoskeleton and nerve cell membranes. Differences between network output and desired (target) outputs are computed at synapses or by synaptic complexes. Biophysical mechanisms are suggested for the summing of errors and the propagation of errors backwards through the cytoskeleton within each neuron of the network. This model argues for the biological plausibility of back-error propagation.

Prior studies regarding biological back-error propagation have assumed that error feedback must be provided by action potentials and axodendritic synapses (Stork, 1989; Hecht-Nielsen, 1989, Churchland and Sejnowski, 1989). This assumption requires a heavy density of bidirectionally connected cells, in which many pairs of cells must be connected in both directions via axodendritic synapses. For each forwards connection to a target neuron, a backwards connection is assumed from the target neuron to the original neuron, to send error difference signals backwards through the network. Because of the lack of evidence for the occurrence of such arrangements, the biological plausibility of back-error propagation has been considered extremely unlikely. For this reason, we take a radically different approach here to the biological plausibility of back-error propagation. We utilize the internal complexity of the neuron to construct a model in which back-error signals are propagated within a nerve cell through the cell cytoskeleton. Thus the assumption of cytoskeletal signaling alleviates the need for bidirectional connections among cells, used in previous arguments against the biological plausibility of back-error propagation.

The model proposed here fits strikingly with a variety of experimental evidence from studies of the cytoskeleton and its associated biochemistry (reviewed in Dayhoff et al, 1992c). Previous authors have suggested that MTs are indeed involved in back-error propagation (Werbos, 1990; Werbos, 1992; Hameroff et al, 1989; Rasmussen et al, 1990) or in neuronal learning (Grossberg 1969), but did not develop a description of the underlying biophysics or suggest anatomical sites at which each of the necessary computations take place. Specific sites and biophysical mechanisms are suggested in this paper as candidate mechanisms for the proposed model.

2 Back-Error Propagation Paradigm

A fundamental challenge today is to explain the possible mechanisms for learning in the brain and in nerve cell assemblies. A variety of learning models have been proposed, including those of "artificial neural networks", which employ processing units that are inspired by biological neurons but are greatly simplified. The leading paradigm in artificial neural networks is back-error propagation, which has led to a large number of applications. Back-propagation has been shown to have powerful mathematical properties with respect to approximation of arbitrary functions and discerning of arbitrary differences among input patterns (Hornik et al, 1990).

In this section we describe a back-error propagation paradigm that appears frequently in artificial neural network applications studies. It is powerful computationally and has considerable capabilities in the learning of arbitrary nonlinear functions and pattern classification tasks (Hornik et al, 1990). Back-propagation networks are non-linear mappers, capable of drawing non-linear boundaries to divide patterns. They were first proposed by Werbos (1974), in his thesis, appropriately entitled "Beyond Regression". Here we follow a specific back-propagating algorithm summarized by Rumelhart, Hinton, and Williams (1986).

We restrict this section to a back-error propagation paradigm for a three-layer feed-forward network. We assume that processing units are organized into layers and that the network is fully interconnected - e.g., the units in each layer send interconnections to all of the units in the next layer. Back-error propagation is not, however, limited to this configuration. This is an important point since biological systems do not have this restricted interconnection configuration. Thus the greater flexibility in interconnection topologies found in biology does not preclude the use of back propagation during biological learning. The model proposed here could potentially be extended to apply to more flexible interconnection topologies.

Each back-propagation iteration during learning consists of a forwards propagation step and a backwards propagation step. In the forwards step, the network is presented with an input pattern (a vector), and produces an output pattern. In the backwards propagation step, the network compares its answer to that of a target answer, and backwards propagates error computations that are used to adjust weight values. Weights are adjusted incrementally to eventually learn the pattern-mapping task at hand (if convergence is successful). A tutorial level explanation of back-error propagation is available elsewhere (Dayhoff, 1990).

Typically, training a network requires many iterations of pattern presentations. Each iteration consists of presentation of a set of patterns known as the "training set". Weights are adjusted after each pattern in the training set ("pattern learning"), or may be adjusted after the entire training set has been presented ("batch learning"). The training set consists of a list of pattern (vector) pairs, with each pair being an input pattern and a target output pattern. This supervised training method is plausible biologically because learning tasks frequently involve the recall of one pattern given the presentation of another; both the initial pattern and the pattern to be recalled (the "input" and "target" patterns) would be present during training. An example would be in teaching a child the letters of the alphabet; a written "A" (input pattern) would be presented at the same time as a verbal "A" (target pattern). An internal neural network would then need to organize a mapping from the neurons that are activated upon seeing a written "A" to the neurons that are activated for a verbal "A".

The notation and equations for the algorithm are as follows. Let n_h be the number of processing units in layer h. Each unit has an activation level, which is a real number. Let $a_{i,h}$ be the activation level of unit i in layer h. Each interconnection has a weight, also a real number. Let $w_{ji,h}$ be the weight to unit j (layer h+1) from unit i (layer h). Note that each interconnection weight can be thought of as a synaptic weight.

In forwards propagation, a vector pattern is presented to the network, and the values of the vector entries are taken on by the input units.

$a_{1,1}, a_{2,1}, \ldots, a_{n_1,1}$

Then the hidden layer calculates its activation levels as follows:

$$a_{j,2} = f(\sum_{i=1}^{n_1} a_{i,1} w_{ji,1}) \tag{1}$$

where f is a "squashing" function. In most applications of back propagation, the squashing function is chosen to be a sigmoid function:

$$f(x) = 1/(1 + e^{-x}) \tag{2}$$

However, any semilinear function will enable gradient-descent learning (Rumelhart et al, 1986).

An alternative squashing function that deserves mention is the ramp function:

$$g(x) = \begin{bmatrix} 0 & \text{if } x \leq 0 \\ sx & \text{if } 0 < x < c \\ b & \text{if } c \leq x \end{bmatrix}$$

The derivative of the squashing function arises in the weight adjustment equations given below. For sigmoids

$f'(x) = f(x)(f(x) - 1)$

For ramp functions

$$g'(x) = \begin{bmatrix} s & \text{if } 0 < x < c \\ 0 & \text{if } x \leq 0 \text{ or } x \geq c \end{bmatrix}$$

Note that the derivative defines an operational range in each case, and multiplication by the derivative corresponds to windowing the operational range. Figure 1 shows these squashing functions and their derivatives.

For a three-layer network the output layer activation is:

$$a_{j,3} = \sum_{i=1}^{n_2} a_{i,2} w_{ji,2} \tag{3}$$

assuming that no squashing function is used by the output units. A three-layer network has powerful and general mathematical mapping properties even when the squashing function is eliminated from the output layer units as above (Hornik et al, 1990). If a squashing function is used at the output units, then the output units activations are instead

$$a_{j,3} = f(\sum_{i=1}^{n_2} a_{i,2} w_{ji,2}) \quad (4)$$

In back-error propagation calculations, error values are computed for each processing unit and then error values are used subsequently to adjust the interconnection weights. These delta values are first computed for the output layer, then for the hidden layer.

Let $\delta_{j,h}$ be the delta value for unit j, layer h. For the output layer, the delta value is

$$\delta_{j,3} = (t_j - a_{j,3}) \quad (5)$$

assuming that the output layer does not utilize a squashing function, otherwise

$$\delta_{j,3} = (t_j - a_{j,3}) f'(S_{j,3}) \quad (6)$$

where f' is the derivative of the squashing function, and $S_{j,h}$ denotes the incoming sum to unit j, layer h:

$S_{j,h} = \sum_{i=1}^{n_{h-1}} a_{i,h-1} w_{ji,h-1}$

Weights associated with interconnections that go to the output layer are changed as follows:

$$\Delta w_{ji,2} = \eta \delta_{j,3} a_{i,2} \quad (7)$$

where η is the learning rate. The value of η is typically set by the user during artificial neural network experiments, and may vary during training.

For the hidden layer, the delta values are

$$\delta_{j,2} = (\sum_{k=1}^{n_3} w_{kj,2} \delta_{k,3}) f'(S_{j,2}) \quad (8)$$

and the corresponding weights to the hidden layer are changed by the amount:

$$\Delta w_{ji,1} = \eta \delta_{j,2} a_{i,1} \tag{9}$$

Equation (8) must be refined into greater detail for the biological model because multiplication of weights times delta values occurs at one site whereas summation occurs elsewhere.

The above description assumes a rigid architectural configuration of units - layered and fully interconnected. It is convenient to use a layered fully interconnected configuration to explain the neuronal model in this paper. However, more flexible and irregular configurations are possible, both in artificial neural networks and in our biological model. For example, neurons need not be organized into layers, and furthermore they may be sparsely interconnected instead of being fully interconnected layered configurations (Werbos, 1988). In addition, learning need not be restricted to pattern or batch learning, but could involve something in between (e.g., where the Δw's are added over a time window before changes are made). Further generalities of the back-propagation network and of the biological model proposed here are possible.

3 Biological Model

In this section we describe a general biological model that utilizes back-error propagation. We propose particular sites where computations are performed and suggest physiological and biophysical mechanisms for their occurrence. In some cases we postulate the existence of second messengers or other mechanisms that are biologically plausible but require postulated substrates. We argue that it is plausible that a back- error propagation paradigm is computed in the various biophysical forms that we describe. Note that the model(s) proposed here are candidate models that must be subjected to experimental verification at a later date.

Figure 2 shows a neuron drawn schematically; dendritic trunks are drawn without the arborizations, for visual clarity. Axons are drawn exceedingly wide to show the highly organized nature of their microtubules, and axons may have branches.

Figure 3 shows the interconnection structure for a layered feed-forward network model. Neurons are interconnected via axodendritic connections. This particular configuration has three layers and is fully interconnected. As in artificial neural network terminology, we will refer to the layers as the input, hidden, and output layers. Our model for back-error propagation through the microtubules will be illustrated for this network, although the model is not limited to layered, fully-interconnected networks, and back-propagation has no such limitation.

3.1 Forwards Propagation

Consider the forwards propagation mode for the network illustrated in Figure 3. The neurons depicted follow typical biological mechanisms, with propagation of signals forwards through the network via action potentials. Axo-dendritic synapses send signals from one layer to the next. Neurons do summation in the dendrites, and propagate membrane potentials to the spike initiation zone where a fire-at-threshold mechanism occurs.

During training, the network is presented with an input pattern. In artificial neural networks, the input pattern is a vector with the length of the vector equal to the number of input units. For a biologically plausible model, we can assume frequency coding of the input vector. Thus, the input pattern $(x_1, x_2, ..., x_n)$ would be modeled as a firing frequency x_i for each input unit i. It is assumed that an external stimulus causes the firing frequency to occur in the input layer neurons. The external stimulus would arise from a particular pattern, such as seeing the written letter "A".

The hidden and output layers sum arriving impulses via normal biological mechanisms, based on post-synaptic potentials, membrane conductances, and spatial locations and changes in membrane potentials. The network's output is "read off" the output layer and is a vector with length equal to the number of output units. Again the simplest biological model is to assume frequency coding. Thus, y_i would be the firing rate of output neuron i, with output vector $(y_1, y_2, ..., y_m)$. The goal of training is to have the output vector of the trained network match a target vector $(t_1, t_2, ..., t_m)$ for the entire training set.

For an artificial neural network the synaptic weights are scalars, either positive, negative, or zero. Biological synapses are complex with many different spatial locations and configurations. In addition there are many different biophysical mechanisms for weighting a synapse. One possibility is to take the synaptic weight equal to the initial height of the post-synaptic potential. This model assumes that the synaptic weight is proportional to the number of post-synaptic receptor molecules.

Such a model is adequate to produce the general pattern-mapping ability of artificial feed-forward networks. This capability has been shown specifically in pulsed networks that are layered and that utilize a post-synaptic potential height as the weight, with a fire-at-threshold mechanism that returns the post-synaptic potential to resting level after a refractory period. General pattern mapping ability has been found with this network, and, in fact, it is mathematically equivalent to a feed-forward network with a ramp squashing function (Dayhoff, 1991).

3.1.1 Alternative Models

More complex temporal structure in nerve impulse trains might be utilized biologically instead of a firing frequency code (Perkel and Bullock, 1972; Dayhoff and Gerstein, 1983a). Although there is considerable biological evidence for the existence of frequency coding, there are also alternative models for neural representation and coding. Alternative neural coding could involve the use of bursts, synchronous firing, temporal patterns, or simultaneously active groups. The mathematical processing of a feed-forward network could probably be duplicated with any of these coding schemes, at least as an approximation. Temporal patterns do appear to be of importance in biological systems from data analysis studies (Dayhoff and Gerstein, 1983b; Abeles and Gerstein, 1988; Frostig et al, 1990; Optican and Richmond, 1987). Our use of firing frequencies does not preclude the use of more complex temporal patterning in alternative models that incorporate the same biologically plausible mechanisms presented in this paper.

Synaptic weights, in addition to or instead of using the number of postsynaptic receptors, could employ the following processes or structures: (1) the area of the synapse and/or density of the post-synaptic receptors, as they influence the overall efficacy of the receptor molecules, (2) the number of synapses, (3) the type of transmitter, (4) the presence of neuromodulators (compounds that influence the transmitter efficacy), (5) the amount of presynaptic transmitter released from each impulse, (6) the spatial effects, such as axon and dendritic branching, whereby synapses at different dendritic locations have different degrees of influence on the cell soma, (7) effects of the dendritic spine (its size and shape), (8) the curvature of the synapse, and (9) density and complexity of the synaptic cytoskeleton (Friedrich, 1990).

3.2 Error Computation for Output Units

In this section, three models that could accomplish the computation of equations (5) or (6) for the back-propagating model are described. These models are shown schematically in Figure 4 (a-c). Figure 4a is based on a reciprocal synapse, whereas Figure 4b assumes the existence of an intermediate neuron. Figure 4c is the most speculative of the models and assumes feedback within a single synapse. The target neurons play the role of transmitting a 'desired' response to the network. For each output neuron there is a corresponding target neuron, whose firing frequency represents the target frequency for the output neuron. Each target neuron corresponds to an entry in the target vector $(t_1, t_2, ..., t_n)$. Then t_i is the firing frequency of the ith target neuron. Equations 5 and 6 become computations of differences between output and target cell firing rates.

The difference between equations (5) and (6) is that (6) contains an additional factor, the derivative of the squashing function. Figure 1d shows the derivative of the ramp function, which is a windowing function that multiplies by a constant in a certain range and by zero elsewhere. This could be imposed by a MT or protein filament that is able to transmit signals only in a given range, corresponding to the window, and that otherwise no signals occur. Figure 5b shows a "soft" windowing effect. A windowing of allowable signal values could correspond to actual biophysical constraints for transport of the signal.

MODEL 1 (See Figure 4a.)

This case corresponds to a reciprocal synapse, here depicted as a pair of axo-axonal synapses, a type of synapse that is not uncommon in the nervous system (Bodian, 1972). G is an output neuron from the network configuration of Figure 3 and H is the corresponding target neuron. The goal of the back-propagation algorithm is for training to bring the firing rate of G to the firing rate of H. G's firing rate is reflected by the post-synaptic activation at H in the region of the forwards synapse. H's firing rate is reflected by the post-synaptic activation of G, in the region of the reciprocal synapse. To implement back-propagation, the difference between these rates must be computed. A signal that is proportional to this difference is assumed to be initiated in G at the MT end and to propagate internally through the MT of cell G.

We assume that the signal value is increased by an increased firing rate of unit H, which causes increased activation at the post-synaptic site of the reciprocal synapse. We assume that the firing rate of G decreases the signal that goes along the MT. For example, the synapse from G to H could be inhibitory or in some way inhibit the release of neurotransmitter across the reciprocal synapse.

A general expression for this type of process is as follows:

$$D = f_1(R_G, R_H, M_{G1}, M_{G2}, M_{H1}, M_{H2}, S_{GH}, S_{HG}, A_G, L)$$

where D is the signal initiated at the MT of cell G, R_X is the firing rate of unit X, M_{Xi} is the set of parameters that govern the membrane parameters and biophysical activities for unit X, synapse i, S_{XY} is the set of synaptic parameters and biophysical activities for the synapse from X to Y, A_G is the set of parameters and biophysical activities that govern the anchoring proteins at unit G as well as signal initiation at the MT, and L stands for any additional parameters of other biophysical processes.

A first-order approximation to the above could plausibly be the following equation:

$$D = \alpha_1(R_H - R_G) + d_1 \tag{10}$$

where d_1 is a baseline value (it is possible for d_1 to be zero). The magnitude of D is thus proportional to the strength of the signal along the MT. The parameter α_1 results from structural factors and relationships that depend on the actual underlying mechanisms. Plausible biophysical mechanisms for the initiation of the MT signal are covered later. Equation (10) implements equation (5), as needed.

MODEL 2 (See Figure 4b.)

Instead of assuming a reciprocal synapse, error computation could be modeled by postulating an intermediate neuron I. Neuron I receives excitatory input from H and inhibitory input from G. The firing rate of I (R_I) then reflects the difference in rates between H and G ($R_H - R_G$), which represents the error difference as given by equation (5).

To initiate a signal within the MT of cell G, there is also an axo-axonic synapse postulated (labelled K in Figure 4b). The post-synaptic membrane activation at K is taken as proportional to the average firing rate of I. In this model a signal is initiated along the MT whose end abuts the post-synaptic membrane at synapse K, and the magnitude of this signal is modulated by the average post-synaptic membrane potential at K. As in the case of the model in Figure 4a, the strength of the signal initiated at the MTs of cell G is proportional to the frequency differences between the excitatory and inhibitory inputs of cell I.

A general expression that reflects this type of error difference may be expressed as follows:

$$R_I = f_1(R_G, R_H, S_{GI}, S_{HI}, M_I, M_G, M_H, L) \tag{11}$$

$$D = f_1(R_I, M_G, , M_I, S_{IG}, A_G, L) \tag{12}$$

where D is the signal along the MT of cell G, starting at synapse K.

A plausible first-order approximation is the following:

$R_I = \alpha_2(R_H - R_G) + d_2$

and

$D = \alpha_3 R_I$

where α_2 is a constant, d_2 is a constant indicating the minimum rate of R_I due to an external source (a possible value for d_2 is zero), and α_3 is another constant. The values of α_2 and α_3 rely on the underlying biophysical mechanisms and parameters.

MODEL 3 (See Figure 4c.)

Another candidate model is shown in Figure 4c, representing a synapse from neuron G to neuron H. The synapse here might be axo-somatic or perhaps axo-axonic located above neuron H's spike initiation zone. The firing rate of G is reflected by the post-synaptic activation of H at the synapse. In addition, the post-synaptic membrane at H reflects the firing rate of H prior to firing because it receives travelling post synaptic potentials (PSPs) that sum to cause spike generation at the spike initiation zone of H. Thus the post-synaptic membrane tends to be activated when the firing rate of H is high. We assume in this model that the two effects tend to subtract from one another, and that the synapse from G to H is probably inhibitory.

In addition to a neurotransmitter that traverses the synaptic cleft from G to H, across the synapse in a forwards direction, there may also be a reverse intermediary, such as arachadonic acid (AA) or nitric oxide (Barinaga, 1991). The reverse intermediary is transmitted from the post-synaptic site to the pre-synaptic site (Williams et al, 1989). In this case, its amount or effectiveness is modeled to be proportional to the difference $R_H - R_G$. This model involves only one single synapse and bears a strong relationship to models recently proposed for long-term potentiation (LTP) in hippocampal neurons (Bliss et al, 1990; Malinow, 1991).

LTP is a relatively long-lasting use-dependent form of synaptic enhancement that can be induced by brief periods of suitable presynaptic activity. LTP is currently throught to underlie some forms of learning and memory (Bliss and Lynch, 1988; Kennedy, 1989; Madison et al, 1991). Although LTP refers to enhancement in the postsynaptic membrane potential, the actual mechanism of LTP is currently still disputed. Both presynaptic mechanisms, either through an increase in the quantal probability of synaptic release or an increase in the actual number of presynaptic releasing sites and postsynaptic mechanisms, such as an increase in the efficacy of the receptor sensitivity, have been suggested (Bekkers and Stevens, 1990). As indicated in Figure 4c one possible mechanism for neuronal signaling of postsynaptic activity to the presynaptic membrane is through receptor-mediated release of "second messengers" that target presynaptic sites. In studies of Aplysia sensory cells (Piomelli et al, 1987) inhibitory synaptic actions of the neuroactive peptide FMRFamide are mediated by lipoxygenase metabolites of arachadonic acid. Thus Figure 4c includes a reverse intermediary which could be AA or nitric oxide (NO), or possibly another chemical (Schuman and Madison, 1991). Since LTP is monotonically related to the number of NMDA receptors activated, it is reasonable to postulate that the amount of the intermediate chemical is similarly related to the membrane potential.

Although higher pre-synaptic activation could increase the amount of the reverse intermediary, this alone does not necessarily imply an increase in the effectiveness of the reverse intermediary at presynaptic sites. In fact, an increased firing rate of G could actually decrease the number of available presynaptic sites at which the reverse intermediary could interact. Then the input signal to cell G's MTs could be proportional to the difference in neurons G and H firing rates. This corresponds to a realization of the model that assumes an excitatory synapse, as is usually observed in LTP experiments in the hippocampus. If we were to assume an inhibitory synapse, then the firing of G would decrease activation at the post-synaptic site and hence decrease the release of the reverse intermediary.

A general expression in this case can be written as:

$$D = f_2(R_G, R_H, S_{GH}, M_G, M_H, A_G, L)$$

where D is the amount or effectiveness of the reverse intermediary in initiating a MT signal in cell G.

We postulate that for a plausible approximation this case can be modeled as:

$$D = \alpha_4(R_H - R_G) + d_3$$

where d_3 is ambient background and allows for negatives to be "coded" as small values (possibly $d_3 = 0$), and α_4 is a constant that is a function of the underlying biophysics.

Here we postulate that the amount or effectiveness of the intermediary is proportional to the activation level of H (e.g. the average firing rate of H) minus the average firing rate of G. Thus, for example, a higher post-synaptic activation raises the effectiveness or amount of intermediary. A higher pre-synaptic activation lowers the amount of intermediary or its effectiveness. We assume this relationship is approximated by first order differences, as above.

3.3 Cytoskeletal Backwards Signals

Since forwards propagation takes place via cell membranes and synapses in this model, using widely known mechanisms, no further explanation is required for the medium of signal propagation. Backwards error signals, however, are propagated inside the cell via cytoskeleton, which is a novelty of our proposed model, and thus requires explanation for both signal initiation and signal propagation. We suggest candidate biophysical mechanisms for signal initiation at MT ends or actin and neurofilaments and for signal propagation along protein polymer strands.

3.3.1 Signal Initiation

Candidate mechanisms for the initiation of cytoskeletal signals in axon terminals are as follows:

1. Material transport. Molecules and particles that can be transported by MTs in the cell cytoskeleton are present at the end of the axons. Their presence and subsequent transport could constitute a signal that carries information to the cell body, and then to the dendrites. Their concentration could perhaps determine the magnitude of the signal. Such molecules would be transported via well-known mechanisms for MT transport (Ochs, 1982; Allan et al, 1991).

2. Phosphorylation / dephosphorylation of MAPs. Since MAPs are bound to MTs, a phosphorylation-induced conformational change could initiate MT signals. For example, protein kinase C (activated by membrane events, such as binding of NMDA and glutamate to receptors) phosphory-

lates MAP-2 in dendrites, and similar events could occur with other MAPs in axons.

3. Calcium - initiated events. Calcium is well-known to be released during synaptic activity, and is capable of binding to calmodulin. Since calmodulin is bound to MTs and MAPs, this coupling could in turn cause conformational or other changes in the MTs which initiate a signal up the MT. Calcium might also directly bind to MTs, initiating tubulin conformational changes.

4. A specialized protein or molecule might bind at the end of a MT, or at the end of an actin filament or a neurofilament. Binding might alternatively take place to a MAP, or to an anchoring protein. Binding would then cause a conformational change that initiates a signal along a MT or protein filament. Particular proteins might even be responsible for initiating different particular signal patterns. Furthermore, such a molecule might be a compound such as AA or NO, that diffuses in a retrograde fashion across synapses, or another compound that is activated by such a retrograde messenger. This mechanism is highly speculative but deserves mentioning.

5. Fodrin and other anchoring proteins might initiate signals at the axonal end of a MT, because they are known to form bridges from the MTs to the synaptic membrane. In this case the signal might be initiated by the membrane potential, membrane proteins, second messengers, or other activity at the membrane, or by modulations in the distance between the membrane and the MT.

6. Other chemical messengers might interact with MTs, MAPs, protein filaments, or anchoring proteins to effect a signal initiation at the end of a MT or filament. Ben Ze-ev (1991) reviews possibilities that involve a receptor bonding to an intermediary which in turn interacts with the cytoskeleton.

3.3.2 Signal Propagation in Cytoskeleton

Candidate mechanisms for signal propagation along cytoskeletal strands are as follows:

1. MTs, together with associated proteins, bring about particle transfer. This transfer could go in both directions, and a variety of specific rates have

been observed. Rates of 400 mm/day and even 2000 mm/day have been reported (Ochs 1982).

2. A propagated conformational wave - a series of conformational changes along a MT or protein filament - constitutes another general type of signal propagation. Propagation of tubulin conformational states are implicated in ciliary MT (Atema, 1973) and by Cianci et al (1986), who claim that MTs are capable of ATP-induced "gelation-contraction" which presumably results from all tubulin subunits assuming shorter conformational states. Sequential shortening of subunits would propagate a wave. In a propagated conformational change, individual tubulin molecules would alter their conformational state in response to neighboring tubulin molecules, causing a signal to propagate down the MT. Energy pumping would be required to counteract energy dissipation, perhaps by GTP hydrolysis and MAP dephosphorylation. Hameroff et al (1989) and Rasmussen et al (1990) considered conformational states (alpha, beta) in each tubulin dimer characterized by a negative charge redistribution towards either the alpha or beta monomer. Dipole coupling among neighboring tubulins and energy pumping via GTP hydrolysis were modeled and resulted in traveling patterns of tubulin conformational state changes. Such traveling conformational patterns are suitable for internal neuronal signaling, and are consistent with models of coherent phonons, solitons, Frohlich depolarization waves or acousto - conformational transitions (Rasmussen et al, 1990; Hameroff et al, 1989; Samsonovich et al, 1992).

The back propagation algorithm imposes the requirement that the signal must carry both a magnitude and a polarity. One possibility is the following model. Tubulin can be modeled as having two conformational states, α and β. The simplest signal would be a traveling cluster of one state (foreground) on a background of another state. For example, a positive polarity could be a signal in state β on a background of state α , and a negative polarity would be a signal in state α on a background of state β. In this case the size of the foreground cluster would correspond to the signal's magnitude. Alternatively, the signal could be a traveling segment that has some percent of the foreground configuration on the background configuration. The percent could then be proportional to the signal magnitude. An alternative way to encode the polarity is to simply have a "baseline" signal size b such that a signal of size D is interpreted as D-b. This would allow us to encode negative numbers with a signal that has only a magnitude.

In the MT molecular automata models developed by Hameroff et al (1989) and Rasmussen et al (1990), specific types of patterns (e.g. "bus gliders") propagate as tubulin conformational changes. They are modeled as cellular automata. Such propagating patterns could represent signals of different polarities and magnitudes. Since the patterns would be discrete entities, each different pattern could stand for a different discrete magnitude being signaled. Quantized magnitudes would be sufficient for learning.

3. Ion transfer. A MT might transfer an ion from one end of the tubule to the other, either inside or outside the MT. This is within the realm of possibilities but has not been experimentally observed. A likely candidate ion is Ca^{++}, which is an important ion that participates in synaptic activity. Quantity, patterns of release or of ion types (e.g., Ca^{++}, Mg^{++}) might be employed as signaling mechanisms.

4. Ionic movements have also been proposed as a signaling mechanism along MTs and filaments. Ions may cluster around a negatively charged strand, such as an actin filament [1-2]. The ions are then "trapped" with respect to the distance between the ion and the center of the cylindrical strand but are not trapped in terms of movements along the length of the strand. Small electrochemical changes at one end of the strand may then propagate an ion-based signal to the other end, based on ions moving a small distance along the length of the strand (Cantiello et al, 1991; Cantiello and Kim, 1992).

5. The actual movement of a MT is a possibility, in a direction towards one of its terminals. This movement alone could be initiated by appropriate anchoring proteins that connect the MTs to the synapse. MTs may be under tension because of the anchoring proteins; thus the cytoskeleton may be a "tensegrity net" (Joshi et al, 1985) capable of end-to-end movements or end-to-end pressure. An alternative form of movement is slow axoplasmic transport in which MTs "grow" by polymerizing at one end and depolymerizing at the other end (1 -3 mm/day) (Kirschner and Michison, 1986).

3.4 Correction of Synaptic Sensitivities / Weights

3.4.1 Models for Synaptic Weights

In artificial neural networks, the weight of an interconnection is presumed to be a simplification for the strength of a biological synapse. In biological systems many factors could influence the strength or sensitivity of a synapse. Potential factors include the spatial locations of synapses, their size, the types of receptors and transmitters, the effectiveness of the transmitters, the number of synapses, etc. We consider first the number of post-synaptic receptors as a model for synaptic strength.

Weight adjustment in back propagation obeys equation (7), which includes the factors of pre-synaptic activation level (firing rate) and the delta (error) value for the target (post-synaptic) neuron. For the network in Figure 3, weight adjustments must be made at the synapses that send signals to the dendrites of the hidden and output layer neurons. In our model, a signal D travels up the cytoskeletal strands to arrive at the dendrites. The arriving signal is then a factor in determining the amount of weight adjustment to take place. We postulate that the signal D is proportional to δ_j, the post-synaptic neuron's error delta value from the back propagation equation (7). This value of D must then be multiplied by R_i, the firing rate of the pre-synaptic neuron, to determine the amount of weight change. A constant factor (η) known as the learning rate parameter is also involved. Note that over time, the average post-synaptic membrane potential can be modeled to be approximately proportional to the firing rate of the pre-synaptic neuron.

Suppose that δ_j is positive, as computed by (5), (6), or (8). Then its effect on the number of post-synaptic receptors should be to increase their number. This increase must be in proportion to δ_j times the post-synaptic membrane activation (on average). For simplicity, we assume that D can implement increased synaptic strength by increasing the number of post-synaptic receptors; alternatively, their sensitivity could be enhanced by altering their conformational states. D may increase the number of active receptor molecules by augmenting transport of nutrients to the axonal terminal. D might also stimulate new synthesis of receptors, because the signal from the axonal end passes through the cell body and the MT lattice connects to the nucleolus where protein synthesis is controlled. D could thereby trigger an increase in synthesis of post-synaptic receptor molecules. For example, a large amount of positive signals, with a high average magnitude, would trigger synthesis near the nucleus. This would make more receptor molecules available to increase the synaptic strength. The positive signal D thereby increases the number of membrane receptors at the post-synaptic site.

D may also act by influencing receptor conformational states. For example, receptor / ion channel complexes (e.g. acetylcholine receptor, NMDA receptor, etc.) involve numerous proteins connected on the cytoplasmic side to fodrin or other anchoring proteins of MTs. There is experimental evidence that anchoring proteins connect to MTs and fasten the receptor molecules in place (Hirokawa, 1991). Different states of these complexes might occur in response to different signals (e.g., polarity and magnitude) arriving via cytoskeletal MTs. Friedrich (1990) has proposed that, in learning, sub-synaptic cytoskeletal receptor complexes become fortified and increase in complexity.

If the arriving signal D is negative, then the number of post-synaptic receptors would need to decrease. This might happen possibly by degradation of fodrin and other anchoring proteins which connect the MTs to the synapse. On the post-synaptic membrane, degradation of fodrin might serve to release these receptor molecules thereby decreasing the number of active receptor molecules available at the post-synaptic site. Instead of degradation it is possible that a deactivation or conformational change in the anchoring proteins could bring about a decrease in the number of active receptor molecules. Receptor molecules are known to constantly "turn over"; thus non-replacement would lead to a dwindling of numbers. Degradation of fodrin has been observed experimentally (Siman et al 1984).

A general expression for this model can be written as:

$$\Delta W = f(P, D, L)$$

where P is the post-synaptic activation level, D is the arriving MT signal, and L denotes other biophysical parameters.

An approximate first-order effect could plausibly be the following

$$\Delta W = \alpha_5 D R_I$$

where R_I is the firing rate of the pre-synaptic neuron, D is the magnitude of the signal arriving up the MT, and α_5 is a parameter that reflects the underlying biophysical processes. Assume

$$P = \alpha_6 R_I$$

approximately represents the relationship that the post-synaptic activation level reflects the pre-synaptic firing rate, with α_6 another parameter that reflects the actual molecular mechanisms.

3.4.2 Additional Candidate Mechanisms for Synaptic Strength

There are obviously many alternative candidate mechanisms for synaptic strength, and the modulation of synaptic strength, which could be factored into a more detailed biological model for back-error propagation. These include: the amount of pre-synaptic transmitter or amount released for a fixed input stimulus; conformational and spatial changes in the postsynaptic dendritic spines (these have been implicated in LTP in the hippocampus) (Desmond and Levy, 1988); curvature and other spatial properties of the synapse; changes in the quantal release probability (this form of presynaptic potentiation has been suggested by Bekkers and Stevens (1990) for LTP; efficacy of receptor molecules (e.g. conductances); possible intermediaries between MTs and membrane, other than anchoring proteins; the amount of neurotransmitter per vesicle; distance between the MT and cell membrane; pre-synaptic enhancement of neurotransmitter release; binding affinity of receptors for neurotransmitter; metabolism and clearance of transmitters; presence of modulators; kinetics of state transitions for channels or receptors; number of synapses; area of synapses, number of receptors; phosphorylation of Ca^{++}/calmodulin dependent protein kinase C (Schulman and Lou, 1989); influences of the anchoring proteins, and density and architecture of the synaptic cytoskeleton (Friedrich, 1990). One of the most interesting of these possibilities is the change in the curvature of the synapse and the shape of the dendritic spines. Anchoring proteins such as actin form bridges between MT ends and synaptic membranes. Actin may contract dendritic spines and thereby influence the synaptic strength; the actin is in an ideal location to receive a cytoskeletal signal that might initiate such a contraction. Weight adjustment at synapses might also be accomplished with backwards transmission at the synapse, such as with arachadonic acid, nitric oxide, or other reverse intermediaries, which would then cause alterations on the pre-synaptic side that could in turn influence the synaptic strengths.

3.5 Sending the Error Back to the Previous Layer

This section addresses the issue of how the hidden neuron receives the error information it needs to compute its own error value. (See equation (8)). Let the hidden unit j have error value $\delta_{j,2}$ according to back propagation. From our biological model, the signal arriving through the MT from the output unit k is $D_{k,3}$ where $D_{k,3}$ is proportional to $\delta_{k,3}$ (in equation (8)). For each synapse from each axon branch in the hidden unit, a signal $D_{k,3}$ is received at the post-synaptic MT end. According to equation (8), a multiplication

$$D_{k,3} w_{kj,2} \tag{13}$$

must take place; in our model the site for this multiplication is the synapse from the hidden unit to the output unit. (See Figure 5.) Later, the summation in equation (8) is modeled to occur within the hidden unit.

After the multiplication of (13) takes place, a signal is initiated up the MTs at the hidden unit's pre-synaptic site. Again, for simplicity, we assume that the synaptic strength is the number of post-synaptic receptor molecules. It is not difficult then to imagine the underlying biophysics for such a computation. Suppose that the value $D_{k,3}$ arrives, and via anchoring protein is communicated to the post-synaptic membrane. If we assume that the amount of anchoring protein present is proportional to the number of active receptors, then it is also proportional to the synaptic weight. We presume then that the signal arriving from the cytoskeleton to the post-synaptic membrane will be proportional to $D_{k,3}$ times the amount of anchoring protein. A reverse intermediary such as AA or NO would then go backwards towards the pre-synaptic membrane, thereby transmitting this signal, with the value in (13). Thus the concentration or effectiveness of the reverse intermediary is the value transmitted.

We assume that a reverse intermediary (e.g., AA or NO) binds to pre-synaptic sites which then interact with anchoring protein and the sub-synaptic complex to initiate a signal within the hidden unit's cytoskeleton (site K Figure 5). The microtubules transmit this signal back to the dendrites of the hidden neurons, where additional weight adjustment takes place.

An alternative model is to assume that the synaptic strength arises from the number of receptor molecules in a particular conformational state. In this case, $D_{k,3}$ would influence, via MT-fodrin interactions, changes in receptor conformational states which in turn effect the release of retrograde transmitters (e.g. AA or NO)

3.6 Summing of Cytoskeletal Signals

In our model, summing of cytoskeletal signals occurs within the axon. This summation is included in equation (8) in the back-propagation paradigm. There are two factors in (8), the first being a sum of weighted error values from the output layer of neurons.

$$\sum_{k=1}^{n_3} w_{kj,2}\delta_{k,3} \tag{14}$$

Multiplication of $\delta_{k,3}$ times the weight $w_{kj,2}$ occurs at the synapse between the hidden unit j and output unit k. Thus, the signal d_k, that goes up the kth axonal branch of hidden unit j, represents the product $w_{kj,2}\delta_{k,3}$. Assume

$$d_k = \alpha_7 w_{kj,2}\delta_{k,3} \tag{15}$$

where α_7 is a constant dependent on the underlying biophysics. We propose a possible explanation in this section of how the summation of these individual terms d_k might occur in the hidden units.

Note that the second factor in equation (8) is $f'(S_{j,k})$, which is the derivative of the squashing function. For a ramp squashing function, this is zero everywhere except for an interval. (See figure 1d.) Its effect is to filter the operating range, and produces 0 for parameter values too large or too small. This corresponds to a biophysical mechanism that works only within a given range of signal values, a plausible assumption for this model.

Figure 6 illustrates a schematic neuron with MTs drawn within each axonal branch. This Figure illustrates a single bundle of MT within the axonal trunk (before branching), with crossbridge MAPs connecting the individual MTs. The bundle divides into smaller bundles with each going into an axonal branch. In the cell body, the lattice-like network of MT is simplified as a converging of specific MT bundles, from the axon and from each dendritic trunk. The MTs are taken to be interconnected via MAPs within each bundle.

In this model, each signal d_k is transmitted to the axonal trunk via MT bundles. The signals are summed in the axonal trunk because the MT bundles gather together in the trunk, and as a result the signal strengths are integrated. Then, the total amount of signal going along the axonal trunk is the sum of the signals along each branch.

A concern arises because the reading mechanism for this sum may be sensitive to variations in the different MT signal values. It is preferable then to have each MT carry the same approximate value signal upon its arrival at the cell body. Such an operation could be accomplished via "probabilistic bus-MAPs", a postulated mechanism whereby a MAP protein transfers activation across MTs. These proteins need only transfer activation some of the time (probabilistically, such as 20 percent of the time). The net result would be that when the signals arrive at the cell body, each MT would be carrying a signal equal to the average of all of the original signals within each microtubule. The average of these signals could then conveniently contribute to compute the sum of the signals by simply multiplying n, the number of branches, by the average signal. The sum would then be

$$S = D_{j,2} = \sum_{k=1}^{n_3} d_k \tag{16}$$

How might the appropriate signal then be transferred back to the dendrites? We propose a model whereby each dendritic trunk has a bundle of MTs that pick up the signal from the axon originating in the cell body. Figure 6 shows a central position where this might occur, but in fact the signal transfer need not necessarily occur at a single position. Furthermore, since each MT filament from the axonal trunk carries the same (average) signal, the dendritic MTs might accept the signals at different locations within the interconnected MT lattice. The resulting signal would then have the value S for each dendritic trunk. Obviously, a variety of detailed models could be constructed depending on specific lattice configurations, based on these general ideas.

The dendritic MTs would then transmit the signal S to the terminal ends of the dendrites. In our model, the entire bundle transmits this signal to each incoming synapse at the dendrite. In contrast to this simplified model, in living cells there is an intertwined lattice of MTs around the centriole which occupies a considerable part of the cell soma area. MTs support each dendritic branch, and thus we assume that the signal reaches each incoming synapse.

The probabilistic bus-MAP is a concept similar to the bus-MAPs proposed in Rasmussen et al (1990). More complex boolean operations in MAPs have been proposed in MAP crossbridges among MTs [Lahoz-Beltra et al, 1992]. In fact, these MAP models can be theoretically constructed to perform BCN (binary-coded decimal) operations such as binary addition and subtraction. Although biological plausibility is not evident for this scheme, it appears to be a powerful construct for future molecular computing engineering designs, and it is inspired by the signal summation model here for MTs.

An important point about this model is that an individual MT does not need to be continuous from axon to dendrite. Each MT can have a length that is shorter than the axon to dendrite distance. Signals can pass from one MT to another via MAPs that interconnect pairs of MTs. Models of polymer lattices have been developed that show arbitrary configurations of protein polymer strands and crossbridge proteins, and that demonstrate signal propagation along such lattices in which the incoming signals arrive at different strands than the strands that carry outgoing signals.

Figure 7 shows such a lattice model consisting of a parallel array of MTs interconnected by MAPs. Each MT strand is represented by a chain of subunits. Each MAP has two connection sites, on different MTs. The set of input MTs consists of the MTs with ends that are placed at the bottom of the lattice configuration, and output MTs have ends near the top of the lattice.

Two conformational states are assumed for each subunit in the MT strand, represented by 0 and 1 in the Figure. Signals were considered to be 1's on a background of 0's. Signals originated at the bottom and moved upwards, moving one subunit per time step s. MAPs acted as buses in a probabilistic fashion, where f_{ac} was the probability that a 1 signal was carried across a MAP in a time interval s. The 1 signal then disappeared from the first MT to which the MAP was connected and appeared at the position on the second MT where the MAP was connected.

MAPs also amplified signals, as MAPS can release energy by changing ATP to ADP. When amplification took place, a 1 was transferred and a second 1 was placed below the 1 that was transferred. Amplification was probabilistic, where f_{amp} was the probability that amplification took place given a 1 signal was transferred by a MAP.

The lattice in Figure 7 consists of 13 parallel-arrayed MTs and 41 MAPs. The MTs appear as vertical strands that communicate signals upwards. The MAPs appear as horizontal crossbridges that connect two adjacent strands. The three lowest strands were inputs and the two highest strands were outputs. MAPs were unidirectional in this model and communicated signals from input strands towards output strands. Part (a) shows the simulation after 53 time steps and Part (b) shows the lattice state one time step later. Most 1 signals have moved upwards one step although some were transferred across MAPs and in one case (the MAP at the bottom left) the transferred signal was amplified. This simulation demonstrates that an individual MT need not be continuous from the bottom to the top of the lattice for a lattice network to transmit a signal.

4 Discussion

This paper presents arguments for the biological plausibility of back-error propagation through intraneuronal microtubules (MTs). We have identified specific sites and biophysical mechanisms that could implement each of the calculations of neuronal back-propagation. Forwards propagation is accomplished through traditional mechanisms, with action potentials and axo-dendritic synapses. Back-error propagation is accomplished through the calculation of error differences (between target and output) at specialized synapses, the backwards propagation of these signals through MTs of the cytoskeletal lattice from the axons to the dendrites, the adaptation of synapses in response to MT arriving signals, and the transport of a MT signal from an output unit to a hidden unit. Biophysical plausibility arguments are given for each step in this process, and for how the biophysical mechanisms might implement the needed computations. The model proposed here should be considered a baseline model; we expect that refinements will be needed as additional experimental and theoretical results become available.

The model covered in this paper is far more general than the layered, fully-interconnected configuration used here (shown in Figure 3). This interconnection configuration was chosen because it would provide a clear explanation. Back-error propagation, however, is not limited to layered configurations, nor to full interconnectivity. Back-error propagation can also incorporate recurrent loops, feedback loops, and time delays in both layered and non-layered configurations (Werbos, 1988; Waibel et al, 1989). The principles used in the model proposed here can be applied to any of these more general configurations. Furthermore, back-propagation is also not limited to the minimization of RMS, as a different performance measure could be optimized by a back-propagating network.

The model here could be extended further through incorporating additional biological complexities, such as multiple synapses between two neurons, different numbers of MTs in each branch of an axon or dendrite, different numbers of MTs arriving at each synaptic site, different lattice and cross-bridge structures for MTs, and more detailed biochemistry. The model could also be extended to incorporate neural assemblies (groups) in place of any of the neurons in Figure 3. Learning does not have to be limited to pattern or batch learning, but updates of weights could be integrated or delayed over time, which seems more plausible biologically. Alternative conduction mechanisms might be employed through actin filaments or neurofilaments instead of MTs, as these filaments are also an integral part of the cytoskeleton.

Biological systems must have maximal weight strengths, as does any physical implementation of a neural network. The magnitude of a transmitted error signal would also have a maximal value possible. Furthermore, biological systems are expected to have a recruitment capability, whereby additional connections are spawned between two neurons, or additional neurons are recruited to participate in a particular network circuit. The cytoskeleton is integrally involved with the formation of new branches, as it supports physically these new spatial structures and defines their spatial configuration. According to the back-error model in this paper, error signals that traverse the cytoskeleton provide information appropriate to a decision to spawn a new axonal or dendritic branch. Suppose that a large error signal along the cytoskeleton actually triggers the production of a new branch, and that this branch would be initiated by cytoskeletal mechanisms. Then the new branch could target to synapse on a neuron within the network or a new neuron. In the first case, there is a new synapse that would probably alleviate the need for such a large error difference. In the latter case, a new neuron would be recruited, which might also alleviate the need for such a large error difference to be transmitted. Thus during training, if an intracellular feedback signal gets too high, the cytoskeleton might respond by spawning a new branch for new interconnections, and this would provide advantages in training the network. In the model proposed here, the information for such a capability is in the appropriate place - the cytoskeleton.

There are models of learning other than back-error propagation in which cytoskeletal signaling within neurons would provide a missing link to biologically plausible models. One such model is Edelman's selectionist "population approach", which invokes heterosynaptic inputs – other dendrites on the same neuron communicating and modifying a given dendritic synapse. The same intra-neuronal cytoskeletal communication we suggest for back-propagation could accomplish the information transmission needed along dendrites for heterosynaptic modification. Another neural learning model that could plausibly utilize cytoskeleton is Adaptive Resonance Theory (Carpenter and Grossberg, 1987; Carpenter and Grossberg, 1988; Grossberg, 1976) in which each connection from the input to the output layer has a reciprocal connection with its own weight. Resonance, or reinforcement of signals, is obtained between the forwards and backwards connections during learning. The forwards connections might be implemented with action potentials and axo-dendritic synapses, and the backwards connections might be implemented with cytoskeletal signals. The pi-sigma architecture (Shin and Ghosh, 1991; Rumelhart et al, 1986), which also utilizes backwards propagation of errors, might also be modeled with MTs. Pribram's cytoskeletal dendritic microprocessing could also be subserved by conformational dynamics and signaling in the cytoskeleton (Pribram, 1991). There are even more possibilities for biological models of other neural network paradigms, in which cytoskeleton would be assumed to provide internal signals.

The neuronal cytoskeleton certainly has a justified existence without the transmission of signals involved in neuronal learning: cytoskeleton mechanically supports the extensive branching structure in both axons and dendrites. These special structures are uniquely complex in neurons, as neurons have extensive development of the cell cytoskeleton. Furthermore, the cytoskeleton anchors synaptic membrane proteins; this is sufficient to explain the relationship of MTs to synapses. Thus one might question the rationale for postulating yet another function for the neuronal cytoskeleton.

On the other hand, the cell cytoskeleton has developed (evolved) more than one role that is critical to the functioning of a nerve cell. Transport of nutrients is critical and is accomplished by MTs and MAPs. Structural support for spatial branching of axons and dendrites is critical to the cell, and depends on cytoskeletal structure and the assembly and disassembly of MTs. Since these different vital functions have evolved for cytoskeleton, why not another function, namely, to participate in neural learning? The cytoskeleton already participates in synaptic processes by attaching to proteins that anchor post-synaptic receptors in place, and therefore might influence synaptic strength through a variety of candidate mechanisms.

Clearly the cytoskeleton is in a key anatomical position to participate in neuronal learning through the transmission of signals. The cytoskeletal lattice extends without interruption from axons to dendrites. When cytoskeletal signals pass near the nucleus, synthesis of new protein molecules, such as receptors, could be triggered. The new receptors could then increase synaptic strengths. MTs anchor to synapses and receptor molecules through anchoring proteins such as fodrin and actin, and so a convenient anatomical pathway exists to influence synapses by cytoskeletal signals. If the cytoskeletal signals carry delta error values, then they are strategically placed to signal information available that could appropriately trigger the formation of new branches and hence new synapses. Thus there is much circumstantial evidence for the plausibility of cytoskeletal signals contributing to neuronal learning.

To study biology is to catch evolution in the act. The process of evolution has put mechanisms in place that could plausibly implement back-error propagation and internal signaling for neuronal learning. Further experimental evidence is needed to determine whether Nature is actually using these mechanisms. If not, perhaps a new step in evolution is about to take place.

5 Acknowledgements

Dr. Judith Dayhoff was supported by the Naval Surface Warfare Center Focussed Technology Program on Molecular Computing, and wishes to thank Ann Tate for encouragement and stimulating discussions about microtubular roles in computing. Dr. Dayhoff received an ONR Visiting Summer Faculty Program appointment (1991-92) through the American Society for Engineering Education (ASEE) for her work at the NSWC. She was also supported by the Systems Research Center at the University of Maryland (NSF Grant CDR-88-03012). Dr. Stuart Hameroff was supported by the University of Arizona Department of Anesthesiology. Dr. Charles Swenberg acknowledges support of the Armed Forces Radiobiology Research Institute under work unit 00145. Dr. Rafael Lahoz-Beltra was supported by the Ministerio de Educacion y Ciencia (Spain) under a Fulbright Scholarship.

6 References

M. Abeles and G. L. Gerstein (1988). Detecting spatiotemporal firing patterns among simultaneously recorded single neurons. J. Neurophys. 60 (3): 909-924.

V. J. Allan, R. D. Vale, and F. Navone, 1991. Microtubule-based organelle transport in neurons. In In The Neuronal Cytoskeleton, ed. R. D. Burgoyne, New York: Wiley-Liss, 5-74.

J. Alvarez and B. J. Ramirez (1979). Axonal microtubules: Their regulation by the electrical activity of the nerve. Neuroscience Letters, 15: 19-22.

L. A. Amos and A. Klug (1974). Arrangement of subunits in flagellar microtubules. J. Cell Sci., 14: 523-550.

A. Aszodi, U. Muller, P. Friedrich, and H-C. Spatz (1991). Signal convergence on protein kinase A as a molecular correlate of learning. Proc. Natl. Acad. Sci. USA 88: 5832-5836.

C. Aoki and Siekowitz (1989). Plasticity in brain development. Sci. Am., 34-42, December.

J. Atema (1973). Microtubule theory of sensory transduction. J. Theor. Biol. 38: 181-190.

H. Athenstaedt (1974). Pyroelectric and peizoelectric properties of vertebrates. Ann. NY Acad. Sci. 238: 68-93.

M. Barinaga, (1991). Is nitric oxide the retrograde messenger. Science 254: 1296-1297.

J. S. Becker, J. M. Oliver and R. D. Berlin (1975). Fluorescence techniques for following interactions of microtubule subunits and membranes. Nature, 254: 152-154.

A. Ben-Ze'ev (1991). Animal cell shape changes and gene expression. BioEssays 13 (5): 207-212.

J. M. Bekkers and C. F. Stevens (1990). Presynaptic mechanism for long-term potentiation in the hippocampus. Nature 346: 724-729.

G. Bensimon and R. Chermat (1991). Microtubule disruption and cognitive defects: effect of colchicine on learning behavior in rats. Pharmacol. Biochem. Behavior 38: 141-145.

D. Bigot and S. P. Hunt (1990). Effect of excitatory amino acids on microtubule-associated proteins in cultured cortical and spinal neurones. Neuroscience Letters 111: 275-254.

T. V. P. Bliss, M. P. Clements, M. L. Errington, M. A. Lynch, J. H. Williams (1990). Presynaptic changes associated with long-term potentiation in the dentate gyrus. The Neurosciences 2: 345-354.

T. V. P. Bliss and M. A. Lynch (1988). Long term potentiation of synaptic transmission in the hippocampus: Properties and mechanisms. In Long-term Potentiation: From Biophysics to Behavior, ed. P. Landfield and S. A. Deadwyler, New York: Liss.

D. Bodian, (1972). Neuron junctions: A revolutionary decade. Anat. Rec. 174: 73-82.

S. T. Brady, and R. J. Lasek (1981). Nerve specific enolase and creatine phosphokinase in axonal transport: soluble proteins and axoplasmic matrix. Cell 23: 515-523.

S. T. Brady, K. K. Pfister, and G. S. Bloom (1990). A monoclonal antibody to the heavy chain of kinesin inhibits anterograde and retrograde axonal transport in isolated squid axoplasm. Proc. Natl. Acad. Sci. USA 87: 1061-1065.

R. D. Burgoyne (1991). Cytoskeleton is a major neuronal organelle. In: The Neuronal Cytoskeleton, ed. R. D.Burgoyne, New York: Wiley-Liss, 1-3.

R. G. Burns (1978). Spatial organization of the microtubule-associated proteins of reassembled brain microtubules. J. Ultrastruct. Res. 65: 73-82.

P. R. Burton (1988). Dendrites of mitral cell neurons contain microtubules of opposite polarity. Brain Res. 473: 107-115.

P. R. Burton and J. L. Paige (1981). Polarity of axoplasmic microtubules in the olfactory nerve of the frog. Proc. Natl. Acad. Sci., U.S.A. 78: 3269-3273.

H. F. Cantiello and D. S. Kim, 1992. Epithelial ion channels are linked by cytoskeletal network. ASBMB/Biophysical Society Joint Meeting, 1992, Abst. 709.

H. F. Cantiello, C. Patenaude and K. Zaner, 1991. Osmotically induced electrical signals from actin filaments. Biophys. J. 59: 1284-1289. G. Carpenter and S. Grossberg (1987). ART 2: Self-organization of stable category recognition codes for analog input patterns. Applied Optics 4919-4930.

G. Carpenter and S. Grossberg (1988). The ART of adaptive pattern recognition by a self-organizing neural network. Computer, March, 77-88.

P. S. Churchland and T. J. Sejnowski (1989). Neural representation and neural computation. In Neural Connections, Mental Computation, eds. L. Nadel, L. A. Cooper, P. Culicover, and R. M. Harnish. Cambridge, Massachusetts: A Bradford Book, MIT Press, 15-48.

C. Cianci, D. Graff, B. Gao, and R. C. Weisenberg (1986). ATP-dependent gelation contraction of microtubules in vitro. Ann. N. Y. Acad. Sci. 466: 656-659.

M. Conrad, W. Guttinger, and M. Dal Cin (1973). Lecture Notes in Biomathematics, Vol. 4, Physics and Mathematics of the Nervous System, Proc. of a Summer School Organized by the Int'l Center for Theoretical Physics, Trieste, and the Inst. for Info. Sciences, Univ. Tubingen.

J. Cronly-Dillon, D. Carden and C. Birks (1974). The possible involvement of brain microtubule in memory fixation. J. Exp. Biol., 61: 443-454.

A. S. Davydov (1973). The theory of contraction of proteins under their excitation. J. of Theoretical Biology 38: 559-569.

J. E. Dayhoff, (1990). Neural Network Architectures: An Introduction. New York: Van Nostrand Reinhold.

J. E. Dayhoff (1991). Pattern Mapping in Pulse Transmission Neural Networks. Analsis of Neural Network Applications (ANNA) Conference Proceedings (ACM Press), 146-159.

J. E. Dayhoff and G. L. Gerstein (1983a). Favored patterns in nerve spike trains. I. Detection. J. Neurophys. 49: 1334-1348.

J. E. Dayhoff and G. L. Gerstein (1983b). Favored patterns in nerve spike trains. II. Application. J. Neurophys. 49: 1349-1363.

J. Dayhoff, S. Hameroff, C. Swenberg, and R. Lahoz-Beltra, A. Samsonovich, 1992a. Biological learning with cytoskeletal signaling. IJCNN-92 Baltimore, II: 45-50.

J. Dayhoff, S. Hameroff, C. Swenberg, and R. Lahoz-Beltra, 1992c. Biological plausibility of back-error propagation through microtubules. SRC Technical Report TR 92-17.

J. Dayhoff, S. Hameroff, C. Swenberg, and R. Lahoz-Beltra, 1992d. The role of microtubules in neural learning. ASBMB/Biophys. Soc. Joint Meeting Abst.

J. Dayhoff, S. Hameroff, C. Swenberg, and R. Lahoz-Beltra, 1992b. Intracellular mechanisms in neuronal learning: Adaptive models. IJCNN-92 Baltimore, I:73-78.

J. E. Dayhoff, S. R. Hameroff, A. E. Tate, and R. Lahoz-Beltra, 1992c. Cytoskeletal lattices as conduits for processing: Neural learning and molecular computing. International Joint Conf. on Neural Networks (IJCNN-92) Beijing, to appear.

M. DeBrabander (1982). A model for the microtubule organizing activity of the centrosomes and kinetochores in mammalian cells. Cell. Biol. Int'l Reports, 6 (10): 901-915.

M. DeBrabander, R. Nuydens, G. Geuens, M. Moermans, and J. DeMay (1986). The use of submicroscopic particles combined with video contrast enhancement as a simple molecular probe for the living cell. In: Cell Motility in the Cytoskeleton 6: 105-113.

N. L. Desmond and W. B. Levy (1988). Anatomy of associative long-term synaptic modification, in: Long-Term Potentiation: From Biophysics to Behavior. eds. P. W. Landfield and S. A. Deadwyler.

L. Finkel, G. Reeke, and G. Edelman (1989). A population approach to the neural basis of perceptual categorization. In: Neural Connections, Mental Computation, Eds. L. Nadel, L. A. Cooper, P. Culicover, and R. M. Harnish. Cambridge, Massachusetts: A Bradford Book, MIT Press, 146-179.

H. Frauenfelder, F. Parak, and R. D. Young (1988). Conformational substates in proteins, Ann. Rev. Biophys. Biophys. Chem. 17: 451-479.

P. Friedrich (1990). Protein structure: the primary substrate for memory. Neuroscience 35 (1): 1-7.

H. Frohlich (1970). Long range coherence and the actions of enzymes. Nature 228: 1093.

H. Frohlich (1975). The extraordinary dielectric properties of biological materials and the action of enzymes. Proc. Natl. Acad. Sci. 72: 4211-4215.

H. Frohlich (1986). Coherent excitations in active biological systems, in: Modern Bioelectrochemistry, eds. F. Gutmann and H. Keyzer New York: Plenum Press, 241-261.

R. D. Frostig, Z. Frostig, and R. M. Harper (1990). Recurring discharge patterns in multiple spike trains. Biol Cyber. 62: 487-493.

L. Genberg, L. Richare, G. McLendon, R. J. Dwayne Miller (1991). Direct observation of global protein motion in hemoglobin and myoglobin on picosecond time scales. Science 251: 1051-1054.

B. Grafstein and D. S. Forman, 1980. Intracellular transport in neurons. Physiol. Rev. 60: 1167-1283.

S. Grossberg (1969). On the production and release of chemical transmitters and related topics in cellular control. J. Theor. Biol 22: 325-364.

S. Grossberg (1976). Adaptive pattern classification and universal recoding: I. Parallel development and coding of neural feature detectors. Biological Cybernetics (23): 121-134.

W. Grundler and F. Keilman (1983). Sharp resonances in yeast growth prove nonthermal sensitivity to microwaves. Phys. Rev. Lett. 51: 1214-1216.

F. Gutmann (1986). Some aspects of charge transfer in biological systems. In R. Gutmann and H. Keyzer (Eds.), Modern Bioelectrochemistry (pp. 177-197). New York: Plenum Press.

M. B. Hakim, S. M. Lindsey, and J. Powell (1984). The speed of sound in DNA. Biopolymers 23: 1185-1192.

S. Halpain and P. Greengard (1990). Activation of NMDA receptors induces rapid dephosphorylation of the cytoskeletal protein MAP2. Neuron 5: 237-246.

S. R. Hameroff (1987). Ultimate Computing: Biomolecular Consciousness and Nanotechnology Amsterdam: Elsevier-North Holland.

S. R. Hameroff and R. C. Watt (1982). Information processing in microtubules. J. Theor. Biol. 98: 549-561.

S. R. Hameroff, S. Rasmussen, and B. Mansson (1989). Molecular automata in microtubules: basic computational logic of the living state? In C. Langton (Ed.), Artificial Life, Santa Fe Institute Studies in the Sciences of Complexity, Vol. VI (pp. 521-553). Reading, Massachusetts: Addison-Wesley.

R. Hecht-Nielsen (1989). Theory of the backpropagation neural network. IJCNN Washington D. C. June 1989. I: 593-605.

S. R. Heidemann, J. M. Landers, M. A. Hamburg, 1981. Polarity orientation of axonal microtubules. J. Cell. Biol. 91: 661-665.

N. Hirokawa (1991). Molecular architectures and dynamics of the neuronal cytoskeleton. In The Neuronal Cytoskeleton, ed. R. D. Burgoyne, New York: Wiley-Liss, 5-74.

K. Hornik, M. Stinchcombe, and H. White (1990). Universal approximation of an unknown mapping and its derivatives using multilayer feedforward networks. Neural Networks 3 (5): 551-560.

H. C. Joshi, D. Chu, R. E. Buxbaum, and S. R. Heidemann (1985). Tension and compression in the cytoskeleton of PC12 neurites. J. Cell. Biol. 101: 697-705.

M. B. Kennedy (1989). Regulation of synaptic transmission in the central nervous system: Long-term potentiation. Cell 59: 777-787.

M. Karplus and J. A. McCammon (1983). Protein ion channels, gates, receptor. In: Dynamics of Proteins: Elements and Function., ed. J. King. Menlo Park, California: Benjamin Cummings. Annual Rev. Biochem. 53: 263-300.

H. Kim, C. G. Jensen and L. I. Rebhund (1986). The binding of MAP-2 and tau on brain microtubules in vitro. Dynamic aspects of Microtubule Biology (D. Soifer, ed.) 218-239.

M. Kirschner and T. Michison (1986). Beyond self-assembly: from microtubules to morphogenesis. Cell 45: 329-342.

D. L. Koruga (1984). Microtubules screw symmetry: packing of spheres as a latent bioinformation code. In D. Soifer (Ed.), Dynamic Aspects of Microtubule Biology, Annals of the NY Acad. Sci. 466: 953-955.

T. Kudo, K. Tada, M. Takeda, and T. Nishimura (1990). Learning impairment and microtubule-associated protein 2 (MAP-2) decrease in gerbils under chronic cerebral hypoperfusion. Stroke 21: 1205-1209.

S. Kwak, and A. Matus (1988). Denervation induces long-lasting changes in the distribution of microtubule proteins in hippocampal neurons. J. Neurocytology 17: 189-195.

R. Lahoz-Beltra, S. R. Hameroff, and J. E. Dayhoff, 1992. Cytoskeletal logic: A model for molecular computation via Boolean operations in microtubules and microtubule-associated proteins. Biosystems, to appear.

R. W. Linck and L. A. Amos (1974). The hands of helical lattices in flagellar doublet microtubules. J. Cell. Sci. 14: 551-559.

G. Lynch and M. Baudry (1984). The biochemistry of memory: A new and specific hypothesis. Science 224: 1057-1063.

G. Lynch and M. Baudry (1987). Brain spectrin, calpain and long term changes in synaptic efficacy. Brain Res. Bull., 18: 809-815.

D. V. Madison, R. C. Malenka, and R. A. Nicoll (1991). Mechanisms underlying long-term potentiation of synaptic transmission. Ann. Rev. Neurosci. 14: 379-397.

R. Malinow (1991). Transmission between pairs of hippocampal slice neurons: Quantal levels, oscillations, and LTP. Science 252: 722-724.

E. M. Mandelkow, R. Shultheiss, R. Rapp, M. Muller, and E. Mandelkow (1986). On the surface lattice of microtubules. J. Cell. Biol. 102: 1067-1073.

R. Manka and B. Ogrodnik (1992). Soliton model of transport along microtubules. J. Biol. Physics, in press.

S. Mascarenhas (1974). The electret effect in bone and biopolymers and the bound water problem. Ann. N. Y. Acad. Sci. 238: 36-52.

G. Matsumoto and H. Sakai (1979). Microtubules inside the plasma membrane of squid giant axons and their possible physiological function. J. Membr. Biol. 50: 1-14.

S. S. Matsuyama and L. F. Jarvik (1989). Hypothesis: Microtubules, a key to Alzheimer's disease. Proc. Nat. Acad. Sci., 86: 8152-8156.

R. Mileusnic, S. P. Rose and P. Tillson (1980). Passive avoidance learning results in region specific changes in concentrations of, and incorporation into, colchine binding proteins in the chick forebrain. Neur. Chem. 34: 1007-1015.

M. Nakanishi and M. Tsuboi (1978). Two channels of hydrogen exchange in a double-helical nucleic acid. J. Molecular Biol. 124: 61-71.

C. Neubauer, A. M. Phelan, H. Keus, D. G. Lange (1990). Microwave irradiation of rats at 2.45 GHz activates pinocytotic-like uptake of tracer by capillary endothelial cells of cerebral cortex. Bioelectromagnetics 11: 261-268.

S. Ochs (1982). Axoplasmic Transport and its Relation to Other Nerve Functions. Wiley-Interscience, N. Y.

L. M. Optican and B. Richmond (1987). Temporal encoding of two-dimensional patterns by single units in primate inferior temporal cortex. II. Information theoretic analysis. J. Neurophysiol. 57: 162-178.

D. E. Parker, (1988). A comparison of algorithms for neuron-like cells, in J. Denker (ed), Proc. Second Annual Conference on Neural Networks for Computing, Proc. Vol. 151, 327-332, Amer. Inst. of Phys, New York.

D. H. Perkel and T. H. Bullock (1968). Neural coding. Neurosci. Res. Program Bulletin 6 (3).

K. K. Pfister, M. C. Wager, D. L. Sternoven, S. L. Brady, and G. S. Bloom (1989). Monoclonal antibodies to kinesin heavy and light chain stain vesicle-like structures, but not microtubules in cultured cells. J. Cell. Biol. 108: 1453-63.

D. Piomelli, A. Volterra, N. Dale, S. A. Siegelbaum, E. R. Kandel, J. H. Schwartz, and F. Belardetti (1987). Lipoxygenase metabolites of arachidonic acid as second messengers for presynaptic inhibition of Aplysia sensory cells. Nature 328: 38-43.

K. H. Pribram (1991). Brain and Perception: Holonomy and Structure in Figural Processing. Hillsdale, N.J.: Lawrence Erlbaum.

M. M. Rasenick, N. Wang and K. Yan (1990). Specific associations between tubulin and G proteins: participation of cytoskeletal elements in cellular signal transduction, in The Biology and Medicine of Signal Transduction, ec. Y. Nichizuka, et al, Raven Press, New York, 381-386.

S. Rasmussen, H. Karampurwala, R. Vaidyanath, K.S. Jensen, and S. R. Hameroff (1990). Computational connectionism with neurons: A model of cytoskeletal automata subserving neural networks, Physica D 42: 428-429.

L. E. Roth and D. J. Pihlaja (1977). Gradionation: hypothesis for positioning and patterning. J. Protozoology 24: 2-9.

D. E. Rumelhart, G. E. Hinton and R. J. Williams (1986). Learning internal representations by error propagation. In Parallel Distributed Processing, eds. D. E. Rumelhart and J. L. McClelland. Cambridge, Massachusetts: MIT Press.

D. E. Rumelhart and J. L. McClelland, 1986. Parallel Distributed Processing, Volume I. Cambridge, Massachusetts: MIT Press.

A. Samsonovich, A. Scott, S. R. Hameroff (1992). Acousto-conformational transitions in cytoskeletal microtubules: implications for neuro-like protein array devices. Nanobiology, in press.

M. V. Sataric, R. B. Zakula, and J. A. Tuszynski (1992). A model of the energy transfer mechanisms in microtubules involving a single soliton. Nanobiology, in press.

E. M. Schuman and D. V. Madison (1991). A requirement for the intercellular messenger nitric oxide in long term potentiation. Science 254: 1503-1506.

A. C. Scott (1982). Dynamics of Davydov solitons. Phys. Rev. A 26: 578-595.

Y. Shin and J. Ghosh (1991). The pi-sigma network: An efficient higher-order neural network for pattern classification and function approximation. Proc. Int'l. Joint Conf. Neural Networks, I:13-18.

R. Siman, M. Baudry, and G. Lynch (1984). Brain fodrin: Substrate for calpain I, an endogenous calcium-activated protease. Proc. Natl. Acad. Sci. 81: 3572-3576.

Siman and Lynch (1985). (Regulation of glutamate binding by fodrin.)

Nature 313: 225-228, 1985.

H. Schulman and L. L. Lou (1989). Multifunctional Ca^{++} / calmodulin - dependent protein kinase: domain structure and regulation. Trends Biochem. 14: 62-66.

H. Stebbings and C. Hunt (1982). The nature of the clear zone around microtubules. Cell Tissues Res. 227: 609-617.

D. Stork (1989). Is back-propagation biologically plausible. IJCNN Washington D. C. II: 241-246.

C. E. Swenberg and J. Miller (1989). Response to 'Are solitons responsible for energy transfer in oriented DNA' Intl. J. Radiat. Biol. 56 (3): 383-386.

H. Teitelbaum and S. W. Englander (1975). Open states in native polynucleotides. I. Hydrogen-exchange studies of adenine-containing double helices. Open states in nature polynucleotides. II. Hydrogen - exchange study of cystosine-containing double helices. J. Molecular Biology 92: 55-92.

W. E. Theurkauf and R. B. Vallee (1983). Extensive cAMP-dependent and cAMP- independent phosphorylations of microtubule associated protein 2. J. Biol. Chem., 285: 7883-7886.

R. Vale (1987). Intracellular transport using microtubule-based motors. Ann. Rev. Cell Biol. 3: 347-378.

M. L. Vallano, J. R. Goldenring, R. S. Lasher, and R. J. DeLorenzo (1986). Association of calcium / calmodulin-dependent kinase with cytoskeletal preparations: phosphorylation of tubulin, neurofilament, and microtubule-associated proteins. Ann. N. Y. Acad. Sci. 466: 357-374.

R. B. Vallee and G. S. Bloom (1991). Mechanisms of fast and slow axonal transport. Annu. Rev. Neurosci. 14: 59-92.

P. Vassiliev, M. Kanazirska and H. T. Tien (1985). Intermembrane linkage by tubulin. Biochem. Biophys. Res. Comm., 126 (1): 559-565.

J. Von Neumann (1966). Theory of self-reproducing automata. ed. A. W. Burks, Urbana: University of Illinois Press.

A. Waibel, T. Hanazawa, G. Hinton, K. Schikano, and K. Lang (1989). Phoneme recognition using time-delay neural networks. IEEE Trans. Acoustics, Speeck, and Signal Processing 37: 328-339.

P. J. Werbos (1974). Beyond Regression: New tools for prediction and analysis in the behavioral sciences. Ph.D thesis, Harvard University. thesis.

P. J. Werbos (1988). Back-propagation through time: What it does and how to do it. Proc. of the IEEE 78 (10): 1550-1560.

P. J. Werbos (1990). A menu of designs for reinforcement learning over time. Chapter 3 in Neural Networks for Control ed. W. T. Miller III, R. S. Sutton, and P. J. Werbos. MIT Press, Cambridge, Ma. 67-95.

P. J. Werbos (1992). The cytoskeleton: Why it may be crucial to human learning and to neuro-control. In press.

J. H. Williams, M. L. Errington, M. A. Lynch, and T. V. P. Bliss (1989). Arachidonic acid induces a long-term activity-dependent enhancement of synaptic transmission in the hippocampus. Nature 341: 739-742.

S. Wolfram (1984a). Cellular automata as models of complexity. Nature 311: 419-424.

S. Wolfram (1984b). Universality and complexity in cellular automata. Physica 10D: 1-35.

S. Yamosa (1984). Solitary excitations in deoxyrybonucleic acid (DNA) doublehelices. Physical Review. A30: 474-480.

C. Zhu and R. Skalak (1988). A continuum model of protrusion of pseudopod in leukocytes. Biophys. J. 54: 1115-1137.

7 Figures

1. Squashing functions and their derivatives. (a) Sigmoid (b) Derivative of sigmoid (c) Ramp function (d) Derivative of ramp.

2. A schematic neuron. Cell nucleus is shown along with a schematic representation of the cytoskeleton. Axonal widths and branches are exaggerated in size to show internal MT structure; dendritic tree has been abbreviated

but is also supported by the MT lattice.

3. Layered feed-forward network, fully interconnected, consisting of an input layer, a hidden layer, and an output layer.

4. Three models for error-differencing computations. (a) Reciprocal synapse. (b) Intermediate neuron. (c) Feedback within a single synapse.

5. Sending the error back to the previous layer. When MT signal D arrives at the synapse, from cell G, a signal proportional to Dw is initiated up the axon of cell E. The parameter w represents the synaptic weight, as implemented by the biological synapse.

6. Summation of delta signal values in the MT lattice. Signals d_i propagate along axon branches to the axon trunk. The axonal fiber between the soma and branches is postulated to average and sum signals to perform $S = \sum d_i$. Signals S then propagate up dendritic trunks.

7. A MT-MAP cytoskeletal lattice model. The 1's are tubulin dimer alpha states, and the 0's are tubulin dimer beta states. Signals are initiated at the bottom of the lowest three strands and exit at the top of the two highest strands. (a) Lattice state after 53 time steps. (b) Lattice state after 54 time steps. From Dayhoff et al. 1992c,

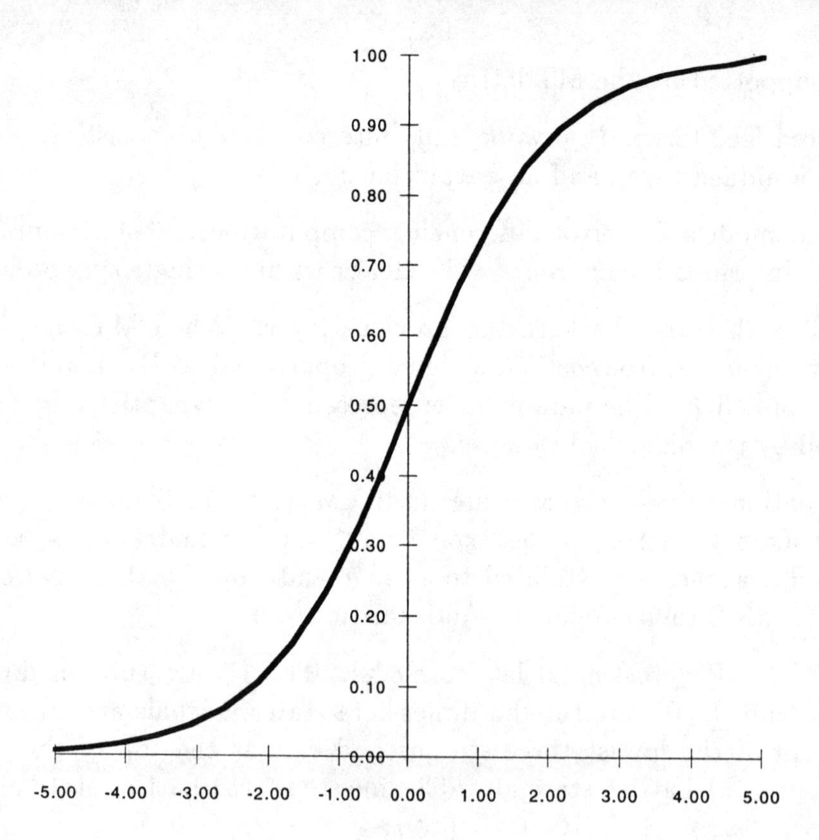

Figure 1a

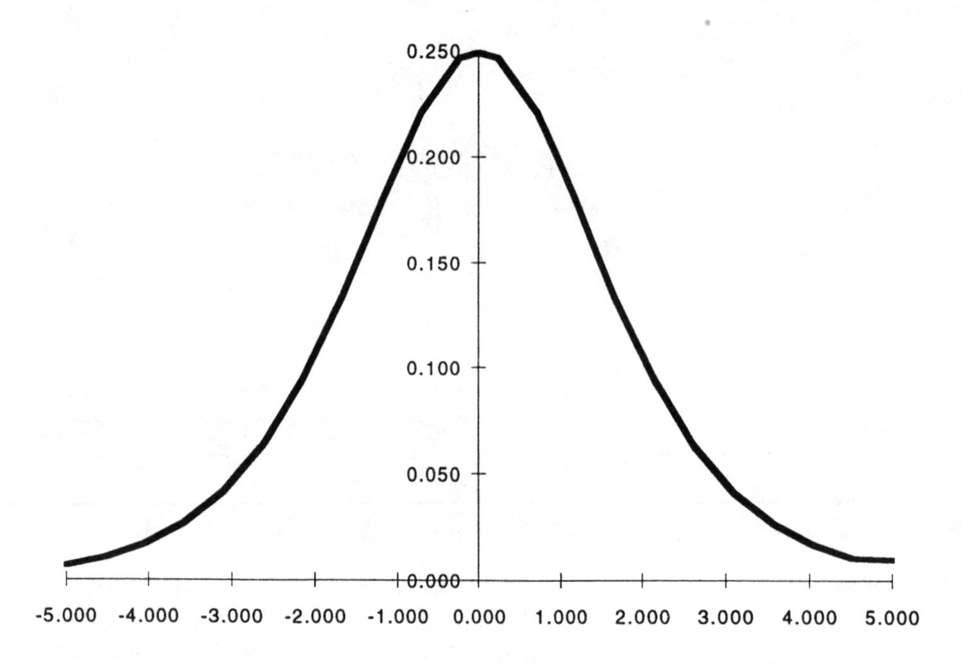

Figure 1b

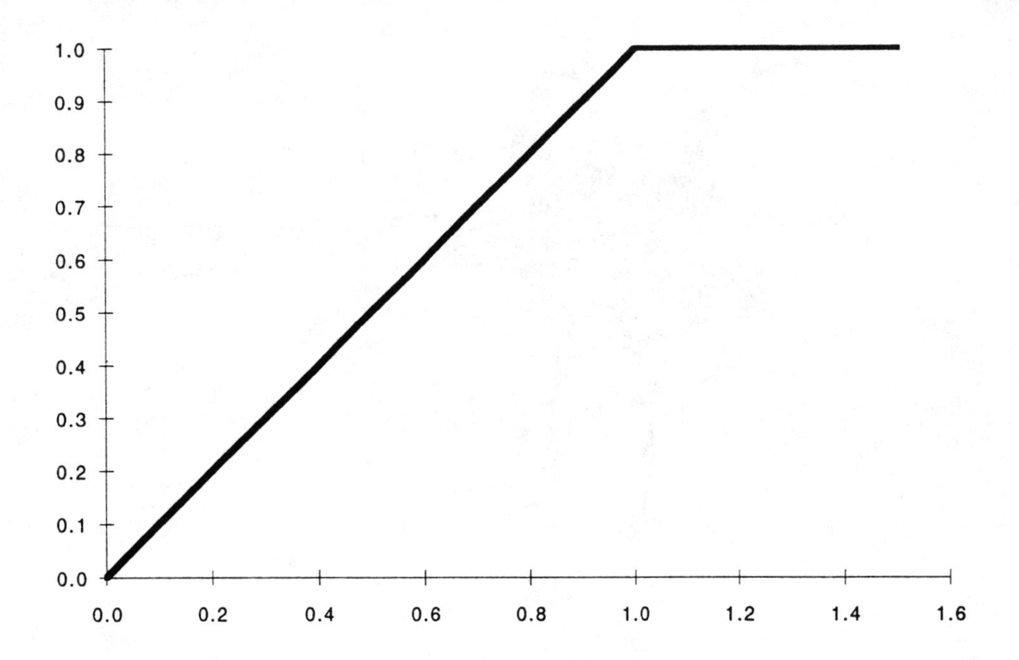

Figure 1c

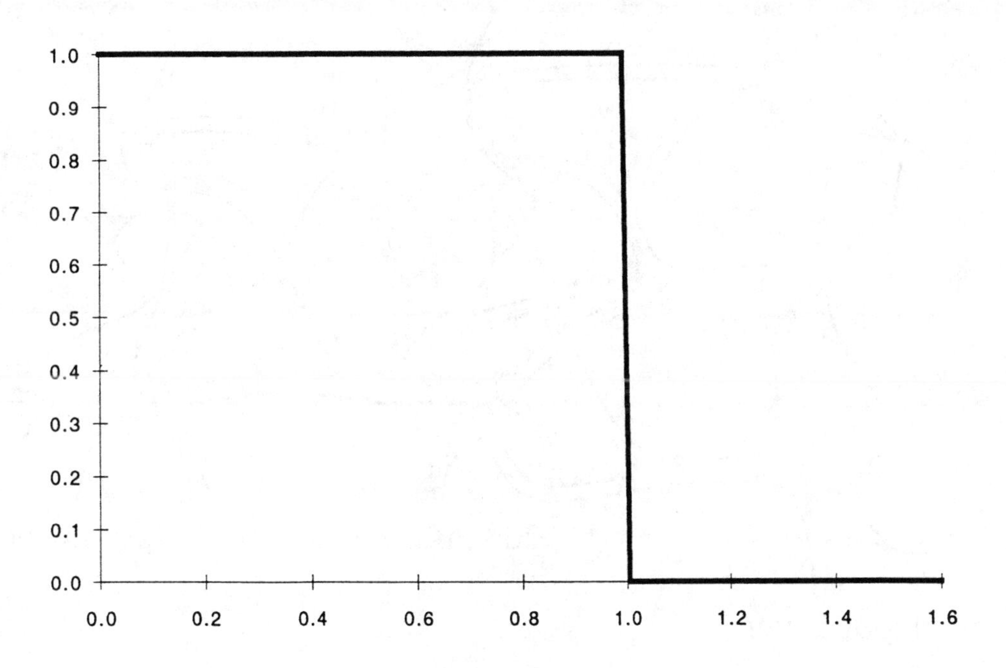

Figure 1d

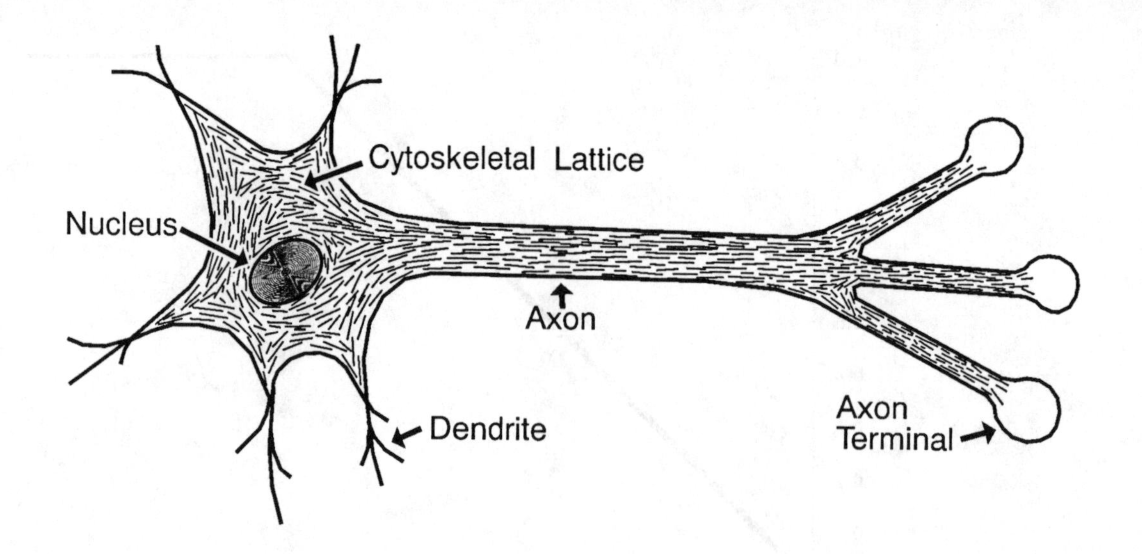

Figure 2

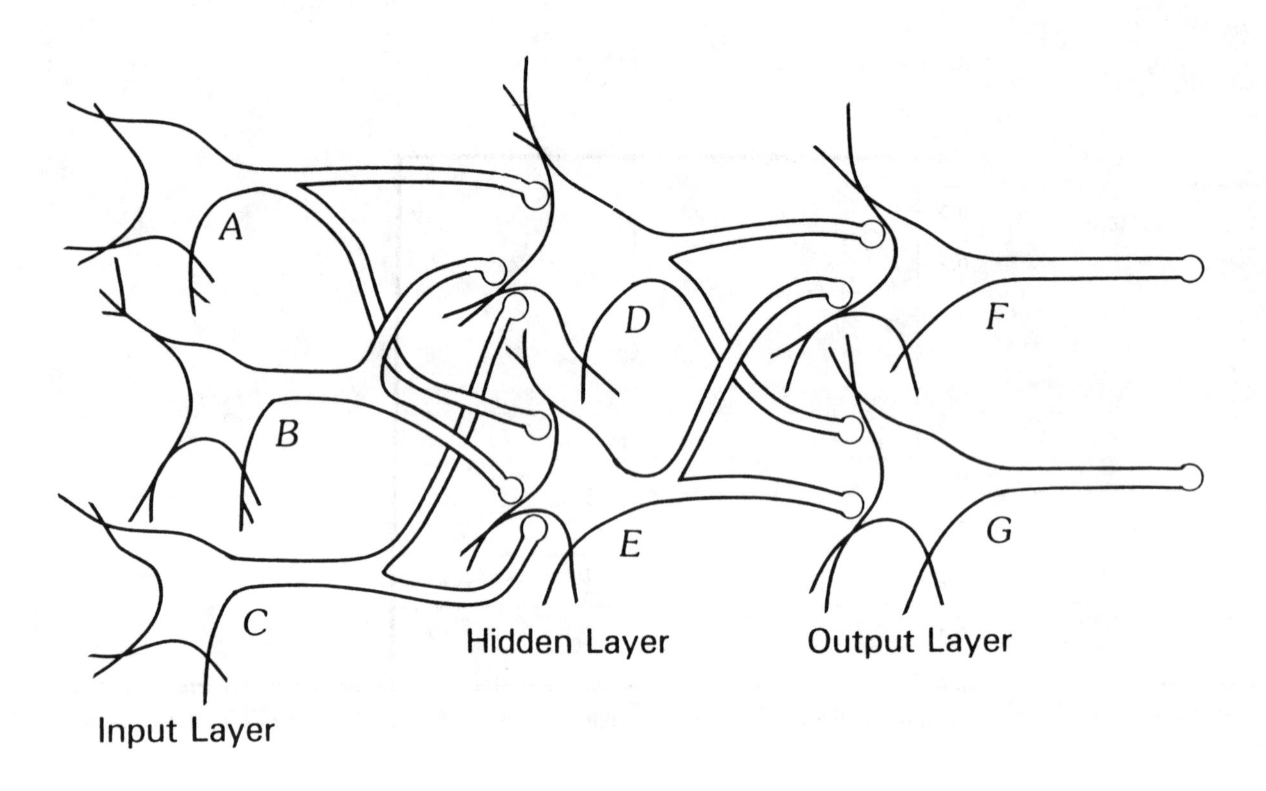

Figure 3

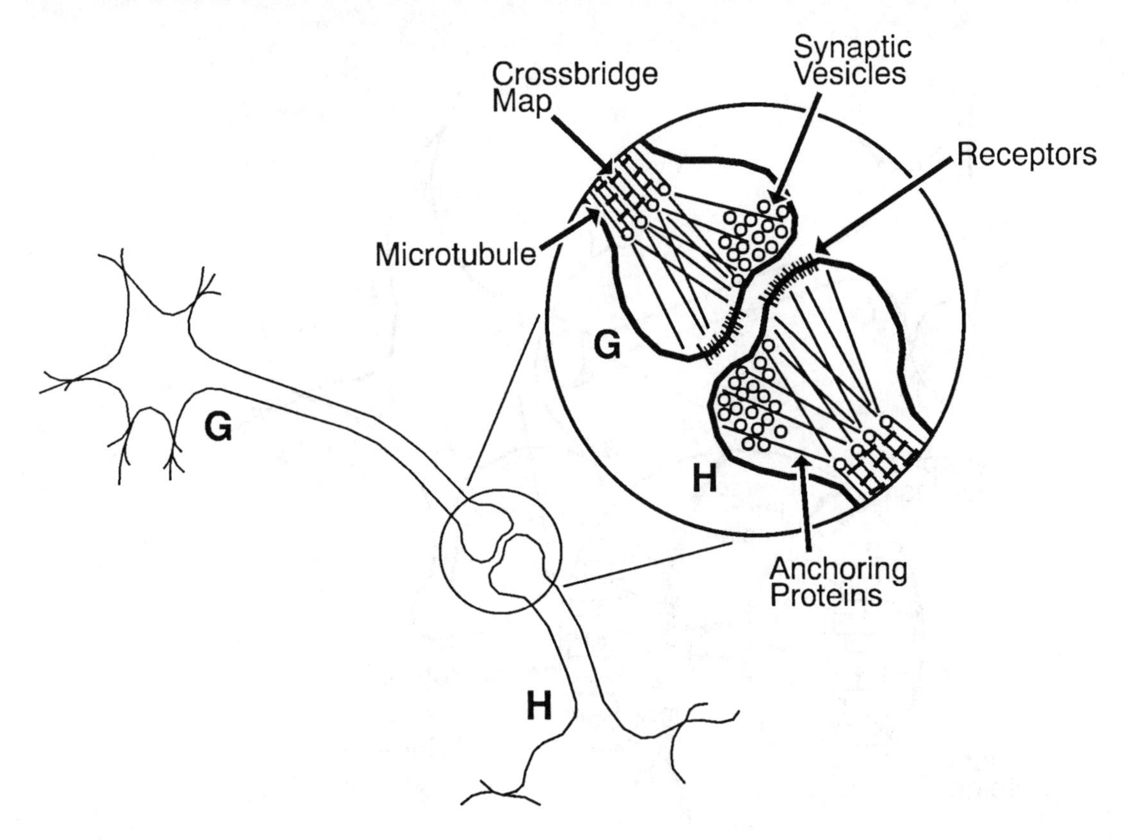

Figure 4a

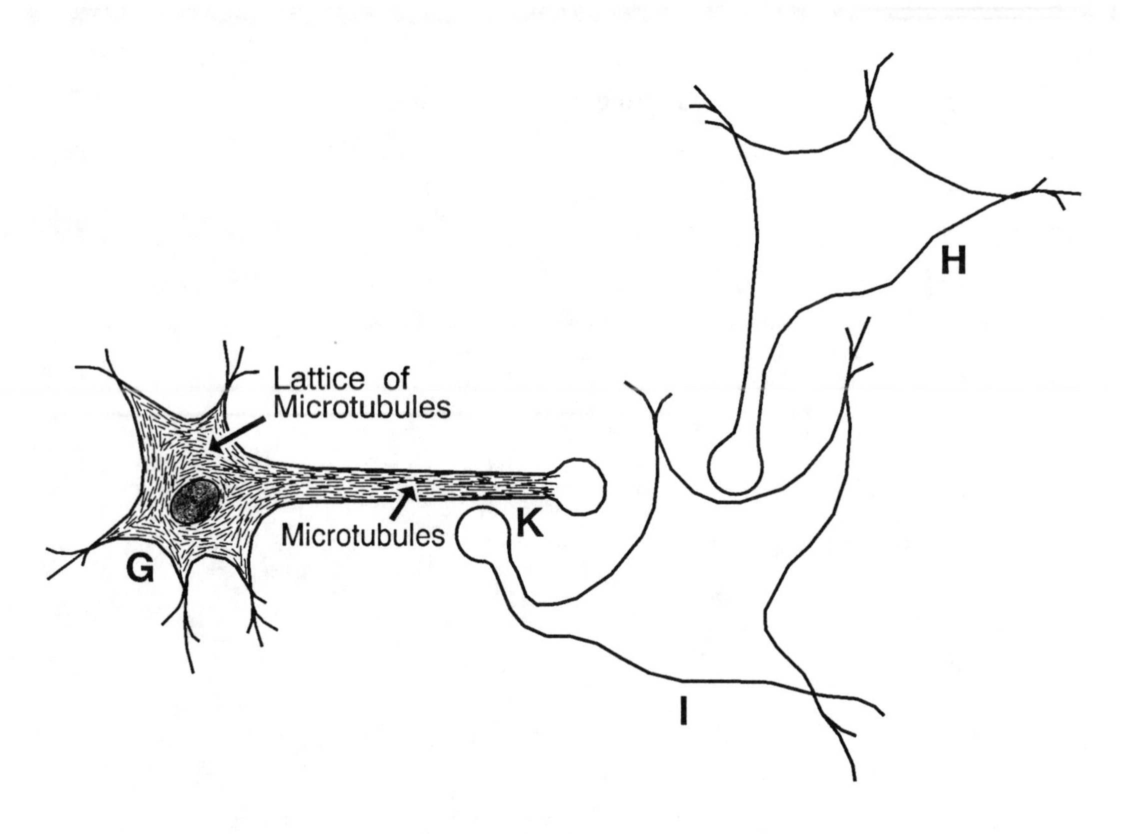

Figure 4b

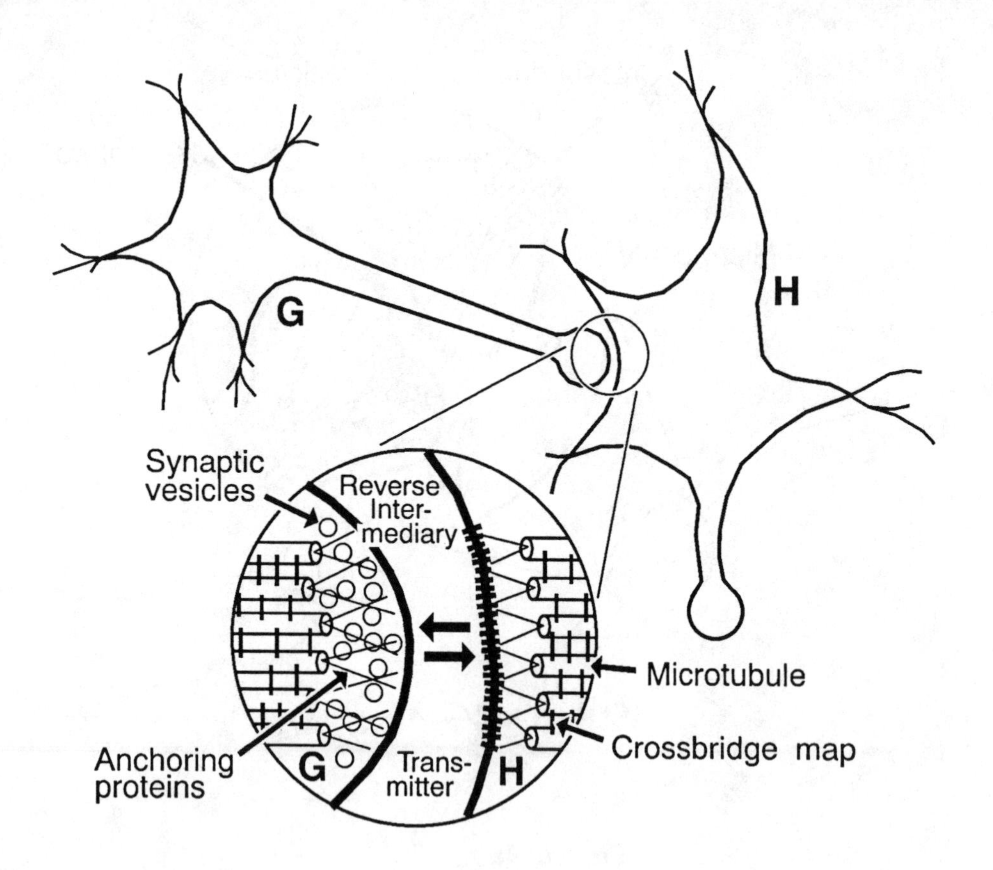

G
H
Synaptic vesicles
Reverse Inter-mediary
Microtubule
Crossbridge map
Anchoring proteins
G
Trans-mitter
H

Figure 4c

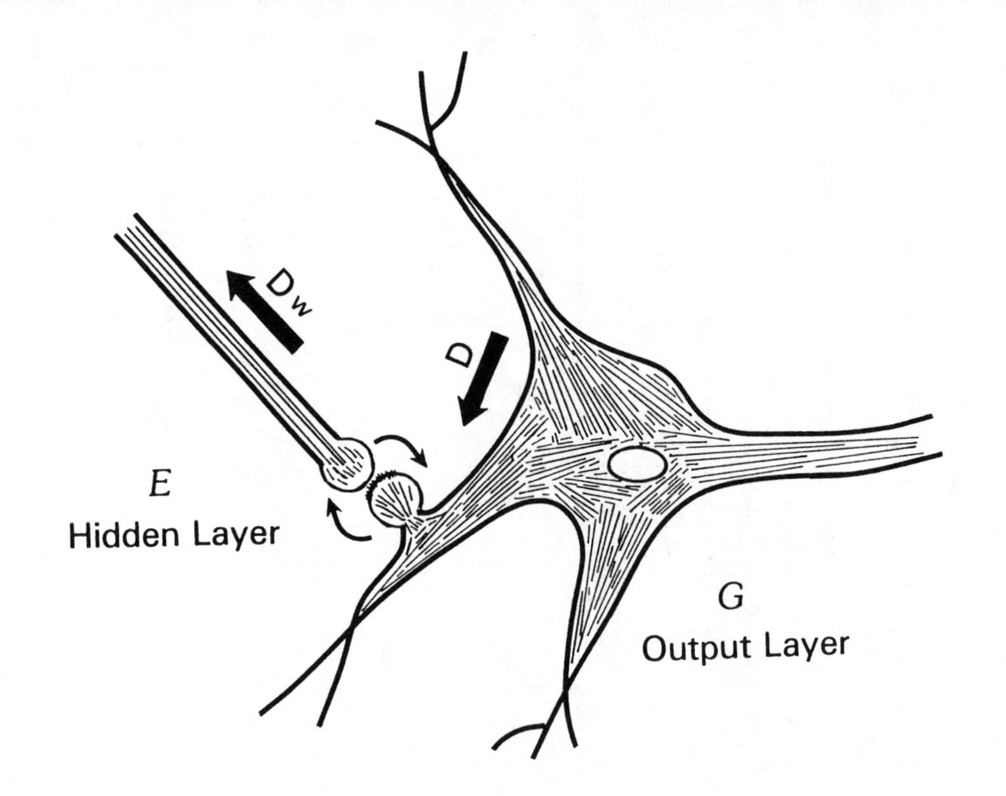

Figure 5

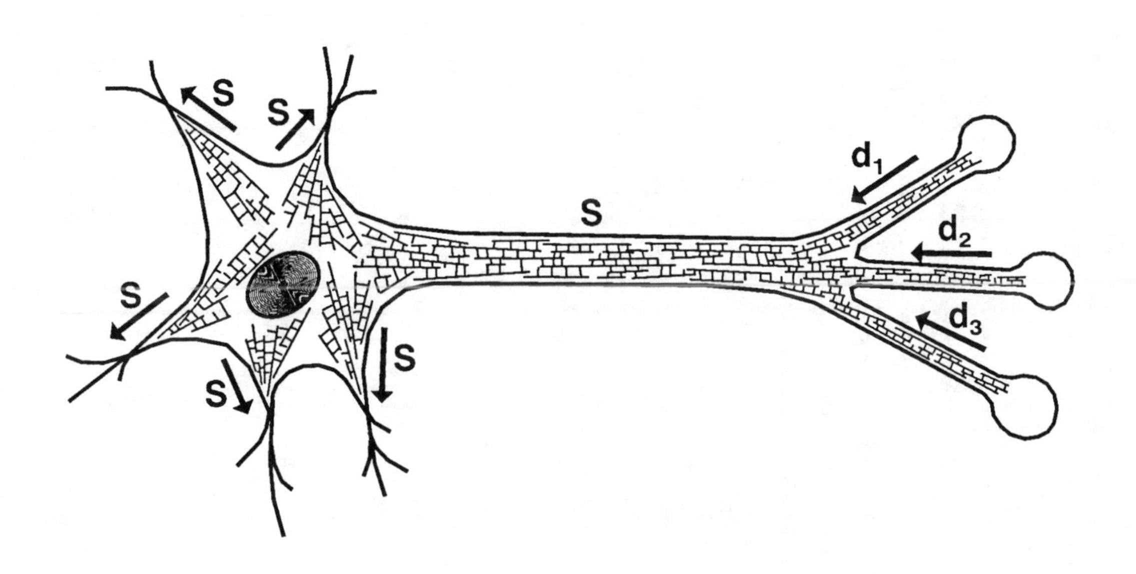

Figure 6

```
.   .   .   1   .   .   .   .   .   1   .   .   .
.   .   .   1   .   .   .   .   .   1   .   .   .
.   .   .   1   .   .   .   .   .   1   .   .   .
.   .   .   1   .   .   .   .   .   1   .   .   .
.   .   .   1   .   .   .   .   .   1   .   .   .
.   .   .   1   .   .   .   .   .   1   .   .   .
.   .   .   1   .   .   .   .   .   1 - 0   .   .
.   .   .   1 - 0   .   .   .   .   1   0   .   .
.   .   0   1   0   0   .   .   0   1   0   .   .
.   .   0 - 1   0   0   .   .   0 - 1   0   .   .
.   .   0   1   0   0   .   .   0   1   0   0   .
.   .   0   1 - 0   0   .   .   0   1 - 0   0   .
.   .   0   1   0   0   .   .   0   1   0   0   .
.   .   0 - 1   1   1   .   .   0   1   0   0   .
.   .   0   1   0 - 0   .   .   0   1   0   0   .
.   .   0   1   0   0   .   .   0 - 1   1   0   .
.   .   0   1 - 0   0   .   0 - 0   1   0 - 0   .
.   .   0   1   1   0   .   0   0   1 - 0   0   .
.   .   0 - 1   0 - 0   .   0   0   1   0   0   .
.   .   0   1   0   0   0   0   0 - 0   1   0   0
.   0   0   1   0   1   0   0   0   1   0   0   0
.   0 - 0   1 - 0   0   0   0 - 0   1   1   1   0
.   0   1   0   0   0   0 - 0   0   0   1 - 0   0
.   0   0 - 1   1 - 0   0   0   0   0   1   0   0
.   0 - 1   1   1   0   0   0   0   0   1   0   0
.   0   1   0   0   1   0   0   0 - 1   0   1   0
0   0   1   .   0   0 - 0   0   0   0 - 0   0 - 0
0   0 - 1   .   0   1   0   0 - 0   0   0   0   1
0 - 1   .   .   0   0   0   0   0   .   0   1   0
1   1   .   .   1   0   0 - 0   0   .   1 - 0   0
0   1   .   .   1 - 0   0   0   .   .   1   0   0
0   1   .   .   1   1 - 0   0   .   .   0   0   0
0 - 1   .   .   .   1   0   0   .   .   .   1 - 0
0   1   .   .   .   0   0   1   .   .   .   0   1
0   0   .   .   .   0   1 - 0   .   .   .   0   0
0   0   .   .   .   0   0   .   .   .   .   0   0
0 - 0   .   .   .   0 - 1   .   .   .   .   0   0
1   0   .   .   .   .   1   .   .   .   .   0 - 1
0   .   .   .   .   .   0   .   .   .   .   .   0
1   .   .   .   .   .   1   .   .   .   .   .   0
0   .   .   .   .   .   0   .   .   .   .   .   1
```

Figure 7a

```
.   .   .   1   .   .   .   .   .   1   .   .   .
.   .   .   1   .   .   .   .   .   1   .   .   .
.   .   .   1   .   .   .   .   .   1   .   .   .
.   .   .   1   .   .   .   .   .   1   .   .   .
.   .   .   1   .   .   .   .   .   1   .   .   .
.   .   .   1   .   .   .   .   .   1   .   .   .
.   .   .   1   .   .   .   .   .   1 - 0   .   .
.   .   .   1 - 0   .   .   .   .   1   0   .   .
.   .   0   1   0   0   .   .   0   1   0   .   .
.   .   0 - 1   0   0   .   .   0 - 1   0   .   .
.   .   0   1   0   0   .   .   0   1   0   0   .
.   .   0   1 - 0   0   .   .   0   1 - 0   0   .
.   .   0   1   1   1   .   .   0   1   0   0   .
.   .   0 - 1   0   0   .   .   0   1   0   0   .
.   .   0   1   0 - 0   .   .   0   1   1   0   .
.   .   0   1   0   0   .   .   0 - 1   0   0   .
.   .   0   1 - 1   0   .   0 - 0   1   0 - 0   .
.   .   0   1   0   0   .   0   0   1 - 0   0   .
.   .   0 - 1   0 - 0   .   0   0   0   1   0   .
.   .   0   1   0   1   0   0   0 - 1   0   0   0
.   0   0   1   0   0   0   0   0   1   1   1   0
.   0 - 1   0 - 0   0   0   0 - 0   0   1   0   0
.   0   0   1   1   0   0 - 0   0   0   1 - 0   0
.   0   1 - 1   1 - 0   0   0   0   0   1   0   0
.   0 - 1   0   0   1   0   0   0   1   0   1   0
.   0   1   0   0   0   0   0   0 - 0   0   0   0
0   0   1   .   0   1 - 0   0   0   0 - 0   1 - 0
0   1 - 0   .   0   0   0   0 - 0   0   0   1   0
1 - 1   .   .   1   0   0   0   0   .   1   0   0
0   1   .   .   1   0   0 - 0   0   .   1 - 0   0
0   1   .   .   1 - 1   0   0   .   .   0   0   0
0   1   .   .   0   1 - 0   0   .   .   0   1   0
0 - 1   .   .   .   0   0   1   .   .   .   0 - 1
0   0   .   .   .   0   1   0   .   .   .   0   0
0   0   .   .   .   0   0 - 0   .   .   .   0   0
0   0   .   .   .   0   1   .   .   .   .   0   0
0 - 1   .   .   .   1 - 0   .   .   .   .   0   1
0   1   .   .   .   .   0   .   .   .   .   0 - 0
1   .   .   .   .   .   1   .   .   .   .   .   0
0   .   .   .   .   .   0   .   .   .   .   .   1
1   .   .   .   .   .   1   .   .   .   .   .   1
```

Figure 7b

Chapter 13

Spatiotemporal Chaos Information Processing in Neural Networks -- Electronic Implementation

Harold Szu, Brian Telfer and George Rogers
NSWCDD
Silver Spring, MD 20903

Desa Gobovic, Charles Hsu and Mona Zaghloul
GWU, EE & CS Dept.
Washington, D.C. 20052

Walter Freeman
Physiology Department
UC Berkeley
Berkeley, CA 94720

Spatiotemporal Chaos Information Processing in Neural Networks---
Electronic Implementation

Harold Szu, Brian Telfer, George Rogers,NSWCDD, Silver Spring MD 20903;
Desa Gobovic, Charles Hsu, Mona Zaghloul, GWU, EE & CS Dept., Wash. D.C. 20052;
Walter Freeman, Physiology Dept., U C Berkeley, Berkeley CA 94720

Abstract: In the framework of the McCullouch-Pitts neuron model we present a simple model which is biologically meaningful and each neuron is capable of generating chaos to be learned in a collective Hebbian interaction among neurons. In the interest of reducing the complexity, we have considered three variations of neuron models: (1) an internal threshold dynamic model of three degrees of freedom of neurons, (2) a smooth N-shape input-output mapping based on a cubic polynomial, and (3) a piecewise negative sigmoidal mapping model. We have derived an asymptotic bifurcation route to chaos where Feigenbaum metric universality is generalized by the antisymmetric cubic polynomial function. Numerically, we have investigated the Hebbian learning of information processing capability of artificial neural networks (ANN) consisting of a large collection of such neuron models. Snapshots of several hundred thousand neuronic outputs of a single layer, called neural images, are generated for the purpose of graphical illustration of the iterative neurodynamics with a global broadcast without a delay in global communication. The fixed-point attractor dynamics, based on the Hebbian learning rule of the synaptic weight matrix among all chaotic neurons, has generated a mean field of the iteration feedback baseline from other neurons, which reveals a spatially coherent neural image as the information content. In the case of N-shape sigmoidal neurons, results of the neural images show psychologically the possibilities of misconception, perceptual habituation or adaptation, novelty detection and noise-generated hallucination. To achieve an exponentially fast pattern recognition inherited from the iterative mapping chaos, a massively parallel design of chaos ANN chip is suggested. Designs toward chaos chips without inductance elements are discussed.

Key Words: Habituation, Novelty Detection, Images, Neural Images, Chaos, Feigenbaum, Nonlinear Dynamics, Neurodynamics

1. Introduction

This paper gives the biological and the engineering perspectives of neural network chaos for the purpose of information processing. In Sect. 1, the biological motivation is succinctly described. In Sect. 2, the reasons for investigating artificial neural network (ANN) chaos are given. In Sect. 3, three mathematical models of chaotic ANN are given. In Sect. 4, neural images are given with discussions. In Sect. 5, chaos chips implementation issues are addressed.

2. Biological Background of Chaos

Sufficient evidence exists to strongly support the hypothesis that brain systems operate in chaotic regions of state space, but it is unclear how global chaos arises in the cortex, and whether it plays essential roles in perception and cognition. If it does, how might we discover and simulate those roles?

How does globally coherent chaos arise? Single neurons are known to have chaotic domains of function. The characteristic Poisson interval histograms, flat autocovariances, and small co-variances between pairs of pulse trains may reflect that mode of operation. Alternatively, each single neuron may operate near a fixed point attractor and be driven by 1,000-10,000 others by re-entrant synaptic pathways with distributed delays. The model proposed here can provide a test bed for this question, because the elements simulating neurons can be easily moved parametrically through their point, limit cycle and chaotic basins of attraction. The spectra, dimensions, and phase portraits of the local and global chaotic outputs of the model can be compared to those with the known properties of units and EEGs from cortexes.

What is the optimal form of the sigmoidal nonlinearity? The most commonly used form is the monotonic, symmetric curve that contributes to the great stability. An asymmetric sigmoid, as revealed in cortical studies, provides a desired degree of instability for rapid state transitions. The N-shaped nonlinearity used in the proposed system is derived directly from studies on neurons, and its properties are consistent with Pavlovian paradoxical inhibition, cathodal block, and the N-shaped performance curves of several types of sensory receptor and central neuron. The present system will enable systematic evaluation of this question.

Is chaos essential for the rapid and complete state transitions that are observed in the sensory cortex during serial perception? The present model can be trained on two or more classes of inputs to be discriminated and can be parametrically shifted quickly and cleanly from a point or limit cycle attractor to one of several chaotic domains to test this hypothesis. Is chaos essential for learning novel stimuli? One hypothesis is that chaos provides unstructured and unpatterned neural activity needed to drive Hebbian synapses during formation of nerve cell assemblies, that enable the cortex to generate novel patterns. The present system can test this by conducting learning in limit cycle vs. chaotic states. Likewise, an essential part of learning is to habituate to irrelevant and ambiguous input (the context) while associative memories are laid down. The system can be used to explore the formation and operation of "negative" images, which are already apparent in preliminary results using chaotic dynamics. Software simulation now in use can give tentative but not definitive answers to these questions, because the solution of the large number of equations by numerical integration is very slow, and the risk is high of being misled by numerical instabilities that might supplant or contaminate the desired chaotic solutions. The proposed hardware embodiment is obviously needed, and it must be designed and constructed so that the parameters relevant to biological hypothesis testing are built in and easy to use. Further, it is only by use of well designed chips that the serial architectures of corticocortical and corticothalamic operations can be simulated. Digital embodiments are too slow for more than one layer at a time.

In the near future, a class of "cortical chips" is foreseen, in which the adjustable parameters are designed and built in, so as to simulate the synaptic and threshold effects of pharmacological agents known to affect cortical function in specific ways, and to test specific hypotheses on how biochemical and genetic diseases of the brain can lead to neurological, perceptual, and cognitive dysfunctioning. That kind of simulation might assist in the development of palliative, remedial, and preventive therapeutic regimens by bridging the gulf between molecular and behavioral abnormalities of brain functions.

Why ANN Modeling of Chaos ?

Based on the (saddle point) control of chaos systems (e.g. in a magnetic ribbon) scientists[1] have recently demonstrated that the wide frequency band chaotic state of a dying rabbit's heartbeats can be restored to a healthy narrow band oscillation measured by the interbeat interval of the monophasic action potential of heart. However, there remains an intriguing question--given biological chaos , whether in hearts or olfactory bulbs [2], how is chaos useful for information processing in general ? Chaos in the Poincare sense is usually exceedingly sensitive to the initial condition, and is usually intractable by rigorous mathematical analysis. This fact becomes even more difficult for a large interacting neural network. Mathematical solutions are based on two approaches: (1) the Complex Processor Model, e.g. Blum and Wang [25], can be mathematically treated in the case of a few oscillator neurons with inhibition-excitation links, and (2) the Complicated Communication Model, e.g. Ross et al. [9], incorporates a bipolar version of a Hopfield network with second order Hebbian interconnects T_{ijk} having a stochastic switch-off probability. While these mathematical analyses are interesting, the relevance to cortical information processing remains to be investigated. Our rationale, similar to the phase transition phenomenon, is that a coherent spatiotemporal structure might happen only in the limit of very large numbers of chaotic neurons, and that the present day computer is powerful enough to investigate chaotic ANNs based on any biologically meaningful neuron models. Thus, we wish to design chaotic neuron models in the framework of the McCullouch-Pitts neuron model and demonstrate in principle the spatiotemporal coherence due to the interaction of several hundred thousand chaotic neurons. However, the spatiotemporal evolutions reported here are computed for 4096 neurons iteratively for 15 time steps. This study of information processing capability is being pursued because:

- ANN Chaos may be an efficient knowledge representation of an external chaotic world.
- ANN Chaos may be a dynamic pattern recognition mechanism, since the chaos could represent a "don't know" state while the other attractors, such as periodic or quasi-periodic attractors, could represent known or familiar states.
- Chaos is known to be exponentially fast to switch from chaos to one attractor basin and back to another.
- Does the individual neuron chaos become collectively more chaotic or more ordered, e.g. quasiperiodic orbits?
- Can we observe such a phase transition and in what sense can we quantify the degree of order or chaos ?
- Does the nonlinear neurodynamics harvest both the advantage of being chaotic and being massively parallel and distributed?

3. Three Simplified Mathematical Models

In the interest of reducing the complexity of the implementation, we have considered three variations of neuron models: (1) an internal threshold dynamic model of three degrees of freedom, (2) a smooth N-shape input-output mapping based on a cubic polynomial, and (3) a piecewise negative sigmoidal mapping model.

3.1 Differential Flow Threshold Dynamics Model: Recently, Szu & Rogers [8] have generalized the threshold value of the McCullouch-Pitts neuron model to be a vector function of <u>three</u> degrees of freedom, consistent with the differential flow requirement of the Kolmogorov-Arnold-Moses Theorem. The sigmoidal outputs v_i are generally defined with an arbitrary slope $1/\tau_i$ as follows:

$$v_i = \sigma(u_i) = 1/\{1 + \exp(-u_i/\tau_i)\}; \qquad u_i = \Sigma_j W_{ij} v_j - \theta_i(t) \qquad \text{(1a,b)}$$

where u_i is net neuron input and θ_i is the the threshold value. Szu and Rogers [8] have generalized the threshold to a vector $\theta_i(t)$ of several components. They showed that when it has only two components, M-P model can produce pulses. This fact is consistent with the Hodgkin-Huxley model where two ionic channels exists for two degrees of freedom. Each freedom may be simplified by employing a first-order fixed-point dynamics, then together two first order equations can account for one second order equation that is mathematically necessary for any oscillation phenomenon involving the replenishment in firing pulses [8]. However for a possible differential flow chaos, a third degree of freedom,a neural housekeeping activity, must be introduced. Its magnitude at the axon hillock θ_i is assumed to be proportional to the value of sigmoidal slope:

$$\theta_i(v_i) = \quad \gamma_i \, dv_i/du_i \quad = 4\lambda_i \, v_i(1-v_i), \qquad (2)$$

where use is made of the slope of the sigmoidal: $(dv_i/du_i)=v_i(1-v_i)/\tau_i$. This is a source of the initial-sensitive and unpredictable chaos in a single neuron model (see Fig. 1).

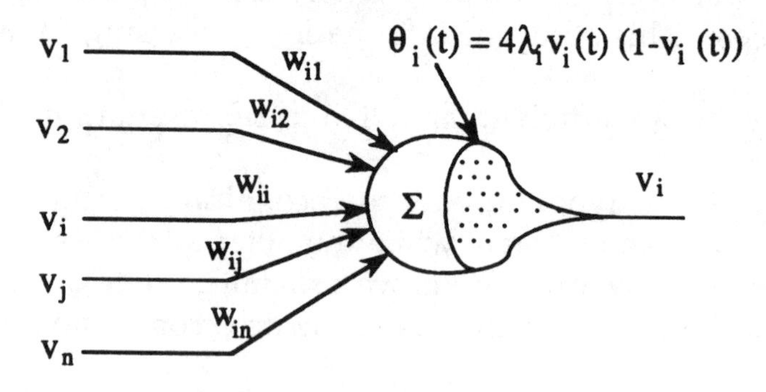

Fig. 1: Threshold Dynamics Neuron Model assumes the threshold to be proportional to sigmoidal slope Eq(2) giving Feigenbaum 's map;

Thus, Feigenbaum's λ–knob is derived for the model to be $4\lambda_i = \gamma_i/\tau_i \leq 4$, which varies according to the slope τ_i of output firing rate v_i Eq(1b). The higher the slope value near the threshold, the more the change of the output v_i value. Thus, more is demanded of the housekeeping logistics to maintain a regulated threshold function $\theta_i(v_i)$, which can give a higher λ–knob value. When the λ–knob value exceeds λ_c=0.8924, the output firing leads the route of bifurcations to chaos. Similar to the population growth of blowflies under a limited food supply, such a neuron model seems to be biologically meaningful, because a larger slope implies a larger change of firing rates and therefore larger demand of housekeeping function.

Unfortunately, the three internal threshold dynamics consumes extensive computing time, an hour per iteration on a Silicon Graphics workstation (see Sect. 6 for detail). This has motivated us to design a chaos chip for massively parallel ANN computing which embodies also a simplified internal dynamics with three adjustable parameters in the following N-shaped sigmoidal function. One is less certain about whether this mapping alone can produce chaos. However, chaos seems to follow when a time-delay is introduced to the discrete mapping because the delay generates an iterative series solution which is composed of discrete mapping of all the previous time steps including the sensitive initial condition. The phase plot of the mapping is quite different. The delay gives rise to two dimensional Henon map, a sign of chaos, while without the delay it gives simply one dimensional Feigenbuam map, a strange attractor. ([29]. figure16-9) This is similar to the Nagumo-Fitzhugh binary model with delay that produces a measure of the Cantor triad, i.e., the devil-staircase plotting the unpredictable frequency ratio jumps against the input strength. Following Harmon's tunneling diode implementation of a neuron[4], Nagumo & Sato [5] studied a binary neuron model with delay for a threshold-refractory period that has also produced the measure of Cantor triad.

3.2 Antisymmetric Cubic Polynomial Mapping

We wish to simplify the 3-D differential flow into an 1-D discrete mapping, such as Feigenbaum logistic map, as well as to preserve the piecewise negative sigmoidal logic. Thus, the following cubic polynomial function is proposed:.

$$v_i = (1/c^2)\, u_i\, (u_i - b)\, (u_i + a) + v_{io} = f(u_i) \qquad (3)$$

where a, b, c are arbitrary real positive constants. The offset constant v_{io} is introduced to keep the output positive. The Feigenbaum peak value λ is related to the roots of the cubic polynomial function. $\lambda = a^3/\sqrt{3}$ for a=b and $c^2=2/3$.

The proposed cubic polynomial mapping is thoroughly explored and many of its interesting and useful properties are discovered. Simulation results for a particular case with $c^2=2/3$, b=0.9, and parameter a changing from 0.7 to 1.4 are shown in Fig. 2.

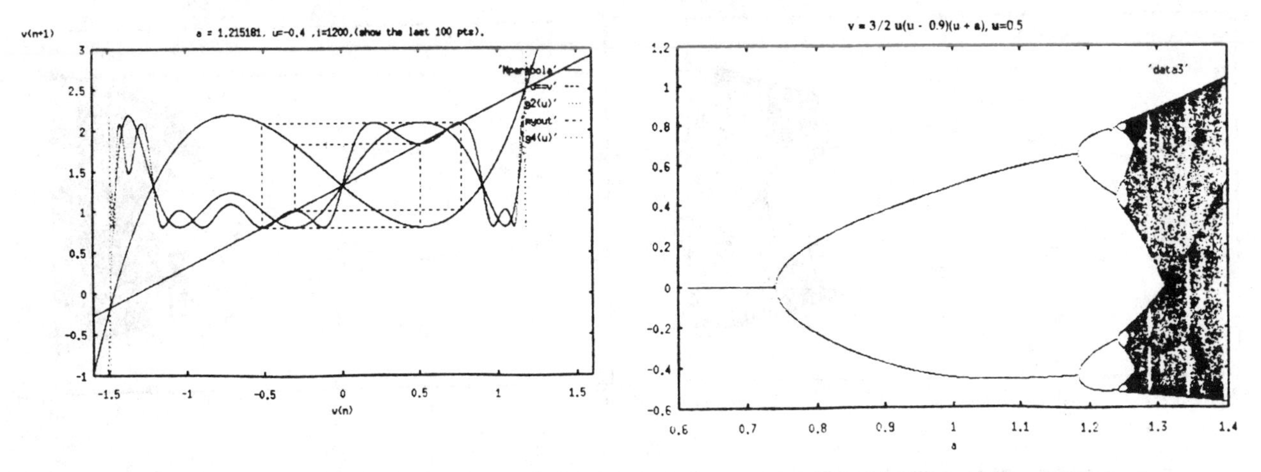

Fig.2 Cubic polynomial mapping: a) Four stable fixed point attractor; b) Bifurcation route to chaos

For example, an attractor of period four is found at a=1.215 (Fig.2a). Note that the fixed points are obtained at the intersections of function $g_4(u)=g_2(g_2(u))$, where $g_2=f(f(u))$, and v=u. Fig.2b portrays the period-doubling route to chaos and the onset of chaos at some critical value a_c. The more beautiful features are observed for the special case of the antisymmetric cubic polynomial function when a=b. A particular case for a=b=1.22 ($c^2=2/3$) is shown in Fig.3a. According to the bifurcation theory [29], the obtained attractor should have four stable fixed points (B, D, F, and H). However, a cycle of two stable fixed points occurs. This is due to the different mapping function which is not fixed at the two ends as the Feigenbaum mapping, and also has the third part which makes the curve antisymmetric. There are two cycles of frequency two, which never occur at the same time. Which cycle of those two is chosen depends on the initial condition (i.e. a seed of chaos) Fig.3. This feature may add more uncertainty in the bifurcation route to chaos as shown in Fig. 4. An example of a chaotic response is shown in Fig. 4c. We have derived an asymptotic bifurcation route to chaos where Feigenbaum metric universality is generalized by the antisymmetric cubic polynomial function.

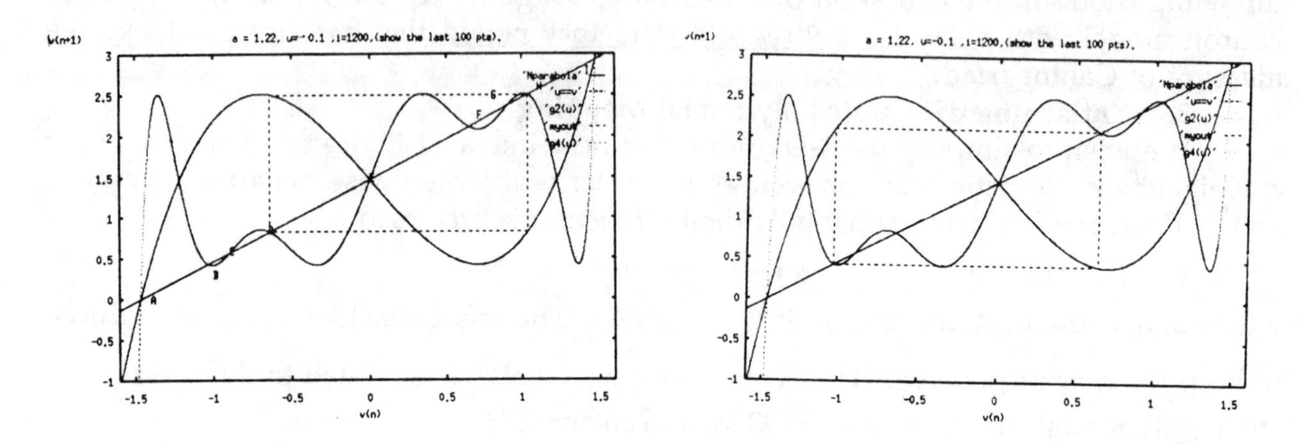

Fig.3 Antisymmetric Cubic Mapping: two different cycles with two fixed points, a=1.22 . a) u=-0.1 b). u=0.1

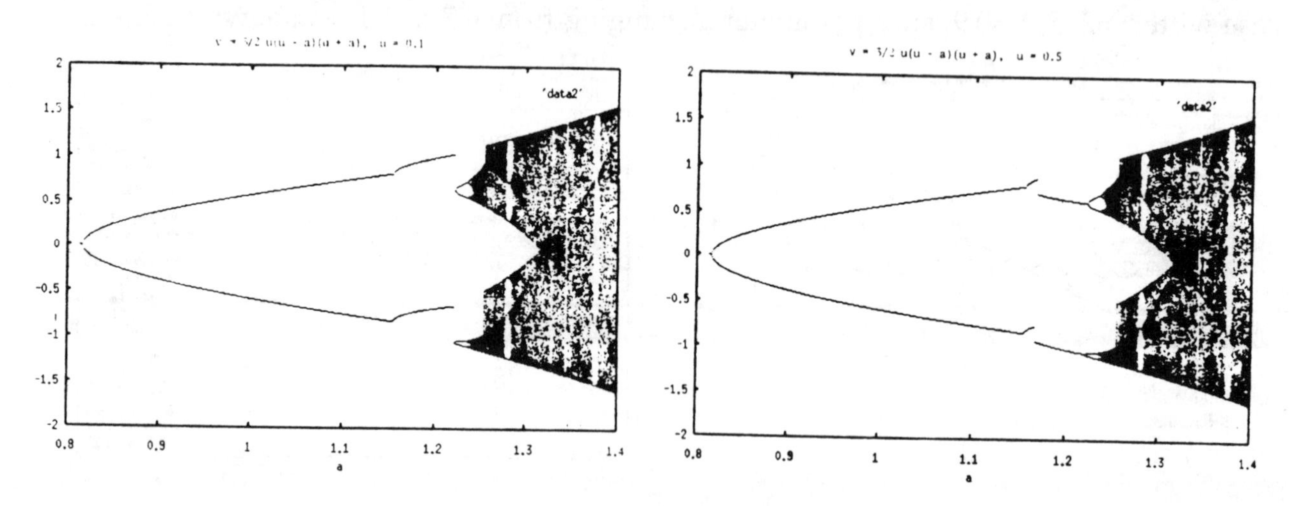

Fig. 4 The antisymmetric cubic mapping bifurcation route to chaos, Seed of chaos: a) u=0.1; b) u=0.5.

The use of the explored cubic polynomial mapping model in the collective neural network is not adequate because of the unboundedness of the function, while the output of the unipolar neuron takes values from 0 to 1. Instead, a new model with an N_shaped sigmoidal function is proposed in the next section.

3.3 Piecewise Negative Logic Model (N-Shaped Sigmoidal Function):

The N_shaped sigmoidal function that allows unbounded input, and yet has piecewise negative logic and the bounded output from 0 to 1 is described by:

$$v_i = \text{N\_shape}(u_i) \equiv \sigma_N(u_i) \tag{4}$$

where piecewise-negative logic N-shape (u) is defined as (using return in C-Program):

```
if (u ≤ -1.0)        return(1/{1+ exp[-(u+1)]});
else if (u<1.0)      return(-(u-1)/4);
else                 return(2/{1 + exp[-(u-1)]} - 1);
```

In terms of neurocomputing, this neuron model has a piecewise-negative logic of which the location is determined by three parameters similar to the threshold dynamics model. The N-shape activation transfer has three branches with a central piece of negative logic near the zero origin, where more input u implies less output v (Fig. 5). The sick region of input is set within ±1, and the recovery begins at u=1 and v=0. These are the three parameters determining the smooth N-shaped input-output function.

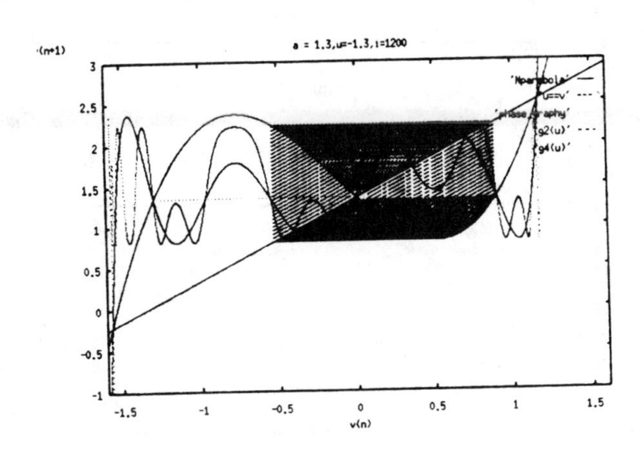

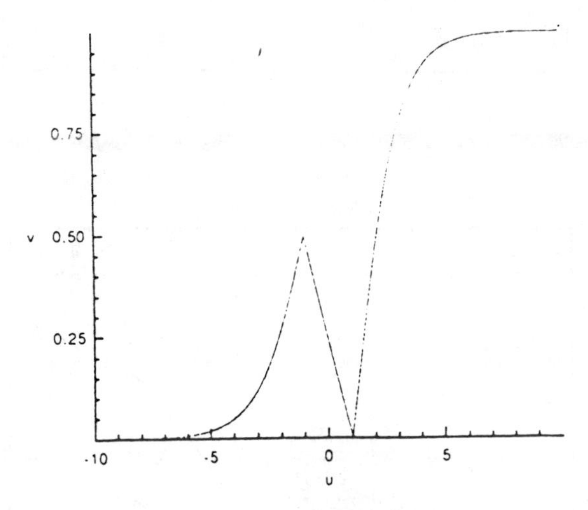

Fig.4 c) Cubic mapping showing a chaotic response **Fig. 5 Analog N-shaped sigmoidal Neuron Model,**

The iterative mapping with the N_shape sigmoidal function in terms of the neurocomputing is considered. A collective neural network is described by a set of equations:

$$v_i = \sigma_N(u_i)$$

$$u_i = \Sigma_j w_{ij} v_j - \theta_i \quad (\text{for the simplicity set } \theta_i = 0) \tag{5a}$$

while the set of iterative mapping for a single neuron is described by:

$$v_{(n+1)} = \sigma_N(u_n)$$

$$u_{n+1} = v_n \tag{5b}$$

where n is the index of iterations. According to the two sets of Eq.(5), the base-line of the iterative mapping, $u_{n+1} = v_n$, should take into account the weight changes following the Hebbian learning rule. Thus, a new base-line is introduced

$$v = \omega u \quad (5c)$$

where the base-line slope is $\omega = 1/w$ for a single neuron. The new mapping with the N_shape sigmoidal function Eq.(4) and the new base-line Eq.(5c) is explored with ω being a changing parameter. The results of such a mapping are shown in Fig.6. The region of chaos is found for certain values of parameter ω. It is interesting to point out that the mapping enters the chaos region almost without going through the bifurcation process.

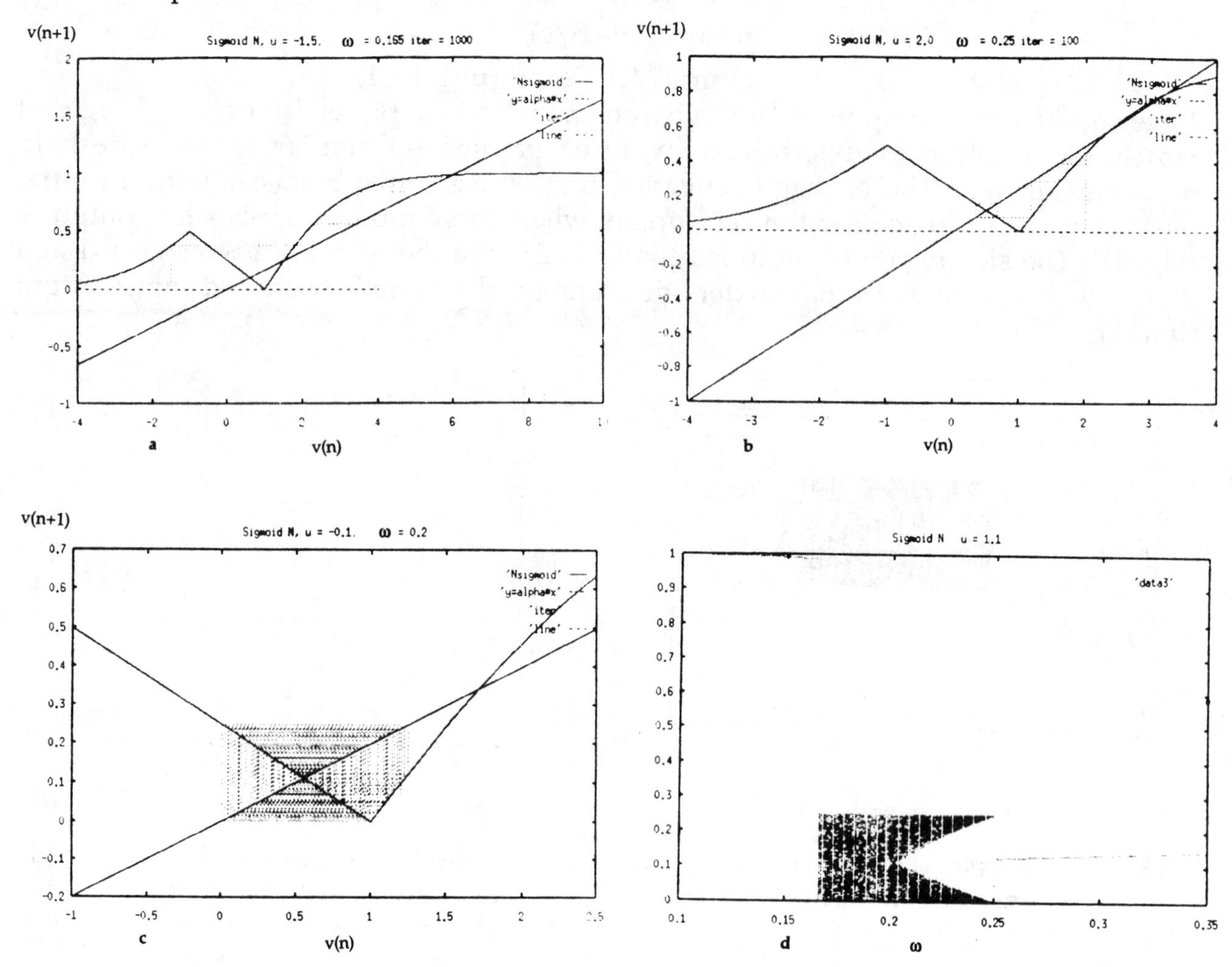

Fig. 6 N_shape sigmoidal mapping with the changing slope of the base-line a) A fixed point response; b) Bifurcation is found only at one value of $\omega = 0.25$ (equal to the negative slope of the N_shape) c) Example of a chaos behavior; d) Chaos region.

The effect and characterization of many neuron iterative mapping is hinged upon the iteration base-line whose slope changes due to the following Hebbian learning. Memory is given at equilibrium by the Hebbian product rule $v_i v_j$. Although the output v_i, due to Eq(4) mapping, is unipolar ($0 \le v_i \le 1$), the memory must be converted into bipolar analog values normalized arbitrarily between ±1 ($1- \leq w_{ij} \leq 1$) in order to provide excitation and inhibition. The diagonal term is set to zero for no self terms. Therefore, the Hebbian product $v_i v_j$ is changed to $(2v_i - 1)(2v_j - 1)$, denoted by

$$x(\mathbf{v})_i \equiv 2v_i - 1, \tag{6a}$$

$$[x(\mathbf{v})_i x(\mathbf{v})_j] \equiv x(\mathbf{v})_i\, x(\mathbf{v})_j - \delta_{ij}\, x(\mathbf{v})_i\, x(\mathbf{v})_i \tag{6b}$$

Then, we postulate the simplest first order attractor dynamics as follows

$$d\,w_{ij}/dt = -\beta\,\{ w_{ij} - [x(\mathbf{v})_i\, x(\mathbf{v})_j\,]\}. \tag{7}$$

The contour plot of Eq(6b) for $i \neq j$ may be called a Hebbian saddle having extrema located at four corners (i.e. evident by rotating coordinates: $x_i\, x_j \equiv (\xi + \psi)(\xi - \psi) = \xi^2 - \psi^2$):

$w_{ij} = 1$ when both output $v_i = 1$ and $v_j = 1$, or both $v_i = 0$ and $v_j = 0$; (8)

$w_{ij} = -1$ when both output $v_i = 1$ and $v_j = 0$, or both $v_i = 0$ and $v_j = 1$; (9)

and the memory vanishes toward the middle output value, 1/2:

$w_{ij} = 1/4$ when output $v_i = 1/4$ and $v_j = 1/4$; (10)

$w_{ij} = 0$ when output $v_i = 1/2$ and $v_j = 1/2$; (11)

Such a Hebbian saddle is 1-1 mapped onto domain $u_i u_j$, via the upper branch of σ_N, Eq(4). But the Hebbian saddle is mapped into three possible branches in the third quadrant ($v_i \leq 1/2$, $v_j \leq 1/2$) corresponding to dark image gray scale values. The exact saddle point has a zero memory Eq(11), at two possible input values: one from the lower branch at the logical breakdown point where $u_i = -1$, $u_j = -1$, and the other from the upper branch where $u_i \geq 1$, $u_j \geq 1$ (see Fig. 5).

Based on the same dynamics, we can take Eq(1a) as the fixed point. Then, we have derived the output dynamics of Grossberg and Pineda (Note that we have taken the alphabetical order to denote **u**-input and **v**-output):

$$dv_i\,/dt = -\delta\,\{v_i - \sigma(\Sigma_j\, w_{ij}\, v_j - \theta_i)\} \tag{12}$$

Alternatively, we can take the fixed point solution of the net input u_i Eq(1b):

$$du_i/dt = -\alpha\,\{ u_i - (\Sigma_j\, w_{ij}\, v_j - \theta_i)\}, \tag{13}$$

which has become known as the Hopfield net. The two approaches Eqs(12,13) are equivalent if w_{ij} is independent of time according to Hopfield model. However, rapid updates of memory Eq(7) by chaotic dynamics imply, by setting both $\alpha = 0$ and $\delta = 0$, and $\beta = 1/2$, using directly fixed point: M-P model Eq(1b), and N-shaped Sigmoid Eq(4).

4. Results of Simulations

The behavior of a neural network composed of 256*256 fully connected N-shape sigmoidal neurons governed by Hebbian learning is illustrated by image processing. We study the perception habituation. Simulation steps are given as follows:

(i) Initiation of Bipolar Memory: Substitution of image **I** (Fig.7a) into Eq(6a):

$$W_{ij} = (x(\mathbf{I})_i\, x(\mathbf{I})_j - \delta_{ij}\, x(\mathbf{I})_i\, x(\mathbf{I})_i) \equiv [x(\mathbf{I})_i\, x(\mathbf{I})_j\,] = w_{ij}(t{=}1) \tag{14a}$$

(ii) N-shaped sigmoidal output of unipolar image (top left 2nd) (Fig. 8) t=1

$$v_i(t=1) \quad = \quad \sigma_N(\Sigma_j\, w_{ij}(t=1)\, x(\mathbf{P})_j) \tag{14b}$$

(iii) Updated w'_{ij} as the average between current $w_{ij}(t=1)$ and image **P** (Fig.7b) at t=1:

$$w'_{ij}(t=2) \quad = \quad \{w_{ij}(t=1)+[x(\mathbf{P})_i\, x(\mathbf{P})_j]\}/2 \tag{14c}$$

(iv) N-shaped sigmoidal output of image (top left 3rd) (Fig.8):

$$v_i(t=2) \quad = \quad \sigma_N(\Sigma_j\, w'_{ij}(t=2)\, v_i(1)_j) \tag{15a}$$

(v) Updated w'_{ij} for iterations between (iv) and (v):

$$w'_{ij}(t=3) \quad = \quad \{w_{ij}(t=1) + [x(\mathbf{v}(t=2))_i\, x(\mathbf{v}(t=2))_j]\}/2 \tag{15b}$$

(vi) Go back to step (iv) for output of image (top left 4th).

Fig. 7a,b,c Three face images (Courtesy of U. of Purdue Image Lab.) denoted as unipolar I, P, K vectors

A glimpse of a new face, Fig. 7b, denoted by vector **P**, is then presented to the network. We observe that after 15 steps in Fig. 8, the image has suffered a contrast reversal of those pixels which have the middle gray scales value below 1/2. This can be explained by the effect of the negative logic located below the middle gray scale value. The final weight $W_{ij}(t \geq 16)$ can be read as the outer product of the final image pixels denoted by $\mathbb{P}_i$. All dark pixels are converted to about -1 values for the inhibition memory, except those brightest pixels that have +1 value contributing to the excitation memory. In other words, the dark pixels (shown in the bottom right of Fig. 8) are of zero value which are mapped to -1 in the memory space. Consequently a uniform dark image is associated with an almost uniform memory $w_{ij} = 1$. Thus, this final image, that has a large contrast shifted toward a zero or one intensity value, yields an almost uniform bipolar memory having a few -1s:

$$W_{ij}(t \geq 16) \quad = \quad [x(\mathbb{P})_i\, x(\mathbb{P})_j] = \pm 1 \tag{16}$$

After such a stable memory has been reached, Eq(16), the glimpse of a second image is applied only once as the initial condition. We consider four possible choices of initial conditions described in the following four cases. All begin with identical Eq(16).

(1) Case 1: the same image, **P** , is presented again. This second introduction of the **P** image (shown in Fig. 4 top left 1st) to the last $\mathbb{P}$ memory Eq(16) induces an adaptation phenomenon that seems to ignore the input image (Fig. 9 top left 2nd).

This can be understood as a consequence of two operations. The first is the (± 1)-averaging having more +1 value over a window size of the image itself. This leads naturally to a low pass blurred image near the 1/2 gray scale value. This is obtained by Eqs(16,1b) ($u_i = \Sigma_j W_{ij}(t \geq 16) X(\mathbf{P}_j) = \Sigma'_j X(\mathbf{P}_j)$). The second operation ($v_i = \sigma_N(u_i)$) occurs near the part of the sigmoidal curve associated with gray values about 1/2. Occasionally (when $u_i < 1$), some pixels which are darker than 1/2 are reversed by the negative logic.

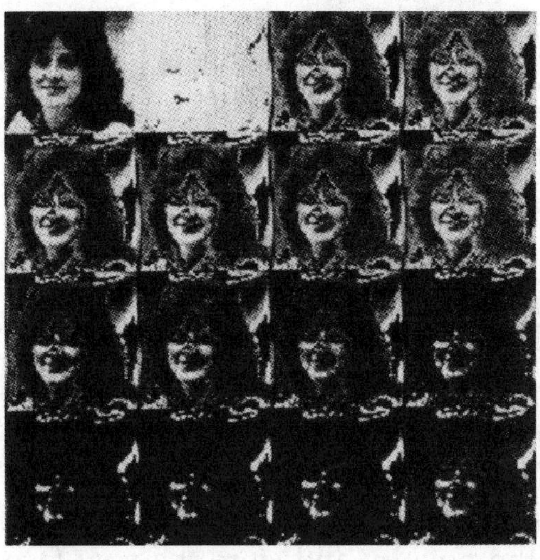

(left) Fig. 8 Perception Habituation shown here 15 steps; (right) Fig.9 Case 1. Consequence of a second look

Therefore, the obtained output (shown in Fig.9 top left 2nd) is a uniform gray image, which is now the input to the second iteration. However, such a uniform gray input that has v_i about 1/2 value does not contribute to the memory w_{ij} (Eq(11)). According to Eq(14), the new memory is the average of the current $W'_{ij} = [x(P)_i x(P)_j]$ and the new input image memory. Since the new input image memory is about zero, then the update memory is about half of the current $W'_{ij} = [x(P)_i x(P)_j]$. That is the reason why the input image P_i recovers quickly in the second iteration (Fig.9 top left 3rd). This fact is also true when the initial input to the network is a new image K_i as in case (4).

(2) Case 2: A part of image P_i is applied to the neural network as the initial condition (hide-and-seek). The hide portion is set at all $v_i = 1/2$ where all $u_i = -1$. We go back to the system that has stored the last memory associated of the IP image (shown in Fig. 3 bottom). The hide-and-seek immediately recalls the hybrid image IP_i. But this case 2 is different than the previous case (1), because the half image has less total intensity to move the (±1)-average value beyond the value $u_i > 1$ where the sigmoidal output image value applies. Thus, more image pixels intensity will be reversed from the IP_i image. The output corresponding to -1 threshold input is a fixed point memory according to Eq(10). Therefore, the equilibrium value seems to remember the uniform output value in the lower half image. Fig.10.

(3) Case 3: The image I_i originally stored in the memory is presented again as the

initial condition of this case. After ignoring the input, the original memory I_i comes back where the medium gray scale value is reversed. Fig. 11.

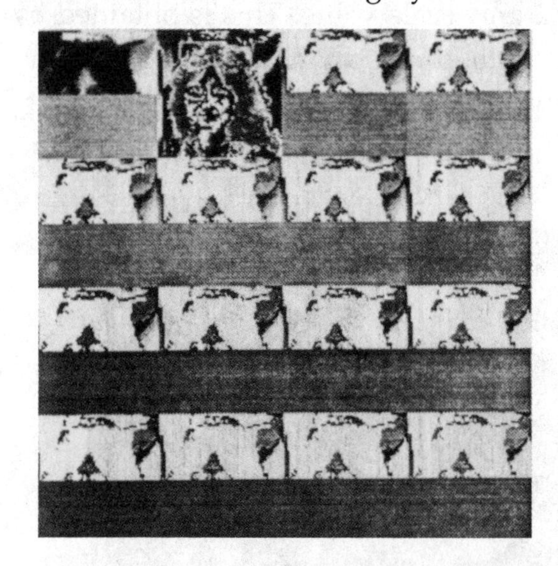

(left) Fig. 10 Hide and Seek Case 2, shows an immediately recall of stored image and then the novelty memory takes over; (right) Fig. 11 presents first image I, it ignores initially, then recalls " deja vu "

(4) Case 4: A new face K_i that has never been seen before is introduced once as the initial condition. After the neutral response of ignoring the input, Fig. 12., it begins to detect the novelty and store the new face into the memory.

Fig.12 Case 4, a new face K is presented after a brief habituation rejection it admits K as a stronger impression, due to the novelty, than that deja vu recalls shown in Fig. 11

Although we have not fully exploited the capability of these models, the neural image is powerful tool to examine some of the cortical functions.

5. Implementation issues of Chaos Chips

Hardware implementation is needed for the parallelism and to demonstrate that using a chip in studying a chaotic network is feasible. The neuron is modeled with an N-shaped characteristic device, realized by the circuit shown in Fig. 13a. In this circuit, the parameters of the three-segment piecewise-linear function of Figure

13b can be controlled by resistors R1, R2, R3 [26]. The resistors may be replaced by an active device as shown in Figure 13a [27] and can be controlled by voltage sources which are easily integrated. Simulation results of the different N_shape neuron characteristics are shown in Figure 14 for different parameter values.

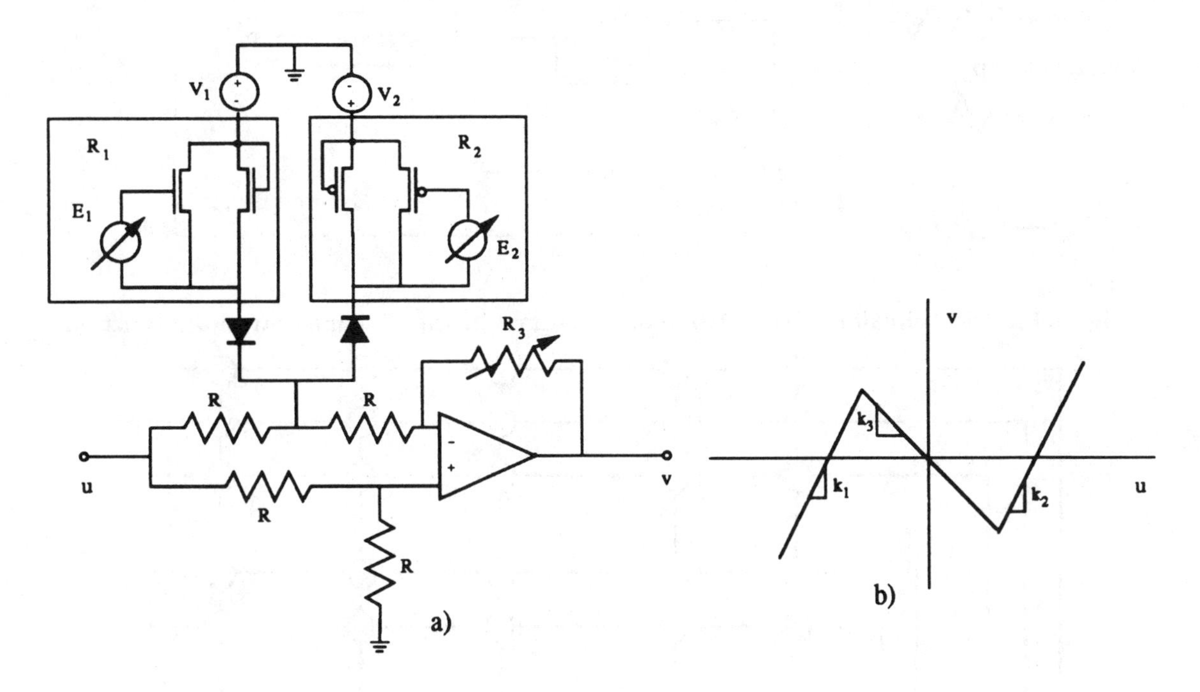

Fig.13 a) The circuit for the N-shape neuron, b) The characteristic of the neuron.

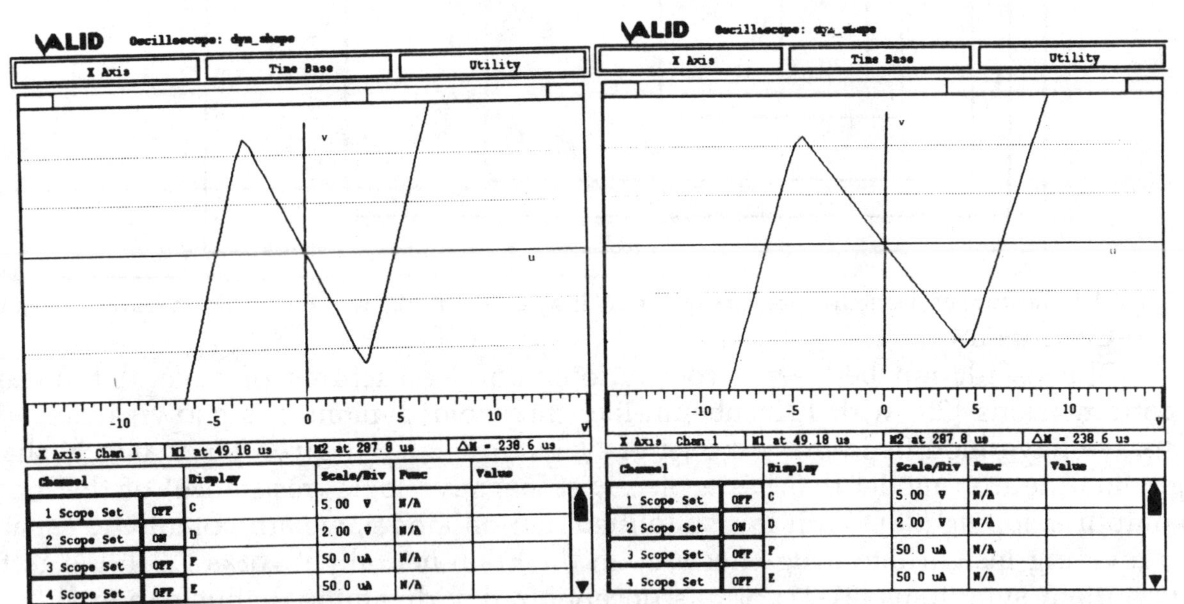

Fig. 14 Circuit Simulation Results using SPICE for different N shape Characteristics

The single neuron and the collective neuron network can be implemented by the circuits shown in Figure 15 and 16.

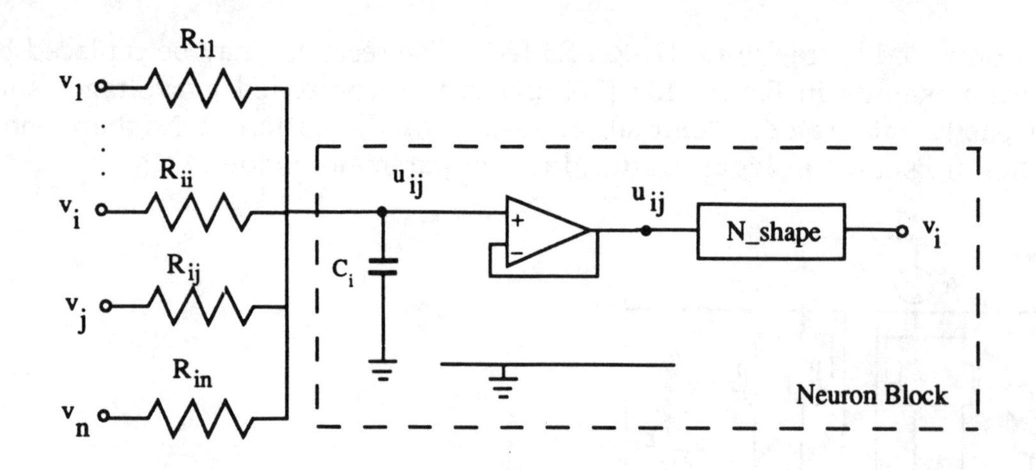

Fig. 15 Electrical circuit implementation of a neuron with the N-shaped threshold function

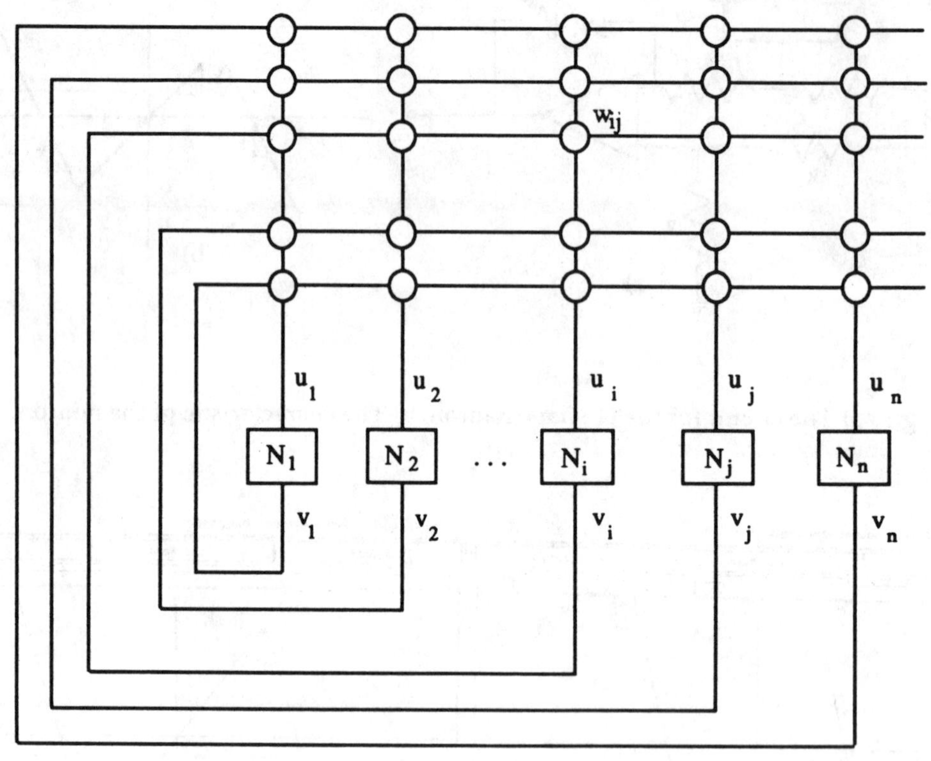

Fig.16 Architecture of the neural network circuit, N is a neuron block, w is the Hebbian learned weight

6. Conclusion

The oscillation between two spatiotemporal structures of several thousand chaotic neurons [28] with Feigenbaum-like threshold dynamics is shown in Fig. 17. Also, we have modified binary model of Nagumo-Fitzhugh given an analog N-shape sigmoidal neuron model that has a piecewise negative logic (resistance) of the input-to-output mapping [28]. With this simplified neuron model, we are potentially capable of providing insight into drug effects upon the brain neural networks [13-19], e.g., the intermittent symptoms [21-21] of misconception, day dreaming, hallucination [12, 28], or other dynamics effects in brain [22] and in neuroscience [23-24]. We expect that collective chaos is informative because (1) an emergent property as evident by the collective oscillations as show in Fig. 17 of neural images in a much lower dimensionality than the degrees of freedom of individual neurons and (2) random noise interference leading to jamming as evident by the collective blackening and whitening effect of neural images as shown in IJCNN-92 Beijing [28].

Fig. 17 While image I is the original memory, image K is presented in the convergent hybrid IK image (left) versus the oscillation between I and K (right).

Our conclusions are:

•collective interaction of nonlinear dynamics can yield an emergent reduction in the dimensionality or degrees of freedom among individual chaos--the switch-on of collective chaos

• noise phenomena can produce a de-locking of the collective chaos-- the switch-off of the collective chaos.

We have introduced the (artificial) neural images as the graphical output of collective behaviors. Indeed, these figures have supported that goal of reduced dimensionality in the collective chaos. Further work [10,11] will be needed to demonstrate mathematically the emergent collective property of neural chaos.

Recently, T. Yamakawa at Kyushu I. T., Japan, has reported a chaos chip Thus, the real time chaos information processing, to control chaos or to process chaos, is becoming imminent.

Acknowledgement

The supports of NSWCDD Independent Research Funds (HS & GR) and the ONR Young Navy Scientist Award (BT) are acknowledged.

References

[1]. A. Garfinkel, M. Spano, W. Ditto, J. Weiss, "Controlling Cardiac Chaos," Science, Vol.257, pp.1230-1235, 28 Aug. 1992.
Dante Chialvo, Robert Gilmour Jr., Jose Jalife,"Low dimensional chaos in cardiac tissue," Nature Vol.343, pp.653-657, 1990;
L. Glass & M. Mackey, "From Clocks to Chaos. The Rhythms of Life 1-248 (Princeton Univ. Press, 1988);
H. Hayashi, S. Ishizuka, K. Hirakawa, Phys. Lett. 98A, 474-476, 1983.

[2]. W.J. Freeman,"petit mal seizure spikes in olfactory bulb and cortex caused by runaway inhibition after exhaustion of excitation," Brain Res. Rev. 11:259-284, 1986
W. J. Freeman, "Simulation of Chaotic EEG Patterns with a Dynamic Model of the Olfactory System," Biol. Cybern. Vol. 56, pp. 139-1150. 1987;
W. Freeman,"The Physiology of Perception," Sci, Am. pp. 78-85, Feb. 1991;
Y. Yao, W. Freeman,"Model of Biological Pattern Recognition with Spatially Chaotic Dynamics," Neural Networks, Vol. 3, pp. 153-170, 1990;
B. Baird,"Nonlinear Dynamics of Pattern Formation and Pattern Recognition in the Rabbit Olfactory Bulb," Physica 22D,150-175, 1986.
[3]. Leon O. Chua, editor of special issue on "Chaotic Systems," Proc. IEEE, Vol. 75, no. 8, August 1987; in it specifically, A. Rodriguez-Vazquez, et al, "Chaos from switched-capacitor circuits: discrete maps,"Proc. IEEE vol. 75, pp.1109-1106, Aug. 1987;
Hao Bai-Lin, Editor of 41 Reprints & 900 Author-indexed References in relation to "Chaos," World Scientific Publishing, Singapore (reprint upto 1985 Vol. 1)
[4]. L. D. Harmon,"Studies with artificial neuron I: Properties and functions of an artificial neuron," Kybernetik Vol. 1, 89-101, 1961;
E.R. Caianiello, A. DeLuca, "Decision equation for binary systems. Application to neuronal behavior, " Kybernetik Vol. 3, pp.33-40, 1966.
[5]. J. Nagumo, S. Sato, "On a response characteristic of a mathematical neuron model," Kybernetik Vol. 10, pp.155-164, 1972;
S. Yoshizawa, H. Osada, J. Nagumo,"Pulse sequence generated by a degenerate Analog neuron model," Bio Cyb. Vol. 45, pp. 23-33, 1982.
[6]. Gen Matsumoto,K.Aihra,Y.Hanyu,N.Takahashi, S. Yoshizawa, J. Nagumo,"Chaos and Phase Locking in Normal Squid Axons, "Phys.Lett.A**123**, 162-166, 1987;K.Aihara,T.Takabe,M.Toyoda,"Chaotic Neural Network,"Phys.Lett.**A144**,333-340,1990.
[7]. G. Basti, A. Perrone, V. Cimagalli, M. Giona, E. Pasero, G. Morgavi,"A Dynamic Approach to Invariant Feature Extraction from Time-Varying Inputs by Using Chaos in Neural Nets," IJCNN-91 San Diego, Vol. III, pp. 505-510.
[8]. H. Szu, G. Rogers," Single Neuron Chaos," IJCNN-92 Baltimore,Vol. III,pp.103-108.
H. Szu, G. Rogers,"Generalized McCullouch-Pitts Neuron Model with Threshold Dynamics,"IJCNN-92 Baltimore,Vol. III,pp.535-540 (June 7-11,1992).
K. Aihara, G. Matsumoto, "Chaotic oscillations and bifurcations in squid giant axons,"In; Chaos,A.V. Holden (ed), Princeton Univ. Press, Chapter 12, pp. 257-269, 1986;
Harold Szu,"A Dynamic Reconfigurable Neural Network", annotated by Walter Freeman, J. Neural Network Computing, Vol.1 pp.3-23,special issue 1989; Harold Szu,"Neural Networks based on Peano Curves and Hairy Neurons", Telematics and Informatics (Pergamon Press), Vol. 7, pp.403-430, 1990.
[9]. A.E. Jackson, "Perspectives of Nonlinear Dynamics," Vol. 1&2, Cambridge Univ.P.;
Lipo Wang, E. Pichler, J. Ross,"Oscillations and Chaos in neural networks: An Exactly solvable model," Proc. Natl. Acad. Sci. USA, Vol. 87, pp. 9467-9471, 1990;
B. Derrida, R. Meir, Phys. Rev. A 38, pp.3116-3119, 1988;H. Sompolinsky, I. Kanter, Phys. Rev. Lett. Vol. 57, pp.2861-2864, 1986. D. Hansel, H. Sompolinsky, "Synchronization and Computation in a Chaotic Neural Network," Phys. Rev. Lett.68,pp.718-721, 1992.
[10]. M. Zak, "An Unpredictable-Dynamics Approach to neural intelligence," IEEE Expert,4-10, Aug. 1991

[11]. T. Hogg, B. Huberman,"Controlling Chaos in Distributed Systems," IEEE Trans, SMC-21, 1325-1332.
[12]. G. B. Ermentrout, J. D. Cowan,"A Mathematical theory for Visual Hallucination Paterns, " Bio. Cyber. vol. 34. p. 137, 1979
[13]. C. Von der Malsburg & E. Bienenstock, " Statistical coding and short term synaptic plasticity: a chime for knowledge representation in the brain," In Bienenstock (Ed.), "Disordered System and Biological Organization," NATO ASI Series Vol. F20, Berlin-Heidelberg-New York, 1986, pp. 247-271.
[14]. J. C. Principe, P. Lo, "Chaotic Dynamics of Time-Delay Neural Networks,"IJCNN-91 San Diego, Vol. II, pp. 403-409.
[15].M.Y.Choi,"Dynamic Model of Neural Networks,"Phys.Rev.Lett.61,2809-2812, 1988.
[16]. Shun-Ichi Amari, "Field Theory of Self-Organizing Neural Nets," IEEE Trans. Sys. Man & Cyb. Vol. SMC-13, pp.741-748, 1983;
S-I. Amari, Proc IEEE Vol. 59, pp.35-46, 1971; S-I. Amari & K. Maginu, "Statistical Neurodynamics of Associative memory," Neural networks Vol. 1, pp.63-73, 1988.
[17]. J. M. Kowalski, G.L. Albert, B. K. Rhoades, G. W. Eioll, "Neural Networks with Bursting Activity," to appear in Neural Networks 1992.
[18]. A. Bulsara, E. W. Jacobs, T. Zhou, F. Moss, L. Kiss, "Stochastic Resonance in a single neuron model theory and analog simulation," J. theor. Biol. **152**, 531-555, 1991.
[19]. A. Longtin, A. Bulsara, F. Moss, "Time-Interval in Bistable Systems and the Noise-induced Transmission of Information by Sensory Neurons," Phy. Rev. Letts,Vol. 67, pp. 656-659.
[20]. A. J. Mandell,"From intermittency to transitivity in neuropsychobiological flows," Am. Physiol. Soc., R484-R494, 1983.
[21]. R. Fitzhugh, "Impulses and Physiological states in theoretical models of nerve membrane," Biophysic. J. Vol. 1, pp. 445-466, 1961.
[22]. Karl Pribram, "Languages of the Brain experimental paradoxes and principles in neuropsychology", Prentice-hall, 1971
[23]. Science special issue:"Frontiers of Neurosciences" 1989
[24[. I. Tsuda,"Dynamic link of memory-choatic memory map in nonequilibrium neural networks," Neural Networks, Vol.5, pp.313,326, 1992
[25]. E.K. Blum and Xin Wang, "Stability of Fixed Points and Periodic Orbits and Bifurcations in Analog Neural Networks," Neural Networks, Vol. 5, pp. 577-587, 1992.
[26]. T. Yamakawa, T. Miki, E. Uchino,"A Chaotic Chip for Analyzing Nonlinear Discrete Dynamical Network Systems," Proc. 2nd. Int'l Conf. Fuzzy Logic & Neural Networks, Iizuka, Japan, 1992, pp.563-566.
[27]. G. Moon, M. E. Zaghloul, R. W. Newcomb, "An Enhancement Mode MOS Voltage-Controlled Linear Resistor with Large Dynamic Range," IEEE Trans. on CAS, CAS-37, pp.1284-1288, Oct. 1990
[28]. H. Szu, B. Telfer, G. Rogers, Kyoung Lee, Gyu Moon, M. Zaghloul, M. Loew,"Collective Chaos in Neural Networks," Int'l Joint Conf. Neural Networks, IJCNN-92, Beijing China, Nov 1-6, 1992.
[29]. D.R. Hofstadter, "Metamagical Themas: Questing for the Essence of Mind and Pattern," Chapter 16 ("Mathematical Chaos and Strange Attractors"), Basic Books: NY, 1985, pp364-395

IV. Perceptual Processing

Chapter 14

Neuronal Encoding of Information Related to Visual Perception, Memory, and Motivation

Barry J. Richmond, Timothy J. Gawne,
Troels W. Kjaer and John A. Hertz

Laboratory of Neuropsychology
National Institute of Mental Health
Bethesda, MD 20892

NEURONAL ENCODING OF INFORMATION RELATED TO VISUAL PERCEPTION, MEMORY, AND MOTIVATION.

Barry J. Richmond, Timothy J.Gawne,
Troels W. Kjaer and John A. Hertz

Laboratory of Neuropsychology
National Institute of Mental Health,
Bethesda, MD 20892.

Introduction.

The brain can be viewed as an information processing system using neurons as the individual information processing elements. Our goal is to learn how the processing done by these individual elements contributes to the complex properties of cognition, particularly perception and memory. We have used our analytic results to form models that describe the functions of individual neurons.

Neurons as Communications Channels.

We have conceptualized neurons as communication channels, so that we could analyze their responses using techniques from signal processing, statistics, systems analysis, and information theory. By formalizing our task in terms of information theory, the stages of processing can be described quantitatively, allowing systematic measurements and thereby providing a basis for comparing the processing in different places in the brain. Originally we developed this approach to analyze data from single neurons. However, it can be applied to any experiment that can be described in terms of an input-output (stimulus-response) relation.

The central quantities in information theory are probabilities. In our experiments the relevant probabilities are those which describe the stimulus-response relation. The mutual or transmitted information is defined as:

$$T(s;r)=\sum_{s} p(s|r)\log\frac{p(s|r)}{p(s)}.$$

Since we control $p(s)$, it is possible to calculate the information a neuron carries about a stimulus set if we can estimate, for each stimulus, the probability, $p(s|r)$, that it elicited a given response. Our work therefore focuses on the problem of estimating $p(s|r)$ from the data.

In our approach, in which we concentrate only on the probabilities and the information we can calculate from them, we do not attempt to define or identify the mechanisms connecting stimulus and response. The complexity of brain structures and mechanisms often makes it difficult to know how these structures and mechanisms are related to information processing. However, understanding the processing done by a neuron or group of neurons provides a necessary framework for inferring and positing the underlying mechanisms.

Stimuli.

Information is always information about something; that is, it depends on the stimulus set used. In order to have a quantity that can be considered generic, we need a large and diverse stimulus set. In our work so far we have used a set of mathematical functions, the Walsh functions, to construct a set of black-and-white stimuli, Figure 1. These stimuli were chosen because they can be considered to be a basic set of picture features. If the stimulus-response relation is approximately linear, the responses to these stimuli can be used to predict the responses to any black and white stimulus of the same or lower resolution. Thus, they have advantages for testing certain types of models.

To apply information theory, we need to represent our stimuli and responses mathematically as codes. For our stimuli, the input coding is very simple. We assign a unique number to each stimulus pattern. If more than one stimulus parameter is varied in an experiment, e.g., the stimulus pattern and its luminance, these variables can be accounted for by choosing codes that incorporate all of the combinations of pattern and luminance.

The choice of output code is less straightforward. In fact it is the heart of our problem. As we measure it, the neuronal response code is an impulse train. We can describe it mathematically by dividing the time course of the measurement into tiny intervals (ca. 1 ms) and indicating whether each one contained a spike. For example, in a response to a stimulus that lasted 300 ms, there would be 300 data points per response at a 1 ms resolution. This would be a 300-dimensional code. The number of responses that would be needed to analyze data of such high dimensionality would be very large, however, and sufficient data are not usually available. Furthermore, we expect that such a code would be highly redundant; it is not plausible that each such neuronal response conveys 300 bits of information. On both these grounds we need to seek a compressed representation or code.

We have shown that the data can be compressed to a small and hence more manageable dimensionality using principal components, Figure 2. This method of compression is optimal in the least-mean-squared error sense (Ahmed and Rao 1975; Richmond and Optican 1987). A few principal components, typically on the order of 5-10 in our experiments, capture most (typically 70-90%) of the stimulus-related variation in the responses (Richmond and Optican 1987; Richmond and Optican 1990; McClurkin *et al.* 1991a; McClurkin *et al.* 1991c). This places an upper limit on the dimensionality of the neural response code.

This is not meant to imply that individual principal components are the intrinsic neural code used by the brain. Any arbitrary combination of the first 5-10 principal components would work as well, and without further studies we do not know the intrinsic structure used by the brain. The point is to determine how many principal components or combinations of them are needed to represent the code.

Most studies of visual processing and related higher functions have assumed that single neurons carry most of their information within a simple one-dimensional code based on the average frequency of the neuronal impulse train. However, there has always been a question as to whether information might be carried in the temporal structure of the firing pattern as well as in the average response strength. Is the average firing adequate, or do we need to account for the temporal variation?

The first principal component has been shown to be closely correlated with the average firing rate in all of the brain regions we have studied. Therefore, any information that is represented by principal components other than the first must be encoded in the temporal variation of the firing, Figure 3.

Treating the principal components as a response code, we calculated the amount of information carried about the stimuli by single neurons at four stages in the visual system: parvocellular layers in the lateral geniculate nucleus, striate cortex, lateral pulvinar, and inferior temporal (IT) cortex. We found that stimulus-related information is carried in several principal components, showing that single neuronal responses can be considered to contain a multidimensional code throughout the visual system (Richmond *et al.* 1987; Richmond and Optican 1987; Optican and Richmond 1987; Richmond *et al.* 1990; Richmond and Optican 1990; McClurkin *et al.* 1991b; McClurkin *et al.* 1991a; Gawne *et al.* 1991). One of these dimensions describes the average firing rate. This conveys more information than any of the others, but other dimensions also carry significant information. Our studies show that the amount of information carried by any one neuron is about the same throughout the visual system, but the proportion carried in the temporal modulation rises the farther the station is from the retinal input, e.g. greater in primary visual cortical neurons than in lateral geniculate neurons, and greater still in IT cortex (McClurkin *et al.* 1991c).

Multiple stimulus-feature encoding.

In general, neurons change their responses as each of several stimulus features are varied. For example, neurons in primary visual cortex are sensitive to both the pattern and brightness of visual stimuli. However, it is not at all clear that the relation of the responses is orderly enough (i.e. linear) so that the response to a particular combination of features can be predicted from studies in which only one feature at a time is varied. Therefore, we thought it important to study how single neurons encode information about the stimulus features as they are all varied. We investigated how much information neurons convey about the luminance and duration of the stimulus as well as its pattern. The finding that single neuronal responses are multidimensional naturally leads to the question of whether information about these different parameters is encoded in specific aspects of the neuronal response.

Using analysis of variance (ANOVA) we found that the effects of stimulus pattern, luminance, and duration on the response could not be described by simply adding their individual effects: they had a significant nonlinear interaction. This interaction means that tuning curves derived by varying each of these parameter alone can not be used to predict the effects that arise when both are varied. Furthermore, varying the stimulus along one dimension will not necessarily affect only one aspect of the response. For example, if the pattern is changed, the amounts of all of the principal components would change; the same would be true for luminance and duration. Indeed, one of the unfortunate aspects of nonlinear systems is that there is no systematic method to describe the nonlinearity revealed by the interaction term.

Finding that the responses had a nonlinear interaction in the ANOVA did not answer the question about how much information was encoded in the responses. Our analysis showed that information about all three stimulus parameters (pattern, luminance, and duration) was encoded in each of the first 3 principal components. The largest amount of information about pattern was found in the first principal component, but the largest amount of information about stimulus luminance and duration was found in the second and third principal components. The amount of information about pattern, luminance, and duration, each considered alone, added up to the amount found when all three were considered together, Figure 4. In spite of the nonlinear effects revealed by the ANOVA, the information about the different stimulus features could be separated by an appropriate decoding mechanism, such as the model used to calculate the information (Gawne *et al.* 1991).

Memory and stimulus context.

Once we had developed methods to study the representation of information by single neurons, we turned to issues that motivated the development of these methods, i.e. higher functions such as memory. We used a simple memory task, the match-to-sample task, to study how information related to the different demands of this task, i.e. seeing, remembering, and matching the remembered pattern, is encoded in the responses of single neurons in area TE of inferior temporal cortex (Eskandar *et al.* 1992). The amount of information about the stimulus being viewed was found to be the same in all three contexts, sample, match and nonmatch. The neurons carry independent information in their responses about which stimulus appeared, about the stimulus context, i.e., whether it was sample, match or nonmatch, and about the stimulus being searched for in the test situation, i.e. the remembered stimulus, Figure 5. Furthermore, information about the stimulus was carried in both the mean firing rate and the temporal structure of the firing pattern, whereas the information about the remembered stimulus and the behavioral context was carried almost entirely in the temporal structure. Thus, the neuronal response can not be interpreted simply as a message about a stimulus feature, but rather as a description of both the stimulus and the conditions under which it is being observed.

By examining the brain sections and relating them to the recording depths, we also found that the amount of information about the stimulus pattern varied with the location of the recorded neuron. Neurons on the inferior convexity of the temporal lobe conveyed substantially more information about stimulus pattern than neurons in the lower bank of the superior temporal sulcus, indicating that area TE can be subdivided according to the type of information carried by the neurons.

Neuronal networks in the brain.

Until recently our work has focused on the responses of single neurons. However, neurons are linked in complex circuits, so we need to study how groups of neurons process information. Most of the investigations into the relations among multiple neurons have depended heavily on cross-correlation analysis of the timings of individual spikes. This approach is valuable for inferring whether neurons share common signals, and whether they might be closely connected within a circuit. However, cross-correlation of the spikes does not directly examine how the information conveyed by different neurons is related.

Therefore, we recorded pairs of neurons simultaneously with a single electrode by separating the spike waveforms using a spike sorting device with modifications that we developed (patent applied for). We wished to determine whether neurons carry (1) independent information, (2) redundant information that increases the reliability of the messages, or (3) information encoded in a joint code that is not present in the response of either neuron considered alone. We isolated the signals from 28 pairs of neurons and found that the information carried by the joint response was nearly equal to the sum of the amounts of information carried by each neuron considered alone, Figure 6. None of the pairs carried information that was essentially the same, i.e. redundant, nor did any pairs carry substantially more information than the amount predicted by adding the information from the two considered individually, i.e. there was no evidence for a joint code (Gawne and Richmond in press).

If adjacent neurons shared the same set of inputs and had identical characteristics, they might be expected to carry the same information, yet they do not. The relative independence of adjacent neurons preserves a rich local description of many stimulus properties. Nonetheless, even a small amount of redundancy places an upper limit on the amount of information that can be carried by a pool of neurons -- a pool of any size can carry no more than 1/y times the amount of information carried by one neuron, where y is the proportion of redundant information, here found to be 0.2. Thus, it is critical that neurons carry information that is as independent as possible to overcome the severe constraints of this redundancy.

Finding that adjacent neurons are largely independent places limitations on how the results of experiments based on population techniques can be interpreted. Because the neurons in local groups may carry out a great deal of independent processing, the activity revealed by averaging techniques, which measure local averages such as optical recording and evoked potentials, can not be easily interpreted in terms of neuronal information processing.

Modeling.

We have studied two types of models, both of which are important for understanding the computations done by the brain. One model we used describes the computation performed by a neuron, or, more accurately, the computation performed by the visual system up through the neuron under study. It represents the mapping from stimulus image (and context) to the neuronal signal. Thus, this type of forward (encoding) model is basically an extension of receptive field models.

Another class of models goes in the opposite direction. Its purpose is to decode the neuronal signal and tell us which stimulus produced it, or the behavioral condition the monkey was in when the response was recorded. This kind of backward (decoding) model arises naturally when we want to calculate the information carried by a response in terms of the conditional probabilities $p(s|r)$. The information calculations described above were based on models of this class.

Response prediction or forward (encoding) models.

For LGN and striate cortical neurons we were able to model the dependence of the responses (as represented in their principal components) on the spatial variation and luminance of the stimulus patterns (Gawne *et al.* 1991; Richmond *et al.* 1989; Richmond and Optican 1992). In these studies we used the responses to the Walsh stimuli to predict successfully the response to other stimuli: a dot in the middle of a uniform surround in the lateral geniculate nucleus, and bars or complex sets of bars in striate cortical complex cells. These models had a simple input pixel array as the input, Figure 7. The models were not linear. For the LGN the only nonlinearity needed was a local (i.e. pixel-by-pixel) sigmoidal transformation of the input pixel luminances. The transformed luminances were fed into 3 arrays of weights rather like receptive field maps, one array being associated with each of the first 3 principal components. The transformed image was multiplied by the weight corresponding to that pixel location, and these were summed for the whole array. The output of each array was used to determine the coefficient of the associated principal component, first, second, or third. These weighted principal components were summed to form a predicted response. When the weight arrays were examined, the first showed a clear center-surround-like structure, which looked like the classical receptive field -- a satisfying result since the first principal component largely represents the average firing, the classical measure of response. The model did not require this to be true! The weight array associated with the second principal component had structures that looked like excitatory-inhibitory dipoles, or deep valleys. It is this structure that gives rise to the temporal modulation that was present. Including this second set of weights significantly improved both the amount of variance explained by the model, and the accuracy of predicting arbitrary stimuli from the responses to the Walsh patterns.

The success of these models established two features of the stimulus-response relation. First, they support our previous conclusion that significant stimulus-related information is encoded in the temporal structure of neuronal responses, because the models fit the data better and make better predictions in the least mean-squared-error sense when higher principal components are included. Second, in these early stages of visual processing, the stimulus-response relation, although nonlinear, is smooth and well-behaved, as shown by our ability to compensate for the nonlinearities relatively easily. However, the LGN model was less complex and hence closer to being linear than that for the complex striate cells.

We have also constructed a nonlinear model of the stimulus-response relation for cells in inferior temporal cortex, but with a new twist: Since IT neurons are involved in memory, we attempted to model not only the dependence of the response on the current stimulus, but also its dependence (if any) on the immediately preceding stimulus (Eskandar *et al.* 1992). We found that the mean squared error was smaller when both the present and past stimuli were used as inputs, confirming that IT neurons are involved in remembering past stimuli.

We used another nonclassical network model to examine the interaction between information about remembered stimuli and information about stimuli currently being viewed (Eskandar *et al.* 1992). This model considered memory to be a 4-step process: (1) Encode the current stimulus. (2) Recall the code for a remembered stimulus. (3) Compare the two codes. (4) Decide whether they are similar or different. To examine the comparison step we had the model generate two waveforms in time, one for the currently viewed stimulus and one for the remembered one. We tried modeling their interaction in two ways: as multiplication or addition of the two responses on a point-by-point basis through time. The multiplication model performed better. Thus, mechanisms that can implement multiplication operations are good candidates for further study.

Neural networks for calculating information.

The calculations of information described in this paper are based on decoding models for $p(s|r)$, the probability of stimulus s, given response r. However, the particular models in our earlier calculations were used mainly to calculate information and were restricted by computational limitations to low-dimensional representations of the response. In practice, we have been limited to working with no more than about 4 principal components. Recently, we have studied new models that overcome many of these limitations.

The modeling procedure has been changed in two ways. First, a more flexible parametrization of the fit using feedforward neural networks has been introduced, Figure 8 (Hertz *et al.* 1991; Hertz *et al.*). Such a parametrization has been shown to be capable of fitting any continuous input-output relation for a sufficiently large number of fitting parameters. These parameters are determined by maximizing a goodness-of-fit measure. Second, the tendency to overfitting (too many parameters, fitting the noise rather than the signal) is controlled by validating the fit on test data not used in making the fit. The number of parameters used is chosen to give the best fit on the test data.

This method yields better fits than the old one and, consequently, more reliable estimates of transmitted information when applied to our previously obtained data. It also permits much higher-dimensional response representations. This allows us to test for effects of finer temporal structure than is contained in the first 4 principal components and to analyze responses from several neurons simultaneously.

In a first test of this method, we made such fits for IT neurons to extract the information in their responses about the behavioral context in which whey were elicited. In the first fit, all the responses used were obtained in either the sample or match condition, and the task was to estimate the probablity that a given response had been elicited under one or the other condition. Similar fits were made for sample-nonmatch and match-nonmatch discriminations. The neuronal responses were represented by 1, 3, or 5 principal components (Eskandar *et al.* 1992).

The results showed three features. First, regardless of the number of stimulus patterns, there was always some information, on the order of 0.1 bits, about the behavioral context of the response, i.e., whether the stimulus was sample, match, or nonmatch. Second, the discrimination between states was better when the identity of the visual pattern had been determined. Finally, the amount of information about the context was substantially greater when 5 principal components were used; a significant amount of this information is present in the temporal firing pattern.

Conclusions.

Neuronal responses have commonly been thought of as one-dimensional, with information carried only in their mean firing rate. This simple concept overlooks the dynamics of the responses. Our work shows that single neurons carry information encoded in multidimensional temporally modulated responses. Thus, the responses can not simply be interpreted in terms of single preferred features, but rather they contain a low dimensional description of the stimulus conditions. Knowing that the responses are multidimensional allowed us to develop models of the stimulus-response relation that account for significantly more of the response variance than can be done with a model using the more traditional mean firing rate model. Finding that adjacent neurons tend toward independent encoding seems at first counterintuitive, since these neurons probably share some common input. However, for individual neurons to contribute to the information processing within ensembles it would be essential that neurons receiving common inputs be as independent as possible because of the severe constraints of correlated noise and redundant information. Without analyzing single and groups of neurons in terms of their information processing many of these issues would be difficult to observe and understand.

FIGURE LEGENDS.

FIGURE 1. A set of black and white pictures used as stimuli. These are based on an orthogonal set of 2-dimensional functions, the Walsh-Hadamard functions, that take the values 1 and -1 over their domain. The value +1 is assigned to white and -1 to black.

FIGURE 2. The average of all of the responses to all of the stimuli and the first five principal components are on the left. The average responses elicited by two Walsh stimuli from a complex cell in striate cortex are at the upper right, and the relative amounts of the first 5 principal components needed to represent them are shown at the lower right. The average response was subtracted from each individual response before the principal components were calculated, and therefore it must be added back to reconstruct the original response.

FIGURE 3. The relation between the average first three principal components and the average firing rate for all of the Walsh stimuli for one cortical neuron. The correlation coefficient is 0.99 for the first principal component in this example. For striate cortical and lateral geniculate neurons the relation has a value of 0.98 or higher, and for inferior temporal neurons it is frequently as low as 0.90.

FIGURE 4. The amount of information about pattern (P), luminance (L) and duration (D), each taken alone, then in pairs, and finally all together. The amounts for the individual features add up to slightly less than the 3 taken together.

FIGURE 5. The amount of information about the stimulus context, sample vs match, sample vs nonmatch, and match vs nonmatch, found for 3 neurons from data collected during a sequential match-to-sample experiment. The white bar shows the amount of information carried in the first principal component, and the total height shows the amount carried by 5 principal components. The different bars show the amount of information carried when asking the neuron to distinguish the condition across more and more stimuli, here 1-32.

FIGURE 6. Histogram showing that the information coded in the response of neurons simultaneously recorded from a single electrode is nearly independent. The values are the amount calculated from the two neurons taken together divided by the amount predicted by adding the information from each neuron taken alone. Note that, although the information is close to that predicted if the neurons were independent, there is, on average, some redundant information.

FIGURE 7. A model of the multidimensional response in a lateral geniculate parvocellular neuron. The response is built from passing the image through a nonlinear, pixel-by-pixel compression, and then calculating a spatial filter that is similar to a receptive field. There are 3 such spatial filters here, each associated with a different temporal response pattern as represented by 3 principal components. The responses from each of these spatial filters are simply summed. When the nonlinearity and spatial filters are fit to model the response to the Walsh patterns, this model succeeds in predicting the responses to a set of small white or dark squares embedded in a dark or light background. The spatial filter associated with the first principal component has a center-surround structure as has been found by many exeriments in the past (Hubel and Wiesel 1962).

FIGURE 8. An artificial neural network that can be used to construct a model of $p(s|r)$. There is one output for each stimulus condition. The inputs are the principal components. The network is trained using backpropogation with a cost function equal to the negative logliklihood, or crossed-entropy. The network is checked for convergence and generalization by cross-validation, i.e., one segment of the data is withheld from the training, and when the cost function reaches a minimum for test data the training is stopped and the information is calculated. The values of the output units may be interpreted as probabilities.

REFERENCES:

Ahmed, N. and K. R. Rao (1975) *Orthogonal Transforms for Digital Signal Processing*, Springer-Verlag, Berlin.

Eskandar, E. N., B. J.Richmond, J. A. Hertz, L. M. Optican, and T. Kjaer (1992) Decoding of neuronal signals in visual pattern recognition. In *Advances in Neural Information Processing Systems*, J. E. Moody, S. J. Hanson and R. P. Lippmann, ed., pp. 356-363., San Mateo, CA..

Eskandar, E. N., B. J.Richmond, and L. M. Optican (1992) The role of inferior temporal neurons in visual memory: I. Temporal encoding of information about visual images, recalled images, and behavioral contex. J. Neurophysiol. *68:*1277-1295.

Eskandar, E. N., L. M. Optican, and B. J.Richmond (1992) The role of inferior temporal neurons in visual memory: II. Multiplying temporal waveforms related to vision and memory. J. Neurophysiol. *68:*1296-1306.

Gawne, T. J., J. W. McClurkin, B. J. Richmond, and L. M. Optican (1991) Lateral geniculate neurons in behaving primates: III. Response predictions of a channel model with multiple spatial-to-temporal filters. J. Neurophysiol. *66:*809-823.

Gawne, T. J. and B. J. Richmond (in press) Adjacent neurons in inferior temporal cortex carry independent messages. J. Neurosci..

Gawne, T. J., B. J. Richmond, and L. M. Optican (1991) Interactive effects among several stimulus parameters on the responses of striate cortical complex cells. J. Neurophysiol. *66:*379-389.

Hertz, J. A., T. Kjaer, E. N. Eskandar, and B. J. Richmond Measuring natural neural processing with artificial neural networks. International J. of Neural Systems *in press:*.

Hertz, J. A., B. J. Richmond, B. G. Hertz, and L. M. Optican (1991) Neuronal decoding. In *Pigments to Perception: Advances in Understanding Visual Processes, NATO ASI Series A*, Lee, B. and Valberg, A., ed., Vol. 203, pp. 437-446, Plenum Press, New York.

Hubel, D. H. and T. N. Wiesel (1962) Receptive fields, binocular interactions and functional architecture in the cat's striate cortex. J. Physiol. (London) *160:*106-154.

McClurkin, J. W., T. J. Gawne, L. M. Optican, and B. J. Richmond (1991a) Lateral geniculate neurons in behaving primates: II. Encoding of visual information in the temporal shape of the response. J. Neurophysiol. *66:*794-808.

McClurkin, J. W., T. J. Gawne, B. J. Richmond, L. M. Optican, and D. L. Robinson (1991b) Lateral geniculate neurons in behaving primates: I. Responses to two-dimensional stimuli. J. Neurophysiol. *66:*777-793.

McClurkin, J. W., L. M. Optican, B. J. Richmond, and T. J. Gawne (1991c) Concurrent processing and complexity of temporally encoded neuronal messages in visual perception. Science *253:*675-677.

Optican, L. M. and B. J. Richmond (1987) Temporal encoding of two-dimensional patterns by single units in primate inferior temporal cortex. III. Information theoretic analysis. J. Neurophysiol. *57:*162-178.

Richmond, B. J. and L. M. Optican (1987) Temporal encoding of two-dimensional patterns by single units in primate inferior temporal cortex: II. Quantification of response waveform. J. Neurophysiol. *57:*147-161.

Richmond, B. J. and L. M. Optican (1990) Temporal encoding of two-dimensional patterns by single units in primate primary visual cortex. II. Information transmission. J. Neurophysiol. *64:*370-380.

Richmond, B. J. and L. M. Optican (1992) The structure and interpretation of neuronal codes in the visual system. In *Neural Networks in Perception, Vol. 1*, H. Wechsler, ed., pp. 104-119, Academic Press, San Diego, CA.

Richmond, B. J., L. M. Optican, and T. J. Gawne (1989) Neurons use multiple messages encoded in temporally modulated spike trains to represent pictures. In *Seeing Contour and Colour*, J. J. Kulikowski, C. M. Dickinson, ed., pp. 701-710, Pergamon Press, Oxford.

Richmond, B. J., L. M. Optican, M. Podell, and H. Spitzer (1987) Temporal encoding of two-dimensional patterns by single units in primate inferior temporal cortex: I. Response characteristics. J. Neurophysiol. *57:*132-146.

Richmond, B. J., L. M. Optican, and H. Spitzer (1990) Temporal encoding of two-dimensional patterns by single units in primate primary visual cortex. I. Stimulus-response relations. J. Neurophysiol. *64:*351-369.

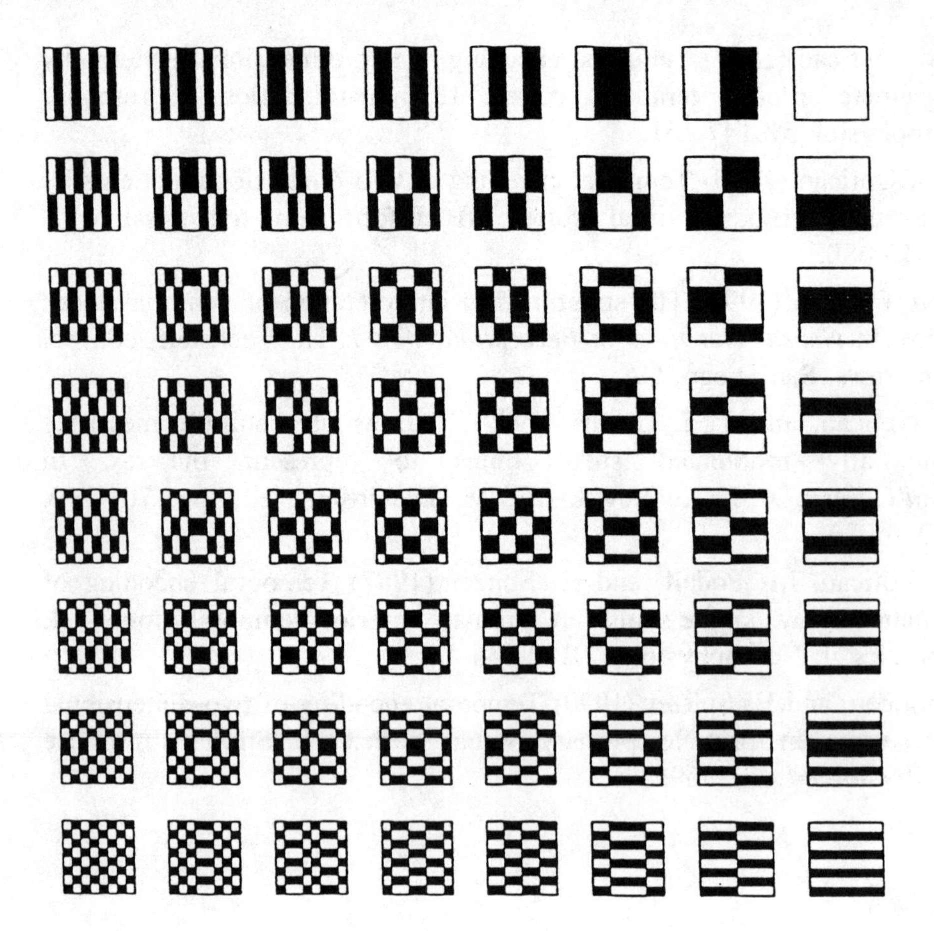

FIGURE 1

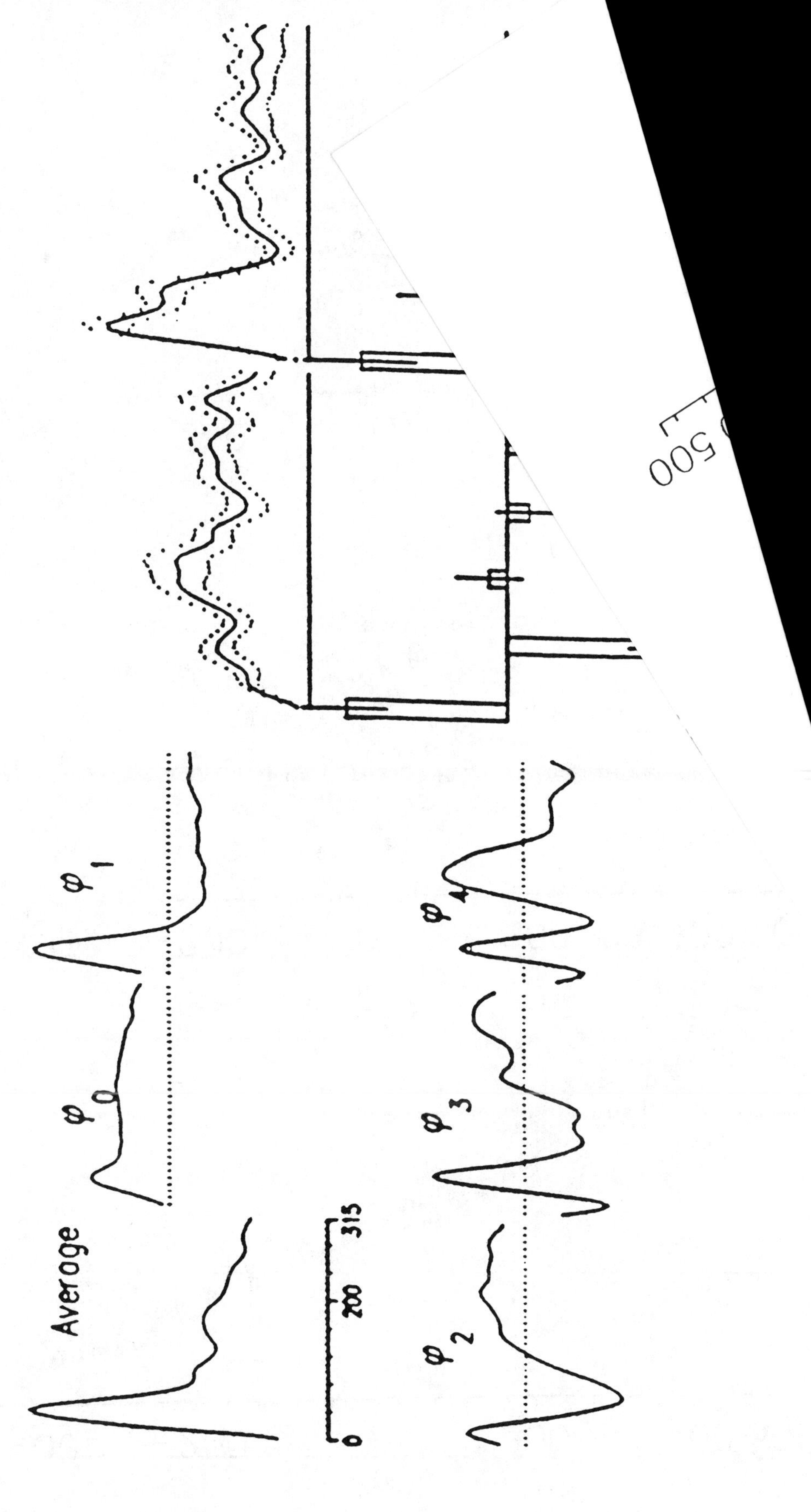
Average
φ0
φ1
φ2
φ3
φ4
0
200
315
500

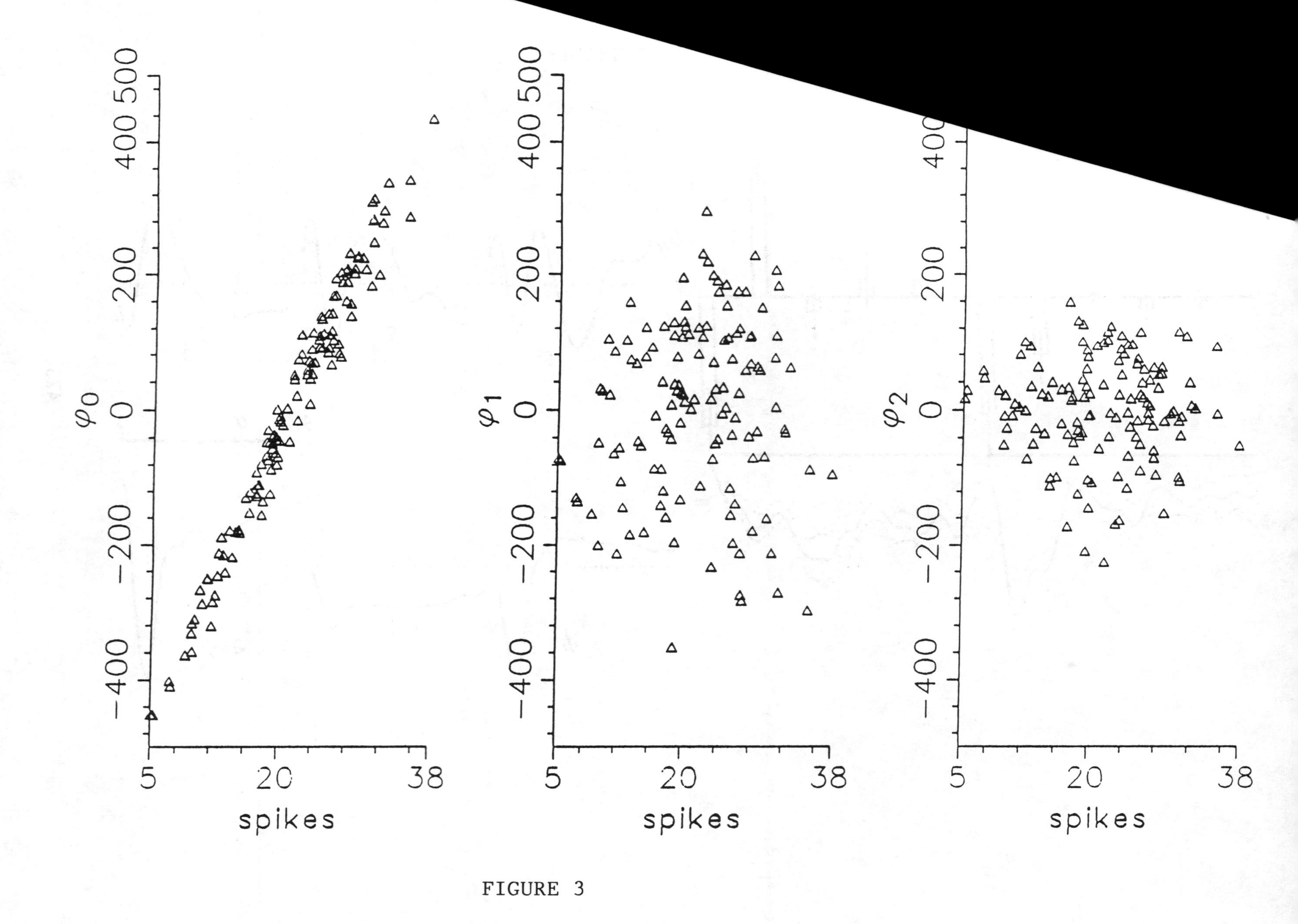

FIGURE 3

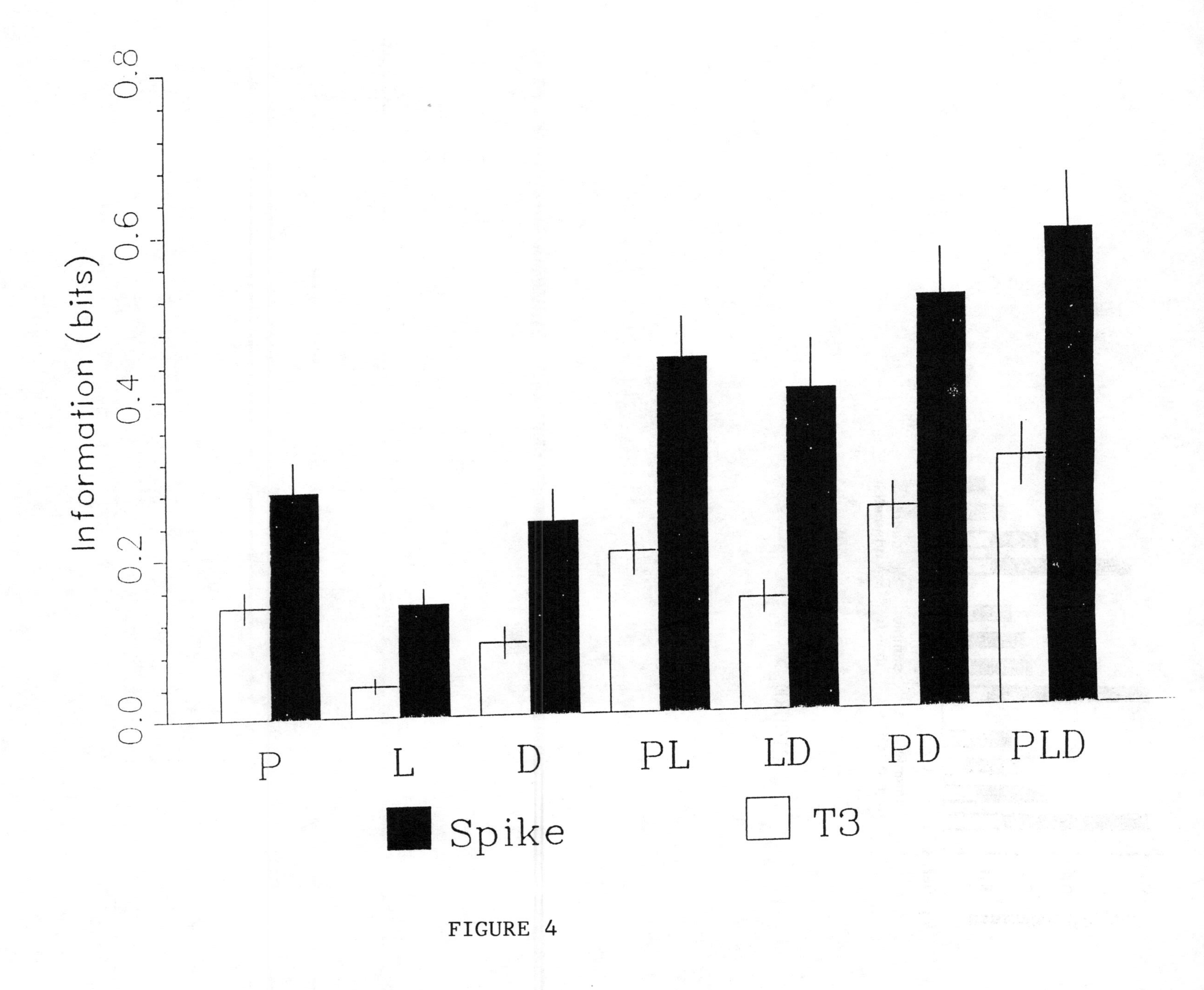

FIGURE 4

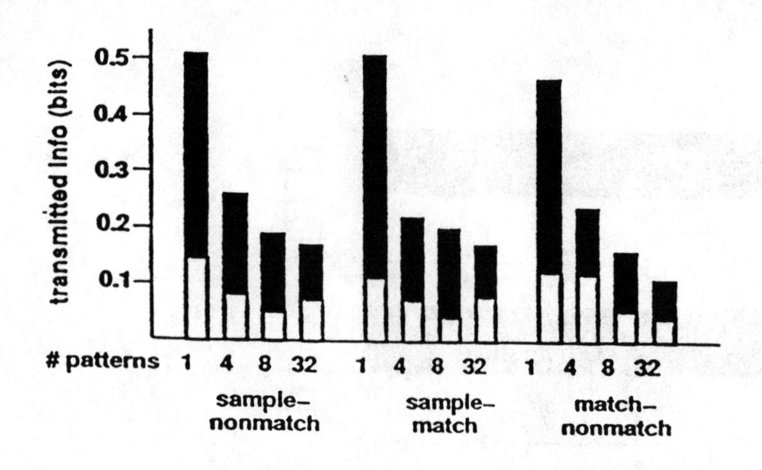
transmitted Info (bits)
0.5
0.4
0.3
0.2
0.1
patterns
1
4
8
32
1
4
8
32
1
4
8
32
sample-
nonmatch
sample-
match
match-
nonmatch

FIGURE 5

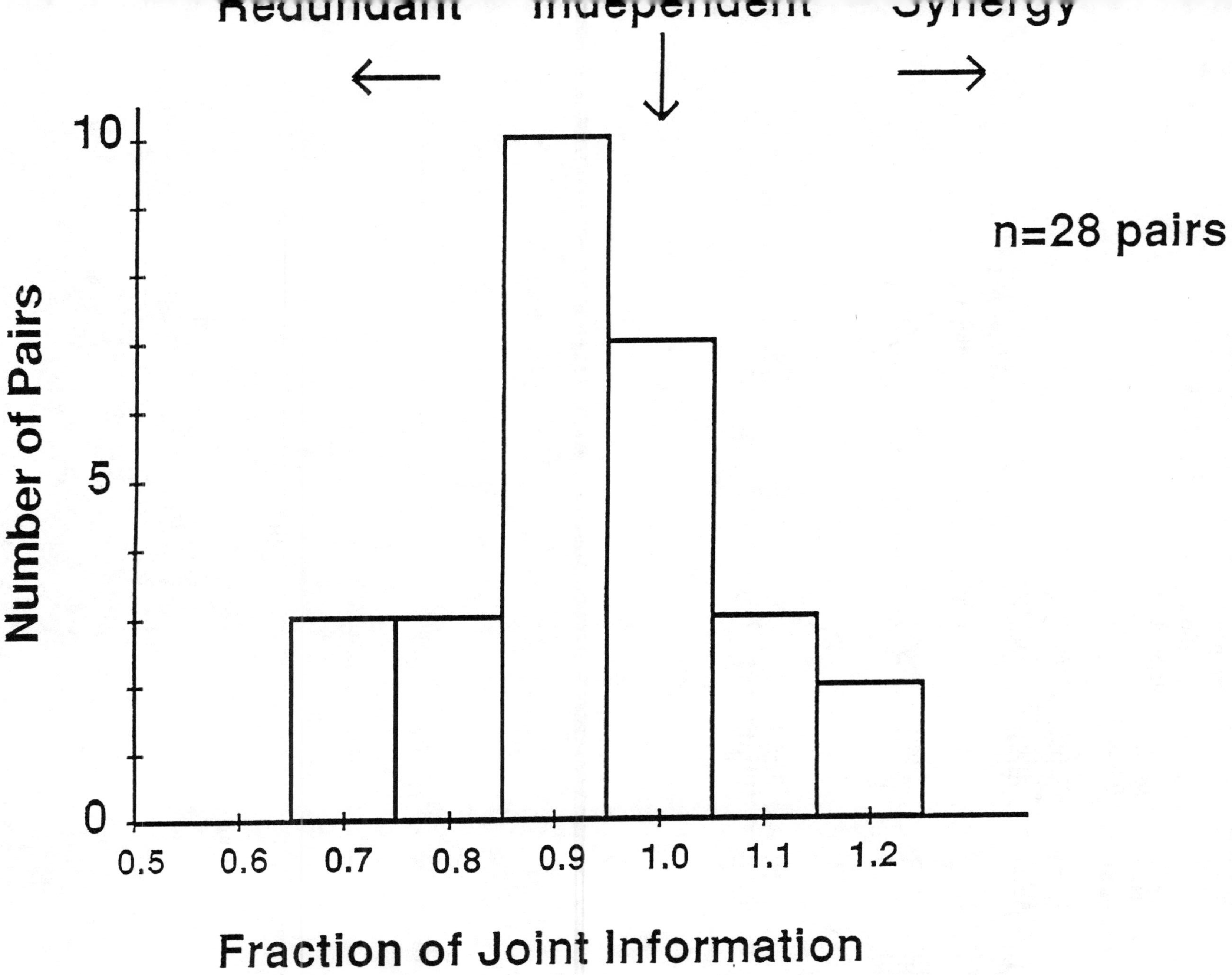

Redundant Independent Synergy

n=28 pairs

Number of Pairs

10

5

0

0.5 0.6 0.7 0.8 0.9 1.0 1.1 1.2

Fraction of Joint Information

FIGURE 6

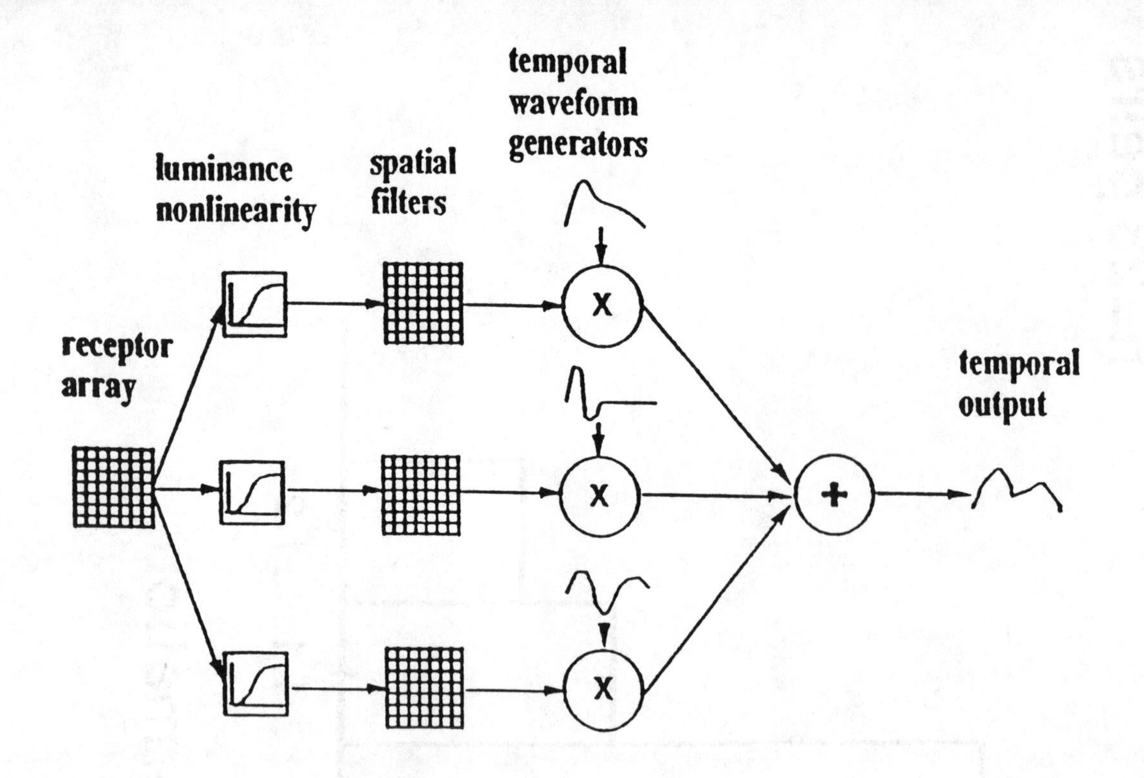
temporal
waveform
generators
luminance
nonlinearity
spatial
filters
receptor
array
X
X
X
temporal
output
+

FIGURE 7

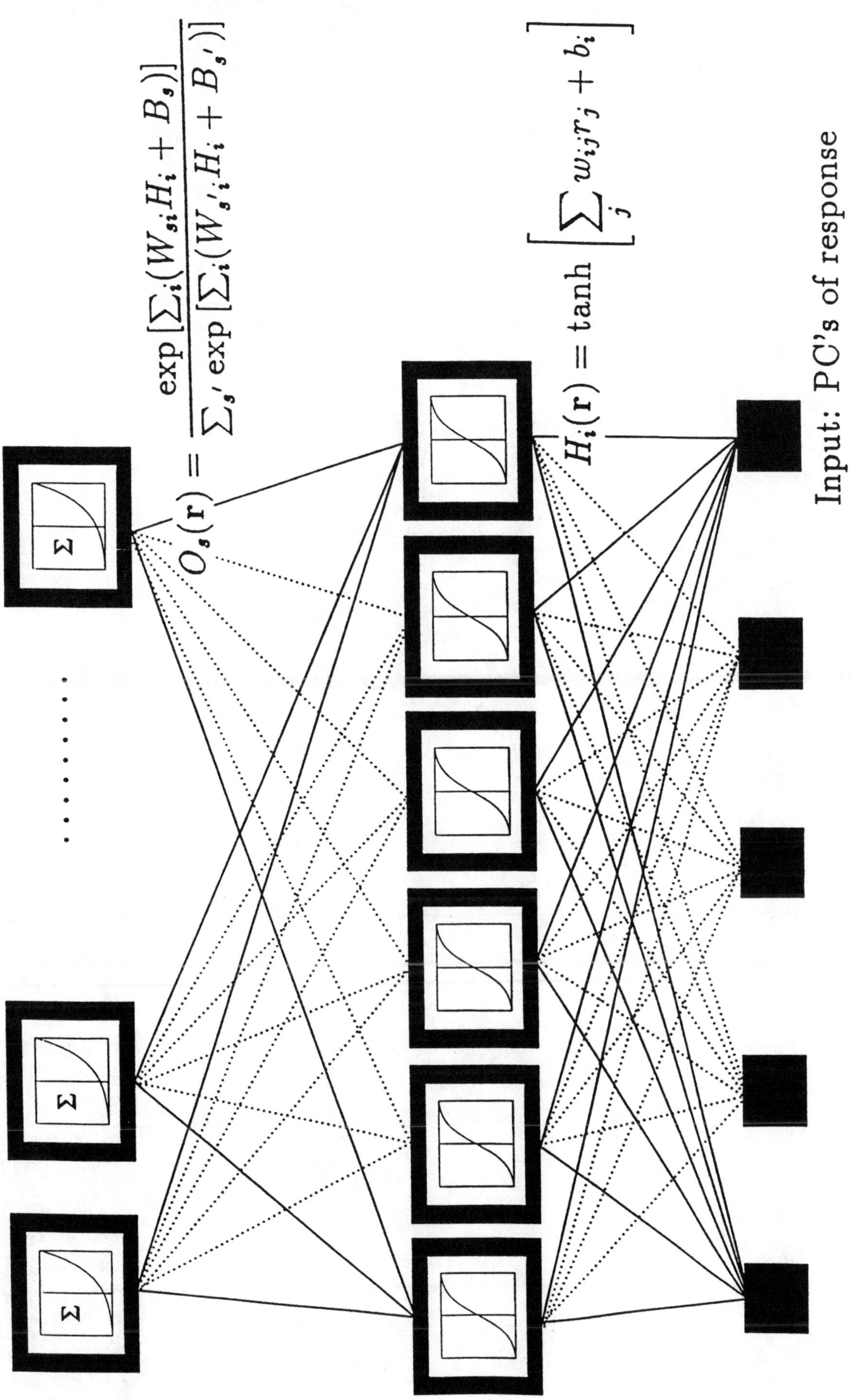

$$O_s(\mathbf{r}) = \frac{\exp\left[\sum_i (W_{si} H_i + B_s)\right]}{\sum_{s'} \exp\left[\sum_i (W_{s'i} H_i + B_{s'})\right]}$$

$$H_i(\mathbf{r}) = \tanh\left[\sum_j w_{ij} r_j + b_i\right]$$

Input: PC's of response

FIGURE 8

Chapter 15

Efferent Programming of the Striate Cortex

Bruce Bridgeman
Program in Experimental Psychology
Kerr Hall
University of California, Santa Cruz
Santa Cruz, CA 95064

Theoretical Approach

Visual perception is more than simply a flow of spatio-temporal patterns from the eyes to the brain: it requires the interaction of patterns from the eyes with stored internal information. The stored information must consist of both supplements to the optical image on one hand, and information about what sorts of patterns are presently needed from vision on the other. A central problem is how these two sources of information, retinal and extraretinal, are combined; a first step in addressing this problem is to determine where and when the combining of the two sources begins.

At subcortical levels, single-cell coding is dominated by image patterns. This paper will show, however, that by the time visual patterns reach the level of the striate cortex, information relating to the task to be performed is already being combined with sensory patterns so that neuronal activity is modified by the organism's requirements for the sensory signals being received. The function of adding context to the visual signal does not happen abruptly, in a single neuronal step, but occurs gradually. Through several successive transformations of visual patterns, context effects play a stronger and stronger role as the signal is transformed from an image of the outside world to an image of what must be done with the information.

The traditional interpretation of coding at the level of striate cortex, the first cortical processing of visual patterns, is that the optical image is elegantly transformed but that nothing further is added (Sakitt & Barlow, 1982). In theory, then, the traditional view holds that knowing the content of the optical image and of the striate cortical transformation should enable one to describe precisely what the activity of the striate cortex neurons will be.

Studies of Firing Enhancement in Striate Cortex

It is difficult to infer the role of the striate cortex in visual experience from most studies of single neurons, because single neurons in primate cortex have usually been studied in contexts where the stimuli that drive the cells have no information value from the animal's standpoint. Information in this context is defined in Shannon's terms as a reduction of uncertainty, in this case a reduction of uncertainty about which of several alternative reward contingencies is present. In single-neuron receptive field mapping studies the animals are usually anesthetized so that they are certain not to be perceiving, or they are paralyzed and unable to use visual input to control behavior. Studies of awake, behaving monkeys have become more popular for this reason. Most of them, however, involve rewarding animals for visual fixation on targets that have no relation to the stimuli being used to probe receptive fields, so that again the neurons under study are not processing information that is relevant to behavior. Such studies are valuable in defining the anatomical inputs to cortical cells and some properties of stimulus processing, but they leave open the question of the role of the cells in visual perception. Studies of receptive fields have generally shown changes in neuronal firing that disappear by about 150 msec after stimulus onset (Wurtz, 1969a, b), and the firing patterns are completely determined by the stimulus properties.

Reports of later secondary bursts of firing in monkey visual cortex are limited to a few examples fortuitously published in illustrations intended to demonstrate other results. A clear example of single cell activity about 200 msec after the primary burst of firing is seen in Wurtz (1969a), elicited by a long bar moving across a receptive field at 900°/sec. The 200-msec latency peak is also visible when the monkey makes a saccadic eye movement across the bar stimulus. The late peak consists of only 1-3 spikes in each trial, however, and is missing completely in some trials, so that it is doubtful that the phenomenon would have been apparent from simply listening to the neuron's activity during recording. The peak is apparent only after averaging, or after displaying single-cell responses to several trials in register. Even the primary response fails to occur on a few of Wurtz's trials, illustrating the labile nature of all responses in the striate cortex of awake monkeys. Clearly, something is modulating the responses of these neurons that is not present in anesthetized preparations.

Further work with awake cats and monkeys in the author's laboratory has revealed neuronal response patterns that are far more complex when behaviorally alert animals use information from the recorded neurons in a learned visual task. In the first of these studies, firing of neurons in monkey striate cortex was modulated both by image patterns and by the demands of a simultaneous brightness discrimination task (Bridgeman 1979, 1980, 1982). In the first 150 msec after onset of a briefly flashed stimulus, neuronal firing was influenced only by the stimulus, as the traditional interpretation predicts. This is the time interval during which the standard receptive field properties are recorded. The animal's behavior had no effect on firing in this interval. In a later post-stimulus interval from 150 to 400 msec, however, firing was increased if the monkey was about to make a correct (rewarded) choice. This is an example of temporal multiplexing of information from disparate sources in single cortical neurons.

The increase in late-interval firing depended not on the physical intensity of the target, but on its apparent brightness measured behaviorally during the single-cell recordings. A visual mask could dim the apparent brightness of the target while leaving its physical intensity unchanged. Under this condition, firing in the late interval was also greater preceding a correct response than preceding an incorrect response (Fig. 1). Apparently, when something goes askew in the information processing scheme, resulting in an incorrect response, most striate cells fail to increase their activity in the late time interval.

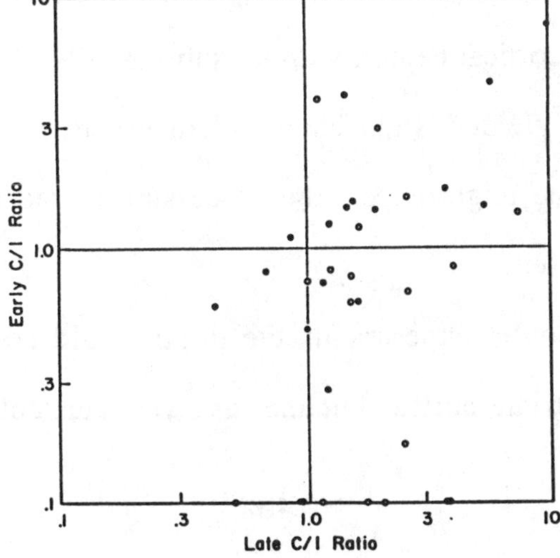

Fig. 1

The possibility remains from these studies that the discrimination was being performed at another level, and that striate cortex neurons were informed only at a later time about the results of the brightness discrimination. Haenny and Schiller (1983) addressed this possibility at least for one noncortical visual center, using a task based on stimuli that could be differentiated by cortical neurons but not by the superior colliculus. Monkeys looked through a circular aperture at an alternating series of vertical and horizontal gratings, and released a key when one of the patterns was repeated on two consecutive exposures. Neurons in the superior colliculus do not have oriented receptive fields, and could not differentiate these two patterns. In this case striate cortex neurons gave an enhanced burst of firing to the second of the two identical gratings, the one containing the critical pattern. In this experiment, then, enhancements of cortical activity are related to behavioral tasks whether or not the stimuli are differentiated in the superior colliculus.

Failures to find information-contingent modulation

This result suggests the alternative that non-image modulation of striate activity is based on the nature of the task to be performed. Wurtz and Mohler (1976b) reported the first tests of modulation of cortical activity by a behavioral task, but obtained only weak and inconsistent relationships between cortical firing and task parameters. Their task, however, did not involve a discrimination; rather, their monkeys were required to track a single luminous spot as it jumped across a tangent screen. The spot could jump into the receptive field of a cortical neuron without substantially affecting its firing pattern. The same task, however, yielded significant enhancement in firing in the superior colliculus (1976a), where one might expect the processing of saccadic eye movements to simple targets to be carried out.

In the Wurtz and Mohler experiments the target could be decoded by either the superior colliculus or the striate cortex, but the task was particularly well suited to the colliculus and the enhancement appeared there. The Bridgeman and the Haenny and Schiller studies, in contrast, used discrimination tasks more appropriate for cortical involvement and found cortical effects.

In another paradigm for assessing the effect of task variables on cortical activity, Moran and Desimone (1985) failed to find any enhancement effects in primary visual cortex. Theirs was a "match-to-sample" task. If two successive stimuli were identical, the animal was to respond immediately to gain reward. However, if two successive stimuli were not identical the animal could still gain reward through a delayed response. It would not be advantageous for the visual system to enhance response to either of these stimuli during the early phases of processing, since both stimuli are potentially rewarding in all situations. In Bridgeman's (1982) discrimination task, early responses from striate cortex were identical while only later time epochs showed differences in response rate dependent on reward value of the stimulus. Because Moran and Desimone did not specify the temporal patterning of their attentional effect, we do not know whether their data would yield similar enhancements at greater latencies.

Taken together, these results suggest that the characteristics of the task are critical in establishing the type of cortical participation in task-related aspects of a behavioral act.

Differentiating Stimulus and Reward -- An Experiment

To further address the question of cortical participation in perception and behavioral choice, we have investigated responses of single neurons in the striate cortex of cat with a stimulus that is physically identical in all trials (Artim and Bridgeman, 1989). The timing of stimulus presentation, rather than image-related variables, determined the appropriateness of behavioral response.

In this design a patterned flash is presented every 10 seconds, and the cat is rewarded if it presses a pedal during a period extending from 0.5 to 1.5 sec after the flash. This flash is informative, telling the cat the reward will be available. In some trials other, uninformative flashes are given, distinguished not by their physical features but by their timing. A flash given 0.5 sec after the first flash, and not rewarded, conveys no additional information to the animal. But the activity elicited by it flows through the visual system when the animal is in an aroused state just prior to responding. Since the animal already has received the flash signalling a reward, the second flash is informationally redundant. These trials are called double-flash trials.

Another kind of flash is given between trials after the close of the reward window, but well before the end of the 10-sec fixed interval. It too is uninformative to the cat, because the cat knows that it is too early for another rewarded flash. It is also unrewarded, and occurs at a time when the cat can be expected to be in a relatively lower state of arousal. These trials are called delayed-flash trials. Thus there are two kinds of uninformative flashes, one presented in a high-arousal context and one in a low-arousal context. With such a paradigm it is possible to isolate the contributions of stimulus information content and arousal to the responsivity of single neurons in striate cortex.

Results

Electrophysiological data were recorded from 48 neurons, of which 44 gave adequate samples from all trial types. The neurons were divided into two categories; (I) those whose firing rate during an arbitrarily defined primary peak window was altered by a criterion amount, and (II) those whose firing rate did not meet the criterion. The primary peak window was 30-70 msec post-stimulus. A cell was included in the primary group if it exhibited either (i) an average increase (or decrease) of firing rate within any one 10 msec bin within the primary window of at least 200% relative to background rate or (ii) an increase (or decrease) of firing rate within any one 10 msec bin within the primary window of at least 300% over background. The background rate was sampled during a 200 msec pre-stimulus recording interval. 27 cells fell into the primary peak group (primary cells) and 17 fell into the non-primary peak group (non-primary cells). None of the primary cells showed a decrease in total number of spikes. These groups had no histological basis (no correlation with depth or location of cortical penetration) nor did their receptive fields differ. Group assignment was probably due to chance matches or mismatches between the constant flashed stimulus and the cell's receptive field.

The first question of interest is whether or not the behavior of the cat covaried with cell firing patterns. For this determination it is important to define the difference between informative and uninformative flashes not in terms of the experimenter's a priori categories, but in terms of the cat's own determination of when a reward would be available. Thus histograms were prepared summarizing the difference in spike rate during trials when the cat pressed (go trials) versus trials when the cat did not press (no go trials).

The key measure is not the absolute firing rate of the neurons, but the differences in firing rate between go and no go trials. This measure reflects the cat's decision about the meaning of the flash. If the animal was about to press the pedal, the primary neurons fired at an increased rate during the 200 msec prior to stimulus presentation. This change may indicate a state of readiness or expectancy, because the fixed interval between rewarded flashes was nearly at an end. The cells fired at a decreased rate during the primary burst, and again at an increased rate during the reward window (Fig. 2). The non-primary cells showed similar through less regular trends.

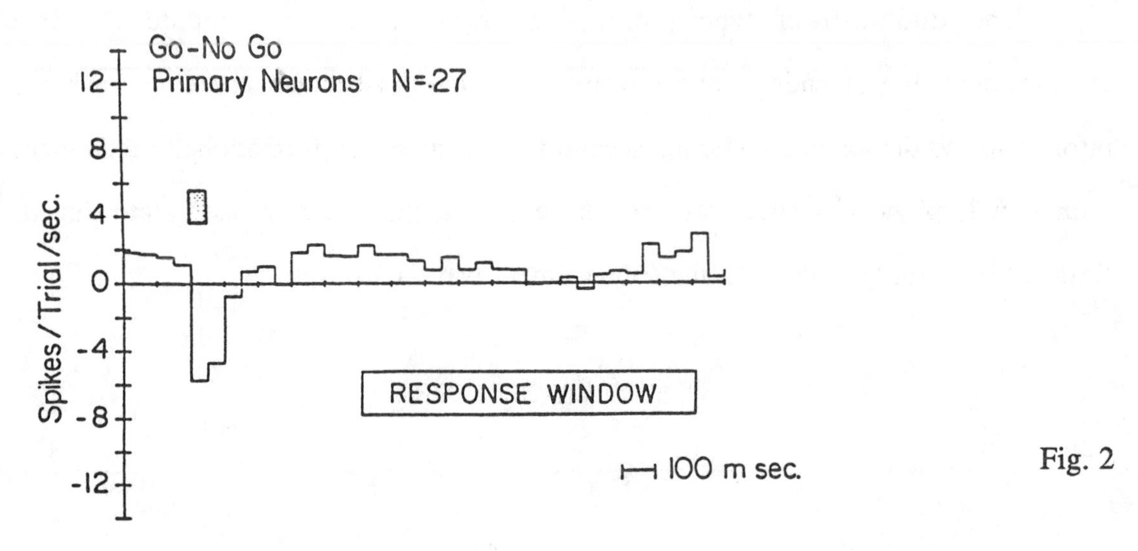

Fig. 2

Background rate was approximately 50% higher when the cat pressed than when he did not. In addition, the primary burst in the primary neurons was reduced by approximately 25% when a press was forthcoming during the reward window.

A second way of examining the data is in terms of each flash's potential for reward. The trials can be collapsed across potentially rewarded flashes regardless of cat's behavior (standard trials, double-flash trials, and 1st flash of delayed-flash trials) versus unrewarded flashes (delayed-flash trials and 2nd flash of double-flash trials). A t-test differences between informative and uninformative trials was not significant at the alpha=0.05 level ($t=0.32$, $p>0.1$, $df=219$). Combining this negative result with the positive results in the previous paragraph shows that responses were differentiated according to the cat's behavior, not according to formal information content.

Greater after-activity to the informative flashes suggests that a more transient response is being transformed into a more sustained response when the stimulus pattern triggers a behavioral response. Primary burst onset is delayed approximately 10 msec.

A split-halves reliability test was performed between the standard-flash trials and the first flash of the delayed-flash trials. These flashes are physically identical and have identical information content from the cat's point of view. The t-test for differences was not significant at the alpha=0.05 level ($t=0.0056$, $p>0.40$, $df=219$). Lack of significance re-enforces the assertion that the two histograms are drawn from the same distribution.

The double-flash type presents an opportunity to compute the level of enhancement due to endogenous information. This is because the first flash presents information to the animal, while the second flash is always informationally redundant even though it is physically identical, and the cat is in the same aroused state during both flashes. In primary peak cells, the enhancement was 21%.

Interpreting the data

This study shows that single striate cortex neurons modulate their activity as a function of the perceptually relevant information flowing through them. The change is too complex to be characterized as a percentage enhancement, and is interpreted more accurately as a temporal repatterning of the neural response to a meaningful target. Analysis of the trials in terms of their formal information content, in the context of the experimental design, gave less dramatic differentiations of activity than analysis in terms of the cat's interpretation of informativeness, as measured by the behavioral responses.

A general account of endogenous modifiability in striate cortex neurons

The single-unit results in cat and monkey reviewed here can be combined with those in the literature to reveal that the neurons are sensitive not only to visual stimuli but also to the behavioral context. The finding that the striate cortex codes more than simply the stimulus pattern present in the optic array confirms earlier results with implanted gross electrodes in monkey (Pribram, Spinelli and Kamback, 1967; Spinelli and Pribram, 1970). Those studies showed differences in evoked responses as a function of the information content of stimulus patterns. But they left open the possibility that different groups of physically intermingled neurons code different aspects of the situation, some reflecting stimulus attributes and others specializing in response or reinforcement.

Differential sensitivity can be conceived in terms either of plasticity or attention; changes due to behavioral context cannot occur in naive animals because stimuli are physically identical, and training changes the attentional state of the animals. But the experiments showed different sorts of modifiability in different paradigms; and some of the experiments in the literature revealed no modifiability at all. How are these disparate patterns to be reconciled?

In the Wurtz and Mohler (1976) work, cortical receptive fields saw little enhancement because the behavioral task could be carried out mainly at the level of the superior colliculus. In the monkey studies reviewed above, Bridgeman (1980,1982) found enhancement only after a delay, because every stimulus was potentially a correct one; it was only the match or mismatch of the stimulus with the behavioral response that defined whether the response would be correct. This information developed only later after the stimulus presentation, as the choice behavior was either driven by the visual system or failed to be driven by it.

In contrast, the Haenny and Schiller (1988) monkeys showed immediate differences in the activity of striate neurons when the informative stimulus appeared. In their design, though, the monkey could know in advance which stimulus would be the informative one. If vertical stripes had just appeared, for instance, the monkeys knew that a second vertical pattern would indicate an opening of the reward window. Thus the cortex could theoretically be "primed" to respond more strongly to the correct vertical stripes. Following horizontal stripes, the horizontal direction could be primed in like manner. The neural response could differ immediately, reflecting the different state of the cortex when new retinally driven activity impinges on it.

The cat results reviewed above can also fit into this framework, for differences between rewarded and unrewarded trials are evident immediately, in the first bins where a cortical response can be expected. Even the background activity, just before the expected rewarded stimulus appeared, was enhanced in trials where the animal responded behaviorally. Correspondingly, at a perceptual level the cat can anticipate in advance which of the several possible stimuli will be the informative one; the cortex can be primed in advance to change its response to the correct stimulus.

Thus the differences in fine structure of enhancements which these studies reveal may correspond to differing task demands, reflecting differences in the brain's programming of the transfer function in the striate cortex. One can conclude not only that the activity of striate neurons is modified by task demands, but also that the pattern of modification is subtly dependent on the nature of the task and the resultant demands upon the visual system. The sorts of contextual distinctions that are important at the conscious level (Bridgeman, 1986) already are beginning to be drawn at the level of striate cortex.

An elaboration of this generalization awaits use of several different kinds of tasks, requiring several kinds of striate cortex modulation, performed by the same animals in a single experiment.

References

Artim, J. and Bridgeman, B. (1989) The Physiology of Attention: Participation of Cat Striate Cortex in Behavioral Choice. *Psychological Research 50,* 223-228.

Bridgeman, B. (1979) Temporal Aspects of Coding in Single Cells of Monkey Striate Cortex. *Society for Neuroscience Abstracts 5,* 778.

Bridgeman, B. (1980) Temporal Response Characteristics of Cells in Monkey Striate Cortex Measured with Metacontrast Masking and Brightness Discrimination *Brain Research 196,* 347-364.

Bridgeman, B. (1982) Multiplexing in single cells of the alert monkey's visual cortex during brightness discrimination. *Neuropsychologia 20,* 33-42.

Bridgeman, B. (1986) Relations between the physiology of attention and the physiology of consciousness. *Psychological Research 48,* 259-266.

Haenny, P. E. and Schiller, P. H. (1983) The behavioral significance of visual stimuli influences the responses of single cells in V1. *Investigative Ophthalmology and Visual Science Supplement 24,* 106.

Moran, J. and Desimone, R. (1985) Selective attention gates visual processing in the extrastriate cortex *Science 229,* 782-784,

Pribram, K. H., Spinelli, D. N. and Kamback, M. (1967) Electrocortical correlates of stimulus response and reinforcement. *Science 157,* 94-96.

Sakitt, B. and Barlow, H. B. (1982) A model for the economical encoding of the visual image in the cerebral cortex. *Biological Cybernetics 43,* 97-108.

Spinelli, D. N. and Pribram, K. H. (1970) Neural correlates of stimulus response and reinforcement. *Brain Research 17,* 377-385.

Wurtz, R. H. and Mohler, C. W. (1976a) Organization of monkey superior colliculus: enhanced visual response of superficial layer cells. *Journal of Neurophysiology 39,* 745-765.

Wurtz, R. H. and Mohler, C. W. (1976b) Enhancement of visual responses in monkey striate cortex and frontal eye fields. *Journal of Neurophysiology 39,* 766-772.

Figure Legends

Fig. 1. Firing of monkey striate cortex neurons dependent on correctness of a brightness discrimination. Each axis plots the ratio of firing in correct vs. incorrect trials. Each cell is indicated by two symbols, a filled circle for brightness discrimination trials and an open circle for trials in which brightness was reduced with masking. If neurons are unaffected by the correctness of the behavioral response, the distribution of points should be symmetrical about a ratio of 1. The 'early' post-stimulus interval, up to 150 msec following the stimulus, shows this pattern (y axis). In the 'late' interval (150-400 msec), cells fire more if the behavioral response is correct, as shown by the clustering of points on the right half of the graph (x axis).

Fig. 2. Difference histogram for neurons in cat striate cortex that fired in response to a flashed stimulus. Greater firing rate during trials with a behavioral response is in the up direction, while greater firing rate during trials without a response is in the down direction. The histogram begins 200 msec before stimulus presentation (hatched rectangle). Bin resolution is 50 msec. The rectangle at the lower right indicates the time window during which the cat could press a pedal to obtain a liquid reward. Neurons fired less spring the early post-response interval and more following that interval, showing a a less transient-like and more sustained-like pattern if a behavioral response was to follow.

Footnote

Experimental work in cats was supported by NIH grant EY04137 and NSF grant BNS79-06853. Preparation was supported by AFOSR grant 90-0095.

Chapter 16

The Emergence of Chaotic Dynamics as a Basis for Comprehending Intentionality in Experimental Subjects

Walter J. Freeman
Department of Molecular & Cell Biology
University of California
Berkeley, CA 94720

The Emergence of Chaotic Dynamics as a Basis for Comprehending Intentionality in Experimental Subjects

Walter J Freeman
Department of Molecular & Cell Biology
University of California, Berkeley CA 94720

ABSTRACT

Simultaneous multichannel recording from the olfactory bulb and cortex has given the following experimental results. 1. The cortical activity that relates to the perception of a sensory stimulus is carried macroscopically by populations of neurons, not microscopically by a small number of single neurons ("units", "feature detectors", etc.). 2. That activity reflects the meaning and significance of the stimulus for the experimental subject and not the stimulus as it is known to the observer. 3. The activity carries the meaning in spatial patterns, not in time series (the difference between a phonograph or radio and a movie or TV). 4. The spatial patterns of activity that accompany previously learned stimuli or responses are changed by the introduction of new stimuli and also by modifications in reinforcement contingencies. 5. The patterns of activity are created by dynamic neural interactions in sensory cortex, not by registration or filtering of stimuli. There is no evidence for storage, retrieval, crosscorrelation, or logical tree search. 6. The dynamics is chaotic, not merely noisy, so that each act of perception involves a new construction by the cortex and not mere information processing. From these findings we infer that chaotic dynamics plays a crucial role in the formation of associational contexts of the memories of experimental subjects, so that intentionality is characteristic of early stages of cortical function, including primary sensory cortexes in lower mammals.

EXPERIMENTAL DERIVATION OF PERCEPTUAL PATTERNS OF EEG

I begin by describing a conceptually simple experiment in sensory physiology. My students and I asked the questions, what is the spatiotemporal pattern of electrical activity that is induced in a sensory cortex, when a stimulus is given which an animal has been trained to discriminate and respond to selectively? And, in what way does the pattern reliably correspond to the stimulus? This is not to ask a more abstract and general question, what is the central "neural code" for "representation" of the stimulus?, but merely, which neurons are reliably and exclusively made active by the stimulus, where are they located, and what is the time course of their activity?

We chose to study the sense of olfaction because its anatomy and electrophysiology are relatively simple in comparison to those of other senses, and they are relatively well understood. We chose the rabbit, because its olfactory modality is dominant, and its olfactory bulb is appropriate in size for spatial analysis. By the existing hypothesis advanced by Adrian (1950) and more recently supported by use of metabolic labeling (Lancet et al., 1982) we predicted that we would find clumps of cells in the bulb that were selectively activated during inhalation, in a manner comparable to the spatial selectivity of discriminative responses in other sensory modalities.

We chose to use electrical recording because, unlike alternative methods such as optical dye recording, metabolic labeling, or magnetic field derivation, it can follow very rapid changes in activity, has a very good signal to noise ratio, and is adapted easily to observation in waking animals over the periods of weeks needed for training to discriminate odors. We surgically prepared rabbits by implanting on or into one bulb a prefabricated array of electrodes with known distances of separation, so that we could get a spatial sample of the bulbar activity,. After full recovery we placed a mask over the muzzle to deliver conditioned odor stimuli, inserted a tube in the cheek to deliver water as an unconditioned stimulus after thirsting, fixed an electrode in the jaw muscle to detect licking, and placed an elastic belt around the chest to monitor respiration and sniffing (Viana Di Prisco and Freeman, 1985).

We first examined the activity of single neurons by their action potentials, as had been done by numerous investigators before us with single electrodes, but we used arrays of 10 microelectrodes that were placed near the mitral cell layer at distances of separation of about 100 microns for simultaneous derivation of action potentials. The results were unsatisfactory (Freeman, 1975), because the variability of response patterns was just as great between repeated measurements with the same stimulus as it was between the measurements with different stimuli. We concluded that the sample size was inadequate by a factor of 100 to 10,000. Our estimates of the variances combined with our anatomical measurements of the numbers of neurons in the olfactory mucosa and bulb (Freeman, 1972) indicated that among its roughly 100 million neurons we should sample at least a few thousands during each sniff, yet at most we were sampling a few tens of axonal pulse trains with the multi-microelectrode approach.

We turned to the recording of local dendritic potentials, which had been pioneered by Adrian (1950) by a single channel electroencephalogram (EEG) of the bulb, but in our hands with multiple electrodes (64 in an 8 x 8 array) forming a 4 x 4 mm window fitted onto the bulbar surface. Our prior work (Freeman, 1975) had already established a close statistical relationship between the spatiotemporal patterns of the EEG amplitudes at the bulbar surface and the distributions of relative firing frequencies of the mitral cells within the bulb. We estimated that each surface electrode gave access to the local mean field of 300 to 500 mitral cells, and that our array accessed about 20% of the bulb in the rabbit. In this way we employed spatial ensemble averaging over neural populations on single trials, instead of time ensemble averaging of measurements from a roving electrode over many trials (Freeman, 1987a).

THE LACK OF INVARIANCE OF EEG PATTERNS WITH RESPECT TO STIMULI

The results were astonishing. We found as predicted that the information serving to classify odors was not in the time domain, where the spectrum was too narrow and the duration of a sniff was too short to support discrimination of many odors, but it was in the spatial patterns of activity averaged over each inhalation, lasting about a tenth of a second in the rabbit. However, each rabbit had its own unique spatial pattern with the familiar scent of the background, and as it learned to discriminate each new odor, its spatial pattern changed uniquely to a new form. Moreover, the information that enabled us to classify these neuroelectric patterns was truly distributed, in that both high and low levels of activity were important, as should have been the case, because the patterns were made of High and low amplitude, comparable to light and dark, but no one channel was any more or less important than any other. This finding of the importance of spatial patterns was consistent with Adrian's (1950) hypothesis, but the behavioral correlates of the patterns were not consistent (Freeman, 1978).

Most strikingly, we found that with each change in training, such as the addition of a new odor to be discriminated, or the introduction of a new unconditioned stimulus, or a change in reinforcement contingency such as the reversal between two odors, one rewarded and the other not, all of the identified spatial patterns were changed for these and for other odors. The affiliated changes were small, about 7% above the level of continual variance in spatial patterns between sessions, but they were undeniable (Freeman and Grajski, 1987; Grajski et al., 1986). Faced with the fact that the central patterns were frequently changing, even though the stimuli and the responses were kept the same, we were led to conclude that the bulbar patterns were signs of the meanings of the stimuli for the subjects, not of the stimuli as we observers knew them. They were dependent on the context, the previous experiences of the subjects, their states of arousal and attention, and their expected responses to the stimuli. In brief, the results manifested a lack of invariance in the storage of mental images of past experience. Any change in stimulus, response, or contingency of reinforcement brought apparently global changes in spatial patterns that were thereafter again induced by previously learned stimuli.

INTERPRETATION OF THE LACK OF PATTERN INVARIANCE

Several conclusions can be drawn immediately from these results. First, in an associative memory system, each new memory must alter the old ones as it becomes tied to them, so that a seamless fabric of contextual memory is incompatible with a store that is invariant with respect to individual stimuli as defined by the observer. Second, the indisputable fact of behavioral stimulus-response invariance we observe in our experimental subjects must be accounted for by simultaneous synaptic changes with associational learning in both sensory and motor systems. There is no difficulty in accepting this for the olfactory system, because we know that functional changes take place throughout its extent (Freeman, 1975; Bressler, 1988) with learning under the influence of the centrally controlled release of global neuromodulators (Gray, Freeman and Skinner, 1986). It follows that S-R congruence must be maintained by the environment, and ,further, that as the environment changes so also will the responses to stimuli adapt appropriately. The greatest surprise here is the intrusion of intentionality at the first synapse in the olfactory pathway. The similarities in neural architectures, dynamics, and carrier wave forms between the olfactory and other sensory systems (Freeman, 1992a) suggest that similar contextual neural constructs should be found in other primary sensory cortexes.

This finding of the lack of central pattern invariance with respect to olfactory stimulus-response configurations has further consequences for epistemology, for the following reason. The read-out of the bulbar neural activity is by transmission in parallel on half a million axons, and the spatial divergence of the axons effects a spatial integration and smoothing of the bulbar output as it is received by the olfactory cortex.

This operation smooths out the sensorily evoked activity of bulbar neurons and allows to be summed only the global cooperative activity as it is most clearly manifested in the EEG. As a result, the only "information" that is successfully transmitted from the bulb more deeply into the brain is the perceptual construct and not the receptor-dependent neural activity (Freeman, 1991, 1992b). We conclude that the brains of our subjects cannot incorporate the raw and infinitely complex environment by the widely postulated "mechanisms of information processing" but only their perceptual constructs based on individual experience. To the extent that this conclusion can be extrapolated to other senses and to other species, including ourselves, we can suppose that neurophysiology can provide an answer to an age-old epistemological question, whether we can or cannot "know" the world by direct sensory input. These experimental results suggest that we can only grasp the constructs that are formed by the cooperative interactions of the neurons in our sensory and motor systems under the influences of sensory bombardment.

These interpretations have already been proposed by many eminent psychologists on other grounds. For example, Sir Frederic Bartlett (1932) wrote from his detailed studies on remembering: "...some widely held views have to be completely discarded, and none more completely than that which treats recall as the re-excitement in some way of fixed and changeless 'traces' " (p. vi) ..."The picture is one of human beings confronted by a world in which they can live and be masters only as they learn to match its infinite diversity by increasing delicacy of response, and as they discover ways of escape from the complete sway of immediate circumstances." (p. 301) "There is one way in which an organism could learn how to do this. It may be the only way. ... An organism has somehow to acquire the capacity to turn round upon its own 'schemata' and to construct them afresh. This is a crucial step in organic development. It is where and why consciousness comes in; it is what gives consciousness its most prominent function. ... I wish I knew exactly how it was done" (p. 206).

CONSTRUCTION OF PERCEPTS BY CHAOTIC DYNAMICS

The wistful last sentence quoted above pinpoints the difficulty we face in accepting the implications of our findings about the fallibility of our memories and our limitation in accessing the world through our senses. Where do the neural activity patterns come from? How are they generated? Our answer is straightforward. A key to understanding brain function lies in the use of nonlinear dynamics to model the perceptual function of the olfactory system. In brief, we conceive that the olfactory system maintains a global chaotic attractor (Skarda and Freeman, 1987; Freeman, 1988, 1992b) with multiple wings or side lobes, one for each odor that a subject has learned to discriminate. Each lobe is formed by a bifurcation during learning, which changes the entire structure of the attractor, including the pre-existing lobes and their modes of access through basins of attraction. During an act of perception the act of sampling a stimulus destabilizes the olfactory bulbar mechanism, drives it from the core of its basal chaotic attractor by a state transition, and constrains it into a lobe that is selected by the stimulus for as long as the stimulus lasts, on the order of a tenth of a second. The activation of the lobe is expressed by the spatial pattern of bulbar activity, which on transmission to the targets of the bulb comparably destabilizes them and enables them to enter into basins of attraction that are appropriate for the percept. In this way the cortical response to a stimulus is "newly constructed" (in the words of Bartlett) rather than retrieved from a dead store. It would be inappropriate to elaborate further on this brief description in the present context, and in any case the theory and its applications have already been developed more fully in several earlier publications (Freeman, 1987b, 1991, 1992b).

A physicist of my acquaintance remarked, "This process is difficult to grasp at first, but once you see it, what else could it be?". What makes it so difficult? Why has this result not been found before? There are several technical reasons. Thorough understanding is required of the neurobiological substrate. The surgical techniques must be developed for long-term placement of a large number of closely spaced electrodes that can be sterilized pre-operatively and positioned quickly. Simultaneous recording is necessary from as many preamplifiers as electrodes, because the unpredictable variation in frequency and phase of central self-organized activity patterns precludes serial sampling with a roving electrode. Extensive investment is needed in computer hardware for data acquisition, reduction, analysis, and modeling. Sophisticated multivariate statistical techniques are necessary for EEG signal decomposition and identification.

However, the paramount barriers to understanding are theoretical. First, it is necessary to grasp the hierarchical nature of neural activity, in which sensory input and motor output are expressed at the microscopic level of single neurons, but perceptual and other higher order events are expressed in macroscopic activity of masses of neurons (Freeman, 1975). This distinction still escapes many neurobiologists, who fail to see the forest for the trees. In part this agnosia seems to be reinforced by a prevalent view that the EEG (also called the "local field potential") is devoid of functional interest or significant information content, often being characterized as "the roar of a crowd at a football game". Second, it is essential to introduce and rely on the theory of nonlinear dynamics and chaos (Thompson and Stewart, 1986: Freeman, 1987b), and in particular to recognize that deterministic chaotic dynamics creates information (in the Shannon-Weaver sense) as well as destroying it. How is it that a mass of interactive neurons can continually generate new spatiotemporal patterns, that have never before existed, yet that conform within definite limits to the constraints imposed by the purposes of the subjects and the environmental conditions in which they must live. Prigogine's (1980) aphorism about "the emergence of order from disorder" captures the essence of the process by which a sought-for and recognizable odorant stimulus forces a change in a chaotic bulbar state and confines the trajectory of the olfactory system into a selected and meaningful orbit.

Further development of the physiology of perception along these lines will be slow and difficult. One reason is that the most interesting perceptual processing takes place in six-layered neocortex, while most of the results I have summarized here have come from three-layered paleocortex. The aperiodic oscillatory carrier waves are quite similar in the two types of cortex (Freeman, 1992a), but the range of spatial coherence is much broader, and the space-time patterns appear to be more complex in neocortex. The deeper three layers of neocortex appear to be responsible for both of these attributes, but we have very little understanding of the neural integrative mechanisms by which these come about. Another reason is that the experimental subjects of greatest interest are obviously ourselves, but the problems of deriving useful EEG data for perceptual studies from scalp recording have not yet been solved. Yet another reason is that expertise is required in several technical disciplines to pursue this work, and the investment needed in computer equipment is not trivial. The planning and team work to coordinate the enterprise must be driven by clear vision, and that is not easy to come by in an area so close to the frontiers of human understanding. Finally, an acceptance of the essential insight, that neural activity exists in global macroscopic forms as well as in action potentials, is slow in coming. Still, what else could it be?

ACKNOWLEDGEMENT

This work was supported by grants MH06686 from the National Institute of Mental Health and N63373 from the Office of Naval Research.

REFERENCES

Adrian ED (1950) The electrical activity of the mammalian olfactory bulb. Electroencephalography and clinical Neurophysiology 2: 377-388.

Bartlett FC (1932) Remembering. Cambridge, England, University Press.

Bressler SL (1988) Changes in electrical activity of rabbit olfactory bulb and cortex to conditioned odor stimulation. Journal of Neurophysiology 102: 740-747.

Freeman WJ (1972) Linear analysis of the dynamics of neural masses. Annual Review of Biophysics and Bioengineering 1: 225-226.

Freeman WJ (1975) Mass Action in the Nervous System. New York, Academic Press.

Freeman WJ Spatial properties of an EEG event in the olfactory bulb and cortex. EEG and clinical Neurophysiology 44: 586-605, 1978.

Freeman WJ (1987a) Techniques used in the search for the physiological basis of the EEG. In: Gevins A, Remond A (eds) Handbook of EEG and clinical Neurophysiology Vol 3A, Part 2, Ch. 18. Amsterdam, Elsevier.

Freeman WJ (1987b) Simulation of chaotic EEG patterns with a dynamic model of the olfactory system. Biological Cybernetics 56: 139-150.

Freeman WJ (1988) Strange attractors that govern mammalian brain dynamics shown by trajectories of electroencephalographic (EEG) potential. IEEE Transactions on Circuits and Systems 35: 781-783.

Freeman WJ (1991) The physiology of perception. Scientific American 264: 78-85.

Freeman WJ (1992a) Predictions in neocortical dynamics that are posed by studies in paleocortex. Chapter 9 in: Basar E, Bullock TH (eds.) Induced Rhythms of the Brain. Cambridge, MA, Birkhaeuser Boston, pp 183-199.

Freeman WJ (1992b) Neurobiology for engineers: From single neurons to chaos. International Journal of Bifurcation and Chaos 2: in press.

Freeman WJ, Grajski KA (1987) Relation of olfactory EEG to behavior: Factor analysis: Behavioral Neuroscience 101: 766-777.

Freeman WJ, Viana Di Prisco, G. (1986) Relation of olfactory EEG to behavior: Time series analysis. Behavioral Neuroscience 100:753-763.

Grajski KA, Breiman L, Viana Di Prisco G, Freeman WJ (1986) Classification of EEG spatial patterns with tree-structured methodology. IEEE Transactions on Biomedical Engineering 33: 1076-1086.

Gray CM, Freeman WJ, Skinner JE (1986) Chemical dependencies of learning in the rabbit olfactory bulb: acquisition of the transient spatial-pattern change depends on norepinephrine. Behavioral Neuroscience 100: 585-596.

Lancet D, Greer CA, Kauer JS, Shepherd, GM (1982) Mapping of odor-related neuronal activity in the olfactory bulb by high-resolution 2-deoxyglucose autoradiography. Proceedings of the National Academy of Sciences USA 79: 670-674.

Prigogine I (1980) From Being to Becoming. San Francisco, W. H. Freeman.

Skarda CA, Freeman WJ (1987) How brains make chaos to make sense of the world. Brain and Behavioral Science 10: 161-195.

Thompson JMT, Stewart HB (1986) Nonlinear Dynamics and Chaos. New York, Wiley.

Viana Di Prisco G , Freeman WJ (1985) Odor-related bulbar EEG spatial pattern analysis during appetitive conditioning in rabbits. Behavioral Neuroscience 99: 962-978.

Chapter 17

The Formation of Live Neural Networks on Electronic Chips

Harold Szu
Naval Surface Warfare Center
Code R44
Silver Spring, MD 20903

Jung Kim and Insook Kim
University of SW Louisiana
Lafayette, LA 70504

The Formation of Live Neural Networks on Electronic Chips

Harold Szu, Jung Kim^, and +Insook Kim,

Naval Surface Warfare Center, Code R44, Silver Spring MD 20903

^Center for Advanced Computer Studies, and +Department. of Biology
Univ. of SW Louisiana, Lafayette, LA 70504

ABSTRACT

Live neuron behavior on an electronic chip was recorded with a time-lapsed video under the microscope. The dissociated chick embryonic brain neurons (telencephalic neurons) were cultured, and individual neurons were placed on silicon glass plates deposited with metal oxide strips about 10 μm width for possible electronegativity neurite guidance.

We have attempted to map biological neural networks (BNN) to artificial neural networks (ANN) to determine whether the connectivity patterns dictate the information processing efficiency, or vice versa. By an image processing technique, we discovered the smallest size of intelligent BNN from those video tapes that happened to fail their neurite guidance experiments. The neurite growth connecting other neurons was accomplished intentionally through selective paring in time rather than mechanically following the external guidance.

Such a dynamic interconnection has inspired a model of energy landscaping, of which a general convergence theorem that has unified early theorems is given, and a nonlinear Hebbian learning is derived capable for self-determination of ANN architecture.

Keywords: Self-Architecture, Neurite Growth, Microtubule, Morphology, VLSI

1. Neuron Cultures and Network Formations, Why Now ?

Recently, live formations of biological neural networks (BNN) on substrates made of electronic chips were pursued by several groups mentioned below for various reasons. (1) Short Term: to measure, in parallel with modern instruments, the sigmoidal function proposed by McCullouch-Pitts five decades ago for the single neuron firing rate transfer function. (2) Mid Term: to characterize the neurite formation pair correlation function proposed recently. (3) Long Term: to determine in vitro the link between the specific BNN architectural topology to the functional efficiency in information processing. It should not be expected from these efforts that one can understand the human intelligence, but rather to be able to eventually endow artificial neural networks (ANN) with somewhat intelligent capabilities. In fact, other than raising a child for truly BNN, to endow a human intelligence to ANN may not be desirable.

The computational properties of BNN can be observed by in vitro systems that consist of the bottom up: electronic chips, the top-down: time-lapsed Video microscopic, and the middle: neurochemical control of synaptic growth (namely phosphoproteins: Synapsin IIb discovered by Han & Greengard in 1991). Toward this goal, it is necessary to set up time-lapsed video imaging through the microscope upon an electronic chip to observe live neuron growth under a controlled environment. The collaboration with NTT began since 1989. This paper describes how in real time dissociated chick embryonic brain neurons (telencephalic neurons) form live BNN on a silica glass plate revealing an intelligent behavior despite the external metal oxide guidance. A minimally intelligent BNN, called Peter-Paul-Mary, is discovered with time-frozen frame analysis and elucidated.

*supported by Board of Regents of Louisiana of Grant LEQSF-RD-A-28, and NSF Grant NSF-ADP-04

The paper is organized as follows. A brief review of international research groups and cell culture techniques is given in Sect.1. Then, a time analysis of live dynamics follows in Sect.2, discussion about mathematical models in Sect.3, and further research perspectives in Sect.4.

Extracellular matrices have been known to guide the growth direction of nerve fibers [Cart67]. Some of the guiding factors have been determined to be bioreactive substances and microtubules, but many factors remain undetermined. Kleinfeld et. al. have reported the hydrophilic guidance of live neural nets on pattern chip substrates [Klei88]. Gross has patterned live neural nets over weeks by trimming the dense interconnections with laser surgery [Gros91].

Based on Taguchi et. al [Tag87] neuron-culture experiments, Kawana et. al.[Kawa90] have successfully applied the electronegativity of the metal (in the metal oxide pattern deposited on a silica glass) to guide live neurons into definite interconnection patterns. Chick brain neurons were cultured as described in [Tag87]. The plating efficiency was approximately 80%. An experiment was made on 5-day-old chick embryos brain neuron cells which were dissociated with 0.125% trypsin at 37° C for 15 min. in the same medium. Tissues were rinsed in F12 medium, supplemented with bovine serum albumin (1 µg/ml), glucose (10mM), insulin (2.5 µg/ml) and antibiotics. Tissues were dissociated in this medium by gentle trituration using a drawn-out Pasteur pipette. Cells ($4x10^{4}$ per well) were plated in 16-mm wells in Costar cluster dishes in 400 ml F12 medium, supplemented with glutamine (2 mM), penicillin (100 IU/ml), streptomycin (100 µg/ml), insulin (2.5 µg/ml) and glucose (10mM). Neurons were then placed on substrates which had metal oxide patterns about 10 mm size. Metal oxide patterns were made by standard optical lithography with lift-off

If the neuron culture could not be cleanly separated by a physical technique, then transferrin, insulin, progesterone, and putrescine could be used to substitute the fetal calf serum, in order to get chemically define medium in which the proliferation and growth of non-neuronal cells were suppressed. Likewise, neurons could be incubated in a medium containing 50 % Dulbecco's MEM(Gibco), 50 % Ham's F-12 medium(Gibco), 33 mM HEPES and 1.9 g/ml of $NaHCO_3$ in the humidified incubator filled with 5%-CO_2/95%-air at a saturating humidity. Nerve growth factor (20 µg/ml of 75 NGF) and the Synapsin IIb (discovered by Han & Greengard in 1991) could be added to the medium to promote the neurite outgrowth and the presynaptic junction formations in a controlled manner.

2. Time Analysis Dynamics

In the video imaging experiment, three dissociated chick brain neurons were seeded on metal oxides on silicon glass plate At time t = 0:00, then the neuron connection patterns was video-recorded under the microscope at a fixed delay, say every 10 or 15 min. The play back rate is compressed at 30 video frames per second. Such a time-lapsed video-microscope-chip technique is proved to be powerful to analyze live neuron dynamics.

Step 1) Figure 1.A shows the culturing process at time t = 3:40. One neuron (named Peter denoted as a) of three dissociated neurons has been producing neurite outgrowth towards another neuron (named Paul denoted as b) located about twenty body lengths away below its own metal oxides strip about ten mm width.

Step 2) At time t = 6:49 (Figure 1.B), the neurite of Peter which has been growing along the axial direction of the metal oxides strip, starts crossing the non-metal oxides strip towards Paul's direction, instead of following the guided axial direction of the metal oxides strip.

This seems to be the first indication that interconnections are formed intentionally rather

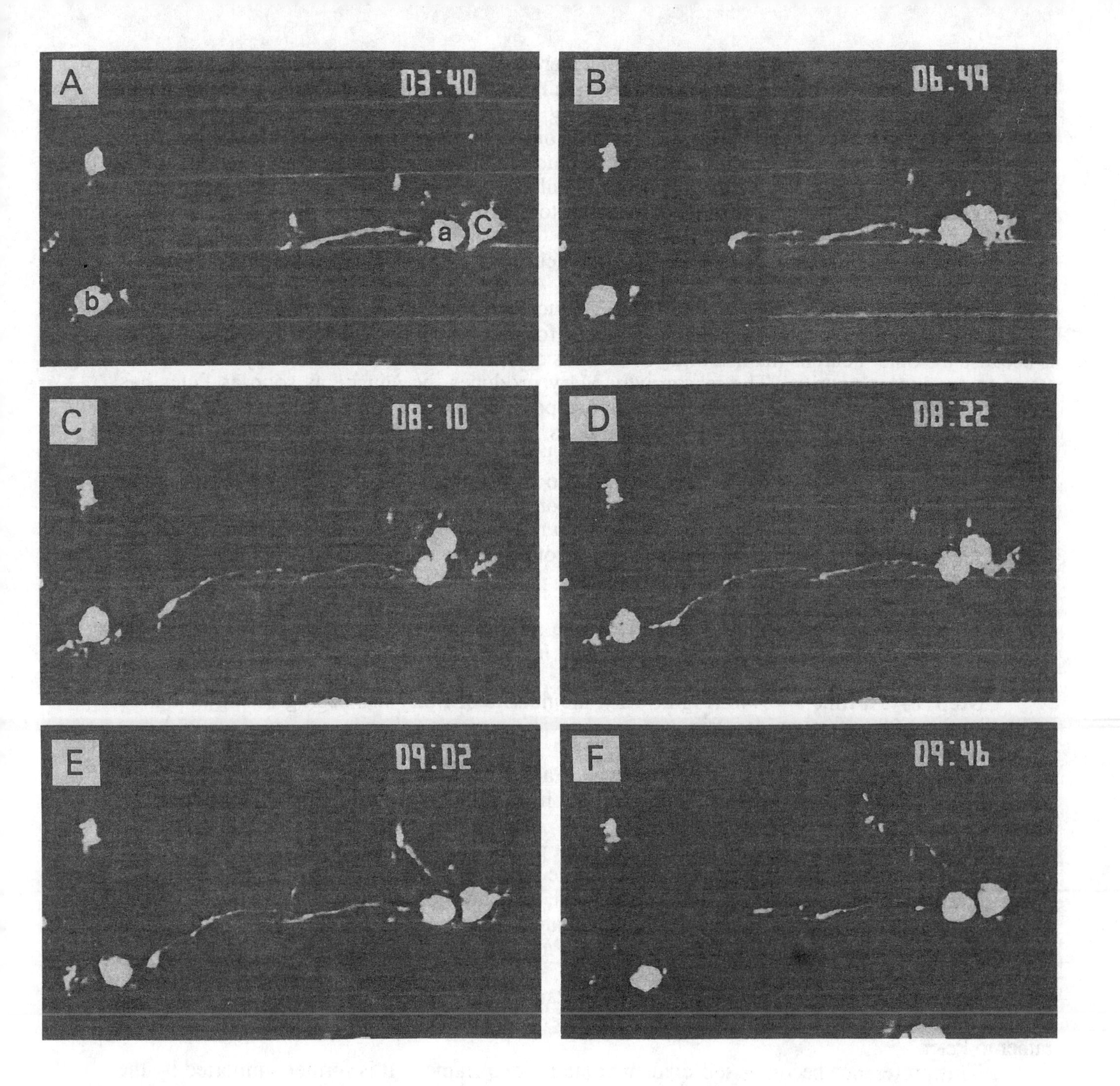

Figure 1. Snapshot pictures taken from a video tape showing the formation of live neural networks from 3 dissociated chick embryonic neurons cultured on a VLSI chip.
(Neuron a is named as Peter; Neuron b is named as Paul; Neuron c is named as Mary.)

than mechanically. What causes the neurite of Peter to cross non-metal oxides strip instead of following the guided direction? It has been known in the nervous system that during the initial part of nerve connection, the growth cone is generally guided by the tissues through which it is passing. As Peter nears Paul and before cell-to-cell contact, it may come under the influence of the target tissue itself through the action of neurotrophic factors that emanate from the target cells [Camp77, Davi84]. It is plausible that the neuron Paul emits some signals or neurotrophic factors, and the growth cone of the neurite of Peter responds to them.

Step 3) At time t = 8:10 (Figure 1.C), the neurite of Peter has just crossed the non-metal oxides strip.

Step 4) At time t = 8:22 (Figure 1.D), Peter-to-Paul contact has been made.

Although the synaptic junction has not been formed, something interesting happens. This is because the other neurons (named Mary denoted as c) which is located immediately next to Peter starts to produce a neurite. The reason why Mary produces the neurite as soon as Peter has connected Paul is not precisely determined with two possible causes given as follows.

The first hypothesis is the instantaneous communication that Mary has constant communications with Peter, thus as soon as Peter-to-Paul contact has been made, Mary knows the presence of Paul and starts producing a neurite toward Paul. The second hypothesis is the shadowing effect that the proper amount of signals or neurotrophic factors which emanates from the distant neuron Paul is no longer used by the growth cone of Peter, because Peter has made the contact, therefore the extra amount of signals or neurotrophic factors becomes available to Mary to produce a neurite. Both are plausible and consistent.

Step 5) At time t = 9:02 (Figure 1.E), the neurite of Mary has crossed the non-metal oxides strip. Interestingly, the initial neurite of Mary is not following the metal oxides strip.

Step 6) At time t = 9:46 (Figure 1.F), the neurite of Mary has been growing along the axial direction of the metal oxides strip.

Step 7) At time t = 11:38 (Figure 1.G), Paul started to produce its neurite outgrowth towards Mary. It took 3:16 time for Paul to initiate its neurite outgrowth, after the contact from Peter.

It has been known that neurons have different preparation time to initiate neurite outgrowth responding to nerve growth factor [Gree84]. These responses can be classified into 2 classes: delayed responses which are transcription-dependent, and early responses which are transcription-independent. It is highly plausible that the initiation latency of the neurite outgrowth of Paul may be transcription-dependent, that is, learning process of Paul from Peter might be gene-related.

Step 8) At time t = 12:57 (Figure 1.H), Paul began the growing of neurites along the existed interconnection pathway built early by Peter-to-Paul and moving quickly toward Mary rather to Peter.

This preference becomes self-evident at later video frames. It is further supported by the detailed time analysis of the neurite outgrowth rate as shown in the sum up Figure 2, where Mary growth time from t = 11:38 to t = 14:03 is reduced about in half compared to that from t = 8:22 to t = 11:38,.

Why should the neurite outgrowth rate of Mary be affected by the other distant neuron Paul? Two possible reasons are given. From the conservation of energy viewpoint, learning from Peter, Paul produces neurites to go after Mary himself secreting no more the neurotrophic factors. Consequently, the outgrowth rate of Mary becomes affected. It is also possible that, as Paul producing neurite toward Mary, Paul emits the inhibitive signal which forces Mary's neurite to reduce its outgrowth speed.

Step 9) At time t = 14:03 (Figure 1.I), the Paul-to-Mary interconnection is intentionally made because Paul has deliberately bypassed Peter and contacted Mary behind him.

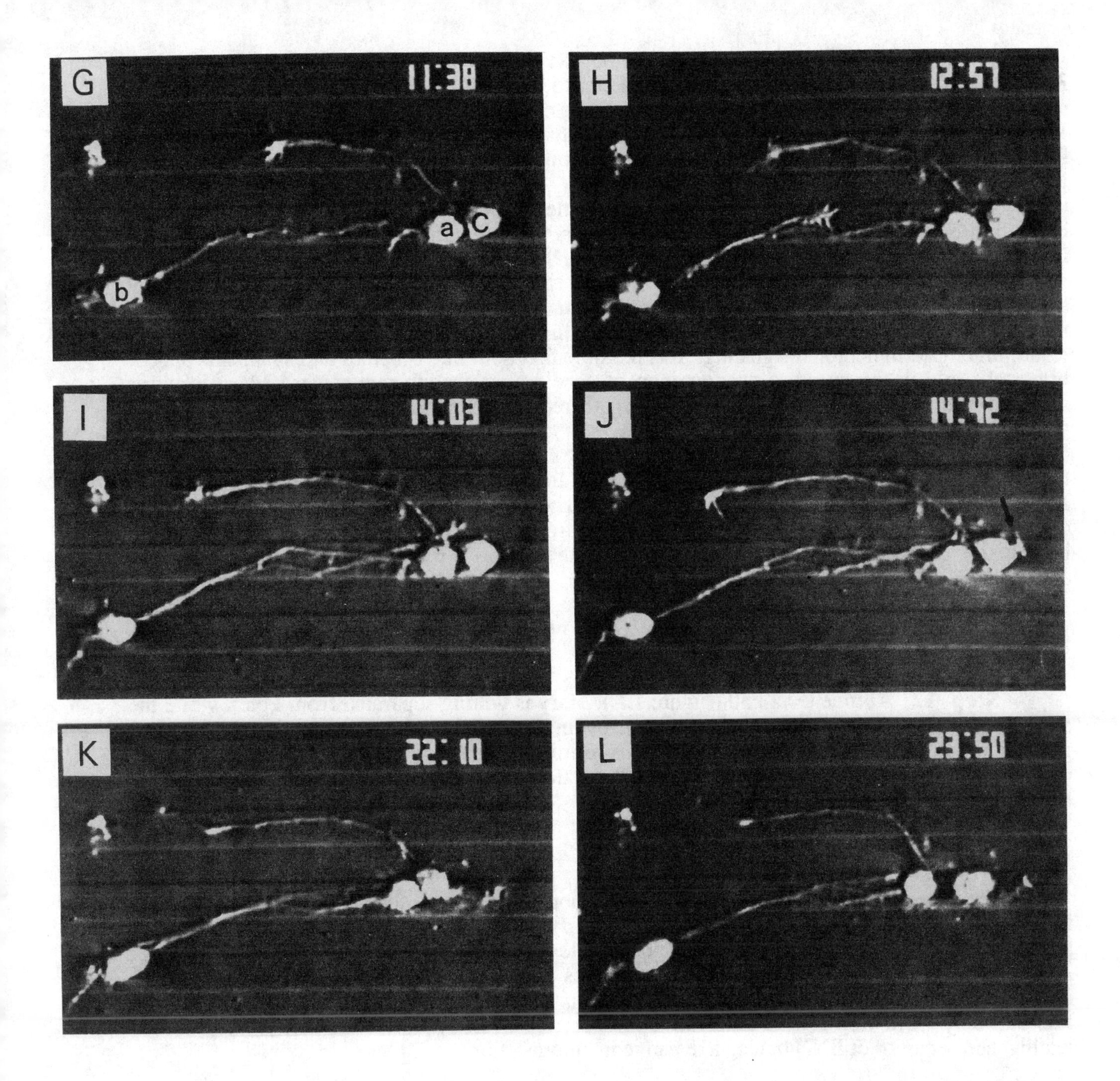

Figure 1.(Continued) Snapshot pictures taken from a video tape showing the formation of live neural networks from 3 dissociated chick embryonic neurons cultured on a VLSI chip. (Neuron a is named as Peter; Neuron b is named as Paul; Neuron c is named as Mary.)

An interesting phenomenon is that the neurite outgrowth rate from Paul to Mary is about 3.5 times as fast as that from early effort from Peter to Paul. While it take 8:22 time for Peter to be connected to Paul, the Paul-to-Mary contact is made only taking 2:25 time, as shown in Figure 2. What makes Paul's neurite grow much faster towards Mary than Peter's neurite towards Paul ? Does Paul learn from Peter how to find its neurite outgrowth path ? If Paul learns, what kind of information does Paul get from Peter ?

It was reported in [Rein91, Tana91] that the neuron spontaneously generates microtubules in the future direction of growth, which suggests that the orientation of microtubules might be an important early step in neural path finding.

It was reported in [Deca90, Han91] that the synapsins (which are phosphoproteins associated with synaptic vesicles) are implicated both in the short-term regulation of the neutrotransmitter release from nerve endings, and in the regulation of synapse formation, as a result, in long-term neuronal signaling. It is possible that both microtubules and synapsins play an important role in the speedup phenomenon of accelerated growth rate toward Mary utilizing somehow the path finding experience that Paul gathered early from Peter.

Step 10) At time t = 14:42 (Figure 1.J), the neurite growth of Mary is almost stopped in the previous direction, and Mary starts to produce another neurite in the new direction (see the arrow in Figure 1.J). Why does Mary stop the neurite growth in the previous direction ?. Mary could have learned its right neurite outgrowth path from Paul when the Paul-to-Mary contact has been made, thus Mary has stopped the neurite in the previous direction and start it in the new direction.

Step 11) At time t = 22:10, Figure 1.K shows that the new nuerite of Mary grows very slowly while the old neurite of Mary is retracting.

Step 12) At time t = 23:50 (Figure 1.L), Mary is getting separated from Peter, while the old neurite of Mary is more retracted (see the arrow in Figure 1.L). Although the reason why Mary gets separated from Peter is not clear, it seems to involve some degree of memory for decision making. Is this a manifestation of intelligence ? we donot know. All those hypotheses mentioned Sect.2 should be investigated further.

3. Mathematics of Self-Architectures

The human intelligence manifesting the memory, abstraction, and generalization leading to imagination and creativity, may require nonlinear dynamics models of interconnections. The absolute sense of human intelligence can not be relevant for the smallest possible nets, BNN or ANN, addressed in this paper, for these attributes happen in the limit of the large complex networks, similar to a phase transition phenomenon. Thus, a linear perturbation Hebb learning rule that may work well for the associative memory on a fixed architecture can not capture the intelligence behavior of BNN having a dynamic interconnection.

Using ad hoc procedure, one can always reduce the interconnections by zeroing out the synaptic weights or eliminating a node entirely, but conversely due to the communication traffic jam the computer code is not intelligent enough to detect a hot spot whose alleviation requires to create new interconnections and nodes in an energy convergent manner.

The minimal intelligence is the ability of comparisons and decision making ranging from the small perturbation of Hebbian learning to the drastic change of nonlinear dynamics of interconnections. A theory that has unified the whole spectrum of learning and integrated three classical neural network models has been synthesized [Szu90]. This hairy neuron model is generalized from (1) fixed energy landscape approach of Hopfield, (2) the synaptic weight descending approach of Werbos, Rumelhart, et al., and (3) the top-down and bottom up adaptive resonance approach of Carpenter and Grossberg. A convergence proof for such a unified hairy neuron model capable of dynamic interconnections is recapitulated.

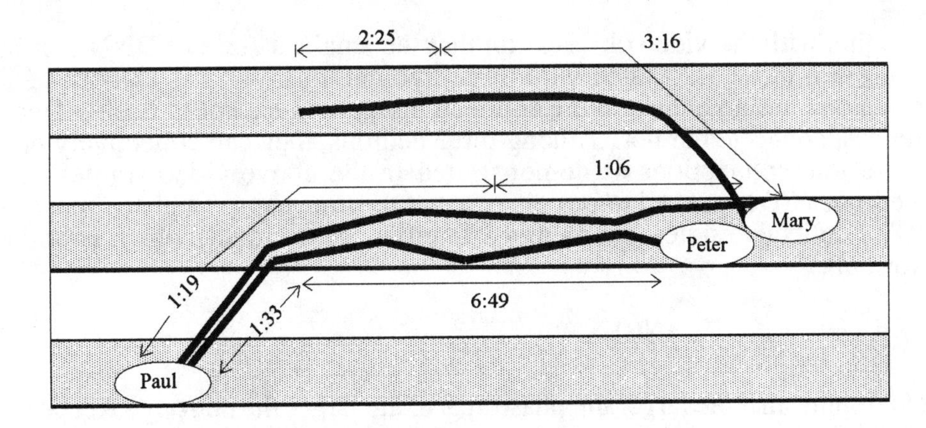

Figure 2. Schematic illustration indicating the time lapse of the neutrite outgrowth of each neuron referring to Figure 1.

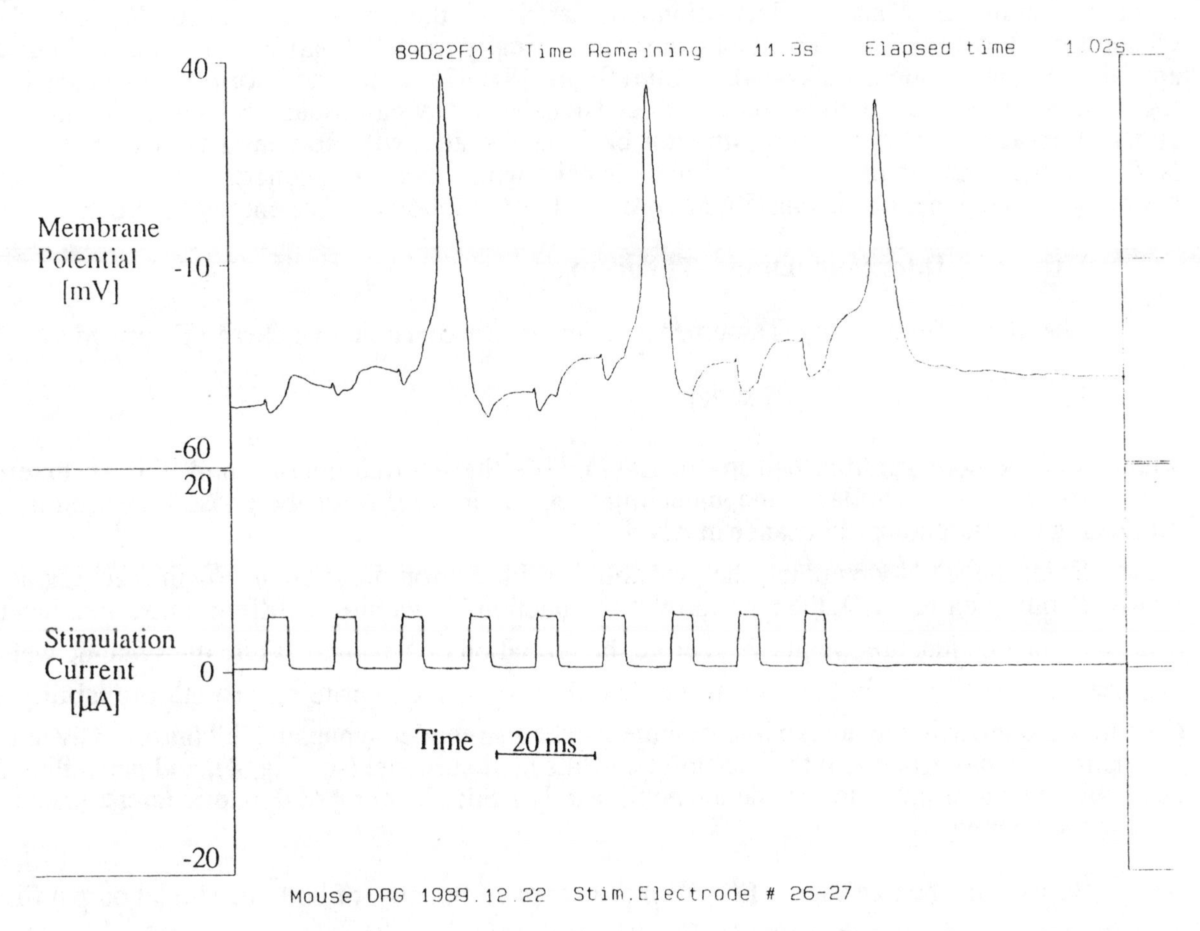

Figure 3 An in-situ meausrement obtained from typical neurons on the chip

We begins with the video observation that the smallest sizes of BNN that has exhibited a self-architecture are those associated with three live neurons. This is elaborated as follows. A single neuron alone has no choice in the connectivity pattern except to itself. Two neurons have only two choices, connected or not. Among three neurons, they can collectively have any one out of six possible interconnections as demonstrated in the above video frames. In general, the number of neurons N(t) happened to be connected at the time t spans a phase space P(N(t)) leading to possibility of collective states (for memory, intelligence, or mind) which is bounded above by the simple formula,

$$P(N(t)) \leq 2^{N(t)}. \tag{1}$$

Eq(1) implies that the larger the phase space, the larger the entropy. According to Shannon and Weaver, the fluctuation of the topology entropy is given as:

$$S = \log P \leq N(t) \tag{2}$$

The question is how does the configuration/topological entropy help the intelligence, or the dynamic interconnections in terms of N interacting neurons at time t. Thus, to answer this, we speculate that each morphology has a local stable energy minimum and a gradient decent converges to a local minimum. Thus, the fluctuation associated with the topological entropy Eq(2) can help escape from local minima. This fact can be numerically modeled, similar to Cauchy simulated annealing mixing random walks with random flights [Szu87]. Since the information entropy is the logarithmic of base 2 which is increased occasionally, ANN can escape a local minimum state either by random flights to a new attractor basin (associated with new inputs) or by the energy landscape reshaping in time (to create an avalanche with a sweeping generalization). This detail has not yet been done, but this insight has provided us the following free energy theorem.

Dynamic Interconnections Theorem.

The total system energy is assumed to be the thermodynamic free energy E defined as

$$\mathbf{E} = U - ST \tag{3}$$

where S is the configuration entropy of Eq(2), U is the internal energy, and T is an external interaction parameter similar to the annealing temperature useful for the phase transition model mimicking the morphological change in ANN.

From the BNN viewpoint, the probablity of ith neuron neurite outgrowth reaching at jth neuron (from Peter to Paul), the pair correlation function T_{ij} requires a different notation than the dendritic synaptic junction weight W_{ij} before the formation of synapse. While the synaptic weight W_{ij} seems to be passively reactive at the dendritic trees, the neurite outgrowth probability T_{ij} describes the growth with active microtubule mechanism under synapsin IIb control. Given that distinction, we have modified the McCullouch-Pitts neuron model (see Fig. 4), and generalize the Hebbian synaptic learning to include the nonlinear dynamics learning of dynamic interconnections as described below.

We assume the free energy $E(v_i, W_{ij})$ is an explicit function of both the singlet output firing rates v_i, and the pair synaptic weights W_{ij}. The weights can be adaptively learned by a top-down supervised manner and by internal adjusment due to architectural changes. The learning rule will be a modified Hebbian derived after proving the following convergence theorem among a set of interacting N neurons described by Eqs(1,2).

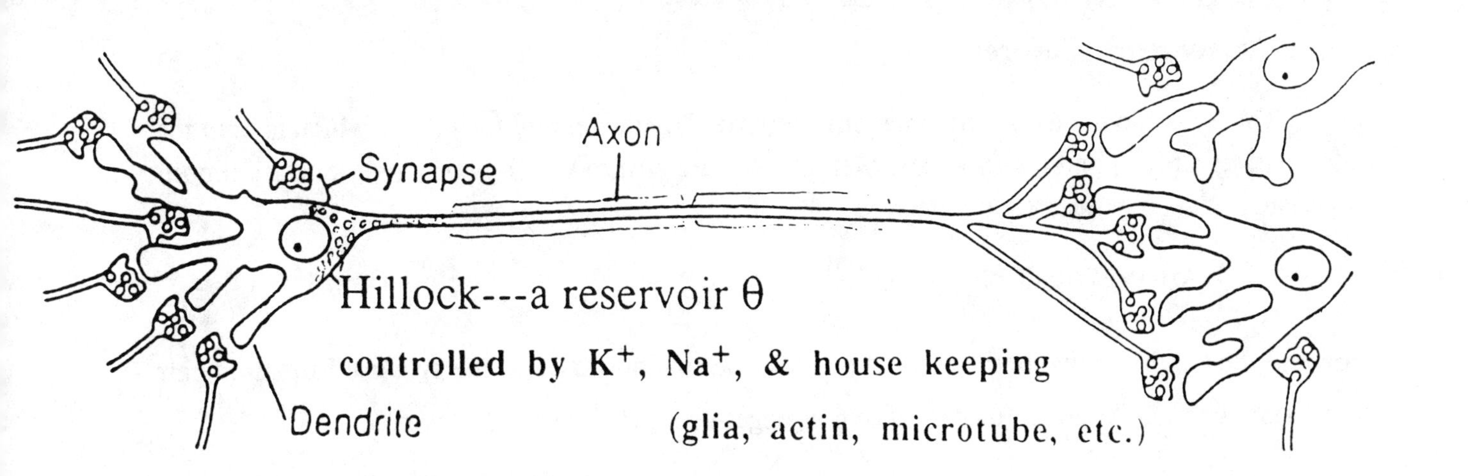

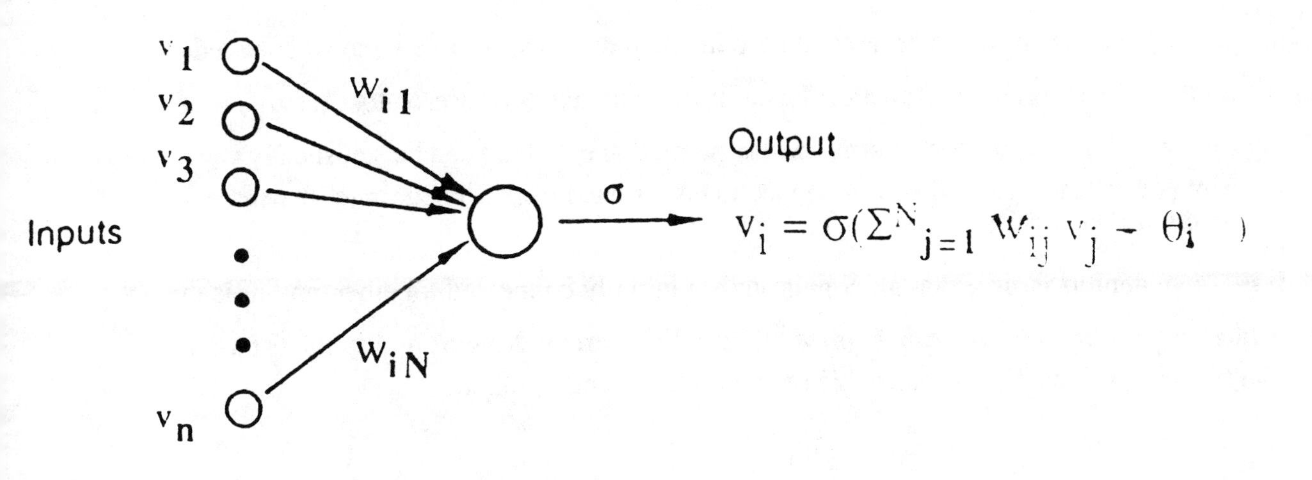

Fig. 4 **Typical Biological and Artificial Neurons**

Convergence Theorem

The dynamic interconnection patterns described by the energy $E(v_i, W_{ij})$ which is both the output firing rates v_i and the synapatic weights W_{ij} are ensured to converge to a local minimum associtated with an N neurons architecture,

$$dE(v_i, W_{ij})/dt \leq 0, \quad (4)$$

provided the condition that both the singlet sigmoidal function σ_1 and the synapse formation pair correlation function σ_2 are defined to have non-negative logic slopes as follows;

$$v_i = \sigma_1 (u_i)=(1+ \exp(- u_i))^{-1}; \qquad \sigma'_1=(dv_i/du_i)\approx G(u_i - \theta_i)\geq 0, \quad (5)$$

$$W_{ij}= \sigma_2(T_{ij})=step(T_{ij}- \theta_{ij})/(1-\theta_{ij});\sigma'_2=(dW_{ij}/dT_{ij})\approx\delta(T_{ij}- \theta_{ij})/(1-\theta_{ij})\geq 0, \quad (6)$$

The sigmoidal slope σ'_1 is known to be a radial base function or Gaussian-like window cnetered around θ_i. Since the pair correlation function T_{ij} has been modeled as a "use-or-loss" step probability function above θ_{ij} properly normalized between 0 and 1which can be statistically estimated about how often an existed pair of connection is ultilized from ith neuron to jth neuron when compared with other pairs.

It is convenient to assume that all N neurons are initially connected together, and u_i is the net input (above the threshold value θ_i) collected initially from all N neuron outputs v_j passing through the synaptic weights W_{ij} whose value may be subsequently pruned.

$$u_i = \Sigma^N_{j=1} W_{ij} v_j - \theta_i, \quad (7)$$

Furthermore, condition (ii) is the local energy descents:

Input firing rate dynamics: $\partial u_i/\partial t \approx - \partial E/\partial v_i$ (8),

Output Axon dynamics: $\partial T_{ij}/\partial t \approx - \partial E/\partial W_{ij}$ (9),

The mathematical proof is based on the universal truth of real positive quadratic expression obtained by chain rule of differentiations and substitution of gradient descents Eqs(8,9) as follows:

$$\begin{aligned} dE(v_i,W_{ij})/dt &= \Sigma^N_{i=1} (\partial E/\partial v_i)(\partial v_i/\partial t) + \Sigma^N_{i,j=1} (\partial E/\partial W_{ij})(\partial W_{ij}/\partial t) \\ &= \Sigma^N_{i=1}(\partial E/\partial v_i)(\partial v_i/\partial u_i)(\partial u_i/\partial t) + \Sigma^N_{i,j=1}(\partial E/\partial W_{ij})(\partial W_{ij}/\partial T_{ij})(\partial T_{ij}/\partial t) \\ &\approx - \Sigma^N_{i=1} \sigma'_1 (\partial E/\partial v_i)^2 - \Sigma^N_{i,j=1} \sigma'_2 (\partial E/\partial W_{ij})^2 \\ &\leq 0 \end{aligned} \quad (10)$$

where the primes denote the nonnegative slopes of singlet and pair correlation functions Eq(5,6). Thus, by definition of nonnegative logic Eqs(5,6) the energy landscape is always monotonously convergent for every quadratic term independent of the energy slope value and the size N. This is a strong convergence that each term is convergent.

One applies the differential chain rule to derive the synaptic weight chnage as follows:

$$\Delta W_{ij} = (\partial W_{ij}/\partial t)\Delta t = (\partial W_{ij}/\partial T_{ij})(\partial T_{ij}/\partial t)\Delta t = -(\partial W_{ij}/\partial T_{ij})(\partial \mathbf{E}/\partial W_{ij})\Delta t$$

$$= -(\partial W_{ij}/\partial T_{ij})(\partial \mathbf{E}/\partial v_i)(dv_i/du_i)(\partial u_i/\partial W_{ij})\Delta t\,. \qquad (11)$$

Substituting these results into Eq(11), one finds that the Hebbian learning rule

$$\Delta W_{ij} \approx v_i\, v_j$$

is modified by means of both Gaussian and weighted Dirac windows:

$$\Delta W_{ij} = -G(u_i)(\partial \mathbf{E}/\partial v_i)v_j\, \delta(T_{ij} - |\theta_{ij}|)/(1-|\theta_{ij}|)\Delta t \qquad (12)$$

Without the synaptic pruning window σ'_2 of Eq(6), the learnig rule Eq(11) is the traditional delta rule,which takes a long computational time to find itself within the Gaussian window of opportunity for a small weight change. That's why the Backprop training is notoriously slow. Furthermore, the change only happens rarely large enough to nullify the interconnection weight in order to prune a specific interconnection weight. Thus, one expects that the modified delta formula, that has divided the backprop delta rule by a samll number $(1-|\theta_{ij}|) \le 1$ and controlled by the second window, becomes efficient. The pair correlation function is also self-updated by

$$\Delta T_{ij} = (\partial T_{ij}/\partial t)\,\Delta t \quad = -(\partial \mathbf{E}/\partial W_{ij})\Delta t$$

$$= -(\partial \mathbf{E}/\partial v_i)(dv_i/du_i)(\partial u_i/\partial W_{ij})\Delta t = -G(u_i)(\partial \mathbf{E}/\partial v_i)v_j\,\Delta t \qquad (13)$$

In a feedforward layer architecture, if a quadratic cost energy is chosen $\mathbf{E} = (d_i - v_i)^2/2$ for the ad hoc supervision training in terms of the actual output v_i departed from the desired output d_i, then

$$(\partial \mathbf{E}/\partial v_i) = (v_i - d_i); \qquad i = 1,2,3, \text{ output layer neurons} \qquad (14)$$

$$(\partial \mathbf{E}/\partial v_i) = -\partial u_i/\partial t; \qquad i = 1,2,3, \text{ all other neurons} \qquad (15)$$

Eq(15) can be further feedbacked via the net input change Δu_i of Eq(7) and synaptic change ΔW_{ij} of Eq(12). Thus, the set of Eqs(11,15) may be useful for the self-organization in an architecture.

There remains to construct an appropriate energy function $\mathbf{E}(v_i, W_{ij})$, knowing the final answer. For example, if input and output neurons are cramped at known conditions, then one should be able to produce several known architectures, in vitro or numerically, for the "Exclusive Or" logic operation, and show that each architecture is associated with a local minimum of the energy landscape $E(v_i, W_{ij})$.

4. Research Prospectives

In this report, the synergism between electronic sciences and live neuron sciences has been demonstrated. We believe that synergism is matured for the greater scientific community to harvest further. Our original motivation was to post-process the vast amount of NTT video records (of different species of live neurons) to seek whether a strong or weak correlation exists between connectivity patterns and information processing capability. In other words, the question of the link between the functionality and the specificity was posed to NTT in 1989. In this preliminary report of our collaboration, we only wish to demonstrate the feasibility of precise and dynamical measurements in time of live BNN formations. Therefore, those unspecialized (but fast growing) chick embryonic neurons have been selected for neural network formations. Consequently, due to the missing link of the functionality and the specificity, our initial goal--to elucidate the self-assembly intelligence behavior--has not yet been completely accomplished. This idea to map BNN to ANN for the sake of the intelligence should be pursued further by the international and interdisciplinary community, using the new discovery of synapsin IIb to control the synaptic formations.

Much more work is obviously needed. One shall investigate functional-specific neurons, such as those associated with hearing, seeing, sensing, moving, controlling, communicating, etc. and to observe the connectivity patterns on chips with real time measurements. As an interesting by-product of the architectural taxonomy study, one can quantitatively measure the single neuron sigmoidal function, that was done early by McCullouch and Pitts almost five decades ago, statistically in parallel via the chip technology. One can also verify the of Hebbian synaptic strength learning rule by parallel and direct measurements of singlet and pair correlation function. These functions might reveal the major learning rule through the morphology change theorem, as opposed to the minor learning via of Hebbian rule upon a fixed architecture. However, given artificial planar substrates, one can never be certain about the neural network connectivity pattern to be meaningful *in vivo*, but it gives the insight of optimum neural network architectures for special classes of information processing.

In order to attract more investigators, we will illustrate these major advances as follows: (1) the new discovery of Synapsin IIb by Greengard et al. [Han91] at the Rockefeller University that made possible a controlled study of synapse formations and memory effects in live neural networks in Fig.5; (2) the underlying microtubule assembly for the nonlinear axon growth unveiled experimentally and theoretically by Kirschner et al. [Rein91, Tana91] at Univ. of San Francisco, that made feasible to trace the growth cone in Fig. 6; (3) usage of the advanced optoelectronic imaging in vitro techniques as shown Fig. 1, and in situ measurement techniques in Fig.3 [Courtesy of Torimitsu & Kawana]. Thus, based on the neural network viewpoint, given the knowledge of both the input (through the linear and distributed dendritic memory trees) and the output (of the nonlinear axon growth cones), one can in principle apply the electronic chip technology to complete the input-output statistics and measure the collective behavior in a controlled manner.

We believe that the trend of modern neural network study will be centered around the learning with dynamic interconnections, which is capable of self-adapting from one architecture to another to accommodate both the hardware fault tolerance and the necessary software inference.

Acknowledgement

Being an Advisor of Int'l. Inst. for Novel Computing, H.Szu wishes to take this opportunity to thank both Hedio Aiso of Keio University (& Profs. Anzai, Yoshi Takefuji & Dr. Yutaka Akiyama), and Isao Idota of JTTAS for the extensive tour in 1989. Since then collaborations have begun, notably with NTT (A. Kawana; H. Kawahara and Mr. Toda, Dir.);

IBM (Szuzuki); TTI (Kitagawa); ATR (Kurematsu); ETL(Matsumoto); Tsukuba(Yatagai); U.T.(Amari).

References

[Camp77] Campenot, R.B. 1977. Local Control of Neurite Development by Nerve Growth Factor, Proc. Natl. Acad. Sci. USA, 74:4516 - 4519.

[Cart67] Cater, S.B. 1967, Haptotaxis and the Mechanism of Cell Motility, Nature 213:256 - 260.

[Davi84] Davies, A. and Lumsden, A. 1984. Relation of Target Encounter and Neuronal Death to Nerve Growth Factor Responsiveness in the Developing Chick Trigeminal Ganglion, J. Comp. Neurol.223:124-137.

[Deca90] Decamilli, P., Benfenati. F., Valtorta, F., and Greengard, P. 1990, The Synapsins, Annu. Rev. Cell Biol. 6:433-460.

[Gree84] Green, L.A. 1984. The Importance of Both Early and Delayed Responses in the Biological Achoins of NGF, TINS 7:91-94.

[Gros91] Gross, G.W. & Kowalski, J.M. 1991 Experimental and Theoretical Analysis of Random Nerve Cell Network Dynamics, Neural Networks: Concepts, Applications, and Implementations, Prentice Hall

[Han91] Han, H, Nichols, R.A, Rubin, M.R, Bahler,M, Greengard, P.1991.Induction of formation of presynaptic terminals in neuroblastoma cells by synapsin IIb, Nature 349:697-700.

[Kawa90] Torimitsu, K. and Kawana A. 1990. Selective Growth of Sensory Nerve Fibers on Metal Oxide Pattern in Culture,Devel. Brain. Res. 51:128-131.

[Klei88] Kleinfeld, D., Kahler, K.H., and Hockberger, P.E. 1988. Controlled Outgrowth of Dissociated Neurons on Patterned Substrates, J. Neuros. 8:4098-4120.

[Rein91] Reinsch, S.S., Mitchison, T.J., and Kirschner, M. 1991. Microtubule Polymer Assembly and Transport During Axonal Elongation, Jour. Cell Biol. 115:365-379.

[Szu87] Szu, H., Hartley, R, 1987, Fast Simulated Annealing, Phys. Lett.A 122:157-162.

[Szu87] Szu, H., Hartley, R, 1987, Nonconvex Optimization by simulated Annealing, Proc. IEEE, 75:1538-1540.

[Szu90] Szu, H.H. 1990. Neural Networks Based on Peano Curves and Hairy Neurons, Telematics and Informatics, 7: 403-430, Pergamon Press.

[Tana91] Tanaka, E.M. and Kirschner, M. 1991. Microtubule Behavior in the Growth ones of Living Neurons During Axon Elongation, Jour. Cell Biol. 115:345-363.

[Tag87] Taguchi, T.,et al.,1987.A Subpopulation of embryonic Telencephalic Neurons Survive and Develop in Vitro in Response to Factors Derived From The Periphery, Devel..Brain Res.37:125-132.

AFTERWORD

KARL H. PRIBRAM

A Convergence :

In concluding this publication I will take up once again a discussion in which Sir John and I have been engaged for well over thirty years. As a confirmed mind/matter dualist, Eccles has, with Karl Popper, (Popper and Eccles, 1977) pioneered an interactionist stance which holds that psychological processes can and do influence what is going on in the brain. I have accepted this view but claim that it is only a part of the total story. My expressed challenge (Pribram 1986) is that epistemologically a dualist position is tenable only at the verbal level of natural languages; that at other levels of interaction -- e.g. at the neural-behavioral systems level -- a multiplicity of cognitive, affective and conative processes can be discerned (a pluralist stance); and, furthermore, that ontologically an identity relation characterizes the elementary neural and elementary psychological (communicative) relationship at the synapto-dendritic level. This identity position leads to a tension between idealism and realism while resolving (in terms of a neutral monism) that between mind and brain: Reciprocally interacting processes are identified which are neither material nor mental and are subject to measurement as quantities of information (in Shannon's and Gabor's terms).

A major step forward in resolving some remaining issues is possible on the basis of Sir John's presentation during this conference. Eccles once again presented his dualist interactionist views. He placed the causal action of mental phenomena at the synapse. The process alters chemical transmission by influencing the probability of opening a channel in the presynaptic vesicular grid. In a paper written with Friedrich Beck (1993), a mathematical physicist, the process is viewed as follows:

> "The interaction of mental events with the quantum probability amplitudes for exocytosis introduces a coherent coupling of a large number of individual amplitudes of the hundreds of thousands of boutons in a dendron. This then leads to an overwhelming variety of actualities, or modes, in brain activity. Physicists will realize the close analogy to laser-action, or more generally to the phenomenon of self-organization."
>
> "Exocytosis is the opening of a channel in the presynaptic vesicular grid and discharge of the vesicle's transmitter molecules into the synaptic cleft. It is as a whole, certainly a classical membrane-mechanical process. In order to investigate the possible role of quantum mechanics in the probabalistic discharge, one has to set up a model for the trigger mechanism by which $Ca2+$ prepares the vesicle of the presynaptic vesicular grid for exocytosis."

And again:

> "Since the resulting excitatory post-synaptic depolarization is the independent statistical sum of several thousands of local excitatory presynaptic potentials at spine synapses on each dendrite, we can concentrate on the process of exocytosis at each individual bouton".

Compare these passages with some by Yasue, Jibu and Pribram taken from Appendix A of Pribram's *Brain and Perception* (1991):

> Once the distribution of charge carriers in the ionic bioplasma evolves due to the distribution of dendritic isophase contours, the pattern of oscillations of

the membrane potentials in each location changes. This is because the amount of charge carriers in each location affects the Ca2+ controlled ATP cyclic process and so the resulting oscillations of biomolecules of high dipole moments. Thus, the fundamental activity of the dendritic network is represented by a reciprocal feedback and feedforward control of the distribution of the dendritic ionic bioplasma due to the oscillating component of membrane polarizations. To summarize, let us recall the idealized case of synchronized oscillations (1):

$$\theta(t) = e^{-i(\omega t+\alpha)} \tag{1}$$

There, $S(x, t) = (\omega t + \alpha)$ and we have a vanishing spatial frequency $k = 0$ and constant angular frequency ?¿ . This highly cooperative oscillating network of membrane polarizations prohibits the flow of ions (i.e., charge carriers).

By contrast, under less idealized conditions, the charge carriers in the dendritic network evolve and distribute as a function of the local phase differences of the oscillating components of the membrane polarization. This less idealized general case describes a holoscape (2). The spatial frequency of the phase relations among

$$\theta(x, t) = e^{i S(x, t)} \tag{2}$$

the contours of the holoscape (3), guides the charge carriers in each location to change with an energy proportional to that frequency. In other words, the dendritic holoscape of contours (2) at any moment controls the further time evolution of charge carriers in the entire dendritic network. According to the theory presented here, this pattern of charge carriers (i.e., ionic bioplasma) in the dendritic network of primary sensory cortex processes sensory input. Thus, the dendritic holoscape (2) of this cortex can be regarded as coordinate with image processing.

$$k(x, t) = \nabla S(x, t) = \left(\frac{\partial S(x, t)}{\partial x^1}, \frac{\partial S(x, t)}{\partial x^2} \right) \tag{3}$$

To return to Beck and Eccles:

"So as to make the model quantitative we attribute to the triggering process of exocytosis a continuous collective variable q for the quasiparticle. The motion is characterized by a potential energy V(q) which may take on a positive value at stage I, according to the metastable situation before exocytosis, then rises towards a maximum at stage II, and finally drops to zero (the arbitrary normalization) at stage IV."

"The time dependent process of exocytosis is described by the one-dimensional Schroedinger equation for the wave function $\Psi(q; t)$

$$i h \frac{\partial \Psi(q;t)}{\partial t} = -\frac{h^2}{2M} \frac{\partial^2 \Psi(q;t)}{\partial q^2} + V(q) \, . \, \Psi(q;t)$$

The initial condition for t=0 (stage I, beginning of exocytosis) is a wave packet left of the potential barrier."

And again, Yasue, Jibu and Pribram:

Because the neural wave equation (4) is linear, analysis of neurodynamics can be performed within the realm of conventional mathematical analysis. For example, the existence of solutions to the neural wave equation (4)

$$i\nu\frac{\partial\Psi}{\partial t}=\left(-\frac{\nu^2}{2}\Delta+U_{ex}\right)\Psi \qquad (4)$$

for a wider class of external static potentials Uex is known (Kato, 1964). The use of the neural wave equation in neurodynamics opens the possibility to represent the dendritic microprocess within a new mathematical framework.

It seems worthwhile to notice here that the formal similarity between neural and quantum processes has been pointed out both in physics and in neurology. In physics, Margenau (1984) has suggested that a process similar to electron tunnelling occurs in the neural microprocess. Hameroff (1987) has developed the theme that soliton waves occurring in microtubules could account for dendritic processing. And in the context of the current appendix, the formulations of Frölich (1975), Umezawa (Stuart et al., 1978; 1979), and Singer (Singer, 1989; Gray & Singer, 1989, Gray et. al., 1989) become especially relevant. Further, as noted in Lectures 2 and 4 of this volume, Gabor developed a communication theory based on psychophysics that used the same formalisms as those used by Heisenberg in his descriptions of quantum microphysics. From the neurological standpoint, the holonomic brain theory is based on these proposals. Neurodynamics as developed in this appendix incorporates this formalism in a mathematical model in which the fundamental equation is of the same form as in the quantum theory.

Finally, from Lecture 4 of Brain and Perception:

"Activity in axons and in other dendrites such as those stemming from reciprocal synapses produce depolarizations and hyperpolarizations in the dendritic spines. The postsynaptic effects are ordinarily invoked by chemical transmitters whose action is modified by other chemicals that act as regulators and modulators."

These postsynaptic effects must overcome an obstacle before they can influence spike generation at the axon hillock.

"The stalks of the spines are narrow and therefore impose a high resistance to conduction (active or passive) toward the dendritic branch. Spine head depolarizations (as well as hyperpolarizations) must therefore interact with one another if they are to influence the action potentials generated at the axon hillock of the parent cell of the dendrite."

Thus the activation of interacting polarizations

"occurs in parallel, is distributed, discontinuous and resembles in this respect the saltatory mode of conduction that takes place from node to node in myelinated nerve' (Shepherd et al., 1985, p2193). In the holonomic brain theory such parallel processing is described as nonlocal and cooperative and is represented by a Hilbert space. The mathematical similarity between the quantum and neural mechanics can [thus] have a basis in neurophysiological reality: For instance, as described in the epilogue to these lectures, the microtubular structure of dendrites can serve to provide cooperativity by way of boson condensation to produce soliton or phonon patterns of excitation practically instantaneously (Frohlich 1968, 1983, 1986; Hameroff 1987)."

The Mind/Brain Relationship:

Despite these agreements as to the details of the relevant synaptodendritic process, there remains an important point of disagreement between Eccles and myself which surfaces only tangentially in these quotations. Eccles views mental processes as unidirectional causal influences on the operation of the synaptic mechanism. By contrast I see the interaction between the physiological and the psychological process as reciprocal. The evidence for such reciprocal interaction at every level (subsynaptic, synaptic, neuronal and neural systems) makes up the substance of the various lectures composing *Brain and Perception* (1991). Reciprocity leads to bootstrapping, that is, self organization, within the brain/mind matrix.

What is missing in Eccles account, is the emergence of mentality (including consciousness) from the operation of the neural process. This is an inconsistency: In the paper presented at this conference, Eccles makes an excellent case for the emergence of feeling and self-consciousness as rooted in the evolutionary development of the very same synapto-dendric cortical architecture which he claims is receptive to psychological influence. In his view, however, this development only "allows" mind to influence brain. Still, Eccles felt sufficiently comfortable with the view that mentality emerges from an interaction between biology and culture to write a book *The Self and its Brain* (1977) with Karl Popper a strong advocate of the emergentist view.

My own stance begins by taking computer programming as its metaphor. At some point in programming, there is a direct correspondence between the programming language and the operations of the hardware being addressed. In ordinary von Neuman configurations, machine language embodies this correspondence. Higher order languages encode the information necessary to make the hardware run in ever more abstract and generally useful languages. When the word processing program allows this Afterword to be written in English, there is no longer any similarity between the user's language and the binary of the computer hardware. This, therefore, expresses a dualism between mental language and material hardware operations.

Transposed from metaphor to the actual mind-brain connection, the descriptions of the operations of the neural wetware made up of dendrites and synapses and the electrochemical operations occurring therein, seem far removed from those used by behavioral scientists to describe psychological processes. But the distance which separates these languages is no greater than that which distinguishes word processing from binary.

What is different in the mind-brain connection from that which characterizes the program-computer relationship is its intimate reciprocal self-organization at every level. High level psychological processes such as those involved in cognition are therefore the result of cascades of biopsychological bootstrapping operations rather than the result of solely top-down programming procedures.

Eccles proposes that the elementary neurophysiological operations of dendrons have a counterpart in elementary psychological operations he calls psychons. He has been severely criticized for failing to delineate what he conceives to be a psychon, that all of his beautifully detailed descriptions are limited to dendrons. If we take seriously the possibility that at the dendron level something is occurring which is akin to a computer being programmed in machine language, it behooves us to delineate the psychon. A reciprocal rather than a unidirectional causal relationship would be more productive, allowing bootstrapping of mind-brain organizations. Beck and Eccles appear to recognize this when they state that "physicists will realize the close analogy to laser action, or more generally, to the phenomenon of self organization." This statement comes pretty close to my own formulation which used the optical laser produced hologram as its initial metaphor for processing at the synapto-dendritic level (Pribram 1966).

Computers process information in terms of Boolian BITS, the amount of processing achieved being measured by Shannon's unit, the reduction of the amount of uncertainty. The holonomic brain theory is based on the evidence that the unit of processing in the cortical receptive dendritic fields, is a quantum of information, a Gabor wavelet or similar Hermetian. But Gabor, as did Shannon, defined his elementary unit to deal with the efficiency with which human telecommunication could proceed. As an hypothesis, therefore, Pribram's *Brain and Perception* takes the idea that a quantum of information describes not only an elementary neural but also an elementary psychological communicative process. In short, the biopsychological language that corresponds to computer machine language is a language based on the quantum of information. In Eccles' terms, the quantum of information, measured in Gabor-like terms, which has been found to describe processing in a dendritic receptive field, is also a measure of the psychon. The contributions to this publication specify various examples of psychons in the biopsychological language of mind-brain interactions at the level of sensory systems.

This conference and its proceedings, therefore, provide an opportunity to examine the convergence of proposals for the how of the mind-brain relation: proposals in detail, not just in philosophic stances. The fact of the influence of psychological process on brain function has been demonstrated in a variety of studies using both micro and macrorecordings of brain electrical potentials. Some of these studies are presented here by Barry Richmond, Bruce Bolster and Walter Freeman. Others were reviewed in Brain and Perception. Still others are in progress in B.R.A.I.N.S. and were shown in preliminary form during the conference. The emergence of the capability of higher order psychological processing as a function of higher order synapto-dendritic organization is the burden of Eccles' presentation, a view most scientists are comfortable with. This is indeed progress. The resolution of remaining differences may not be far away.

References:

Beck F. & Eccles J.C. (In Press). Quantum aspects of brain activity and the role of consciousness. *Procceedings of the National Academy of Sciences.*

Eccles, J.C. (1986). Do mental events cause neural events analogously to the probability field of quantum mechanics? *Proc. R. Soc. Lond.* Great Britian.

Pribram, K.H. (1966). Some dimensions of reemembering: Steps toward a neuropsychological model of memory. In J. Gaito (Ed.), *Macromolecules and behavior. New York: Academic Press*, pp. 165-187.

Pribram, K.H. (1986). The cognitive revolution and mind/brain issues. *American Psychologist, Vol. 41*, No. 5, pp. 507-520.

Pribram, K.H. (1991). *Brain and Perception: Holonomy and Structure in Figural Processing*. Lawrence Erlbaum Associates, Inc. New Jersey.

Yasue, K., Jibu M. & Pribram, K.H. (1991). In *Brain and Perception: Holonomy and Structure in Figural Processing*, Appendix A. Lawrence Erlbaum Associates, Inc. New Jersey.

List of Authors Cited

Facts About INNS

What Is INNS?

- INNS is a professional and scientific association which is dedicated to promoting scientific understanding about models of brain and behavioral processes and exploring the application of neural modelling concepts to technological problems.

Who Can Join?

- Any individual with an interest in learning about or contributing to this dynamic scientific field is invited to join INNS. INNS' 3,000+ members represent a diversity of disciplines, including computer science, neuroscience, psychology, engineering, physics, mathematics, business, and law to mention just a few.
- INNS members span the globe. The Society has active members on all continents except Antarctica.
- Students are especially welcome. INNS gives full-time students special discounts on membership dues and other benefits.

What Does My Membership Include?

- One year subscription to the journal Neural Networks.
- Discounts on registration fees for the annual World Congress on Neural Networks. Congresses are currently planned for 1993 in Portland and 1994 in San Diego.
- One-year subscription to the INNS newsletter, Above Threshold.
- Free Special Interest Groups (SIGs) focused on aspects on neural networks and based worldwide.
- Discounts on subscriptions to other scientific publications related to the field.
- Opportunities to participate in special professional education and development workshops on neural networks.
- Use of an on-line electronic message/bulletin board system devoted to the exchange of information about neural networks.

How Do I Join INNS?

- Complete the membership application and return it to INNS at the address above.
- Questions? Call 202-466-4667 or fax 202-466-2888 (both numbers are in the United States) or contact us via e-mail: 70727.3265@compuserve.com

Membership Application

Check one: ☐ **Regular** (US$60) ☐ **Student** (US$40)

Students - Please verify status by providing:

Expected Degree: __________ Graduation Date: __________

Faculty Signature: ______________________________

Dr./Mr./Ms.: ______________________________

Affiliation: ______________________________

Mailing Address:

____

____

____

____

Telephone: ______________________________

Fax number: ______________________________

E-mail: ______________________________

Check your areas of interest in neural networks:

- ☐ Biomedical applications
- ☐ Electronics/VLSI
- ☐ Expert Networks
- ☐ Finance/Economics
- ☐ Geology/Geophysics
- ☐ Higher Level Cognitive Processes
- ☐ Mathematics/Theory
- ☐ Mental Function & Dysfunction
- ☐ My Local City/State/Country SIG
- ☐ Neuroscience
- ☐ Optics
- ☐ Philosophy/Evolution
- ☐ Power Engineering
- ☐ Pulsed Networks
- ☐ Robotics/Automation
- ☐ Speech
- ☐ Standards
- ☐ Vision/Motion Analysis

Mailing List: INNS rents its mailing list to earn additional income. If you do not want your name used, check below:

☐ I DO NOT authorize INNS to use my name/address for non-neural network mailings.

Membership Fee Payment: I would like to pay for my membership with:

☐ Check (drawn in US funds)

☐ MasterCard ☐ Visa

Account number: ______________________________

Expiration Date ______________

Signature: ______________________________